THE WORLD'S GREATEST
ARCHITECTURE

PAST AND PRESENT

D.M. FIELD

Published in 2005 by
Regency House Publishing Ltd
24-26 Boulton Road
Stevenage
Hertfordshire
SG1 4QX
United Kingdom

www.regencyhousepublishing.com

ISBN 1 85361 506 4

Printed in China

PAGE 2: Fontainebleau.

TITLE PAGE: Taj Mahal.

*OPPOSITE: Doge's Palace,
Venice.*

PAGE 6: Reichstag, Berlin.

*CONTENTS PAGE: Saint
Peter's, Rome.*

Contents

*A*rchitecture is the one art that we cannot avoid. It is constantly before our eyes, indeed we live in its works, in the sense that all buildings are designed or planned, if not by Brunelleschi or Sir Norman Foster. At the same time architecture is probably the least highly regarded of the visual arts. This is partly due to the fact that it is functional, it serves a practical purpose, which in the West, though not in other cultures, is regarded as somehow downgrading. It becomes a 'mere' craft, and subject to compromises imposed by economic, political or social constraints, though the greatest artists also worked for patrons, and aimed to earn a living. But to some extent, the inferior status of architecture is due to popular disillusionment with the works of Modernism – all those sub-Miesian glass towers and mock-Corbusier concrete blocks that disfigured many a European cityscape in the years after the Second World War. Architecture of earlier periods is, for most people, more easily categorized as art, largely because age is considered to confer virtue. But, at the beginning of a new millennium, there are signs that the popular prejudice is changing. It is not, we are discovering, necessary to revert to a pastiche of the past to avoid the ugliness of the present. The 20th century may not have produced many indisputably 'great' buildings but it did produce an unparalleled number of, if not all 'good' ones, creative, innovatory, and visually spectacular buildings.

The aim of this book is to offer a panoramic view of the marvels of world architecture by looking at nearly 300 individual buildings. Inevitably, Western examples far outnumber those of the East, because of their greater variety, number, influence and, not least, durability; in eastern Asia, the traditional building material was wood, with the result that very few buildings in China have survived from earlier than the Ming dynasty, 1368–1644. If the subjects highlighted in this book had been chosen on aesthetic criteria alone, probably the European majority would have been smaller and the Islamic section larger. In general, the buildings have been chosen because they are, for one or several reasons, outstanding in themselves or typical of an important type; but no strict qualifications have been demanded and some are present (or absent) largely as a result of personal preference. Although one or two family houses are here, in general large, spectacular or monumental buildings – cathedrals rather than churches, skyscrapers rather than bungalows – are preferred.

The buildings are arranged first by geographical region, second by chronology, but with exceptions in both cases. For instance, Islamic buildings in India, something of a special case, will be found under South Asia, but Islamic buildings in Europe will be found under Islam. Most modern buildings in Asia, even if designed by Western architects, are placed in the appropriate region unless, for example, they are closer to international Modernism than indigenous tradition. But there are some borderline cases. A few small liberties have been taken with chronology too, when it is desirable to place two buildings together for purpose of comparison although, if strict dating were adhered to, one would appear earlier or later. However, it is in any case difficult to put a precise date on many buildings, as they were often built over many years, even centuries.

This book is designed for the general reader. Abstruse theories and technical terms have been excluded as far as possible. Sometimes they cannot be avoided, in which case the term may be found in the glossary at the end.

The Ancient World

Chapter One

Stonehenge

Great Pyramid, Giza

Ziggurat, Ur

Abu Simbel

Temple of Amun, Karnak

Ishtar Gate, Babylon

Knossos

Persepolis

Pyramid of the Sun, Teotihuacán

Machu Piccu

Mesa Verde

Architecture is usually considered an activity exclusive to the human species, but building is not, since many animals practise it with remarkable aptitude. The bowerbird, indeed, decorates his alluring arbour with flowers and shells in a display, were the bowerbird human, of what might be called taste. Still, we would not describe the bowerbird as an architect.

Building is an ancient human activity. Even Palaeolithic hunter-gatherers, constantly on the move, must have made shelters of leaves and branches. But serious building, meant to last, only became possible when people settled down in one place, something they could not generally do until they had learned how to grow crops and keep animals. When buildings were no longer merely temporary expedients, they ceased to be merely functional and acquired other characteristics. They became architecture. As Vitruvius defined it in the 1st century AD, architecture is building that fulfils three criteria: it is useful, soundly built, and venustas, *meaning delightful, attractive or – a work of art.*

Until quite recent times, the buildings that have survived are almost exclusively temples, palaces, castles, and the like. Ordinary houses were built of less durable materials such as adobe or wood and naturally received far less care and expenditure than was lavished on the homes of gods and rulers. It is no surprise that the earliest works of architecture were predominantly religious buildings, such as the great temples of ancient Egypt or Greece. Increasingly, other kinds of building became prominent as time passed, but spiritual motives have generally been responsible for the peaks of architectural achievement: think of the cathedrals of medieval Europe, the Baroque churches of the Counter-Reformation, the mosques and madrasas of Islam, the Hindu and Buddhist temples of south and south-east Asia. The decline of religion in the contemporary West may explain why today, although we have an unprecedented number of fine architects, we have no indisputably great buildings.

Stonehenge

Stonehenge, which stands amid the bleak expanse of Salisbury Plain in southern England, is the most famous megalithic monument in Europe. The earliest construction began before 3000 BC, and the building remained in use, sporadically at least, for nearly two millennia. It consists basically of an incomplete circle of roughly worked standing stones up to 22ft (7m) above the ground and arranged in a ring.

Archaeologists distinguish three main periods of construction. In Period I, Neolithic workmen using picks made from antlers dug a circular ditch nearly 327ft (100m) in diameter, backed by a circular wall. Two large stones, one still surviving, marked the entrance. In Period II,

about 2100 BC, two concentric circles of 80 bluestone pillars weighing up to four tonnes each were erected in the centre. Period III, 100 years later, saw the erection of the circle of sarsen uprights capped by sarsen lintels, fashioned with stone hammers, which largely form the monument as it is today, after centuries of climatic erosion and pillage by builders. There is no natural stone nearby. The sarsen stones came from the Marlborough Downs, about 20 miles (32km) away, but the only known source for the huge bluestones is South Wales. Numerous theories, many patently absurd, have been put forward to explain how the monument was constructed and what its purpose was. It certainly had nothing to do with

the Druids, who did not appear on the scene until centuries later, and this puzzle is unlikely to be solved, though it is generally accepted that Stonehenge was a place of worship. The construction of Period II is aligned with the rising sun at the summer solstice, which is clearly not a coincidence, but its significance remains a mystery. It has been widely supposed that the bluestones were brought overland to the site by rollers and by water on a raft. An attempt to reproduce this operation in 2000, however, ran into serious difficulties. Another theory holds that the bluestones were a relic of the Ice Age, deposited on Salisbury Plain thousands of years earlier by glaciation.

Stonehenge: the slightly controversial reconstruction has made it appear less of a ruin than it once was.

The Great Pyramid, Giza

Although Egyptian architecture remained remarkably constant for nearly 3,000 years, there were changes. Pyramids, built chiefly to contain the bodies of pharaohs, were restricted to the Old Kingdom (c. 2575–2134 BC). They developed from the earlier, low, flat-topped *mastaba* but, due partly to the menace of thieves, were replaced in about the 18th century BC by tombs cut deep in the rocks, which were unfortunately not thief-proof either.

About 100 pyramids are known today, but the great majority are no more than piles of rubble. The earliest is the Step Pyramid, or Ziggurat, of Zoser, a king of the 3rd Dynasty of about 2800 BC, which was originally about 200-ft (60-m) high. The true pyramid, with four smooth sides on the plan of a square sloping inwards to a point, developed in the 4th Dynasty. There is reason to think, however, that the most notable survivals, the three pyramids at Giza on the outskirts of modern Cairo, are the finest. They are regarded as one of the Seven Wonders of the Ancient World, and are the only survivor of the seven.

The largest and oldest of the three is the Great Pyramid of Khufu (Cheops). Measuring 756ft (230m) along each side at the base, it rose originally to a height of 482ft (147m). It covers an area of about 13 acres (5 hectares), more than the five largest European cathedrals put together, and is said to contain about 2,300,000 blocks of stone with an average weight of 2.5 tonnes. Buried deep within were three separate chambers, reached by intimidating, angled passages and heavily buttressed against the oppressive weight of stone.

Though still an awe-inspiring sight, it is not untouched by time, and the encroachment of the city is a growing threat to its integrity. Today, it has lost about 39ft (12m) of its original height, and it lacks its outer layer of smooth and dazzling limestone, appropriated by the builders of Cairo. Though about 4,500 years old, the Great Pyramid remains one of the largest and most splendid of human works.

OPPOSITE
The three pyramids at Giza.

BELOW
The outer facing of the pyramids has largely disappeared except for a section towards the top of the Great Pyramid.

generally dry climate such material, which would be practically useless in more temperate regions such as northern Europe, lasts a remarkably long time, although, of course, it does not last as well as stone. The reason why the ziggurat at Ur is comparatively well preserved is that its sloping walls were carefully faced with sun-dried bricks set in mortar made from mud. An interesting feature is that the facing of the wall is interrupted at intervals by shallow vertical channels which, experts suggest, were made to allow the mud-brick core to 'breathe', preventing cracking during the wet season. The remaining lower stages have recently been restored to their original appearance.

The ziggurat was originally built by Ur-Nammu, a king of the 3rd Dynasty, during the last two centuries of the 3rd millennium BC, when Ur was the leading Mesopotamian power. It is roughly 1,000 years later than the earliest giant temples of the Sumerians such as those at Eridu and Uruk. The form of the earlier buildings – basically a monumental temple with buttressed sides raised on a huge platform – led to the ziggurat, or temple tower, which was the essential form at Ur. Ziggurats were often built on the same sites as archaic temples and have many features recalling them in form.

The great ziggurat at Ur is essentially a truncated pyramid, built in a series of platforms of diminishing area, and accessed by stairways. On the topmost platform would have been the temple of the Moon god Nanna, the chief god of Ur, although there is no trace of it now. The large temple enclosure includes royal residences and the royal tombs, which have yielded treasures of extraordinary sophistication.

The restored lower section of the Ziggurat of Ur.

Ziggurat, Ur

The Sumerians in southern Mesopotamia (roughly modern Iraq) are generally credited with being the earliest of ancient civilizations, followed closely by those of Egypt, China and the Indus valley. The focus of Sumerian life was the temple, the house of the god who ruled the city, the king at that time being merely his agent. In southern Mesopotamia, little stone or wood was available for building, but what did exist in huge quantity was alluvial mud, from the frequent flooding of the river. In the

Abu Simbel

Abu Simbel lies about 174 miles (280km) south of Aswan, in ancient Nubia. The region was first conquered by the Egyptians during the Middle Kingdom (2134–1786 BC), and was ruled by them, with intervals, until the late 8th century, when the position was reversed and the Nubians briefly ruled Egypt, until driven out by the Assyrians.

The great temple of Abu Simbel was built during the long reign of Ramses II (1304–1237 BC) and proclaims the formidable power of that mighty pharaoh. On the rock-cut façade are four colossi of Ramses, each about 65-ft (20-m) high, accompanied by comparatively tiny figures of his family, who cluster at his feet like satellites around a planet. The plan of the temple is in the customary form, with two large, hypostyle (pillared) halls, surrounded by other chambers and apartments. The temple was built so that at the most important festivals of the year, 20

Ramses II built seven major temples at Abu Simbel, including the Great Temple. The so-called Small Temple (left) was associated with his Great Royal Wife, Nefertari, who appears inside being crowned as a goddess. Below are details of the exterior and interior decorations at Abu Simbel.

February and 20 October, the rays of the sun would shine directly along the main axis to illuminate the sanctuary. The inner walls were

decorated with painted low-reliefs celebrating the activities of the divine king, including his famous battles against the Hittites in Syria, the first military campaign in history that can be reconstructed from surviving records. There is also a rather more attractive, smaller temple, dedicated to Ramses' chief wife, Nefertari.

The proposal to build the Aswan High Dam in the 1960s threatened Abu Simbel with inundation, and a remarkable rescue effort was mounted under the auspices of UNESCO. The entire complex was dismantled in pieces and raised to a position 200-ft (60-m) higher, where it was reassembled and protected from the vast piles of rock introduced to emulate its original setting by a gigantic concrete dome. The whole operation took four years and cost over $40 million, a modern technological achievement to match the skill and effort of the original temple builders.

Temple of Amun, Karnak

Little remains to be seen of the ancient city of Thebes, capital of Egypt during the New Kingdom (c.1550–1070 BC), but the two great temples of Luxor and especially Karnak, which stand close by on the east bank of the River Nile, are notable exceptions.

The temples of ancient Egypt were not places of worship but dwelling places for the gods. Few temples earlier than this have survived, and it can often be assumed that the surviving building, as at Karnak, replaced an earlier one, perhaps dating back to the Old Kingdom, and for about 1,500 years the style hardly changed. These temples are huge, Karnak in fact being the biggest, and are built along an axis. The main entrance takes the form of a pylon gateway, leading to a colonnaded court and a hypostyle hall. Walls bear rich decorations, typically in low-relief, representing rites of the cult, deeds of the pharaoh, and sometimes more domestic scenes. They form an integral part of the building.

The Egyptians were not interested in experimenting with interior space, and the vast hall is somewhat cramped by the profusion of columns. But it was merely a 'hall', in the sense of an anteroom. Beyond lay the holiest chamber, the sanctuary, comparatively dark and narrow, where the cult statue in which the god resided was housed within a shrine. Ordinary people were not admitted, but at festivals, which were extremely elaborate, the images of the gods were carried outside the temple to make contact with them. The annual ceremony at Karnak, when the image of the god was

carried by water to Thebes, lasted for a month. It was conveniently celebrated during the Flood season, when no work could be done in the fields.

The great temples, something like medieval monasteries, were substantial, largely self-contained units, containing craftsmen's workshops and schools. In the 12th century BC, the Temple of Amun at Karnak employed about 10,000 people.

Ishtar Gate, Babylon

Although the city of Babylon existed in the 3rd millennium BC, it only became important in the first half of the 18th century BC, when Hammurabi made it the capital of an empire comprising most of Mesopotamia, from the Persian Gulf to the borders of Anatolia. It was raided and sacked by the Hittites and others in succeeding centuries and was dominated by Assyria from the 9th century until the fall of Assyria in 612 BC. Under a dynasty of Chaldean kings, notably Nebuchadnezzar II (602–562 BC), it again became a major political power in the Near East.

The new Babylon, whose ruins, first seriously excavated at the beginning of the 20th century, can still be seen on the River Euphrates about 55 miles (90km) south of Baghdad, was essentially the creation of Nebuchadnezzar. Straddling the river and guarded by a three-part wall, it covered an area of up to 12 miles (19km) in circumference, and contained such fabulous structures as a seven-staged ziggurat that has been popularly identified with the Tower of Babel and Nebuchadnezzar's palace with its alleged Hanging Gardens, one of the Seven Wonders of the Ancient World. In fact, excavations have shown that the palace was much smaller than might have been expected.

The main entrance to the city was through the Ishtar Gate, which led to the Processional Way, the main central avenue that bisected the city. The glazed brickwork, decorated with heraldic animals, sometimes in relief, adorned the Processional Way and Nebuchadnezzar's palace, as well as the Ishtar Gate which, carefully restored, is now in the National Museum in Berlin. The animals, not only real ones such as lions and bulls but also obscure mythical ones, were originally modelled on a large panel of soft clay. The panel was then cut into bricks, fired, and reassembled on the wall. Colours, on a deep blue background, are bright and varied. The technique was not new, but it had never been employed on such a large scale before. It so impressed the Persians, who under Cyrus the Great captured Babylon in 539 BC, that they took Babylonian craftsmen back to decorate their capital at Susa.

The Ishtar Gate, preserved and restored, is now in Berlin.

Knossos

The Bronze Age Minoan civilization of the Aegean was one of the most remarkable discoveries of the 20th century. Excavations in Crete began under Sir Arthur Evans in 1900, and although the palace of the legendary King Minos had practically disappeared, some parts, especially the alleged royal apartments on the eastern side, were restored in a bold attempt to recreate their original appearance, some say rather insensitively, the characteristically short, heavy, red-painted columns, which were originally of wood, being made of concrete.

The first palace was built soon after 2000 BC, and apparently consisted of a series of individual buildings grouped around a courtyard. In about 1720 BC it was destroyed by an earthquake and was rebuilt in a more elaborate form, while retaining the large central courtyard. This is the building whose remains are visible today. The palace occupies a hilly site and the buildings, which vary in height between two and five storeys, were connected by shady colonnades and flights of stairs. They were surmounted by an emblem representing the horns of a bull, a sacred animal in Crete as the famous painting of the intriguing rite of 'bull-dancing' confirms. Carved in stone and gilded, these images, mounted on the outward

edge of the flat roofs, must have produced a brilliant effect in the Mediterranean sunlight.

The palace was virtually a city in itself: it contained thousands of rooms, and the site would have comfortably accommodated two full-sized football pitches. It must have been almost as confusing a place for the newcomer in the 2nd millennium as it is today for the tourists, as they wander through endless rooms and corridors, surrounded by the evidence of a sophisticated society which remains largely unknown, despite the evidence, unfortunately fragmentary, of the surviving wall paintings. The effort to recapture the decorative scheme was taken farthest in the Throne Room. The great frieze of mythical beasts around the walls is modern, but based on fragments discovered during excavation. The high-backed throne of alabaster is original.

Knossos survived the Mycenaean takeover in the 15th century BC, but was destroyed early in the next century by fire, probably the result of a natural disaster.

ABOVE
One of the pillared halls at the Palace of Knossos, thought to have been private apartments.

LEFT
A restored section in the eastern part of the palace; the red columns are concrete replicas of the wooden originals.

FAR LEFT
Some of the storage jars or pithos*, many with sophisticated decoration, found at Knossos.*

Persepolis

In the 6th century BC the Persians, under Cyrus the Great, rapidly swallowed up all the territories of the various earlier empires of the Near East. The ceremonial capital at Parsa, better known by its Greek name of Persepolis ('City of the Persians'), was founded by Darius I in the late 6th century BC, and completed by Xerxes and his successors. It was an unsuitable administrative capital, being remote and inaccessible, but for nearly two centuries it was the chief royal residence.

Although the Greeks had never heard of Persepolis until Alexander the Great conquered it in 331 BC, it bears traces of Greek influence, although it is thoroughly unGreek in spirit. Figures from the processional frieze in the palace of Darius I show Greek influence in the drapery, but are more closely related to Assyria than to Athens.

The Achaemenids, the founders of the Persian royal family, were not great originators, but expertly exploited and refined the achievements of their predecessors. As in Assyria, the whole complex is raised on a huge limestone platform, creating a level surface on sloping ground. In the east, it is backed by the Kuh-e Rahmat (Mount of Mercy), which also provided the greyish stone from which the complex was built. The other three sides were guarded by a wall that ranged up to 41ft (12.5m) where the ground level is lowest. A magnificent stairway on the west led to the top. The colossal royal palaces were built according to the trabeated technique of post and lintel, like the Greek temples. The lofty stone columns that survive from the Audience Hall of Darius rise from a curved base to a

complex decorative capital, to support wooden beams. Besides the palaces of Darius I, Xerxes and Artaxerxes III, the buildings included a treasury, a harem, and the Hall of One Hundred Columns, Xerxes' Throne Room. Extremely large stone blocks were used, meticulously masoned, and parts still stand without the aid of mortar.

Persepolis was largely destroyed by a vengeful Alexander, when it remained as capital of a Macedonian province, but gradually declined. The south wall still bears Darius' inscription, 'God protect this country from foe, famine and falsehood'. He didn't, but enough of Persepolis remains to make it one of the world's most impressive monuments.

OPPOSITE
This overall view reveals the vast scale of the monumental Persian citadel.

BELOW
Part of the ceremonial staircase of the Tripylon.

Pyramid of the Sun, Teotihuacán

About 2,000 years ago, a little-known people (whose language is still not understood), who had settled in what was then a fertile offshoot of the Valley of Mexico about 400 years earlier, began to build a massive ceremonial complex north-east of modern Mexico City, which grew into the greatest city of Mesoamerica. At its height in the 6th century AD, it covered about 8sq miles (20sq km), housed over 100,000 people, and outposts of Teotihuacán's empire eventually stretched to the Gulf Coast and Guatemala. The city was planned on a formal grid pattern, with even the streams channelled to conform to the rectilinear layout. The manner in which streets and buildings are aligned suggests some astronomical significance. The main north-south thoroughfare is called the Avenue of the Dead because the buildings that lined it, probably residences of the great, were once thought to have been tombs. It runs south from the Pyramid of the Moon, with the somewhat larger Pyramid of the Sun standing to the east. Both date from the earliest period of construction.

Like all the temples of Teotihuacán, the Temple of the Sun has disappeared; but the gigantic ziggurat that supported it remains, along with its ceremonial plaza. It measures roughly 735ft (225m) on each side and is 240-ft (73-m) high, consisting of five great 'steps' with sloping sides, the fourth stage being much smaller than the others. On the west, facing the Avenue of the Dead, a grand staircase rises from three stepped terraces. The core of the pyramid is earth – nearly 1 million cubic metres of it. It is faced with a red volcanic stone found locally and lime-plastered.

Teotihuacán began to decline after about 600 and it was sacked by the Toltecs, probably soon after 650. Later settlers, impressed by its grandeur, respected the place, though it never recovered its former power or population. The Aztecs, who would have recognized many of the gods portrayed in murals and sculpture, believed that the city had been built by the gods and made occasional pilgrimages there.

ABOVE
Head of the god Quetzalcoatl, in high relief.

RIGHT
A general view of the Pyramid of the Sun with the Avenue of the Dead in the foreground.

quite how the Incas managed to overcome the communications problem, there being no conventional written language, remains something of a mystery.

Another mystery surrounds the exact function of Machu Piccu, today the most-visited of the Inca sites, which is set in a spectacular position on a high precipice surrounded by almost sheer mountain peaks. In fact the Spaniards never knew it was there: abandoned for centuries, it was first rediscovered by the American archaeologist, Hiram Bingham, in 1911. There may have been some religious association responsible for its location, and its architecture supports this supposition, as it seems too substantial to be merely a frontier strongpoint. A notable feature of the site, the carved, natural stone Intihatana, enclosed by

curving walls, must have had some ritual significance, no doubt connected with the Sun god. The careful planning and orderly layout suggests that this was probably a state enterprise, perhaps organized from Cuzco, which is about 50 miles (80km) away to the south-east.

As well as fine stone buildings the city also combines extensive agricultural terraces. The extraordinary skill of the stonemasons and engineers is famous, for they worked with primitive tools and without mortar, yet managed to fit the stone blocks together with extraordinary precision, building on simple lines, generally based on squares and rectangles. They did not employ the arch, and the buildings of Machu Piccu are quite devoid of sculpture.

Two views of Machu Pichu. The site is in serious danger from erosion: in 2001, a survey reported that a large section was in imminent danger of destruction.

Machu Piccu

The dominance of Andean civilization by the Incas, whose empire at the time of the Spanish conquest extended over most of South America west of the Andes, from Ecuador to central Chile, was a recent achievement. Inca legends go back no further than AD 1200, and it was not until the mid-15th century that the power of the Incas, the 'Children of the Sun', was established in Peru. The greater empire was won in the last quarter of the century, only to be extinguished by the arrival of the Spaniards under Pizarro in 1532.

The Inca empire was a notable triumph over its topography, most of its cities, including Cuzco, the capital, being situated far up in isolated mountain valleys. Good roads, though never travelled by wheeled vehicles, connected the towns and outposts, although

The Cliff Palace at Mesa Verde. The circular structure in the foreground is a kiva, revealed by excavation.

Mesa Verde

The Mesa Verde National Park in Colorado, south-west USA, was established in 1906 to protect the ancient dwellings of the Pueblo people, which had been cut into the sheer cliffs. Long deserted, they were rediscovered in about 1890 by cowboys. Nearly 2,000 years ago, the site was occupied by Basket Makers who were able to raise crops such as maize, beans and squash on the green (*verde*) table tops (*mesa*) of the cliffs. They made circular pits for storage which, lined with stone and roofed, they later adapted as dwellings. Later they built stone houses, sometimes of two or more storeys, above ground.

The famous cliff dwellings were constructed by their descendants between the 12th and 14th centuries, probably as a defence against marauding Navajo and Apache. The ground floor had no doors or windows, and access to the higher floors could only be reached by ladders, easily removed when danger threatened. Access to the ground floor was through a hole in the ceiling, and upper storeys were reached by the same means. There were also sacred chambers, called *kivas*, below ground level.

The main construction material was hand-cut stone, fashioned with great skill, and adobe (mud) mortar. Ceilings were built by laying cross-beams which supported laths made from smaller branches, plastered over with adobe. Ascending storeys were recessed, creating a terraced effect, like a ziggurat. Living rooms average about 194sq ft (18sq m). A large number of different groups combined to build these massive communal residences, the most spectacular of the ruined buildings being the so-called Cliff Palace, which was inhabited between about 1100 and 1300. It contains about 200 rooms, plus 23 *kivas*.

The buildings were abandoned early in the 14th century, when the people moved farther south to construct smaller *pueblos* with better access to water. The move may have been prompted by the raids of nomadic tribes or dissension among the different tribal groups, but archaeologists have identified a severe drought between 1272 and 1299 which may also have contributed to the abandonment of Mesa Verde.

A general view of the site, tucked into the cliff. The population must have been well in excess of 400.

The Classical World

CHAPTER TWO

Temples of Paestum

Temple of Apollo, Bassae

Parthenon, Athens

Erechtheion, Athens

Theatre, Epidaurus

Stadium, Olympia

Pont du Gard, Nîmes

Maison Carrée, Nîmes

Colosseum, Rome

Pantheon, Rome

Baths of Caracalla, Rome

Diocletian's Palace, Split

The driving force of ancient Greek architecture was religious: the search for the perfect temple, the home of a god, which they believed was a matter of proportions, in fact a mathematical enterprise. Although not immune to foreign influence (the Ionic Order was ultimately of Eastern origin), the Greeks had a profound respect for tradition, and were in general conservative. Decorative details such as metopes and triglyphs derived from functional aspects of a wooden structure, the ends of the cross-beams and the spaces between them, and their stone or marble buildings followed the same form as their wooden predecessors, being based on the post and lintel. This is an architecture of straight lines, though, in fact, owing to the Greek grasp of entasis, perfectly straight lines are rare in, for instance, the Parthenon. This Athenian temple is often called the nearest thing to a perfect building and represents the culmination of about 150 years of evolution of the Classical Doric Order. Other beautiful buildings, such as theatres, were built in Classical Greece, and in the Hellenistic era, from the late 4th century BC, different types proliferated. Gifted artists were even engaged for private houses, and decoration became more elaborate, with the Corinthian Order displacing the pure simplicity of the Doric.

The Greeks were not ignorant of the arch, it was simply irrelevant to

them. The arch makes possible the vault and the dome, and where Greek architecture is based on straight lines, Roman architecture is rounded. The Roman answer to the Parthenon is the Pantheon: although strongly influenced by Greece, Roman architecture is remote from Greek in both spirit and technique, although, ironically, the actual architects of Roman buildings were often Greeks. The chief structural element in Greece, the column, in Rome became merely decorative. In a basilica, the most characteristic Roman building, the columns are inside, their structural function taken over, as in the Maison Carrée in Nîmes (p. 39), by walls. Types of Roman building are more varied, including palaces, baths, amphitheatres, etc., often of colossal size, ingenious design and in later times elaborately decorative, as at Split in Croatia (p. 44–45). The Romans were excellent technicians who were willing to experiment. What made their domes and vaults, and hence their vast interiors, as in the Baths of Caracalla, (p. 43), possible, was their development of concrete, often used together with brick. Their technical ability produced many utilitarian structures, some, like the apartment blocks of Rome, to poor standards; others, like the Pont du Gard (p. 38), ageless monuments to their style and efficiency.

Temples of Paestum

Paestum, the Roman name for the Greek colony of Poseidonia in southern Italy, on the shores of the Tyrrhenian Sea, about 60 miles (100km) south of modern Naples, flourished during the 6th–4th centuries BC. It sometimes happens that Classical Greek remains in Italy and Sicily are better preserved than counterparts in Greece; at Paestum there are two large, early Doric temples of about 460 BC, almost contemporary with the Temple of Zeus at Olympia, plus a smaller, slightly later one. Although there have been losses since Piranesi engraved the remains of the Temple of Hera (formerly called 'the Basilica' because its patron was unknown) in the 18th century, both this and the so-called Temple of Neptune (the Roman Poseidon) are still remarkably well preserved. The exterior columns are standing and, inside, there are survivals of both tiers of the two storeys.

Work in the colonies was generally less refined than in Greece, and the Paestum temples are built of travertine stone, common in Italy, though they would have been covered with marble stucco. The Temple of Neptune has 14 columns, while the Temple of Hera has 18, and nine on the ends, an unexpected number in relation to the dimensions, but no doubt planned to create an effect no longer evident. The columns in the *cella* have a considerable convex curve (*entasis*), greater than in any other known temples. That makes them seem taller and stronger but, compared with the Parthenon, these temples have a rather heavy look.

Another characteristic of buildings outside Greece was that the builders felt less strictly bound by convention, for instance in introducing Ionic features in the Doric Order. The flutes of the columns of the Paestum temples end in a semicircle, usually an Ionic characteristic, and they have an almost unique feature in the rounded band of the capitals, known as the *echinus*. Normally plain, they are carved with a decorative pattern, each one different from its neighbours. The only other known example of this occurs in the small temple, usually called the Temple of Ceres, built a generation or two later.

The former Greek colony was taken over by Latins (Romans) in 273, whereupon the Temple of Poseidon (below) became the Temple of Neptune.

The site at Bassae with archaeological excavations in progress.

Temple of Apollo, Bassae

The Temple of Apollo at Bassae is remarkable in representing all three of the Classical Greek Orders. A hexastyle temple, with six columns across the front of the porch, and 13 columns along the sides, it was built in about 430 BC, in grey limestone with a marble frieze and *metopes*, by the little state of Phigalia as thanksgiving for deliverance from plague. The architect was Ictinus, architect of the Parthenon. Although there is a family relationship to the Parthenon, in some respects the temple at Bassae, though probably built later, harks back to earlier traditions. A possible explanation is that it was influenced by the earlier Temple of Apollo at Delphi, the god's chief shrine, a theory supported by the unusual orientation of the temple, which faces north, towards Delphi. It is Doric outside and Ionic inside, but it also had at least one Corinthian capital (the earliest known) on a solitary free-standing column, which supported the frieze between *cella* and *adytum* (the inner sanctuary), where there is usually a wall, and probably others on adjacent half-columns. (It may be significant that the Corinthian Order is better suited to angles than the Ionic.)

High in the mountains of Arcadia, the temple was unknown except to locals until it was discovered by a French architect in 1765. His investigation was cut short by murderous bandits, but his report aroused widespread interest and resulted in the first major international archaeological expedition (British, Germans, Scandinavians and others) in 1811–12. Given the early date, it was carried out in a responsible, scientific manner and was a great success; the archaeologists seem to have enjoyed themselves eating roast kid, drinking rough wine from goatskin flasks, and watching rustic dances. Some of the marbles eventually found their way to the British Museum, but the Corinthian capital was unfortunately not among them. Though there are more colourful explanations of its disappearance, it was probably inadvertently left behind on the site.

Parthenon, Athens

The Parthenon, the shrine built by the Athenians for their patron goddess Athena is possibly the world's most famous building, and is as near as possible to perfection. It represents the climax of the Doric style, the first of the three Orders, and the one that engaged the Greeks longest and most intensely. Aesthetically, the main criticism of the Doric Order is that it is inclined to be heavy, but the Parthenon, though much the largest temple in Greece, demonstrates by the beauty of its design that this effect is not inevitable. Unusually, it has eight (not six) columns across the porch, and 17 along each side. The temple stands on the highest point of the Acropolis, and would have been visible from any spot in Periclean Athens. Built in Pentelic marble (the whitest) between 447 and 436 BC, its architects were Ictinus and Callicrates. The sculpture was by Pericles' friend, the genius Phidias, though naturally many hands were employed. Originally it contained an image of the goddess 40-ft (12-m) high, by Phidias, in gold and ivory.

At close quarters, the sheer size of the temple is a surprise, being disguised by the perfection of the proportions and subtle devices such as the slight convex curve of the columns (*entasis*) to correct the optical illusion that makes straight columns look concave. Such devices required extraordinary mathematical calculation as well as building skill. The columns are over 34-ft (10-m) high and measure 74in (188cm) in diameter at the base. A well-built man leaning against one fits into the curve of a single flute.

Renaissance drawings show that the Parthenon survived two millennia in good condition, but in 1687 it was partly destroyed by an explosion during war between Venice and the Ottoman Turks, who had turned it into a mosque and were currently using it as an arsenal. Thereafter it deteriorated steadily, a process currently accelerating due to atmospheric pollution. In 1801–05 Lord Elgin rescued, though the Greeks say stole, the famous Elgin marbles (now in the British Museum), including substantial fragments of Phidias' masterpiece, the frieze, which was 524-ft (160-m) long. The frieze was 40ft (12m) above the floor and therefore quite hard to see so, in order to compensate, Phidias designed it with the background to the figures tilted slightly forward.

The Parthenon is a larger, subtler and more refined version of the Paestum temples and represents the climax of the Classical Doric Order.

BELOW
Detail of the frieze.

Athenian heroes Erectheus, for whom the temple is named, and his brother Butes. It was sited, according to legend, where Poseidon, brother of Zeus and god of the sea, who first claimed possession of the city, thrust his trident into the ground. The result was that a salt-water well sprang up within the precincts of the Erectheion. (Zeus later granted precedence to Athena on the grounds that the olive tree she had planted predated Poseidon's well.)

The decorative sculpture of the Erectheion is of the same superlative quality as that of the Parthenon. The best-known feature of the building is the south porch, associated with the cult of Athena, in which the columns are replaced by *caryatids*, sculpted female figures, which are slightly more than life-size and combine the Classical attributes of strength and beauty. As the temple appears today, the second *caryatid* from the left is a copy, cast in Portland cement, the original having been removed by Lord Elgin. (One of Elgin's associates planned to deconstruct the whole temple and take it back to England but was frustrated by lack of available shipping.)

The Erechtheion, with the caryatid porch to the right. This remarkable little Ionic temple flaunts the rules with perfect assurance.

Erechtheion, Athens

The Erechtheion belongs to the great reconstruction of the Acropolis of Athens, set in motion by Pericles after the Persian Wars, and stands to the north of the Parthenon. The finest building in the Ionic Order, which, having originated in the cities of Ionia, was just becoming fashionable in mainland Greece, it is sometimes attributed to Mnesicles, who designed the Propylaea, the monumental gateway to the Acropolis. It was built in marble between 421 and 406 BC, and its plan is peculiar and unique, since it has three façades or porches, east, north and south. All of these are at different levels, the result of a sloping site and a profusion of divinities, for the temple was dedicated to not one but three – Athena, Poseidon, and Hephaestos – as well as to the

Theatre, Epidaurus

Most Greek theatres were radically changed in later times: the large theatre at Epidaurus is the best surviving example that retains its original form, though it has been considerably restored in recent times. It was probably built around 300 BC and is ascribed to Polykleitos the Younger, who also designed the Tholos, a rare circular building with a cone-shaped roof, in the same area.

Greek theatres were built in the open on a hillside, exploiting the natural slope to provide clear sight lines for a large audience. The audience sat on benches, first wooden, later of stone, in a semicircle. A central block of seats at the front, originally occupied by the priests of Dionysus, whose rites were the starting point for the development of Greek drama, was reserved for important persons, but otherwise seating arrangements seem to have been democratic. Entrance was at one time free, and even after admission charges were introduced the poor did not have to pay. 'Tickets' in the form of bronze tags have been found. The performance took place in a large circular, later semicircular, space called the *orchestra*. The altar to Dionysus, once placed in the centre, had been removed by the 4th century BC, though its position can still be seen in the theatre at Athens. Behind the *orchestra* was a permanent structure, the *skene*, somewhat resembling a temple façade. It contained the actors' dressing rooms, the few props and stage machinery, the main item of which was a kind of crane enabling an actor impersonating a god to descend from the sky – the original *deus ex machina*. The theatre at Epidaurus had a raised stage with a ramp

connecting with ground level. The *orchestra* and the seating have been restored, but not the buildings.

The theatre measured about 390ft (119m) across: though large, it was not unique, having a similar audience capacity to the theatre at Syracusa of about 14,000, a figure to make contemporary impresarios blink. Its acoustics are famous, and it is still in use for the annual summer festival of the Greek National Theatre.

The theatre at Epidaurus was one of the last to preserve the circular orchestra (not visible here).

Stadium, Olympia

Olympia was the centre of the biggest religious festival of ancient Greece, and of the associated Olympic Games which, according to tradition, were first held in 776 BC. The Olympia complex is something of a jumble as town planning did not interest the Greeks; but at its heart was the Temple of Zeus, built between 470 and 456 BC and at that time the largest building in Greece. The stadium was originally next to it, but was later moved farther east, out of the sanctuary precincts. Events, in which only men took part, though women's races were probably held in the Archaic period, included wrestling, boxing and chariot-racing, as well as track and field events, especially foot races.

What was then just a slight depression in the ground became the centre of intensive German archaeological exploration in 1936, inspired by the Olympic Games in Berlin that year, and continued, after a gap imposed by war, until the 1960s. The end result was the virtual restoration of the stadium to the form it had taken in the 4th century BC. Races were not run, as now, on an oval track, but in a straight line, so that the main area of the stadium was a narrow rectangle, measuring about 208 x 33yd (190 x 30m). The athletes began from a starting gate and ran from end to end. The shortest race was the *stade* (the origin of the word stadium), which was one length. There was also a medium-distance (two lengths) and a long-distance (20 lengths) race, the athletes rounding a post at each end. Athletes competed naked, but there was also a race for armed men. The excavations revealed the foundations of other details, including bathhouses with hot-air furnaces to heat the water and provide underfloor heating, the umpires' box about halfway down one side, hand weights held by long-jumpers to gain momentum, and a 4th-century BC building that appears to have been something like a luxury hotel for the richer competitors. Access to the arena was through a tunnel passing under the sloping bank where spectators sat, latterly on tiers of stone benches.

Pont du Gard, Nîmes

The Romans regarded nature as a challenge to be overcome in much the same way as they regarded their enemies. The straightness of their roads is often remarked upon, and although the Romans were not so foolish as to build a road up and over a hill if there was an easier way around it, they did take satisfaction in overcoming natural obstacles. Armies would ford rivers, or build a temporary 'bridge' of boats, but it was preferable to demonstrate mastery over water by building bridges. Permanent bridges and aqueducts were usually built of stone, and many still stand.

A good water supply was essential in any Roman town, where the liking for frequent bathing raised consumption, and sometimes water had to be brought from a very long distance – ideally by tapping a mountain spring from which it would run for miles downhill. Aqueducts best demonstrate the skill of the Romans as construction engineers. The aqueduct at Segovia is over 900-yd (820-m) long with two tiers of arches made of granite blocks without mortar. The Pont du Gard, in the south of France, is one of the most impressive sights imaginable. It is a relatively short section of an aqueduct that was nearly 15-miles (24-km) long, built by Agrippa (also responsible for the original Pantheon in Rome) around 14 BC to supply the thriving settlement of Nemausus (Nîmes).

The bridge that carries the aqueduct across the gorge of the River Gard for about 300yd (275m) consists of two tiers of arches each about 65-ft (20-m) high, with a third tier of much smaller arches. The channel on the top of that, about 180-ft (55-m) above the river, is about a 3-ft (1-m) wide and has cemented sides covered with stone slabs. The first tier carries what until recently was the main road, and it is also possible to walk along the water channel, providing you are not affected by vertigo.

The Pont du Gard is a testament to the Romans' determination to ensure a constant supply of clean water.

Maison Carrée, Nîmes

Roman temples, up to about the 1st century BC, generally followed Greek design, at least in principle, and were indeed sometimes built by Greek architects. However, there were also differences: the Romans were less inclined to respect the Greeks' strict purity of style or order, and they were given to elaborate on ornamentation, sometimes to a fault. It is not surprising that the Corinthian Order was their favourite because it offered greater decorative opportunities than Doric, which the Romans disdained, or Ionic. Many of the differences, however, were more fundamental, and can be traced to native Italian, especially Etruscan, sources.

Some of these are demonstrated in the little temple known as the Maison Carrée, in Nîmes (Roman Nemausus), in Provence, a place that in the 1st century AD, when the temple was built, has been described as 'more Roman than Rome'. The large raised platform or podium is over 11-ft (3-m) high, with a flight of steps providing access to the façade, features found in Etruscan temples. The *cella* is set well back, the porch being three columns deep in the common Greek manner, and is broad enough to cover the entire width, so that the lateral columns are engaged with the *cella* wall and the peristyle, or colonnade, disappears. This too is characteristic of Etruscan temples.

It is a particularly beautiful building: its harmonious proportions and the fine sculptural decoration of the entablature and Corinthian capitals have been ascribed to the fact that a Greek colony existed here before the town, founded by well-subsidized Roman army veterans. However, the temple has imperial

associations. It bears an inscription to the sons of the Emperor Augustus, and it is likely that the architect was an imperial appointee.

The Maison Carrée, which would have stood originally in the forum, is a gem, a perfect example of its type; but it owes its fame to some degree to the fact that it is so miraculously and uniquely well preserved, the exterior remaining virtually unchanged since it was built.

The Maison Carrée from the side, showing the high base and the engagement of the flanking columns with the cella *wall.*

The Colosseum was used as a handy quarry by local house builders until the pope declared it a Christian shrine in the 18th century.

OPPOSITE
The floor has disappeared to reveal the maze of subterranean rooms.

Colosseum, Rome

It is difficult to imagine the people of Periclean Athens enjoying the kind of entertainment that occurred in the Colosseum in Rome, at any rate in later imperial times, and the amphitheatre, though with obvious similarities to a theatre, is a type of building not found in ancient Greece. At least three Roman amphitheatres have survived in a fair state of preservation, good enough still to be used, though not for gladiatorial combats or mass slaughter, in Arles, Nîmes and Rome itself.

They are all similar, but the Roman Colosseum is the largest and finest. Besides its aesthetic merit, it is of great structural interest because of the special problems facing the builders, such as security and access, and the ways in which they solved them. It is sometimes said that an architect who could build an amphitheatre could build anything.

The Colosseum, built in AD 70–80, is about 160-ft (49-m) high and 615-ft (187-m) across at the widest point, and held nearly 50,000 people. Much of the four-tiered exterior arcades is still standing, and demonstrates the Roman method of building a massive structure with a combination of order and arch – Greek decoration and Roman construction. The three main tiers illustrate the three Greek Orders, Doric, Ionic and Corinthian in ascending rank. The fourth, walled tier was added later and was originally of wood, and statues once stood in the open arches of the first three tiers. The walls are brick or stone, but the carved decoration and seating is marble. Staircases within the walls give access to passages separating blocks of seats, and each tier has two adjacent circulating corridors. The vaulting problem alone was

enormous, as changing levels, tapering diameters and varying angles, caused by the oval plan, had to be catered for. There was a retractable canvas roof to keep the sun off, which was maintained by professional sailors. The arena itself, 278ft (85m) by 180ft (55m), was supported on joists. Underneath was space for gladiators and wild animals.

ABOVE and BELOW
Details of the rotunda.

BELOW RIGHT
Façade of the portico.

Pantheon, Rome

The Pantheon is probably the most admired of all Roman buildings for its combination of aesthetic quality and structural brilliance. A circular temple with a rectangular porch, it was built from AD 118–c.128, probably supervised by that most cultured of Roman emperors, Hadrian, and was a replacement for another older building built in 25 BC by Agrippa, the son-in-law of Augustus. The original inscription to Agrippa was retained, which caused much confusion over the dating of the Pantheon for many years.

Considering what it has suffered, the Pantheon's very existence is something of a miracle. It survived the Barbarian invasions and the vandalism of early Christians. It was plundered by rulers such as the Byzantine

Emperor Constans II, who stole the gilded bronze plates from the dome and re-covered it in lead, and Pope Urban VII, who removed the bronze beams of the porch in 1625 because he had another use for them.

Unusually for a Classical temple, the interior is far more spectacular than the exterior, and the one obvious design fault is the clumsy junction of porch and *cella*. The porch has 16 columns, each cut from a single block of grey granite, with the rear ones red. Capitals and bases, in the Corinthian Order, are in Pentelic marble and, before the temple was converted into a Christian church, a bronze relief of Zeus crushing recalcitrant Greeks filled the tympanum. The bronze doors, almost unparalleled for their workmanship, were originally gilded.

The *cella* is a brilliantly planned masterpiece of lighting and proportions. The diameter is 142ft (43m), and the total height is the same, divided equally between wall and dome. The dome, which is slightly larger than that of St Peter's, was made possible by the Romans' command of building in concrete. Above the coffered panels, it consists of alternate layers of concrete and brick, about 21-ft (6-m) thick at the base, diminishing to less than 5ft (1.5m) at the crown. Weight, which is further diminished by reducing the specific gravity of the mortar towards the top, is concentrated on four massive but unobtrusive piers. The only natural light comes from the circular opening, or *oculus*, at the centre of the dome.

Baths of Caracalla, Rome

In Roman society, the public baths fulfilled a variety of social functions that it would be difficult to find nowadays all in one place, if within one city, and could certainly not be obtained so cheaply, sometimes, indeed, for nothing. There were over 800 such establishments in imperial Rome, though they varied greatly in size and quality. Roman citizens went to the baths for many purposes, besides bathing: they were a place of leisure, for general social gossip or perhaps for conducting important business affairs. After bathing, the client could have a massage, perhaps medical treatment, and he (rarely she)

could eat and drink, play games and sports, and enjoy live entertainment. The larger establishments included restaurants and theatrical performances, gardens and fountains, perhaps a sports stadium, and large public halls for lectures and debates.

The bathing itself, in a society which placed bodily and spiritual health on a roughly equal footing, was quite a complex process. One might start in the hot room (*caldarium*), have a rub-down with a strigil (scraper), then into the cold swimming bath, followed by a massage and a rub-down with scented oils.

Many emperors built public baths, but the finest surviving are the Baths of Caracalla (AD 212–216), ruined of course, but less than others, and with a graphic record going back to the Renaissance, when more was intact. They

covered an area of over 270,000sq ft (25,000sq m), including the huge central hall of 183 x 79ft (56 x 24m), which was covered by intersecting barrel vaults and supported on massive piers. Being higher than the surrounding buildings, it was lit by a clerestory. The moderately heated *tepidarium* and the hot *caldarium*, heated by hot air from furnaces blown though openwork bricks, were covered by a dome, while the *frigidarium*, which had plenty of room for spectators, was open to the sky. While the exterior was rather plain, constructed of brick and stucco, the interior was lavishly decorated, with marble floors and walls and a great deal of sculpture, some of it from Greece, which was to be thoroughly plundered during the Renaissance.

The sheer scale of the ruins of the Baths of Caracalla, which were not the largest in Rome, Trajan's baths being larger, strikes the visitor with awe.

Diocletian's Palace, Split

The Palace of Diocletian at Spljet (Split, or Spalato), on the Dalmatian coast of Croatia, was more than a residence, being more like a small, fortified town. Nevertheless, besides being a statement of imperial power and prestige, one of Diocletian's purposes for building it was as a retirement home, and he moved there on abdicating his imperial office in 305.

Like a Roman fort, the palace (and, today, the medieval town) is contained within a rectangle measuring about 700 x 580ft (213 x 177m), and is guarded by walls and projecting square towers on the three landward sides. At the centre of each wall was a gateway flanked by octagonal towers, the main gateway being the Porta Aurea (Golden Gate), still in reasonable condition on the north side. The south side, fronting the Adriatic, was occupied by the Grand Gallery, where the imperial apartments were located beyond a colonnade. A seaward gate in the centre gave access to the interior via an underground passage. Intersecting cross-streets met at the centre of the rectangle, and the most sacred buildings, including the barrel-vaulted Temple of Jupiter and the Emperor's domed, octagonal Mausoleum, were in the southern half.

Over the centuries, Split has been subjected to the usual ravages of time and unsympathetic inhabitants, and much has been lost or obscured. Some has gone since the great English Neoclassical architect Robert Adam visited it and made the careful drawings engraved for his book on the palace in 1764. More recently, painstaking archaeologists have disinterred and restored other parts. The Mausoleum, the most important building,

probably benefited from being turned into a church around the 9th century, the Romanesque bell tower that now looms over it being raised in the 13th century. Much of the Temple of Jupiter, built of finely cut limestone blocks, also survives, in particular the coffered vault and some marvellously rich sculptural decoration in the Corinthian capitals and entablature. Otherwise, little of the imperial apartments of the palace – baths, halls, temples, libraries, gardens – can now be seen, having succumbed to medieval building when Split was a prosperous commercial entrepôt for Balkan-Venetian trade: but the extensive basements remain, preserved by centuries of rubbish-dumping.

OPPOSITE
The peristyle of
Diocletian's palace.

RIGHT
The 13th-century
Romanesque bell tower.

THE MEDIEVAL WORLD

CHAPTER THREE

Santa Maria Maggiore, Rome

Hagia Sophia, Constantinople (Istanbul)

San Vitale, Ravenna

Charlemagne's Cathedral, Aachen

Mont-Saint-Michel, Normandy

Gravensteen, Ghent

Strasbourg Cathedral

Château de Chillon

Saint Sophia, Kiev

Durham Cathedral

Ely Cathedral

Canterbury Cathedral

Tower of London

Abbey of Cluny

Mainz Cathedral

Worms Cathedral

Windsor Castle

Wartburg

Edinburgh Castle

Krak des Chevaliers

Laon Cathedral

Chartres Cathedral

Notre Dame, Paris

Bourges Cathedral

Royal Chapel, Palermo

Salamanca Cathedrals

Amiens Cathedral

Leaning Tower of Pisa

Reims Cathedral

Beauvais Cathedral

Santiago de Compostela

Borgund Church, Norway

Château de Blois

Brussels Cathedral

Cloth Hall, Ypres

Palazzo Pubblico, Siena

Burgos Cathedral

Castel del Monte, Apulia

Château d'Angers

Marienburg Castle

Rochester Castle

Doge's Palace, Venice

Caernarvon Castle

Cologne Cathedral

Rouen Cathedral

Münster Cathedral

Regensburg Cathedral

Salisbury Cathedral

Toledo Cathedral

Florence Cathedral

Palace of the Popes, Avignon

Cathedral of St Vitus, Prague

Ulm Cathedral

Rambouillet

Guarda Cathedral

Vienna Cathedral

Milan Cathedral

Kremlin, Moscow

Old Hospital, Beaune

Seville Cathedral

Frauenkirche, Munich

Palaces of Sintra

Christiansborg

When Christianity became the religion of the Roman Empire in the 4th century, church-building began on a large scale. Two main types emerged: the West favoured the Roman basilica, a rectangular building that in time produced transepts and became cruciform. The East preferred the round church, dramatically, in the miraculous Hagia Sophia in Constantinople (p. 50–51), an early example of Byzantine architecture which was not equalled in the next millennium. It was also an early example of the principle of the pendentive, which solved the problem of erecting a dome on a square base. Byzantine architecture had interesting offshoots in Armenia and in Russia, while in the West there was little of note until the Carolingian period (8th–10th centuries), of which the most notable survivor is Charlemagne's church at Aachen (p. 53).

The Romanesque style was established by the 10th century (some would include Carolingian) and is especially associated with the Abbey of Cluny (p. 64) and its offshoots. The Christian religion was the main unifying factor as, like its successor, Gothic, the Romanesque style was subject to marked regional variations. The English variety is known as Norman, being associated with the Norman Conquest of 1066. Another complication is that builders were becoming more willing to experiment, and constant rebuilding meant that comparatively few purely

Romanesque buildings have survived.

Romanesque is the architecture of the round arch and the barrel vault. Churches are clearly planned, sometimes with a series of apses in the east, or with chapels off an ambulatory. Shafts or piers, often with geometric patterns, are heavy, and interiors tend to be dark. Gothic, which first appeared in the mid-12th century abbey of St-Denis, near Paris, is by contrast an architecture of light, with huge windows of stained glass, made possible by the pointed arch in accompaniment with weight-reducing features, such as the rib vault and the flying buttress. None of these features was entirely unknown in the Romanesque period and to a large extent the changes were motivated by aesthetic as much as structural considerations. There is no functional reason for the immensely high vaults to which Gothic builders aspired.

Gothic architecture covered a wider area than Romanesque and, while the great Gothic cathedrals stand supreme as the finest achievement of European art in any period, with the growth of towns and a wealthy merchant class, the ever-changing Gothic style was adapted for secular buildings. The Cloth Hall at Ypres (p. 86) and the Doge's Palace in Venice (p. 94–95) are examples, not only of different types of building, but also of the great stylistic differences contained under the umbrella of 'Gothic'.

Santa Maria Maggiore, Rome

Christian churches began to appear in the Roman Empire after the Emperor Constantine adopted Christianity in 313. Two types developed, the basilica, a rectangular hall with lower side aisles to allow for a clerestory, and the round or octagonal church. S. Maria Maggiore (c. 432–440) is an example of the first type, which came to be almost universal in the West, while S. Vitale in Ravenna is an example of the second type, which was preferred in the Byzantine Empire and produced the astonishing Hagia Sophia in the 6th century.

One of the advantages of the basilica church was that it offered the opportunity for a splendid colonnade dividing the aisles from the nave. In S. Maria Maggiore, lines of Ionic columns form stately margins to the broad nave. They carry a Classical entablature and, above, the upper walls of the clerestory have muted Corinthian pilasters between the windows, below which are mosaic panels illustrating incidents from the Bible. Mosaics also cover the arch that extends into the apse.

The church is an example of a recurring phenomenon in the history of Western architecture, the revival of Classicism. At one time scholars thought that the building must date from the 2nd century because in style it resembles the architecture of the reign of Trajan (AD c. 53–117). (Methods of dating have since improved; for instance, it has been possible to date early brick churches in Rome by the width of the mortar between the bricks.) S. Maria Maggiore is associated with a revival of an earlier, Classical style of about the time of Pope Sixtus II, and was one of several

large religious foundations in what was a time of prolific church-building.

Although it is not hard to visualize the original appearance, the church has been considerably altered since the 5th century. The apse was rebuilt and a transept added in the

13th century. The coffered ceiling and aisle vaults belong to the Renaissance, the *baldachino* over the altar to the 18th century. Much of the rest of the fabric has been restored, but in the original style.

Santa Maria Maggiore has been much altered, but behind the Baroque façade the early Christian church is still recognizable.

Hagia Sophia, Constantinople (Istanbul)

Early in the reign of Justinian (527–565), riots broke out in Constantinople, in the course of which several important buildings were destroyed. They included the Church of Divine Wisdom (Hagia Sophia), which was both the cathedral church of Constantinople and the palace church of the emperor. Imperial prestige demanded rapid reconstruction; moreover, the new church was expected to be far more magnificent than the one it replaced, a building to astound the eye of the beholder. Justinian entrusted the job to Anthemius of Tralles in Lydia, a scholar not known to have ever produced another building, and his nephew, Isidorus of Miletus. In just five years, between 532 and 537, they had built what is universally regarded as the supreme masterpiece of Byzantine architecture.

The crowning glory of Hagia Sophia is the dome. Here Anthemius' background in geometry was undoubtedly useful. Built in brick and measuring 106ft (32m) in diameter, it was an extraordinary feat of engineering, though it collapsed after an earthquake in 568 and was rebuilt by another Isidorus. Of course, the Romans had built domes and they had also used brick, though not for domes. But to build a dome on circular walls, as in the Pantheon, is comparatively simple compared with raising a dome over a square. Anthemius overcame the problem by the device of the pendentive, a concave, triangular section with the point at the right-angle of two walls or arches, rising to form a quarter-circle at the height of the arches. Such a structure transmits the weight of the dome evenly to the main supports at the

Views of the interior and exterior of Santa Sophia. The Church of Divine Wisdom is an example of a work of genius that, springing almost from nowhere, was imitated but never equalled. The church became a mosque in the 15th century.

corners. Screened aisles and galleries were employed to conceal the supports, so that the dome appears to float miraculously heavenward, a mysterious effect enhanced by the contrast between the well-lit central space and the dark surrounding aisles. The glittering mosaics, carved capitals and coloured marble

helped to justify Justinian's boast, when he first entered the finished building, that he had 'triumphed over Solomon'.

When the Ottoman Turks took Constantinople in 1453, Hagia Sophia became a mosque, and a model for other mosques. Today it is a museum.

San Vitale in Ravenna, the first great monument to the Byzantine style.

San Vitale, Ravenna

The city of Ravenna, about 60-miles (100-km) north-east of Florence, first flourished when its port became the main base for the Roman fleet in the Adriatic under Augustus. In the early 5th century, it was the imperial capital, and Theodoric the Goth made it his seat as ruler of Italy. When the generals of the Byzantine Emperor Justinian reconquered the West, Ravenna became Byzantium's western capital. The architecture of 6th-century Ravenna reflects a mixture of Italian and Eastern influences, notably in the characteristically Byzantine art of mosaics, which remained in fashion for 1,000 years. They are the most famous element of S. Vitale (built c. 540–48).

Sometimes called the first truly Byzantine Church, S. Vitale is Justinian's greatest monument after Hagia Sophia in Constantinople. In the 4th century, the earliest Christian churches had followed the general plan of the Roman basilica, but S. Vitale is centrally planned. The general form is octagonal, with a second, smaller octagon rising above the first, topped by a dome. The outline is broken by an apse in the east, a porch in the west, and several attendant chapels. Built in brick and plaster, its exterior appearance is plain, with understated buttressing pilasters at intervals along the walls and otherwise little decoration. Inside, it is a different story. The overall impression is of space and light, an effect enhanced by the pale marble columns and lofty arches. The Byzantine love of ornament is given full reign, with richly carved capitals and, especially in the presbytery, mosaics occupying every suitable space. Some of them depict the Byzantine court, including hierarchical portraits of the Emperor and his equally famous wife, Theodora, whose jewellery is represented in mother-of-pearl. The advantage of wall-mounted mosaics over their traditional use for floors, was that the artists could make more use of coloured glass cubes, too fragile to be satisfactory under foot. The effect of the stately procession, with figures ranged from left to right and the pale, large-eyed, solemn faces framed in a marvellous arrangement of brilliant colours, represents the apogee of Byzantine art.

Charlemagne's Cathedral, Aachen

The imperial chapel of Charlemagne is the finest surviving example of Carolingian architecture. When, in the late 8th century, Charlemagne chose Aachen (Aix-la-Chapelle) as his capital, he planned to create something that would rival the great imperial centres of Rome or Ravenna, both places he had visited. He attracted to Aachen such men as the Frankish scholar Einhard and the learned Englishman Alcuin, together with the finest available artists, craftsmen and scholars, which included Italians, Greeks, Provençals, Jews and even Arabs.

The basic form of the building is an octagon with a projecting apse. It is usually said to have been modelled on the Church of S. Vitale in Ravenna (opposite), although its simple strength is more Roman in spirit than Byzantine. The interior of the octagon, with its three tiers of arches and marble-columned arcades, appears much as it did in Charlemagne's time, and the simple, marble throne on which Charlemagne sat and later Holy Roman emperors were crowned, is still in place.

Otherwise the building has been greatly altered. The Carolingian apse was replaced in the 14th century with a lofty Gothic choir, the tall outer roof of the octagon was added in the 17th century, and the western steeple dates from 1884.

Its founder endowed the church with many relics and sacred objects, now housed in the treasury with other, later precious objects. In the 13th century, Charlemagne's remains were transferred to a shrine of gilded silver and copper, decorated with coloured enamels and gems. The figure of the emperor is shown holding the church in his hand, his crown informally tilted, and is in contrast to the solemn saints flanking him. In the 14th century, a silver and gilt bust was made to contain Charlemagne's brain case. An interesting addition to this piece, of unknown origin, reminds us that Charlemagne is claimed to be a founder of both the German and French nations; the shoulders of the bust bear a jewelled costume with German eagles, while a plinth on the base of it is studded with the French *fleur-de-lis*.

Gothic additions to the Carolingian chapel.

Mont-Saint-Michel from the landward side.

Mont-Saint-Michel, Normandy

The steep, rocky island of Mont-Saint-Michel, less than 3,280ft (1000m) in circumference and accessible overland at low tide, though the sands are treacherous, is crowned by the ancient abbey. It is one of the most famous sights in France, familiar to those who have never been there from tourist posters and advertising. Seen across a calm sea in the evening sunlight, it is a breathtaking sight.

According to legend, the Archangel Michael instructed Bishop Aubert in a dream to build the original chapel on the mount in the 8th century, when it attracted pilgrims then, as it still does today. It became a Benedictine abbey in the 10th century, and the oldest structure found is a Carolingian church of that time. Construction of the present buildings, originally in the Norman Romanesque style, dates from the early 11th century, but part of the abbey and the village below were burned by the Bretons in 1203, the monks later successfully defending themselves against English attacks during the Hundred Years War. Later buildings are Gothic. Part of the 13th-century reconstruction was La Merveille, which became the main monastic building. Because of the limited space, it was necessary to build upwards rather than out, and La Merveille is on three storeys. The vaulted Knights' Hall (Salle des Chevaliers), a beautiful specimen of Norman Gothic that was originally the Scriptorum, is on the second storey, with the refectory and cloister above it. The choir of the church was rebuilt in the Flamboyant style in the 15th century, and the tower and spire, topped by a gilded St Michael and the Dragon, 570-ft (174-m) above the sea, were erected in the 19th century.

The abbey gained a reputation for learning in the 12th century and held a famous library, which may explain why it was not damaged by the vandals of the French Revolution. However, monastic life had declined disastrously, and when the monastery was dissolved in 1790 there were only seven monks at Mont-Saint-Michel. It became a state prison under Napoleon, until it was rescued in 1863 and subsequently restored.

Gravensteen, Ghent

The people of Ghent have always manifested a sturdy desire for independence or, in the words of a medieval chronicler, an 'overbearing arrogance'. Their revolt of 1539, for example, brought upon them the vengeance of the Emperor Charles V who, in spite of having been born in the city, executed the leaders and quartered his underpaid troops all over town, with no instructions to be kind to their hosts.

The Gravensteen was the medieval stronghold of the counts of Flanders, and though now near the city centre, it would have been outside the town in the 9th century when it was first built. The site offered no natural topographical advantages, and the castle was protected by a wide moat which, however, failed to prevent two successful sieges in the 14th century. By 1539, however, the counts had moved out and the castle had passed into the hands of the dukes of Burgundy. Thereafter the history of the Gravensteen was less important and less violent. Various parts were converted into government offices and, for a time in the 19th century, even a factory.

The castle has an unusual appearance, chiefly due to the hanging turrets along the curtain wall, providing covering fire for the walls, which may have derived from experience of the Crusades. There are other indications of familiarity with Byzantine practice and the chapel has an unusual window in the form of a cross; but there is no known architectural prototype. Another striking feature is the gatehouse, defended by machicolated towers, which is large enough to suggest a kind of subsidiary castle in itself. The

keep, with large halls on two floors, is massive, and still dominates the city. The castle contains the usual horrors, a torture chamber and an *oubliette*, which was entered only by a trapdoor in the ceiling (and rarely left again).

There are some remains of the original

building in the base of the keep: otherwise, the Gravensteen today looks like an unusually well-preserved 13th-century castle, though this is chiefly due to a careful restoration in the late 19th century.

A restorative spruce up in recent times cannot conceal the turbulent heritage of the Gravensteen.

Strasbourg Cathedral

When the cathedral, of which only the crypt and parts of the east end remain, was first built in the early 11th century, Strasbourg was a powerful German city, and German architecture was approaching its zenith. The original building was destroyed by fire in 1176 and the cathedral was subsequently entirely rebuilt, changing in the course of the 13th century from heavy Romanesque into an harmonious example of High Gothic, whose aspiration to height, perhaps augmented by the comparatively tall houses of medieval Strasbourg that crowded around it, gives it a particular dynamism. In 1439 the spire eventually rose to 480ft (146m), the highest in Europe, and was a structure as bold, it was said, as the Tower of Babel. The impression of soaring growth is heightened by the tense upward momentum of towers, buttresses and gables, although the nave is less high than in most French contemporaries. Much of the design is credited to Erwin von Steinbach, who probably planned the sculpture of the west front, though it was not completed until the late 14th century. Building still continued thereafter, but in spite of the great span of years, Strasbourg maintains a remarkable artistic integrity.

During the Reformation, Strasbourg became Protestant, and many of the figures of saints were removed from the interior along with tombstones and a number of altars, making it today seem comparatively austere. The greyish sandstone, quarried locally, has also darkened with time. Strasbourg returned to Roman Catholicism when Alsace was ceded to France in 1681 but suffered more damage during the French Revolution, when many sculptures on the exterior were torn down and a law, fortunately disobeyed, was passed calling for the demolition of all church steeples. Of the surviving sculpture, perhaps most notable are the tympanum of the Death of the Virgin and the figures of the Church and the Synagogue. They flank the south transept, which inside contains the unusual, sculptural Judgement Pillar, marking the place where the bishop dispensed justice and mystery plays were performed. Like the Church and Synagogue figures, it was apparently the work of a group of itinerant craftsmen who were in Strasbourg in 1225, having previously worked at Chartres. Surprisingly, a good deal of medieval glass has survived, including two rose windows from the 12th century.

Château de Chillon

From a distance, the Castle of Chillon, with its cluster of turrets and pitched roofs, has a picturesque appearance that belies its strength as a fortress. Once the stronghold of the dukes of Savoy, whose territory straddled the French-Italian border, it stands on a rocky island not far from the shore of Lake Geneva, near Montreux, with the mighty slopes of the Alps providing a suitable backdrop. It was first built in the 10th century, and the lower portion of the donjon, or keep, dates from that time. It was expanded in the 11th century, and the Tower of the Dukes was built at the northern end. There was further, extensive rebuilding in the 13th century and, bar a few later accretions, it is the building which we see today.

Besides the surrounding water, the castle is guarded on the landward side by a double wall, with the outer walls interrupted by round, machicolated towers. The drawbridge has been replaced by a permanent bridge, leading through a gatehouse into the outer courtyard. A second gate gives access to the inner courtyard, which is virtually divided in two by the bulky keep. On the far side are two great halls, with magnificent 13th-century vaults and, to the north, the ducal apartments and Tower of the Dukes, including the red-ceilinged *camera domini*, or lord's chamber, the most interesting room in the castle.

Although the dukes moved their chief residence to Chambéry in the 13th century, and the castle was taken over by the city of Berne in the 16th century, it remained in occasional use. Lord Byron visited Chillon in 1816 and subsequently wrote his poem, *The Prisoner of Chillon*, which commemorates François

Bonnivard (1496–1570). A political enemy of the Duke, Bonnivard was held for six years in the impressive vaulted cellar, partly carved from the rock under the Great Hall, chained to a pillar. Byron scratched his name on what he believed to be the pillar in question.

The Castle of Chillon, exceedingly well preserved, is enhanced by its site, with the lake on one side, the mountains on the other.

The 13 domes of the cathedral, some of which are just visible above the trees, set a style which spread throughout Russia.

Saint Sophia, Kiev

In 988 Prince Vladimir, ruler of the old Russian state of Kiev, under the influence of Byzantium, adopted Greek Orthodox Christianity. When he returned to Kiev, bringing Byzantine icons, crosses and other sacred objects, he ordered the pagan idols of Kiev to be thrown into the river, where a few days later his people came to be baptized. These events mark the beginning of the Christian Middle Ages in Russia, in which Byzantine art and the Orthodox Church together formed the major theme of Russian culture.

The earliest churches of Kiev have not survived, though we know they were Byzantine in character and based on the form of a Greek cross. The Cathedral of St Sophia, founded in 1037, is probably the oldest survivor, but there is not much evidence of its original appearance, which is now that of a fine example of Ukrainian Baroque. A reconstruction of the original building shows a basilica with a brick dome and five aisles terminating in round apses, with cloister-like arcades on the other three sides. The exterior was banded with alternating horizontal courses of brick and pinkish mortar, producing a novel effect. Another striking feature, not derived from Byzantium, was the total of domes which, including the large central one, numbered 13, representing Christ and the Twelve Apostles. But the addition of new aisles and domes in the Baroque period obscures the 11th-century church.

It was designed to rival Hagia Sophia in Constantinople, whose dedication it shares, and inside, the immediate impression is of the skill with which the Byzantine architects handled the admission of daylight, a notable feature of the earlier Hagia Sophia. The chief decorative

features are frescoes and mosaics, the Orthodox alternative to the stained glass and sculpture of the Latin Church. Most famous is the powerful, almost intimidating mosaic of Christ Pantocrator ('Ruler of the Universe') in the central dome, which is lit by windows below. The largely glass mosaics illustrate the painstaking detail employed in their creation: in the huge mosaic of the Virgin Orans ('praying Virgin'), more complex parts such as a human face contain about 26 cubes per square inch.

Durham Cathedral

Durham Cathedral, built from 1093–1133, together with the bishop's palace and castle – a powerful combination of lay and ecclesiastical power in Norman England – share a spectacular site, high on a wooded, cliff-like peninsular all but circled by the River Wear far below. Seen from the west, the three great towers of the cathedral convey an impression of massive invulnerability and which nearly 1,000 years of history confirms.

Durham is the finest example of the Anglo-Norman version of the Romanesque style. Not only does it contain more Norman work unaltered by later generations, it is also the one Romanesque cathedral in England of truly remarkable design. It contains all the main Gothic features – pointed arches, ribbed vaults (probably the earliest in Europe) and flying buttresses (concealed above the vaults of the aisles), but remains essentially Norman in character and possesses a stylistic unity rare among English cathedrals. The massive central tower, for example, was built in the late 15th century but, lacking the usual pinnacles, it confirms the Anglo-Norman character of the whole structure.

Durham contains a famous relic, the body of St Cuthbert (died 687), once believed to work miracles, which was brought here by the monks of Lindisfarne in 995 to save it from the depredations of the Vikings. An elaborate shrine was built to house it, and the Chapel of the Nine Altars built around it. The unusual Galilee porch was built in about 1170 at the west end, after a previous attempt to build it at the eastern end was thwarted by cracking, interpreted as a sign of St Cuthbert's disapproval.

The interior, perhaps unexpectedly, is scarcely less impressive than the exterior. Great round columns decorated with geometric patterns, combining power and vigour, march down the nave alternating with composite piers, each about 10ft (3m) in diameter. Among the most interesting furnishings are the Neville Screen, carved in Caen stone with alabaster images.

Durham, untypical and in advance of its time, is one of the outstanding buildings of medieval Europe. Today, it is sited in what may seem a rather remote region, but in St Cuthbert's time and later, the early Anglo-Saxon kingdom of Northumbria was one of the most civilized places in Europe. The cathedral is a reminder of that heritage.

Durham Cathedral, high on a bluff above the River Wear, has some very advanced features which influenced architectural developments elsewhere.

Ely Cathedral

Driving north from Cambridge through the dead-flat fens of eastern England, the Cathedral Church of the Holy and Undivided Trinity appears above the ground-clinging mist like a heavenly apparition. This magnificent building is situated within a market town of little more than 10,000 people which has changed comparatively little in essence since the cathedral was built.

Of the Saxon original, developing from a 7th-century religious foundation endowed by a daughter of an East Anglian king, there is no trace, except for the 7th-century Cross of St Ovin, unearthed in archaeological excavations, and a window in the *triforium* (below the clerestory). The house was later destroyed by

the Vikings, but a new Benedictine monastery was founded on the site in the late 10th century, and the present cathedral was begun under the first Norman abbot in the 1080s. The nave, characteristically lengthy, at 208ft (63m), the lower part of the grand western tower that replaces the common arrangement of twin towers, the southern transept, and the superb Prior's Door with its tympanum of Christ in Glory, are Norman, all in place before the end of the 12th century, though the tower fell in the early 14th century and was rebuilt by Alan de Walsingham, who appears to have been responsible for the innovation that makes Ely Cathedral unique. The cruciform plan of most English cathedrals had the disadvantage that the central crossing, with four massive columns and arches at the corners to support a tower or steeple, was rather cramped. The solution at Ely, credited to Walshingham, was an octagon, in the Decorated style, with the arches of the nave and choir set obliquely, to open up the central space. The late 14th-century lantern at the top of the western tower repeats the octagonal form, with four long sides and, at the angles, four shorter ones.

After the octagon, the most famous feature of Ely is the beautiful, airy Lady Chapel, by a pupil of Alan de Walsingham from among the monks of Ely, and built in the second quarter of the 14th century. From 1566 to 1938 it served as a parish church.

Canterbury Cathedral

Canterbury Cathedral incorporates the entire history of the Christian Church in England since Pope Gregory I sent St Augustine to convert the English in Kent in 597. There are no visible traces of the original building, although the world of demons and monsters encapsulated in the capitals of the crypt embodies pre-Christian superstitions, and there are some fragments of the early Norman Benedictine abbey.

The double transepts of Canterbury were to influence other English cathedrals, such as Salisbury; but the most remarkable feature of the building is the length, especially of the eastern end, begun by William of Sens in 1175 and completed ten years later by William 'the Englishman', which was nearly twice as long as the 197-ft (60-m) nave of the 1390s. The latter is the work of a great 14th-century architect, Henry Yevele, and its slender piers and high arches make it one of the most spacious and distinguished interiors in the whole of medieval architecture. Despite this and other examples of the 14th-century Perpendicular style, Canterbury belongs predominantly to the Norman and Early English Gothic styles. It was constructed mainly in the warm stone imported from Caen in Normandy, but Purbeck marble was extensively employed inside, particularly in the choir, transepts and the Trinity Chapel, where the shrine of Thomas à Becket once stood.

Due to Canterbury's position as the seat of the English primate and importance as a place of pilgrimage, more of the stained glass, some of it from the same workshop as that of Chartres, has survived here than anywhere else in England. The windows of the Trinity Chapel, having escaped iconoclasts, 'improvers' and

German bombs, depict the miracles associated with the cult of Becket, the former chancellor and friend of King Henry II, who appointed him archbishop in the hope of securing his co-operation in subordinating the Church to the royal will. Becket's unexpected and bitter defiance led to his martyrdom at the hands of four of the King's toadying vassals in 1170, and the king himself, who understood public relations as well as any modern politician,

inaugurated the tradition of pilgrimage by walking barefoot to Canterbury to seek absolution. After him came thousands of pilgrims, guided by the long-vanished gilded angel on the top of the central spire, which was replaced by the lovely Bell Harry Tower, the crowning feature of this emotive building, built in the 1490s by John Wastell, architect of King's College Chapel, Cambridge.

BELOW LEFT
The Bell Harry Tower, which replaced the famous angel steeple that guided pilgrims from afar.

BELOW
One of the figures of English kings that give Canterbury a marked association with royalty.

Tower of London

The strategically placed castles of the early
Norman period in England were built as a
defence not so much against enemies as against
the Anglo-Saxon population. The Tower of
London is the most famous of these, erected on
the Thames at the south-eastern corner of the
old walled city. William the Conqueror was
responsible for the White Tower, whitewashed in
the late 12th century, hence its name, which has
changed very little since, except for the
somewhat dubious onion domes and the
windows, which were enlarged in more peaceful
times by Sir Christopher Wren. The remainder of
what is probably the greatest medieval fortress
in Europe, dates mainly from the 13th century,
although no intervening century has passed
without additions and alterations.

The Tower has served many purposes. It
was a royal palace until the 17th-century Civil
War, an arsenal and, for over 400 years, home
of the Royal Mint. In the 13th century it was
also a zoo, begun when the Emperor Frederick
II gave Henry III three leopards, and the
animals were only moved when London Zoo
was opened in 1834. The English Crown Jewels
were lodged there in a secure vault below the
19th-century Wellington Barracks, and the
unparalleled collection of weapons and armour
includes the codpiece of Henry VIII, which
childless women once stuck pins into in the
hope of conceiving.

But the Tower is popularly remembered as
a prison, especially for traitors, of whom about
50 were executed on Tower Hill. The most
recent internees were spies captured during the
Second World War. The princes who were
confined there in the 15th century by their
uncle, Richard III, were probably held in what
was later named the Bloody Tower. The Bell
Tower was the final residence of several of
Henry VIII's victims during the Reformation, and
Elizabeth I was briefly held there by her
Catholic half-sister, Mary I. A few prisoners
endeavoured to escape. A rebellious Welsh
prince made a bid for safety in 1244 but fell to
his death; more fortunate was Lord Nithsdale, a
supporter of the exiled Stewart dynasty, who
slipped away the night before his appointed
execution in 1716, disguised as a girl.

Old traditions are zealously maintained,
including the nightly Ceremony of the Keys,
over 700-years-old, the Yeomen Warders, or
'Beefeaters', in their pantomime Tudor uniforms,
and the daily feeding of the ravens, whose
departure from the Tower will foretell its fall.

A single tower is practically all that remains of the greatest abbey in Europe.

Abbey of Cluny

As the centre of the great reforming movement in monasticism in the 11th century, the Abbey of Cluny in Burgundy was one of the most influential places in Europe, with some 2,000 religious houses affiliated to it. It was virtually independent of any secular authority, and its church, the largest in Christendom, with its huge basilica and vast cluster of towers and chapels, must have had a dizzying effect on pilgrims setting eyes on it for the first time.

The abbey was originally founded in 910 and built (the second or third rebuilding) in its final form between 1088, when the foundation stone was laid by the Pope's emissary, and 1130. The finely ordered Burgundian Romanesque style that it typified was to be echoed, even imitated, in later Cluniac houses and can be seen today, especially on the pilgrims' route to Santiago de Compostella, in Spain, which Cluny supported.

According to Abbot Hugh, the abbey was built at the direction of St Peter and St Paul, who outlined its dimensions on the ground with a long rope. The speed with which the buildings were completed confirms that Cluny was extremely well endowed, as the costs must have been enormous. The church, whose nave was about 200-ft (60-m) long, could hold thousands of worshippers, and its size provoked some criticism, possibly the cause of Abbot Hugh's insistence that he was only following the saints' instructions. There was also controversy over the results of the Cluniac belief that the House of God (the 'lobby of the angels', as Hugh described it) should testify to his glory and be sumptuously adorned with the finest works that artists could provide. Such ostentation was fiercely attacked by St Bernard of Clairvaux, who joined the new Cistercian Order (1112).

Today it is possible to trace the outline of the abbey on the ground; but of the actual structure, all that remains besides traces of the basilica is one solitary tower and the south transept. The abbey was badly damaged in the French Wars of Religion and closed during the Revolution. The building was then demolished.

Mainz Cathedral

The three great Romanesque cathedrals of the Rhineland, Mainz, Speyer and Worms, form a close-knit group, perhaps because it would be possible to see them all in one day, though a less hectic schedule is preferable. They have obvious affinities: all are constructed of the same reddish sandstone from local quarries and, though Worms is later, all were built in roughly the same period. They make it easy to see why the Romanesque was less easily displaced by Gothic in this region than elsewhere.

The Romans noticed the strategic significance of the site where the Rivers Rhine and Main come together; Mainz is one of the oldest cities in Germany. Though frequently damaged by restless 'barbarian' tribes, it was an early centre of Christianity, and St Boniface, the first archbishop and primate of Germany, set out from there to convert the pagans in the 8th century. During the High Middle Ages, it was a rich imperial city, known as 'Golden Mainz', with a population not much smaller than it is today.

The cathedral is a memorial to the ecclesiastical patronage of the emperor Henry IV (1056–1105), though his cathedral building arose largely from his dispute with the pope. Of the three Rhineland cathedrals, Mainz is perhaps the grandest and certainly the most spacious, partly through the effect of later restorations and partly through certain Gothic features. Among these are the dominant western twin towers, usually considered a characteristically Gothic arrangement. In fact, the west end of the cathedral was built in the 13th century, but in the same style as the east end of over 100 years earlier. Gothic additions, such as the upper stages of the polygonal towers, appear sympathetic to the character of the building.

The cathedral has a turbulent history. The original basilica burned down on the day it was dedicated in 1009, and it was destroyed again in 1081. Fires, earthquake, a hurricane, shortage of finance, local riots and political quarrels, all interrupted construction of the present building. By the Renaissance it was set on a long decline, not arrested until Napoleon, shocked at its disrepair, ordered a major restoration in 1814

Mainz Cathedral, one of the great kaiserdome *(imperial cathedrals), has been much restored. The two crossing towers are 19th century.*

65

Worms Cathedral

Worms was the seat of a bishop in the 7th century, and perhaps earlier. There was also a palace where Charlemagne stayed and his daughter Emma was allegedly courted by the great Carolingian scholar, Einhard. The present cathedral was founded in the 11th century by Bishop Burchard, a powerful figure in the region, but the citizens of Worms (the name probably comes from the German *wurm*, a worm or maggot) later gained a degree of independence as a free imperial city. Worms was a frequent meeting place of the imperial diet, or legislative assembly, where in 1521 Martin Luther took his famous stand before the emperor Charles V. The citizens subsequently embraced Lutheranism, the cause of much damage during the Thirty Years' War, though the cathedral is now Roman Catholic.

Lacking limestone, most German cathedrals were built of materials such as sandstone that are much less durable, with the result that frequent restoration was necessary. There is very little that remains from the 12th century, but despite many later alterations, additions and restorations, the cathedral of St Peter and St Paul remains a noble example of German Romanesque architecture.

The plan is simple. The doubling up of major elements conveys a pleasing sense of order. A distinguishing feature, derived from the Carolingian style, is an apse at each end, though the eastern apse is concealed by a straight wall. This plan rules out a grand western façade, as in French Gothic cathedrals, and also a western entrance, the doors instead opening into the aisles of the nave, north and south. Another common feature is the twin round towers at each end. A shorter, octagonal tower over the central crossing is again echoed by a similar tower in the west, flanked by the slimmer round towers. Certain Italian features, such as the open galleries in the two octagons and the western twin towers, can be explained by the inclusion of Italy in the emperor's domain.

The interior is cool and stately, with scarcely any ornamentation, the tall, cliff-like walls and solid piers ascending austerely into Romanesque shadows.

The round towers of Worms Cathedral, with the octagonal tower between them, and Gothic additions in the foreground.

Windsor Castle

Windsor Castle has been a residence of the English monarchy for nearly 1,000 years, which makes it unique. There was a royal residence nearby in Saxon times, but William the Conqueror selected a site 2-miles (3-km) away, on a loop of the River Thames, when he came to build a *motte* castle here, one of several similar strongholds guarding, or threatening, London.

In plan, the figure-of-eight outline, stretching half-a-mile (1km) from east to west, reflects the 12th-century castle. A central *motte*, or mound, later surmounted by the Round Tower, or keep, divides the Lower Ward, in the west, from the Upper Ward, in the east. The modern entrance leads into the Lower Ward via Henry VIII's Gate.

Norman castles, which had to be put up fast, were originally wooden, though some believe that Windsor was stone from the start. Little, it seems, had been built by William's death in 1087, and little more was done until the reign of Henry II (1154–89), who built spacious royal apartments and started the enclosure wall and towers. Under John, the castle was twice besieged by rebellious barons, but not taken. It has never suffered another siege, although it was occupied by Parliamentary forces, who indulged in minor acts of anti-royalist vandalism during the Civil War of the 17th century. Later monarchs restored and expanded the castle over the centuries. Edward III founded St George's Chapel for his order of the Garter, though the present chapel dates from 1528.

The biggest reconstruction took place during the reign of George IV (1820–30). The architect was Sir Jeffrey Wyatville, who raised the Round Tower by nearly 32ft (10m), rebuilt the royal apartments and created many of Windsor's present splendours, including the Waterloo Chamber, scene of state banquets. Comparing the present castle with pre-Wyatville prints reveals enormous differences. What one sees now is predominantly his work.

Wyatville was less interested in domestic comforts, and Queen Victoria complained about the smell from the ancient cesspools. Bathrooms were also extremely scarce. The castle contains a variety of attractions for the hordes of tourists, besides its architecture. Here are housed the Queen's collection of Leonardo drawings and a remarkable doll's house belonging to Edward VII's queen. A disastrous fire, by no means the first, destroyed the north-east corner in 1992, but the contents were saved and restoration was completed within five years and, remarkably, under budget.

LEFT
The so-called Norman gateway, actually dating from the 14th century.

BELOW
The Round Tower, the upper part of which is a 19th-century addition.

Wartburg

The Wartburg is the name of a rocky peak south of the town of Eisenach in Thuringia, and of its crowning castle, once the residence of the landgraves of Thuringia. At first appearance, little about the castle suggests a defensive function. With its half-timbered, red-roofed buildings, it looks more like a prosperous late-medieval village or manor; but the site gives the game away.

It was probably founded by an obscure ancestor of the future landgraves in the mid-11th century, but was considerably enlarged in the late 12th century, when the landgrave, a cousin of the emperor, Frederick Barbarossa, was at the height of his power, ruling Hesse and the Palatinate as well as Thuringia. During the 13th century the Wartburg was the centre of the *minnesingers*, predecessors of the *meistersingers*, who celebrated chivalry and courtly love. A contemporary poem describes a poetry competition supposedly held at the Wartburg in 1207. It was the home of Elizabeth of Hungary who, after the death on crusade of the landgrave, her husband, devoted her life to the care of the poor and was later canonized, and briefly, of Martin Luther, in flight from pope and emperor after the Diet of Worms (1521), who stayed at the Wartburg under the transparent disguise of 'Junker Jörg'.

Such events contributed to the almost mythic awe the Wartburg inspired in Romantic German nationalists in the 19th century. By then the castle was in decay, and a huge programme of reconstruction took place, much of it directed at satisfying Romantic conceptions rather than historical accuracy. Some of this was corrected when a second major restoration took place

A half-timbered penthouse structure covers the wall-walk of romantic Wartburg. In the background is the reconstructed belfry; the landgrave's house is just visible on the extreme left.

under the auspices of the East German government in the 1950s.

The most impressive building is the landgrave's residence, now restored to its medieval state and one of the finest secular Romanesque buildings in Europe. It stands east of the main courtyard on an awkward, sloping site, with arcades running the full length of the

main storeys, providing light. Rooms include the deeply vaulted Rittersaal (knights' hall), where the capitals of the abbreviated columns are carved with bizarre eagles and, on the next floor, the Sängersaal (singers' hall), its massive timber ceiling supported by a pair of stone pillars, where, presumably, the *minnesinger* contests took place.

Edinburgh Castle

Edinburgh Castle looks as though it has grown out of the vast rock of volcanic basalt that raises it over 300ft (90m) above the city streets. The site, dominating the entrance to the River Forth, was fortified in the 6th century, probably by Edwin, king of Northumbria, who is sometimes credited with giving his name to Edinburgh but, having been continually occupied throughout the past 13 centuries, there is no archaeological evidence until much later times. The oldest surviving building is the little chapel of St Margaret, English queen of Malcolm III Canmore (Ceann Mor), who died a few days after her husband in 1093. The chapel, still occasionally used, dates only from the early 12th century, though it may contain elements from an earlier chapel contemporary with Margaret, a great ecclesiastical patron.

It must be admitted that Edinburgh Castle is notable more for its historical heritage than its architecture. Always a working castle, frequently in English hands, destroyed by Robert Bruce when he finally captured it in the year of his victory at Bannockburn (1314), it has been constantly reconstructed according to the needs of the moment, and the bulk of it dates from the 16th century or later. King David II added what appears to have been a characteristic Scottish tower house in the south-east in 1367. The base of it was incorporated into the Half Moon Battery, originally built in 1574 but subsequently reconstructed. The palace buildings date from the time of James IV (1488–1513), who was also responsible for the Great Hall with its fine hammer-beam ceiling; but the building of Holyroodhouse and the susceptibilities of

Mary, Queen of Scots, whose son, the future James I of England, was nevertheless born in the castle, ended its long career as a royal residence two generations later. The esplanade was levelled in the mid-18th century as a parade ground, 'a bow-shot wide'. It is now the scene of the floodlit Military Tattoo held annually at the time of the Edinburgh Festival.

Among interesting artifacts are 'Mons Meg', a five-ton 'bombard' or cannon, with a 20-inch (500-mm) calibre, made for James II in the 15th century, and the 'Honours of Scotland', the crown jewels, more venerable though less costly than those of England.

LEFT
Edinburgh Castle floodlit for the popular Military Tattoo.

BELOW
The buildings of the castle seem to have grown directly out of the rock.

Krak des Chevaliers, Gebel Alawi

Krak des Chevaliers is the most famous of the castles of the Christian Crusaders in the Near East. It stands at the edge of the Syrian desert, commanding a pass between the desert and the coast and guarding the road to Tripoli. On a low rocky hill between converging *wadis*, the site is well defended by nature. It was already fortified when the Crusaders arrived in 1096.

In 1142 the Christian Count of Tripoli sold the castle to the Knights Hospitallers of St John, the military order which, with the Knights Templar, provided the most effective Christian forces during the Crusades. Over the next 140 years, and interrupted by various setbacks, including an earthquake, the Hospitallers created the castle as it appears today.

Krak is an outstanding example of the concentric plan, a double ring of fortifications, in castle architecture. The original 12th-century castle was contained within what became the inner wall when the outer one was built after 1202. The main gate, in the east, was approached up a steep and rocky slope, and in the second construction a vaulted ramp, with 'murder holes' in the vault, was built between inner and outer walls, presenting attackers who broke through the outer gate with a virtually impossible passage to the inner gate. The most vulnerable side was the south where another formidable defensive structure was created, a massive, outward-sloping stone bulwark, ending with a 32-ft (10-m) sheer drop to a ditch. On the south, the ditch was enlarged and lined with stone, creating a combined moat and reservoir. Within, other elements, such as the Great Hall, its adjoining cloister and the large chapel, were more elegant.

Krak was virtually impregnable to mining or siege. Capable of holding 2,000 men, it was latterly seriously undermanned. After the failure of the Eighth Crusade (1270), no reinforcements could be expected and the castle was besieged by the determined Sultan Baybars in 1271. A letter from the Grand Master of the Hospitallers, whether or not it was recognized as a forgery, persuaded the Knights to abandon a hopeless cause, and Krak became a mosque.

RIGHT
The chapel at Krak with a Muslim minbar *(pulpit) visible on the right.*

FAR RIGHT
Overall view of the greatest of the Crusaders' castles.

Laon Cathedral

Driving along the autoroute towards the Channel ports, through the blessedly deserted countryside of northern France, the distant view to the south of the early Gothic Laon Cathedral, perched on a steep hill, rises like a welcome beacon.

Its history is, of course, less tranquil. Its predecessor was partly destroyed by fire in 1112 during a violent revolt against a notorious bishop, who had revoked the citizens' charter. A new bishop sent out the canons far and wide to collect funds for reconstruction, one group venturing as far as England. The building was soon functioning again, but 50 years later the canons were out again, collecting for a complete rebuilding, which began in 1160 and was largely completed by 1230.

In some ways the result was an innovatory structure, as is immediately evident from contemplation of the vigorous west façade, a prototype much imitated throughout the 13th century, with its deeply recessed arches and gabled porches, and the extraordinary openwork pattern of the towers. The interior, with comparatively slim columns, is unusually light, lively, and uncommonly long, especially by French standards, and the choir, is also unusual in being square-ended, though its predecessor was polygonal, which became the typical form. Although the orderly arrangement of ascending stages derives from the Norman Romanesque style, the contrast with a building such as Durham, only a couple of generations older, with its massive piers, is striking. The design of the transept apses is, in the light of the development of the Gothic style, the most advanced feature of Laon. Polygonal in form, the boldly projecting buttresses that separate the

windows virtually eliminate the wall. An advantage of the polygonal over a semicircular form is that the glass of the windows is flat and more manageable for stained glass. At one time Laon dazzled with 2,000 stained-glass windows, though few remain.

The most charming, and probably most famous features of Laon are the carved stone oxen, commemorating those that hauled the stone up the hill, which look out placidly from high in the western towers over the quiet countryside.

BELOW LEFT
Detail of figures in one of the portals.

BELOW
The west front conveys a sense of strongly sculptural energy with its deeply recessed porches, bold relief and open towers.

Chartres Cathedral

Chartres has become a symbol of the Gothic age, a name that conjures up an image of the Middle Ages which, if more poetically than historically accurate, still makes an impact on the modern mind.

At first glance, Chartres is not particularly spectacular. Approaching from the west, the portals seem rather cramped and the unmatched spires strike a dissonant note. Yet, if one imagines the later Flamboyant spire in the same form as its southern partner, with its assured proportions and brilliant switch from square to octagonal at roof height, the integrity of the building would not be enhanced and something would certainly be lost. After five centuries of close association, even unlikely partnerships seem to work.

Chartres is really the first incontrovertibly Gothic cathedral. The chunkiness of the flying buttresses, characteristic of the general geometry of Chartres, suggests Romanesque influence, but more importantly they form, for the first time, an integral part of the structure. The quadripartite (four-part) vaulting was also new, and set the common pattern for High Gothic churches.

The cathedral was built quickly in a burst of civic enthusiasm and all but the transepts were completed in a single generation by 1220. The master mason based his elevation on the Golden Section of antiquity: the height of the shafts corresponds exactly to the width of the nave between the columns, bestowing a sense of divine equilibrium. Chartres was a centre of pilgrimage (relics included the Virgin's shift) in the Middle Ages and was also the greatest cultural centre in northern France outside Paris. It is a testament to the spirit of northern humanism which is displayed in the beautiful sculpture and, above all, in the stained glass which, then and now, is frequently likened to jewellery. Most of the windows date from the 12th and 13th centuries, and the earliest predate the fire of 1194 that necessitated reconstruction. Not only do they represent the highest achievement of this medieval art, but they are also pleasingly simple to understand. The dominant colour is a deep, mystical blue, which modern technology has failed to reproduce, nor can photographs recapture its effect. Chartres is undoubtedly a building that must be visited to be appreciated.

Notre Dame, Paris

The Cathedral of Notre Dame de Paris is one of the world's most familiar buildings, rivalled only by the Eiffel Tower as a symbol of its favourite capital. For centuries a centre of Parisian life, housing market stalls, minstrels, a hostel for the homeless, even an employment exchange, it has witnessed momentous events, and few churches have suffered such affronts at the hands of men. Execrable alterations were made in the 18th century, which had no sympathy for the Gothic. The stalls were destroyed, the columns overlaid with marble slabs and the stained glass knocked out of the windows to give more light. Worse came with the Revolution, when an actress was crowned Goddess of Reason on the high altar and the cathedral was auctioned to builders for its stone, a disaster prevented by Napoleon's seizure of power. Notre Dame was saved by the great planner of 19th-century Paris, Viollet-le-Duc, who carried out the restoration of the building – even the gargoyles are his. He recalled that he had wandered there as a boy and thought how the great rose windows seemed to break into song when the organ began to play. His work is not universally approved, but on the whole we should be grateful.

The cathedral was begun in 1163, and at the time it surpassed all rivals. It owed much to a remarkable bishop, Maurice de Sully, a forester's son, who appears in the tympanum of St Anne's portal that shows him with a kneeling King Louis VII at the dedication of the cathedral. A double-aisled plan was adopted, necessitating the fabulous array of flying buttresses which do so much to create the impression, remarked on by so many, of a great oared ship sailing up the Seine towards some heavenly harbour. From the west, the cathedral presents a strong, squarish front 164-ft (50-m) wide, growing steadily lighter in texture as it moves upward from portals to towers, and seeming to proclaim the resilience of medieval French culture. It might be difficult, as the saying, attributed to Zola goes, to 'teach the towers of Notre Dame to dance', but that is not their purpose. What they do convey is a calm image of noble strength.

LEFT
Notre Dame viewed from across the Seine.

RIGHT
The powerful towers of Notre Dame de Paris.

Bourges Cathedral

Bourges is almost at the dead centre of modern France, about 125 miles (200 km) south of Paris. It is dominated by the Cathedral of St-Étienne, one of the most remarkable of French Gothic churches. The archbishop and moving spirit in the construction of the present building was a brother of the founder of Notre Dame de Paris and there are obvious affinities, although the end result is quite different. The building was mainly completed in the first half of the 13th century, though significant additions appeared in the centuries following.

Approaching from the west, the visitor is confronted by a façade of battered majesty with two asymmetrical towers, the southern tower of the 13th century and the northern tower in 15th-century Flamboyant style. But the most striking impression is of sheer width. Above the broad steps, five large and splendid portals march across the front. Walking around the building, one is almost shocked by the total absence of transepts (already minimal at Paris), which results in a long, straight, uninterrupted line of flying buttresses that may be regarded as slightly monotonous.

It is the interior that makes Bourges unique. Here there is no jumble of styles but perfect unity and, most remarkably, an almost springlike atmosphere of light and space. The significance of the breadth of the building, which like Paris adopts the double-aisled pattern, contributes, though the exhilarating effect owes even more to the extraordinary height of the arches, and thus of the vault which, at 125ft (38m), is only 10ft (3m) short of the breadth. The inner aisles reach an unprecedented height of 69ft (21m), abundantly admitting the light lacking in Paris, whose obstructing galleries are absent from Bourges.

There is not much decoration, and not much wall to decorate; but the other outstanding feature of Bourges is its stained glass, which is second only to that of Chartres. As was usually the custom, the windows were presented by various guilds, the beautiful window of the Good Samaritan being the gift of the weavers.

FAR RIGHT
The absence of transepts gives Bourges its slightly parade-ground air. In fact the nave broadens imperceptibly towards the choir, while the aisles narrow proportionately, a device to correct the optical illusion of parallel lines converging.

RIGHT
Detail of the outstanding stained glass.

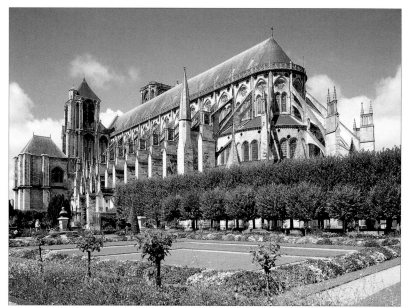

Royal Chapel, Palermo

Medieval Italy was a country which experienced frequent upheavals that left a complex, mixed heritage. In the 11th century, the country contained provinces of the Byzantine empire, Lombard duchies, a claim to overlordship by the Holy Roman emperor, the empire-building Normans in the south and a Muslim state in Sicily. Muslims from North Africa had launched a persistent series of attacks on Sicily in the 9th century, gradually driving out the Byzantine forces. In 1016 a Lombard ruler invited the Normans to Italy as mercenaries, a dangerous move when, playing off their employers against one another, they soon began to conquer the country for themselves. In the late 11th century they drove the Muslims from Sicily, and in 1139 Roger II was recognized as king of Sicily by the pope.

The interchange of cultures in Sicily is almost unique and produced a complex artistic style, broadly a mixture of Western, Byzantine and Muslim influences, which suggests a greater degree of cultural unity in the 12th-century Mediterranean region than might be expected from the general picture of mutual hostility.

The finest example of this style is the Capella Palatina, or royal chapel, the jewel of Roger II's palace in the west of the Old Town of Palermo. Besides the fine marble of the lower walls and floor and the wonderful mosaics, probably the work of Sicilian artists working in the Byzantine tradition, the crowning glory of the chapel is the ceiling, below a dome and small cupolas, which dates from about 1140. This shimmering work of art, its beaded stalactite at first glance suggesting an almost abstract pattern, is of inlaid and painted wood.

The painting, of both decorative and figurative subjects, is probably by Fatimid artists (the Egyptian Fatimids were culturally the leading Islamic dynasty), and gains added importance as it is almost the only major surviving example of Fatimid painting other than on pottery. Since Roger was apparently well pleased, the decoration of the royal chapel confirms the identification of the hard-headed northern Europeans with the fascinating culture of medieval Sicily.

Detail of the Byzantine mosaics in the Royal Chapel, Palermo.

Salamanca Cathedrals

There are two cathedrals in the fabled, golden city of Salamanca. The old cathedral, built in the 12th century, presses against the southern flank of the new cathedral, dating from the late Gothic era, which, being larger, higher, and more ornate, tends to dominate, perhaps over-dominate: to make space for it, the northern transept of the old cathedral was demolished, and the only entrance to the Romanesque building is via the new cathedral. The celebrated, domed and turreted Romanesque Torre del Gallo is diminished by the Renaissance cathedral looming over it.

The bold, square, western tower has an interesting history. Its core belongs to the old cathedral, as the much-restored frescoes inside confirm; but when the new cathedral was begun in 1512 it was refaced in more contemporary style. The old wooden belfry remained, but in the 18th century it was destroyed by lightning. A new belfry and lantern were built but proved too heavy, and the earthquake of 1755 caused cracks and an ominous twist to the spire. Experts advised demolition, but their advice proved so unpopular that a compromise was reached in which the entire structure was encased in stone. Thus the old tower was preserved, though totally invisible!

The plan of the new cathedral is basically a rectangle, the transepts extending no further that the appendant chapels. Although construction continued over two centuries, the final effect is homogeneous. But passage into the old cathedral may cause slight culture shock. Founded in 1102, this solemn building represents the transition from Romanesque to Gothic. The nave was meant to be barrel-vaulted in the Romanesque manner, but by the time that stage was reached, the builders opted for a quadripartite vault. The large human and animal heads above the capitals are not merely decorative: they support the ribs of the vault.

One of the greatest treasures of Salamanca is the 15th-century curved *reredos* of 55 wooden panels painted with scenes from the Life of Christ by a Florentine artist, who also painted the marvellous Last Judgement in the curve of the apse above.

The old cathedral is dominated by the vast Gothic pile erected in the 16th century,

Amiens Cathedral

The cathedral at Amiens, which could have held the entire medieval population of about 10,000, represents the peak of the High Gothic style of the 13th century. If one were trying to choose a single building to stand for all the great cathedrals of France, Amiens would be a candidate.

The environment of the cathedral has changed a great deal since the Middle Ages and the heart of the city has moved. The best approach is through the narrow streets to the south-east, when the cathedral springs dramatically into view, a perfectly proportioned, though not quite as originally built, vision of slender but steely vertical forms, whose dramatic effect depends on lightness and precision. Contemporary glass-walled buildings sometimes contrive to look heavy: the stone of Amiens appears scarcely heavier than the air. The pigeons fly freely through the flying buttresses, and even the tracery of the windows is minimal. Walls are relatively thin and the vault, the highest in France after neighbouring Beauvais, is supported by slim, uninterrupted shafts. Among its other virtues, the cathedral might be cited as a fine example of economy in the use of materials.

The foundation stone was laid in 1220 by Bishop de Fouilloy, whose bronze tomb is in the nave, and the first master mason, in charge for nearly 30 years, clearly had Reims in mind, though Amiens is altogether more slender. It was the fourth church on the site, and construction began, unusually, at the west end, so that the church to the east could be used until the last moment. Despite a serious fire in 1258, the cathedral was basically complete 11 years later.

For many people, Amiens Cathedral represents the peak of High Gothic art.

The famous figure of the Vierge Dorée was probably already in place on the south transept. The Virgin is frankly portrayed as a fashionable lady – 'the soubrette of Amiens' – Ruskin called her, and though no longer gilded (*dorée*), her charm remains irresistible. In general, the sculpture is hardly excelled anywhere, even at Reims, partly because so much has survived. The serene assurance of the building is finally expressed by the welcoming figure of Le Beau Dieu at the west door.

Leaning Tower of Pisa

The Cathedral of Santa Maria Maggiore and its attendant buildings allegedly owe their origin to the gratitude of the citizens of this powerful medieval city for a naval victory in 1063, though work was not begun until about 15 years later. The entire Romanesque complex, favoured by perceptible Byzantine and Lombard, as well as Classical, influences, forms one of the most rewarding architectural vistas in a country not short of them. Despite a period of construction of over 200 years, with the exception of the Baptistery, given Gothic additions in the 14th century, it displays a pleasing conformity.

The campanile (bell tower), better known as the Leaning Tower of Pisa, is probably the best-known architectural phenomen in the world, familiar to schoolchildren everywhere. Because it is so famous for its tilt, it is easy to overlook the fact that it is also the most beautiful Romanesque tower in southern Europe, eight circular storeys of arcaded perfection, with the final stage, the belfry, of lesser diameter than the superb cylinder it surmounts.

It was begun in 1174, and was only half built when, towards the end of the 13th century, the anxious citizens of Pisa observed that it was shifting slightly from the vertical, the result of a soggy site and insufficient foundations. Experts were consulted, without, it seems, much effect, and building optimistically continued. The belfry was not installed until 1350. In a sense, the optimism proved justified, since the tower stood for centuries. Nevertheless, the tilt continued imperceptibly to increase, until it became evident that, eventually, the tower would fall. Numerous schemes were proposed over the years and some of them were ineffectively implemented, at least one actually aggravating the situation. Bold new techniques in the 1990s, which were completed in 2000, appear to have averted the imminent disaster, and are designed to reduce the tilt to a less dangerous angle without restoring the tower to the vertical, which would now be unacceptable. The Leaning Tower must lean.

RIGHT
The campanile at Pisa owes its fame not to its exquisite design but to the fact that it tilts.

OPPOSITE
The tower in context.

Reims Cathedral

Clovis, the ancestor of the Merovingian dynasty, adopted Christianity at Reims nearly 1,500 years ago, and Reims became the coronation church of later French kings. Appropriately, the cathedral, which has benefited from the clearing away of buildings that used to crowd it, is perhaps the grandest in France. It proclaims a proud, if battered, majesty. The addition of blind portals flanking the three main porches, a device copied from an earlier Reims church, gives it a feeling of solid width lacking at, for instance, Amiens, which is actually a slightly larger building.

It was begun in 1211 after the earlier building had been destroyed by fire, and that may account for the uniformity not only of the structure but also of the sculpture, in spite of the fact that construction, slowed by the Hundred Years War, took over 200 years. The upper stages of the towers were completed in 1427, and two years later Charles VII was anointed king at Reims in the presence of Jeanne d'Arc. The battered appearance of the cathedral is chiefly due to damage in the First World War, when, perilously near the Western Front, it received direct hits from German artillery. Looking at photographs of the damage, it seems remarkable that so much was rescued.

The chief glory of Reims is the sculpture of the west façade. The sheer quantity of the sculptural decoration is extraordinary, although it is arranged in perfect symmetry with no sense of clutter. Almost the first thing that strikes the observer on examination of the sculpture is its affinity with Classical models. The frieze of figures rising from their coffins on the Day of Judgement gives the lie to the common

The west front of the royal cathedral of Reims.

supposition that Gothic artists could not convincingly portray the human nude. The larger, draped figures include some of the most famous examples of medieval sculpture anywhere. The impish Smiling Angel (Le Sourire de Reims), the first successful attempt at such an expression, is entirely convincing, and altogether at Reims we see a new spirit of naturalism where Classical balance, pagan identification with Nature (over 30 plants have been identified in the lavish decorative foliage), and Christian charity are wonderfully combined.

Beauvais Cathedral

The devout builders of the medieval cathedrals aspired to Heaven, and the hallmark of Gothic ecclesiastical architecture is verticality, upward movement. We may well find the results of this aspiration equally inspiring, if in a different way. But among all the citizens of the still-small French kingdom, except for the poorest classes, more than spiritual aspirations were engaged. They wished to outdo their neighbours. Higher and higher rose the columns and the vaults. Laon set the record, Paris exceeded it, Chartres just topped that, then Amiens leapt ahead by nearly 17ft (5m).

At Beauvais, begun around 1220, 30 miles (50km) south of Amiens, the limit was reached. The choir of the Cathedral of St Peter rose to the fantastic height of 157ft (48m), a jump of nearly another 17ft. A building of 25 floors could have been placed inside without touching the vault. For sheer daring, the builders of Beauvais are unparalleled.

In 1284, the walls of the choir began to bend outwards, and the roof sagged and fell to the ground. But such disasters were not uncommon, and the ambitions of the citizens of Beauvais remained undiminished. Nearly 300 years later a huge spire was erected, in spite of the fact that the nave was still incomplete because the money for construction had been spent restoring the choir, now rebuilt with additional, strengthening piers. A few years later the spire collapsed, and the choir had to be rebuilt again.

The cathedral was never finished. The central tower was not replaced and the nave was never completed. Today, Beauvais remains, a splendid, wounded giant, held together internally by iron rods and externally by massive, three-tier buttresses. The beauty of the stained glass and the heavenly vault (still a record) remain and, in its permanently incomplete state, Beauvais has assumed a unique if unusual appeal of its own.

Beauvais, a wounded giant, and a monument to spiritual endeavour.

Santiago de Compostela

The popularity of the pilgrimage in medieval Europe is easily understandable. The purpose might be a solemn one, but there was no reason why people should not have enjoyed themselves on the journey in a unique opportunity to take a long holiday. All kinds of people, like those in Chaucer's *Canterbury Tales*, became pilgrims.

Although God is present in any church, or, as the priests say, anywhere else, to most worshippers the most vivid presence was the patron saint, a presence powerfully enhanced if the church possessed actual relics of the saint. Some pilgrimages were undertaken for the purpose of securing relics, but less ambitious pilgrims brought back a token of their journey

in the form of a little metal badge. Many of these have survived, and one of the most common is the scallop shell of St James of Compostela, whose shrine is in the north-west corner of Spain.

The Apostle James the Great was said to have brought Christianity to Spain and after his martyrdom his body was returned there, eventually reaching Compostela. By the 10th century his shrine was the greatest centre of pilgrimage in Europe apart from Rome.

The Romanesque pilgrim churches have a certain similarity: long, barrel-vaulted naves, tall arcades with spacious galleries, aisles circling the apse to allow the pilgrims to circulate, with the main artistic emphasis on the shrine in the east. They later acquired various accretions, chapels off apse and transepts, and the Romanesque structure at Compostela, built between 1075 and 1128, is not at first apparent. What meets the eye is a stately, twin-towered Baroque façade, begun in 1667. It overlooks the plaza, built in the Churrigueresque style, like the central section of the façade. Inside, St James's remains are enshrined in a tremendous, gilded Baroque sanctuary. Otherwise, the interior is austerely Romanesque. The 12th-century Portico de la Gloria, with its figures of apostles and others, just west of the nave, has been called 'one of the greatest glories of Christian art'.

FAR LEFT
The sensational Baroque façade of the pilgrimage church of St James.

LEFT
Detail.

Borgund Church, Norway

In regions, such as China, where the chief building material was wood, old buildings are understandably uncommon; thus there are few buildings of great antiquity in China. In Europe, similarly, domestic buildings built more than 200 years ago are rare except when built by those who could afford stone or brick. Not only does timber tend to rot, it is also highly inflammable, and fires in stone churches, which of course also contained much wood, were surprisingly common: Old St Paul's in London was merely one of many casualties.

Timber was used as the structural material for churches only in the forested regions of Scandinavia and Romania. Fortunately, several wooden churches whose foundation dates to within a few generations of the acceptance of Christianity have survived in Scandinavia, chiefly Norway. The Borgund Church in western Norway dates from the mid-12th century, although little, if anything, of the existing material is original. For those accustomed to Romanesque basilicas, the church on first appearance must have been a shock. It seems to bear little resemblance to contemporary churches in the rest of Europe and the dragon heads (probably 13th-century) that launch themselves from the gables are a disconcerting reminder of the warships of the pagan Vikings.

These buildings are called stave churches, and the structural technique resembles barrel-making. The walls are made up of slightly curved vertical timbers that fit into horizontal beams at top and bottom. This method has the advantage of keeping the wall members clear of the ground and therefore making them less liable to rotting. Although the profusion of steep, shingled roofs is confusing, the basic plan is actually a simple rectangle, based on four tall central posts set in a square. Sometimes, as at Borgund, there is a small square chancel, sometimes aisles were added to the nave, with further elaborations as time advanced; timber churches continued to be built into the 13th century. These churches also contained extensive carved decoration, most famously at Urnes, not far from Borgund, which has given its name to the style.

The Norwegian stave churches are unique, but, being wooden, few have survived, Borgund, exceptionally, being the outstanding exception.

Château de Blois

The counts of Blois were powerful figures in medieval France who became the ancestors of later kings. Sons of Count Estienne (d. 1102) included Henry, a future bishop of Winchester, and Stephen, a future king of England. It was from Blois that Jeanne d'Arc set out in 1429 to dispel the English besiegers of Orléans, and in the 16th century the 'city of kings' was virtually a second capital. The old château has witnessed sensational events, including the escape down a rope of the portly queen mother, Marie de Médicis, when confined by her son Louis XII, and later the assassination of the Duc de Guise on the orders of Henri III (1588).

In the centre of the château country of the Loire valley, Blois is in many ways typical. There are substantial medieval remains, including the 13th-century great hall where the States General twice met during the reign of Louis XIII, although the main elements of the château, seen from the central courtyard today, date from the 16th and 17th centuries. During the 15th century, Charles d'Orléans demolished part of the old castle to build more comfortable accommodation, which included that part of the east wing now turned into a museum. Renovations by Louis XII included the gallery along the front linking the rooms, a comparatively new idea in 1500 when it was normally necessary to move from room to room. The wing added by François I is little more than a decade later, but in the meantime the Italian Renaissance had made itself felt. Perhaps the most striking feature of the whole château is its exterior staircase in an attached, highly decorated, octagonal tower. Originally the centrepiece of the façade, it was displaced by the ambitious plans of François Mansart on behalf of Gaston d'Orléans in the 17th century. Had they been fulfilled, Blois would have been grander than the Luxembourg Palace, but finance called a halt. As it is, Mansart's block is a minor masterpiece and displays probably the first example of the type of double-sloped roof named after him.

ABOVE
An equestrian statue of King Louis XII over the entrance gate of the Château de Blois.

LEFT
François I's striking exterior staircase tower.

Brussels Cathedral

St Gudule was a rather obscure saint of the 7th century, and the 13th-century church dedicated to her is popularly known as Brussels Cathedral. It stands on the slope of what was once called Mont-Saint-Michel, St Michael being the second patron saint; a gilded copper figure of him, twice life-size, is mounted on the spire of the hôtel de ville in the Grand-Place. The church was founded in 1220 after its predecessor had been burned down, and most of the east end appears to have been completed by 1273, although the nave was not finished until the 15th century, closely followed by the towers and west façade, which have a uniformity somewhat lacking elsewhere.

This is practically the first significant Gothic building in the Low Countries, where the style arrived slightly later than in France, and there are remaining traces of the Romanesque, notably in the apse. There are no fundamental distinguishing features of the Brabantine Gothic, at least until the 15th century, as seen at Brussels or in the cathedral of Antwerp, though churches tend to be shorter and wider than in France which, obviously enough, was the dominant influence. However, the southern Netherlands was included in the diocese of Cologne, and considerable German influence, strongest in the Romanesque period, continued to percolate. At St Gudule's, moreover, it is possible to detect slight affinities with the Early English Gothic style, though this could be a matter of chance rather than imitation.

The mixture of influences, the time of construction, and the many restorations make the architecture of St Gudule's rather complicated. The general plan of abbreviated transepts without aisles, and wide chapels flanking the choir on both sides, is typical of the Low Countries, and the style of the carved foliage on the capitals of the circular columns is characteristically Brabantine. Notable features of the interior are the 16th-century oak pulpit, carved with a scene of The Fall, and some very fine medieval stained glass, some of which was restored in the 19th century.

The Cathedral of St Gudule, or Gertrude, is characteristic of the mixed influences at work in the southern Netherlands.

Cloth Hall, Ypres

The biggest industry in the Middle Ages was clothmaking and the wool trade. As early as the 12th century the cities of Flanders, such as Ghent and Ypres, were important clothmaking centres, partly because the country raised many sheep and partly because urban enterprise was encouraged by the counts of Flanders. As it grew, the Flemish clothmaking industry soon came to depend largely on high-quality English wool. Merchants of all countries came to the great Flemish fairs, and the wealthy Flemish towns had few rivals. It was a serious blow when, in the 14th century, the English began to make their own, albeit generally inferior cloth, though political factors, not to mention reactionary efforts by the towns to preserve their monopoly, also contributed to the gradual decline.

It is therefore not surprising that Flemish architecture was generally most distinguished in civic buildings, in the weavers' guild halls, town halls and lofty bell towers. Structurally, Gothic was more obviously suitable for churches than secular buildings, but in the Netherlands, the churches were usually outshone by sumptuous secular buildings, even though these sometimes lost sight of constructional needs on which the Gothic style depended. There are several spectacular examples, such as Ghent's guild houses or the 300-ft (90-m) belfry and market hall of Bruges; but perhaps the most distinguished architecturally is the Cloth Hall at Ypres.

Sober, restrained, and perfectly proportioned, the Cloth Hall was built as an exchange for the cloth industry between 1201 and 1304. It has been called 'Europe's outstanding secular medieval building'. Its plan is a relatively narrow rectangle, with small spires at each corner; the façade is 440-ft (134-m) long, broken only at the centre by a large and dignified tower.

What is now the small town of Ypres was the scene of some of the most hideous fighting in the First World War, in which the Cloth Hall was destroyed. It has since been carefully and thoroughly restored.

In medieval Flanders, as in northern Italy, civic and commercial buildings rival the architectural dominance of the Church.

Palazzo Pubblico, Siena

During the 13th century, the city of Siena, already becoming an important centre of banking, was a self-governing commune. It was not altogether a peaceful development, and was marked by a long struggle for ascendancy between the nobles, who at first controlled the government, and the increasingly powerful – and vocal – burghers, who resented the nobles' exemption from taxation.

The city was also prone to plague and wars, notably against its neighbour and rival, Florence. A great victory of the Sienese and their allies over the Florentines in 1260 crushed Florence for many years, which roughly coincided with a long period of good government by the burghers, after they had overcome the power of the nobles.

The influence of French Gothic was more acceptable to Siena than it was, for instance, to Florence. The cathedral, in black-and-white marble, which if ever completed as planned would have been one of the largest in Europe, is a fine example. Another is the Palazzo Pubblico, the seat of government.

It was built between about 1290 and 1310, and its most distinctive feature is the bell tower, called the Torre del Mangia, which at 334ft (102m) is the highest in Italy and a splendid expression of the pride of Siena's merchant class. The palazzo itself, though massive and palatial, with its curved façade and whimsical crenellation, is the reverse of overbearing. It is built of brick except for the ground floor, which is stone and lined with characteristic Sienese arches in which a round arch is set within a pointed one.

There are many treasures of Sienese art within, including a fountain by the sculptor Jacopo della Quercia. The panoramic frescoes in the Sala della Pace on the apposite theme of the effects of just and unjust government were painted by Ambrogio Lorenzetti in the 1330s. One of the two halls on the ground floor has a fine Resurrection by the Renaissance artist known as Il Sodoma, while in the Sala del Mappamondo is the *Maestà* (1315), a Virgin and Child with attendant saints, of Simone Martini, after Duccio the prince of Sienese painters.

The campanile of the Palazzo Pubblico rivalled the spires of church and cathedral.

The west front of Burgos Cathedral. The great size and exuberant ornamentation are characteristics of Spanish cathedrals.

Burgos Cathedral

Burgos Cathedral stands on a steep slope below the castle of the old city, approached by steep cobbled streets or stone steps. It is closely integrated with its surroundings, with various outbuildings clustering around the massive pile from which emerge intensely ornamented towers and spires.

Burgos, the city of El Cid, and in more recent times the headquarters of General Franco, was the capital of Old Castile, a state that grew from the struggle of the Christians to reconquer Spain from the Muslims. The cathedral, in one sense a gesture of triumph, was founded in about 1221 and, like León and Toledo, was based on French models, with early master masons coming from France or England. Construction continued off and on until well into the 16th century; its original French High Gothic appearance almost disappeared in the wealth of decorative additions of the late 15th and early 16th centuries, which include no less than 22 ornately crocketed spires and pinnacles. This was the work of three generations of the

Colonia (Cologne) family. The western steeples were built by Juan de Colonia (Hans of Cologne), the beautiful Constable's Chapel to the east by his son Simon in the 1480s, and the present, almost too exuberantly Flamboyant, central tower with its swarming sculpture, by his grandson Francisco in the 1540s, which replaced an earlier version by Juan himself.

The decoration, inside and out, which of course owes a great deal to Islamic tradition, is what chiefly distinguishes the cathedral; it coincided with the period of the city's greatest prosperity. Visiting in the 19th century, Théophile Gautier was dazzled by Burgos, which he regarded as the finest cathedral in the world. Standing in the crossing, he looked up at 'a giddy abyss of sculptures, arabesques, statues, miniature columns, ribs, lancets and pendentives. One might look at it for two years without seeing everything'. He was puzzled by 'a great staircase of most beautiful design, with magnificent carved chimeras'. In fact, the staircase connects the north transept, which was built on a higher level to accommodate the slope, with the body of the church.

Castel del Monte, Apulia

Castel del Monte, dating from around 1240, is probably the most famous and most attractive of the castles of the Emperor Frederick II, king of Sicily (1197–1250), where he grew up and preferred to live, and was emperor from 1220. It has been called the Crown of Apulia, a name suggested by its shape and situation, on a low hill commanding the surrounding plain, near the Adriatic coast. Well-preserved, modest in scale, and the colour of pale honey, it is supposed to have been designed by Frederick as a place of leisure, but it is a much more formidable stronghold than it appears. The elegant Classical doorway was probably protected by a portcullis, and the building itself may have been planned as the keep of a larger structure whose walls were never built. Aspects of the building deriving variously from Classical, Christian and Islamic traditions, and its strict mathematical plan, lend strength to the notion that Frederick himself, a man of wide and eclectic knowledge, had a hand in the design.

The highly symmetrical plan is a double octagon around a central courtyard, with the plan repeated in the octagonal towers at each angle of the outer wall. (There may have been special significance in the fact that an octagon can be seen as midway between a square, representing the Earth, and a circle, representing Heaven.) Towers and wall are now the same height, but originally the towers would have been 6½ft (2m) higher. The mixture of styles is evident at the doorway, where a Gothic window appears above the Classical pediment. Further evidence of Gothic principles exists plentifully within, in ribbed vaulting, column capitals, etc., although at this time the Islamic influence is more evident, and would have been more easily appreciated when the original furnishings – marble floors, tapestries, Eastern carpets, as well as sculpture – were in place. The plumbing was advanced, with running water for baths and latrines supplied from cisterns in the roof.

In fact, the Emperor seems to have seldom used the castle, and may never have stayed there at all. In later times Castel del Monte was used as a prison.

FAR LEFT
Its perfect symmetry largely explains the appeal of Castel del Monte.

LEFT
The Classical entrance.

Château d'Angers

The town of Angers on a tributary of the Loire is still dominated by the remains of the castle, which is a genuine medieval fortress rather than a decorative palace of the type generally associated with châteaux of the Loire.

The original fort was built around 1000, but no trace of it remains. Its successor was built during the reign of that most admirable of medieval monarchs, Louis IX, Saint Louis (1214–70). Its purpose was to defend Anjou, recently regained after long possession by the kings of England. Construction began in 1228 and was largely completed within ten years.

The site is raised above the land around it, and this rocky platform was exploited to raise the effective height of the curtain wall and its towers, the line of plinth that supports them continuing through natural rock. The plan is an irregular heptagon. One side faces the river, the others are guarded by the massive curtain wall and its frequent towers. The towers are round, and made from layers of slate, sandstone and granite, giving a striking banded effect that is the one concession to decoration. The entrance, in the east, was via a drawbridge across the deep moat to a gatehouse. To the north is the Tour de Moulin, which would once have housed a mill, the only one of the towers that stands at its original height, the rest having been reduced to the level of the walls during the French Wars of Religion (1562––98). There is scarcely anything left of the original structures within, though there is a 15th-century chapel with a charming little gatehouse to the gardens.

A major attraction of Angers is the tapestries, now housed within a special gallery. They were commissioned by Count Louis I of Anjou in the late 14th century and fashioned in the workshop of the premier *tapissier*, Nicolas Bataille of Paris. Based on the unusual but visually rewarding theme of the Apocalypse, in the Book of Revelations, they once hung in the Great Hall, and although not all survive, the whole work, which was about 470-ft (143-m) long and 18-ft (5.5-m) deep, can be reconstructed from records.

Marienburg, home of the Teutonic Knights, was largely rebuilt in the 19th century.

Marienburg (Malbork) Castle

The Polish town of Malbork was formerly in East Prussia, and better known historically by its German name, Marienburg. The castle was built for the Teutonic Knights, and was their headquarters for over a century.

The order was founded by merchants from Bremen and Lübeck to provide medical services during the Third Crusade and took its name from the Hospital of St Mary of the Germans, or Teutons, in Jerusalem. It soon developed into a military-religious order like the Templars and Hospitallers, its membership restricted to German nobles who took monastic vows of poverty, chastity and obedience. After the loss of Acre, the order, under the leadership of Hermann von Salza, became involved in German colonization of the east, the *Drang nach Osten*, and embarked upon the conquest of what became Prussia. The headquarters of the order was moved from Acre, via Venice, to Marienburg in 1308. It was independent of all political authorities except the papacy from which, at its own instigation, it held its extensive lands as a fief.

The castle was founded a generation earlier on a hill near the River Nogat. As the headquarters of the Grand Master of the Teutonic Knights, in the 14th century it became one of the largest and most powerful castles in Germany. It was built of brick, with steepish red-tile roofs and turrets in a recognizably 'Baltic' style, seen also in the cities originally responsible for the founding of the Order. The Grand Master ruled his Baltic empire in some style, and great banquets were held under the immensely high vault of the great hall. This is one of the most impressive buildings of the old

castle, along with the chapel. This was, after all, the home of a religious order, and the knights never entirely forgot their religious responsibilities.

The castle's heyday was short. The defeat of the knights by the king of Poland at Tannenberg in 1410 marked the beginning of their decline.

In 1466 Marienburg passed to Poland, and later Polish kings occasionally resided there. It returned to Prussia as a result of the partition of Poland in 1772, and was largely rebuilt in the 19th century by the Prussians. After the destruction of the Second World War, it was restored by the Poles.

Rochester Castle

The English town of Rochester, between London and Canterbury, is full of literary and historical memories. There is a memorial to Charles Dickens, who lived on Gad's Hill, in the cathedral, and the house that was a model for Miss Havisham's in *Great Expectations* can still be seen. The city's eventful history is largely due to its situation at the lowest point at which the River Medway can be forded, on the route followed by the invading Romans. The original cathedral was founded by St Augustine in the 7th century, destroyed by the Vikings and rebuilt in the late 11th century by Bishop Gundulf, who also started the Norman castle.

Though there are earlier remains, including parts of the Roman walls, the core of Rochester castle, which still stands, was the massive great tower, or keep, one of the finest survivals of its type in England. It belongs to the years 1127–42, after the castle passed to the archbishops of Canterbury. Practically square in plan, about 70ft (21m) along each side, it has towers at each corner and a fortified entrance on the north side. The walls are over 10-ft (3-m) thick at ground level and rise 113ft (34m) to the parapet, with the flanking towers another 10ft higher.

During the rebellion of the barons against King John in 1215, the castle was held for the barons and became the object of a famous siege. The south-east tower was successfully mined after a large number of fat pigs had been used as incendiary devices to fire the timbers that supported the sappers' tunnel. However, the attackers were held up by the inner wall, and the garrison held out until it was eventually starved into surrender. The castle was restored and a round tower replaced the casualty on the south-eastern corner. Besieged again in 1254 by Simon de Montfort, it was restored under Edward III, damaged during the Peasants' Revolt (1381) but once again patched up. By the 18th century, years of neglect had rendered it liable to demolition, but it was rescued by the City corporation and restored in the late 19th century.

Rochester Castle was built at the lowest fordable point of the River Medway.

Views of the west façade (below and opposite) from the Grand Canal. The walls of the upper storeys have the appearance of a fine silk fabric. The ornamental window (below right) has the Lion of Venice (symbol of St Mark) superimposed above it.

Doge's Palace, Venice

According to tradition, the first doge of Venice was elected in 697. However, his powers were subject to constraints and by the time Venice became a rich empire, due to accessions from the defeated Byzantines, he was little more than a figurehead.

The first palace was built in the early 9th century, though even its form is now uncertain, and the present building, arguably the most spectacular secular building in Europe's most beautiful city, was built in about 1340, largely as a meeting place for the Venetian Assembly, and was completed by the early 15th century. The most familiar image of the palace is its unique façade, which overlooks the lagoon. A masterpiece of Italian Gothic, it is also a brilliant combination of East (Byzantium) and West, as befits a city poised between the two. Above the spacious arcades at ground level are delicately ornamental arches, while the upper half, basically a flat wall, has a colourful geometric pattern of pink and white marble. The most novel element of the design, it is pierced by seven widely spaced windows, the central one ornamented and with a small balcony. Closer examination of the fine, mainly 14th-century sculptural decoration reveals portraits of two Byzantine emperors as well as Venetian contemporaries. Between the palace and the basilica of St Mark a gateway, the Porta della Carta, opens into the courtyard, flanked by rich and various buildings, mostly Renaissance though with some Gothic remnants, with a sight of the domes of St Mark's beyond. The overall effect is slightly disorderly by comparison with the façade. At the top of the monumental Staircase of the Giants, with Jacopo Sansovino's flanking figures of Mars and Neptune (1554), the doge used to stand to receive his cap of office.

Among the impressive state rooms, the Sala delle Quattro Porte contains Tintoretto's frescoes celebrating Venice's maritime supremacy. Veronese's vast painting of the Battle of Lepanto, a famous naval victory over the Turks (1571), and Tintoretto's paintings in tribute to various doges, are in the Sala del Collegio, where the doge met important visitors. A fire in 1577 destroyed many earlier masterpieces, but the Doge's Palace is still a treasure house of Venetian art and history.

Caernarvon Castle

Of the four great castles built by the English King Edward I (reigned 1272–1307) to subdue the Welsh, Beaumaris is aesthetically the most satisfactory, Harlech the most picturesque, and Conwy the most threatening. But the grandest is certainly Caernarvon, as befitted the intended seat of royal government in North Wales. The polygonal towers, which perhaps owe something to Constantinople (a city that Edward had visited when on Crusade), may have been a deliberate attempt to add a touch of distinction to Caernarvon compared with his other castles, which lack them.

Although the remains of a Roman fort can be seen on rising ground beyond the medieval town, the first fortifications in Caernarvon were the work of the Norman Earl of Chester in about 1100. Edward's castle, nearly 200 years later, was built on a flat spit of land projecting into the Menai Strait, dividing mainland Wales from Anglesey. Originally it had water on three sides, but the river that used to flow into the Seiont east of the castle has since been built over. The medieval town on the north was entirely enclosed by the walls extending from the castle, which still stand.

The plan is unusual, like an irregular figure-of-eight, with the residential quarters located in the 13 massive towers along the walls, no two of which are exactly alike. The largest is the Eagle Tower, named for the stone eagles adorning the turrets. This would have been occupied by the justiciar, or royal governor, of North Wales, who as the king's representative lived in some style. The Eagle Tower is large enough so that, after deducting the great width of the walls, there remains an apartment about 40-ft (12-m) across. According to legend it was in the Eagle Tower, in reality not yet built, that Edward I scored a propaganda coup by presenting to the Welsh people his newborn son, a prince 'born in Wales who speaks no English'.

Caernavon Castle at night, with the Eagle Tower at left.

Cologne Cathedral

Cologne Cathedral is one of the most awe-inspiring buildings in Europe, rising above the city almost as if it belonged to another planet where everything is larger and proportions are different. It is the largest Gothic church in northern Europe, its heritage is ancient, and it contains many magnificent treasures, including the gold shrine of the Magi, a supreme example of the art of the medieval goldsmiths, and a superb early-15th-century painted panel of the Adoration above the altar. Yet Cologne has never attracted the admiration or affection often lavished on apparently lesser buildings. There may be many reasons for this, but undoubtedly the proportions are slightly jarring. The cathedral is uncommonly broad in comparison to its length (275:466ft/84:142m), and the vault of the nave is almost as high as Beauvais. The two western towers, 512-ft (156-m) high, are so massive that not only do they exclude a central window, they also seem to be preparing to shoulder one another aside.

Medieval Cologne was a wealthy city whose ruling prince, the archbishop, was one of the seven imperial electors. Conflict between archbishop and citizens was frequent and often violent. Of the cathedral, started in 1284, little more than the choir was built in the following two centuries. A stationary crane sat on the base of the south tower for over 100 years, and during the Napoleonic Wars (1800–15) the cathedral was used as a barn or a military prison.

The surge of nationalism provoked by French occupation provided the impetus the cathedral needed. A special tax was levied to pay for the work, and luminaries like Goethe and the king of Prussia contributed. Remarkably, the original plans were discovered and between 1820 and 1880 the cathedral was finished, more or less in the style originally intended. It was severely damaged by bombing during the Second World War but has since been completely restored.

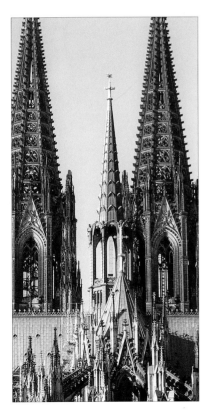

BELOW
From a distance, the vastness of Cologne Cathedral suggests a structure from another dimension.

BELOW LEFT
An unusual view, from the roof, of the twin spires.

Rouen Cathedral, showing the Butter Tower. The famous spire is obscured by the tree.

Rouen Cathedral

Notre Dame de Rouen was one of the subjects which spurred the painter Monet to produce a series of paintings (1892–95), made in different conditions and at different times of day; he is not alone in finding it a building of diverse effects. The present cathedral was begun in 1202, but not finished until 1509, and the overall impression is of a later Gothic style.

The old Norman capital was the seat of an archbishop in the 4th century, and for a long time it was the largest city in France outside Paris. Its historical importance is reflected in the size and splendour of the cathedral, which also reflects the many conflicts in which the city has suffered, most recently from international warfare. Bombs, while wreaking havoc with the existing structure, sometimes reveal

archaeological surprises, and at Rouen revealed traces of a very early church, dating back perhaps to Roman times. The cathedral contains survivals from before 1202, such as the base of the Tour St-Romain on the north-west; but otherwise most of the immense west front is Late Gothic, including the Flamboyant south-west tower, the Tour de Beurre (Butter Tower). Normandy is, of course, a great dairying region; the Tour de Beurre is so named because the cost of its construction was raised by sale of dispensations allowing butter to be eaten during Lent.

Perhaps the most interesting part of the interior is the early 14th-century Lady Chapel. It contains an outstanding example of Renaissance sculpture in the memorial to two cardinals d'Amboise, in black-and-white marble 26-ft (8-m) high.

Although spires were nearly always planned for Gothic cathedrals, few survived long, and the present, enormously tall spire of Rouen – at 512ft (156m) the highest in France – is made of cast iron and replaces the original, felled by lightning in 1822. It has attracted much criticism on the grounds of excessive height and because of the curious lantern-like structure at its tip. But, altogether, Rouen Cathedral is a building with many extraordinary and beautiful parts that do not quite make up a coherent whole.

Münster Cathedral

Münster, the old capital of Westphalia, became the seat of a bishop at the instigation of Charlemagne in 800. The cathedral is basically Romanesque but was largely rebuilt in the 13th–14th centuries and today combines elements of Romanesque and Gothic. Besides the Romanesque twin towers at the western end, the chapel next to the cloisters has a fine Romanesque tympanum, while the porch in the south contains admirable Gothic sculptures of scenes in Paradise.

The people of Münster are said to be more religious than most, and the cathedral today is seldom empty of worshippers who come for a few minutes of private prayer or to pay respects to the tomb of Cardinal Galen, opponent of the Nazis. The cathedral is of relatively modest proportions, solidly rooted in the town, adjoining a square packed with market stalls. There is a pleasing scent of cooking sausages in the air. But for all the appearance of solid conservatism, the religious history of Münster is exotic, for this was the town ruled briefly by an extreme and aberrant group of the otherwise pacific Anabaptists.

By the Reformation, the citizens of Münster had, after years of conflict, acquired some independence of their bishop, and the council was dominated by Lutherans. Two Anabaptist missionaries arriving from the Netherlands received an unexpected welcome, and they saw Münster as the New Jerusalem. Under the leadership of Jan Bockelson of Leiden, who aspired to rule the world preparatory to the Second Coming of Christ, they rapidly gained control of Münster, killing or driving out opponents. Private property was abolished and

all books except the Bible were burned. Since there was a superfluity of women, Münster being a haven for apostate nuns, Bockelson introduced polygamy. In the cathedral, many images were destroyed and, given the violence of Anabaptist rule, it is surprising that any

survived. For a time, the bishop was powerless, but besieged by the combined forces of the Catholic bishop and the Lutheran landgrave of Hesse, resistance collapsed, and the Anabaptists were destroyed with a cruel efficiency that more than equalled the ferocity of their regime.

Münster Cathedral is basically Romanesque but today contains elements of Romanesque and Gothic.

Regensburg Cathedral

The Bavarian city of Regensburg, sometimes called Ratisbon, is situated at a crucial crossing of the River Danube and was the site of a Roman military base. It became the seat of a bishop in the 8th century, when the first church was built on the site of the cathedral. Its 11th-century Romanesque successor, damaged by fire, was largely pulled down for the present cathedral in 1273, but some remnants survive, notably St Stephen's Chapel and All Saints' Chapel, a little octagonal tower with attached semicircular chapels, which still bear Romanesque murals in fair condition.

Regensburg was prosperous in the 13th century. It was a free imperial city and a major commercial entrepôt; much of the trade of Venice and the East passed across its famous stone bridge which was a century older than the cathedral but also still standing. Given the city's prosperity, financing construction of a new cathedral was not too daunting, and the east end rose quickly. The ground plan closely followed that of its predecessor, but the style was now the High Gothic of Strasbourg. Thereafter progress slowed down. Regensburg was still a famous city, the seat of the imperial diet, but it was suffering from increasing competition from booming Bavarian neighbours such as Augsburg and Nuremberg. Nevertheless, building continued according to the original plan until 1530, when the west side was completed, except that the towers rose only to the height of the nave. Like Cologne, Regensburg had to wait until 1867 for the final element and, as with Cologne, it is arguable that the building would be better off without its heavily and rather monotonously crocketed Flamboyant spires.

The interior was refashioned in the late 17th century in the contemporary style of Bavarian Baroque. The high altar remains an undulating dazzle of gilding, but a disapproving King Ludwig I ordered other Baroque embellishments to be removed in the 1830s. Though now rather austere, at least by Bavarian standards, the cathedral contains some 14th-century stained glass, and in particular, some naturalistic sculpture of ethereal charm by the artist known as the Erminhold Master.

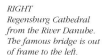

Salisbury Cathedral

Most medieval cathedrals were for obvious reasons built over a very long period; that is especially true of English cathedrals. Salisbury is an exception, since the bulk of it, choir, transepts and nave, was completed in a very short time, between 1220 and 1258, in the so-called Early English Gothic style. It is thus architecturally 'pure' in a way that few others are, and typifies English Gothic in the same way that Amiens typifies French.

A Norman cathedral existed in Old Sarum, on the top of a hill with a poor water supply and a royal castle uncomfortably nearby; when the decision to rebuild was taken in the early 13th century, a site was chosen on the plain close to the River Avon. That solved the water supply, but resulted in occasional flooding. The old cathedral was freely plundered for building stone, perhaps a factor in speeding construction. It is a very English setting, and the view of the cathedral from the water meadows, as painted by Constable, is an icon of the heritage industry.

Salisbury is one of the largest English cathedrals, slightly larger than Canterbury, which it resembles in adopting a double-transept plan. The west façade, an out-of-key add-on, the least successful part of the building and not helped by 19th-century replacements for the sculpted figures, was completed in 1266 and the octagonal chapter house about the same time. The perfectly proportioned steeple (tower plus spire), at 404ft (123m) much the tallest in England, was added in 1334.

The interior is cool and a trifle aloof. Many of the images, such as the statues of kings from the beautiful choir screen, disappeared in the Reformation or during other disturbances, and the stained glass was discarded during a disastrous 'restoration' in the 18th century, which also demolished the detached *campanile*. But the dimensions and proportions are impressive and the bold, coloured Purbeck stone of the columns is arresting. The Lady Chapel, with its plunging vaulting, was a structure of special importance because it contained the shrine of a saint. As an example of the Early English style at its best, it is perfect.

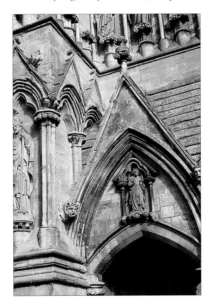

ABOVE
Detail of a side door on the west front.

RIGHT
The well proportioned steeple, seen from the cloisters.

Toledo Cathedral

According to legend, the city of Toledo was founded by Hercules: at any rate, it is a very old city. A Visigothic church was consecrated here in 589, and the early history of the city is closely bound up with the history of the Church in Spain. It was the scene of many early Church councils, and the long struggle between Spanish Catholicism and Arianism was fought out here. The archbishop of Toledo is still recognized as the primate of Spain, though the city itself declined in importance in the 16th century, especially after Philip II decided to make his capital at Madrid. One happy result is that to an unusual degree Toledo has retained its attractive medieval appearance.

The former church, which had served as a mosque under Muslim rule, was demolished by Ferdinand III of Castile (St Ferdinand) in order to build the present cathedral, which was founded in 1227. In spite of common misfortunes, such as despoliation by French soldiers in the Napoleonic era, the cathedral is one of the finest and richest in Spain. It follows the double-aisle plan and is somewhat similar to Bourges in plan, although it is much wider in relation to its height. Construction continued into the 16th century, with additions later, and the basic Gothic design is augmented by Renaissance and Baroque features. Except for the tower, the exterior has none of the extravagance of

Burgos, with very little decorative detail on the main body of the church; but it is equally sturdy and seemingly rooted to its site, 'clothed in russet tones, the colour of a browning roast or of a skin tanned like that of a pilgrim from Palestine'. The interior, thanks largely to its great space, is imposing, with much more sculptural decoration. Because of the space, the mass of powerful piers, each made up of 16 attached columns, do not seem to crowd the nave. Light percolates through the blue-and-red filters of the stained glass and gleams on gilded altarpieces, alabaster tombs and the dark wood of the finely carved choir stalls, all adding to the air of solemn luxury.

RIGHT
The south door of Toledo Cathedral.

FAR RIGHT
A view of the medieval city of Toledo, with the tower of the cathedral visible on the left.

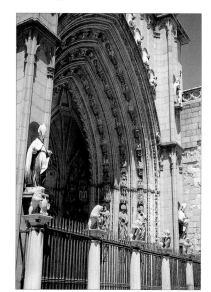

Florence Cathedral

The great Gothic cathedrals of northern Europe were created largely by craftsmen whose very names are often unknown. In 13th-century Florence, artists received more credit, and those who contributed to Santa Maria del Fiore included many of the most famous names of the early Renaissance, from Giotto to Michelangelo.

The cathedral (*duomo*) consists of several units, campanile, nave, domed octagon and baptistery, mostly built between 1296 and 1462. The interior is surprisingly plain, not overflowing with masterpieces as might be expected, and with little of the brilliant decorative effects of the marbled exterior. The original plan was by Arnolfo di Cambio, though it was expanded in the course of construction by Giotto, Andrea Pisano and other masters of the works. Giotto designed the campanile, though only the first stage was built in his lifetime, and his planned spire was never built at all. The Baptistery, in the west, is the oldest building of the group and may have originally served as a church in itself. Apart from the great dome, its most famous features are the bronze doors, a staple of any book on Renaissance art, the south door by Pisano from the 14th century, the others by Ghiberti a century later, which represented the winning design in a competition in which he tied with Brunelleschi, who backed out.

Brunelleschi's dome is one of the most discussed and, though itself unique, influential structures in the history of architecture. Brunelleschi had studied ancient architecture in Rome, including the Pantheon, but he was a more practical architect than many of his successors, more interested in engineering problems than reviving the antique; the pointed and ribbed dome of Florence is basically constructed on principles more Gothic than Classical. Given that the octagon on which the dome would rest could not be changed, and the distance that had to be spanned was nearly 141ft (43m), the general opinion was that the task was impossible. But Brunelleschi built his dome – strictly two domes, since there is an inner and outer shell of differing curvatures – without exterior buttresses or timber centring by binding the base with timber and iron rods, employing tension to prevent the dome from splitting outwards. The work took 14 years (1420–34).

The Cathedral of Florence, with the detached campanile and Brunelleschi's dome, one of the most emotive structures in the history of European architecture.

BELOW
The truncated Pont d'Avignon, with its chapel, a frequent feature of medieval bridges.

BELOW RIGHT
Attached turrets above the main entrance to the palace.

OPPOSITE
Machicolated tower: the formidable construction suggests the popes were prepared for trouble.

Palace of the Popes, Avignon

In 1305 the Bishop of Bordeaux was elected pope as Clement V, although he was not a cardinal and not an Italian. He immediately appointed a number of French bishops, showed no desire to go to Rome, and in 1309 finally settled in Avignon with his papal court. The 'Babylonian Captivity', as it came to be called, a period of absentee popes under French control, was a disastrous period for the authority of the papacy because it was so prolonged. Gregory XI did return to Rome in 1377 but on his death two rival popes were elected, one in Rome and one in Avignon, and the Great Schism did not come to an end until 1417, having done much over the previous century to encourage heretical thinking among disillusioned Christians.

The Palais des Papes in Avignon, now a museum and exhibition centre, is a monument to the near-failure of the medieval papacy. It is a rather severe assembly of Gothic buildings, its cliff-like walls giving it the appearance of a fortress rather than a palace. Inside, the absence of furnishings and lack of natural light make it even gloomier. Still, it does form an impressive setting for Avignon's annual international festival.

The palace, dwarfing the nearby cathedral, dates from the 14th and early 15th centuries and as the former citadel of the papal state of Avignon, it is a huge complex, with numerous public chambers, chapels, courtyards, towers and gardens. Like the famous bridge with its little Romanesque chapel that no longer crosses the Rhône, the palace has suffered severe damage at various times. It was used as a barracks for Napoleon's soldiers, who left nothing movable behind them and, it is said, even hacked off sections of frescoed wall. However, among other frescoes, they missed a remarkable work in the Oratory of St Michael which is attributed to the school of Duccio.

Cathedral of St Vitus, Prague

The site of Prague Cathedral, within the precincts of the castle, was formerly occupied by a Romanesque basilica, some parts of which can be seen in the crypt. The Gothic cathedral was founded in 1344 to mark the promotion of the bishop of Prague to archbishop. This was the city's golden age, when it was the capital of the Emperor Charles IV and the greatest city in northern Europe. The designer of the cathedral was a Frenchman, Matthias of Arras, but he died in 1352, having seen the east end almost finished. Charles then hired a Swabian, Peter Parler, whose statue may be his self-portrait, whose family played an important part in the

adornment of Bohemia and southern Germany in the 14th–15th centuries and made Prague a temple of the late, courtly style sometimes called 'International Gothic'. Building continued until the Hussite revolt in the early 15th century brought it to a stop, with the nave and most of the main tower unbuilt. A temporary wall was built to close off the nave.

Little progress was made for three centuries. The onion-topped tower, which is nearly 325-ft (100-m) tall, was built in the 16th century, though the Baroque roof dates from about 1770. Otherwise, the cathedral had to wait for another period in the 19th century, when national enthusiasm was high and there was the added inspiration of Cologne. Some of the work, such as the bronze doors depicting an episode from the life of St Wenceslaus, is of high quality. The western spires went up in 1892, and the building was completed just in time to celebrate the millennium of the death of St Wenceslaus in 1929.

The cathedral contains a vast collection of treasures; there are, for example, 24 chapels in the cathedral and few do not contain objects of interest. Perhaps the most notable is the statue of the saint himself in the Wenceslaus Chapel, which is a product of the Parler workshop. A pleasant surprise is the stained-glass window in the New Archbishop's Chapel by Alphonse Mucha, master of the art nouveau poster.

The Cathedral of St Vitus was a product of Prague's golden age, when it was the greatest city in northern Europe.

Ulm Cathedral

Ulm, the city of the *meistersinger*, had been a free imperial city, answerable to no one except the emperor, since 1155. Its great church was founded in 1377, partly as a mark of gratitude for a further boost to its prosperity resulting from victory over the rival city of Württemberg. The church was to hold 30,000 people, probably more than the population of the city at that date, but Ulm was expanding, and by the early 15th century the population was nearer 60,000.

The advanced German Gothic style known as Sondergotik ('special Gothic') developed partly from the rise of the individual artist-craftsmen who are often known by name and by the buildings on which they worked. The Parler family, encountered also in Prague and elsewhere, were engaged on the choir at Ulm, and the master mason from 1392 was Ulrich von Ensinger, member of another well-known family. He is also known to have worked at Strasbourg and Milan, but Ulm is his masterpiece.

The Gothic style in Germany had developed quite differently from France. The German passion for tall spires led to the custom of building one giant steeple, instead of two, at the west end. Ulm minster is the outstanding example, its spire topping out at 529ft (161m) above the ground, the tallest in Germany or anywhere else. To reduce weight, Ulrich employed elaborate tracery and openwork: from some angles one sees more sky than stone, which helps to prevent the spire from seeming too overbearing. However, Ulrich did not, of course, see it finished. He did complete the first stage of the tower, though even that ran into

problems forcing a change of plan; but the spire was only finished in the 1880s. The roof was then strengthened with iron and, when the brick walls protested, the flying buttresses were installed along the sides.

Inside, the minster's finest treasures are Hans Multscher's realistic figure, Christ as Man of Sorrows (c. 1429), and the fine, humanistic, wood-carved figures of the choir stalls by a renowned Swabian artist.

Ulm Cathedral at night. Its spire is the tallest in Germany or, indeed, anywhere else.

Rambouillet

Rambouillet, about 28 miles (45km) south-west of Paris, belongs to that class of French château that began life as a medieval fort and survived into a more peaceful age to become a luxurious country house or hunting lodge, a function that Rambouillet, with its extensive forest, has fulfilled for kings, emperors and more recently, for presidents of the republic.

The château was built in the 14th century and was owned for 300 years by the D'Angennes family, one of whom, in the 17th century, was the husband of the Marquise de Rambouillet, arbiter of Parisian taste. Though strongly defended, it was more a fortified house than a castle, and it changed hands more than once during the Hundred Years War. The only obvious medieval relic now is the great, machicolated Tour François I, named after that Renaissance monarch because he is supposed to have died there after being taken ill while hunting. Other parts were rebuilt during the Renaissance, but the greatest changes were made in the 18th century when Rambouillet came into the possession of the Comte de Toulouse, a son of Louis XIV. He enlarged the place considerably, and built Classical façades that concealed the medieval walls. An unusual feature for which he was also responsible is the decoration of carved wood, in which oak, though an intractable material, is transformed into lacy patterns almost as if it were plaster.

Rambouillet passed to Louis XVI in 1784, who made some changes required by Marie Antoinette, including a small dairy (though in agricultural history Rambouillet is more famous as an early centre of sheep breeding), and it was fortunate to escape the Revolution if not unscathed, in sufficient order for Napoleon to restore it for his own use. He demolished one wing, rebuilt the main gate and the east turret and had his own suite of rooms built next to the Tour François I. The imperial bathroom is a splendid Neoclassical chamber in which the actual bath may be easily overlooked.

RIGHT
Except for its ivy-covered towers, Rambouillet betrays small sign of its origins as a fortress.

OPPOSITE
The garden front.

Guarda Cathedral

Guarda is the highest town in Portugal, almost 3,280ft (1000m) above sea level in the Serra da Estrela; its breezy climate is said to be healthy and its hospital was founded as a sanatorium for consumptives. The region is rural, sparsely populated, and off the tourist track, but the town contains a ruined castle and several other medieval buildings, of which the most interesting is the cathedral.

The Romans built a fort here, but there is no evidence of substantial settlement until the town was founded by Sancho I in the 12th century. The older buildings, in rough granite, look as if they have been there much longer. As its name implies, the town was a defensive outpost, keeping watch on the borders of Muslim – and for that matter, in later times, on Christian – Spain. It is said that one of the gargoyles looking towards the Spanish border makes a rude gesture, but this is not apparent from ground level.

The cathedral was founded in 1390 and completed by 1540. It derives from the well-known monastic church of Batalha, near Leira, which was inspired by French and Norman examples; but Guarda is an altogether tougher customer, built of harsh, rusty granite, which looks well prepared to withstand a siege. Except for the west door, there is virtually no external decoration. The octagonal west towers are not much higher than the roof and the tower over the crossing was never built. Yet the appearance of plainness is misleading. The building has a subtle symmetry, best appreciated from a raised viewpoint such as the towers of the Baroque church nearby, and the design is both rich and complicated. Inside, the lofty vault is supported by rectangular columns, with the end pair surprisingly in a cable-twist pattern, a familiar device of the Portuguese late Gothic style known as Manueline. The florid furnishings in the Manueline style strike an undeniable note of nationalistic grandeur, issuing a reminder that, when the cathedral was built, tiny Portugal was leading Europe in establishing a worldwide maritime empire.

RIGHT
Statue of King Sancho I (reigned 1185–1211), known as the Builder of Cities, among them the frontier town of Guarda.

FAR RIGHT
The stalwart cathedral, from the north.

Vienna Cathedral

Stefansdom, the cathedral church of St Stephen, is a great monument of godliness and Gothic architecture in a city not especially renowned for either. It predates the Habsburgs, having been founded by Ottokar the Great of Bohemia in the 13th century shortly before he surrendered Vienna to Rudolf I, the first Habsburg emperor, in 1273. However, most of the present building is of a later date.

Like many medieval cathedrals, St Stephen's is architecturally a mixture, and one in which time has not altogether succeeded in achieving a harmonious blend. The cathedral has many beautiful things, but as one critic remarked, it is a building that should be appreciated according to humane rather than architectural standards.

It is basically a very large example of the *hallenkirchen* ('hall churches') of characteristic German Gothic type, with nave and aisles of equal height. In Vienna they are covered by a single, immense, steeply-pitched roof decorated with an audacious zigzag pattern of black, green, white and yellow tiles and, over the

choir, a huge Habsburg eagle rather suggestive of modern advertising hoardings. All this is 19th-century work. Of course, the plan of the building rules out a clerestory, which makes the interior rather dim, though there is light enough to admire the rich Baroque decoration, the magnificent tomb of the Emperor Frederick III, the great organ, and the Late Gothic pulpit carved from a single block of stone by Anton Pilgram, who carved his own portrait below the steps.

The oldest part is the west front, which includes parts of the Romanesque original. The tall main door is flanked by two unusual, rather oddly proportioned, octagonal towers that terminate in spires. The transepts act as entrance porches, and above the south transept rises Vienna's finest feature, the great spear-like steeple, 450-ft (137-m) high, which was raised in the early 15th century, though its intended northern twin was never built. Unusually, there is little openwork, but proportion and filigree modelling prevent a sense of heaviness.

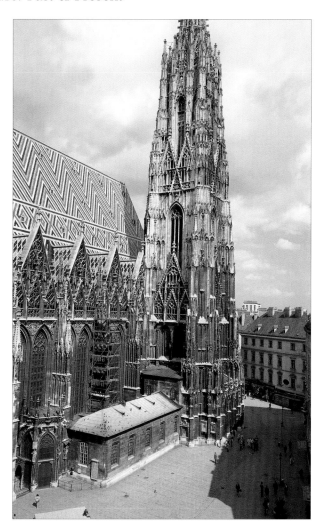

The great steeple of St Stephen's Cathedral, over the south transept, still awaits its twin on the north.

*Milan Cathedral is
without doubt a
magnificent artistic
achievement, yet it is
also, in its way, a failure.*

Milan Cathedral

The Italians tended to remain faithful to their
Classical heritage, the Gothic style being less
suitable in the south, where large windows are
not desirable, than in the north. It is sometimes
said that there are no true Gothic buildings in
Italy, which is to take too French a view of
Gothic, but even those who make that
generalization allow one exception, Milan
Cathedral. Gothic did offer one advantage that
Italian architects recognized – greater interior
space – and Florence and Pisa are examples of
a new spaciousness. Milan and other cities also
produced quite individual styles.

Started under the Visconti dukes in the late
14th century, Milan Cathedral was the largest
building project of its time, and its construction
was spread over many generations. The project
enjoyed widespread popular support, and on
occasions when money ran short the citizens
provided free labour. Progress was still slow.
The façade was not begun until the 17th
century, the 15th-century lantern did not get its
spire until the 18th century, and the north side
was not completed until the 19th century. What
emerged was a building with a decidedly French
flavour, although it can also be alleged to
demonstrate the Italians' basic lack of sympathy
for French Gothic. The usual ingredients are
present – flying buttresses, huge windows, a
forest of pinnacles; but there is a very unGothic
emphasis on horizontals, the pitch of the roof is
low, and the building does not soar like the
cathedrals of the Île de France. It is a very
sophisticated design, with the elevation built on
a series of equilateral triangles, a concept alien
to the French masters. Besides learned residents
like Leonardo, many advisers from north of the
Alps came to resolve technical problems at
various times, but most stayed only briefly and
left in frustration, even rage.

It remains one of Europe's most remarkable
buildings. It is built of brick faced with pinkish
marble, and its great bulk is offset by the rich
and complex exterior decoration – 'lacework
in stone'. The lantern is a triumph of Renaissance
engineering, the polygonal apse is inspired, and
the array of sculpture provides a detailed lesson
in the history of European sculpture through
five centuries.

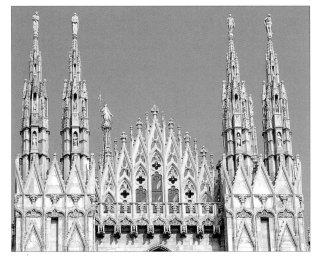

Kremlin, Moscow

Most old Russian cities have a 'kremlin', which comes from a word meaning fortress or citadel. The most famous one, in Moscow, consists of a walled enclave covering an area of about 90 acres (36 hectares) on a hillside above the Moskva river, and adjoining Red Square. It has been, besides a fortress, the residence of tsars and patriarchs, the seat of government and the centre of Russian religious and political life. It contains a wealth of ecclesiastical and palatial buildings, and from across the river it is a glittering array of gilded cupolas and stone towers.

First mentioned in the 14th century, when some of the buildings would still have been of wood, it was reconstructed by Ivan III in the late 15th to early 16th centuries. Problems arose when a rebuilt church collapsed before the

vault was completed, and Ivan was forced to call in Italian architects. They studied the principles of Byzantine architecture before they began, but more than a trace of the Italian Renaissance made itself evident in their work, sometimes called 'Lombardo-Byzantine' in style, and it proved a persistent influence.

The old buildings are grouped around the cathedral square, several of which are based on earlier churches. The cathedral of the Assumption, for example, was modelled on the 12th-century cathedral in the city of Vladimir, though with Lombard affiliations. The Archangel Cathedral (1505–09), where the tsars are buried, bears signs of the Italian Renaissance, especially in its decorative devices. Of Ivan's Grand Ducal Palace, called the Granite Palace, only the magnificent vaulted hall now survives, along with his 266-ft (81-m)

bell tower, the oldest, and tallest, of several.

Three grand palaces in the Russian Baroque style survive from the 17th century, when defence ceased to be a prime consideration and cupolas were added to defensive towers. Construction continued in the 18th century although Moscow had ceased to be the capital. Several older buildings were demolished to make way for the vast Great Kremlin Palace, fronting the river, which was built in the mid-19th century under Nicholas I and later used as a parliamentary assembly. It can hold 20,000 people, surely a reasonable capacity for even the tsar's court. In the Soviet era, two substantial but unattractive buildings were added and some necessary restoration took place. The Kremlin was opened to the public in 1953.

OPPOSITE
The Great Kremlin Palace is said to contain 700 apartments, most of them of substantial size.

BELOW
The gilded cupolas of the Kremlin churches and the old Terem palace (right).

Old Hospital, Beaune

Among the finest masterpieces of the Louvre is a painting known as *Madonna with the Chancellor Rolin*, by the greatest master of the early Dutch school, Jan van Eyck. It is a sumptuous painting, its colours still glowing as richly as they did when freshly painted nearly 600 years ago, thanks to Van Eyck's mastery of the medium he was once thought to have invented, and in particular to the quality of his varnish. Van Eyck was court painter to Philip the Good, duke of Burgundy, from 1426, and spent several years in and out of the wealthy, aristocratic, cynical Burgundian court with which, as a painter, he showed such affinity. His painting of the worldly Cardinal Rolin, the duke's chancellor, is dated to about 1435.

Rolin was a remarkable man, intelligent, rich, powerful, ruthless, feared, but he was a generous patron. He founded the hospital of St-Esprit in Beaune, which was also known as the Hôtel-Dieu, God's House, which was opened in 1452. Rolin owned valuable vineyards on the Côte d'Or, still the mainstay of Beaune's economy, but the town was also the birthplace of his mother, and his foundation may well have been a form of spiritual insurance, an act of retribution, and a gift to the people he had exploited. He certainly showed himself willing to spend freely, and the building, ranged around a broad courtyard, might well today be an expensive resort rather than a refuge for the poor and sick. Its steep roofs are covered with coloured tiles arranged in geometric patterns and pierced by dormer windows. Below is an open gallery supported by neat, faceted columns that form a colonnade for the lower floor. In the courtyard is a well with contemporary ironwork and an outdoor pulpit.

Part of the hospital is still in use, though other wards have been converted into a museum. Exhibits include an altarpiece of The Last Judgement commissioned by Rolin from Rogier van der Weyden, who at the time was an even more popular painter than Van Eyck.

ABOVE
The famous Giralda,
once a minaret and the
most notable feature of
what is possibly the
largest cathedral in the
world.

RIGHT
Seville Cathedral,
because of its structure
and great size, was
responsible for
transforming the later
architecture of central
Spain.

Seville Cathedral

Great size is a characteristic of Spanish cathedrals in general and the most obvious distinction of the Cathedral of Santa Maria de la Sede in Seville is that, depending on what measurements are involved, it is the largest not only in Spain but anywhere else in Europe.

According to legend, the 15th-century builders held the opinion that anyone looking at their finished building would be so amazed by its size and shape that he would think them mad; in spite of such a gloomy forecast, the building was finished in remarkably short time, between 1402 and 1520. There is no reason to doubt the sanity of the builders, if only because the size and shape of the building are difficult to perceive on the congested site without the advantage of a helicopter. One tends to see the cathedral only in glimpses, and the situation is further complicated by numerous additions, including a Baroque parish church north of the cathedral, which disguise the original form.

Overall, the roughly rectangular plan measures about 427 x 263ft (130 x 80m). The height of the nave is 131ft (40m) and of the central crossing 184ft (56m). The unusual overall dimensions result from the fact that the site was originally occupied by a mosque; the cathedral has followed the mosque in choosing area over axis. More concrete signs of the mosque remain, notably the famous campanile or bell tower known as the Giralda, which was once a minaret and still bears Muslim decoration below the elaborately Classical belfry.

The hugely spacious, double-aisled interior, with 32 enormous but finely articulated piers and over 70 windows, contains many rich and artistic objects: paintings by the Spanish masters,

fine Renaissance metalwork and carving, and the marvellous Late Gothic screen of gilded wood with scenes from the Life of Christ. There is also a wooden image of the Virgin with movable arms and hair of spun gold, which was presented to St Ferdinand (Ferdinand III of Castile, conqueror of Seville) by his fellow monarch and saint, St Louis, in the 13th century.

Frauenkirche, Munich

Munich is not a city dominated by a particular style or period, like Romanesque Regensburg. Comparatively modern by Bavarian standards, founded by Henry the Lion in the 12th century, Munich contains a wide variety of different sorts of buildings. Much of their magnificence is due to the enthusiasm of King Ludwig I of Bavaria, though there were many losses to Allied bombs during the Second World War, when about one-third of the city was destroyed, including the Wittelsbach palace, but not, ironically, the large and hideous headquarters of the Nazi party. The Frauenkirche, a cathedral since only 1817, also survived, though was seriously damaged; however, most of its valuable furnishings had been removed and stored somewhere safer for the duration.

Rather unusually for Munich, the Frauenkirche, built in the 15th century, is an indigenous building, designed by a local architect, Jörg von Halsbach, known as Ganghofer, who is otherwise unknown. Nor can it be said that he was particularly inspired, though he was certainly more than competent. He was a follower of Hans Stetthaimer, builder of the earlier St Martin's Church at Landshut with its 436-ft (133-m) brick tower. The Frauenkirche is fairly typical of the large south German hall church, which always tends to achieve its spacious interior at the cost of a rather dull exterior. The main structure was complete by 1479, when the vast roof, whose timbers must have depleted the Bavarian forests, was finished. The towers were added later, and they are far the most important feature, responsible for the familiarity of the Frauenkirche as a symbol of the city. As in other examples of architectural landmarks, the appeal is not easily accounted for in architectural terms, for the twin red-brick towers, though matching the rest of the building in mass, are not in themselves particularly spectacular despite their individual bulbous cupolas. They are, however, unmistakable, and that must account for their symbolic status.

BELOW LEFT
Munich's cathedral is a fine example of a south German hall church, a design that gains in interior space but loses in light.

BELOW
Detail of the unusual towers.

OPPOSITE
The Palacio da Pena.

*BELOW and BELOW
RIGHT
The Palacio Nacional de
Sintra.*

Palaces of Sintra

The attractive little town of Sintra is set among the hilly woodlands of the Sierra de Sintra, about 15 miles west of Lisbon. Its charms were celebrated by the great Portuguese national poet Camoes, and later by Lord Byron in *Childe Harold's Pilgrimage.* For centuries it was the summer refuge of the Portuguese royal family. Among their memorials are the royal palace in the Old Town, partly wrecked in the earthquake of 1755 but afterwards restored, and the spectacular Palacio da Pena, which crowns a hilltop.

The royal palace, brusquely described by one writer as Moorish and debased Gothic, and by an 18th-century English visitor as this confused pile, is not a prepossessing building from the outside. The first one is likely to see of it is the enormous conical chimneys of the kitchens. It was once thought to be an old Moorish palace, but it seems to have been built from scratch in the reign of John I (1385–1433), though with many Muslim characteristics and on the site of a Muslim building. It has also many features of the curious Portuguese late-Gothic style known as Manueline, which itself owed something to Muslim tradition.

The extraordinary Gothick Palacio da Pena incorporates the Monastery of Our Lady of Pena, which was built about 1500. The monastic ruins were bought in 1839 by Ferdinand of Saxe-Coburg-Gotha, first cousin of both Queen Victoria and Prince Albert, who had married Maria II of Portugal in 1836, receiving the title of king-consort. With the advice of a Prussian engineer, Ludwig von Eschwege, he greatly enlarged it and turned it into a Romantic medieval, palace, part monastery part castle, as a gift for his wife. Opinion on such a building is bound to be highly subjective, but Ferdinand's project, judged on his terms, is a dramatic success. The intensely Romantic atmosphere is heightened by the richly exotic furnishings and, in the chapel, a fine Renaissance altar piece. Today, the palace is the scene of concerts and other cultural activities.

Christiansborg

Christiansborg, the royal slot (castle) in Copenhagen, has been rebuilt at least five times in the course of over 800 years of stormy history, and although it still contains traces of the original 12th-century building, most of what one sees today is less than 100 years old.

Bishop Absalon, founder of Copenhagen, erected his 'harbour castle' in 1167. It played a vital part in the development of the little fishing and trading port during the Middle Ages as it strove to exploit and control the prosperous Baltic trade. The castle was captured twice in the 13th century, when Denmark was weakened by constitutional conflict, and was destroyed and built again. The growing strength of the Hanseatic League, which did not believe in free competition, resulted again in destruction in 1370, when the Danish king was forced to sign the Treaty of Stralsund confirming the dominance of the Hanse. It rose again, and by 1500, with the power of the League fading, Denmark regained its position as the leading North European power. Under Christian III (reigned 1534–59) the castle was much enlarged and became a royal residence. The first tower was added by Christian IV in the 17th century.

In the 18th century much of the existing castle was demolished, and a new one, the first to be called Christiansborg, arose between 1731 and 1745. The Rococo remains suggest a splendid palace, but unfortunately they are few, as it burned down in 1794. Its successor was in Neoclassical style, but lasted only a short time longer and perished by the same means in 1894. The present Christiansborg, founded in 1907, is the work of Thorvald Jörgensen. It is an unpretentiously elegant building, mainly of granite with a copper roof and with an unconventional central tower, which is about 330-ft (100-m) high and is a famous landmark in Copenhagen. As well as being the official residence of the monarch, Christiansborg contains parliament, the supreme court and ministries.

RENAISSANCE TO BAROQUE

CHAPTER FOUR

Medici-Riccardi Palace, Florence	Saint-Germain-en-Laye	Versailles
Pitti Palace, Florence	The Louvre	Royal Palace, Amsterdam
Ducal Palace, Urbino	Longleat	Royal Palace, Turin
Quirinal Palace, Rome	Villa Rotonda, Vicenza	Drottningholm Palace
Barberini Palace, Rome	The Escorial	Charlottenburg
Ducal Palace, Mantua	Rialto Bridge, Venice	Nymphenburg, Munich
Wawel Castle, Cracow	Teatro Olimpico, Vicenza	Schönbrunn, Vienna
King's College Chapel, Cambridge	Saint Basil's Cathedral, Moscow	Blenheim Palace
Segovia Cathedral	Saint Peter's, Rome	The Belvedere, Vienna
Fontainebleau	Il Gesù, Rome	Superga, Turin
Château de Chambord	Santa Maria della Salute, Venice	Royal Palace, Stockholm
Hampton Court	Mexico City Cathedral	Saint Nicholas, Prague
Château de Chantilly	Saint Paul's Cathedral, London	

The revival of Classical learning and Classical values in the Renaissance was one aspect of fundamental changes in European society which happened, more slowly than appears in retrospect, over the course of many generations. No new development was more important than the invention of printing, which allowed ideas to spread more quickly and to more people. Printed books helped to undermine the totalitarian authority of the medieval Church and promote the growth of humanism, again inspired by ancient – and of course pre-Christian – civilization, which the

humanists saw as a cultural golden age. Printing also made widely available two written works which, together with the discovery of the law of perspective (perhaps by Brunelleschi, the first true Renaissance architect), had enormous influence on architecture. The treatise of Vitruvius, De architectura, written in the 1st century BC and almost unknown even to scholars until the 15th century, was printed in Rome in 1486. Leon Battista Alberti's equally famous, and more lucid, book on architecture, De re aedificatoria, clarified the mathematical principles of design and proportion which, correctly followed, lead to perfect harmony. Though written in about 1452, it was not printed until 1485. It had many successors, notably Vasari's Lives (1550–68) and Palladio's Four Books, I quattro libri di architettura (1570). For the first time, architecture became, if not yet quite a profession, a serious occupation and an admired art,

with established theoretical texts.

Renaissance art and architecture began in Italy in the early 15th century and did not spread to other countries until the 16th. Elsewhere it took different forms, and the first result of the spread of Italian ideas and Italian artists was usually some kind of mixture of Medieval and Classical, as in the châteaux of the Loire, or the elaborate Spanish style known as Plateresque. The influential School of Fontainebleau encouraged a further proliferation of complex styles in different countries; the great houses of Elizabethan-Jacobean England are one example. They were akin, if at some distance, to Italian Mannerism, a more self-conscious style exemplified by Michelangelo in Rome and Giulio Romano in Mantua, which emerged from Classicism in the mid-16th century. Great houses and palaces rose to challenge churches as the pre-eminent buildings of European civilization.

In the 17th century Mannerism, always more of a variant than a distinct style, gave way to Baroque. Like 'Gothic', this was originally a term of abuse, meaning 'misshapen', for a new, vigorous, often emotional interpretation that, while recognizing the authority of the antique, offered greater freedom to the individual artist. Outside Italy, it resulted in so rich a variety of styles (e.g. very restrained in England, very ornate in Spain) that the name 'Baroque' is more apt as a description of the age than as a specific style.

Medici-Riccardi Palace, Florence

Generally known as the Palazzo Riccardi, after its more recent proprietors, this rather forbidding building was the home of the Medici rulers of Florence in the 15th and 16th centuries. It was commissioned by Cosimo the Elder (1389–1464), who ruled as a despot without holding any major office, and was built between about 1444 and 1460. Here beat the heart of the Florentine Renaissance, where Lorenzo the Magnificent kept his brilliant court, Michelangelo first tried out his sculptor's chisels and the Platonic academy was lavishly entertained. It was also the headquarters of the Medici commercial empire.

These Italian Renaissance palaces, built around a courtyard, derived from ancient Roman forms. In the Palazzo Rucellai, built at the same time by the most influential contemporary architect, Leon Battista Alberti, the three Classical orders were employed as pilasters on the three floors in the manner of the Colosseum, though this example was not widely followed as it posed problems of proportion. The huge Medici palace was designed by Michelozzo di Bartolommeo, a follower of Brunelleschi, and is his best-known work. Elsewhere, Michelozzo is renowned for the lightness of his style, but that is certainly not evident here. The impression the palace makes is one of immense strength, emphasized by the pronounced rustication of the lowest storey. These early princely residences were almost fortified houses: they were not expected to withstand a siege, but angry, stone-throwing mobs were a more likely hazard. The second storey is faced with lightly channelled stone, and the top storey is smooth.

The building is crowned by an elaborate cornice incorporating Classical motifs.

The interior is more gracious: the rooms are arranged around an open, arcaded courtyard and the main apartments are on the *piano nobile*, the principal floor (second storey), reached by a splendid staircase. Among the treasures of the palace are the frescoes by

Benozzo Gozzoli, painted in 1463, in the little chapel, which illustrate the Journey of the Magi and incorporate several Medici portraits.

The palace was sold to the Riccardi in 1659 and was later altered and extended (there used to be ten, not 17, windows on the second storey). It became state property in the 19th century.

The palace, commissioned by Cosimo the Elder, was once the home of the Medici rulers of Florence in the 15th and 16th centuries.

The rear façade of the Pitti Palace by Ammanati, with the octagonal Fountain of the Artichoke in the foreground.

Pitti Palace, Florence

Formerly the residence of the grand dukes of Tuscany, the Medici and their successors of the house of Lorraine, the Pitti now houses one of the world's great collections of Renaissance art, second only to the Uffizi across the river. The palazzo was built on rising ground near the Ponte Vecchio for Luca Pitti, an ambitious adherent of Cosimo de' Medici, beginning in 1458. Tradition says that the original plans were by the great Filippo Brunelleschi, best known for the dome of Florence cathedral, which is possible although he was dead before work began.

Luca Pitti had chosen an inauspicious moment to commemorate the prestige of his family; within eight years, with the building barely half finished, the decline of the Pitti put an end to its construction. Having passed to the Medici, it was completed and enlarged 100 years later in the time of of the Medici Grand Duke Cosimo I, on the initiative of his wife, Eleanor of Toledo. The architect was Bartolommeo Ammanati, perhaps best known for the charming Ponte S.Trinità over the Arno. He built the slightly grotesque, though often copied, rusticated façade of the Pitti that overlooks the famous Boboli Gardens. Further minor additions were made in the 17th century, and in the 18th century the projecting outer wings were added. They rather spoiled the symmetry of the building but contributed to its appearance as probably the largest and the most imposing palace in Italy outside the Vatican.

The fame of the Pitti as an art gallery dates from the late 18th century, when the public was first admitted to view the paintings. The gorgeous rooms of the Galleria Palatina, each named after one of the planets, contain some 500 Renaissance paintings, mainly Florentine, naturally, but include many of the finest Venetians, several Raphaels and Rubens. There are really five museums in the Pitti, which also contains the treasures collected by the Medici grand dukes, a gallery of modern Tuscan art, and a coach museum.

Ducal Palace, Urbino

The most attractive of all early Renaissance palaces, Urbino is a monument to Duke Federigo da Montefeltro, a model 'Renaissance man' whose hooked nose and square, intelligent head are familiar from several contemporary paintings. His court at Urbino was perhaps less glamorous that those of the Medici in Florence or the Este in Ferrara, but it was one of the liveliest centres of Renaissance culture in Italy.

The palace is very large, spacious, and irregular in plan, largely due to its adaptation to a hilltop site. The transformation of the original medieval building began in 1468 and, thanks to the tall, turreted towers that flank the entrance, and notwithstanding their rather unconvincing machicolation, the first appearance is Gothic. There are also medieval inclusions in part of the east wing and elsewhere, but within the great courtyard, surrounded by its graceful Corinthian colonnade, all is cool Classicism. The architect was the Dalmatian Luciano da Laurana, whose command of delicate detail was unrivalled. He had numerous assistants and advisers, not the least of them perhaps the man responsible for the basic conception, the Duke himself; but they also probably included Piero della Francesca, to whom is attributed the well-known painted panel of an ideal city, and possibly the young Bramante, who was born near Urbino in 1444.

The ducal apartments were beyond the towered west façade, and a passage led to Laurana's 'secret garden', with geometric flower beds and a central fountain. The largest room is the Throne Room in the east, where all the windows face north to provide a pure but subdued light. The decoration everywhere – sculptures, friezes, paintings – is all of a very high order. But perhaps the most fascinating room is a quite small one, the study of Duke Federigo, with its brilliant, illusionist marquetry, said to be based on designs by Botticelli, its carved and pierced wooden panels and brightly coloured ceiling.

View of Urbino, with its twin towers on the right, shows the rather cramped site that partly dictated the plan of the palace.

Quirinal Palace, Rome

The former summer home of the popes is only about 15 minutes' walk from the Vatican, but as it is set on the Quirinal hill, it is usually appreciably cooler, and commands a fine view of Rome. The palace, which is very large and rather complex, was begun by Pope Gregory XIII in 1583 and continued under his immediate successors. The finest Roman artists of the Mannerist and early Baroque periods were employed in its construction and decoration, and it also includes antique and Renaissance works, such as the Classical figures of the Horse-Tamers, found originally in the Baths of Constantine.

The original buildings are mainly the work of Carlo Maderno and Domenico Fontana, who built the main front and the façade overlooking the piazza (except for the entrance portal, designed by Flaminio Ponzio with later embellishments by Bernini). Ponzio also designed the Pope's private chapel (Capella del'Annunciata), which contains beautiful paintings by Guido Reni and other members of the Bolognese school. The highly elaborate Sala Regia (or Sala de Corazzieri) designed, together with the adjoining public chapel, by Maderno, is without doubt the most arresting chamber. It contains ornamental contributions by Bernini and Agostino Tassi, and its marble floor reflects the gilded stucco ceiling and Tassi's painted frieze, in which human figures appear to be leaning out of windows overlooking the room. Among other rooms of special interest are the 18th-century Mirror Room in the Chinese style and a beautiful little library of the same period with inlaid ivory and mother-of-pearl in a delicate Rococo arrangement.

The gardens, little changed since the early 17th century, have statues, fountains, palms, orange trees and lawns enclosed by box hedges cut with military precision, as well as a little Palladian coffee house and an organ played by water.

The Quirinal palace was used by popes hoping to escape the heat and malaria of the Vatican until the late 19th century, when it was appropriated by the King of Italy. Today it is occupied by the president of the Republic.

The former summer palace of the popes on the Quirinale.

The Sala Regia.

Details of atlantes, *Barberini Palace.*

Barberini Palace, Rome

The Palazzo Barberini, now the Italian National Gallery, though popularly still known as the Barberini Gallery, is in terms of ostentatious Baroque splendour, one of the most magnificent palaces in Rome. And so it should be, given the reputation of the architects who worked on it. The Barberini family was established in Florence in the 14th century and settled in Rome in the mid-16th century (it seems very profitably). In 1623 Mafeo Barberini was elected pope as Urban VIII. He was an effective ruler but notorious for nepotism and plunder. He was responsible for removing the bronze beams from the Pantheon, provoking the acid witticism, *Quod non fecerunt barbari, fecerunt Barberini* ('What the Barbarians did not do, the Barberini did').

The Palazzo Barberini, opposite the Quirinal Gardens on the Via delle Quattro Fontane, was begun during Urban VIII's pontificate. Three architects are primarily associated with it, Maderno, Bernini and Borromini, which, as someone remarked, is like having a baptism conducted by the Holy Trinity. Exactly who was responsible for what is a matter of argument, but the general consensus is that the original plans of Maderno, who died in 1629 when construction had barely begun, were carried out fairly faithfully by his exalted successors. The most notable feature, however, the great central portico with its two upper rows of large arched windows, is probably the work of Bernini, as is the more orthodox, rectangular staircase. The subtle oval staircase on the other side of the building is likely to be one of Borromini's contributions.

The basic plan is unusual for a Roman palace, since it is in the form of an H, like a country villa, thus lacking a central courtyard. The famous ceiling fresco of the great hall, called an *Allegory of Divine Providence and Barberini Power*, in which the figures seem to float above the room, is the masterpiece of Pietro da Cortona, a client of the Barberini and the exponent of illusionist Baroque decoration at its most extravagant.

Ducal Palace, Mantua

The Gonzaga family gained control of the fortified island city of Mantua in Lombardy in the early 14th century and held it for nearly 400 years. Their court was a centre of princely patronage as early as 1350, and in the 15th century it attracted such major figures of Renaissance art as Alberti and Mantegna, who is buried in Mantua. It reached the height of its reputation during the time of Isabella d'Este (1474–1539), wife of the Gonzaga marquess, and his successor, Federigo II (1500–40). He became the first duke and presided over a court that outclassed even the Medici in Florence.

During this period, several palaces and villas were built, notably the Palazzo del Te (1525–35), the summer villa and honeymoon home (hence the erotic frescoes), which was designed by Giulio Romano. Mantua attracted many of the greatest names of the High Renaissance, including Leonardo, Raphael and Titian.

The vast ducal palace contains about 500 rooms and has stabling for 600 horses; some staircases were designed for horses, to spare their riders the fatigue of climbing on foot. The building goes back to the early 14th century, predating the Gonzaga takeover, and still retains its 14th-century Gothic façade. Many additions, and most of the interior, were undertaken under the Gonzaga, especially during the reign of Federigo, by Giulio Romano and his successors. Their frescoes, woodwork and stucco ornament by Primaticcio, busts by Bernini and some fine Venetian glass remain to be admired, though many of the Gonzaga treasures have been dispersed. Among other remarkable features are an enormous roof garden, a highly informative astrological clock, which recommends the best

time to go on a journey or have one's clothes mended, and a group of apartments built to a small scale for the dwarfs of whom the Gonzaga, themselves subject to a hereditary tendency to deformation of the spine, were so fond. Some later decoration is less attractive: the inspired

taste of the Gonzaga during the Renaissance declined towards the end of the 16th century and degenerated into mere extravagance.

The palace of the dukes of Mantua is probably the largest and grandest of all the Renaissance princely palazzi. This is the view from the cathedral.

Wawel, home of the Jagellion dynasty.

Wawel Castle, Cracow

When Poland was reunited by Wladyslaw I in the early 14th century, Cracow (Kraków) became the capital, the place where the Jagellion kings of Poland were crowned and buried for over 200 years. The dynasty ended in 1572, the capital was moved to Warsaw soon afterwards, and Cracow entered a decline. The royal castle, which dates from the 12th century, is sited on Wawel hill, overlooking the city and the River Vistula, which seems to have been the citadel in very early times.

Essentially, the building is a Polish medieval castle that between 1507 and 1536 was turned into an Italian Renaissance palace by craftsmen imported from Italy. This gave rise to some odd conjunctions, such as the little tent-like pavilion that rests on a convenient Gothic battlement, but the overall effect is quite harmonious. The large and impressive central courtyard is surrounded by distinctive three-tiered arcades, the two lower stages of which together equal in height the third stage. Interestingly, one of the four blocks surrounding the courtyard is a dummy. There are no habitable rooms behind its façade; it was built for the sake of symmetry alone.

Some of the state rooms were decorated with considerable splendour at no small expense. The Senate Chamber has famous Flemish tapestries illustrating the story of Noah, and the ceiling of the Chamber of Deputies is equally famous for its panels inset with realistically carved and painted heads. Throughout the palace, which is now a museum with an internationally notable collection of armour, there are fine wooden doors carved in the Late Gothic style, and some of the rooms are still heated by handsome tiled stoves.

Adjoining the castle is the cathedral, the third, possibly fourth church on the site. It was begun soon after the castle, though like its secular neighbour it is a blend of successive styles and includes a very fine Renaissance chapel by Bartolomeo Brecci. The cathedral contains many royal tombs, including a fine effigy of Casimir the Great (1333–70) in pink marble, and the ornate Baroque mausoleum of St Stanislaus.

King's College Chapel, Cambridge

King's College was founded by the English King Henry VI in 1440 and work began on the chapel a few years later. Owing to the upheavals of the Wars of the Roses, little progress was made until more secure times, and in 1505 the work was renewed under Henry VII, first of the Tudor dynasty. It was completed about ten years later under his son, Henry VIII.

The chapel is the most successful example of the astonishing English Late Gothic style known as Perpendicular. Earlier Gothic builders had learned how to achieve great height and lightness by supporting the walls with flying buttresses that permitted very large windows, and at King's the windows seem to occupy the entire wall, bathing the interior in the beautiful light filtered through the stained glass, which is still largely original. This extreme effect is achieved by the use of fan vaulting, in which a fan-like cluster of fine stone ribs distributes the weight of the vault.

Regardless of aesthetic judgments, which are not universally approving, this is an extraordinary demonstration of craftsmanship and engineering skill. The master mason responsible for the vaulting was John Wastell, who had worked at the Abbey of Bury St Edmunds, possibly his home town, and at Canterbury Cathedral, where he became master mason in succession to Simon Clerk. He probably died in the year that King's College Chapel was finished.

The Perpendicular style as seen at King's, and in the Chapel of Henry VII (completed 1519) in Westminster Abbey, represents the end of the road. At King's, amid that purity of glass and stone, the hearty vigour of earlier versions of English Gothic seems to be missing.

Significantly, when Wastell became master mason in Cambridge, Bramante was working on his plans for St Peter's in Rome.

King's College Chapel, the west end. Irreverent students have likened it to a sow lying on its back.

Segovia Cathedral

The large size of Spanish cathedrals reflects the aggressive spirit of the successful Crusaders which, when the cathedral of Segovia was being built, was being directed to the acquisition of an empire in the New World. This is the last monumental church in the great age of Spanish building, in which the Late Gothic style mingles with new influences from Renaissance Italy. Perhaps the best view of it is from the north, late on an autumn afternoon, when the sinking sun lights up the golden stone. As travel posters proclaim, there is something quintessentially Spanish in the view of the city of whitewashed houses, the huge stone church, and the towers and pinacles of the Alcázar, against the distant backdrop of the Sierra de Guadarrama.

During the Revolt of the Comuneros in 1520–21, Segovia was besieged and captured and the old cathedral badly damaged. Some items were retrieved – the choir stalls and the figure of the Virgen del Perdón come from the old cathedral – but total reconstruction was necessary. Work began in 1525, and was directed by Juan Gil de Hontañón. He had worked at Salamanca since 1513 and the plan of Segovia closely resembled that of Salamanca. The work was largely completed under his son, Rodrigo, who died in 1577, though due to the speed of its construction Segovia is stylistically consistent.

The site makes the most of the great size of the building, but it is not particularly heavy or overpowering. The Spanish Late Gothic style tends to indulge in a profusion of Plateresque decoration that can look more like an excrescence than an adornment, and although this is not wholly absent at Segovia, the general impression of the exterior is of a relatively plain building. There is little external sculpture and the main, western entrance, which was usually the subject of the most extravagant decoration, is simple and restrained. The great tower, which is nearly 295-ft (90-m) high and about 52ft 6-in (16-m) square, is plain below the domed octagon and lantern. For those energetic enough to climb its 306 steps, the view is wonderful.

Fontainebleau

The rambling palace of Fontainebleau has been described as a group of châteaux that have met by chance. Situated in a large forest only 30 miles (50km) from Paris, the forest was popular with medieval kings for its hunting. The oldest surviving part of the château is the 13th-century tower or keep, now the centrepiece of the Oval Courtyard. Although additions were made in many different periods, often involving demolition of older parts (the famous Gallery of Ulysses by Primaticcio vanished in the 18th century), there was never a total reconstruction. The most crucial period, when Fontainebleau first emerged as a grand royal palace, was in the reign of François I (1515–47), who commissioned the finest artists and craftsmen to decorate the palace in the 1530s.

A general view reveals buildings erected over three centuries but all are in the same local sandstone and appear comfortably related. The old core of the palace, the Oval Courtyard, is only one of five courtyards. The Gallery of François, which links it to the White Horse Courtyard on the south side, exemplifies the brilliance of the decoration for which Fontainebleau is famous. It was built in 1531 and decorated by the Florentine artist, Giovanni Batista Rosso, one of the founders of the School of Fontainebleau, in 1533–41. The scheme is built on a masterly combination of woodwork, stucco and fresco, of mainly mythological subjects. The way in which paintings are combined with sculpture, though not entirely without precedent (Rosso may have known similar work by Perino del Vaga in the Doria Palace, Genoa), is characteristic of the Fontainebleau school and had a powerful influence on French Renaissance art. After Rosso's death in 1541, his work was continued by Primaticcio, whose female figures in stucco that flank the frescoes in the bedroom of the Duchesse d'Étampes express the Fontainebleau ideal of female beauty. Work continued in the next reign, when Primaticcio was aided by a fellow pupil of Giulio Romano, Niccolò dell'Abbate, but fresco came to dominate stucco.

Later additions included new wings and courtyards and the over-elaborate Horseshoe Staircase in the Baroque period, the 18th-century Salle du Conseil decorated by Boucher among others, and the refurnishing in the Empire style when Napoleon adopted Fontainebleau as his chief residence.

Château de Chambord

Chambord is one of the largest, most famous and beautiful châteaux in the Loire valley, a vision of Renaissance splendour in pale stone. Unlike its near neighbour at Blois, or the even larger royal palace of Fontainebleau farther north, it is stylistically uniform; the original hunting lodge was completely rebuilt by François I. Later alterations were comparatively few, and Chambord remains the outstanding building of the early French Renaissance.

Although the Italian influence is strong – the chief designer was Domenico da Cortona – the successive master masons were French, and the basic plan is that of a medieval castle, with the buildings grouped around a large, rectangular courtyard about 525 x 394ft (160 x 120m), and the main block or tower centred in the north-west façade. At each corner of the main building are large round towers, and another pair flank the main façade. A staggering

riot of turrets, towers and chimneys, a final flourish of the Gothic style, breaks out at roof level. François had a moat created by diverting the little River Cosson, a tributary of the Loire, but it proved troublesome to maintain and was later filled in. The park is enclosed by a wall over 18-miles (30-km) long.

Inside the château, the most remarkable feature is the central staircase, which ascends through four floors at the point where four lofty barrel-vaulted halls meet. It takes the form of a double spiral so that a person going up never meets anyone coming down; contained within

four narrow columns, it offers a view of the whole of each floor.

Louis XIV visited Chambord on several occasions and witnessed there a first performance of a play by Molière. His successor gave it to Stanislas Leczinski, the dethroned king of Poland, and later to the victorious marshal, Maurice de Saxe, after the battle of Fontenoy (1745). Chambord survived the Revolution but lost all its furnishings, and despite some restoration, the interior is still rather bare. The entire property, including the village of Chambord, was purchased by the state in 1932.

OPPOSITE
Chambord, seen from across the moat, is perhaps the most successful of François I's architectural projects.

LEFT
The staggering sky line of the château, from the south. Foreshortening creates a misleading impression: there is a space of about 100ft (30m) between the low building in the foreground and the main block or donjon.

FAR LEFT
Detail.

Hampton Court

The palace of Hampton Court, on the River Thames south-west of London, is a comparatively unpretentious building by comparison with its contemporaries in France. The original builder was Cardinal Wolsey, the humbly born minister of Henry VIII, who presented it to the king in 1529 in vain hope of buying back Henry's good will. As enlarged and completed by Henry, it became the grandest residence in England. Henry brought his various wives here, and it was the favourite residence of his successors, enjoying its most festive days in the reign of Elizabeth I.

It is the Tudor palace, with its forest of decorated chimneys, that the visitor first sees on approaching the towered main gateway. Beyond are two courtyards (a third was later demolished) surrounded by buildings which in both style and material (brick) resemble old colleges of Oxford and Cambridge. The building belongs basically to the English domestic Gothic tradition, but some awareness of the Italian Renaissance is evident, for instance in the terracotta roundels of Classical heads set in the walls.

The palace was greatly enlarged in the reign of the Dutch king, William III (1689–1702), who found it healthier than Whitehall and commissioned Christopher Wren to rebuild it. Wren wanted to sweep away most of the Tudor palace, plans thwarted by dwindling finance, and as things turned out, his cool, English version of Baroque complemented the more rugged Tudor palace rather well. However, Hampton Court soon afterwards fell from favour as a royal residence.

Among the most remarkable features of Hampton Court are the early Tudor royal chapel, which has an extraordinary vaulted ceiling of wood aping stone, and Great Hall, with its magnificent hammer-beam ceiling. The 'real' tennis court is still in use, though rebuilt since Henry VIII played there. The kitchens, imaginatively restored, could cater for 500 guests. Gardens, where Elizabeth I worked in the mornings, have been restored to their appearance in the 16th and 17th centuries. The splendid wrought-iron gates were designed by Jean Tijou in about 1690. A colossal vine, planted in 1769, is still fruiting.

OPPOSITE
The main entrance to Hampton Court is essentially Gothic but with Renaissance roundels on the gateway.

RIGHT
View across the restored Tudor gardens, with part of Wren's wing on the right.

Château de Chantilly

A many-faceted Baroque château, beautifully sited on a small island in an artificial lake 25 miles (40km) north of Paris, Chantilly was the domain of the princely Condés, a branch of the Bourbon dynasty who were leaders of the Huguenots during the French Wars of Religion. It was to Chantilly that the Duc d'Enghien, known as 'the Great Condé' (1621–86), retired towards the end of his hectic military career.

Earlier, the lordship of Chantilly belonged to another famous house, the Montmorency. In the 16th century Anne de Montmorency, Constable of France, reconstructed the medieval castle. He also built the *châtelet* ('little castle') nearby, which still survives, but the château itself was again rebuilt, partly by François Mansart, when the Prince of Condé took possession in the 17th century. The gardens were laid out by André Le Nôtre. King Louis XIV stayed at Chantilly in 1676 and hunted a stag by moonlight, but his visit was spoiled by the suicide of the steward who had been told that the fish had not reached the table on time. Louis, surely well accustomed to eating his dinner cold, was distressed and implored his host for less lavish entertainment next time.

The French Revolution brought disaster, and the main building was completely destroyed, along with Le Nôtre's landscape. However, in 1830, with the Condés extinct, Chantilly was acquired by another branch of the Bourbons in the person of Henri, Duc d'Aumale, a son of the Orléanist King Louis-Philippe. He had the means to indulge his zeal for art, amassing not only paintings, particularly of the Italian and French Renaissance and including most of the known court portraits of Jean Clouet (died c. 1540), but also manuscripts, sculpture and tapestries. The château was rebuilt according to Mansart's plans, and the duke bequeathed it and his collections to the Institut de France, to form what is now the Musée Condé.

The famous race course was instituted in 1834, but the great stables of Chantilly, which accommodated 240 horses, date from the 18th century.

Saint-Germain-en-Laye

While Versailles was being built, the favourite residence of Louis XIV was St-Germain, on the River Seine nearly 12 miles (20km) west of Paris, now virtually a suburb though still on the edge of the forest. The move to Versailles was not popular with all of Louis's courtiers, but when James II of England took refuge in France in 1688, the recently vacated St-Germain was made available to the exiled Jacobite court.

The present château, renovated as the national museum of antiquities under Napoleon III, is a fragment of what was once an enormous complex. The original castle was built by Louis VI in the early 12th century. It was destroyed more than once by the English and rebuilt, but was largely neglected under the early Valois kings in the 14th–15th centuries. It was converted into a royal palace by François I (1515–47), who had been married there. A notable medieval survival is the gem-like Chapel of St Louis, which resembles the Sainte-Chapelle in Paris and may have been the work of the same man.

The Renaissance reconstruction was planned by Pierre Chambiges, and although most of the work was not completed until after his death in 1544 (many famous architects worked subsequently at St-Germain), it faithfully reflects his early French Renaissance style. A remarkable feature is the terraced roof of great stone slabs, which had to be supported by large stone buttresses reinforced with iron. The plan follows the outline of the medieval castle, incorporating a 14th-century tower at the north-west corner, which does impose certain limitations. Along the edge of the roof runs a balustrade with slender stone vases between the windows, a feature echoed above the second storey with a pleasingly harmonious effect. The superb terrace planned by André Le Nôtre in the 17th century, 'the finest promenade in Europe' and over 1¼-miles (2-km) long, offers a distant view of Paris across the Seine.

The Château of Saint-Germain-en-Laye, from an 18th-century engraving.

The Louvre

Now one of the world's greatest art museums, the Louvre began as a small fort in about 1100; by 1200 it controlled shipping on the Seine with the aid of an iron chain stretched across the river. As Paris grew, the fort expanded and eventually became a palace, the decisive conversion taking place in the 16th century, when it became the seat of the royal court in the capital, though the court usually preferred to be elsewhere. The artists responsible were Pierre Lescot, whose buildings ranged around a square court influenced the development of French Classicism, augmented by the refined work of the sculptor Jean Goujon. Cathérine de Médicis built the Tuileries palace (destroyed in 1871) to the west and Henri IV completed the gallery on the river to link it with the Louvre. Two wings of the old chateau were demolished to enlarge the quadrangle, but without jettisoning Lescot's conception. The palace continued to grow in the 17th century, under Louis Le Vau (when he could spare time from Versailles), and the original and impressive colonnaded eastern front was built by Claude Perrault in co-operation with Le Vau and others, and perhaps influenced by a rejected design by Bernini. After the Louvre narrowly avoided destruction during the Revolution, it was turned into a museum, its collections benefiting from the sack of less fortunate palaces and, later, from Napoleon's acquisitions (though most were returned to their former owners). The 'Nouveau Louvre' on Place Napoléon III was built in the 1850s.

Besides the contents that are its chief claim to fame, the architecture of the Louvre embodies work from the Middle Ages to 1993, when the glass pyramid of I.M. Pei was completed. One of the motives for President Mitterand's determined pursuance of this project, which at first aroused ferocious opposition, was to continue the Louvre's tradition of incorporating new construction from each new age. The pyramid, 75-ft (23-m) high, has a network of cables and girders supporting 800 large glass panels, and is situated in the great quadrangle and surrounded by water. It forms the entrance to the expanded 'Grand Louvre', made possible by the evacuation of the finance ministry from its offices, which resulted in almost doubling the exhibition space.

I.M. Pei's steel-and-glass pyramid, which provided the great museum with a new entrance in 1993 and nearly caused a revolution when the plans were published. However, despite some technical problems, it has since gained widespread approval.

Longleat, a Renaissance palace in the English countryside, has survived with remarkable success in the possession of the same family, now headed by the Marquess of Bath.

Longleat

Apart from a few decorative touches, as seen at Hampton Court, the style of the Renaissance made little impression in England before 1550, and even then, in the new Elizabethan country houses, it mingled idiosyncratically with traditional English Gothic into the 17th century.

At Longleat in Wiltshire, though a comparatively early example (begun 1568), Renaissance concepts are obvious. On the long and elegant façade (the third storey and parapet are slightly later than the rest; there was originally a pitched roof), the three Classical orders are prominently displayed, perhaps

based on engravings in John Shute's *First and Chief Grounds of Architecture*, published in 1563, which in turn borrowed from an earlier book by the influential Italian architect, Sebastiano Serlio. The strapwork decoration on the parapet derives from the Low Countries. However, the plan of the house, though Classical in its symmetry, is traditional, the building arranged around two courtyards. The great hall, which is entered directly from the main entrance, was a feature common to medieval castles and did not go out of fashion in England until the 17th century. Yet the house, which almost demands the name palace, is an undoubted success and is now regarded as one of the finest adornments of the Elizabethan age. For all its French, Italian and Flemish connections, it is thoroughly and uniquely English.

It was built by Sir John Thynne, a rich and well-placed courtier who was associated with the design of several other houses. This one, however, was for his own use, and his descendants still live there. His master mason was Robert Smythson, and Longleat is the first recorded commission of the man who became the foremost, if not the only, architect of the period. Among his other so-called 'prodigy' houses are Wollaton Hall and, probably, Hardwick Hall, where the large windows notable at Longleat are even larger, hence the quip, 'Hardwick Hall, more glass than wall'.

Palladio's famous villa has been one of the most influential buildings in the entire history of European architecture.

Villa Rotonda, Vicenza

Andrea Palladio (1508–80), trained as a mason and bricklayer in Padua, was probably the greatest and most influential architect of the 16th century, who aimed to capture the splendour and idealism of the Classical past. A wealthy patron encouraged his intellectual interests, nicknamed him Palladio after Pallas Athena, goddess of wisdom, and took him to study in Rome, where he also read the works of Vitruvius and Alberti. He became a scholar as well as a craftsman and, many years later, published his own, equally influential *I quattro libri dell'architettura*. Meanwhile, he had acquired great practical experience, designing handsome but practical farmhouses in the Veneto, subtle churches in Venice, impressive public buildings and palaces, and one of the first permanent

theatres since Roman times, the Teatro Olimpico in Vicenza.

Palladio represents the epitome of the Classical virtues of balance, harmony and cool clarity, his work combining ancient Roman splendour with his own airy elegance. Those virtues are evident in what is probably his most famous building, the Villa Rotonda, also known as the Villa Almerico-Capra after a later owner, on a small hill outside Vicenza where, as the architect himself observed, 'wonderful views can be enjoyed from every side'. It was built in the 1550s as a country house for a wealthy gentleman, then a novel concept and quite unlike the working farmhouses Palladio had built hitherto in the region, although, like the architecture, the concept recalled ancient Roman models. The villa has four equal façades facing

each point of the compass, with a porch like that of a Roman temple – six columns and a pediment, approached by a broad flight of steps. Palladio believed, wrongly, that Roman houses also followed this design. At the centre of the building is the rotonda, crowned by a dome recalling that of the Pantheon, richly decorated with frescoes and stucco and illuminated by indirect light, suggesting constrained luxury.

Imitation is said to be the sincerest form of flattery and Palladio was perhaps the most imitated of architects. During the 18th-century Palladian revival, his buildings were copied in countries as far apart as Russia, England, where Lord Burlington's Chiswick House is partly modelled on the Villa Rotonda, and North America, on which Thomas Jefferson's Monticello is based.

The Escorial

Philip II of Spain founded the Royal Monastery of St Lawrence about 30 miles (50km) from Madrid in 1557 in gratitude for a victory over the French. The setting is stark but magnificent, 3,300-ft (1000-m) above sea level in the Sierra Guadarrama. The complex of buildings includes monastery, palace, seat of learning and mausoleum. They are set within a huge walled rectangle, 655 x 525ft (200 x 160m), internally divided into courts on a grid pattern resembling the plan of Diocletian's palace at Split and dominated by the large church, a domed basilica resembling St Peter's in Rome. The palace acquired its name from the village that housed the workmen, which means 'the slag heap', and it was completed with extraordinary speed between 1563 and 1585. Most later monarchs added something to the Escorial, but without altering its main features.

From the outside, it is easiest to admire it from a distance, assimilated into the landscape. Its austere grandeur is not incidental. Philip demanded 'simplicity in construction, severity in the total effect; nobility without arrogance, majesty without ostentation', and his architects did not fail him. But the result has not been widely admired. Théophile Gautier, predictably unsympathetic, was not alone in remarking its resemblance to a barracks.

The contents are more rewarding. They include paintings by the Dutch masters, of whom Philip was unexpectedly fond, as well as Titian, El Greco and Velázquez. The library, with its wonderful painted barrel vault is, despite losses, probably still the greatest Renaissance library in Europe, and includes many Arabic manuscripts. The Hall of Battles, a

gallery over 165-ft (50-m) long, is painted with Spanish feats of arms and has a vaulted ceiling with 18th-century designs inspired by Pompeii. The Pantheon of Kings contains the remains of Habsburg and Bourbon kings.

The Escorial has survived several catastrophes that reduced its treasures (including a feather from the wing of the Archangel Gabriel). In 1671 a fire burned for two weeks before it was extinguished, French troops looted the palace in 1808 and another fire in 1872 destroyed part of the library. It remains the most impressive monument of Philip II's Spain which, financed by American silver and fortified by the faith of the Counter-Reformation, became the greatest kingdom in Europe.

Rialto Bridge, Venice

Given their vulnerability, especially in time of war, it is surprising how many Renaissance bridges have survived in Italy. (The Ponte San Trinità in Florence was destroyed in 1944 but has been rebuilt with some of the same materials, rescued from the riverbed.)

Bridges naturally assumed special importance in Venice, a city of canals as well as streets, and the earliest bridges were made of wood. Stone began to replace them in the 12th century, when streets began to be paved, though wood remained the preferred material for short bridges into the Renaissance; Palladio designed several on the principle of the truss. The development of the stone-arch bridge is one of the outstanding engineering achievements of the Renaissance.

The Rialto is the commercial heart of Venice. A wooden Rialto Bridge over the Grand Canal at its narrowest point was built in 1178, on pontoons. It was replaced in the mid-13th century by another wooden bridge carried on beams, which could be raised and lowered like a drawbridge. The present stone-arch bridge was built in 1588–91 by Antonio 'da Ponte' (1512–95), who probably earned his nickname from earlier, now-unknown bridges. It is an ornamental, single-arched span of two segments, covered with shops in the traditional manner. Many features were required by the commission, including the shops (still there), the open arch in the centre (where earlier bridges usually had a chapel) and the side pavements. The span is 89ft (27m) and the rise is 21ft (6.4m), the dimensions of the bridge dictated by the need to accommodate shipping on the Grand Canal. From the day it opened, the Rialto Bridge became a Venetian landmark.

The architect-engineer faced serious structural problems because of the soft, wet soil. He overcame them by driving in 6,000 wooden piles under the abutments on each side. The masonry was then so arranged that the stones were bedded at right angles to the line of thrust of the arch, a technique that has been used ever since.

The enchanting Rialto Bridge rests on sound engineering.

Teatro Olimpico, Vicenza

No permanent theatres were built during the Middle Ages. Drama, where it existed, was performed in churches, on temporary wooden stages in market square or inn yard, and later in some kind of temporary accommodation in royal courts and grand houses. Even the rise of professional companies of actors did not necessarily imply a permanent, purpose-built theatre.

By 1500 the desirability of a central, self-contained acting space was recognized in Italian courts and elsewhere, but this only required minor modifications to the existing arrangements. A wooden theatre is recorded at Ferrara early in the 16th century, but when it burned down it was not rebuilt. As late as 1556 a book on stage design took it for granted that the stage would be a temporary structure. One catalyst for change was Vitruvius' *De architectura*, which first appeared in an Italian translation in 1531. Vitruvius provided the first description of what a Classical, specifically a Roman, theatre looked like, and provided the basis for the works of theatre designers such as Sebastiano Serlio (1475–1554).

The Teatro Olimpico at Vicenza was one of the first permanent theatres. It opened in 1585 with a production of *Oedipus Rex*, and it is still standing today. Designed by Andrea Palladio for a group of scholarly classicists, like himself, it is his last building. He died in 1580 and construction was supervised by his disciple Vincenzo Scamozzi, who took over several of his projects and may have been responsible for the design of the stage at Vicenza.

Palladio's theatre was intended as a reconstruction of a Classical Roman theatre on a smaller scale, with a curved auditorium, a small orchestra, and a magnificent architectural set pierced by doorways and backing a very narrow stage. Unlike the theatres of ancient Greece and Rome, however, it was roofed, so the ceiling was painted to look like the sky! Although a magnificent building, its influence on theatre design was slight: a more significant innovation appeared in 1618 in the Teatro Farnese at Parma, which provided more acting space and introduced the proscenium arch, a device that was to dominate theatre design for over 300 years.

Part of the vestibule of the splendid Teatro Olimpico, one of the earliest modern examples, but essentially an academic exercise, something of a dead end in theatre design.

Saint Basil's Cathedral, with, centre, the view from Red Square and, right, decorative details of the astonishing towers.

Saint Basil's Cathedral, Moscow

Christianity came to Russia from Byzantium, and along with the religion, the Byzantine style of ecclesiastical architecture was also imported. The standard form was a plan of a Greek cross (equal arms) within a square. It was topped, typically, by five domes. However, the Russians introduced their own variations, notably the onion-shaped dome, adopted after too many normal domes had collapsed under the weight of Russian snow. Early Russian churches were also chunkier, with minimal openings near ground level, since for 300 years they also served as strongholds to protect the people against the attacks of the Mongols.

By the 16th century, when the old principality of Moscow was transformed into the Russian empire, a basically simpler plan, with a tall central steeple, had emerged, and over time became increasingly decorative. St Basil's Cathedral, opposite the Kremlin, belongs to this tradition, but it introduced another novel development. The central tower is surrounded by eight, not (as hitherto) four, subsidiary spaces, or chapels. It was built in the 1550s to celebrate the victories of the first tsar, Ivan IV (the Terrible), with additions in the 17th century and later. The eight chapels are dedicated to saints whose anniversaries coincided with the dates of Ivan's victories against the Tatars; each one is independently treated, and the eight domes have different designs. Nevertheless, like a basket of tropical fruit, they achieve a recognizable unity. The effect is exotic, but the original building looked quite different; it was whitewashed, the brilliant colours of the domes added in the 18th century.

By the time St Basil's was built, the Renaissance had already reached Russia. When Ivan III had begun to reconstruct the Kremlin at the end of the 15th century, he had relied largely on Italians. But St Basil's was a thoroughly Russian building, built by Russian craftsmen and strongly indebted to traditional wooden architecture, in which Russian architects were expert. St Basil's itself was to inspire many later churches, such as the great Cathedral of the Resurrection in St Petersburg, built in the late 19th century.

Saint Peter's, Rome

The 1,000-year-old St Peter's, then and now the most famous Christian church and the shrine of St Peter, was in need of extensive restoration or rebuilding in the 15th century, as several popes remarked. The energetic and determined Julius II (1503–13) finally embarked on the task, with the clear intent of creating a symbol of the power of the Christian faith and, no less, of the magnificence of the papacy, which would rival the buildings of imperial – and pagan – Rome. The man for the job was at hand in Donato Bramante, who planned a Greek cross with a very large central dome. Work began in 1506 but had not gone far when Bramante died (1514). Several famous artists were subsequently employed, including, briefly, Raphael, who proposed a plan in the form of a Latin cross. Antonio da Sangallo (d. 1546) produced a curious compromise, attempting to combine Greek and Latin crosses. He was succeeded by the septuagenarian Michelangelo, who returned to Bramante's central plan but in a brilliantly modified form that largely overcame the drawbacks of such a plan in catering for elaborate ceremonies and large numbers of people.

Michelangelo also designed the famous dome, the chief splendour of the whole Vatican complex. It was not built until 25 years after his death, by Giacomo della Porta, and is probably slightly different in form. Carlo Maderno, who took over as architect in 1603, faced ecclesiastical pressure for more space, which resulted in his major revision of Michelangelo's design, which abandoned the central plan and created a long nave and an immense façade. The final addition was the

The demands of prestige, requirements of ceremonial, and the profusion of architects, all combined to make St Peter's, as a building, less than harmonious.

*OPPOSITE
The west front.*

more successful design of the piazza with its elegant curved colonnades created by Bernini in the mid-17th century.

It is not easy to comprehend St Peter's as a unit, and the exterior offers little guide to what lies within, where there appears to be not one but several churches, and the atmosphere changes from one part to another. Under the

soaring dome, the impression is of lightness and delicacy, and the sheer space in the nave permits Baroque adornments that might seem excessive in a lesser building. Among the works of art, most famous are Michelangelo's Pietà, and Bernini's dazzling throne of St Peter, with its brilliant use of light as a sculptural element.

The imposing interior of Il Gesù, a church designed for preaching to a large congregation.

Il Gesù, Rome

The Jesuit Church in Rome was begun in 1568, 34 years after the founding of the Society of Jesus by St Ignatius Loyola, who is buried here, and was the spiritual base of the Jesuits, especially during the missions in the New World. It provided a model for many later churches in Europe as well as the Americas, and probably had more influence on church building during the next four centuries than any other.

The builders, both members of the Jesuit order, were Giacomo da Vignola, who was responsible for the plan, and Giacomo della Porta, who took over on Vignola's death in 1573 and designed the façade. The latter was a follower of Michelangelo, and succeeded him as architect of the Capitol and of St Peter's, being partly responsible for the dome. The façade of the Gesù is well proportioned but rather plain and flat, even severe, predating the dynamic Early Baroque rhythms soon to be introduced by Maderno and others.

The design of the interior is more significant. Vignola was the finest architect in Rome on the death of Michelangelo and the first to build a church (the Tempietto di S. Andrea, c. 1550) on an oval plan. The Jesuit church has some affinity with Alberti's S. Andrea in Mantua, 100 years earlier. (Like Alberti, Vignola was the author of an influential text on architecture.) The Gesù had to fulfil special functions. Jesuit preachers attracted huge congregations, and to accommodate them Vignola's plan, basically a Latin cross, provided a short, very wide nave with no aisles but chapels opening directly off it, with shallow transepts and choir. A central dome provided plenty of light and promoted good acoustics, so that everyone should hear.

The interior of Il Gesù was redecorated with no expense spared in the High Baroque style in about 1670, with elaborate gilding and frescoes by the Genoese master of illusionism, Baciccia (Giovanni Battista Gaulli). The ceiling of the nave bears a staggering *trompe l'oeil* painting of Christ overcoming the Devil, Baciccia's greatest work.

restraint, the 'trademark' of Santa Maria della Salute confirms its Baroque sense of movement. This unique feature is the huge *volutes* that circle the dome. Although decorative, they were originally coloured, in contrast to the white limestone of the rest, but have faded; they also have an important functional purpose, helping to distribute the weight of the dome more evenly.

OPPOSITE
The dome of Santa Maria della Salute from across the Canale della Giudecca.

LEFT
The side chapels (one partly obscured to the right) have their own exterior façades, like separate churches. The unique volutes *are here clearly visible.*

Mexico City Cathedral

Mexico City Cathedral, whose impressive dimensions make it the largest church in the country.

Those of Classical sympathies generally regarded the ecclesiastical architecture of Spain and Portugal as degenerate: in the Spanish empire, things were even worse. Today, the novelty and vigour of an architecture that combines traditional Spanish styles with strong local influence, particularly in its riotous sculptural decoration, its sheer invention, and the atmosphere created by the intimacy of worshippers with their saints, are more appreciated.

The cathedral of Mexico City is the largest church in the country, a formidably imposing structure whose dimensions alone are impressive; 387-ft (118-m) long, 177-ft (54-m) wide, the western towers are 203-ft (62-m) high. Standing on the site of an Aztec temple, it dominates the large expanse of the Plaza de la Constitución, or Zócalo. Basically it is a reasonably typical example of the colonial Baroque style associated with (but in various individual ways different from) southern Spain, which was employed in many other Mexican churches. In fact it is, overall, more restrained and less unorthodox than most. It was begun in about 1560, consecrated in 1656, and not finished until the beginning of the 19th century.

Owing to the long time span of construction, it displays many architectural and decorative features of virtually all the styles of Spanish colonial art. Some of the vaulting is Gothic, while each bay of the side aisles is domed. The western façade, with white marble statues posed against the warm brown limestone, is broadly Neoclassical. This is largely the work of an underrated Creole architect, José Ortiz de Castro, in the late 18th century,

though much of the decorative work, like the dome and lantern, was designed by Manuel Tolsá of Valencia in the early 19th century. The view of the cathedral from the west, enhanced by the open space of the Zócalo, is the most impressive, particularly when floodlit in the evening.

For sheer ornamental abundance, the altarpiece (c.1730) in the Chapel of the Three Kings is unequalled. A central painting of the Adoration is surrounded by a tropical riot of sculpted and gilded ornament, with exuberant use of a favourite Spanish device, the *estípite*, a truncated, vase-like pilaster.

Saint Paul's Cathedral, London

The old St Paul's, the cathedral of London, was a vast Gothic pile nearly 650-ft (200-m) long. It was the most notable casualty of the Fire of London in 1666, when the heat reached such a pitch that the stones of the old church exploded like shells. But the fire, like other disasters, had certain compensations. It created opportunities for rebuilding at a moment when Christopher Wren was available, though his plan to redesign the City fell foul of special interests.

Though Wren's style is nowadays often described as English Baroque, it is very different in spirit from the work of, say, Mansart or Bernini, though he knew, and was not unmoved by both. But Wren's style is essentially academic, moderate, even staid. The famous spires of his City churches are exceptional, and most were probably designed by others, though Wren approved them.

Gothic was currently despised, and Wren's idea for St Paul's was a domed, Classical building on the plan of a Greek cross. The ecclesiastical authorities, wanting more space for processions, demanded a traditional cruciform plan with a long nave. Two plans were rejected, before a compromise was reached, and even that was later altered by Wren, with the connivance of King Charles II; but the plan was basically a Latin cross. With a huge circular space under the dome, the final result could be said to have possessed the best of both worlds. The foundation stone was laid in 1673 and the building was more or less complete by 1711.

St Paul's is often compared with St Peter's, Rome, and there are obvious superficial similarities, but it is an altogether more harmonious building. The division of the west façade into two tiers is very successful, while the dome, with its supporting drum and even the gallery, forced on Wren against his will, is not only a masterpiece of elegance but also of structural engineering, where Wren's true genius lay. The stone lantern is supported by an internal brick cone which is independent of both the inner and outer shells of the dome. Wren employed a team of artists and craftsmen of high calibre, notably the wood carver Grinling Gibbons, who made the choir stalls.

St Paul's from the south. Wren's original plan was for a Greek Cross with the four arms linked on the exterior by concave curves.

RIGHT
Louis XIV's Versailles.

OPPOSITE LEFT
*Le Vau opted for low
roofs, breaking the hard
horizontal of the skyline
with statues.*

OPPOSITE RIGHT
*The north wing, flanking
the main approach via
the Cour d'Honneur, with
the chapel to the right.*

Versailles

The palace of Louis XIV, 'the Sun King', at Versailles, is and was meant to be the grandest in Europe. Foreign visitors were first staggered by its sheer size – it could allegedly hold the entire, numerous, French nobility – then overwhelmed by its magnificence. It was a modest château until the 1660s when Louis decided to make it the home of his court, resisting pressure to reside in the Louvre. Here he planned a new citadel to symbolize the eminence of France which was to be manifested in her monarch.

The grounds, described by Saint-Simon as swampy yet waterless, were planned by André Le Nôtre, greatest of the French landscape designers. Vast engineering works were needed to compensate for the drawbacks Saint-Simon mentioned and to supply over 1,000 fountains, which were turned off when the King was absent. Louis Le Vau was responsible for the building, incorporating the existing château. He opted for terraced roofs, breaking up the stark horizontals of the cornice with grand sculpture, but died in 1670. He was succeeded in 1675 by the capable Jules Hardouin-Mansart who, with his team of talented assistants, contributed most

to the building. He vastly extended Le Vau's palace to the north and south and created, under Louis' personal supervision, the royal chapel and the famous Galerie des Glaces (Hall of Mirrors), still the most splendid chamber in the palace, though Louis was compelled to melt down its solid-silver furniture to pay for his wars.

Life at Versailles was grotesquely formal and ritualistic. The unfortunate monarch can never have eaten a hot meal, and the public were admitted, for a fee, to watch him eat, though he could sometimes give private parties for a few cronies in the pavilion of the Grand Trianon. In his depressed later years, Versailles was rather a gloomy place, but it revived under Louis XV, when many rooms were decorated in the lighter, consciously graceful, Rococo style. It was sacked, but not seriously damaged, during the Revolution. Louis-Philippe turned it into a museum full of dull history paintings. Serious restoration began in the 20th century and is ongoing. Much of the glory of the palace in the days of Louis XV and the attractive Mme de Pompadour has been reclaimed, and Versailles is, as intended, an illustrious memorial to the greatness of the French monarchy.

Royal Palace, Amsterdam

What is now the Dutch royal palace in Amsterdam dates from the same period as the Versailles of Louis XIV of France, the huge power that frequently threatened the viability of the little Dutch republic yet, after a Dutch prince had become king of England, came off worse. The symbol of autocratic monarchy in France and the repository of commercial enterprise in Holland are rather different buildings.

Built after the end of the Thirty Years' War in 1648, the Dutch palace was originally Amsterdam's city hall, replacing an earlier building that had burned down. It is a splendid example of Dutch civic architecture in the Classical style, unassertively assured, with minimal Baroque influence. It stands on the west side of the Dam in the heart of the city. Rectangular in plan, it measures about 305 x 245ft (93 x 75m). The architect was Jacob van Campen, the foremost Dutch architect of the period, also responsible for the Mauritshuis in the Hague (1633). The façades are simple and uncluttered and it still looks more like a city hall, though a splendid one, than a palace. However, the pediment is filled with sculpture, representing the Merchant City surrounded by Neptune, tritons and sea nymphs, by Artus Quellin, member of a notable family of Dutch sculptors. The capitals of the pilasters are also decoratively carved, and there are simple swags under the windows. Above the pediment, a tall lantern makes a faintly subversive effort to escape from strict and sober Classicism.

The Dutch were at the height of their mercantile prosperity in the mid-17th century, and everything about this building, from the weather vane in the form of a Dutch cog or trading ship (the badge of the city) to the handsome chimney pieces and the allegorical paintings within, suggests a confident community of wealthy burghers. When Louis Napoleon, brother of Napoleon, became king of Holland, he ordered the city hall's conversion to a royal palace, and it retained that role under the house of Orange.

RIGHT
Detail of the sculpture of the pediment and the lantern.

FAR RIGHT
The palace from across the Dam. Originally the town hall, it was built on boggy ground, supported on over 13,000 piles. To the right is the 15th-century Nieuwe Kerk, where Dutch monarchs are crowned.

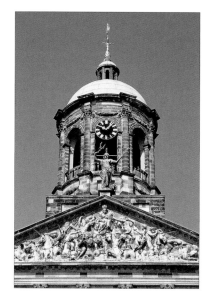

Royal Palace, Turin

The former residence of the kings of Sardinia stands in the centre of Turin. It is a massive building, but its exterior appearance is plain and uninspiring. Inside it is a different matter, for it contains rooms decorated in as luxurious a manner as can be seen almost anywhere else in Europe. It was begun in the mid-17th century, at the beginning of a rich period in Piedmontese art, with Juvarra the outstanding figure; construction continued into the 19th century.

Standing at a distance from the façade, just visible above the roof line is an amazing structure, striking the sort of contrast one might expect if a Martian spaceship landed next to a 1950s office block. This is the dome of the royal chapel, the Capella della S. Sindone where the Turin Shroud is kept, and is the work of Guarino Guarini (1624–83).

Guarini was one of the most imaginative architects of the age, or of any age, beside whom Borromini, whom he admired and borrowed from, seems quite orthodox. He was an intellectual and a well-known mathematician, and his exhilarating but complex designs, with their interlocking spaces, are essentially works of advanced geometry; their appeal is intellectual as well as artistic. Fortunately Guarini's work, which in terms of actual buildings is small, is very well documented, and has fascinated architects of every age since his own. Besides S. Sindone, he is represented by only one church, S. Lorenzo, also in Turin which, though utterly distinctive, has been somewhat spoiled by later additions.

Guarini turned the dome into an object of fantasy. In S. Sindone, the dome is cone-shaped,

built up in a series of overlapping segmental arches that decrease in width towards the crown. Filtered light from grids encourages the air of fantasy. Such structures had no obvious precedent in Christian architecture, but

something like them appears in certain medieval Spanish churches and is probably of Muslim origin; the vault of the Great Mosque of Cordoba provides suggestive evidence.

The Royal Palace, Turin, formerly the residence of the kings of Sardinia.

Drottningholm Palace

The former summer palace of the Swedish monarchs, on a small island near Stockholm, was inspired, like so many others, by Versailles. Of course it is on a more modest scale, but it is distinctly grand nonetheless, reminding us that Sweden was the major power in northern Europe in the 17th century. The plan of a central block with projecting wings is clearly of French inspiration, and the formal terraced gardens are in the manner of Le Nôtre, but there is evidence of Italian and Dutch influence as well; altogether the palace has a Baroque style of its own.

Construction began on the site of a smaller, earlier building in the 1660s. It was directed by members of three generations of the famous family of statesmen and architects, the Tessins, the original design being the work of Nicodemus Tessin the elder, whose son built the royal palace in Stockholm. The palace contains interesting features, including Gobelin tapestries, fine furniture, a ceremonial staircase with frescoes by D.K. Ehrenstrahl, and a state bedchamber resplendent in blue and gold. There is a delightful Rococo pavilion in Chinese style in the grounds.

But the most interesting part of Drottningholm is the theatre, one of the oldest in Europe. A fire destroyed it in 1762 and the present one dates from 1766. Its most brilliant period was the reign of the theatrically inclined Gustav III (1772–92), himself a dramatist. After him it ceased to function and was used as a store room, which explains how it survived. It was restored to its original state, but with the addition of electric lighting, in the 1920s. It seats over 400, and is still used occasionally.

RIGHT
A pavilion in the grounds of Drottningholm Palace.

OPPOSITE
The garden façade of Drottningholm, gleaming brilliant white in the sunshine.

The 18th-century stage machinery for changing the wings is a unique survival, and still working. Much painted scenery of that time also survives.

Even earlier stage designs can be seen in the museum housed in the royal apartments.

Charlottenburg by night and by day. The unusual dimensions of the drum certainly give it originality.

Charlottenburg

Schloss Charlottenburg stands near the edge of the Spandauer forest about 5 miles (8km) along the Charlottenburger Chaussée from Berlin's Brandenburg Gate. The original building was a country mansion which the Elector, and future king, Friedrich III, a ruler more interested in cultural and courtly affairs than mundane administration, built for his wife, Sophie Charlotte, in about 1690. Its first name was Lietzenburg but when Sophie Charlotte died in the palace in 1705 it was renamed in her memory. The original building was then enlarged on an E-shaped plan around a large courtyard under a Swedish architect, Johann Friedrich Eosander, who is said to have taken advice from the recently appointed imperial architect in Vienna, the great Fischer von Erlach (1656–1723).

The most striking feature of the building is the dome, which surmounts an unusually high, octagonal drum and is topped by an elaborate lantern and large gilded statue of the goddess Fortuna. Many observers have commented critically on the disproportionate height of the dome, which is slightly exaggerated by the wrought-iron railings that, from a distance, mask much of the ground floor of the comparatively modest central block, but this idiosyncrasy has been sanctified by time. The palace was at its most splendid in the reign of Friedrich II (Frederick the Great), who was responsible for its magnificent collection of paintings, including masters of the French Rococo such as Boucher and Watteau. Frederick also commissioned the most famous feature of the palace, the Goldene Gallerie, which was carefully photographed as insurance against war damage in 1943, and destroyed in an air raid less than 24 hours later. Later adornments to the park and gardens include the Classical mausoleum by Karl Friedrich Schinkel (1781–1841), and statues of Prussian and German heroes, including a splendid equestrian statue of the Great Elector (father of Friedrich I) by Andreas Schlüter (d. 1714), who, though unsuccessful as an architect, was to Berlin almost what Bernini was to Rome.

Nymphenburg, Munich

The 'castle of the nymphs' on the outskirts of Munich was the summer palace of the Wittelsbach electors, later kings, of Bavaria. Like Versailles, it is essentially a collection of buildings in which some parts are of greater interest than others. The original building, the five-floor central block, was built in 1664 by the Bolognese architect, Agostino Barelli, who introduced the Italian Baroque to southern Germany. In fact it looks vaguely like an Italian villa. The matching blocks on either side, linked by arcaded galleries, were built in the next reign, and the famous gardens were laid out in 1701 by Carbonet, a former pupil of Le Nôtre at Versailles. At about the same time, the original interior was reconstructed to accommodate a great hall three storeys high, for which the arched windows in the façade were installed. The addition of two further buildings on the wings in the mid-18th century, almost matching their neighbours, completed the scheme. The architect chiefly responsible for the final arrangement was Josef Effner, a gardener's son sent to study in Paris by the Elector Max Emanuel.

In the 1720s Effner also built two of the Rococo pavilions in the park, which are more famous than the palace itself. They included the Badenburg, or bath house, more a small swimming pool, and the Pagodenburg, an early example of the taste for 'Chinese' decoration, or chinoiserie. The Magdalenenklause was built about the same time as a kind of hermit's retreat, as a grotto encrusted with stucco seaweed and shellwork.

But the most fascinating of the Nymphenburg's pavilions is the Amalienburg

(1734–39), intended as a hunting lodge. It is the masterpiece of François Cuvilliés, who joined the household of the exiled Elector and returned with him to Munich in 1714 as court dwarf before becoming, with Effner, joint court architect. The Amalienburg is a small building of one storey with a large circular room in the centre. Its vibrant but delicate decoration in gilded stucco and wood seems to float over walls and ceiling. This gem of a building has been described as 'the supreme secular monument of the Rococo'.

Due partly to its longitudinal span, the harmonious assembly of the Nymphenburg is not easily captured in photographs.

Schönbrunn, Vienna

Its great size notwithstanding, the Schönbrunn palace is not an intimidating building. That may be due partly to its mellow golden colour, also to the arrangement of the façade, in which the broad wings are brought forward in a welcoming manner. A third reason is the absence of the three imposing domes which the architect, Johann Fischer von Erlach, placed over the main entrance, though their removal plays havoc with the general proportions.

On the outskirts of Vienna, the Schönbrunn was the summer palace of the Habsburgs during roughly the last third of their 600-year reign in Austria. A hunting lodge stood here, where the Emperor Maximilian had his

menagerie in the early 16th century; there is still a zoo, founded in 1752 and one of the oldest in Europe. The house was destroyed during the siege of Vienna by the Turks in 1683, but the Emperor Leopold nevertheless decided to replace it with a palace on a grand scale. Fischer von Erlach was then approaching the height of his fame, but his original design of 1690, which aimed to challenge Versailles, was rejected as too costly even for the Habsburgs. A second plan was put into effect in 1696 and the building was largely completed by 1711. It was subsequently modified somewhat, first by Fischer von Erlach's son, Josef Emanuel, and again by Nikolaus Pacassi, who removed the domes in 1744. Probably its

most famous resident was the Empress Maria Theresa, who spent nearly every summer of her reign (1740–80) here. The palace and grounds were first opened to the public in 1918.

The Schönbrunn contains an alleged 1,440 rooms, most of them of an ornate magnificence striking even by the standards of Austrian Baroque. Among the showpieces are the Great Gallery, with its staggering painted ceiling, huge chandeliers and inlaid floor, the adjoining Hall of Ceremonies, and the sparkling Hall of Mirrors. Smaller rooms, such as the Yellow Drawing Room, are equally splendid in their way and, being on a more human scale, perhaps more attractive to the modern visitor.

Despite its size, the Schönbrunn is not a forbidding building. The sad disappearance of Fischer's domes, however, has not improved its proportions.

Blenheim Palace

Blenheim Palace in Oxfordshire, among the most thoroughly Baroque of English buildings, is a very large and rather pretentious structure designed more as a public statement than a comfortable residence. The means to build it were a gift from a grateful nation to the Duke of Marlborough after his victory over the French at the battle of Blenheim (1704). Although Wren, England's outstanding architect, was at his peak, the Duke chose Sir John Vanbrugh, equally famous as a playwright, to design it, assisted by Nicholas Hawksmoor. Both men had great talent and originality, but did more admirable work elsewhere, Vanbrugh at Castle Howard, Hawksmoor in several London churches.

The plan is of three wings, each with its own internal courtyard, grouped around a larger one and linked by colonnades. The fourth side of the main courtyard was to be filled by a grand entrance front, which was never built. The material is the attractive local stone. Outstanding features are the four bulky towers at the corners of the main block, which hold together the wide and complex spread of buildings, making an impressive sight from a distance, and the arrangement of the entrance where, behind the pediment of the portico, a second, higher pediment appears over the main hall. The skyline is richly arrayed with sculpture by Grinling Gibbons and others, but the formal gardens or *parterre* laid out by Vanbrugh disappeared later in the 18th century when the park was redesigned in the English manner by Lancelot 'Capability' Brown (1716–83). The interior, though grand, is not particularly memorable. The large saloon has frescoes by

Louis Laguerre, one example of the employment of French talent in spite of the context of the structure, and the most attractive room is the Long Library, or gallery.

The project was not entirely a happy one.

The funds proved insufficient and the Marlboroughs were themselves left with substantial bills. Vanbrugh retired in high dudgeon after quarrels with the Duchess, and Hawksmoor was apparently never paid in full.

Blenheim Palace was the birthplace of Winston Churchill, descendant and biographer of the 1st Duke of Marlborough.

The Belvedere, Vienna

It is amusing to go from Blenheim Palace, where guides may mention a loyal ally and subordinate commander of the Duke of Marlborough called Eugene of Savoy, to the Belvedere, residence of Prince Eugene, where the guides are vaguely aware that in his victories over the French the great imperial general had some assistance from an English milord.

The Belvedere is two fine but different Baroque palaces, the unpretentious Lower Belvedere, completed in 1715, where Eugene actually lived, and the Upper Belvedere, completed in 1723, a magnificent showpiece used on festive occasions. The architect was Lukas von Hildebrandt, who had fought in Prince Eugene's army and was the greatest Austrian Baroque architect after Fischer von Erlach, whom he succeeded (1723) as chief architect to the court. Hildebrandt was more Italian than German, having studied in Italy, and the influence of Borromini is evident in the Belvedere, which has been described as 'a rare blend of Teutonic solidity and Mediterranean caprice'. The interior of the Upper Belvedere is a dazzling assemblage in marble, gold and inlaid wood, created by a team of architects gathered by Hildebrandt. Like most Baroque architects, Hildebrandt rubbed his hands when he came to designing a staircase, which was treated as an individual work of art. In the Upper Belvedere, *putti* play around the almost Rococo lamps and vaguely Michelangelesque *atlantes* appear to support the vault and also appear elsewhere. The white marble marvellously lightens the whole structure, which has similarities with an even more attractive

staircase (1711) at Pommersfelden in Bavaria, which Hildebrandt placed within a spacious hall with three tiers of galleries.

The Belvedere later passed to the Habsburgs: Marie Antoinette left from here on her way to become queen of France. The composer Bruckner lived in the caretaker's

lodgings in his last years, and it was the home of the Archduke Franz Ferdinand, assassinated in Sarajevo in 1914. Today it contains the Austrian Gallery (modern art). Medieval Austrian art can be seen in the orangery of the Lower Belvedere.

The Belvedere is perhaps the finest example of the Italian-influenced yet thoroughly Austrian style.

Superga, Turin

Filippo Juvarra (1678–1736) is often seen as the successor to Guarino Guarini in the context of north Italian Baroque, but, although both were based in the same country and both were gifted with extraordinary imagination, otherwise they have relatively little in common. Juvarra, who came from a family of silversmiths and was trained in Rome under Carlo Fontana, was invited to Turin by Victor Amadeus II of Savoy

The Superga, Juvarra's ecclesiastical masterpiece, combines church and monastery in a single unit.

in 1714, over 30 years after Guarini's death. He remained there for 20 years, although he also worked on commissions elsewhere. He spent a year in Portugal, was more briefly in London and Paris, and died in Madrid where he was building a royal palace for Philip V.

Juvarra began his professional career as a stage-designer and continued to carry out work in furniture design and other fields. Nonetheless, as an architect he was hugely

prolific. In the area of Turin he built five large churches, at least eight palaces, besides numerous villas, and redesigned substantial sections of the city itself. His greatest secular work and most original building is the Stupinigi, officially a hunting lodge, in reality a magnificent palace, which balances Juvarra's gift for exciting theatrical design with the restrained Classicism that he learned in Rome.

Juvarra's ecclesiastical masterpiece is the Superga (begun 1716), one of the grandest of all Italian Baroque churches, which stands on a marvellous hilltop site dominating Turin, an indication of Juvarra's keen eye for topographical advantage. Juvarra was thoroughly eclectic, his work gives little sense of a coherent stylistic development, and a notable feature of the Superga is that, besides exploiting many aspects of Italian architecture, it also demonstrates more northerly influences. It is often compared with the great Austrian abbey of Melk (built a decade earlier), and echoes the way in which the body of the church is subsumed in the buildings of the monastery. The church protrudes beyond flanking towers, with a high, elegant dome soaring above the low monastic building, fronted by a grand Classical portico suggestive of the Pantheon in Rome. The commanding position is enhanced by the podium on which it stands, reached by steps on three sides. Inside, Juvarra's sure-footed and sophisticated design is marked by the skilful way in which he handles the transition from octagonal drum to round dome, and the achievement of a simple, spacious, integrated, two-storey structure. As always, he was assisted by some of the most gifted artists and craftsmen in Italy.

Royal Palace, Stockholm

In the middle of the 17th century, Sweden was a great power, and clearly the royal house of Vasa required something more impressive than the ramshackle old castle that then occupied the site of the royal palace, or slot, on Stads Island in the heart of Stockholm. A plan to enlarge and extend the castle was put into effect, but in 1694 the whole building was destroyed by fire; the body of King Charles XI, who had just died, was barely rescued from the flames.

There was not much doubt who would design the new palace. Nicodemus Tessin the Younger (1654–1728) had succeeded his father and namesake as Stockholm city architect, and completed his father's work at Drottningholm before moving to France, where he hoped to gain employment from Louis XIV at Versailles or the Louvre. Disappointed, he returned to Stockholm to undertake his finest achievement, and create what has been called the finest monument to French art outside France.

It is a very large, grand, block-like and unbending building with extended wings which, although it certainly manifests a French heritage, also appears to owe something to the *palazzi* of Renaissance Rome. The interior is more thoroughly, and lavishly, French of the Louis Quinze period, and is largely the work of French artists and craftsmen who would be better known had they worked in Paris. Some of the tapestries were designed by Boucher, and imported direct.

Construction did not go smoothly. On the throne from 1697 was Charles XII, the Swedish meteor, who apart from being hostile to everything French, had no money to spare outside his sensational military campaigns. The statues that were meant to decorate the pediment in the manner of Versailles were among the casualties; they would have made the façade less stark. Work petered out entirely after Charles's defeat at Poltava (1709) and was not resumed until after Tessin's death. Subsequent directors of the works were French-trained, and the building was largely completed by 1754, though it has been altered since.

The Royal Palace, detail of the south façade.

St Nicholas is a grand church, skilfully fitted to the cramped and uneven site.

RIGHT
The dome and drum.

OPPOSITE LEFT
Detail of the bell tower.

OPPOSITE RIGHT
Detail of the west front.

Saint Nicholas, Prague

The church of St Nicholas and the Jesuit College in Prague, in the Malá Strana or Lesser Town between the castle and the river, is the finest of all Bohemian Baroque churches. Like others, it owes much to the Italian Baroque of Borromini and especially Guarini. The Jesuits decided to rebuild their Gothic church at the end of the 17th century and the first period of construction lasted from 1703 to 1711. The architect was Christoph Dientzenhofer (1655–1722), a member of the second generation of a famous Bavarian family, settled in Prague. He completed the west façade and much of the nave before work was interrupted, no doubt by money problems. Work resumed in 1737 under Christoph's famous son, Kilian Ignac, who was responsible for the mighty dome and drum and the adjacent tower that dominates the Malá Strana, likened by the irreverent to a fat lady dancing with a thin man. The structure was largely completed by 1755, after Kilian Ignac's death. The reason for building from west to east was to preserve the Gothic sanctuary until the last moment.

Even by the standards of the Late Baroque, this is one of the most dramatic of churches, largely the result of the striking colour scheme of pink, green and cream and the flowing, rhythmic quality characteristic of the whole building. The walls almost disappear in the wealth of galleries, balconies, niches and doorways. There is no insistent point of focus, but the eye is drawn to the fabulous Rococo pulpit by the Prachners, a local workshop, the immense, almost threatening figures of Church Fathers, and the massive high altar with the figure of St Nicholas, a popular church patron

in Prague. Above, the dome over the choir is, in contrast, restrained and ethereal, while in the nave Johann Lukas Kracker's huge illusionist fresco of the Life of St Nicholas, painted in the 1760s (with a self-portrait in one corner), has been described as 'one of the finest expressions of Baroque monumental painting north of the Alps'.

The decoration was only completed in 1775, just two years before the Jesuit Order was, temporarily, dissolved.

BAROQUE TO REVIVALISM

CHAPTER FIVE

The Residenz, Würzburg

Royal Palace, Madrid

Royal Palace of Caserta, Naples

Vierzehnheiligen

Ottobeuren

Die Wies

Sans Souci

Royal Palace, Aranjuez

Royal Palace, Queluz

Spanish Steps, Rome

Tsarskoe Selo, St Petersburg

Winter Palace, St Petersburg

Monticello, Virginia

Syon House, Middlesex

Four Courts, Dublin

Strawberry Hill, Middlesex

Brighton Pavilion

Ducal Palace, Weimar

Iron Bridge, Coalbrookdale

Malmaison

Buckingham Palace

Houses of Parliament, Westminster

Royal Palace, Corfu

Trinity Church, Wall Street

United States Capitol, Washington, DC

Forth Railway Bridge, Edinburgh

Eiffel Tower

Arc de Triomphe, Paris

Washington Monument

Saint Pancras Station, London

Schloss Linderhof

Herrenchiemsee

Sacré Coeur, Paris

Glasgow School of Art

Sagrada Familia, Barcelona

Post Office Savings Bank, Vienna

Secession Building, Vienna

The origins of Baroque were associated with the Catholic revival of the early 17th century and it always tended to be strongest in Catholic regions. Late Baroque grew self-consciously decorative and spawned the Rococo, essentially a decorative style and related to Baroque, much as Mannerism was related to Renaissance Classicism. It seemed a secular, even frivolous style, yet the finest examples of Rococo are to be found among the Late Baroque

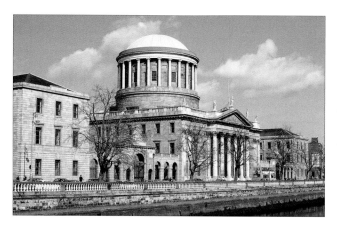

churches and abbeys of south Germany, notable examples being Ottobeuren and Die Wies.

When it became clear that Baroque and Rococo had nowhere else to go, the result was a revival of Classicism. In some countries, such as England and France, Classicism had never really gone away, but the Neoclassicism of the 18th century was different from the Classicism of the Renaissance. Knowledge had advanced, ancient Roman sites were now the target of upper-class tourists as well as artists, and techniques and building methods had also improved. However, Neoclassicism was also a revival of the Renaissance style: the designs of Palladio were especially influential in 18th-century England and the USA. The Classical style proved adaptable to all sorts of buildings, not only churches and civic buildings, but structures that had no parallel in Classical times.

As a counter to Classicism, other divergent styles emerged towards the end of the 18th century, including the English 'Picturesque', which embraced exotica like the Brighton Pavilion and the monumental Gothic house of Fonthill. Developments in the 19th century were largely dictated

by social and economic changes, which required new types of building (hospitals, hotels, factories) and by the new materials and techniques made available by the Industrial Revolution. A dramatic example was the Chicago School and the rise of the skyscraper. Meanwhile, historical styles flourished. The Greek Revival reflected increasing knowledge and the results of archaeological research; previously, Classicism had been predominantly based on Roman models. The Gothic Revival was strongest in England where, besides being adapted to new types of structure, it came to be the only acceptable style for churches. But virtually every historical style, from Ancient Egyptian to Neo-Baroque, cropped up somewhere, and some models were drawn from non-European sources. Architects were sometimes faithful to the original sources, sometimes not, and quite often two or more disparate styles mingled in the same building, in which case the result was not always dreadful: the Houses of Parliament in London mixed Classical planning with Gothic decoration to achieve a very satisfactory result.

Innovations derived from new materials, particularly iron (later steel) and glass, were perhaps the most interesting aspect of 19th-century developments, but towards the end of the century a reaction against 'historicism' appeared, influenced by movements such as the Arts and Crafts movement in England and the Werkbund in Germany, in the styles known generically as Art Nouveau. Initially a purely decorative style, Art Nouveau, coloured by differing national and political ideas, proved significant for architecture also.

The Residenz, Würzburg

The early 18th century was a fertile period for building, both religious and secular, in the German lands. A religious revival in the Roman Catholic Church prompted the building of new pilgrimage churches such as Vierzehnheiligen. The wealthy rulers of Germany's numerous principalities competed to build the richest palaces, resulting, as Ian Sutton puts it, in buildings 'that can still astonish by their scale, verve and vitality'. Perhaps the finest secular building in the Baroque style in Germany was the palace of the prince-bishops of Würzburg, begun in 1720.

The splendour of the Würzburg Residenz rests on the work of many people, but chief among them are the architect Balthasar Neumann (1687–1753) and the painter Giambattista Tiepolo (1696–1770). The Czech-born Neumann was a comparative tyro in 1720, so the Prince-Bishop consulted other experts besides his protégé, including Hildebrandt and the Frenchmen de Cotte and Boffrand, who are presumably responsible for the strong flavour of the Rococo at Würzburg. Neumann was an architect of catholic sympathies who seems to have benefited from these influences. He was to gain fame for his new and complex ways of handling space, and the most magnificent feature of Würzburg, the ceremonial staircase, is probably entirely his work.

The structure was completed by 1744, and the decoration of the interior was carefully considered. Unlike Neumann in 1720, Tiepolo in the 1740s was already at the height of his fame, and correspondingly expensive. However, the resources of the Prince-Bishop were considerable, and the great Venetian painter

arrived, together with his two sons, late in 1750. Within three years he had completed the decoration of the Great Hall and the vault of the staircase, where the theme chosen was the Four Continents; some of the sculptures in the gardens amusingly parody Tiepolo's figures. The Kaisersaal or Great Hall has historical scenes, not always particularly relevant to the

Würzburg rulers, and comprises a brilliant display of the Baroque artists' combination of frescoes (Tiepolo), stucco (Antonio Bossi) and architecture (Neumann). Tiepolo's brilliant exploitation of light, his magical, fizzing colours, and his ever-fertile imagination were never more splendidly displayed than at Würzburg.

The Residenz, Würzburg, represents the work of the architect Balthasar Neumann and the painter Giambattista Tiepolo, among others.

Royal Palace, Madrid

Although there was a walled town here under Muslim rule in the 10th century, Madrid is comparatively new and comparatively small – more a *villa* (town) than a *ciudad* (city) – as the capital of a major European country. Although several earlier kings of Castile spent some time here, and the Emperor Charles V (Carlos I) found its dry air and high altitude, 2,100ft (640m) above sea level, assuaged his gout, it was not until 1561 that Charles's son, Philip II, moved his court there, and it did not become the official capital until 1607.

The grand and costly Buen Retiro palace was built in the 1630s, rather too quickly, it seems, as the cost of maintenance proved intolerable, and nothing now survives except the park. The original Palacio Real in Madrid was badly damaged by a fire at Christmas time in 1734, and Philip V decided to build a completely new palace in closer accord with Bourbon tastes. A scheme was drawn up by the great Juvarra, chiefly active in Turin where he built the famous Stupinigi and the Superga, but he died a few months after he arrived in Madrid and the building was completed by his former pupil, Giovanni Battista (Juan Bautista) Sacchetti. He enlarged the building and made considerable alterations, deriving to some extent from Bernini's plans for the Louvre in Paris, but the palace is really Sacchetti's work. He also planned the immediate environment of the palace. The huge ceilings were painted by Tiepolo, who spent his last years in Madrid.

It is an impressive, powerful edifice, its great height partly the effect of a sloping site; it is built of a whitish granite that resembles marble. In style it belongs rather to the North Italian Baroque than to any Spanish tradition. Notable among the contents is the library of ancient books and manuscripts. Huge statues of Spanish monarchs were commissioned to stand on the balustrade, but when the time came to erect them, nerves failed, and they were positioned more safely at ground level, around the Plaza de Oriente, created by clearing about 60 buildings, including several religious houses.

OPPOSITE
The elevated site adds a sense of grandeur to the palace.

LEFT
The façade from the Campo del Moro.

Royal Palace of Caserta, Naples

Caserta was conceived as a challenge to Versailles, and though it did not compare is was certainly vast.

Caserta, north of Naples, is one of those monumental royal palaces that aimed to challenge Versailles. It was built for Charles III of Naples, a great-grandson of Louis XIV. The architect was Luigi Vanvitelli (1700–73), born in Naples of Dutch descent, who had studied with Juvarra and earned a reputation in Rome before returning to his birthplace in response to a royal summons in 1751.

The palace consists of a rectangular block 492 x 623ft (150 x 190m), with four internal courtyards. It is larger even than the Escorial, and the great length of almost uninterrupted façade is slightly depressing. Vanvitelli's original plan, which included towers at the corners and a central dome on a high drum, might have been more attractive but, though somewhat smaller, it was judged too costly.

This is almost the last major building in the Italian Baroque style, and the plain, repetitive exterior already signals the revival of Classicism. Inside there is more evidence of Baroque energy and panache, notably in Vanvitelli's theatre and the great double staircase. There are one or two Rococo rooms, like the Queen's Bathroom, but the state apartments, which are now open to the public, date from much later and, except for the magnificent Throne Room of 1845, are relatively severe. The palace was to be linked with Naples by an avenue 19-miles (30-km) long. The park was designed to be even larger than it is now, with a watercourse and a variety of fountains supplied by an aqueduct 25-miles (40-km) long and with elaborate sculptural groups such as Diana and Actaeon dotted about the sward.

In the end, perhaps the most remarkable thing about Caserta is its sheer size. It is said to be possible to walk around it all day without passing the same spot twice. This vastness is the more staggering when one remembers over what a wretchedly poor country the preposterous Bourbon kings of Naples reigned.

Vierzehnheiligen

In the wake of the Counter-Reformation, religious architecture in central Europe in the Baroque period reached a peak only previously equalled in the late medieval centuries and never since. The sheer size of such buildings as the abbey of Melk, commanding the Danube valley west of Vienna, is staggering, and raises problems for conservation in a secular age. In almost every church, it seems, there is a creative striving for something unique in the handling of space and form.

Vierzehnheiligen ('Fourteen saints'), on the River Main in Bavaria, is a pilgrimage church, the site of a miraculous vision in 1445, and which incorporates the shrine. The decision to replace the Gothic chapel with a sensationally grand Baroque church was taken in 1730, but there was a quarrel over who should design it. The bishop of Bamberg, who eventually won, was a Schönborn and therefore an admirer of Balthasar Neumann, to whom the commission was transferred in 1743. Besides the shrine, Neumann also had to adapt to work done by his predecessors.

Neumann is sometimes called an 'architect's architect': his work seems light-hearted, easy, almost instinctive, but was based on extraordinarily careful and complex planning. The connection often made between German Baroque architecture and the music of Bach is particularly apt in Neumann's case.

From the outside, Vierzehnheiligen is largely a building of straight lines; the lofty, twin-towered west façade, though articulated with the Classical Orders, is undeniably Gothic in shape; moreover the basic plan is a Latin cross and there are other debts to the still

unfashionable Gothic tradition. However, the interior is designed on the basis of intersecting circles and ovals, and there is not a straight line to be seen – even the columns are concave. The emphasis is cunningly diverted away from the crossing towards the shrine in the nave by innovatory handling of vaulting and light sources. The Rococo decoration employs columns of coloured *scagliola* (versatile, plaster-based material resembling marble) and sparkling stucco work. The church was not finished until the 1770s, after the death of Neumann and of his former pupil, Jacob Küchel, who succeeded him and was largely responsible for the interior. It was struck by lighting in 1838 and has been restored more than once.

The exterior of Ottobeuren (opposite) is plain, though assured. However, the Rococo interior is somewhat different. Here, Fischer overcame the slightly cramped effect evident in his other building, Zwiefalten.

Ottobeuren

In the early 18th century plasterers enjoyed an unprecedented demand for their services. A vast amount of sculpture was required in the grand new churches springing up in such numbers in southern Germany, and increasingly it was in plaster rather than marble, partly because plaster was much cheaper, partly because it was better suited to the flying draperies and flamboyant poises of Rococo decoration. Sculptors were displeased, and a compromise was arranged (1725) in which for independent sculptures the plasterer had to follow models provided by a sculptor. This seems to have worked well at Ottobeuren, where J.M. Feichtmayr followed models by the sculptor J.J. Christian.

The abbey of Ottobeuren, just south-east of Memmingen in Bavaria, was originally founded in the 8th century. The decision was taken to rebuild the church in about 1730, but the abbey's masons did not give satisfaction and in 1744 Johann Michael Fischer (1692–1766) was called in. Fischer, born in Bavaria, had served his apprenticeship in Bohemia and knew the Dientzenhofers. Although highly gifted, he is considered to be not quite in the same class as Hildebrandt and Neumann, perhaps partly because he was so prolific: he is said to have designed no less than 22 abbeys and 32 churches. His appointment to Ottobeuren followed his work at the abbey of Zwiefalten, though in plan that church, where Fischer had to follow the medieval foundations, is very different.

Ottobeuren has been described by James Lees-Milne as 'probably the noblest of all 18th-century German churches'. Here too Fischer was limited by pre-existing foundations, but he altered the design of the interior by increasing the size and significance of the central piers and emphasized the diagonal axes with additional altars. It is an enormous building, with a soaring façade, but is most renowned for its breathtaking decoration. The gorgeous Rococo decorative scheme creates an effervescent riot of coloured *scagliola* (columns in pale-grey and pink), frescoes (by J.J. Zeiller), and plasterwork, all on a dazzlingly white, gold-banded background, in which structural elements seem almost to dissolve.

Die Wies

Whereas J.M. Fischer concentrated on abbeys, the speciality of Dominikus Zimmermann (1685–1766) was pilgrimage churches of which Die Wies is his finest. Zimmermann was originally a plasterer, often working with his brother, Johann Baptist (1680–1758), who became a painter around the age of 50 and was so successful that he was called in to help Cuvilliés at Nymphenburg. The most thoroughly Rococo of south German architects, he established his style at another pilgrimage church, Steinhausen (begun 1727), not far away, which appears rectangular from the outside but inside turns out to be oval, like Die Wies. Such a plan is convenient for circulating pilgrims.

Zimmermann was of peasant stock and appropriately Die Wies (begun in 1745) was built not for some princely bishop or wealthy abbot but for ordinary people. The name means 'the meadow', and the church even today stands isolated among fields. It originated in events that illustrate the deep piety of the times, a piety that Zimmermann shared. For this was not, as was most common, a medieval shrine; in fact the miracle that attracted pilgrims to the little chapel that preceded Zimmermann's church had occurred as recently as 1738. It involved a crude wooden figure of Christ, painted a horrible green, which had been seen to weep tears; the money for the church was raised in a few years entirely from the offerings of devoted pilgrims.

At Die Wies, Zimmermann combines the spacious oval of the 'nave' (customary terms are not so appropriate for Baroque churches), circled by a wide ambulatory for pilgrims, with a rectangular 'choir'. The dominant colours are white and gold, with carved wooden figures and paintings, including Johann Baptist's spectacular vault frescoes, red *scagliola* columns around the high altar, bright blue ones at the opposite end, unusually grouped in pairs, and windows of disparate shapes that admit plenty of light. Colours and motifs are symbolic, their meaning not always obvious in a less religious age. Because the church was based on a solid wooden frame, Zimmermann did not have to worry much about structural restrictions and was free to exploit to the full the freedom of Rococo decoration.

OPPOSITE
The Church of Die Wies retains its isolation in the fields. The tower is attached to the choir, and the clergy houses are to the left.

BELOW LEFT
The vault fresco of Johann Baptist Zimmermann.

BELOW
Detail of the interior.

Sans Souci

Sans Souci is the North German equivalent of the Amalienburg, and this fanciful summer palace of the cultured Frederick the Great of Prussia, who personally sketched at least the general design, seems a little unexpected in a stern, northern, Protestant land. It is a one-storey building with a low central dome but, because of its hilltop site in Potsdam, it commands a fine view from the floor-length windows. Again like the Amalienburg, it is only one element in a large complex, though not so large as the more conventional Neues Palais, also built by Frederick, and set among a variety of smaller structures, some contemporary some later. These include some surprises, such as the whimsical fantasy of the 'Chinese' pavilion, with columns in the form of palm trees.

Sans Souci was built by Georg Wenceslaus von Knöbelsdorff (1699–1753), Frederick's court architect and close friend, and a man of similarly cultured and eclectic tastes. He was also responsible for the most intensely Rococo additions to Charlottenburg in the 1740s, and for the Classical Berlin Opera House. He began work on Sans Souci in 1745 but in the following year quarrelled with the king over the designs, with the result that he was dismissed from his post and never produced another building.

Apart from some slightly obtrusive sculpture, the exterior is attractive and inviting but not especially striking, so that the brilliant Rococo decoration of the rooms beyond comes as something of a surprise. The little library, the music room, the so-called Voltaire room, display an unparalleled fantasy of ornament, employing almost every conceivable material. Delicate leafy and gilded forms by Johann August Nahl and others clamber over door panels, around windows and asymmetrical frames and mirrors, and across walls and ceilings. It sounds too much, but the German craftsmen did not overstep the bounds of good taste. The effect is undeniably stagy, but not vulgar.

The King's bedchamber and sitting room, completed after his death in 1786, is in Neoclassical style, suggesting that in his later years Frederick was abandoning the French frivolities of the Rococo in favour of a more austere style. The armchair in which he died is still here.

It is easy to sympathize with Philip II's fondness for Aranjuez, after the rigorous formalities of the Escorial.

Royal Palace, Aranjuez

In spite of the magnificent façade of Santiago de Compostela, architectural historians hesitate to describe the style of Spain or Portugal in the 17th–18th centuries as 'Baroque'. Although there are obvious similarities, such as the love of ingenious and spectacular effects, there is no real affinity with the principles of Bernini and Borromini. The ultra-decorative, specifically Spanish 'Baroque' style is often called Churrigueresque, after the Churriguera family of sculptors-architects from Barcelona.

The palace of Aranjuez is on the River Tagus about 30-miles (50-km) south of Madrid. Superficially, it appears pleasingly uniform, though as so often is the case, its history is more complicated. There was a castle on the site in the Middle Ages, held by the Knights of Santiago, a military order active in reconquering Spain from the Muslims. It passed into royal possession around the end of the 15th century, and Carlos I (the Emperor Charles V) converted it into a hunting lodge. Under Philip II it grew into a palace, built by those who had worked on the Escorial, though here they were in lighter mood. It was subsequently seriously damaged by fire, and the present building largely dates from the reconstruction for Ferdinand VI by an Italian architect, Santiago Bonavia, in the mid-18th century.

The long low buildings around a large courtyard, only two storeys high except for the central main block, were built over a longish period. The wings, with terraced roofs and galleries, were completed after Bonavia's time but followed his subdued Rococo style quite faithfully. The main block consists of three units, with shallow domes at the corners that suggest the influence of Juvarra. Topped by lanterns and placed on drums pierced with circular windows, they augment the general air of quiet distinction. The interior is more of a mixture, and besides many treasures it contains some odd features such as the pseudo-Moorish smoking room in over-bright colours that was added in the 19th century. Of greater interest is the dazzling porcelain room, with tiles and mirrors from the Buen Retiro factory near Madrid.

Royal Palace, Queluz

The palace of Queluz, north of Lisbon on the road to Sintra, was begun in 1747, and much of it was completed by 1752. This attractive Rococo residence, one of the few royal palaces one would like to live in, was designed for a younger son of the Portuguese royal family and was financed out of the profits of the gold and diamonds produced by Brazil. Although not finished at the time of the great Lisbon earthquake of 1755, it suffered comparatively little. It was badly damaged by fire in the 1930s but subsequently restored.

The palace itself, set amid flower gardens, is the masterpiece of a Portuguese architect, Mateus Vicente de Oliveira (1710–60), and has an unpretentious charm and a sense of easy assurance. The stucco of the walls is pink, with white stonework and lime-green windows and doors. Among the main rooms is the Sala des Mangas, with panels of *azulejos* (decorative tiles) in the 'Chinese' manner covering most of the walls, predominantly in blue and gold. The Hall of Mirrors glitters with glass and gilt. In the Ball Room, also with shimmering chandeliers, the Rococo decoration is most lavish, and the room is planned on an elliptical oval.

Other architects and designers, including a Frenchman, Jean Baptiste Robillon, were engaged on other buildings and features of the gardens which augment Oliveira's perfectly proportioned central block. Robillon planned the hanging gardens; the extensive topiary was the work of a Dutchman, Gerald van den Kolk, and the lead statues, a fashion also stemming from the Netherlands, were by an Englishman, John Cheeve. The extraordinary little western pavilion, reached by the dramatic Lion's Steps, is by Robillon. From a staid Classical colonnade, Rococo statuary breaks into a riot against the sky. The eastern pavilion, with its scrolled pediments, is also interesting, but its designer is unknown.

The Palace of Queluz combines fine proportions with exuberant decoration.

Spanish Steps, Rome

In Rome, by about 1700, though palaces were still being built, there was increasing emphasis on public projects, as if to turn the whole city into a Baroque monument.

Except in Venice, Rococo did not make much impact in Italy, least of all in Rome, where it was simply too far removed from the honoured principles of Classicism. However, traces of the Rococo did appear here and there, not only in the window frames of 18th-century palaces, but also in some public monuments, such as the Trevi Fountain and the Spanish Steps, which are based on flowing Rococo curves.

In the 16th century, the only way to climb the steep slope between the Piazza di Spagna, where Bernini would later build a fountain, to the church of S. Trinità dei Monti was by a treacherous footpath (the Spanish Steps would provide firm footing but not safety from thieves and bandits). The long delay before the project was realized was largely the result of a territorial dispute between the pope and the French embassy. Compromise was eventually reached, and the French provided money for construction, hence the presence of the French *fleur-de-lis* on the Steps, though they were named after the nearby Spanish embassy.

The Steps, built in 1723–25, were designed by Francesco de Sanctis (1693–1740), who is otherwise little known. This huge and fabulous monument, which has featured so often in literature (the poet Keats died in a room overlooking it), achieves one of the objectives of Rococo by provoking surprise in the viewer, at first at the sheer scale, then by the diverging curves of steps and balustrades. Walking up,

wrote Michael Kitson, 'it is as if the architecture has taken charge, controlling one's movements in ways that are hard to resist or understand yet are gentle enough to be delightful rather than disturbing.'

Tsarskoe Selo, St Petersburg

Bartolomeo Francesco Rastrelli (1700–71) was the leading architect of the Late Baroque/Rococo period in Russia. Though Italian by birth, he trained in Paris and his style is thoroughly French, which suited the cultural aspirations of the Russian aristocracy, though with a few traces of Russian influence. He arrived in St Petersburg in 1716 as an assistant to Jean-Baptiste le Blond, builder of the massive Peterhof, and was appointed court architect to the Tsarina Elizabeth Petrovna in 1741. He was responsible for many buildings, including the Smolny Convent in St Petersburg, the style of which has been described as 'Russo-Rococo'; but the most successful were the Great Palace of Tsarskoe Selo, 'village of the tsar', later called Pushkin, which became the favourite residence of Catherine the Great, and the Winter Palace. Paradoxically, Rastrelli, remembered for enormous buildings which required so many labourers that the workforce was partly recruited from the army, was at his happiest working on a small scale.

The Great Palace, started in 1749, was built around a colossal quadrangle, and is only slightly smaller than the Winter Palace. The main façade is about 330-ft (100-m) long, and is highly decorative in blue, white and gold, with a powerful, rhythmical arrangement of columns, pilasters, balustrades, balconies, *atlantes* and broken pediments. Few of Rastrelli's interiors survive today, though his delicate little pavilions still grace the grounds.

Under Catherine the Great, considerable alterations were made by the Scottish architect, Charles Cameron (d. 1812), trained in Rome, who arrived in Russia in 1774. He was an admirer of his countryman, Robert Adam, though his own brand of Neoclassicism is less delicate and refined, the plasterwork more elaborate. His interiors at Pushkin are possibly his finest work. He employed rich but delicate materials, the colours mostly pale, pastel shades, with much use of glass and, in some rooms, inlaid Wedgwood plaques specially commissioned from the famous English pottery. Some further changes took place in the 19th century, but they were insignificant compared with the disasters of the Second World War, when St Petersburg was besieged for 900 days and the palace suffered looting as well as fires. It was splendidly restored after the war by the Communist regime.

The effect of the exterior of Tsarkoe Selo is like a highly decorated Rococo version of Versailles.

Winter Palace, St Petersburg

When Peter the Great founded his new capital to give Russia a 'window on Europe', a royal palace was built on the bank of the mighty River Neva. This building was soon replaced, and the Winter Palace (now the Hermitage Museum) that now occupies the site is the result of several later reconstructions of which the most important is that of 1754, by Bartolomeo Rastrelli for the Tsarina Elizabeth. Rastrelli was still involved with Tsarskoe Selo, begun five years earlier, and the two palaces have much in common, besides sheer size.

Rastrelli was remarkably successful both in overcoming planning restrictions and in avoiding monotony. To fit in with the rest of the city he was limited to a maximum height of 65ft (20m). The length, however, is nearly 495ft (150m) on the longer sides. He avoided the monotony of, for instance, the palace of Caserta, by designing a highly ornamental exterior that is broken up by pairs of columns and alternating projections and recessions. The colour scheme, similar to Tsarskoe Selo, is white, greenish-blue and gold, although it seems that Rastrelli originally specified orange and white; during the 19th century, the palace was painted a darker, reddish colour. Work on the interior continued throughout the reign of Catherine the Great and beyond, especially after a fire in the 1830s. As a result, Rastrelli's Rococo interiors have mostly disappeared, although the state rooms have

been restored, with gorgeous velvets and marbles, to something like their original appearance; his grand double staircase remains as testimony to his theatrical style.

Besides war, one event that might have been expected to cause serious damage was the coup d'état of the Bolsheviks against the Kerensky government, in the Winter Palace, in 1917. The palace was defended by a handful of army cadets, a women's battalion, and a few half-hearted Cossacks. They were no match for Trotsky's Military Revolutionary Committee, backed by the guns of the cruiser *Aurora* in the Neva, and the Revolution was almost bloodless.

Rastrelli, who went to Russia as a youth, had studied in Paris, and the distinctive, graceful, Rococo style he brought to the Winter Palace was more French than anything else.

*OPPOSITE
Today tourist boats, not warships, cruise the Neva.*

Thomas Jefferson was largely responsible for the adoption of Neoclassicism as more or less the official style of the USA. It was familiar, yet not too English (i.e. not Georgian, an impossible term in view of recent events). His own Palladian villa, Monticello, was the most distinguished of the colonnaded mansions of eminent American gentlemen.

Monticello, Virginia

Appropriately, the Classical revival of the 18th century took strongest root in the USA, perhaps because it was associated with republican virtues, and it became virtually the only acceptable style for great public buildings. Leadership in this respect, as in others, came from Thomas Jefferson, author of the Declaration of Independence, Enlightenment polymath and third president of the USA. He deserves the credit for establishing what became in effect a national style that lent great distinction to simple domestic architecture – the 'clapboard classicism' of New England and elsewhere.

Jefferson, the son of a landowner who was also a trained civil engineer, took architecture very seriously, was genuinely gifted, and would collect much the biggest library of architectural books in the country. Inheriting a large estate east of the Blue Mountains near Charlottesville, Virginia, he built his own house, Monticello, on a carefully chosen, elevated site. Though begun in 1770, the basic plan came to be derived largely from Robert Morris's *Select Architecture* (1775), modified by Jefferson's study of Palladio's villas. Jefferson altered and greatly enlarged the house after his spell in Paris as minister to France (1784–89), increasing the height of the rooms (eventually there were 35) and building the octagonal dome over the hall. During that period, with some help from the French Neoclassical architect Charles-Louis Clérisseau, also associated with William Chambers and the Adam brothers, Jefferson designed the state capitol in Richmond on the model of the Maison Carrée at Nîmes, but larger and with unfluted Ionic, instead of Corinthian, columns. He would later design the University of Virginia at Charlottesville, the buildings representing several Classical variants and culminating in a splendid pantheon.

Monticello is the result of long thought and careful planning, not only in its adaptation of Palladian design but also in its – some would say – characteristically American concern for comfort. Jefferson incorporated various labour-saving features of his own devising, such as revolving shelves to speed the serving of food, and had his bed in an alcove between dressing room and study so that he could move easily from the one to the other.

Syon House, Middlesex

Robert Adam (1728–92), the greatest British architect of the late 18th century, is perhaps best known as a decorator, author of the ultra-elegant, Neoclassical 'Adam style', because in so many cases he was working on a pre-existing building. He represented the opposite pole of Neoclassicism from his contemporary, William Chambers, designer of Somerset House in London, with whom he shared the position of royal architect. Chambers regarded him as frivolous.

Syon House, seat of the dukes of Northumberland, was a 16th–17th-century house around a square courtyard. The Duke was cultured, rich, and prepared to spend, although Adam's planned rotunda proved too much even for his pocket. In reconstructing the interior in 1762–69, Adam, fresh from his researches in Italy and Split, created what Sacheverell Sitwell described as 'among the greatest works of art in England', in which, however, practically everything derives from Classical prototypes. In fact there are only five rooms. The monumental, basilica-like hall in the Doric Order has painted medallions on the curved ceiling of the apse that decrease in size to lengthen the perspective. The spectacular anteroom is a rectangle which is converted to a square by a line of free-standing columns. Huge Ionic columns of green marble line the walls and are topped by athletic figures in gilded plaster, with panels of gilt trophies and a multicoloured *scagliola* floor. The largely white dining room and the red drawing room, with its unusual decorated coving, as well as ceiling, where the pattern of medallions suggested to Chambers dinner plates thrown at the ceiling, offer contrasting examples of Classical splendour that is also comfortable.

The whole of the east side, overlooking the Thames and Kew Gardens, is occupied by a very long and very narrow Jacobean long gallery. Here Adam displayed imagination and finesse in overcoming the tunnel-like appearance with Corinthian pilasters that break the line and suggest depth, while the lozenges that decorate the ceiling are interrupted by the walls as if they continue beyond. The overall impression is of what Adam described as 'a style to afford great variety and amusement'. It is the quintessence of the Adam style.

Syon House retains its original appearance of a 17th-century, square-planned, castellated mansion.

*OPPOSITE
Gardens and conservatory: the house is just across the river from the Botanical Gardens at Kew.*

Four Courts, Dublin

Dublin became an elegant, largely Neoclassical city during the 18th century, with the old Parliament Building, Leinster House, the Classical façade for Trinity College, and streets and squares of pleasant Georgian houses. Although the English associations of much of its architecture caused mixed feelings in nationalists, few would now condemn it as a symbol of English imperialism.

Among the finest buildings are the Custom House and the Four Courts building, both the work of James Gandon (1743–1823). English-born, of French descent, Gandon was a pupil of William Chambers. He arrived in Ireland in 1781 to design the Custom House. He had to deal with many difficulties during construction, including the threat of violence, but was not deterred, and in 1786 took over the Four Courts building on the north bank of the River Liffey, begun ten years earlier but with only the west wing already built.

Although Gandon rejected the Adam style as too frivolous, he was not exactly Chambers' disciple either. His style, described by Brendan Lehane as 'Palladian with Baroque and Neoclassical additions', also seems to owe something to his French connections, and he had studied Wren's riverside buildings at Greenwich and Chelsea (London). But his imaginative and original style was essentially personal.

The entrance to the Four Courts is a hexastyle Corinthian portico, but the most distinctive feature is the central colonnaded drum, surmounted by a very shallow dome, originally even flatter than today, which gives the building its striking originality and contributes so splendidly to the Dublin skyline. It is one of those structures familiar because it is so distinctive, indeed unique. Below it is the circular central hall from which radiate, on diagonal axes, the chambers that contained the original 'four courts' (Exchequer, Common Pleas, King's Bench and Chancery).

During the Irish Civil War in 1922–23, mines and artillery destroyed all but the shell of the building, and much of the invaluable and irreplaceable archives of the adjoining Public Record Office. The building was restored in 1932.

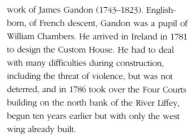

Strawberry Hill, Middlesex

In 1747 Horace Walpole (1717–97), younger son of a British prime minister, leased 'a little plaything house' near the river in Twickenham, south-west of London. Two years later he bought it, and began its conversion into a kind of miniature Gothic castle. Walpole was a cultured, slightly 'precious' bachelor, a dilettante but a learned one. He was the author of an early Gothic novel, *The Castle of Otranto* (1764). His house was a forerunner of the Gothic Revival, but it was conceived in an entirely different spirit, more frolicsome than the studious 'archaeologizing' of the next century, as displayed in the 19th-century addition to Strawberry Hill. It seemed to

Walpole that the Gothic style was well suited to the kind of small country house he required. Completed between 1749 and 1766, Strawberry Hill is a romantic, make-believe place, and Walpole always spoke of it in that way, while privately taking it more seriously than he was prepared to admit.

Walpole was a stickler for authenticity, studying medieval engravings and if possible visiting sites for design sources, and consulting the group of friends he called his 'Committee of Taste'. Among them were the poet Thomas Gray, John Chute and Richard Bentley, who designed a great deal of the house, and for a short time Robert Adam, who designed one of the rooms, although under Walpole's

supervision. The emphasis on accuracy was oddly eclectic. The models for bookcases and fireplaces came from tombs and screens in French and English churches: the chimney piece in the Little Parlour is modelled on the tomb of a 13th-century bishop in Westminster Abbey. The overall effect is neither incongruous nor vulgar, but graceful, delicate and endearing. The whole place is on a small scale: Bentley's delightful staircase would fit in a modern suburban house. After Walpole's death Strawberry Hill was neglected and his furniture dissipated, but the house enjoyed a new lease of life when reopened and enlarged by Lady Waldegrave in the 1860s.

There is something rather precious about Walpole and his Committee of Taste, but his precocious little Gothic villa is a delight. It was expanded in the 19th century, in broadly the same style but in a different spirit.

Brighton Pavilion was something of a royal folly. Among English monarchs, none but George IV would have contemplated such a costly frivolity.

Brighton Pavilion

On the whole, English monarchs were less extravagant builders than many of their European contemporaries, but one exception was the Prince Regent, later George IV (1820–30), whose expenditure infuriated parliament when called upon to pay his bills. Later generations may be thankful for George's fecklessness, in particular for his greatest 'folly', the fairytale 'oriental' palace known as Brighton Pavilion.

In the mid-18th century Brighton was a small fishing village on the south coast of England, about 50 miles (80km) from London. The Prince first visited it in 1783 and built a small but delightful brick villa there with the result that Brighton soon became fashionable, and the Brighton Road became dangerously crowded with speeding coaches. In 1806 George decided to extend the villa and hired Humphrey Repton, best known as a landscape gardener, to submit plans. Repton had recently worked on a house for a retired Indian nabob and had 'discovered new sources of beauty and variety in Indian architecture'. His plan was for a building based vaguely on Indian sources. The Prince was delighted, but when work began ten years later Repton had been superseded by the more fashionable, and more gifted John Nash, his former partner.

Nash's building, though indisputably oriental in flavour, mixes Hindu, Islamic and Chinese styles, without being faithful to any. The exterior, with its sparkling white domes (provoking one contemporary critic to remark that 'St Paul's has gone down to Brighton and pupped'), minarets, fretted balconies and arcading, and creamy walls, suggests at first glance a backdrop for a pantomime Aladdin. The relative fragility of the building masks extensive use of iron, invisible except in a spiral staircase. The interior contains the finest display of *chinoiserie* in England, and some of the finest furniture in the style termed (after the Prince) 'Regency'. As well as intense disapproval, the Pavilion, seldom actually lived in, aroused great popular interest in England and elsewhere, and it is said to have been pictured in 19th-century books more frequently than any other English building.

Ducal Palace, Weimar

The medieval town of Weimar in Thuringia became the capital of a duchy in the 16th century under rulers of the Saxon house of Wettin, and though never powerful, Weimar has a distinguished history. After the post-war revolution of 1918–19, the German National Assembly met here and drew up the constitution of the short-lived state known as the Weimar Republic, overthrown by Hitler in 1933. In the history of architecture, Weimar is remembered as the site of the Bauhaus, the most important school of art and design in the 20th century, which originated in the school of arts and crafts founded by the Grand Duke in 1906. He appointed as director the Belgian Henri van der Velde, who was responsible for the policy of teaching through workshops rather than studios; when he left Germany during the First World War, he suggested Walter Gropius as his successor.

But Weimar's greatest period was the late-18th and early-19th centuries, when it was the unrivalled intellectual capital of Germany. Under the Grand Duke Karl August, Goethe, Schiller, Herder and others were attracted to Weimar. The many memorials to them include the Goethe-Schiller Mausoleum and Archives and the bronze monument in front of the German National Theatre, where Goethe was director for many years, though the theatre was later rebuilt.

Schloss Weimar, the ducal palace, is the most important building in Weimar, although not perhaps the most interesting or the most beautiful. An English visitor described it as only 'imposing from its extent'. It was largely rebuilt after a fire, from 1789 until 1803, when the Napoleonic Wars interrupted progress, and was not finished until much later. The major survival from the earlier castle is the tall clock tower, buttressed by adjoining later buildings. Herder, Goethe and Schiller have their own named rooms with scenes from their works, and the gracious private apartments contain Italian Renaissance paintings. The Neoclassical hall is the most distinguished part of the 18th-century building, whose construction, according to tradition, was supervised by Goethe himself.

Schloss Weimar, the ducal palace, is the most important building in Weimar, once the intellectual capital of Germany.

Iron Bridge, Coalbrookdale

Iron was used in architecture from early times to strengthen structures, but it was exclusively functional and usually invisible. No one considered it might be beautiful in itself, and that was not widely accepted as such until very recently: some local people considered the Iron Bridge a monstrosity only 30 years ago. Completed in 1779, the Iron Bridge was the first large structure made wholly of cast iron, and signalled the beginning of the end of timber and stone as the materials for bridge construction and eventually for other utilitarian buildings. It gave its name to the village and rapidly achieved worldwide fame.

It was no accident that this innovation occurred in Shropshire, north-west England, a centre of iron founding since the 16th century and a cradle of the Industrial Revolution. The original design was by Thomas Farnolls Pritchard (1723–77), though he died before the final plan was approved. The builder, who probably had a hand in the design too, was Abraham Darby the Third (1750–91). His grandfather, who died in 1717, was one of the first to use coke rather than charcoal in his Coalbrookdale iron foundry, a vital step towards the great industrial take-off.

The bridge is an arch spanning 100ft (30m). The deck is supported by iron ribs passing through vertical pillars set in the stone abutments, five across and in five reducing tiers. They are reinforced by cross-stays and diagonals. The roadway is based on iron plates each 24-ft (7-m) wide, i.e. the width of the roadway, and lined by a cast-iron balustrade. As inevitably happens when new material or new types of structure are introduced, the builders

naturally adapted existing techniques. The details of the Iron Bridge thus resemble those of the carpenter and the stonemason – mortise and tenon and dovetail joints, iron keys, screws and wedges rather than rivets and bolts, which were

yet to be invented. The iron circles that link vertical pillar, topmost rib and deck reproduce the pierced spandrels of stone bridges, a technique to reduce weight that had only become common a generation earlier.

Coalbrookdale's Iron Bridge lies at the heart of the birthplace of the Industrial Revolution.

Malmaison

Malmaison, 45 minutes from Paris on horseback, is chiefly famous as the home of the Empress Josephine. It barely merits the name of château, being merely a comfortable country house in pleasant grounds. The original 17th-century house was a simple building consisting of a three-floor central block with short protruding wings. It was looted during the Revolution but escaped serious damage. Josephine bought the house and gardens in 1799 while Napoleon was in Egypt, and he was not at first pleased.

It was subsequently enlarged, and the demolition of the original wings weakened the structure and necessitated the unfortunate buttresses topped by vases. Josephine, divorced in 1809, loved the place and lived there for the rest of her life. For Napoleon it had been a relaxing country retreat, where he was able to forget strategy and government and indulge in games of blind man's bluff. He returned, after Josephine's death from a chill caught when showing the Tsar around the park, to contemplate his bleak future after his defeat at Waterloo. He left at five o'clock on 25 June, 'gave a long lingering look at the house and gardens connected with his happiest hours, and left them for ever'.

During the 19th century Malmaison passed though many hands, and most of the park, where Josephine's greenhouses had supplied botanical gardens throughout France, was sold off. The house was presented to the nation in 1904 and was opened as a museum soon afterwards. It remains a monument to the French Empire style; but the pompous furniture contradicts the spirit of the place. Many of Josephine's pictures were bought by the Tsar, perhaps to ease the financial plight of her worthy son Eugène, and found their way to the Hermitage in St Petersburg. One may still feel the presence of that oddly attractive woman under the spreading cedar that she planted to mark the victory of Marengo in 1800, in sympathy with the words of the poet: 'Malmaison is only a sigh ... a place of great languor, an urn for the ashes of the heart ...'

At Malmaison, at five o'clock in the evening of 25 June 1815, Napoleon put on a costume de ville, un habit marron, tenderly embraced the persons present, gave a long lingering look at the house connected with his happiest hours, and left forever.

FAR LEFT
The main façade of Buckingham Palace.

LEFT
Detail of the Victoria Memorial (1912), a flamboyant work by Sir Thomas Brock incorporating 2,300 tons of white marble.

Buckingham Palace

Buckingham Palace, in the heart of London, has been the chief residence of the British monarchy for about 150 years. It is not an old building: most of what the public sees today was completed less than 100 years ago, and nothing is left of the original 18th-century building, which was called Buckingham House after its original owner, the Duke of Buckingham. It was sold to King George III in 1762, and when George IV became king (1820), he commissioned John Nash, designer of Brighton Pavilion, to extend it. He estimated that the job would cost £50,000 – nearly three times more than the government was willing to spend and predictably much less than then final cost.

Nash did a great deal to make London more elegant, but Buckingham Palace is not among his greatest successes. His original design was a three-sided court with an ornate triumphal arch forming the entrance. Both style and cost were heavily criticized. Nash was eventually forced to appear before a hostile committee of parliament but, perhaps bored with the project, and certainly with the questions, he returned eccentric answers, and was eventually removed. His successor, Edward Blore, enclosed the courtyard by building the familiar east front, overlooking the Victoria Memorial and the Mall. Nash's far more attractive garden front, despite a rather timid dome, is generally seen only by guests at royal garden parties. Blore also moved

the marble arch from the palace to its present site at the northern end of Park Lane.

Inside, besides Nash's Grand Staircase, probably the most splendid of the 600-odd rooms is the Blue Drawing Room, formerly the Ball Room, containing Napoleon's porcelain table with portraits of military heroes and a clock allegedly designed by George III. Some of the paintings from the royal collection can be seen in the adjacent Queen's Gallery.

The palace was not completed in time for George IV, nor for his successor William IV. But Queen Victoria, succeeding to the throne in 1837, was keen to move in regardless of doors that would not close and windows that would not open.

Houses of Parliament, Westminster

Westminster became the main residence of English monarchs in the 11th century and eventually the capital of England, developing alongside the City of London. Medieval parliaments met in Westminster Hall (1097, rebuilt c.1400). Accommodation was always makeshift, and the fire that in 1834 destroyed most of the old palace (though not Westminster Hall) provided the opportunity to create a purpose-built legislature.

Despite the claims of Classicism, acknowledged, for example, not only in Washington but in nearly every state capitol in the USA, it was agreed that the style should be Gothic, recalling the Tudor Age and the foundations of English liberties. The architect chosen, Charles Barry (1795–1860), was by inclination a Classicist, but he was assisted by the fervent genius of the Gothic Revival, Augustus Pugin (1812–52), a Catholic convert who identified the Gothic style with the Christian religion. He designed everything from the architectural details to inkwells and coat hooks.

Construction began in 1837: the House of Commons was finished by 1847, the Clock Tower, popularly known as Big Ben, by 1858, the larger Victoria Tower by 1860, and the whole complex by 1865. The final result is Classical in plan and overall design but authentically Gothic in appearance, a 'great and beautiful monument to Victorian artifice', and the product of one of the most successful architectural partnerships in British history. It established Gothic as a suitable style not only for parliaments (e.g. Budapest, Ottawa), but for all public buildings.

Encouraged by Prince Albert, the royal consort, no effort or expense was spared on statues and paintings to augment Pugin's gorgeously rich interiors. The Robing Room, a large chamber 54-ft (16-m) long, is a good example of both Pugin's fertile imagination and devotion to 19th-century painting on a large scale with frescoes by William Dyce of the legends of King Arthur. The House of Commons was destroyed by bombs in the Second World War and rebuilt (1945–50) by Giles Gilbert Scott on the original plan but with less rich decoration.

OPPOSITE
View from the river, with the Victoria Tower on the left and the clock tower containing Big Ben in the distance.

LEFT
Detail from New Palace Yard. In a sense the building was more daring than any contemporary example.

The main façade of the Royal Palace in Corfu, with its fine Doric colonnade.

Royal Palace, Corfu

When the Ionian Islands became a British protectorate in 1815, a suitable residence was required for the High Commissioner. At the same time, a meeting place had to be found for the legislative assembly and a headquarters for the British Order of St Michael and St George.

Founded in 1918, its membership was at that time bestowed on those who had performed special service in the Mediterranean region, but which is today more widely spread. The palace was officially known as the Palace of St Michael and St George.

The architect was George Whitmore, at that time a colonel in the Royal Engineers attached to the British garrison in Corfu. A Neoclassical design was inevitable, given the time and place, and the most distinguished feature of the façade is the fine Doric colonnade that marches across it. It is flanked on either side by large arches that are, of course, more Roman than Greek, one of them accommodating what was once the main road; the central pediment of the palace contained a figure of Britannia. The material used was a creamy Maltese stone, which did not weather particularly well. The state rooms on the second storey consist of an elegant central, circular chamber with a dome decorated with plaques of Wedgwood jasperware (white figures raised on a blue ground), and Classical statues.

After Corfu was handed back to Greece in 1864, the palace was sometimes used as a summer residence by the Greek royal family. Corfu suffered during the Second World War from bombing and separate occupation by Italians and Germans, and as a result many buildings and other landmarks were destroyed. The former palace survived both that man-made disaster and the earthquake of 1953. It was rather dilapidated, but it was later sympathetically restored by a local architect and is today a museum of Asian art (founded 1927).

Trinity Church, Wall Street

The Gothic Revival, perhaps stronger in England than anywhere else, first reached the USA as a Romantic fashion but became more serious under the influence of Pugin and others in the second quarter of the 19th century. One of the most enterprising and most active architects of the Gothic Revival in North America was the English-born Richard Upjohn, founder and first president of the American Institute of Architects. His first Gothic building was a picturesque mansion in Maine, but he became most famous as the designer of at least 40 churches, of which one of the earliest and best, and far the best known, was Trinity Church in Wall Street, New York, built between 1836 and 1846.

When it was built, and for many years afterwards, Old Trinity Church was the tallest building in Wall Street, or indeed in Manhattan, and parts of the wall that gave its name to the street and marked the northern boundary of the early Dutch settlement, could still be seen. Though now so thoroughly overshadowed by the looming skyscrapers of 20th-century capitalism that a full view of the steeple is only possible from the middle of the street, it still strives to assert a spiritual presence in the midst of modern materialism.

There was an earlier church on the site, erected, legend says, with block and tackle supplied by Captain Kydd, another kind of pirate, which burned down; when its successor proved structurally unsound it was replaced by Upjohn's building. Upjohn generally followed English models and favoured the Decorated and Early Perpendicular phases of English Gothic (late 13th–14th centuries). Trinity Church is admired for its clean lines and stylistic authenticity, and its stained glass is said to have been among the earliest made in North America. Its capacity is unnecessarily large for today's congregation, though some correlation is said to exist between the number of worshippers and the state of the markets; the church filled up at the time of the Wall Street Crash.

Trinity Church, Wall Street: it is difficult to suppress the feeling that God has been overtaken by Mammon.

United States Capitol, Washington, DC

The need for large and imposing government buildings which would replace palaces as the major type of very large secular building, roughly coincided with the return of Classicism in the mid-18th century, not that, in some places, it had ever gone far away. Capital cities increasingly boasted rather similar buildings, with central, columned porticoes, long façades and flanking pavilions. In North America Classicism was firmly established due largely to the influence of Thomas Jefferson, on whose advice the state capitol in Richmond, Virginia, took the Maison Carrée in Nîmes as its model. The prime example, if only on grounds of size, is the Capitol in Washington, D.C.

The competition for the design of the building in 1792 was won by William Thornton, an English-born physician, and the foundation stone was laid by George Washington the following year. Thornton never in fact superintended the actual construction, which proceeded slowly over many years with many modifications by different hands, though on the whole they were sympathetic in spirit to the original Palladian conception. Under James Hoban, architect of the White House, the Senate wing was completed in 1800. Benjamin Latrobe, the foremost American architect of the day, took over in 1803 and within eight years he had completed the House of Representatives wing. In 1814, British troops burned much of Washington, including the White House and the

Capitol, which Latrobe proceeded to reconstruct in a revised form. His plan, with only minor modifications, was completed by Charles Bullfinch by 1830; but before long Congress had outgrown the building, and between 1851 and 1863 the whole complex was reconstructed on a massive scale. Thomas U. Walter's Capitol, which adopted the Greek Revival style and used marble instead of the original sandstone, has overall measurements of 702 x 350ft (214 x 107m). In 1960 the east façade was lengthened by another 33ft (10m). Walter's massive 224-ft (68-m) cast-iron dome, which nods across the Atlantic to St Paul's in London, was topped by a correspondingly massive 20-ft (6-m) statue, Armed Freedom with the inscription *E Pluribus Unum*.

OPPOSITE
The grand approach to the Capitol, an outstandingly distinguished building which shows no trace of its rather turbulent construction history.

RIGHT
Details of the lantern and drum.

Forth Railway Bridge, Edinburgh

The railway bridge across the Firth of Forth just west of Edinburgh is a structure so vast it makes the trains it carries look like toys. A masterpiece of Victorian engineering, it revolutionized bridge-building and still inspires structural engineers today.

The original plan was for a suspension bridge designed by the builder of the Tay Bridge, but when that collapsed in 1879, the plan was hastily dropped. Benjamin Baker, a prominent engineer, then produced a cantilever design, more stable than a suspension bridge, but still relatively novel, though the principle was known and utilized by ancient civilizations.

The main members are tubes 12ft (4m) in diameter and the span of 1,710ft (521m) between piers was a record unbroken for many years. The material was mild steel, not iron as in the Tay Bridge. Use was made of a rocky islet in the middle of the Firth, but otherwise the foundations of the massive piers were built in the turbulent currents of the estuary in caissons, providing a working chamber on the bottom from which water is excluded (the method was used by the Romans and described by Vitruvius). The bridge employed the unheard-of quantity of 58,000 tons of steel, and the total cost of construction, about £33 million, was also a record. The area of painted surface is 653,406sq yd (546313sq m), giving rise to the

common expression for an unending task, 'like painting the Forth Bridge'. Construction took seven years and, after testing with two 900-ton trains, the bridge was opened in 1890. In 1964 it was joined by a road bridge, a suspension bridge with a 3,300-ft (1000-m) span.

Although admired then and since by engineers, the views of others were more mixed. The artist-designer William Morris called it 'the greatest specimen of all ugliness', but few would agree with that verdict today, now that it has become perhaps Scotland's most popular and recognizable image, a Caledonian equivalent of another great monument in steel, the Eiffel Tower.

The Forth Railway Bridge was immediately recognized as a triumph of engineering, but aesthetic approval took longer to achieve.

*Views of the Eiffel Tower.
It still lords it over Paris
and is likely to do so for
the forseeable future, a
building not for a
lifetime, not even for a
bicentenary, but for a
millennium. The arched
base derived from Eiffel's
experience of bridges.*

Eiffel Tower

International exhibitions that became
fashionable in the second half of the 19th
century were often the occasion for new ideas,
in architecture as well as manufacturing and
engineering. The now-legendary Gustave Eiffel
(1832–1923), the 'magician of iron', designed
the influential Gallery of Machines for the
Paris Exhibition of 1867, long before his
famous tower.

Eiffel began his career in 1855 working for
French railway companies, especially in the
design of bridges. By 1880 he was at the height
of his powers, involved in projects in a dozen
countries, designing dams, locks, reservoirs,
casinos, department stores, even churches, and
the frame for the Statue of Liberty in New York
harbour. Were it not for the tower, his bridges
might be better known, especially his
masterpiece, the Garabit Viaduct over the
Truyère river, in which the viaduct carrying the
railway is supported by a parabolic arch,
tapering in section towards the peak, which
spans 530ft (162m). While being purely
functional, is is also artistically satisfying, and
the form appears again in the base of the Eiffel
Tower, though the arches there are semicircular.

In the competition for a monument to
commemorate the centennial of the French
Revolution in 1889, Eiffel's plan was accepted
ahead of over 100 others. It proposed a tower
984-ft (300-m) tall, by far the highest building in
the world, of open iron latticework. Many
people thought it was impossible; still more
thought it would be hideous. The engineering
problems were certainly formidable, but Eiffel's
experience, especially in calculating wind
forces, in which, along with the builders of the

Forth Bridge, he was a pioneer, and his unrivalled knowledge of the behaviour of iron arches and trusses under the various types of force action produced by loading, ensured the success of the structure. It heralded a revolution in civil engineering and, to some extent, also in architectural design. Aesthetically, it soon came to be accepted and indeed admired, superseding Notre Dame as Paris's most familiar building, its attractions enhanced by the glass elevators which, owing to the arched base, had to move through a curve.

The Arc de Triomphe, derived from ancient Roman examples.

Arc de Triomphe, Paris

The 19th century was a fruitful time for national monuments, a type of structure invented by the Romans. They employed three types – the triumphal arch, the column and the equestrian statue – which were never forgotten, even in the Middle Ages, though they were seldom repeated until the Renaissance. The equestrian statue, such as Giovanni da Bologna's figure of Cosimo in Florence, was preferred then but later, other types were invented, though they were not necessarily built, an example being Étienne-Louis Boullée's colossal monument to Isaac Newton in the form of a globe over 500-ft (150-m) high.

Napoleon was responsible for several monuments in Paris. The Madeleine, a church begun in 1806 in the form of a large Corinthian temple, was at Napoleon's decree turned into a Temple de la Gloire, a military shrine, though it later returned to being a church; the Colonne Vendôme, based on Trajan's Column in Rome, had a statue of the emperor on top, like Nelson's Column in London. The largest and most famous is the Arc de Triomphe de l'Étoile, symbol of French valour, dedicated to 'the glory of the imperial armies'. Designed by Jean François Thérèse Chalgrin, a former pupil of Boullée, it was begun in 1806 though not finished until 1836, when Napoleon was but a memory. It is a vast structure, 162-ft (50-m) high, in the heart of Paris. At the foot of the Champs Élysées, it forms the hub from which 12 avenues radiate like the spokes of a wheel.

It too has a London equivalent in Marble Arch, and the ancestor of both is the Triumphal Arch of the Emperor Septimius Severus in Rome. But the Arc de Triomphe is not merely a copy and in fact is markedly different in that it is more monumental, more bulky and less decorative. The lack of columns and comparatively little relief decoration give it the quality Niklaus Pevsner described as 'blockiness'. Since 1920 it has contained the tomb of France's Unknown Soldier.

Washington Monument

George Washington led the colonial armies that won independence for the United States and became the republic's first president. As a national hero he ranks with Moses or Charlemagne.

Discussion of a public monument took a long time to germinate. The first actual commission was issued by Benjamin West, American president of the British Royal Academy. George Dance, the most original English architect of the age, submitted a design of two large pyramids flanking a vaguely Eastern temple. It got no further. The first monument in the USA was erected in Baltimore in 1815–29. A round column 130-ft (40-m) high and topped by a statue, it belongs to the

tradition of Napoleon's Colonne Vendôme and London's Nelson's Column. The designer was Robert Mills, who claimed to be the first professional, native-born American architect. In 1836 he became official architect to the federal government. He built the Treasury Building, among several others in Washington, and designed the Washington Monument.

Mills forsook his Baltimore column. His original design began with a Doric rotunda, from which arose, unexpectedly, an Egyptian obelisk. The rotunda was abandoned soon after work began in 1848, and all work stopped in 1855. It did not resume until 1877, and was finished in 1884.

The monument is 555-ft (169-m) high, with sides tapering from 15ft (4.5m) at the base to

18in (46cm) at the top, and is the largest in the world. Many other plans, of varying extravagance, in every style and in none, had been rejected, but even Mills' simple obelisk attracted hostile criticism. The architect Henry van Brunt compared it unfavourably with the Giralda in Seville. The sculptor Horatio Greenough, who made the colossal statue of Washington now in the Smithsonian Institution and was also the designer of the monument, an obelisk, at Bunker Hill, objected to that design, though on grounds that actually seem to justify it. 'The obelisk,' he said, 'has to my eye a singular aptitude in its form and character to call attention to a spot memorable in history. It says but one word, but it speaks loud ... It says Here! It says no more.' Exactly.

The custom of celebrating a famous person with a column goes back to imperial Rome, though, in this case, the choice of an Egyptian obelisk aroused lively controversy.

Saint Pancras Station, London

The three great railway terminals in north London displayed a variety of 19th-century styles. Euston, before its reconstruction (or vandalization) in 1967, was Classical, with a tremendous Doric portico (1838) 75-ft (23-m) high and splendid Roman Great Hall (1849). Lewis Cubitt's King's Cross with its simple, misleadingly modern, twin arches and plain 112-ft (34-m) tower, might have been built a century later than it was (1851–52). St Pancras, fronted by the Midland Hotel, now offices, in the form of a medieval castle (1868), represented the Gothic Revival at its most romantic, though some threw up their hands in horror at the whole idea of industrial buildings in the Gothic style.

St Pancras remains one of London's most spectacular sights: a 'great Gothic phantasmagoria ... drawing up with complete confidence into its sky-assaulting range of turrets' (David Piper), the clock tower reaching a height of 270ft (82m). The architect was Sir George Gilbert Scott (1811–78), one of the ablest exponents of High Victorian Gothic, who won the competition in spite of the fact that his was the most costly design. It seems an extraordinarily exotic building for a railway station and hotel, and Scott himself admitted that 'it is possibly too good for its purpose'. Some years earlier he had submitted, unsuccessfully, a design for government offices in Whitehall, and the plans show that it would have borne a close resemblance to St Pancras.

Tucked away behind Scott's fairy-tale façade is an equally remarkable building, the train shed (1868) of William Barlow. It is a great arched roof of iron and glass, 689-ft (210-m long, 242-ft (74-m) wide and 98-ft (30-m) high, held in place by iron rods passing below the platforms. In 1868 it was the world's largest single span. The arch is slightly pointed, as if in acknowledgment of the Gothic front, and although the conjunction seemed distasteful to many at the time, today the two buildings seem a perfect partnership.

An extravagant gilded fountain plays before Ludwig's Linderhof. On windy days the fountain is turned off.

Schloss Linderhof

Linderhof is the most modest of the architectural 'follies' of King Ludwig II of Bavaria. Like Herrenchiemsee, but on a much smaller scale (it is more villa than palace), it can be regarded as a tribute to Ludwig's ideal of Grand Monarchy epitomized by Louis XIV; it was modelled on the Neoclassical Petit Trianon (1762), the masterpiece of perhaps the finest French architect of the 18th century, Ange-Jacques Gabriel (1698–1782), although Linderhof is much more ornamental. It is said to have been Ludwig's favourite residence, and he had plenty from which to choose.

When first built between 1870 and 1879, Linderhof aroused more contempt than admiration, but attitudes have changed somewhat and the excesses of Linderhof, such as the carefully modelled stalactites in the grotto, the strange little 'Moorish' pavilion, the gilded nymphs gallivanting around the fountain, or the lavishly overdecorated rooms, do not prevent it from being seen as a work of art. Its modest size – there are only four windows across the main façade – is an advantage, and it is not merely a slavish imitation of the French Baroque style. No more than at Herrenchiemsee can one imagine finding tranquillity and ease in the royal bedroom, and in general the Rococo interiors owe more to the south German than the French tradition. The craftsmanship is impeccable, and it is difficult to imagine such a building existing in any other time.

Another asset is the site, a wooden valley with mountains rising beyond. Nature, especially the trees, seems to moderate the excesses of Man. A double flight of marble steps rises through terraced gardens to a little

Classical rotunda below the rock face, and the ancient lime tree which probably gives Linderhof ('Lime Court') its name was left in place by Ludwig's builders.

Herrenchiemsee

This is the largest of the never-never-land castles of Ludwig II of Bavaria who, deprived of real power, compensated by building extravagant and redundant palaces where he could indulge his nostalgia for a romanticized past. His indulgence in German myth and legend was most extravagantly expressed in the fantasy castle of Neuschwanstein, but at Herrenchiemsee he pursued another obsession, with Louis XIV of France, the absolute monarch that Ludwig would have liked to have been. He paid several visits, incognito, to Versailles, of which Herrenchiemsee was supposed to be a copy. Building began in 1878 and progress was swift, although the palace was still unfinished when, eight years later, Ludwig was declared insane and his building projects halted.

This dinosaur, though magnificent, is bogus, a palace for a kind of ruler who did not exist, built on an island in a lake, remote and empty. In some ways, it does indeed rival Versailles. The Hall of Mirrors is nearly 330-ft (100-m) long and required an army of servants merely to light the candles. There are many remarkable objects, but it is difficult to contemplate so much anachronistic regal extravagance without a flicker of revulsion. Who could get any sleep in the royal bedroom? In fact, Ludwig only spent 23 nights there. Here is Baroque gone mad, a mass of gilded figures, scrolls, leafwork, emblems, with velvet hangings and various decorative conceits that obliterate the dimensions of the room. In the dining room the table sinks below the floor, so that it can be cleared and replenished without servants appearing in the room, a device copied from Louis XIV. Ludwig dined alone on the 23 nights

Another great fountain fronts Herrenchiemsee, perhaps the most grotesquely inappropriate of all poor Ludwig's excesses.

he spent at Herrenchiemsee, but the table was set for four. The guests who never arrived were Louis XIV, Mme de Maintenon and Mme de Pompadour.

Ludwig preferred his Wagnerian castle of Neuschwanstein (an inspiration for Disneyland) where, amid grand scenes from Germanic legend, he spent his last years alone and mad.

Sacré Coeur, Paris

Revivalism in 19th-century Western architecture was not entirely new; after all, the Renaissance had been a revival. The chief difference was that 19th-century architects were much better informed not only about earlier European styles but also about those of other civilizations, so a wealth of possibilities were open to them. Arguments between advocates of Classical and Gothic were sometimes fierce, but even the most conservative architects tended to experiment, and some of the most extraordinary buildings of the late 19th century employed a mixture of styles in the same structure (though this was not entirely new either, e.g. Nash's mixture of Chinese and Mughal in the Brighton Pavilion).

The Church of the Sacred Heart (Sacré Coeur) commemorates the pain and suffering endured in the national disaster of the Franco-Prussian War (1870–71) and, though sponsored by private subscribers, it was quickly adopted by the National Assembly. The site is high on the 'butte' or hill of Montmartre and is, in the words of a guidebook, 'only too visible' from any part of Paris. The building, described as 'neo-Romanesque-Byzantine', has not had a good press: 'vulgar and bizarre' is the description of one modern critic, and everyone agrees that the best view of the Sacré Coeur is from a distance, when the dazzling effect of the stone, which whitens with age, is effective. But it seems to lack exactly the quality that this pilgrimage church should have, a sense of soul and spirituality, and instead communicates a strange deadness.

Basically a basilica, it is large – 328-ft (100-m) long and 246-ft (75-m) wide across the ambulatory. The curious dome rises to 272ft (83m). The square campanile contains a bell, the Savoyarde, that weighs nearly 20 tons. The architect was the elderly Paul Abadie (1812–84), and the church is based on his controversial restoration of St-Front at Périgueux. The church is heavily decorated with mosaics by Luc-Olivier Merson and others. Building started in 1876 but it was not finished until 1918, although it was first used in the 1890s.

Glasgow School of Art

The Scottish architect and designer Charles Rennie Mackintosh (1868–1928) was a man of singular gifts. His buildings are comparatively few, in view of his later influence and reputation, deplorably few in the British Isles, one of the few complete examples being the Hill House, near Glasgow, now a museum, and he is probably remembered first as a designer of furniture and interiors (e.g. The Willow Tea Room), usually in collaboration with his wife, Margaret Macdonald and her sister, Frances. His universally acknowledged masterpiece is the Glasgow School of Art, begun in 1897 to replace the building he had studied in himself.

Some Mackintosh chairs, graceful and slender, do not look as if they are designed primarily with comfort in mind, but a notable characteristic of the School of Art is its combination of strikingly novel design with thoroughly practical functioning. The centrepiece of the building is a highly original piece of fancy, owing something perhaps to Scottish tradition, with which Mackintosh was not in general much engaged; but in spite of its deliberate asymmetry the plan and the general exterior form of the building, with its large, north-facing studio windows, is highly rational. It is not that far removed from the late 19th-century Arts and Crafts movement, and the so-called English Domestic Revival, led by Philip Webb and Charles Voysey among others.

Mackintosh's interiors were generally more adventurous. The library has some inexplicable decorative details and un-library-like features, but it has gained the approval of generations of working students. Another aspect of the Mackintosh style is that, while it belongs thoroughly in spirit to Art Nouveau, and employs characteristically languid Art Nouveau curves, this is predominantly a building of straight lines and verticals. It is hard to imagine personal styles less alike than those of Mackintosh and Gaudí, and Mackintosh has more in common, in spirit if not in detail, with Otto Wagner, the designer of the Post Office Savings Bank in Vienna.

All architecture is derivative, some more derivative than others; but Gaudí's is in a class of its own.

Sagrada Familia, Barcelona

The ultimate exponent of the plant-like curve in the Art Nouveau period was the Catalan, Antoní Gaudí (1852—1926). A devout Roman Catholic, Gaudí reworked the old observation that there are no straight lines in nature: 'The straight line belongs to man, the curve to God'. His extravagant, sometimes grotesque buildings have struck some observers as more devilish than divine, but they are indisputably fascinating and undeniably original. Influences may include Gothic (in the case of the Sagrada Familia), Muslim and Classical, but Gaudí's style was utterly personal and he owed less to any historical style than all previous architects.

Many of Gaudí's most exciting schemes came to nothing, but it seems remarkable that so many of his designs were fulfilled. He was assisted by the faithful patronage of a wealthy industrialist, Eusebio Güell, for whom, besides other buildings, is named the well-known Parc Güell, with its undulating mosaic-collage of a wall that also backs a bench, a probable influence on Picasso, also a resident of Barcelona. Another asset was his identification with the cause of Catalan nationalism; all his buildings are in the Catalan capital. Had he been a foreigner, perhaps Barcelona's wealthy middle class would have been less ready to take up residence in apartment buildings such as the Casa Batlló, in rooms with no straight walls and balconies reminiscent of the jaws of a shark.

The Church of the Holy Family (Sagrada Familia) was originally intended to be a conventional Neo-Gothic edifice, and Gaudí, who took over the project in 1883, retained a Gothic general outline, while introducing Art Nouveau curves; the tall spires ('like the homes of giant termites' says Ian Sutton) are convex and elaborately ornamented. The façade, completed in Gaudí's lifetime, suggests a 13th-century French church overgrown by vaguely vegetable forms. There are some almost 'pure' Gothic features, and some that owe nothing whatever to Gothic or any other style. The building is an important marker in the gradual abandonment of historicism in architecture, and also a testament to Gaudí's craftsmanship and understanding of structure. Only a relatively small part was built in the 1890s, and the project was then practically abandoned for nearly 100 years until another era of intense Catalan nationalism provided the motivation to embark on its completion.

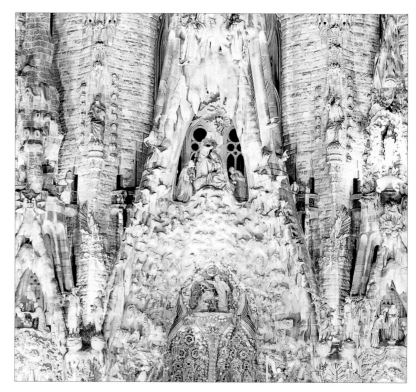

The massive, relatively conventional exterior of Wagner's Post Office Savings Bank bears little relation to the sleek lightweight interior.

Post Office Savings Bank, Vienna

Otto Wagner (1841–1918), one of the apostles of Modernism, was the most influential Austrian architect at the turn of the century, at first as a teacher, later by example. His early work was broadly in the Neoclassical tradition, which remained a presence in his later style. He was appointed professor at the Academy of Fine Art in Vienna in 1894 where, in his inaugural lecture he called for a newer, rational approach to architecture, abandoning historicism and asserting that 'nothing can be beautiful if it is not practical'. He was also head of the city's transport planning department, and designed stations for the Vienna Metro. In 1897 he became the leading architectural influence in the Viennese Secession, a new group founded by mainly younger men, including Josef Olbrich and the painter Gustav Klimt, who were united in rejecting academic art and favoured contemporary movements.

Like Charles Rennie Mackintosh, who exhibited at the Secession exhibition in Vienna in 1900, Wagner, and the Viennese architects he influenced, avoided the undulations of the so-called 'Belgian line' and generally remembered that architecture is supposed to be an art of line and space; but Wagner was not averse to decoration, sometimes rich and exotic. His Post Office Savings Bank (1904) has been consistently admired for a century and is one of those buildings that have never gone out of date, its use of glass making it particularly apt today. It displays with complete success the achievement of clarity, space and expression of function, aimed at by the Secessionist architects. The main banking hall is a large open space

with a glass floor, admitting light to the basement, and a vaulted glass ceiling. The aluminium bolts fixing the marble panels to the monumental façade are repeated in the banking hall, where the heads are polished to attract attention to them.

The building escapes the stricture

sometimes applied to the architecture of the Vienna Secession that it is too heavy and forbidding, a trait that is not absent from Wagner's second most famous building, the monumental, domed Church of St Leopold at Steinhof, outside Vienna.

Secession Building, Vienna

The outstanding architects of the Vienna Secession influenced by Otto Wagner were Josef Hoffmann (1870–1956), who built the luxurious Palais Stoclet in Brussels, and Joseph Maria Olbrich (1867–1908). They carried further the more geometrical form of Art Nouveau initiated by Wagner and Mackintosh towards an architecture of volumes and masses.

Olbrich studied at the Vienna Academy and, like Hoffmann, worked under Otto Wagner in the 1890s, becoming a founder member of the avant-garde Secession group. He made his reputation by designing their headquarters, the Secession Building, in 1896. This small, blocky, cubic building is surmounted by a curious gilded, openwork, wrought-iron dome, known as the Golden Cabbage, a symbol of the Secessionist journal, *Ver Sacrum*. The whole building could be regarded as an irreverent gesture towards the entire Classical tradition, but the combination of solid, simple shapes with inventive decorative detailing is characteristic of Olbrich's work in general. Much of the decoration was in fact designed by other members of the group, including the painter Gustav Klimt.

In 1899 the Grand Duke of Hesse invited Olbrich to Darmstadt, introducing the style of the Vienna Secession to Germany, and he remained there for the rest of his short life. Darmstadt was the home of an artistic colony, whose members included Peter Behrens, later the architect of the AEG Factory in Berlin, and other distinguished industrial buildings. Several of the artists designed their own houses. Olbrich designed his, and also several others, as well as the Artists' House, the communal building of the

artistic colony. In a ground-breaking event, the whole settlement was presented as a standing exhibition in 1901. Later, Olbrich also built the tower known as the Hochzeitsturm, and the following year began his last building, a department store in Düsseldorf. By then, Art

Nouveau had passed its inspirational peak. Hoffmann would move in a different direction, but what direction Olbrich's career might have taken we cannot know.

Olbrich's Secession Building, with the Surrealist Golden Cabbage (in fact foliage) just visible.

241

The Far East

CHAPTER SIX

Great Wall of China

Wild Goose Pagoda, Sian

Temple of Heaven, Beijing

Cheng-te

The Forbidden City

Kyongbok Palace, Seoul

Potala Palace, Lhasa

The Horyuji, Nara

The Todaiji, Nara

Himeji Castle

Byodoin, Uji

Golden Pavilion, Kyoto

Katsura Villa, Kyoto

Saint Mary's Cathedral, Tokyo

Great Hall of the People, Beijing

Olympic Stadia, Tokyo

Having developed in relative isolation, the Chinese arrived very early at their preferred basic forms of building, which appear to have altered little in style over the centuries. To some extent this apparent lack of change is merely the view of an alien and inexpert eye; nevertheless, basic forms remained similar from one dynasty to the next, and architecture, which was never seen as a fine art among the Chinese, became highly ritualistic, subject to strict religious or social conventions. Since the structural material was invariably wood, except for pagodas, there are few buildings in China today dating from before the Ming dynasty (1368–1644) although, since the Chinese style spread all over eastern Asia, equivalent buildings of earlier periods can sometimes be seen in Japan where, for instance, the Horyuji pagoda represents the style of T'ang China.

From very early times the Chinese adopted the trabeate style, the architecture of post and lintel as in ancient Greece. Walls were never a structural element, and the outstanding feature of Chinese buildings came to be the roof, usually tiled, with its curving lines and overhanging eaves. Buildings were typically of one storey only, again with the exception of pagodas. Without any form of truss, to make buildings larger it was necessary to increase the number of columns, which thus constricted the open space. This problem was overcome by an intricate system of brackets, which increased the breadth of support afforded by each column and thus reduced the number of columns required for a given space. Carved brackets came to be the chief evolutionary feature of Chinese architecture as well as a major decorative feature. In time, the clusters of brackets, expanding as they ascended and supporting a range of beams, became extremely intricate, bewildering to the casual observer (about 60 different types are employed in the Yinghsien pagoda), and demonstrating refined carpentry skills – perhaps most notably in Japan. This gave rise to the need for a constant unit of measurement, based on the standard measurement of the bracket and thence the proportionate size and spacing of beams and pillars. This modular system was described by Li Chieh in 1103 in his book on architecture, actually a craftsman's manual, which like all Chinese books on architecture, is silent on questions of aesthetics.

In general, Japanese architecture followed the Chinese example, although Japan had its own traditions, dating from before the advent of Buddhism in the 5th century BC and which continued to exert some influence into the modern age. Broadly, Japanese architecture tends to be less grand and more decorative, with greater empathy with nature, reverence for tradition, and thus continuity of style. The simple, natural, Zen-inspired buildings of the early modern period in particular had a powerful influence on the Modern movement in the West.

The invasion of Western influence in the Far East in the late 19th century introduced dramatic changes, the resulting Sino-European compromise architecture seeming to lose more than it gained. Eventually, International Modernism produced no less thorough a revolution in the East than it did in the West although, in Japan particularly, ancient traditions were not entirely abandoned.

Chinese names are given in either the old Wade system of transliteration or the Pinyin system (or both) according to which is likely to be more familiar.

Great Wall of China

The Great Wall of China (Wanli Changcheng) is often called the largest man-made structure in the world; including all its branches, its total length is about 4,000 miles (6400km). It stretches across northern China from Po Hai on the Yellow Sea (Huang Hai) far into Central Asia.

When the Qin emperor Shih Huang-di united China in 221 BC, some sections already existed, made largely of rammed earth. Shih Huang-di ordered it to be linked up and rebuilt to form a single system. Its purpose was to defend the settled communities of China from the predatory, nomadic Ixongnu (Hsiung-nu). It was often rebuilt, sometimes on a different route, in succeeding centuries. The empire-building Han extended it to the Jade Gate (Yumen) in Gansu, and the present structure belongs predominantly to the Ming dynasty in the 15th–16th centuries. It consists of a complex of fortified walls (a traveller entering by the Xifengkou Pass would actually pass through four gates and three sections of wall), and is constructed of masonry on an earth core, though the original was sometimes faced with brick. Manned signal towers at regular intervals communicated by smoke (daytime) or flame (night). Dimensions vary, but in general the wall is about 30-ft (9-m) high, the towers about 40ft (12m). The wall is up to 12ft (3.75m) across, enabling a column of ten men wide to march along it.

The Qin emperor could conscript vast numbers of labourers for building programmes that exceeded even the pharaohs'. They included a network of roads, for swifter troop movement, a canal through the mountains to the southern coastal region, never completed, and, famously, a posthumous 'bodyguard' of about 7,000 life-size, individualized, clay soldiers and servants.

The effectiveness of the Great Wall is hard to judge. It no doubt deterred raiding parties, but it did not prevent large-scale invasions. The main problem, especially in unsettled periods, was keeping it manned. After the Manchu conquest (1644), the frontier moved farther north and the Wall became redundant. It deteriorated over the years but since China has become accessible to international tourists, large parts have been restored.

*LEFT and OVERLEAF
The Great Wall, wrongly reputed to be the only man-made feature on earth visible from space, but still the world's largest.*

Wild Goose Pagoda, Sian

Sian, or Xian, is the former Chang'an (Changan), ancient Chinese capital. In the 7th century AD, it was the abode of the monk Hsüan-tsang, a hugely famous figure after his amazing travels, also known as Tripitaka, 'Master of the Law'. He crossed the desert and the Hindu Kush into India, where he learned Sanskrit, traversed most of the subcontinent and returned in 645, after 15 years' absence, with 700 books and a large collection of sacred Buddhist artifacts. A few years later he suggested the construction of a stone building, described as a 'stupa', in which to store his treasures, the study of which occupied his remaining years. He stipulated that it should be 300-ft (90-m) high, to be worthy of so great a kingdom and to stand as a monument to Buddhism. According to contemporary accounts, his proposal was put to the Emperor who immediately ordered construction to begin, in or about 652. The Wild Goose Pagoda, more pedantically the Great Gander Pagoda, which has survived to this day, however, is a slightly later building, dating from 701–705 and containing Hsüan-tsang's ashes.

The appearance of the original building has provoked considerable interest, since accounts report that it was built 'in the form adopted in India'. It was actually only 175-ft (53-m) high, had five storeys and was topped by a cupola or stupa. It probably resembled the Indian Buddhist shrines that Hsüan-tsang had visited (there are quite close affinities between some later styles of pagoda and Indian temple towers).

The new building, square in plan (the octagonal plan, eventually universal, appeared in the late 8th century), has seven storeys separated by corbelled cornices, and is 190-ft (58-m) high. The form of construction closely resembles the timber towers of the Han period (206 BC–AD 220), which are known from survivors in Japan. It is built of yellowish brick on a rammed-earth core and has little space inside (it could not have served Hsüan-tsang's original purpose), although there is a staircase with vaulted openings leading off it. The Pagoda is powerful rather than decorative, but the potential tedium of the walls is relieved by dividing them into very shallow bays.

The Wild Goose or Great Gander Pagoda contains the ashes of the monk Hsüan-tsang, also known as Tripitaka, 'Master of the Law'.

Temple of Heaven, Beijing

The Temple of Heaven (T'ien-t'an) contains probably the most familiar building in China, after the Great Wall. The entire complex covers about 690 acres (280 hectares) to the south of the Forbidden City in Beijing. It illustrates the Chinese love of symmetry, particularly strong in Ming China (1368–1644), and it follows the same symbolically significant north-south axis as the Forbidden City, though in fact slightly off-line, while also duplicating it. The splendid geometry of the whole site is most easily appreciated from the air. From the blue-roofed

Hall of Prayers on its high marble platform in the north, a raised processional way leads via another circular building, 'the Imperial Vault of Heaven', to the larger enclosure in the south of the Altar of Heaven, or Circular Mound Altar, with its circular marble walls encircling ascending terraces and four sets of double gates in the square enclosing wall.

The whole layout dates from 1420; the Altar of Heaven and the Imperial Vault were built in 1530, but the design was older and would have been familiar under the Han dynasty (206 BC–AD 220). Most of what one sees today is actually the result of extensive renovation in the 18th century; in the case of the Hall of Prayer the late-19th-century timber for the pillars came from the Pacific North-West of the USA. Nevertheless, it would have looked no different in Ming times. The three-tiered, drum-shaped Hall of Prayer, housing 'the Altar where Prayer for Grain is Offered', is sometimes described as the most sacred building in China. Its form is dictated by cosmological concepts and it stands on an ancient site where once the emperor offered animal sacrifices. The building is about 125-ft (38-m) high and 100ft (30m) in diameter. It is supported by 28 massive wooden columns, four in the centre symbolizing the four seasons. The remaining 24 form two concentric rings, representing respectively the months of the   year and the old division into 12 of the day and night. There are no structural walls, only latticework partitions. The beauty of the building lies partly in its shape, but also in its intense colours, gold, white and red, with the tiles of the conical roofs a deep midnight-blue, and the topmost roof crowned with a golden ball.

Cheng-te

Cheng-te (Chengde), in rugged countryside north-east of Beijing and not far from the Great Wall, was an old Manchu town, rediscovered by the famous K'ang-hsi (Kangxi) Emperor (1662–1722) of the Manchu or Ch'ing (Qing) dynasty. It offers one of the finest displays of imperial architecture in China.

In 1703 K'ang-hsi, keen to escape the summer heat of Beijing and gain easy access to old Manchu hunting grounds, undertook to build a summer palace there; a subsidiary reason was to impress the Mongol tribes to the north. Work continued under his successors, notably Ch'ien-lung (Qianlong, 1735–95), and by the end of the century the complex included over 70 buildings. In general not a particularly extravagant ruler, K'ang-hsi pulled out all the stops here, drawing craftsmen from every part of the empire to construct a complex of pavilions and palaces, temples and pagodas within a huge, walled park dotted with pools, lakes, islands and ornamental bridges, an assembly that blends perfectly with the natural landscape. Engravings by one of the Jesuit missionaries whom K'ang-hsi both welcomed and employed, reached England in 1723 and are said to have stimulated the 18th-century revolution in garden design. Lord Macartney, who led a humiliating British embassy to China in 1793, remarked, as he waited to be summoned as a barbarian tributary to the Emperor's presence, on the resemblance of his surroundings to the park of an English country house.

The buildings themselves, though they are far more elegant than the Manchurian village that K'ang-hsi is said to have wished to imitate (the palace buildings themselves have 120 rooms!), are much less grand than, for instance, the imperial palaces of Beijing. Some appear quite dark, with little decoration and muted colour. However, K'ang-hsi's successors were less economical, and some interiors, such as the Hall of Frugality and Sincerity, are decidedly sumptuous.

Some fine temples outside the park, whose numbers have been depleted since the 18th century, suggest Tibetan influence, an acknowledgment of the Ch'ing emperors' interest in Tibetan Buddhism; a model of the Potala was made at Cheng-te in honour of a visit by the Panchen Lama in 1786.

Besides the exquisite buildings of K'ang-hsi, Cheng-te includes more utilitarian structures.

The Forbidden City

The imperial palace, or palaces, within the Forbidden City (forbidden to all commoners and foreigners) were built by the Ming emperors in the early 17th century. Though extensively restored under the Ch'ing (Qing) in the 18th century, with some decorative additions, the original style was faithfully repeated in accordance with the tradition, in Beijing particularly, of preserving both the detail of buildings and the symmetry of the city plan, on its north-south axis inherited from Han times. This array of huge gates, terraces, halls, gateways and courtyards, in brick, marble and wood, which has now been restored as a museum, presents an unparalleled display of imperial magnificence.

The main entry is via the monumental Meridian Gate (Wumen), formerly reserved for the emperor alone, which also served as a platform for imperial announcements. Beyond is a vast courtyard, crossed by a balustraded stream with five marble bridges, and the Gate of Supreme Harmony, guarded by an imperious row of bronze lions and flanked by galleries and pavilions. It leads into another, even larger courtyard, about 656-ft (200-m) wide. On the far side is the greatest of the three ceremonial halls, the Hall of Supreme Harmony, where the Emperor presided from his golden Dragon Throne. It stands on a three-tiered platform and is approached by stairways and ramps in white marble. Here, as throughout the Forbidden City, while the decoration is sumptuous almost beyond belief, the basic plan is very simple. It is rectangular in plan, with the supporting columns arranged in double rows. The overhanging, tiled roof protects the open colonnade and is surmounted by a second roof, more steeply curved.

Farther along the axis stands the Hall of Middle Harmony, a lesser audience hall, and the Preserving Harmony Hall, used for the famous civil-service examinations, which contains carvings of dragons on a marble block weighing 250 tons, brought to the site by skidding it along roads artificially flooded in winter so that they froze. Farther north are the imperial living quarters, buildings of mind-boggling extravagance but on a smaller scale.

Within walls 2.5-miles (4-km) long, the buildings of the Forbidden City are said to contain 9,000 rooms, the sort of statistic that no one can confidently contradict.

A temple in the extensive and beautiful gardens of the Kyongbok Palace. This is a modern reconstruction, but a faithful one.

Kyongbok Palace, Seoul

In spite of a sprinkling of stone pagodas over 1,500-years-old, historic buildings in Korea are rather few, not only as a result of perishable materials but also of the wars and invasions that have ravaged this peninsula over the centuries.

Historically, Korean architecture is an amalgam of chiefly Chinese, Japanese and native traditions. Differences are due partly to climate but mainly to different sensibilities. Simplicity and naturalism are the key to Korean architecture, which avoids the excessive

decoration sometimes found in China; indeed the influence that flowed from China and Japan also moved in the opposite direction.

The Choson dynasty, also called Yi, after its founder, seized power in Korea in 1392, and unified the country under its rule, which lasted until the Japanese annexation of 1910. The early kings established Confucianism as a kind of state religion, which encouraged a period of artistic renewal. The oldest of five palaces in Seoul, the Kyongbok Palace (Kyongbokkung) was begun in 1395 as the seat of government and the royal residence. It is a collection of graceful and varied pavilions and other buildings set among beautiful gardens and pools, and lies at the north end of the broad avenue of Sejongno in central Seoul. There are few finer examples of man's sensitive awareness of the beauties of nature.

The Japanese invasion of 1592 resulted in the burning of the palace, and the royal family moved to the Changdok Palace (begun 1405). They did not return to Kyongbok until after the reconstruction of 1867, and were driven out for good in 1910 when Japanese annexation was confirmed. The Japanese authorities tried to obliterate Korean culture and of the 200-odd buildings that made up the Kyongbok Palace, all but about ten were ruined, and a vast concrete Japanese headquarters was built in its southern courtyard. This building was demolished when a major restoration, scheduled for completion in 2020, was begun in 1995. Within five years the royal residences had been completed and the complex was on the way to reclaiming its former glory.

Potala Palace, Lhasa

Named after the sacred Mount Potalaka, the Potola Palace was the official summer residence of the Dalai Lama, the spiritual and political leader of Tibet. Under the current Chinese regime, which is hostile to Tibetan culture, the Dalai Lama is in exile, his summer palace has been turned into a 'Pleasure Park', and the Potala itself is a museum. Its 13 storeys, which once made it possibly the world's tallest building, compete with ugly concrete tower blocks, though it still dominates Lhasa, and its golden roofs greet the approaching traveller from afar.

The first palace was built in the 7th century, and at least one small chapel in the Red Palace is believed to date from that period. It was entirely rebuilt, on the same site and two storeys higher, in the 17th century by the Fifth Dalai Lama (1617–82) in a style that blends Chinese, Indian, Central Asian and Tibetan traditions although, in Tibet more than anywhere else, architecture is subordinate to religion. Considerable renovation and restoration has taken place since, most recently under Chinese authority. The building is 387-ft (118-m) high, and the area of the interior has been calculated at 155,500sq yd (130000sq m). Altogether it contains about 1,000 rooms and about 200,000 works of art, including murals, sculptures, tapestries as well as scrolls, books (the Potala contains a printing press with 18th-century wood blocks), sacred relics, painted banners (*tanka*) and religious images, especially of the eleven-faced Avalokiteshvara, the *bodhisattva* of mercy associated with Mount Potalaka.

The outer section, known as the White

Palace, contained the Dalai Lama's residence, the offices of government, as well as a school and living quarters for the monks. The inner section, the Red Palace, which rises from the centre of the White Palace, contains religious buildings, including the tombs of former Dalai Lamas in the form of golden stupas. The largest chamber of the White Palace is the hall where the Dalai Lamas were enthroned, with murals

illustrating scenes from Tibetan history and the lives of the Dalai Lamas. Still larger is a pillared chamber in the Red Palace, with 17th-century murals depicting the Fifth Dalai Lama and Tibetan kings. Murals on the second floor of the Red Palace are of particular interest since they portray the construction of the Potala in the 17th century.

BELOW and OVERLEAF The Potala Palace was once the home of the Dalai Lama, the spiritual and political leader of Tibet, before he was forced into exile.

The Horyuji, Nara

Chinese culture and Buddhism arrived in Japan, via Korea, in the 6th century and received a powerful impetus from Prince Shokotu (572–622), whose reforms were largely responsible for transforming a basically tribal society into an imperial state, based on the model provided by T'ang China. He is also credited with the construction, close to his palace, of the monastic complex of the Horyuji, the earliest in Japan, which became the centre of a popular cult identifying Prince Shokotu with the Buddha. The Horyuji, built mainly in 601–607, was burned down in 670 but promptly rebuilt. Not everything was destroyed: among the many treasures of the Horyuji are early 7th-century bronze Buddhas of Korean workmanship. The monastic buildings in 670 were confined to the present western precinct, the Teaching Hall in the north being later. The eastern precinct, containing the octagonal Hall of Dreams dedicated to Prince Shokotu, dates from the Nara period (8th century).

The main enclosure is surrounded by a gallery or cloister, open but for lattice panels between the outer pillars. It contains two main buildings, raised on masonry platforms. The Golden Hall, which was equipped with its huge mural paintings during the 670 reconstruction, has columns showing slight *entasis* that some scholars rather improbably ascribe to distant and indirect Western influence (support for the roof is supplied, of course, through brackets, not capitals!). The other, outstanding building, known to millions through photographs, is the five-storeyed pagoda (Gojunoto). It is the oldest surviving pagoda in Japan and valued all the more as an example of the T'ang style, of which none comparable remains in China itself. Square in plan, it is 105-ft (32-m) high, with deeply projecting eaves. Each ascending storey is slightly smaller than the one below, giving it a sense of balance and stability. At the top is a tall pinnacle of bronze rings, deriving ultimately from the umbrella symbols of Indian temples.

One of the buildings in the Horyuji complex, which dates back to the time of Prince Shokotu.

261

The Todaiji, Nara

During the Nara period (710–784) in Japan, a permanent capital was established for the first time at Heijo (Nara), modelled on the T'ang capital of Chang-an. Buddhism became more strongly established, due to court patronage, and numerous monasteries were built or rebuilt.

In 745, prompted by an outbreak of plague and other disasters, the Emperor Shomu called for the founding of a new monastery, the Todaiji or Great Eastern Temple, which would house a massive new Buddha figure, the Daibutsu, (Great Buddha) or Buddha Vairocana, an enormous cast-bronze figure over 53-ft (16-m) high, and also serve as the headquarters and training centre of the numerous provincial monasteries and nunneries that the devout Emperor had founded at state expense all over the country – a Japanese Cluny. With the aid of many people – the Emperor had called upon everyone to contribute 'at least a twig' – much of the vast complex of the Todaiji was completed by 752, when an Indian monk, with a brush attached by a cord to the hand of the Emperor below, painted in the irises of the eyes of the Great Buddha, thus giving the statue life. The total area of the Todaiji covered an area about 2,460-ft (750-m) long and 1,970-ft (600-m) wide. It included two pagodas and living accommodation for thousands of apprentice monks. The whole place was destroyed in one of the wars of Minamoto and Taira in 1180, and over the years fire and other disasters wreaked havoc. The only substantial building left today is the Hall of the Great Buddha, which itself has been rebuilt several times. Most of the present structure dates from 1709, the roof from 1980. It is said to be the

world's largest wooden building, 225-ft (69-m) long and 150-ft (46-m) high, and derives from the typical T'ang palace, although with a recognizably Japanese aspect. The Great

Buddha has also survived, an immense and calming presence, although not a scrap of the material of the original statue remains.

Japanese temples, like the Todaji, usually consist of a number of buildings, with the main one in the centre of a series of enclosures.

LEFT
The interior of the Hall of the Great Buddha.

Himeji, the 'White Heron Castle', was originally built by a warlord in the 14th century, but it was rebuilt and greatly enlarged from the late 16th century.

Himeji Castle

With the virtual collapse of the authority of central government in medieval Japan, those who could carved out their own domains and prepared to defend them; even the great monasteries had large armies of fighting monks. The *daimyo* or warlords who dominated medieval Japan built their forts or castles on easily defended hilltop sites These medieval castles were of course built of wood, but with the arrival of guns and cannon, they became suddenly vulnerable. At the same time the civil wars of the 15th–16th centuries, in which the constant strife between warring *daimyo* was finally ended and the Tokugawa shogunate established, encouraged the building of large castles (*hirajiro*) of stone, at least the lower storeys, often on artificial mounds commanding the valleys. Eventually, these castles served other purposes besides war, notably for encouraging trade and serving as centres of local government; they were often decorated with painted screens and other furnishings of great magnificence.

Japanese castles, which have no equivalent in China, were unique in adapting the style of a one- or at most two-storey building, with its curved, projecting eaves and gables, to a building six- or seven-storeys high. Several examples of these buildings, which so impressed visitors from Europe, still remain, including Himeji, Kumamoto and Matsumoto, which was built by Hideyoshi in about 1595.

Himeji, the 'White Heron Castle', was originally built by the Akamatsu *daimyo* in the 14th century. It was rebuilt and greatly enlarged from the late 16th century by Hideyoshi and later owners. It is set on a lowish hill and

protected by a moat, in some sections by double moats, and a complex of earth ramparts. The lower parts are protected by a formidably battered, inward-sloping wall. From the outside, the main keep or donjon has five storeys, but from the main enclosure on the inward side it

has seven. It is linked with several other, smaller blocks. Altogether, the castle, which dominates the modern city of Himeji, looks impregnable, yet its upper parts, in gleaming white with grey-green roofs, manifest considerable elegance.

Byodoin, Uji

One of the many aspects of Japanese culture that profoundly impressed Westerners was the art of the garden. They were intrigued by the aesthetics of landscape-garden design as illustrated in the medieval Zen Buddhist temples of Kyoto, particularly the famous drystone gardens typically consisting of raked sand with strategically placed rocks and few if any plants. But there were other traditions, some of them older than Zen, that influenced the art. One was the cult of Amida known as the Pure Land Buddha, who originated in India and later flourished in China from the 5th century AD, reaching Japan by the 11th century. Pure Land Buddhism has some obvious parallels with Christianity, for instance in its emphasis on enlightenment, or salvation through the intervention of the compassionate Buddha Amida (Amitabha), a name that can be translated as Eternal Life, and the promise that eventual access to the Land of the Western Paradise (the Pure Land, Gokuraku) requires only faith and devotion.

The Byodoin at Uji, a few miles south of Kyoto, is a temple and garden that represents an earthly representation of the Pure Land. It was originally a Fujiwara palace, converted into a temple in 1053, a generation after it was first built. The main construction, built on an island, is the Phoenix Hall, one of the most elegant buildings in the whole of Japanese architecture. It is the only original building among the whole assembly of the Byodoin, and is named after the two gilt-bronze birds that stand on its roof. Viewed from across the tranquil lily pond, there is something bird-like about the whole building, with its swooping roof apparently preparing for

flight, and wings on each side that culminate in smaller, projecting pavilions, a plan deriving from the typical aristocratic palace. The whole façade is nearly 160-ft (49-m) long, although from a distance it does not appear so large. Inside is a gilded wooden Amida figure by Jocho, the most famous sculptor of the Heian

period (784–1185), who developed the versatile technique of joining several blocks rather than carving from a single piece of wood.

The swooping roofs of the Amida, or Phoenix Hall, Byodoin.

Golden Pavilion, Kyoto

Columbus's men, sailing west from Europe in 1492, expected to find their way to the fabled lands of Cathay (China) and Cipangu (Japan) where, they had heard, the very roofs of the houses were made of gold. Possibly the origin of this tale was a rumour, passed to the West by who knows what mysterious means, of the Golden Pavilion.

Like the earlier Phoenix Hall at Uji, the Temple of the Golden Pavilion (Kinkakuji) is an elegant building on a lake in an exquisite setting. The gardens here are on a magnificent scale, and include aspects of the typical Zen garden as well as the water gardens of the Heian period associated with the villas of the aristocracy, who liked to do some fishing from a comfortable lodge. They offer several carefully calculated views of the glittering pavilion, in a manner associated with the Zen monk Muso Soseki (1275–1351) who built small shrines with 'natural' gardens on his wanderings through the countryside, until he was taken up by the Ashikaga shoguns. The Golden Pavilion was built in 1397 and was originally part of the palace built after his official retirement by the Ashikaga shogun Yoshimitsu, the most powerful governor of the dynasty and patron of the Noh drama. He received visits from the Emperor here, and it was converted into a temple after his death. It has three storeys, the top one smaller, and its light, airy, even joyful appearance, with wide balconies under the extending eaves, is enhanced not only by its reflection in the lake, on which it seems to float, and by the lovely setting, but also by the glitter of the gilding. (It proved influential: one of Yoshimitsu's successors built a Silver Pavilion.)

With occasional restorations, the building survived wars, bandits, earthquakes and other threats for over 550 years, only to be burned to the ground in 1950. It was reconstructed immediately and, after some delay, regilded.

The Katsura Villa complex celebrates the poetic marriage of house and gardens in the intimate sukiya *style.*

Katsura Villa, Kyoto

A number of splendid residences were built in or around Kyoto towards the end of the 16th century. One of them gives its name to the brief Momoyama period (1573–1615), which roughly coincided with the ending of the wars between the *daimyo*, the unification of Japan, and the establishment of the Tokugawa shogunate, marking the beginning of the Edo period, when the capital moved to the future Tokyo. Probably the best-known is the Katsura Rikyu, named after the river on whose bank it stands, southwest of Kyoto. It was originally authorized by Hideyoshi in about 1590 for Prince Toshihito, brother of the emperor, and after his death in 1629 it was enlarged further by his son, Prince Toshitada. The original designer of the beautiful gardens and the layout of the villa was Kobori Enshu, a master of the tea ceremony.

Both princes, not to mention Hideyoshi himself, were enthusiasts of this hugely influential convention. With its emphasis on rustic simplicity, it did not encourage artistic innovation, though Hideyoshi built himself a large and luxurious tea house. Katsura's tea houses (there are no less than four) are made of simple materials – plain wood, thatched roofs, etc., used in a sophisticated way.

The whole complex, on a sloping site, covers about 16 acres (6.4 hectares) and is surrounded by a high bamboo hedge. There are three main, interlinked buildings or halls and many other smaller, pavilion-like buildings, self-consciously simple with an almost total lack of furniture and ornament, designed to admit a maximum of light and set in a largely artificial landscape. The older ceremonial *shoin* style is still evident in the main Old Hall; otherwise, the villa represents the more domestic *sukiya* style, in which house and garden are one, of the Edo period. Interior floor space is variable, thanks to sliding paper screens, and is based on the fixed unit of the straw floor mat (*tatami*). The buildings are connected by paths which wander among streams and pools supplied by the Katsura river, with a constant provision of well-calculated views from the open pavilions and verandas, Japanese gardens, of course, being designed to present a view, not for strolling around.

Saint Mary's Cathedral, Tokyo

Modernism finally swept away historical styles even in the ecclesiastical field, and one result of the globalization of architecture in the mid-20th century was that the best architects were commissioned to design buildings for societies of a different culture from their own, often with highly satisfactory results. It could be said, for instance, that many of the best modern Christian churches were designed by non-Christian architects.

The cathedral in Tokyo, designed by the great Japanese architect, Kenzo Tange, was built between 1961 and 1964 and is therefore contemporary with his more famous Olympic buildings. It combines a novel concept of structure with traditional symbolic form, being on a cruciform plan. (This was partly dictated by the site, since it replaces the former cathedral destroyed by bombing during World War II.)

The cathedral dominates the low-rise houses of the Bunkyo district of Tokyo like a huge silver bird. It hardly has conventional walls or roof, but vast, shimmering sails or shells, clad in ribbed stainless steel, which rise to repeat the cross form at roof level, angling upwards from the centre, more sharply so over the chancel. A broad ribbon of skylight runs along each arm, interspersed with cross-beams bracing the shells. When it reaches the peak at the end of each arm of the cross, it descends as a long vertical window to the ground. The architect has made something almost abstract out of a traditional Gothic form, and this impression is strengthened by the lack of sculpture and the tall, tapering concrete needle of the bell tower, 197-ft (60-m) high and set well apart from the cathedral, from

which one might expect to hear electronic music rather than bells. People enter through two low annexes that skirt the nave like aisles. Inside, the light is muted by louvres on the skylights. The soaring concrete shells still bear the marks of the shuttering, perhaps surprisingly in view of Tange's identification of beauty with function, but their clear if dizzying upward sweep recalls the ideals of medieval builders.

St Mary's is the creation of the great Japanese architect Kenzo Tange and is contemporary with his famous Olympic buildings.

The Great Hall of the People contrives to fulfil the conflicting demands of several sharply contrasting traditiions, and does so with more success than might have been expected.

Great Hall of the People, Beijing

During the second half of the 19th century, foreign, mainly Western, influence threatened to swamp China culturally, as well as economically and politically. The buildings of the foreigners were in their own style, and few were distinguished. Chinese imitations were even

worse, giving rise to the hybrid style of the so-called Chinese Renaissance or Revival. Progressive, reform-minded Chinese recognized that traditional architecture had to adapt to modern needs, and that reform implied Westernization. But the 'Eclectic' buildings of the interwar period were essentially Western – 'foreign buildings with Chinese roofs on', as one famous scholar called it, or 'pigtail architecture'. Political disarray and economic weakness did not help matters.

After the Communist victory of 1949, Russian influence was understandably strong, but the 'Soviet wedding-cake' style was no great improvement, and eventually ideological differences made it less popular. The alternative was a slow and cautious move towards the International Modern style, though there were ideological difficulties there too, as it was strongly associated with the USA.

The most memorable building that resulted was the Great Hall of the People (1959), a gigantic edifice on the south-west side of Tiananmen Square in Beijing. It is chiefly memorable for its size rather than its beauty, though it has a certain almost Classical sense of order and, built within one year, was an impressive symbol of the strength of the Communist Republic. It is an immense, flat-roofed building, 1,100-ft (335-m) across the façade, capable of seating 10,000 people, and surprisingly colourful, with grey marble columns set in red bases, a gold cornice, the lower parts of the building in pinkish stone and the walls a warm yellow. Inside, walls and ceiling are rounded and the main light source is a red star set in sunflowers. The main floor space, over 6,050sq ft (562sq m) in area, could

house all the buildings of the Forbidden City.

More recently, the Chinese in their mushrooming industrial cities have abandoned the ancient tradition of building spaciously but horizontally, not vertically. The pagoda was the only exception and that has now been replaced by the tower block.

Tange's audacious twin stadia, or sports halls, for the Tokyo Olympic Games of 1964 were perhaps his greatest masterpiece.

Olympic Stadia, Tokyo

Japanese architecture was extremely lively and imaginative in the post-Second World War era, with Kenzo Tange as its outstanding exponent. He took a leading part in the debate concerning tradition in the 1950s and was the dominant influence on, though not really part of, the movement called Metabolism, propounded by a group of young Japanese architects who produced some highly futuristic buildings in the 1960s, though they soon broke up and went their separate ways.

Tange was more adept than most at combining tradition with the International Modern style. He expressed his hope or belief that the belated achievement of a democratic society in Japan would release great national energies and create something new and exciting. Sympathetic to Shinto and Buddhist tradition, in his Tokyo City Hall he imitated, not altogether convincingly, the techniques of the very early Jomon culture in Japan, which ended in about 300 BC. More successful was his widely praised Kagawa Prefecture building in 1955–58, which mingled concepts drawn from the Heian period (9th–12th century) with the characteristic forms of the International Modern style, reworking details of traditional wooden architecture in concrete.

His hugely audacious twin stadia, or sports halls, for the Tokyo Olympic Games in 1964 were perhaps his greatest masterpiece. Their sweeping, curved, steel-covered concrete roofs, forming vast ellipses suspended like tents above the arena, seemed in line with Japanese tradition, not because of any direct borrowing but through their brilliant asymmetrical arrangement and siting, a demonstration of how

thoroughly Tange had comprehended historical aesthetics, not to mention the latest engineering techniques. These buildings proved as 'functional' as they were spectacular and set a high standard for future designers of such Olympian structures. They showed, too, that

modern architecture did not necessarily have to be Western, although this particular road did not take him very far; Tange's interests subsequently changed as he became absorbed by urban planning and he largely abandoned his concern for preserving tradition.

SOUTH ASIA

CHAPTER SEVEN

The Great Stupa, Sanchi

Ajanta

Kailasanatha Temple, Ellora

Mamallapuram (Mahabalipuram)

Bhubaneswar

Temple of the Sun, Konarak

Khajarao, Madyha Pradesh

Jama Masjid, Fatehpur Sikri

Humayun's Tomb, Delhi

Udaipur, Rajasthan

Gul Gunbad, Bijapur

Golden Temple, Amritsar

Red Fort, Delhi

Taj Mahal

Badashi Mosque, Lahore

Victoria Terminus, Bombay

Viceroy's House, New Delhi

Chandigarh, Punjab

National Assembly Building, Dhaka

Borobudur, Java

Angkor Wat, Cambodia

The architecture of the Indian subcontinent, reflecting historical conditions, is unique in several respects; in spite of centuries of conflict and upheaval, there is overall a remarkable sense of continuity. It can be broadly divided into three periods. The first is that of the 'native' tradition, sometimes called 'Hindu', a term that is strictly speaking both anachronistic and inaccurate, although it does describe most of the great surviving monuments. It began well over 2,000 years ago and continued up to about the 12th century (longer in some regions), spreading beyond the subcontinent to Indonesia and south-east Asia. The second is the era of Islam which dominated North India, and under the Mughals most of the subcontinent, when it produced perhaps the most beautiful buildings in the world. After the collapse of the Mughal empire in the 19th century, the British became the dominant power in India. Imperial European powers generally followed their own architectural styles, and the British were no exception although, in the late 19th century, many British architects endeavoured with varying success to incorporate local traditions in their still essentially Western buildings. By the time India and Pakistan became independent (1947), they, like practically every other ex-colony, attempted to establish a new identity under the ubiquitous influence of the International Modern style.

The earliest architecture was wooden, but nothing survives. The earliest surviving buildings are the Buddhist stupas, which, like later

Hindu temples, betray their origin in wooden structure and carving. The first stone temples were excavated or rock-cut, as at Ellora and Mamallapuram: those built by the more common method, by assembling stone blocks, first appeared in the 7th century. Styles steadily evolved, though they continued to suggest the tradition of woodcarving, being more sculpture than architecture. Not until quite late in the period did Hindu architects learn how to create large internal spaces.

Muslim attacks, and eventually conquest, from the north-west resulted in the destruction of Hindu temples throughout northern India, although a few regions, such as Orissa, escaped. But Muslim rulers, whose architectural traditions came from Persia and Central Asia, naturally employed Hindu workers and adopted Hindu architectural features. The Indo-Islamic style existed long before the arrival of the Mughals, but reached its peak under Shah Jahan (1628–58), builder of the Taj Mahal. Nor was this exclusively a Muslim style. Hindu princes in Rajasthan built their palaces in the same style as the Mughal emperors in Delhi.

The British created some strange buildings in what was called the 'Indo-Saracenic' style, but eventually achieved a fairly successful blend in Viceroy's House, New Delhi. Independent governments, seeking a new, national style, perhaps inevitably tended to employ top Western architects, notably Le Corbusier (Chandigarh) and Louis Kahn (Dhaka).

The Great Stupa, Sanchi

The monuments at Sanchi, on a hill in Madhya Pradesh, form one of the most important Buddhist sites in India. Together they represent a potted history of Buddhism and a museum of the development of techniques in architecture and sculpture, encompassing the transition from wood to stone.

The stupa is not intrinsically a structure of commanding architectural interest, and the Great Stupa at Sanchi is not the most impressive. Although it is one of the largest in India, measuring 121ft (37m) in diameter and 52ft (16m) in height, the stupas at Anuradhapura in Sri Lanka are far larger. It is not one of the eight stupas to which the ashes of the Buddha were distributed, but its core dates from the time of the Maurya emperor, Asoka (273–232 BC), the wise ruler who adopted Buddhism without threatening its egalitarian appeal.

The Buddhist stupa derived from the funeral mounds of earlier times, and had a similar function in that it contained Buddhist relics (one of the smaller stupas at Sanchi contained relics of famous disciples of the Buddha); but eventually the stupa itself became an object of worship. Early Buddhism was unconcerned with appearances, the structure itself was not important, and the Great Stupa was originally much smaller and plainer – a mound of earth and stone covered with bricks and plaster, with a small space in the centre for the relic, niches for lamps set in the dome, and a circling ambulatory. As Buddhism grew in wealth and the monks in influence, the material world intruded. The Great Stupa doubled to its present size in the 2nd century BC, wood was replaced

by stone, and sculpture made its appearance, reaching its peak around 50 BC with the four magnificent *toranas* (gates) of the Great Stupa, one of the glories of Indian art.

Neglected for 600 years, Sanchi was rediscovered by a British officer in 1818.

Unfortunately, treasure-hunters and amateur archaeologists caused considerable damage (Asoka's pillar was used in a sugarcane press) before the British government took steps to protect it.

The Great Stupa at Sanchi is India's most famous Buddhist monument.

Ajanta

A year after the 'discovery' of Sanchi, a British hunting party stumbled on the rock-cut Buddhist sanctuaries (*chaityas*) and monks' houses (*viharas*) of Ajanta, in the Sahyadri Hills about 230 miles (370 km) north-east of Bombay and not far from the later site of Ellora. Overgrown by dense forest, they had apparently been undisturbed for centuries. There are 29 caves at Ajanta, dating from the 2nd century BC to the 8th century AD. Cut in a U-shaped hillside above a ravine, they would have originally been reached from the river by steps.

Strictly speaking, these are works of sculpture rather than of architecture, since they were carved from solid rock, a volcanic lava comparatively easy to cut; but they are of special architectural interest because the freestanding buildings on which they were modelled were made of wood and have therefore long disappeared. One of the oldest, Cave 10, from before 100 BC, measures 98 x 41ft (30 x 12.5m) and is 36-ft (11-m) high. The method of work was to start at the top, the roof being completely finished before moving down, thus avoiding the need for scaffolding. Covering such a long time span, the caves also show how the skills of the 'builders' advanced. Whereas the early sanctuaries closely follow existing models, the later ones show the development of more inventive design. The impressively sculpted façade of Cave 19, a large *chaitya* hall which belongs to the Gupta period (early 6th century), although it retains the customary large, almost-circular opening, the only source of light, is unlikely to have duplicated a freestanding building.

The greatest glory of Ajanta, however, are the paintings, which besides the life of the Buddha, depict life and culture in almost every imaginable aspect, with buildings, street scenes, court and domestic life, as well as astonishingly realistic paintings of animals. Some, like the famous Bodhisattva Padmapani in Cave 1, are of unsurpassable quality, which is extraordinary given the working conditions, with the only light reflected from metal mirrors mounted outside.

OPPOSITE
Overall view of the cave sanctuaries of Ajanta in the cliffs above a curve of the River Waghora.

LEFT
One of the Gupta façades. The circular opening is the main source of light.

Detail of the
Kailasanatha temple.

Kailasanatha Temple, Ellora

The earliest rock-cut sanctuaries at Ellora are contemporary with the later ones at nearby Ajanta, but work continued much later, well after the time when freestanding temples were first built in stone elsewhere in India. There are 34 caves: from south to north, 12 Buddhist, 17 Hindu and 5 Jain. Chronologically, they were made in roughly that order, but some Buddhist and Hindu work was going on simultaneously, although there are also signs of a Hindu takeover in places: the Hindu Cave 15 was probably originally a Buddhist *vihara*, or monastery. Of the Buddhist caves, the most impressive is the Tin Thal ('three-storeyed') Cave 12, with its rich sculpture, but on the whole they are less impressive than those at Ajanta.

The outstanding work at Ellora is the Hindu Kailasanatha Temple which, although cut from the rock, is not enclosed but open to the elements. Work started with trenches cut in the top of the cliff, eventually isolating an immense block of stone over 200 x 150ft (60 x 45m) in plan and over 100-ft (30-m) high. The top was completed first, with the main shrine on what became the upper storey, as work continued steadily downwards. Other large blocks were left intact, to be fashioned later into separate shrines and pillars, and a life-size carving of an elephant. The temple, which as a giant sculpture has been called the most impressive single work of art in India, is dated to the late 8th century, but work must have continued for many years. The name of the temple means 'Lord of [Mount] Kailasa', and it is supposed to represent the sacred mountain beyond the Himalayas that was the home of Shiva. As elsewhere, Shiva himself is represented in an inner sanctuary in the form of a large *lingam* (phallus).

The whole creation, a marvel of craftsmanship and imagination, is a proclamation of Hinduism resurgent and, by implication at least, a symbol of its victory over Buddhism. Because of its situation, closely hemmed in by the surrounding rock face, it is difficult to appreciate its magnificence as a whole, and it is notoriously impossible to photograph effectively.

Some of the rock-cut
temples at Ellora.

Mamallapuram (Mahabalipuram)

Mamallapuram, on the coast of the Bay of
Bengal south of Madras (Chennai), was
established as a major port by the commercially
minded Pallava dynasty in the 7th century.
Besides merchants, it also became, and
remains, an attraction for pilgrims. Nothing of
the old port has survived except for the
magnificent collection of rock-cut temples in
the Pallava, or early Dravidian, style, which was
to be influential throughout India and in
Cambodia and Java. Most of the temples were
carved from outcrops of rock on the seashore.
For architectural historians, they provide
evidence of the influence on Hindu temples of
earlier Buddhist architecture, particularly the
chaitya hall.

The rock-cut architecture consists of ten
mandapas (open halls, or 'caves'), and eight
rathas (monolithic temples whose form suggests
a chariot, i.e. *ratha*). Five of the *rathas* are
named after the Pandava heroes of the
Mahabharata and their wife, Draupaudi. Among
the most interesting are the Arjuna *ratha*, with
its curious tower, and the Bhima *ratha*,
rectangular and barrel-vaulted, clearly deriving
from the Buddhist *chaitya* hall. The *mandapas*
are comparatively small, none more than 25-ft
(7.6-m) deep, and are like open art galleries,
where pilgrims can contemplate in shaded
leisure the accomplished sculptures of gods and
mythological scenes.

The sculpture of Mamallapuram is its
greatest glory. It includes one of the world's
most famous bas-reliefs, called the Descent of
the Ganges (the precise subject is a matter of
argument), carved in the serene yet vigorous

Pallava style on the surface of two large,
adjacent rocks, 95-ft (29-m) long and 23-ft
(7-m) high.

The most striking architectural feature is the
Shore Temple, built – and it is 'built', not cut –
in the early 8th century, after work on rock-cut
temples petered out. Its square towers, rising in
diminishing horizontal bands like a ziggurat, are
an early example of the typical southern Indian
temple tower (*vimana*), which is distinct from
the smooth and rounded *sikhara* of the north.
The towers of the Shore Temple clearly derive
from the earlier, carved Dharmaraja *ratha*.

Parasuramesvara and all other Bhubaneswar temples, is the even smaller Vaital Deul, which clearly derives from the Buddhist *chaitya* hall. Possibly the architect came from the south, though equally he may have been following local Buddhist traditions. The temple has Tantric connections, suggested by a frightening image of Durga in her aspect of an eight-armed Chamunda, sitting on a corpse and garlanded with human skulls.

The full blossoming of the Orissan style appears in the esteemed 10th-century Muktesvara Temple, again a relatively small structure, about 45-ft (14-m) long, but with its own sacred pool and a unique *torgana* (gateway), apparently the work of some individual and unknown genius. The porch, hitherto a rather squat, flat-roofed building, has now acquired a pyramidal roof and is unusual in having sculptural decoration inside as well as out. The whole temple is so encrusted with fine sculpture that is more jewel than building.

In the Lingaraja Temple (c. 1000), contrarily, sculpture is subordinated to architecture in this the largest temple in Bhubaneswar. Its sanctuary tower, the Sri Mandir, is 177-ft (54-m) high and dominates the town; in the sanctuary Shiva himself is to be found in the form of his symbol, a giant stone *lingam*. The temple consists of what became the standard four units, Tower, Porch, Dancing Hall and Hall of Offerings, the last two added a century or more later. The temple stands in an enclosure measuring 242,000sq ft (22,500sq m), which contains a number of freestanding shrines built by pious worshippers, their form often reflecting that of the temple itself, and is surrounded by a defensive wall.

ABOVE
The Muktesvara Temple beside the Sacred Pool.

OPPOSITE
The Lingaraja Temple.

Bhubaneswar

Bhubaneswar, the great temple city of Shiva in Orissa, eastern India, bears much the same relationship to medieval north Indian architecture as Mamallapuram does to the south Indian style.

The temples that survive today, out of the hundreds, even thousands, that tradition asserts were once present, date from the late 7th to the 12th century. The earliest is the Parasuramesvara, quite small, only 48-ft (15-m) long with the tower 44-ft (13-m) high, but remarkable for its extensive, small-scale sculpture which negates the potential heaviness of the slab-like construction. Somewhat later, but quite different in form from the

European sailors called the Surya Deul the Black Pagoda to distinguish it from another coastal landmark, the White Pagoda, at Puri.

Temple of the Sun, Konarak

The huge Surya Deul, or Temple of the Sun, which stands on its platform among sand dunes on the Bay of Bengal at Konarak, represents the culmination of the Orissan style and is one of the greatest art treasures of India. Its popular name, the Black Pagoda, derives not, as some suppose, from its frankly erotic sculpture, but from Calcutta-bound sailors who used its dark bulk as a landmark. It represents the chariot of the Sun God, and has 12 pairs of giant wheels along each side of the platform and seven realistically straining horses to pull it.

Rescued from the sands in the early 20th century, the temple is largely ruined, though still hugely impressive. The great sanctuary tower (*deul*) is no more, and was possibly never completed, though legend insists it was. The best preserved element is the porch (*jagamohana*), which still has its distinctive pyramidal roof topped by the characteristically Orissan flattened sphere. A third element, either a Hall of Offerings or, as the sculpture of female dancers suggests, a Dancing Hall, stands separately and is also now roofless.

Built in the 13th century, the temple is said to have occupied 1,200 masons and sculptors for 16 years at a cost of 12 times the annual revenue of the kingdom. Most of it is in a pale softish stone, though doorways and major sculptures are of hard greenish chlorite, suggesting bronze. Mortar was not used, and the stones were hauled into place up earth ramps; as further reinforcement the builders added iron girders, which are unknown outside Orissa.

Practically every inch of this monumental building is covered with sculpture of extraordinary variety and of a universally high standard. The imagination of the sculptors was unlimited; for example, a continuous plinth running around the base of the temple is carved with elephants. There are over 1,700 of them, and no two are alike!

Khajarao, Madyha Pradesh

The temples of Khajarao were built by the dynamic Chandela Rajputs at the peak of their power in the 10th–11th centuries. The remoteness of the site, no doubt chosen for safety, resulted in its passing from general awareness until 'discovered' by a British officer in 1838. Having been built all within about 100 years, there is little stylistic variety in the temples which, interestingly, are dedicated to both Vishnu and Shiva and some to Jain saints, suggesting a marked degree of religious tolerance.

There were originally 85 temples, of which 25 remain in reasonably good order. Generally, they represent a refined and fully developed version of the style that evolved at Bhubaneswar, and this is the near-perfect culmination of a magnificent tradition. Building techniques may still be relatively simple, but these are highly sophisticated buildings by any standard.

Among innovations are the high platforms on which the temples stand, and the integration of the four basic units – which are separate structures at Bhubaneswar – into a single building, often on a cruciform plan. Each temple has a number of towers rising to the *sikhara* over the sanctuary, like mountains rising to a peak. The finest example is the magnificent Kandariya Mahadeva, the largest temple, with a tower nearly 115-ft (35-m) high and 84 smaller towers and turrets. The towers are more rounded than at Bhubaneswar, and windows are set back from projecting balconies, creating dramatic contrasts of light and shade.

The sculpture, largely of human or divine figures, is in high-relief, occasionally in the round, and is of extremely high quality. Again in contrast to Bhubaneswar, the temple interiors are also highly decorated, and the utmost skill is deployed on areas that, in normal light, are invisible. The sculpture engenders an atmosphere of contentment and good feeling, as if the sculptors fully shared the success and prosperity of the art-loving Chandela Rajputs. The effect is in striking contrast to the imagery of, for instance, a medieval Christian church with its demons, gargoyles and scenes of hell. There is a good deal of energetic sexual activity, but the sensuousness of the female musicians and entertainers is accompanied by a calm serenity which reminds us that, however sexy, these are heavenly beings. Michael Edwardes remarked that 'the men who carved these statues had very little to learn from anybody'.

One of the many magnificent temples at Khajarao.

Jama Masjid, Fatehpur Sikri

Concerned by the absence of an heir, the Emperor Akbar took the advice of a sage, Salem Chisti, that a son would be conceived at Sikri, the sage's village about 25 miles (40km) south-west of Agra. When this advice proved correct, in 1569, Akbar in gratitude declared he would make Sikri his capital, adding the name Fatehpur ('Victory') after his conquest of Gujarat. In about a decade a spectacular palace complex (hardly a town, there were no streets) was constructed. A vast army of workers was required, and although the style is generally uniform, it is sometimes possible to detect from particular details whereabouts the craftsmen came from.

The main buildings are the royal palace assembly and the Great Mosque, or Jama Masjid. In the palace, the most interesting room historically is the Diwan-i-Khas, or Hall of Private Audience, where Akbar would listen to the debates of representatives of various religions, including Portuguese Jesuits who hoped to convert him. There is ample decorative evidence of Akbar's open-mindedness in motifs of the lotus (Buddhist or Hindu), *chhatris* (Hindu), and Tree of Life (Muslim).

Chhatris also adorn the Buland Darwarza, the magnificent triumphal arch or gateway to the Jama Masjid complex. Approached by the broad flight of steps, the Buland Darwarza, which is 176-ft (54-m) high excluding the steps, looks like an octagon, the gate itself flanked by narrower elements receding at an angle. This is misleading: on the other side it tumbles away from the mighty façade in disappointing steps. The main entrance to the sanctuary, the King's

Gate, is less assertive, though high, and possibly served in place of a minaret. It is flanked by cloisters with domes rising behind. The mosque itself may be intended as a copy of the Great Mosque at Mecca, but here too there are Hindu motifs, as well as elaborate and colourful though faded floral decoration, carved, painted and inlaid. Beautiful vistas extend on all sides. Among the buildings within the enclosure is the

Tomb of Salem Chisti, a low building in white marble of such light-hearted charm that one might almost expect to buy exquisite ice cream there. Altogether, Fatehpur Sikri is a splendid monument of the mixture of Persian and Indian elements that formed the Mughal style. But a monument it remained. Akbar left in 1585, and Fatehpur Sikri was abandoned.

The characteristics of the
Mughal style are already
established in the
magnificent Tomb of
Humayun, seen from the
ceremonial gardens.

Humayun's Tomb, Delhi

Humayun was the second Mughal emperor,
who inherited a shaky empire on the death of
Babur in 1530 and was swiftly forced out by
rivals. He took refuge with the Safavids of
Persia, and was understandably impressed by
the splendour of Persian art and culture. He
restored his authority with Persian help and a
predominantly Persian court, but only regained
Delhi in 1555, a year before his death.

Although the first mosques in India were
built before 1200, the artistic and architectural
traditions of Islam and India could hardly have
been more different. For instance, the pointed
arch and the dome were alien to Indian
architecture, and so was the use of concrete.
Hindu craftsmen adopted Islamic traditions
successfully, but also introduced Hindu
traditions of ornamentation. The Tomb of
Humayun is a splendid, early example of that
mixture of Persian and Hindu traditions that
formed the so-called Mughal style, which would
reach its peak with the Emperor Shah Jahan and
the Taj Mahal.

Like most tombs, the building is set in
lovely water gardens, representing Paradise,
here divided into quadrants with the tomb, one
of the finest funerary monuments ever built, in
the centre. The plan is octagonal, with two tall
and powerful gateways. In red sandstone
outlined with white marble, the complex
occupies a podium 156-ft (48-m) square. The
dome, which rises to 125ft (38m), is the first
double-skinned dome in India. There are fine
inlays, and marble lattices (*jalis*) in the recessed
windows, but in general the decoration of the
complex is restrained, and the tomb itself, in
glistening marble, is unadorned, without even
an inscription. There is much evidence of Hindu
architectural traditions, for instance in the
kiosks, or *chhattris*, above the central gateway,
as well as decorative details such as the twin
stars above the arch of the central gateway. The
tomb was built between 1564 and 1573 by
Humayun's chief wife, Hamida Begum, mother
of the great Akbar, who camped on the site to
keep a closer eye on the workmen and is
herself buried here.

*The City Palace, from the
landward side. Its many
pavilions and balconies,
some of later date, were
for the use of the women
of the royal harem.*

Udaipur, Rajasthan

The walled city of Udaipur on the shores of
Lake Pichola was the capital of the princely
state of Mewar in Rajasthan, founded in 1567.
Continuing conflict with the Mughals destroyed
most of the original city, but when peace came
in the 17th century the capital was rebuilt in a
style that reflected it, though the vast blank
walls of the City Palace fronting the lake, parts
of which date from earlier times, are clearly
defensive. The architecture of Udaipur reflects
the blending of Indian and Islamic styles that, in
Rajasthan particularly, long predates the Mughal
era; the early work largely resists the influence
of the Mughal court style current elsewhere.

The tradition of wall painting in
Rajasthan is prominent in the courts of the
massive City Palace, actually several palaces
combined. The style varies from the bold and
colourful Rajput style to a later, more
sophisticated, courtly style which has an almost
Rococo charm, extending over architectural
boundaries. Elsewhere the decoration is jewel-
like, sometimes actually employing semiprecious
stones; a famous feature is the remarkable use
of glass, mirrored, coloured or plain, which in
some rooms covers walls, ceilings and even
floors. One 19th-century ruler was so
impressed with the material that he ordered a
suite of glass furniture, made in France, and
topped the pinnacles of the palace with
diamond-cut glass globes.

In general, 17th-century Udaipur was up to
50 years behind the current fashion until after
its occupation by the last effective Mughal
emperor, Aurangzeb, in 1679. In the 18th
century a new, distinctly Mewar style
developed, fully employing the techniques and
conventions of Mughal art but in a restrained,
ordered style, with exquisite use of white
marble. The pavilion erected on top of the City
Palace, from gigantic blocks somehow hauled
up the walls, is the outstanding example.

The famous Lake Palace, on an island
overlooked by the City Palace, offers one of the
most romantic vistas in India. It is often likened
to a great white ship floating on the lake. Most
of it is now a hotel and comprises a mixture of
styles from Mughal to modern.

Gul Gunbad, Bijapur

Bijapur, a town in northern Karnataka, formerly Mysore, southern India, was the capital of a substantial medieval kingdom or sultanate, which was ruled from 1489 until 1686 by the distinguished Adil Shahi dynasty, whose domain briefly included Goa.

The dynasty had an admirable reputation for religious toleration, cosmopolitan culture and support of the arts, and their legacy is Bijapur's outstanding collection of Islamic buildings – tombs, mosques and palaces – perhaps the finest in the Deccan and more typical of a northern city. Among them are the Jama Masjid, with its shallow, onion dome and graceful, arcaded court, built by Ali Ardil Shah I (1557–79), and several large mausoleums, of

which the 17th-century Tomb of Ibrahim Rawza is the most elegant.

The largest and most remarkable building is the Tomb of Muhammad Adil Shah, known as the Gul Gunbad (Gol Gumbaz), meaning 'Round Dome', built in 1625–56. Muhammad is buried here along with members of his family and his favourite court dancer. The dome is said to be the second largest in the world and to span the largest floor area unsupported by pillars, 59,795sq ft (5555sq m). Its form is a huge cube, with a hexagonal porch or gate and octagonal turrets eight-storeys-high on all four corners. The turrets are crowned with their own galleried cupolas.

If not a particularly beautiful building, Gul Gunbad is certainly an engineering marvel. The

immense weight of the dome is skilfully transferred to the square building by a system of arches, but the springing of the dome is invisible from below because the arches also support a projecting and concealing platform, 10-ft (3-m) wide. This is said to be an effective whispering gallery which will carry a whispered message 11 times across the span of 125ft (38m). Unfortunately, conditions are seldom quiet enough to test it. The decoration is incomplete due to the early death of the builder, though it includes characteristic Bijapur motifs, such as leafy points to arches. The grave itself, besides the usual screen, has a canopy of mother-of-pearl.

The massive foursquare tomb of Muhammad Adil Shah is topped by one of the world's largest domes.

Golden Temple, Amritsar

The Golden Temple, or Harimandir, is the central shrine of the Sikhs, first built in the late 16th century on land given by the Emperor Akbar, whose eclectic attitude to religion the Sikhs shared. It was built on an artificial island in the Pool of Nectar (Amrit-sar), by the fifth guru, Arjan, who also compiled the original version of the Granth Sahib, the Sikh 'bible', now kept in the Temple under a golden canopy studded with emeralds and diamonds. In the 1760s the temple was destroyed by the Afghans but swiftly rebuilt. This building survives, though is largely obscured by alterations and additions made after Ranjit Singh, the 'Lion of the Punjab', united the Sikhs under his rule in 1802.

A white marble causeway leads to the temple, the lower parts of which are also of white marble. The upper parts, including kiosks and cupolas, are covered with gilded copper plates, Ranjit Singh having contributed 220lb (100kg) of gold for the purpose in 1830, and are inscribed with words from the Granth Sahib. The building has four entrances, one in each side, representing the four Hindu castes, all equally accepted by Sikhs, the doors of which are silver-plated, enhancing the brilliance and luxury of the temple. On top of the temple is a domed pavilion, the Shish Mahal or Mirror Room, topped by the royal umbrella symbol, such as appears on the Great Stupa at Sanchi.

The interior is richly decorated with painting, inlays and gilding. It is generally Mughal in spirit, but the largely floral and abstract designs contain occasional images of animals and human beings, which is rare in Mughal decoration. In the past, Sikh art and

architecture was often disregarded, seen as the work of untutored folk aping courtly styles, if it was not literally stolen (some of the marble for the Temple was supposed to have been taken from the Tomb of Jahangir near Lahore). The marble floors and the immense pavement

around the pool were created by workmen from Jaipur, where the Mughal style had been adopted comparatively early. In any case, the status of the Harimandir as a work of art is irrelevant, since it is a shrine, and a hugely important one, rather than a museum.

Red Fort, Delhi

The Red Fort (Lal Qila), is the great citadel built by Shah Jahan within his projected new capital, Shahjahanabad (Old Delhi). Though requiring restoration, it is an immense achievement, a statement of imperial power and wealth that, by its combination of grandeur and delicacy, avoids vulgar pomp and equals, perhaps exceeds, that of any civilization.

A feature of the late Mughal style of Shah Jahan was the replacement of traditional sandstone by marble, previously used mainly for ornamental effect, as in Humayun's tomb, so the name, deriving from the walls and the massive Lahore gate, is slightly ironic. The palaces within, backing on to the river front and open on the inward-looking side, are marble, though some buildings, such as the Diwan-i-Am (Hall of Public Audience) are also of red sandstone. This hall, over 13,000sq ft (1200sq m) in area, is fronted by an arcade of double pillars with cusped or engrailed arches, and decorated with designs in *pietra dura* (marble inlaid with semiprecious stones), both characteristic features of the Red Fort. A panel of birds and flowers behind the raised throne is Florentine, which was once taken as evidence of European craftsmen in India but was more probably imported.

The Diwan-i-Khas (Hall of Private Audience) is, by contrast, of marble. It has the same arches, though here on square piers rather than faceted pillars. The silver plates that covered the ceiling were torn off by the Marathas in the 18th century, and the fabled Peacock throne was carried off to Teheran by Nadir Shah in 1732, later destroyed and now known only from written descriptions. Another

treasure in the Diwan-i-Khas illustrative of a Mughal speciality has survived, the Scales of Justice, a fretted screen of marble 4-in (10-cm) thick. The painted or inlaid decoration is mainly of flowers, and in spite of the losses this is still an impressively luxurious chamber. Who would quarrel with the verse, written in gold on the arches at the end, that proclaims, 'If there is a

Paradise on Earth, then this is it'. Some of the palaces, notably the Rang Mahal (Painted Palace), are, though restored, no less luxurious.

Of many other superb buildings, one of the most attractive is the Moti Masjid, or Pearl Mosque, built in white marble with less decoration as a private chapel by Shah Jahan's son, the more austere and devout Aurangzeb.

OPPOSITE
The buildings of the Red Fort mix the transitional sandstone of the early Mughal emperors with the glittering marble introduced by Shah Jahan.

LEFT
The Pearl Mosque, built by Aurangzeb as his private chapel.

Taj Mahal

The Taj Mahal at Agra, which marks the acme of the Mughal style under Shah Jahan, has often been called the world's most beautiful building, and few who have seen it by dawn light would contradict. It was also one of the world's most expensive buildings, and contributed to Aurangzeb's decision to overthrow its extravagant builder, his father Shah Jahan, who spent the last eight years of his life a prisoner in his palace at Agra.

The Taj, which Rabindranath Tagore described as 'a tear on the face of eternity', was built to demonstrate the Emperor's love for his wife, Mumtaz Mahal, who died giving birth to their fourteenth child in 1631. The mausoleum, in a luminescent white marble that was carried from quarries 186-miles (300-km) distant by 1,000 elephants, took nearly 20 years to

complete. It employed thousands of workmen from all over Islam, and precious materials from a similarly wide area. A miracle of symmetry, it stands on a platform nearly 22-ft (7-m) high and 312-ft (95-m) square, with tall minarets at each corner, an arrangement introduced in the Tomb of Akbar. The minarets were set at an indiscernible outward slant so that, in the event of an earthquake, they would fall away, not onto, the tomb. The central, pearl-shaped dome, actually a double dome, rises to 187ft (57m) at its brass finial. Exterior decoration is of calligraphic reliefs and *pietra dura*.

In the centre are the tombs of Mumtaz Mahal and Shah Jahan himself, placed here by Aurangzeb and the one asymmetrical element in the entire complex. They are guarded by an octagonal screen of fretted marble, each section carved from a single piece, inlaid with precious stones. Some flowers contain 60 or more pieces. This masterpiece of craftsmanship was also installed by Aurangzeb, who feared the original solid silver screen would be looted, as was the case with some other furnishings.

The building is set in water gardens, such an important feature of the Mughal style, which though well maintained, can only suggest their former symbolic glory. The Taj was neglected after Mughal authority collapsed; it was nearly dismantled and auctioned off by an early British governor, but was restored by Lord Curzon in about 1900.

The Badashi Mosque presents a striking contrast to Aurangzeb's other creation, the Pearl Mosque in the Red Fort.

Badashi Mosque, Lahore

An important feature of Islamic architecture is the enclosed space, with the result that houses were generally built around a courtyard with few or no windows on the outside. The courtyard mosque, though less inward-looking, derives ultimately from the house of the Prophet in Medina. Its primary purpose is, of course, to accommodate a large number of worshippers.

The Badashi Mosque is attached to the royal fort in Lahore. One of the most splendid examples of Mughal architecture in today's Pakistan, as well as the biggest, it was built by Aurangzeb in 16733–74 and presents a striking contrast with the Pearl Mosque in the Red Fort at Delhi. It is by far the largest building of the reign of Aurangzeb, the last of the great Mughals, and in area it is the largest mosque in the Indian subcontinent, the enclosure measuring approximately 492ft (150m) on each side. The pool in the centre confirms the effectiveness of a fountain in a rectangle of open water as a visual experience, aside from its purpose of providing facilities for washing.

Raised on a high platform and approached by steps, it broadly resembles the Friday Mosque built by Shah Jahan in his new capital, adjoining the Red Fort, in Delhi, though the Badashi Mosque is altogether a grander structure. The Prayer Hall has a bold central portal with three domes, tucked into low cylindrical drums, in white marble, contrasting with the red sandstone of the façade and the four minarets at the corners, themselves topped by white marble cupolas, which here are octagonal in plan. Together with the large arcaded courtyard, it is in general characteristic of the plan of Friday mosques in South Asia.

The relief decoration employs semi-abstract floral mouldings in painted plaster and inlays worthy of comparison with the Taj Mahal. The sense of harmony is enhanced by the delicacy of the cusped arches.

Victoria Terminus, Bombay

The Chhatrapati Sivaji Terminus, formerly Victoria Terminus and still known popularly as 'VT', is the main railway station of Bombay (Mumbai), used in the 1990s by over half a million passengers per day. Perhaps India's most remarkable piece of Gothic-Revival architecture, it was completed in 1887 in the year of Queen Victoria's Golden Jubilee, hence its name.

Under British rule, public buildings in India generally reflected the fashions of Victorian Britain – racial architecture, some would say. Bombay, where a building boom followed the opening of the Suez Canal in 1870, contains the greatest number and variety of Victorian eclecticism, with examples of everything from Neo-Gothic (French and Venetian as well as English) to Renaissance Classical. However, a vocal minority of architects in the late 19th century held that the most appropriate style should at least draw on Indian architectural tradition, giving rise to the curious style

sometimes called Indo-Saracenic. The architect of the Victoria Terminus, Frederick Stevens, while influenced by St Pancras station in London, was sympathetic to this argument, as he also demonstrated in his vaguely Byzantine Churchgate Station and in several other Bombay buildings.

These 'Anglo-Indian' buildings, as Michael Edwardes observed, 'with their demented Mughal motifs [convey] a pleasant zaniness which was not in the minds of their designers'. Stevens' plum pudding of a building looks almost as if it might have been built for some eccentric maharaja impressed by medieval Venice. It commands affection rather than respect. The large central block is flanked by matching wings, and the central dome is topped by a large statue of Progress by Thomas Earp, who also designed the two great cats, an Imperial lion and an Indian tiger, on the gateway pillars. Inside, the influence of Scott's St Pancras is evident in the arcades and stained glass of the booking hall.

Purists may blanch, but Bombay's Victoria Terminus, suggestive of Venetian Gothic as well as mixed Eastern styles, has, at least, a certain presence.

Prospect of Rashtrapati Bhavan and the Jaipur Column.

Viceroy's House, New Delhi

Viceroy's House, now the presidential residence (Rashtrapati Bhavan), is the centrepiece of the new capital that the British embarked upon, south of the old city, in 1912. Like the Romans, they built for durability, assuming that their empire would last longer than it did. The architect was Edwin Lutyens, the ablest and most original English architect of the day. As a symbol of imperial might, solemn monumentality was required, and Lutyens planned a Classical palace with a faint flavour of India.

Monumental, it was at 630-ft (192-m) wide and 530-ft (162-m) deep, of local brick faced with sandstone from the Mughal quarries. The floors were concrete, covered with stone slabs or marble, and underfloor heating was included. The main approach is up a rise, peaking at the Jaipur Column, so that the building rises slowly into view, first the dome, then its drum, the wide colonnade, and finally the steps before the portico. The plan cunningly obscures the presence of windows of disparate shapes in the façade behind the columns, and thus achieves an impressive unity and symmetry. Closer to, the building has a slightly stark and menacing air, not alleviated by the shining copper dome with recessed apertures in the drum that according to common gossip concealed machine-guns. The garden façade is less formal. The overhanging eaves suggest the Mughal style, and the buttress on the drum, topped by cupolas, recalls the familiar form of Mughal *chhatri*.

The chief and most splendid state apartment is the Durbar Hall, which derives ultimately from the Pantheon and gains natural light only from the *oculus*. It is grand but plain, since Lutyens counted on the colourful uniforms of British officers and Indian princes to provide colour and ornament on ceremonial occasions. Indeed, all the public rooms, even the ballroom, show cool restraint, but for all the imperial solemnity, Lutyens included touches of humour.

A fireback has an Indian elephant above a row of Tudor roses, but one of the roses is only a stalk, as the flower has been plucked by the elephant.

This splendid structure was officially inaugurated in 1931, when the Raj was 16 years short of extinction.

Chandigarh, Punjab

When India and Pakistan became independent in 1947, the Indian government decided to build a new capital for the Indian state of the Punjab, since Lahore, the former Punjabi capital, was now within Pakistan. After the death of one of the original US architects in 1950, Le Corbusier took over the project, together with the British partnership of Maxwell Fry, Jane Drew and a team of Indian architects. Le Corbusier's role was to supervise the general layout and design the government buildings of the Capitol, though he completed only the Law Courts, Assembly and Governor's Residence, with assistance from his brother, Pierre Jeanneret.

Prime Minister Nehru called for 'a new town symbolic of the freedom of India, unfettered by the traditions of the past'. Neither the general plan, which was influenced by Le Corbusier's urban master plan of 1935, called the Ville Radieuse, nor his individual, modernist buildings, truly reflect Indian traditions, although they do not contradict them. They are well adapted to the climate and landscape, and Le Corbusier, who admired Lutyens's Viceroy's House at Delhi, included certain acknowledgements such as the symbol of the umbrella, which appears in various guises. The most admired buildings, lapped by a large artificial pool, are the Law Court (1952–56), with its solid, concrete sun screens, and the Assembly Building, with its great, boat-shaped concrete roof that recalls the contemporaneous chapel at Ronchamp.

Religious and linguistic differences have complicated the political background: Chandigarh is currently the combined capital of Punjab and the new Hindu state of Haryana, but this may change. It is administered by the central government. There are other problems typical of utopian new capitals, including a severe disparity between the sexes (10 men to 1 woman) and increasing scarcity of land. Regardless of the merits of Le Corbusier's Capitol, Chandigarh is more concrete desert than garden city. And a city depending on the car in a country where most people cannot afford a bicycle adds weight to the accusation that the messianic genius Le Corbusier 'never understood other people' (Russell Walden).

Chandigarh: garden city or concrete jungle?

National Assembly Building, Dhaka

Louis Kahn was born in Estonia in 1901 but emigrated to the USA as a child. He taught for some years at the University of Pennsylvania and elsewhere, only achieving international fame comparatively late in life. His major commissions all came within a period of about 15 years. Formidably intelligent (his writings are not always easy to follow) and imaginative, he opened up new directions for modern architecture. Although some regarded him as a reactionary because of his affinity with the tradition of the French École des Beaux-Arts, the great *bête noire* of the avant-garde, and his desire to restore a certain historical grandeur to architecture, he was seen by others as not only the most creative pioneer of Postmodernism and of 'Rational Architecture' but also perhaps the most influential US architect of the 20th century after Frank Lloyd Wright.

Few would dispute that the formidably powerful, almost fortress-like and highly complex National Assembly Building in Dhaka (Dacca), in what was then East Pakistan (now Bangladesh), is his masterpiece. He began work on it in 1962 but actual building did not begin until shortly before his death in 1974. A truly monumental complex, it is really several buildings, secular and religious (it includes a mosque) that are both connected and separate, and illustrates Kahn's principle of the 'house within a house' and dividing 'service' from 'served'.

Kahn explained that what guided his work was 'not belief, not design, not pattern, but the essence from which an institution could emerge...' The complex is built of concrete, which Kahn, in spite of his association with the 'New Brutalism', had already demonstrated, with his attention to detail and finishing, was a less 'brutal' material than it had seemed, combined with marble, and red-brick exterior walls. It is based on simple geometric forms, but they are deployed in an endless variety of ways; there is much to remind us of another of Kahn's axioms: 'silence and light'. For all the aesthetic, even mystical qualities that informed Kahn's work, of course he did not ignore such practicalities as the need to withstand the extreme heat of the region.

Borobudur, Java

The Buddhist temple-stupa of Borobudur in central Java is one of the world's most impressive man-made structures. It was built in about 800, conceived as a whole and completed in a comparatively short time; but the circumstances of its construction are a mystery. Although there is emphasis on the legend of the royal *bodhisattva* (Buddhist saint), it does not appear to be associated with any great ruler or local cult. Though it must have been directed by some individual or group with considerable resources, it seems to have been a popular shrine.

It occupies the top of a mountain and can be thought of as a kind of ziggurat, rising through terraces that diminish in area as they ascend. The lowest terrace was built later, and is in effect a giant rampart no doubt constructed to prevent the structure slipping away down the slope under its own weight. Above it are five terraces basically square in plan, though each side is stepped out twice between corner and centre. The comparatively narrow path is lined by a sculptured wall high enough to conceal the terraces above and below. Above these are three more terraces that are circular, not square (in the Buddhist *mandala*, the Earth is a square contained within the circle of Heaven). They are occupied by 72 stupas in stone latticework through which it is sometimes just possible to make out a Buddha figure within. At the upper levels the slope becomes less steep, space opens out, and the summit is crowned by a single large, bell-shaped stupa 103ft (30m) above the lowest terrace.

The whole structure represents progress from primitive, everyday reality to a state of enlightenment, *nirvana*, illustrated in the relief sculpture along the walls. Thus, a pilgrim circling the building in a clockwise direction, as custom dictated, would complete nine circles to reach the summit. He first sees scenes from the earthly life, mostly carrying a warning message, such as the dire results in the next life for one who kills and eats fellow animals, then scenes from the life of the Buddha, ascending to more philosophical themes from the Buddhist scriptures. The lowest stage of reliefs was obscured when the retaining wall was added.

By 1000, the site was overgrown, having apparently been neglected for nine centuries until it was 'rescued' by the Dutch colonial authorities. It has recently been more thoroughly restored.

Detail of one corner of the temple-mountain of Borobudur. The hefty wall and terrace prevents the whole structure toppling down the hillside.

Angkor Wat, Cambodia

The spread of Indian culture to other lands produced two religious structures of mind-boggling size, Borobudur in Java and Angkor Wat in Cambodia, which is equal to any of the great temple complexes of India both in size – it is usually described as the largest religious structure in the world – and beauty. It was built by the greatest of the Hindu rulers of the Khmer empire, Suryavarman II (reigned 1113–c.1150). It was dedicated to Vishnu and was probably also intended to be the tomb of Suryavarman, who appears frequently among the sculpture as Vishnu himself. As in India, the pyramidal temple symbolizes the sacred mountain, home of the gods.

A broad stone causeway, with monumental balustrades in the form of the universal serpent, leads to the great cruciform gateway to the temple complex, itself nearly 650-ft (200-m) long. The courtyard beyond is divided into four by beautifully decorated galleries. Staggeringly steep steps lead to the second level, lined by galleries, with towers at each corner. Another breathless ascent leads to the central court, again divided into four, with corner towers and, at the centre where the galleries intersect, the central tower containing the shrine. It rises 215ft (66m) from the stone platform on which the vast pyramidal temple stands.

Although the Khmer style ultimately derives from India, it is far from identical, and the inventiveness and imagination of the Khmer builders, not to mention their technical skill, amounts to something much more than a variant. The curved form of the towers, of which only five of the original nine survive, may derive ultimately from Bhubaneswar, but is quite different, and so is their overall effect – like growths from a common stem. The main structural principle is based on the corbel, pillars having broad capitals to support weighty architraves, and though iron dowels are used, there is no mortar. The sculpture, originally painted and gilded, which even extends to roofs, is mainly in low-relief, yet it portrays scenes of vigorous action, mostly deriving from Hindu mythology, with rare accomplishment. Significantly, figures in the round show less assurance.

Angkor was sacked soon after Suryavarman's death, and though his successor restored the Khmer empire, the Hindu gods were discredited and the Wat became a Buddhist temple. Angkor was abandoned by the 16th century and largely overgrown. It was unknown to the world for centuries, and the first European visitors felt much like the aliens in the science-fiction story who stumble on the long-ruined towers of Manhattan.

ISLAM

CHAPTER EIGHT

The Great Mosque, Mecca

Dome of the Rock, Jerusalem

The Great Mosque, Cordoba

The Great Mosque, Samarra

Mosque of Qairouan, Tunisia

Masjid-i Jami, Isfahan

Citadel, Cairo

Caravanserai, Aksaray

Citadel, Aleppo

Alhambra, Granada

Tomb of Timur, Samarqand

Selimiye, Edirne

The Great Mosque, Djenné

Süleymaniye, Istanbul

Topkapi Palace, Istanbul

Masjid-i Shah, Isfahan

Khwaju Bridge, Isfahan

Khan of Azad Pasha, Damascus

Madrasa of Mir-i-Arab, Bukhara

Islamic architecture here is intended to include all structures built by Muslims, whether religious or non-religious, throughout the many lands that make up Islam. An exception is South Asia, where the cultural circumstances are different because other religions, notably Hinduism, existed alongside Islam and the interaction of the two resulted in a distinctive architecture of mixed heritage.

The qualities that distinguish Islamic architecture are quite different from those of European, or Christian, architecture. In general, Islamic buildings are inward-looking, typically surrounded by walls, with no interest shown in outward appearances;

however, there are many exceptions, such as tomb towers and other 'monumental' buildings. It is often difficult to tell what kind of building lies behind them; while, for example, a great gateway or a dome may be visible, it could belong to either mosque or palace, or to some other type of building. It is the interior space that matters, and to experience a building, you have to get inside it.

Islamic buildings are surprisingly adaptable: a Gothic cathedral can scarcely be anything else, but in Islam, the plan of the courtyard mosque could be, and was, employed for many other types of building at one time or another.

Islamic buildings often appear to have no specific axis or direction, or they have two contrary ones, and there is generally no particular central point or focus. Patterns repeat themselves, with no clear start or finish. Nor were Islamic architects interested in large-scale planning; new buildings were added without regard for the scale or situation of older ones so that, where growth is ongoing for a long time, the result can be something of a jumble, as in the Topkapi Palace in Istanbul.

Another, perhaps the major disparity between Islamic and other architectural traditions, is the attitude to structure. Instead of emphasizing the form and structure – the actual mechanics – of a building, Islamic architects are intent to disguise it. They wish to make it light and insubstantial: domes float, vaults and walls disappear, thanks to the panoply of decorative techniques – mosaic, painting, cut stone, modelled plaster and, above all, glazed tiles – available to obscure their mundane solidity. Decoration is not only astonishingly rich but, at least in religious buildings, predominantly abstract or floral-based, with striking use of calligraphy and geometrical patterns although, of course, this kind of effect has other motives than the purely decorative. The symbolism may be less easy for non-Muslims to comprehend, and without that knowledge a full understanding of the buildings is impossible, because, apart from the many traditions, Arab, Turkish, Iranian, involved, what makes Islamic architecture so distinctive, so different from other traditions, is that it is an expression of Islamic culture, deeply rooted in religion and society.

Umayyad caliphs and decorated with mosaic. An Abbasid caliph built the colonnades. It was rebuilt again by the Ottomans, on a grander scale, and most recently by the Saudis.

The Ka'aba is a stone building which stands in the centre of the courtyard. It is almost a cube, 42 x 36ft (13 x 11m) in plan and about 52-ft (16-m) high, and is oriented so that its corners face the points of the compass. It is believed to date from the days of the Prophet Abraham (Ibrahim), whose grave is also in the courtyard. It has been rebuilt many times, in the same form, and is normally hung with black silk, renewed annually. In one corner is the Black Stone, an object of veneration for the pilgrims who walk around the Ka'aba seven times, which is probably of astronomical origin. There is a door in the Ka'aba high up on one side, its frame sent by the Ottoman sultan when it was rebuilt in 1627.

Views of the Mosque of the Haram at Mecca, Islam's holiest site.

The Great Mosque, Mecca

The Great Mosque at Mecca, or Masjid al-Haram, is the most sacred place in Islam. It contains the very centre of the Muslim religion, to which the *mihrab* of every mosque in Islam is oriented, and every Muslim is expected to make a pilgrimage there, at least once during their lifetime.

The origin of the mosque, the most familiar of Islamic buildings, was the house of the Prophet Muhammad in Medina, a square courtyard with rooms around two sides for his wives. When some of the Companions complained of the heat, an arcade was made with palm trees to provide shade. Many other features of the mosque originated there. The *minbar*, or pulpit, derived originally from the pillar that Muhammad leaned on when preaching, like teachers in a *madrasa* to this day, though later he had one made of cedar, with three steps (he stood on the top step; all imams since put their feet on the second step).

The mosque at Mecca was already a religious building, with the Ka'aba already present, long before Muhammad cleared out the idols in 630. It was much enlarged by the

Dome of the Rock, Jerusalem

The Dome of the Rock is the third most sacred shrine of Islam (after the Ka'aba at Mecca and the Mosque of the Prophet in Medina). Its site could hardly be more holy, for it was here that Abraham nearly sacrificed his son, Isaac. Later the site was occupied by the Temple of Solomon and later still by a Roman Temple of Jupiter. This had disappeared along with the Hebrew Temple when the Caliph 'Abd al-Malik ordered the construction of the shrine (690–692) on the the rock that represents Mount Moriah, whence the Prophet is said to have taken flight to heaven.

One of the world's best known and most beautiful buildings, it is a highly unusual, indeed unique, building in Islamic terms since, apart from its plan, it is as decorative on the outside as it is on the inside. It owes something to the Byzantine tradition and something also to the tradition of Near Eastern builders.

The ground plan is almost a perfect octagon, slightly narrower on two sides. It produces the double octagonal ambulatory beyond which, at the centre, a circle is formed around the rock and below the drum by four piers with three pillars between each pier. Above the round drum of masonry is the semicircular dome, in fact a double dome of wood, which is said to have been covered, when built, with gold plates. Inside it demonstrates a fine sense of proportion, the height from the floor to the springing of the dome being approximately the same as the diameter of the central space, and the octagonal ambulatories about half that height. The diameter of the octagon is about 164ft (50m). The upper part of the octagon and the drum are

decorated with mosaics, the dominant colours being gold and greenish-blue. The dome is now covered by gold-anodized aluminium. The original decoration was replaced under the Ottomans in the 16th century, and the present version is recent. Inside, however, the original decoration has survived more or less intact, though the columns of the octagon have been faced with marble.

OPPOSITE and ABOVE
This exquisite building has survived many centuries despite its contentious site.

313

The Great Mosque of Cordoba, one of the most magnificent buildings in the whole of Islam, was founded by 'Abd ar-Rahman I in 784, having escaped to Spain where Muslims were already established and where he founded a dynasty with Cordoba as its capital.

The Great Mosque, Cordoba

When the Umayyads were supplanted by the Abbasids in 750 and the centre of Islam moved from Damascus to Baghdad, one Umayyad prince, 'Abd ar-Rahman I, escaped to Spain, where Muslims were already established. He founded a dynasty with Cordoba as its capital, and the kingdom flourished, lasting for nearly 300 years (756–1031). In 929 a restored Umayyad caliphate was set up in Cordoba, in rivalry with the Abbasids in Baghdad: by any standard, Cordoba, where Christians and Jews were at least tolerated, was the richest, most sophisticated city in Europe.

The Great Mosque of Cordoba, one of the most magnificent buildings in the whole of Islam, was founded by 'Abd ar-Rahman I in 784. It followed the customary Arab plan, a large courtyard with a prayer hall on the south side. It was substantially enlarged on three subsequent occasions, making it today the largest mosque in Islam outside Samarra. The *qibla* wall (nearest Mecca) and the minaret date from the 10th century. The extensive arcades, which eventually quadrupled in number, amounting to 19, or 18 rows of arches, follow an unusual pattern which was faithfully followed in each successive extension. Roman columns were used but, as they were not tall enough, rectangular piers were placed on top, supporting a semicircular arch that in turn supports the roof. The *voussoirs* of each arch are alternately red brick and white stone, creating, as one looks along the aisles, a striking striped effect. This is repeated in the complex cusped arches before the central *mihrab*, a space sometimes called the sanctuary or the *capella del mihrab*, where stone of two

contrasting colours is employed. This elaborate and intricate chamber dates from 965 and is almost a separate artwork, unusually large and deep, with introductory trios of three-tiered arches. The decoration here is at its richest,

basically floral with inscriptions from the Qur'an in carved plaster, marble and glass and gold mosaic. The vaults whose intersecting ribbed arches support the domes are so complicated they challenge eye and brain.

The famous 'winding tower' or minaret at Samarra.

The Great Mosque, Samarra

The architectural heritage of the Abbasids (750–1258) has been sadly depleted. Nothing survives of their great capital city in modern Baghdad, and Samarra, which extended 19 miles (30km) along the River Tigris and, as suggested by Ernst Grube, was 'probably the most magnificent city the Muslims ever built', was deserted by the 13th century and fell into ruins. One of the few surviving, though largely ruined, buildings is the Great Mosque of al-Mutawakkil, the caliph who founded it in 847. It is said to be the largest mosque in the world and probably the largest ever built. Al-Mutawakkil later built another mosque, that of Abu Dulaf, in Samarra which was almost as large.

All that survives of the Great Mosque is the vast fortified rectangle of brick wall, with half-round bastions at intervals, which surrounds the whole enclosure, and the minaret, a famous landmark, to the north of the enclosure. The wall measured about 784 x 512ft (239 x 156m) and is still about 30-ft (9-m) high. The mosque followed the established pattern of the Umayyad period, but the material here is brick. The prayer hall, in the south, had no less than 25 aisles, and was covered by a flat wooden roof. The *mihrab* was rectangular and decorated with mosaic.

The minaret, for obvious reasons, is known as *al-malawiya*, 'the winding tower'. Over 90-ft (27-m) high, it is set on a solid, square base but the tower itself is round and tapers towards the top. It is ascended by an exterior spiral ramp, circling the tower anticlockwise five times in decreasing circles, giving it a suggestion of a scroll uncoiling. Since symmetry is preserved by keeping the same distance between each circle, the climb grows steadily steeper towards the top. The purpose of a minaret is, of course, to facilitate the muezzin's call to prayer, but clearly a tower of these proportions is not necessary. It is also a symbol of the authority of Islam; al-Mutawakkil's minaret was imitated elsewhere, notably in the Mosque of ibn Tulun in Cairo.

Mosque of Qairouan, Tunisia

The mosque at Qairouan in Tunisia was founded soon after the Arab Conquest of 670, on a site that had formerly been occupied by a Roman building. It was completely rebuilt in 836 and although it has been partly rebuilt or restored several times since, its form has not changed greatly since the 9th century, unlike the Great Mosque of Sfax, which was originally modelled on it. The 9th-century builders were a local dynasty, the Aghlabids, the first native North African dynasty. They had cultural ties both to Umayyad Spain in the west and to the Abbasid caliphate in the east, as well as to Roman predecessors.

The simple clarity of this impressive building, the first 'monumental' mosque in North Africa, was to prove influential throughout the Maghreb, although it is not particularly distinguished architecturally and is comparatively lacking in decoration (the 9th-century painted wooden ceiling has not survived). It follows the established plan for a large, courtyard mosque, consisting of a huge rectangular prayer hall divided into 13 aisles by columns, which were appropriated from Roman remains, a common practice in Muslim North Africa. A double arcade, added later, lines the other sides of the courtyard. The central aisle of the prayer hall, leading from the entrance to the *mihrab* and thus bisecting the hall, is wider and higher than the others – an Umayyad feature. It is surmounted by a fluted dome on a drum on a square base, these elements being plastered white; there is a second dome over the marble *mihrab,* which is decorated with plant-based carving and lustreware tiles imported from the East. The minaret, on the same axis, is built

within the outer wall. It is a strikingly large, square tower in three sections, the upper ones again white, and is closer in form to a Christian church tower than to the slender minarets of Ottoman Constantinople. The top storey is crowned with a cupola and is probably of 11th- or 12th-century date. The porches at the eight entrances also belong to that period.

FAR LEFT
The massive minaret is the most impressive feature of the mosque at Qairouan.

ABOVE
The courtyard.

LEFT
A small tower over a gateway.

Masjid-i Jami, Isfahan

The Seljuk Turks, named after the founder of their fortunes, were one of the semi-nomadic groups of Turkic people in Central Asia who converted to Islam in about the 10th century. They moved into Iran, the cultural heartland of a much wider region and, by the mid-11th century, they controlled it. They upheld the caliph in Baghdad, officially at least, and took the title of sultan. In the next century they conquered virtually all of Asia Minor, defeating the Byzantines in the process.

In spite of the cultural unity of Islam, a slight division between east and west had been evident since the Umayyad-Abbasid rivalry, and the Seljuks, great builders with powerful ideas on architectural form, introduced new ideas which had great influence not only in the Iranian cultural sphere but in most of Islam. Their innovations included the round minaret; the plan of four *iwans*, vaulted halls open on one side and placed on each side of the courtyard, associated especially with *madrasas* (religious teaching colleges similar to mosques);

greater emphasis on the exterior of the building; and the creation of complex patterns in brick.

The Masjid-i Jami or Friday Mosque, i.e. a mosque designed for the main weekly services, was originally founded in the 8th century; the present mosque contains some remnants of the 10th-century rebuilding. The Seljuk mosque consisted of a courtyard with arcades, a prayer hall and four *iwans* attached to the arcades. The main dome, erected in 1080 above the prayer hall forward of the *mihrab*, is of classic form, entirely undecorated, with a polygonal base, all in magnificent brickwork. The inside of the dome bears a Kufic inscription commemorating Malik Shah (1072—92, also in brick. There is another splendid domed chamber directly opposite on the far side of the courtyard.

Later rulers added new elements, most of the glazed tiles and the twin minarets on the principal *iwan* dating from Safavid times, so that the final form is complicated and less well integrated, but it offers a practical encyclopaedia of Iranian style over many centuries.

The Seljuk Friday Mosque at Isfahan is almost a textbook of Iranian architectural styles.

Today, the Citadel of Cairo is dominated by the gigantic 19th-century mosque of Muhammad Ali.

BELOW RIGHT Domes of the mosque.

BELOW Detail of interior calligraphic decoration.

Citadel, Cairo

The Fatimids, whose name derived from their claimed descent from Fatima, daughter of the Prophet, were Shi'ite Muslims who gained control of most of north-west Africa in the 10th century. Already Egypt, in effect Cairo, was rich and vigorous, and its comparative security from invasion made it a pre-eminent centre of Islamic architecture throughout the late Middle Ages. The Fatimids aimed to supplant the Abbasid caliphs, who had already surrendered all meaningful power. They extended their rule to Syria and founded the district called al-Qahira (Cairo), which became the nucleus of the Egyptian capital. They also introduced an architecture of stone, rather than of brick.

Between 1087 and 1092, the Fatimid vizier replaced the existing mud-brick fortifications of the city with stone. The works included several powerful, monumental gates of similar design but with different-shaped towers, the Gate of Victory, Gate of God's Help, etc, which,

according to tradition, were designed by architects from Anatolia. This seems to be confirmed by marked similarities with Seljuk structures. However, by that time, Fatimid power was also fading under the impact of the Seljuks and the Christian Crusaders, and Egypt came under the remote control of a Damascene dynasty. In 1171 the Damascus-appointed governor Salah ad-Din (Saladin) overthrew the last Fatimid caliph and seized power himself, establishing the Ayyubid dynasty.

Salah ad-Din built the Citadel as the centre of government, while simultaneously extending and restoring the city fortifications, with the aim of enclosing all the disparate parts of Cairo. This huge project was incomplete at his death, and much work continued in later times. Cairo is the best preserved of all Islamic cities, and substantial parts of Salah ad-Din's structures remain today. In spite of the impregnability of the defensive towers, the Cairo Citadel is, from a military point of view, slightly less substantial than the Citadel of Aleppo, but it remains one of the most notable existing examples of Muslim military architecture. The skilful masonry work, and the impressive vaulting in particular have no precedent in Egypt.

Caravanserai, Aksaray

People in Muslim society tended to be comparatively mobile. The relative cultural unity of Islam allowed an educated traveller like Ibn Battuta, inspired largely by curiosity, to spend years travelling all over Islam, and beyond, in the 14th century and, as son of a *cadi*, meeting like-minded people, and gaining employment, almost wherever he went. Apart from the movements of merchants and armies, all Muslims, given the means, were supposed to undertake the *hajj* once in their life, and there was considerable movement of scholars and of pilgrims to other places besides Mecca. Since these long journeys often passed through inhospitable country, the need for stopping places providing food and shelter was obvious. Resthouses, called caravanserais (long-distance travellers usually travelled in caravans), were therefore built along the main routes. They were commonly 'prestige projects', built and endowed by a ruler or some rich dignitary and, if so, sometimes no charge was made for a limited stay. Although they existed much earlier, the development of the caravanserai as an architectural type is chiefly associated with the Seljuks in Anatolia; nowadays, unfortunately, they are often in a ruined state, though some have been restored and a few converted into modern hotels.

The usual plan was a walled rectangle with a single gateway wide enough to admit a heavily laden camel. Rooms, stalls and workshops of various kinds, often on two storeys, were ranged along the inside walls and provided accommodation for travellers and their servants, livestock and their fodder, and merchants' goods. Resident staff were housed in the gatehouse. Water was available for drinking and ritual ablutions, and usually there was a prayer hall. Larger buildings had pillared halls and acquired many extensions and annexes, eventually becoming almost self-contained villages.

One of the largest and grandest Seljuk caravanserais is on the road between Aksaray and Konya, built in 1229 by the Sultan Kayqubad I. It covers an area of 48,000sq ft (4500sq m). The impressive stone-faced gatehouse is over 40-ft (12-m) high, and intricately decorated, with *muqarnas* (corbelled brackets) in the vault of the entrance. The hall, entered through the central courtyard which contains a central prayer room, has five aisles and a dome. The general air of luxury proclaims that it is a *Sultan Han*, or Royal Caravanserai.

Although much has been recently restored, parts of the Caravanserai of Aksaray are in ruins. However, they do give some idea of the scale of the building.

The formidable main gate is the best-preserved survival of the Citadel at Aleppo.

Citadel, Aleppo

A feature of major cities throughout most of Islam was the citadel (*qal'a or qasaba*), a fortified, largely self-contained centre of power, a city within a city, like the kremlins of Russia. They varied considerably in size and importance, some being largely military in character, others, like Cairo, mainly political and containing comfortable buildings for gracious living. Militarily, much the most impressive survivor is the spectacularly sited citadel of Aleppo, in Syria, which withstood a siege by the Christian Crusaders in 1124–25.

It is built on top of a steep, exposed hill, which is partly the work of nature and partly of man, and is surrounded by a moat. What remains today is the citadel of the Ayyubid governors built over a long period, but mainly in the early 13th century, together with alterations and additions made under the Mamluks (1260–1517). Inside the rough oval of the walls were a palace, mosque, baths and various other buildings, forming something of a jumble, probably the result of problems posed by the terrain and the different periods of construction. Though the walls and the minaret of the mosque still stand, most of the other buildings are now in ruins.

What does survive in good order is the most impressive structure of all, the entrance gate; few buildings make a more forthright statement of power. On the town side of the moat is a barbican, which leads via a handsome, upward-sloping stone bridge to the main gateway, a substantial fortress in itself. It presents a squarish face of limestone with battlements, machicolations, arrow slits, and a plain, narrow entrance to a vaulted passage. Beyond this façade, the building is more relaxed, with a large hall for receiving visitors built over the entrance. Sculpture and decoration in inlaid stone dates from the end of the 13th century.

Alhambra, Granada

The Nasrid dynasty was established in Granada in the 13th century, after Muslim Spain had broken into separate states. The founder of the dynasty, Muhammad I, also founded the citadel of the Alhambra, probably the best-known Muslim building after the Taj Mahal. Construction continued under his successors, and the palace itself was largely built in the reigns of Yusuf I (1333–54) and Muhammad V (1354–91). The contrast between exterior, with the mighty stone walls and square towers innocent of decoration, and interior, with the richly decorative refinement and delicacy of courts and chambers, is nowhere more startling.

The general layout is rather confused, no doubt partly the result of different periods of building; the hilltop site does not explain the arrangement. The palace is divided into separate units, each with a central courtyard, though the units bear no obvious relationship to each other and the axis changes from west-east to north-south (the Hall of the Ambassadors and Court of Myrtles), then back to west-east, around the well-known Court of Lions. With its elegant arcades, palm-shaded pools and fountains, its fine-cut stucco, tiles, and geometric, calligraphic and floral designs, the Alhambra has often been likened to an oasis, or a dream world emerging from dour reality. Like a dream world, it is easy to get lost in, being both highly intricate and in total area very large. The compulsion of Muslim architects to make solid buildings dissolve before the eyes is seldom more successfully realized. Standing in the Chamber of the Two Sisters, probably the most magnificent single room, the view up into the cupola, the amazing vault with its myriads of *muqarnas*, is like some

optical illusion, achieved by the skilful manipulation of light.

This is a highly sophisticated building but, unfortunately, little is known of its builders. There are evident connections with North Africa, but the serene spaces and subtle decoration of the Alhambra surpass any building in the Maghreb. Once, it would have looked even finer. The Lion Court, with its central fountain supported by sculpted lions, a rare example of freestanding sculpture in Islamic art, was once a mass of blossom and foliage, and the roof, which is modern, would probably have avoided seeming rather too heavy for the slender arches and columns below.

Muhammad I established his Nasrid dynasty in Granada and established the Alhambra as his seat of power, construction of it continuing during the reigns of his successors.

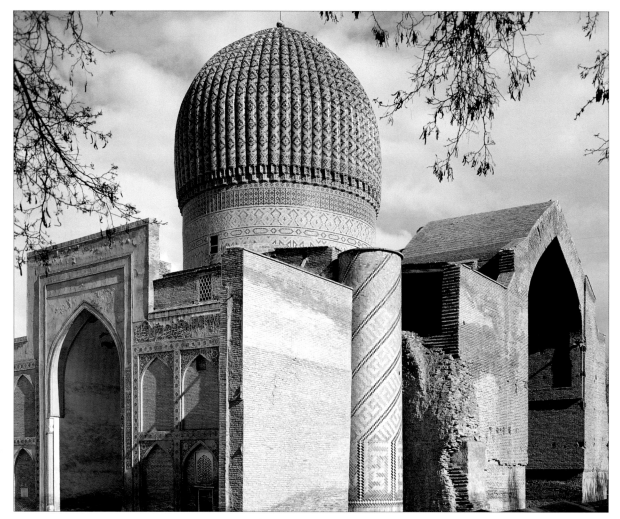

Tomb of Timur, Samarqand

The invasion of Timur (Tamerlane) put an end to Mongol culture in eastern Islam in the late 14th century, but did not immediately introduce any dramatic new directions in art and architecture. Timur made his capital at Samarqand, now in Uzbekistan, and although his successors preferred Herat, Samarqand remained an important centre of art until the 16th century.

The family mausoleum of Timur is part of a complex of buildings, the Gur Emir, that includes a mosque, a *madrasa* and other buildings ranged around a courtyard. The tomb that Timur ordered to be built here was originally intended for his heir, Muhammad Sultan, who was killed fighting the Ottoman Turks in 1402. However, the building was completed just in time to accept the body of Timur himself, who died in 1405. Unlike most Timurid buildings, including the gigantic palaces known only from contemporary descriptions, it is well preserved.

It follows a well-established plan for the tomb tower, an octagonal chamber, though square on the inside, with a dome; it is similar to tombs of the mid-14th century in the nearby necropolis of Shah-i Zinda, where the tall drums and fluted domes are clearly related to Timur's tomb. The double-shelled dome, about 110-ft (34-m) high is, at its base, the same diameter as the drum and swells outward slightly before curving inward towards the finial. The outstanding feature, however, is the decoration, which consists of glazed bricks and tiles and of carved marble. Around the tall drum is an inscription in huge Kufic script, while the octagon walls are covered with irregular panels in a diagonal pattern, that are filled with a different, highly stylized, type of calligraphy. A monumental gateway to the courtyard was erected by Timur's grandson, Ulugh Beg, in 1434. Inside, the square tomb chamber, covered by the rising curve of the inner shell, is decorated in gold leaf and onyx. The dark-green sarcophagus of Timur, and others of marble, are surrounded by a carved marble barrier, though the bodies are actually under gravestones in the crypt below.

The Gur Emir at Samarqand. It has a double dome, the outer one being raised on a very high drum.

Selimiye, Edirne

Edirne (Adrianople), near the point where the modern boundaries of Turkey, Greece and Bulgaria meet, was the Ottoman capital for nearly a century before the capture of Istanbul (Constantinople) in 1453. The complex of the Selimiye, begun in 1569, was built, almost 20 years after the similar Süleymaniye, in the reign of Süleyman I's son and successor, Selim II (1566–74), although here the mosque itself is even more dominant.

Most experts, including, it is said, the architect himself, regard the Edirne mosque as Sinan's masterpiece. It is the final result of years of development in making the most of the central space of the mosque, which here conveys a perfect sense of order and calm. The dome is 104ft (32m) in diameter, approximately the same size as Hagia Sophia, and 137-ft (42-m) high. It is buttressed by a circle of walls and half-domes, and the main thrust is skilfully distributed via arches to eight columns, but they are positioned so close to the walls that they appear to be part of them. The result is that, seen from the floor, the dome seems to float effortlessly without obvious support, and the sense of weightlessness is amplified by the numerous, relatively large windows. The minarets, which at over 230-ft (70-m) in height are even taller than those of the Süleymaniye, are shifted from the usual position at the corners of the courtyard to the corners of the mosque itself, and thus help to emphasize its compactness and upward movement. They each have three balconies, with separate staircases. The decoration is of the highest standard, with outstandingly fine Iznik tiles in the apse of the *mihrab*.

Sinan died within a few years of the completion of the Selimiye, and Ottoman art and architecture would lose its originality and dynamism in the 17th century, but his heritage lived on in the early 17th-century mosque of Sultan Ahmet I, in Istanbul, by a possible student of his, Sedefkar Mehmet Agha.

The Selimiye is widely regarded as Sinan's masterpiece. He died within a few years of its completion.

The Great Mosque, Djenné

Islam, 'the religion of trade', percolated through to West Africa via the Sahara trade routes around the 10th century but made little progress until the rise of Mali under a black Muslim dynasty in the 13th–14th centuries, when it spread swiftly through a large region of the Sahel, especially around the towns of the upper Niger, Djenné (Jenne), Timbuktu and Gao. Both Timbuktu and Djenné later acquired a

considerable reputation in western Islam for Muslim scholarship, and inaccurate legends concerning the riches of Timbuktu circulated in Europe.

It was in that area that the characteristic type of mosque, built of clay reinforced with timber, evolved as a mixture of Islamic influences of Arab origin and pre-Islamic West African architectural traditions. Buildings of clay lasted a considerable time in the arid climate, but were nevertheless often restored or rebuilt, usually, it is assumed, in the same form. On his journey to Mali in the 14th century Ibn Battuta mentioned many mosques, although he said nothing about their structure. The mosques at Djenné and Timbuktu were seen by the French explorer, René Caillié, in 1827, though he is little more enlightening and his picture of Timbuktu, in which the mosque appears in the distance as a long, buttressed building with the typical square, tapering minaret deriving from indigenous conical shrines or pillars, was criticized as inaccurate by the next European visitor, Heinrich Barth. The mosque seen by Caillié was demolished soon after his visit.

The large and impressive mosque of today, one of the most striking monuments in the whole region, dates from 1909, and received considerable input from the French, conscious of establishing an official ethnic architectural tradition. Archaeological and other evidence suggests that the previous building may have been rather different. The original building was probably built in the 14th century, possibly the 13th. It was rebuilt in the 15th century, and restored at many later dates.

In the West African architectural tradition, timber horizontals provide support for the relatively frail adobe. During actual construction, they act as scaffolding.

329

Süleymaniye, Istanbul

After the decline of the Seljuks in Anatolia, a
brief interlude followed before another dynasty,
the Ottomans, began to subjugate their
neighbours in the 14th century. Overcoming the
setback of Timur's invasions, within the next
two centuries they came to dominate western
Islam as well as conquering south-east Europe,
including the old Byzantine capital of
Constantinople, which became the centre of
western Islamic civilization.

The Ottomans introduced new
developments in architecture. Their great
achievement was the monumental domed
mosque plan, in which a central dome spans a
uniform space, the perfect circle on the perfect
square, with a uniform system of vaulting. An
early step was taken at Bursa, the old Ottoman
capital, in the late 14th century, where the
rectangular Great Mosque has 20 domes in four
rows of five. Following the capture of
Constantinople in 1453 the great dome and
spacious interior of Hagia Sophia exerted some
influence. After two centuries of development,
the scheme was fully realized in the Ottoman
'golden age' of Süleyman I (Suleiman the
Magnificent, 1520–66), in the hands of the great
architect Sinan, who finally, in the Selimiye in
Edirne, achieved the final resolution of the
problem of supporting the domes while
maximizing the spatial concept.

The earlier Süleymaniye complex covers
an area of about 650,000sq ft (60,000sq m)
and includes colleges, hospitals, hostels, tombs
and many other features as well as the great
mosque. It was founded in 1550 and built by
Sinan; it is his largest building and many
consider it his greatest, and it has been the
chief mosque of Istanbul ever since. Süleyman
had already reigned for 30 years when he
commissioned the building and he clearly
intended it to be a monument of unparalleled
magnificence. The overall proportions,
observing strict ratios, indicate unusually
careful planning. The main dome is 174-ft
(53-m) high and it is surrounded by a cluster
of cupolas, arches, and semi-domes: there are
more than 500 subsidiary domes in the whole
complex. The workmanship is peerless and
the decoration, though that is secondary in
Sinan's geometrical masterpieces, is of a
similarly high order, and includes tiles from the
famous Iznik potteries.

In Ottoman buildings such as the Süleymaniye, the priority of structure and space over decoration and detail was derived from Seljuk tradition.

Topkapi Palace, Istanbul

The Topkapi Palace of the Ottoman sultans, now a museum, was begun in 1462 and remained the residence of the sultans into the 19th century. Originally it was two palaces, a summer palace by the water and a winter residence on the hill above, overlooking the city, where it occupies the northern tip of the peninsula south of the Golden Horn. The buildings date from the 15th century onwards and some have disappeared in recent times, for instance to make room for a railway. Islamic buildings, especially palaces, were seldom designed as a single coherent unit and the original plan has been obscured by later changes; this is a site in which the parts amount to more than the whole. There is certainly no statement of imperial power and glory such as one would expect in the West.

The palace consists rather of a series of comparatively small buildings, not arranged in any particular pattern but mostly ranged around two large courtyards, actually Second and Third Courts, the Throne Room being situated in Third Court, opposite the handsome and well-named Gate of Felicity. Some of the quite small buildings are of exquisite appearance and many contain furnishings and decorations of the richest kind imaginable. A notable example is the domed bedroom of Murad III (1574–95) in gold, white and blue, with a beautiful Kufic inscription on a deep blue background running in a band around the walls. Next door is the handsome building known as 'the Cage', with a central courtyard and iron grilles. It was the residence of the Sultan's brothers, a dangerous class to belong to.

One of the most attractive pavilions is the Chinili kiosk which, although dating from 1473, is actually outside the palace walls. It is square in plan, with a dome and an elegant and refined arcaded portico. Its form was influential on later Ottoman architecture, but it is chiefly famous for the glazed earthenware tiles from Iznik with which it is covered. The open-sided Baghdad kiosk, built by Murad IV to celebrate his capture of that city in 1638, has its own pool and stone fountain, surrounded by a marble terrace. The women's quarters (*harem*), a warren of small buildings and chambers with small domes and pinnacles, form a palace within a palace on the north-east.

LEFT
The main gateway to the Topkapi Palace.

OPPOSITE RIGHT and LEFT
In the astonishing maze of the Topkapi, the eye is constantly caught by fascinating sights and structures. It contains about 100 individual buildings.

Masjid-i Shah, Isfahan

The Safavids, a native dynasty, reunited Iran in the early 16th century and reached a peak in the reign of Shah Abbas I, called the Great (1587–1629). He moved the capital to Isfahan and, in a rare example of Iranian town planning, reorganized the whole city in a series of interlinked squares according to the grandest plans conceivable. The largest square, in the north, is the Maidan-i Shah, a vast open space big enough for polo, with a major building complex on three sides. One of these is the Masjid-i Shah, or Royal Mosque, the greatest building in a magnificent city. Its monumental gateway, with minarets 110-ft (34-m) high,

occupies a substantial part of the southern side of the *maidan*. In order to align with Mecca while maintaining the integrity of the square, the mosque is set at an angle of about 45 degrees to the gateway, yet this is hardly apparent on the ground. The same plan was followed in the slightly earlier Mosque of Shaykh Lutfallah on the east side of the square.

The building largely follows Seljuk tradition, conforming to the four-*iwan* plan, each leading to a domed hall and flanked by double-storey arcades with pointed niches of the Seljuk type. The largest *iwan* is on the *qibla* (i.e. nearest Mecca) side and has a truly massive portal and dome, itself set on a large drum. Beyond the

iwans east and west of the courtyard are *madrasas* or religious colleges. The whole complex was completed in only four years, 1612–16, though the decoration took longer.

The visible exteriors of the mosque are largely covered with ceramic tiles, in colour predominantly blue or turquoise, cool colours contrasting agreeably with the warm tones of brickwork and landscape round about. The interior tiling is mainly polychrome; up to seven colours were fired at the same time. Designs are varied and fluid, mostly based on stylized floral devices. The concentration on decorative façades is a departure from Seljuk tradition which was less determined to conceal structure.

The Khwaju Bridge represents the culmination of the Seljuk tradition. Not only is it a means of crossing the river, it is a delightful place to pause and enjoy the beauty of the situation.

Khwaju Bridge, Isfahan

Muslims are historically great travellers, partly because of the popularity of the pilgrimage, partly because of the importance of trade in Islam. Good rulers were almost invariably builders of roads, bridges and caravanserais, although, for the most part, the roads of Islam followed the ways trodden out by earlier people, such as the Sassanids in Iran, while in the Near East and North Africa there was the example of the Romans. Former structures, or parts of them, were often incorporated. Bridges are also unusual in Islamic architecture because, being totally functional, no attempt is usually made to disguise their structure.

In Anatolia a number of Seljuk bridges not only survive today but, though heavily restored, are also still in use. These brick or stone arch bridges represent an advance on their Roman predecessors because the Seljuks were able to span a greater width by widening (and raising) the central arch, which is slightly pointed. (The famous single-arch Ottoman bridge at Mostar, destroyed in the recent Yugoslav wars but rebuilt, is similar.) There was often a caravanserai built close to the bridge, as at the particularly fine, five-arched bridge east of Antalya in ancient Pamphylia, southern Turkey.

Probably the most famous bridge in Islam is the Khwaju Bridge over the Zayandeh river in Isfahan, built by Shah Abbas II in the mid-17th century, which is exceptional in that aesthetic as well as practical ideas plainly governed its design. The river here is too shallow to be navigable, and the bridge, about 443-ft (135-m) long, is really a weir, the water deeper on the upstream side, with a road and superstructure. The latter is in essence a two-storey arcade, similar to those flanking the courtyard of a mosque, and is suitable for social gatherings as well as for crossing the river, with arched niches lining the roadway and larger structures in the centre and at each end. The passer-by may also descend steps down to the water.

Khan of Azad Pasha, Damascus

A *khan*, or *han* in Turkish, was the name given to a caravanserai in a city or town. They differed in several respects from caravanserais, which were usually situated in comparatively remote spots. They did not need a high, fortified wall, and had greater capacity for storing merchants' goods while not requiring to stock so much food and fodder. They often functioned as an exchange or market, and even a manufacturing centre, no doubt as a convenient social centre too. Comparatively few have survived to the present, being vulnerable to urban renewal as well as to the variety of disasters, natural and man-made, that have demolished most of the caravanserais; they sometimes seem to have been almost indistinguishable from markets (*suqs*). The famous market at Fustat on the Nile, destroyed in the 12th century, had tall houses lining the streets, reported to be up to 14-storeys-high, no doubt an exaggeration, which combined the functions of living accommodation and warehouses. A later successor was the 16th-century Khan al-Khalili, which was the primary market for luxury goods in Cairo. Later still, the important port of Suakin on the Red Sea had an immense *khan* equipped to handle caravans of 100 camels or more. The buildings around the courtyard were three- or four-storeys-high, with two sides of the square occupied by stores and warehouses.

Damascus was another great centre of trade and contained many *khans*, of which the largest was the Ottoman Khan of Azad Pasha, built around the mid-18th century. The courtyard was roofed and covered by nine domes, and the surrounding buildings were organized on the common system, with living quarters above storerooms and stables. The columns and arches that supported the domes, and that are still standing, were built in alternate bands of light and dark marble, as in the Great Mosque of Cordoba and elsewhere. The main stone gateway into the *khan* from the *suq* (*souk*) next door is decorated with colourful *muqarnas*.

The mightiest khan in this great trading city of Damascus, the coutyard was once roofed and covered by nine domes; the surrounding buildings were organized on the common system with living quarters above storerooms and stables.

Madrasa of Mir-i Arab, Bukhara

Education is closely linked with worship in Islam and distinguishing between a mosque and a *madrasa* (literally school) is often difficult because early mosques, beginning with the Prophet's house in Medina, were used for either purpose. When the *madrasa* became established as an institution – it is believed to have originated in Seljuk Khorasan – it closely resembled the four-*iwan* mosque in plan. Minor differences included the absence of a minaret. Teaching, which was often conducted in an informal way with the students forming a circle on the ground and the teacher leaning on a pillar, took place in the *iwans*, and accommodation for students was ranged along the intervening walls. Rooms might be rather spartan, though some *madrasas*, such as the Madrasa-i Shah in Isfahan, are extremely elegant.

The ancient city of Bukhara, already flourishing when the Arabs conquered it in 709, is famous as a seat of learning. Its *madrasas* include the Mir-i Arab, built about 1535, when Bukhara was entering its most glorious period as capital of an extensive Uzbek state. It was one of only two *madrasas* allowed to function in the Soviet Union (the other was in Tashkent). Founded by a Yemeni sheikh, for whom it is named, it was built (possibly under the Sheikh's direction since he is described as an architect) on the four-*iwan* plan, with 100 cells for students studying Islamic literature, law and Arabic. It is not open to non-Muslims, who can admire from a distance the calligraphy and mosaic around the drums supporting its two blue domes but are said to be missing some of the finest ceramic decoration in Bukhara.

Among other *madrasas* of Bukhara are the 15th-century Madrasa of Ulugh Beg and, standing opposite it, the later Madrasa of Abdal-Aziz Khan, begun in 1645, which resembles it in plan though it is much larger. Apart from its great size, its most notable feature is the great *pishtaq* (gateway), which is beautifully decorated with mosaic, plaster relief work and painting. Immediately south of the Mir-i Arab Madrasa is the 19th-century Madrasa of Amir Alim Khan, which breaks with architectural tradition and seems to have been primarily used as a library.

The Madrasa of Mir-i Arab was built according to a four-iwan plan, with 100 cells to accommodate students.

THE 20TH CENTURY

CHAPTER NINE

Auditorium Building, Chicago

Guaranty Building, Buffalo

The Exchange, Amsterdam

Flatiron Building, New York

AEG Turbine Factory, Berlin

Grand Central Station, New York

Helsinki Railway
Station

Einstein Tower, Potsdam

Chilehaus, Hamburg

Selfridge's Department Store

Bauhaus, Dessau

Sydney Harbour Bridge

Golden Gate Bridge, San Francisco

Church of the Sacred Heart, Prague

Fallingwater, Pennsylvania

Johnson Wax Building, Racine

Chrysler Building, New York

Empire State Building, New York

Rockefeller Center, New York

Seagram Building, New York

Eames House, Santa Monica

Ford House, Illinois

Unité d'Habitation, Marseilles

Chapel of Notre Dame du Haut,
Ronchamp

The Atomium, Brussels

Coventry Cathedral

Guggenheim Museum, New York

Maracaibo Lake Bridge, Venezuela

Gateway Arch, St Louis

TWA Terminal, New York

Palace of Labour, Turin

Brasilia Cathedral

Marina City, Chicago

Lake Point Tower, Chicago

Habitat, Montreal

University of East Anglia, Norwich

Sydney Opera House

Neue Staatsgalerie, Stuttgart

Pompidou Centre, Paris

Lloyd's Building, London

High Museum of Art, Atlanta

Commerzbank, Frankfurt

Reichstag, Berlin

Petronas Towers, Kuala Lumpur

Guggenheim Museum, Bilbao

The 20th century was dominated by what is called the Modern Movement, a name that will grow increasingly inappropriate as time goes on. Influenced by such figures as Gropius and Mies van der Rohe, patriarchs of the Bauhaus, the cradle of Modernism, and less obviously but no less importantly by the prodigious genius of Le Corbusier, a new international style which, though it cannot be pinned down in a sentence or two, developed from several basic ideas. They sprang first from technological advance and new materials, iron, glass and reinforced concrete, which created such possibilities as the skyscraper, and a fairly rigid devotion to the idea that the function of a building should define its form; 'form follows function', in the words of the doyen of the Chicago School, Louis Sullivan. In other words, buildings should be 'honest'.

Architects looked to the future, not the past. They rejected historical styles and sought a new kind of architecture adapted to a new age, an architecture that was useful, democratic and universal, which led to what came to be called the International Modern style. Its spread was facilitated by the great advances in communications and mobility, comparable to the effect of the invention of printing in movable type on the spread of knowledge in Renaissance Europe. Architects all over the world knew exactly what their colleagues were up to. Paradoxically, the effect of the Nazis' closing down of the Bauhaus was actually to increase its international influence, notably in the USA, where many of its leading figures took refuge. However, within the general criteria of Modernism, great variations existed, national differences did not altogether disappear under the impact of the International Modern style, and it is increasingly obvious in retrospect that many of the best 20th-century architects were 'modern' without being 'Modernist'. Hence, perhaps, the rigid dogmatism of Modernists, manifested at its

most extreme in such statements as that of Adolf Loos, back in 1908, that 'Ornament is crime', and more subtly by Mies, 'Less is more'.

While classic buildings such as Mies van der Rohe's Seagram Building are likely to command respect indefinitely, the proliferation of inferior glass and concrete blocks after the Second World War, many of them highly non-functional in that they were loathed by the people who lived or worked in them, caused increasing restlessness. But what next? By about 1970, architects in general were rejecting the strict tenets of Modernism, but no clear idea had emerged of what should replace it. Post-Modernism is something of a bran tub: one ingredient is the High Tech style of, for instance, the Centre Pompidou, a transparent building that emphasizes the engineering. Concrete, previously admired for strength and honesty, is often used in freer, more sculptural forms, often precast. There is more colour, sometimes in startling tones, and some masquerade, forms pretending to be something other than they are; there is deliberate provocation, such as hefty columns combined with fragile walls, and calculated bad taste, like Disneyland. There is more symbolism, not always easy to interpret. There is often humour too, a well-known example being the AT & T building (1978) of the American veteran Philip Johnson, which has a broken pediment like a Chippendale bureau; but the trouble with architectural jokes on that scale is that they quickly stale. And of course architects haven't all gone to California to get high. Most of them are serious and committed, and a firm like Norman Foster and Partners has produced a succession of innovative and effective buildings, making use of the unstoppable advance of technology, including computers. One thing is certain. Although architecture inevitably remains international, it is far more varied. Style has returned.

Auditorium Building, Chicago

In the last quarter of the 19th century, Modernism arrived, though not at once and not everywhere. New man-made materials and new engineering techniques on the one hand, and the failing of the dynamic of architectural style on the other, gave rise to a growing awareness that the future belonged to the new methods and new materials, and that the primary consideration in designing a building should be, not its appearance, but its purpose. Or, in the words of Louis Sullivan, the leading figure of the Chicago School, 'form follows function'.

Iron had been used to strengthen buildings, and the idea of using iron as the frame of a building was current as early as the 1850s though not until later were such buildings regarded as 'architecture'. This technique resulted in a completely new type of building, the skyscraper. But that only became a practical proposition after other developments in the 1850s: the spread of Bessemer's convertor, which sharply reduced the cost of steel-making, and the invention of a successful elevator, or lift, by Elisha Otis.

This was also the era of architectural partnerships, with architects often working in teams such as (in Chicago) Adler & Sullivan, who were responsible for the Auditorium Building (1886–89), Burnham & Root, and Holabird & Roche, architects of the Tacoma Building (1886–88).

The Auditorium Building was a revolutionary concept, one of the first multi-use structures, and included a hotel, offices and a large performance hall.

Although Buffalo's Guaranty Building obeys Sullivan's dictum that form follows function, he was equally interested in ornament, which at least one contemporary scholar regards as the area of his greatest genius. The feathery foliage (right) is characteristic.

Guaranty Building, Buffalo

The leading figure of the Chicago School was Louis Sullivan (1856–1924), by birth and upbringing a New Englander of part-Irish descent, who moved to Chicago in 1873. He worked first for William Jenney, whose Home Insurance Building of 1883, with iron beams and girders, was one step away from the metal skeleton, and spent a year in Paris at the École des Beaux-Arts before joining Dankmar Adler in the firm that became known as Adler and Sullivan.

Sullivan's first metal-skeleton building was the ten-floor Wainwright Building in St Louis (1890); it was followed by the the Guaranty Building in Buffalo (1894), 14-storeys-high, both notable landmarks among the first large office blocks. As in the Wainwright Building, the structure is quite evident in the exterior appearance, a grid-like arrangement of identical cells, and uncompromisingly vertical. The

ground floor is more spacious and is suggestive of the future fashion for raising buildings on *pilotis* or pillars. But in spite of his emphasis on function, Sullivan was not at all averse to decoration, in fact he was hardly less interested in decoration than he was in the expression of structure. It is most evident in the brick cladding of the Guaranty Building, especially on the topmost floor below the overreaching cornice. Sullivan's delicate, abstract, decorative patterns, which tend to vanish at any distance, place him unexpectedly close to Art Nouveau, though he later came to feel that current ornamentation of buildings was retrograde. But then the notion that 'form follows function', while it may look forward to the Bauhaus, also looks back to the 'truth to materials' principles of William Morris and John Ruskin and the Gothic Revival.

The work of the Chicago School effectively rejected dependence on historical styles. That did not mean that the past ceased to have any influence on the present, far from it; but the heavyweight revivalism of the mid-19th century which Sullivan so deplored was finally and no doubt permanently abandoned.

Berlage's massive Exchange Building, a very personal structure displaying its architect's profound knowledge of historical forms, was of seminal influence in the development of Modernism.

OPPOSITE
Detail of the clock face on the tower, showing Berlage's close attention to detail.

The Exchange, Amsterdam

This massive brick building has three large trading halls, of which the Commodities Exchange is the largest, with a glass roof supported by parabolic iron beams and broad but unobtrusive arcades on the lower levels. Around the halls are grouped offices and other smaller rooms; the Amsterdam chamber of commerce met in the large room above the entrance.

The original design won an open competition in 1884, though the building when finished (1903) was somewhat different. It is the masterpiece of the influential Dutch architect, Hendrik Berlage (1856–1934), and is one of the icons of what is sometimes called the 'proto-modern' movement that includes Art Nouveau, where Berlage is sometimes placed. His influence depended largely on his writing and lecturing, and he was the first great European champion of Frank Lloyd Wright, even before he had seen any of Wright's buildings. Yet he was essentially a traditionalist, sympathetic to the Romanesque especially, and influenced by Viollet-le-Duc's insistence that even the Gothic style was essentially practical and logical rather than spiritual in motivation. Berlage's liking for historical materials and his emphasis on 'honesty' in architecture went so far as refusing to apply plaster to a brick wall, even in a domestic interior. He was not against historicism, but only against that aspect of it called eclecticism, the selective exploitation of historical styles that marked the 1880s and 1890s. 'What is modern?' he asked, 'Usually something ... without a distinct character ... modern Gothic, modern Renaissance, and even modern Norse, Indian, Japanese ... If

it weren't so sad one could laugh at it.'

Berlage's Amsterdam Exchange is a testament to his mastery of past styles, especially the Romanesque, evident in the use of round arches as well as the massive scale, and to his love of brick (there are some details in stone); but he also openly embraces contemporary technique, for instance in the iron trusses supporting the roof of the main hall, which are left exposed.

351

Flatiron Building, New York

The proper name for this heroic survivor of the first age of the skyscraper, whose place in popular affection should safeguard it from demolition, is the Fuller Building; but it was called the Flatiron Building from the time it was built, in 1901–03, and is a comment on its unusual shape. It occupies an awkward triangular site on 23rd Street where it is crossed by Broadway and Fifth Avenue. It was built by the firm of Daniel H. Burnham (formerly Burnham and Root, pioneers of the steel-frame building in Chicago); but at this time Burnham was occupied with his town-planning schemes and the architect credited with the design of the Flatiron Building is Charles B. Atwood.

A certain amount of myth has accrued to the Flatiron Building. City guides sometimes maintain that it was the first steel-frame building, which of course it was not, and that it was New York's first real skyscraper, which

people feared would fall over. In fact it was not the tallest building in New York in 1902, and any fears that it would tumble probably arose from its shape. It is essentially a three-sided building but unlike, say, the Chilehaus in Hamburg, the 'sharp' end is rounded off and is about 6.5-ft (2-m) wide at the narrowest point.

The building is 285-ft (87-m) tall and 21-storeys-high and, when built, loomed mightily above its neighbours. Described by one critic as 'an energetic mix of Gothic and Renaissance styles', it obeys the Classical three-tier division of base, tall middle section and top, it is clad in rusticated stone, with dirt-collecting terracotta reliefs of flowers and busts, and is altogether unashamedly decorative. The central section is also divided into three by vertical lines of slightly bowed pairs of windows. With its great height and dramatic shape, it impressed even New Yorkers.

New York City has always displayed a sometimes breathtaking readiness to pull down the old, however honourable, in order to build something bigger, if not necessarily better; but the Flatiron building has survived.

Paradoxically, modern architecture was largely pioneered in industrial structures that were not then regarded as architecture at all, a result of the hierarchical divide between art and craft.

AEG Turbine Factory, Berlin

Peter Behrens (1868–1940) was originally a painter and designer sympathetic to the Arts and Crafts movement and Art Nouveau. His career took a new direction when in 1900 he was invited to the artists' colony at Darmstadt where, like Josef Olbrich, he designed his own very original (despite debts to Charles Rennie Mackintosh) Art Nouveau house. In 1907 he and Olbrich were among the founding members of the Deutscher Werkbund, which embraced industrial design as well as craftsmanship, and in the same year he was appointed architectural adviser to the progressively minded AEG company, for whom he designed everything from office blocks and manufacturing plants to office stationery and electric toasters. But what,

above all, makes him one of the most admired of the immediate precursors of Modernism, was his industrial buildings.

Behrens's massive, monumental Turbine Factory (1909) was part of a vast industrial complex. It was his first and most important industrial building, the first basically steel-and-glass structure in Germany and one of the first anywhere to proclaim that a factory is or can be 'architecture'. A highly functional building, which employed the most sophisticated engineering methods, it was built on a light steel frame, and its powerful-looking (in fact thin) concrete corner elements, a common Behrens characteristic, are clearly not load-bearing. Although there is no obvious connection with any historical style, the Turbine

Factory has a certain timeless monumentality that suggests a Classical heritage; the front has the general form of a Classical temple, while columns march along the sides. (Some of Behrens's later, non-industrial buildings, such as the German Embassy in St Petersburg, had more obvious Neoclassical attributes.) It is also, in spite of the architect's arts-and-crafts sympathies (others see a greater resemblance to a barn than a temple), an anthem to industry on a massive scale, as Behrens, reluctantly or not intended, for in an article published in 1908 he defined 'monumental art' as an expression of whatever is the dominant force of the time. He became an extremely influential teacher, with no less a trio than Le Corbusier, Gropius and Mies van der Rohe among his students.

RIGHT
Disgust at the destruction
of Penn Station,
generally regarded as the
finer structure, saved
Grand Central from a
similar fate, though not
from the looming
presence of the 1960s
Pan-Am Building.

OPPOSITE
The concourse of Grand
Central, before its recent
restoration.

Grand Central Station, New York

In the early 20th century, before the challenge of motor vehicles had made itself felt, railways were still very big business, especially in the USA, for whose booming prosperity they were largely responsible. The railway companies not only had the resources to build grand new stations but, relatively progressive in spirit, they were one of the few patrons for adventurous architectural schemes on a large scale. The two outstanding products of these circumstances were both in New York City, where Pennsylvania Station (1902–11) and Grand Central (1903–13) were built at roughly the same time.

Both were inspired by the monumental structures of ancient Rome: the Baths of Caracalla are frequently mentioned as a source for Penn Station. Equally, they were a total success from a functional point of view, and made use of the latest engineering techniques. Penn Station was the work of the outstanding firm of McKim, Mead and White, which was also responsible in New York for the Washington Triumphal Arch and Columbia University. Sadly, and to the irritation of thousands, the station was needlessly demolished in 1963. Grand Central only escaped a similar fate after a defensive campaign that ended victoriously in the US Supreme Court.

In 1900 trains ran by steam, and it was an accident caused by a build-up of steam underground that led to the reconstruction of the station, with electric engines replacing steam. This allowed more freedom in placing about 100 platforms, on two levels, below the streets of Manhattan. The original architects

were a Mid-Western firm that concentrated on railways, but in 1911 Warren and Whitmore, former students, like McKim, at the École des Beaux-Arts in Paris, took over the project; they were responsible for the famous concourse,

perhaps the world's most famous rendezvous, a gigantic and astonishingly quiet space over 27,000sq ft (2,500sq m) in area and 125-ft (38-m) high. If the traveller is delayed, there is no more attractive place to wait for a train.

357

Helsinki Railway Station

Nationalism is often a spur to architectural innovation, not necessarily in the best of taste. Finland, a country that has produced a disproportionate number of brilliant architects in the past century, was looking towards emancipation from Russian control in the early years of the 20th century, and this encouraged a return to traditional, solid and simple methods and materials of building, based on the abundance of timber and rugged granite. The National Romantic style also bore an affinity with the masculine style of the great American architect, Henry H. Richardson (1838–86), with his shingled houses and solid Romanesque masonry, whose buildings, incidentally, included a number of small railway stations.

In partnership with others, Eliel Saarinen (1873–1950) built the Finnish Pavilion for the Paris Exposition Universelle in 1900, and by himself, the National Museum in Helsinki in 1905, a fairly typical product of the Finnish national style. His railway station, which won a competition in 1904 and was built, after a series of revisions, in 1906–14, also belongs basically to the Finnish National Romantic school, with a flavour of Art Nouveau, but advances a large step forward. This self-assured and monumental building made a considerable impact far beyond Finland, establishing Saarinen on the international scene and easing his future move to the USA in 1923, when he had become more of a Modernist.

The Helsinki Station is both massive and sleek. Its powerful, greyish granite is elegantly sculpted, and the tall clock tower, soon to spawn progeny in both Europe and North America, is almost slick. The massive round

arch of the main hall, delicately scalloped in outline, is famously flanked by pairs of vast, decorative *atlantes*, each holding a large lamp. Saarinen, who had studied painting as well as architecture, was married to a sculptress, Louise

Gesellius, and collaborated with her and other sculptors in later buildings. This interest was to be inherited by his son, and for a time his partner, Eero.

Façade of the elder Saarinen's most famous building (opposite), with (below) a detail of the light-bearing figures flanking the entrance.

Einstein Tower, Potsdam

Erich Mendelsohn (1887–1953), starved of commissions for a considerable period of his life, was one of the major European architects of the 20th century, though the quality of his imitators was not always impressive. The Einstein Tower is one of his most famous buildings, though one of his least influential. He was fascinated by buildings whose form is not dictated by function, which are more like Expressionist sculptures, moulded rather than built; he designed, or at least sketched, many of them while he was stationed on the Russian Front during the First World War. The drawings made a stir at an exhibition in Berlin after the war, but the Einstein Tower is the only one that was ever built, mainly in 1917–21. It originated in a project encouraged by an assistant of Einstein, then a professor in Berlin, to test the theory of relativity. It had an observatory on top and a laboratory in the basement. The government presented the land at Potsdam, and the official inauguration took place in 1924.

One acknowledged influence was the theatre (1914) for the Deutscher Werkbund, the design-oriented group founded in 1907 by Behrens and Olbrich among others, by the Belgian Henry van der Velde, which Mendelsohn admired for its 'concrete used in the Art Nouveau style, but strong in conception and expression'. Unfortunately, German industry was in ruins after the destruction of the First World War; as Mendelsohn was unable to obtain the flexible material he needed – reinforced concrete – he was forced to use brick, steel and concrete, disguising this amalgam by covering the whole building with plaster to suggest uniformity of material. Nevertheless, the result, which faintly resembles some futuristic form of transport, is highly dramatic and uniquely original. One curious effect remarked on by many is that the building appears to be larger than it actually is.

The form of the Einstein Tower was to some extent affected by the exigencies of the German post-war economy, but it is one of the most interesting structures of an immensely fertile architect.

Awkward sites often generate interesting solutions, as in Höger's Expressionist masterpiece in Hamburg, with its spear-like leading edge.

Chilehaus, Hamburg

The influential Deutscher Werkbund, an association of craftsmen, designers and others founded in 1907, had obvious affinities with the earlier English Arts and Crafts movement, although it was more sympathetic to machines and mass-production, which, by 1907, had clearly come to stay. One of the founders of the Werkbund, Hermann Muthesius, had spent some years in England and was an expert on the Arts and Crafts movement. He in turn influenced younger German architects like Fritz Höger (1877–1949). As a result, the revivalist English domestic architecture represented by Philip Webb, Charles Voysey and others makes itself felt in the building that is generally considered to be one of the architectural masterpieces of German Expressionism, the Chile House in Hamburg, which was built in 1922–23 and somehow survived the carnage of 1943.

In fact, Höger's earlier private houses exhibit that connection more closely. He was the best known of a group of architects who revived the North German tradition of dark red brick in the years after the First World War. The Chilehaus, built for a shipping company engaged in the nitrates trade with Chile is, like the Flatiron Building in New York, a fine demonstration of how to turn an awkward, roughly triangular site to advantage. At the sharp angle, one might almost say the prow, the roof line sweeps up to a sharp point. The ocean-liner impression is furthered by the exaggeration of perspective resulting from the shape, and confirmed by the audacious, asymmetrical 'wave' in the long south façade. The base is a round-arched arcade, occupied by shops, with odd but effective twin porches

flanking the angle; the walls of the top three (of eight) storeys are recessed in an unusual and highly effective way, both vertically and horizontally, the breaks marked by a change

from rectangular to rounded windows below projecting balconies. Altogether, the Chilehaus is a triumph and a startlingly original design, perfectly suited to its place and function.

Selfridge's Department Store

Oxford Street, London, is one of the world's great shopping centres, full of 'shops as big as towns'. In recent years, the numbers of the big stores have been depleted as less costly means of retail selling have been developed, but Selfridge's, the first, the biggest and the mostest, still flourishes.

H. Gordon Selfridge, though British-born, was a junior partner in Marshall Field of Chicago, the first great American department store, who in 1906 decided to try something similar in England. He had backing from the furniture firm of Waring and Gillow on condition that Selfridge's did not sell furniture, and some mind-blowing schemes for this vast temple of consumerism were put forward; the end result, though more sane than some, was exotic enough, though subtlety was not on the brief. The original scheme was apparently by Daniel Burnham, the famous pioneer of the Chicago School, but the architect on the spot was Frank Swales, together with others. Although the store opened in 1909, when the western part of Oxford Street was largely neglected and unvisited, the building was not entirely finished until 1928; the huge central tower that was part of the original plan remained unbuilt.

The store looks like an oversized Roman palace, in an approximation of the Ionic Order and on a steel frame. The base contains the all-important shop windows, between piers, with the hefty columns rising from the second storey. The *pièce de résistance* is the clock above the entrance, with a robed, winged, female figure in bronze, by Gilbert Bayes, standing on a stone ship's prow and attended by tritons. The open-

plan interior was a novelty in Edwardian Britain. Customers could stroll about, freely inspecting the wares without being pressured by salesmen or stared at by security guards; there were other amenities such as restaurants and wash rooms, as well as 'events' and exhibitions, like the first demonstration of television.

Detail of the clock and sculpture group above the main entrance of Selfridge's.

Gropius's designs for the
Bauhaus buildings at
Dessau proclaimed the
doctrines of what became
the International Modern
movement.

RIGHT
The tower containing
student accommodation
(right), looking towards
the main block
containing workshops.

OPPOSITE
The main entrance, with
the two-storey office block
above the road and the
teaching block to the left.

OVERLEAF
The main entrance seen
from the front.

Bauhaus, Dessau

In 1919 Henry van der Velde resigned as director of an arts-and-crafts school in Weimar and recommended Walter Gropius (1883–1969) as his successor. Gropius was a former student of Peter Behrens, an advocate of mass-production in housing, and one of the originators of the International Modern style exemplified in cubic blocks, glass walls, no extraneous decoration, asymmetrical composition and little colour other than white. The Bauhaus ('Building House'), as Gropius renamed it, aimed to encourage all kinds of artists to work together to 'build the future'. Perhaps his greatest achievement was to make a potentially difficult group of the finest contemporary artists and designers co-operate so successfully.

The Bauhaus was originally dominated by Expressionism and the arts-and-crafts tradition, but soon became oriented more towards technology and industry. It became the heart of the International Modern Movement, and when it moved to Dessau in 1925–26, after its left-leanings had prompted the Weimar government to withhold funds, Gropius designed new buildings that were intended to represent the 'new unity' of art and technology, as proclaimed by Gropius in a 1924 memorandum. The complex comprised the impressive main building with its huge glass walls, several other buildings including a two-storey structure that bridged a street and housed Gropius's office and homes for teachers. The students' (originally called 'apprentices') block included a gymnasium as well as classrooms, dining hall and living accommodation. There was also a theatre. Function is the guide to form, and the

buildings, which have recently been restored, are no less visually impressive for being well-adapted to practical purposes.

Gropius resigned in 1928 and was eventually succeeded by Ludwig Mies van der Rohe. As at Weimar earlier, the school fell from political favour and was shut down in 1932.

Mies restarted it on a private basis in Berlin, but when the Nazis gained power in 1933, they closed it for good. In a way this was the making of the Bauhaus, because its staff and ideas were scattered abroad, to the USA in particular, and its influence thus greatly expanded.

RIGHT and OVERLEAF Practical considerations apart, the Sydney Harbour Bridge gave Australia's chief city a landmark to compare with Big Ben, the Eiffel Tower or the Statue of Liberty.

Sydney Harbour Bridge

The desirability of a north-south crossing (some favoured a tunnel) of Sydney Harbour became increasingly pressing as the city underwent rapid expansion in the late 19th century. The project was first put out to local tender in 1900, but all 24 designs were considered wanting and over 20 years passed before work began.

The presiding genius of the bridge was the chief engineer John Bradfield, the builders the British firm of Dorman and Long. As an arch bridge carrying a heavy load, including a railway, careful planning was needed to avoid making costly changes later; Ralph Freeman of London, the consulting engineer, filled 28 books with calculations. As it was, the bridge would be expensive to maintain, needing constant repainting. A suspension bridge would have been less expensive both to build and maintain, but it would not have been the grand monument that Sydney was expecting.

About 800 houses had to be demolished before construction began in 1924. About 1,400 workers were employed and 16 were killed in accidents. The span of the main arch between the pylons is 1,650ft (503m) and clearance above the water is 170ft (52m), allowing free passage to the largest ships. The total length is 3,770ft (1149m). The arch was built out from the sides, held by steel cables, and with hinges at each end to spread the load and the permitted substantial sway in high winds. When the two sides of the arch were finished, the cables were slackened off over 12 days to bring them together. The deck was then built from the centre outwards.

The bridge opened in 1932. The opening ceremony did not go quite according to plan, because the Labour prime minister's cutting of the ribbon was pre-empted by a royalist militia officer who rode up and slashed through it with his sword, 'for King and Empire' (he was charged with damaging government property). Today, although assisted by the Gladesville Bridge (opened 1964, the world's longest concrete span) and the Sydney Harbour Tunnel (1992), the bridge can barely cope with the unanticipated increase in traffic, more than ten times what it was in 1932.

Golden Gate Bridge, San Francisco

Although in recent years its span has been many times exceeded, the Golden Gate Bridge was for years the longest suspension bridge in the world. It is one of the engineering marvels of the 20th century and, due largely to its superb situation, is a magnificent and evocative spectacle.

The Golden Gate is the strait between San Francisco Bay and the Pacific Ocean, about 3-miles (5-km) long and up to 2-miles (3-km) wide. Though the bridge was first proposed in 1872 as a great maritime asset, it presented a serious obstacle to overland communications in a fast-developing area. The idea was revived in 1916 and the city polled leading engineers. Many considered a bridge impossible, others put the cost at over $100 million; but one veteran, Joseph B. Strauss (1870–1938), believed not only that it was possible but that it could be done for only $30 million (the actual cost was £35 million). Strauss was an experienced bridge builder and specialized in long spans; his earlier bridges included the George Washington Bridge over the Hudson at New York City.

Lacking state or federal funding, capital was raised by a bond issue secured against tolls. The statistics were daunting. The main span was 4,200ft (1280m), a world record and, as this was a major shipping lane, the roadway had to be 220ft (67m) above the water at high tide. The towers for the suspension cables were 500ft (152m) above the bridge deck, and the load of the main cables on each tower was 61,500 tons.

In spite of strong opposition from the ferry companies, the project was approved in

1923–24 and Strauss's scheme accepted in 1930. Construction began in 1933. Safety precautions were elaborate, and included a net suspended under the deck, which saved the lives of 19 men, though not of 12 on a section of

scaffolding that fell and broke the net. The bridge was formally opened in 1937, just six months after the San Francisco–Oakland Bay Bridge, which was built with government funding at almost double the cost.

The romantic Golden Gate Bridge by night and by day.

Plecnik was a little-known figure until quite recently, but his remarkable, uniquely personal style and his inexhaustible fund of ideas are now seen as indications of a true genius.

Church of the Sacred Heart, Prague

Josip Plecnik (1872–1957) is something of an odd man out among 20th-century architects. A few years ago, few people had heard of him; now, he is increasingly seen as a remarkable genius, with an apparently inexhaustible fund of ideas, but with little sympathy for his own time. He belonged to no school and left no followers. His architecture seems to be an attempt to express the whole process of civilization, which led him to use the styles and ideas of the past, but in a thoroughly imaginative way.

Born in Ljubljana, Plecnik was a devout Catholic and a committed Slav who worked mainly in the Slav lands. He trained in Vienna under Otto Wagner and arrived in Prague in 1911 as head of the School of Decorative Arts, remaining in the Czech capital for over 30 years. He was employed at the castle under President Masaryk, though arguments over his alterations led to his departure in 1935. His most notable building is the Church of the Sacred Heart (1928–32) in Zizkov, a district somewhat removed from the tourist-packed historical area. Elements of Plecnik's romantic nationalism, religious devotion, historicism, rationality and not least of all his bravura gift for design are all displayed in this extraordinary church, which, if it had been built 40 or 50 years later might be described as Postmodernist.

It is most remarkable from the outside. The first, immediate shock is the slab-like tower, almost as wide as the basilica it adorns, and whose restrained pediment it repeats. In the centre of the tower, in a touch of Surrealism, is a huge circular opening which contains a see-through clock. The lower part of the basilica

and of the tower is brick, the upper parts, together with doorways, plastered white. The building is simple yet decorative, with Classical

swags above the rows of small, almost-square windows, and vertical lines of projecting stones on the brick walls.

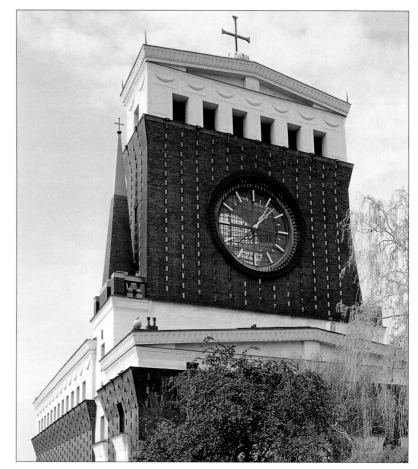

Fallingwater, Pennsylvania

Frank Lloyd Wright (1867–1959), the most famous American architect of the 20th century, lived the best part of a century himself and remained extraordinarily prolific for most of that time, designing a great variety of different types of building, finding his own solution to the problems posed by each one, never repeating himself, and never losing his creativity. He was very much his own man, subscribing to no school or style but relying on his own inspiration. As a young man he worked with Louis Sullivan, one of comparatively few architects he respected; he remained thoroughly American, negating his affinities with the Modern style, which in origin at least, was a European invention.

He first gained a reputation as a designer of houses for the rich in the Chicago area, the type he called 'Prairie Houses', low and spread out, with rooms opening into each other and with cantilevered roofs and terraces that merge with the landscape. Although larger projects began to come his way after about 1905, he continued to design private houses for the rest of his career, including his own, Taliesin in Wisconsin, which had three incarnations, a community of disciples over which he presided like a rather demanding guru. The most famous of his houses is Fallingwater (1936–39), at Bear Run in Pennsylvania.

Here Wright carried out the integration of house and landscape most successfully. The house is set among woods on a steep hillside; the ground floor is set on piers, with projecting terraces over a waterfall immediately below. There is a high vertical core in stone, while the remainder is in concrete and glass, which makes up most of the walls. Horizontal elements interpenetrate in a complex and inventive way. Thoroughly modern, this is also a romantic house (Wright's claim that it was partly based on a Mayan temple does not seem very significant), built as a country retreat for a city entrepreneur and retailer. Today it has become such an icon that, in summer at least, it is rather well frequented.

Fallingwater, probably the 20th century's most famous private house, combines Modernism and Romanticism.

Johnson Wax Building, Racine

The late 1930s was possibly Frank Lloyd Wright's most fertile period. The Johnson Wax Administration Building (1936–39) was built at about the same time as Fallingwater, and showed that he could bring a new vision to the design of offices as well as houses. This building is almost square in plan and basically a single-storey, with an executives' penthouse on top. It has rounded corners and the attractive brick walls are uninterrupted on all sides, except for the entrance. The lack of windows is the only obvious outward sign of a highly unconventional interior.

The office is open-plan, then still a novelty, and is lit by a continuous glass band round the top of the walls. The glass is in the form, not of panes, but of layers of Pyrex tubes, which are translucent but not transparent, though too high to look out of anyway. The other striking feature is the manner in which the roof, also a light source, is supported – by concrete columns with a reverse taper (thinner at the base) which, at the top, expand into flat mushroom forms. This system worried the building inspectors, and before he could get a permit Wright had to demonstrate that the columns could actually support six times as much weight as was required. The lofty 30-ft (9-m) office is too spacious to induce claustrophobia; Wright insisted that 'you catch no sense of enclosure whatever at any angle, top or sides... Interior space comes free, you are not aware of any boxing in at all'. He also designed the movable furniture, which included three-legged chairs for the typists that tipped up if they deviated from their correct posture.

At a time when some of the finest architects in Europe were arriving in the USA as refugees from Germany, there is something faintly uncomfortable about this building, brilliant though it is. The main later addition was a 15-storey tower (1944–50), which matched the brick and glass arrangement of its horizontal companion, even to the rounded corners. Inside, alternate floors are mezzanines cantilevered from the tower's concrete core, which contain elevator and services. Additional offices were also built adjoining the 1936 Administration Building.

RIGHT
The suggestion of a space rocket from early science fiction is even stronger when the Chrysler building is lit up at night.

OPPOSITE
Though increasingly challenged, the Chrysler Building remains a distinctive landmark among the towers of Manhattan.

Chrysler Building, New York

In the early years of the 20th century, there was a vogue for skyscrapers in the Gothic style, headed by New York's Woolworth Building (1913). Curious as this may seem to us, for historicists it had some logic, since a skyscraper is by definition a vertical building and verticality was the essence of Gothic. William van Alen in his building for the Chrysler Corporation also featured a spire, but a spire of an altogether different style and spirit. The gleaming, stainless-steel spire, with its arcs of sunbursts, is an Art Deco creation which, for no obvious reason, appears absolutely right. It also makes the building quite unmistakable (this is the one skyscraper that everyone recognizes, even though some may still regard it as frivolous). Art Deco, which has been described as a sort of pop-Modernism, had limited applications in architecture. Although there was a brief vogue for Art Deco skyscrapers, they lack the appeal of the Chrysler Building. The style did, however, prove ideal for the new pleasure palaces, the movie theatres.

The 77-storey Chrysler Building (1928–30) was originally commissioned by a construction company, but was taken over by motor magnate Walter P. Chrysler, who wanted a building to make people stop and stare. It was planned to be the highest in the world, exceeding the Eiffel Tower, and in the process tested the current technology to the limit. It included several decorative motifs referring to automobiles, such as the gargoyle-like radiator tops, although it was never occupied by the car company. It achieved its aim at a height of 1,046ft (319m), but held the record only for a matter of months before the Empire State Building outclimbed it. The architect, William van Alen (1883–1954), finds little coverage in textbooks and seems to have faded from view after his one great success. Among his other gifts, however, he was a showman: the steel-faced spire, seven-storeys-high, was put together inside the tower, so that no one except the workers saw it until, on the appointed day, it was raised through a hole in the top and fixed in position – all in 90 minutes.

Though outreached, since the 1970s, by the twin towers of Minoru Yamasaki's unappealing World Trade Center (1,350ft/411m), the Empire State Building is still the king of Manhattan's skyscrapers.

Empire State Building, New York

The USA, as we all know, is a country of wide open spaces, where small towns tend to spread themselves across the landscape in a way that seems profligate to visitors from the Old World. In the big cities, however, the opposite occurs. Office and apartment blocks shoot upwards, claiming the maximum possible space from a given site. The obvious explanation is that in cities like Chicago and New York, prime metropolitan building land is scarce and expensive. But is that the whole story? Perhaps the impulse to create ever more spectacular skyscrapers may have been rooted in a desire to pit human technology against the abundance of Nature. And there was a more mundane reason: a spectacular building carried more prestige and therefore higher rents.

No sooner had the spire of the Chrysler Building appeared to dominate the Manhattan skyline than the Empire State Building, a few blocks south, rose to challenge it. Whereas Chicago skyscrapers could go straight up from the street, New York's building restrictions demanded that very tall buildings be stepped back, to prevent streets and neighbouring buildings from being cast into permanent darkness. This was a rare example of planning regulations acting, on the whole, to enhance appearances.

The Empire State Building of 1929–31 was built at the beginning of the Great Depression. The architects were the firm of Richmond H. Shreeve, William Lamb and Arthur L. Harmon. It is a handsome, even elegant tower but, because it is set back, it is only visible from a distance; when Le Corbusier said he could lie down on the pavement and stare at it all day, he would have been disappointed by the view. In any case, the building acquired its immediate and lasting fame by its sheer size. At 1,250ft (381m), not including the mast, intended, apparently seriously, to provide mooring for airships, it was easily the tallest building in the world and held the record for over 40 years. Its steel frame is clad in stone and its Art Deco decoration is less assertive than that of the Chrysler Building. Well over 1 million people have been up to look at the view since 1931.

Views of the Rockefeller Center.

RIGHT
Hercules brandishing a skeletal globe.

OPPOSITE LEFT
A pedestrian area.

OPPOSITE RIGHT
The former RCA Building, whose extreme verticality makes it seem even taller than it is.

Rockefeller Center, New York

The Rockefeller Center was built between 1931 and 1940 in a consistent style, with strong verticals, belonging really to the Art Deco period. Although it could be said to be slightly out of date by the time the last building was completed, it represents the peak of high-rise construction in the interwar period and, although its heights mean nothing to the man and woman on the street, it has become an attractive area. One of the first great high-rise urban ensembles, it consists of ten major units (14 buildings altogether) occupying three city blocks between Fifth and Sixth Avenues in midtown Manhattan. A variety of architects, including Raymond Hood (1881–1934), architect of the Modernist McGraw-Hill Building not far away, worked on the buildings.

The Art Deco style is best displayed in the six-storey foyer of Radio City Music Hall, by Donald Deskey and others, which opened in 1932, the first building to be completed. The world's largest (6,000 seats) and technologically most advanced theatre, it soon became an international attraction. Predominantly, however, the Rockefeller Center was a commercial venture, sponsored by John D. Rockefeller Jnr, and the chief ingredients of the ensemble are office blocks. The largest is the former RCA building, with 70 storeys, which, being very thin, was found to require special bracing. It governs the axis of the other buildings, parallel or at right-angles, resulting in an interesting handling of space. There were also shops, restaurants, a second theatre (since demolished) and, most famously, a skating rink in an outdoor plaza, overlooked by a slightly comical golden Hercules. This is one of the most attractive public places in New York City on a winter evening, but it was something of an afterthought. The plaza was originally intended to be an area for small shops, but it attracted insufficient tenants. Recent advances in refrigeration techniques led someone to suggest, as a rather forlorn hope, a skating rink. Serendipity!

Seagram Building, New York

Ludwig Mies van der Rohe (1886–1969) was, with Le Corbusier, among the greatest exponents of the Modern style, and cannot be held responsible for the sometimes unfortunate influence he had on later, less talented builders of high-rise offices and apartments. Mies was director of the Bauhaus for the last three years before it was shut down by the Nazis. Soon afterwards he went to the USA and became a professor at the Illinois Institute of Technology in Chicago, for which he designed a new campus. Although his reputation was extremely high, at least among fellow-architects and designers as early as the 1920s, his buildings are comparatively few until after 1945, when he was nearly 60 years old.

By that time, Mies's austere style ('Less is more') was fully matured, and had already been displayed in his buildings for the Illinois Institute. His buildings are basically cubic or box-like in form, on a revealed steel frame, predominantly glass-walled, clean-lined and marked only by vertical and horizontal lines, with very precise detailing and virtually no decoration. (His first glass skyscraper was designed in 1921, though technology was not then up to building it.) In practical terms, they are very adaptable: the interior has no effect on the exterior, and Mies soon demonstrated that they were equally suitable as apartments or offices. In outline, it sounds a simple recipe, but the fact that his numerous imitators were responsible for so many awful buildings suggests that it was not. One of their more obvious failings was a lack of the acute awareness of proportion that is what Mies signally possessed.

The Seagram Building (1954–58), built by Mies with Philip Johnson for the big Canadian distillers, is by general consent the prime example of the Miesian office tower, and one of the finest buildings of the past half-century. The building, the largest of its kind when built, occupies only one-third of the site, rising from a broad plaza that introduces welcome space in a congested area east of Park Avenue. It rises in smooth lines, cliff-like, for 38 storeys, its seductive colour deriving from the fact that it is clad in bronze (one advantage that Mies enjoyed over inferior imitators was that he could usually spend more): the Seagram Building was notoriously expensive. Even the slightly earlier Lever Building (Skidmore, Owings and Merrill, 1951–52), a near neighbour and another superior example of the International Modern style, looks outclassed.

The rectangular office tower, based on simple principles (grid construction, mass-production of units, central service core, etc.) was an all-too-popular format. But the Seagram Building was not a signpost to the future, it was more of a ne plus ultra.

A dramatic street sculpture outside the Seagram Building.

Eames House, Santa Monica

The husband-and-wife team of Charles (1907–78) and Ray (1916–88) Eames was among the best design collaborations of the 1950s, from which came the famous moulded-plywood chair. California-based, they had Californian attitudes, a laid-back approach, no great high-art aspirations, and an amiable, sometimes inspired, eclecticism. Their house, No. 8, Pacific Palisades, tucked into woods on a hillside, was their only building. Though they lived in it, it was commissioned by *Arts and Architecture* magazine in 1947 as part of an effort to convince the house-buying public that modern designers had as much to offer as conventional builders.

The house (1945–50), its long and narrow plan dictated by the site, includes living quarters and a studio divided by a courtyard. The light and airy main living room ascends through two storeys and opens on to a roofed terrace. This means that the upper floor is only about half the area. But its most important characteristic is that it is a DIY house, made up of machine-made, mass-produced components selected from catalogues, and put together on what might be called the Meccano principle. It was no more expensive, and far more attractive, than a mass-produced, lowest-common-denominator developer's house, and far less expensive than a one-off, architect's house. Despite its steel frame, the house looks, and indeed is, extremely light and insubstantial, with a pronounced Japanese flavour; yet it has proved solid enough. The Eames House was designed to grow, or rather change, along with the tastes and requirements of the occupants. It is a negation of Classical order: there is no symmetry; parts were meant to be added or taken away without damaging the whole, something you cannot do with a Greek temple!

Though ideal for its place, time and purpose, the house has obvious limitations. The sunny climate is essential, and it is not suitable for young children as there is no rail on the spiral staircase. After completing it, the Eames turned to films and never built another house, thought they did design one. They had great influence internationally, not for the architecture of the house itself, but in the approach to building that it represented.

Goff designed and built a large number of remarkably disparate houses. The Ford House is one of his most successful.

Ford House, Illinois

Bruce Goff (1904–82) began his career in Chicago in the 1930s but moved to the south, teaching for some years at the University of Oklahoma. His buildings, almost exclusively private houses, make a strange and varied collection. It is difficult to imagine him finding so many clients in any country other than the USA, for Goff was an eccentric. His early work may show the influence of Frank Lloyd Wright, with whom he had studied, and he also shared Wright's tendency towards the bizarre in later years. He has been called an Organic Expressionist Modern, all relevant terms, but rather too inclusive to be helpful. For all that, his houses are technically very well planned, and many, like the Wilson House (1950) at Pensacola – wholly timber-built, while employing avant-garde devices – now look almost traditional.

An early building, Colmorgan House (1937) in Glenview, near Chicago, is in fact fairly conventional, in that it is a wood-frame house with projecting roofs and the massive masonry central block of the chimney, redolent of Wright. Nevertheless, it hints at the more audacious, open-ended approach of Goff's later houses.

Of these, the Samuel Ford Residence (1949) is perhaps the most successful. It is a low, round, domed building, 166-ft (51-m) across, with a red-painted steel frame. The steel dome is covered with dark shingles and admits light through a central lantern with spectacular effect inside, where the upper floor takes the form of a gallery. Construction is simple, much is prefabricated, and the house illustrates Goff's liking both for simple materials and complex forms. It also looks forward 20 years or so to the types of house devised by and for the ecologically-minded.

Designed a year or two later, the spiral Bavinger House at Norman (1950–55) is probably the most famous or controversial. The length of time building it was the result of construction being largely DIY. It looks very odd, and the upper rooms are supported by tension cables from a central mast; but it is in fact an exposition of sophisticated theories, and was described by Goff as 'a continuous study in contemporary architecture'.

Unité d'Habitation, Marseilles

This is probably the most famous work of the 20th century's most famous architect, Le Corbusier (Charles-Édouard Jeanneret, 1887–1965). Regarded as the great hero of the Modern movement (or great villain, according to taste), Corbusier, like most geniuses, is hard to categorize because of his sheer fertility, the great cornucopia of his creativity.

Soon after the end of the Second World War he was invited by the French government to build housing for 1,600 people in Marseilles. He accepted, on the characteristic condition that he could ignore building regulations. Since urban planning and large housing schemes had exercised him for many years, he welcomed the commission, but in the post-war circumstances skilled workers were few and many materials were hard to come by: a steel frame had to be abandoned on grounds of cost.

The Unité d'Habitation (1946–52) is a single concrete block 540-ft (165-m) long and 184-ft (56-m), or 17 storeys, high, raised on mighty stilts, for Corbusier believed that traditional architecture wasted land; a raised building offered more space, if only for car parking. It contained 337 apartments and much besides, including shops, a hotel, school, gymnasium, swimming pool, etc., and was virtually a self-contained settlement. It represented Corbusier's belief in community as opposed to the concept of family that characterized contemporary 'garden cities'. The flats were slotted into the skeleton grid like small drawers in a cabinet, which makes them blessedly soundproof. Living rooms rise through two storeys, with the outside wall glazed and a balcony beyond; but the effect is to make the main 'bedroom' a gallery

over the living room, an unsuitable arrangement for families. The flats, comparatively long and thin and partly two-storey, slot in alternately, one facing east, the next west. Since two flats occupy three storeys, space is left for a rather dark, because windowless, 'interior street'.

Concrete was by this time a familiar material, but it was normally smartly finished, plastered and painted. Corbusier left the concrete rough, with the marks of the wooden shuttering into which it had been poured still

evident. However, the decision, which reduced costs significantly, was largely forced on him. It did produce a pleasingly rugged effect, and had a powerful impact, not always favourable, on the numerous architects who visited the construction site; but it was to become tiresome when overused by imitators. But nobody dared imitate the extraordinarily inventive array of features, again in rough concrete, that turned the roof into a kind of playground for adults.

This famous block is another example of a seminal building whose influence on later architecture was sometimes unfortunate.

Chapel of Notre Dame du Haut, Ronchamp

Two predecessors of the pilgrimage chapel at Ronchamp (1951–55), high in the Vosges, were successively destroyed in the two world wars. Their replacement is unlike any other significant modern building, and unlike any other building by Le Corbusier, yet for many people it is his finest work. It is, at least, a relief from the severity and logic of the International Modern style, although it does apparently conform with the system of proportional dimensions that Le Corbusier called the modulor, and its architectural significance lay not in inspiring imitations (there were some) but in demonstrating that even the most 'rational' of architects could design a building that is essentially personal and poetic, a work of sculpture in concrete which springs from faith, not reason. As the architect wrote to the bishop when it was finished, 'I sought to create a place of silence, of prayer, of peace and inner joy.' It

is hard to see how his achievement of those aims could be improved.

The design was clearly influenced by the landscape; Le Corbusier visited the site several times, making drawings of the ruins of the earlier chapel, though he also asserted, very plausibly, that the design was inspired by a seashell he had picked up on the beach: he is known to have made small-scale models before he drew up the plans.

Within the great, curving concrete walls that reflect the line of the hills, the interior is lit by small windows, seemingly placed at random,

some of them with coloured glass, some clear. The extraordinary, boat-like roof, which would be echoed later at Chandigarh, is in fact a hollow shell and quite light: it rests not on the massive concrete walls but on thin steel columns rising from them, which leaves a narrow band of glass between roof and wall. The roof also extends over an outdoor altar, where mass for hundreds is celebrated. Inside, the cult figure of the Virgin, the object of the pilgrims' devotion that was rescued from the ruins, is set before a clear window, against the heavenly blue of the sky.

The Atomium, Brussels

The Atomium (1954–58) in north Brussels, bestriding the Boulevard de Centenaire and not far from an earlier scientific architectural marvel, the Laeken Glass Houses, was built as the symbol of the 1958 World Exposition. It is a model, on a vast scale, of an atom of iron, and sprang originally from a notion put forward by a representative of Belgium's metal industries. Many Belgian designers and engineers worked on the project.

The somewhat banal theme of the Exhibition was Progress and Mankind; the motif of the atom seemed suitable in spite of the fact that to most people it stood for massive destruction or possibly a future menace to the planet, nuclear power. Still, the 'atom', in approximately this rather misleading form, was a fashionable motif in the 1950s, and in fact an earlier, smaller version had been seen at the Festival of Britain (1951).

The total height of the structure is 335ft (102m). It consists of nine giant steel spheres, each about 60ft (18m) in diameter and weighing about 200 tons, and with two floors. The topmost sphere contains a restaurant; the others, each with seating capacity for about 200 people, stages special events and exhibitions. The spheres are linked by tubes, representing the bonding power of the atom, which contain elevators and provide passage from one sphere to another. The central shaft contains an 'express' elevator.

The Brussels Atomium, as it loomed above the city, was considered an almost miraculous structure. It could be imagined as a cube balanced on one corner; but unfortunately fire regulations demanded the steps which appear to prop up two of the flanking spheres, rather spoiling the effect and, at a certain angle, giving it the disconcerting appearance of a science-fiction machine about to advance menacingly on the spectator. The Atomium was cleaned and restored for the millennium and some spheres are still open to the public. The view at least repays a visit.

LEFT
The Atomium may be kitsch, but it is kitsch on a very grand scale.

RIGHT
Detail of the interconnected spheres.

Coventry Cathedral

The city of Coventry lies at the geographical centre of England. Unlike its neighbour, Birmingham, offspring of the Industrial Revolution, it is an ancient city (Lady Godiva's famous protest ride through the streets took place before 1066). In November 1940, Coventry was the target of an 11-hour German bombing raid which destroyed much of the old city, including the Perpendicular Cathedral of St Michael. A competition in 1950 to design a replacement was won by Basil Spence (1907–76), who later became a very successful 'establishment' architect, though he has never found great favour among architectural critics and scholars.

It was, perhaps, a relief that the Church of England authorities did not insist on the Gothic style. But Spence's Coventry Cathedral (1954–62) is not exactly modern, although proclaimed in a slightly defensive pamphlet at the time of its consecration as being 'definitely and sincerely of the present day'. It is built largely in an attractive pinkish-grey sandstone. The cliff-like walls of the large and blocky nave perform a kind of zig-zag, with the thinner edge forming an uninterrupted vertical series of window lights. The roof, of copper-covered concrete, is invisible from the ground. Inside, slim columns rise to form a kind of ribbed vault, as if Gothic leanings were not entirely dead.

A pleasant feature of the construction was the opportunity for contemporary artists and craftsmen to contribute works of a kind for which there were few other opportunities. Best known are the enormous tapestry of Christ behind the altar designed by the painter

Graham Sutherland, and the 25-ft (8-m) bronze of St Michael and the Devil by Jacob Epstein next to the porch. The curious, detached Chapel of Unity has a pleasing mosaic floor by a Swedish artist, Einar Forseth.

One aspect of this building that finds more general approval is the way in which the architect combined it with the ruins of the old, whose fine Gothic spire still stands.

The windows in the zig-zag walls (opposite) direct light towards the altar and the enormous tapestry of Christ by Graham Sutherland (below).

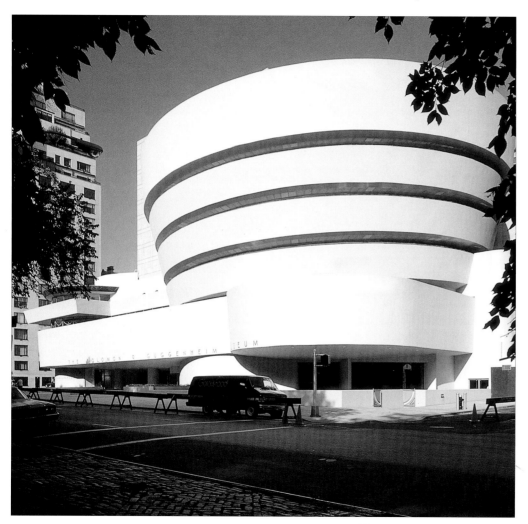

Guggenheim Museum, New York

Although it has not quite succeeded in dethroning the Statue of Liberty as the symbol of New York City, the Solomon R. Guggenheim Museum (1956–59) on 89th Street and Central Park is probably the city's most easily recognized building.

Its patron, who had inherited a vast industrial fortune, originally founded the museum to house the collection under another name, in 1937. When considering a new building, Guggenheim and his agents favoured something appropriately avant-garde; why, otherwise, should they have hired Frank Lloyd Wright? But in 1943, when he was commissioned, Wright was 76, not an age associated with radicalism; but once again, he surprised them all. In a letter to Guggenheim's agent advising that he was bringing the plans for inspection, he wrote: 'The whole thing will either throw you off your guard entirely or be just about what you have been dreaming about.'

Though startling, the building is simple in form. It is essentially a giant concrete drum which grows steadily larger in diameter as it rises, looming out over Fifth Avenue. Inside, a spiral ramp against the wall ascends from the ground to the top, which is covered by a flattish glass dome unseen from the outside at ground level. The pictures are ranged along the wall, the spectator viewing them while descending the ramp, having gone up in an elevator. Only Wright, who had first experimented with spirals in a planetarium designed in 1925, would demand that visitors contemplate paintings in a museum where you are forced to stand with feet on different levels!

Construction was delayed for over a decade, and some contractors were wary of getting involved, doubting, like other Wright contractors before them, whether the structure would be viable. By the time it was officially opened, both Wright and Guggenheim were dead; its reception was mixed, though predominantly favourable. Like most architectural landmarks, it attracted good-natured epithets that signified popular acceptance, but it did not inspire any significant successors. A ten-storey annexe, forming a kind of backdrop, was added in 1992.

The bold Guggenheim Museum in New York introduced a completely new way of arranging pictures in a gallery.

This dramatic but foreshortened view of the Maracaibo Lake Bridge shows the main (300-ft/92-m) high, V-shaped supports of the cantilevered main spans and (foreground) the H-shaped trestle piers.

Maracaibo Lake Bridge, Venezuela

Maracaibo, Venezuela's second city and seaport, lies close to some of the richest oil reserves in the world. By the 1950s the ferries could not cope with the volume of traffic across Lake Maracaibo, which, though the largest lake in South America, draws to a bottleneck only about 5-miles (8-km) wide approaching the sea. The Venezuelan government resolved to cross it, either by a bridge or tunnel or a combination of the two, as in the Chesapeake Bay Bridge Tunnel under construction at the same time. Twelve tenders were submitted, of which 11 proposed a bridge with a superstructure of steel. The government commission recommended acceptance of the twelfth, for a concrete bridge. It was based on a design by Riccardo Morandi (1902–89), second only to Pier Luigi Nervi among 20th-century Italian engineer-architects; but its construction (1959–62) became a large international enterprise involving Portuguese geologists, Swiss technicians, German contractors, and others.

The commission gave several reasons for choosing this design, among them cheaper maintenance (steel needs frequent painting) and visual appeal: it was aesthetically the most satisfying. Another reason was that it would give the Venezuelan construction industry experience of prestressed concrete, a development of reinforced concrete with the steel rods replaced by wires, running in ducts, which can be tensioned after casting. This material permitted much more slender, and therefore economical structures, as had been demonstrated in the lightweight bridges and airship hangars of Eugène Freyssinet (1879–1962).

The bridge, over 70 per cent of which was prefabricated, is made up of three sections, two landward sections of prestressed concrete beams on plain, V- or H-shaped piers, and a central section, to accommodate shipping, of five main spans of 780-ft (238-m) each. These consist of a pair of cantilevers which, to reduce the depth of the box-section beam carrying the road, are supported by inclined ropes from 300-ft (90-m) towers. These six simple and economical structures are reminiscent of the Forth Railway Bridge near Edinburgh, which Morandi acknowledged as an influence.

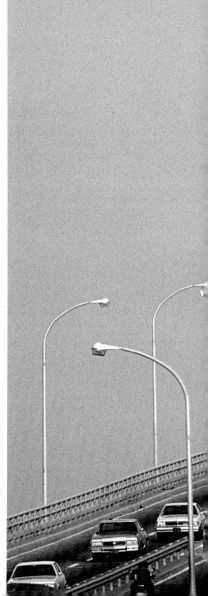

The sleek and shining, stainless steel parabolic arch on the riverfront of St Louis, the Gateway Arch, as it came to be called, justifies its claim to be the tallest memorial in the USA.

Gateway Arch, St Louis

St Louis, Missouri, is proud of its heritage as the 'Gateway to the West', when it was not only the biggest centre of trade on the Mississippi but also the main crossroads for westward expansion in the half century or so following President Thomas Jefferson's Louisiana Purchase (1803). It retained its dominance in the railway age. A competition for the design of the Jefferson National Expansion Memorial was instigated in 1947, and the winning design was by Eero Saarinen, who was virtually unknown and whose work up to that time had all been done in association with his then more famous father, Eliel. The design drew on a ten-year-old project by Adalberto Libera (1903–63) for the gateway to an Italian international exhibition that was planned for 1942 but which was submerged by greater events.

A sleek and shining, stainless steel, parabolic arch on the riverfront of St Louis, the Gateway Arch, as it came to be called, was built between 1963 and 1965; all survey work was done at night to avoid distortion caused by the rays of the sun. It is 630-ft (192-m) high, which justifies its claim to be the tallest memorial in the USA, and is gently tapered towards the crown. The height is the same as the distance across the base, and takes the structurally sound form of a catenary curve – the shape formed by a chain when held at both ends. It weighs 17,246 tons and sways about half an inch in normal weather; it is calculated that it could sway safely up to a maximum of 18in (46cm), and that a 150-mph (240-km/h) wind would be required to make it do so.

The city authorities have shown some enterprise in making the Gateway Arch, which cost $13 million to build, a major tourist attraction. According to the Arch's web site, it is 'the fourth most visited tourist attraction in the world', a claim which, sadly, induces a certain amount of scepticism.

From some angles, Saarinen's airport terminal has a shark-like appearance. Like railway stations before them, airports called forth some innovative designs from architects in the late 20th century.

TWA Terminal, New York

Eero Saarinen's unashamedly symbolic terminal for Trans World Airlines (1956–62), at New York's Kennedy (then Idlewild) Airport, has been described alternatively as a late Expressionist and an early Postmodern building. Equally, it could be said to signify Saarinen's emergence as a Mannerist, or to reflect his early interest in sculpture. The design, of which there had been a foretaste in Saarinen's skating rink for Yale University (1956–58), represented a more flexible attitude to space and form that became increasingly evident in the 1950s, encouraged by Le Corbusier's chapel at Ronchamp.

The building created a sensation at the time. It was criticized by purists of the Modern movement (a declining breed) but greeted enthusiastically by others and, unusually for a controversial building, by the general public. Saarinen said he was aiming to capture the 'excitement of flight', and passengers might have been forgiven for thinking, on seeing the terminal, that it could transport them through the air all by itself, though they would have revised their opinion on entering the vastness of the interior space.

From the air, the four concrete shells of the roof look like a pair of gigantic and slightly distorted butterflies in close conference – distorted because the shells are not identical. They are supported by large, athletic, Y-shaped buttresses that almost strike a pose, with a line of skylights running between them. Free, curving forms are repeated throughout the interior: the Arrivals and Departures screens are housed in an 'organic' structure with a hint both of Art Nouveau and the science-fiction hero ET.

An enclosed concrete walkway conveys passengers direct to the aircraft and makes Saarinen's building the most passenger-friendly as well as the most exciting terminal in the airport. There were reports that its introduction resulted in a rise in TWA's ticket sales.

Saarinen designed another, even more audacious terminal building for Dulles Airport in Washington, DC, almost his last, completed in 1963. Even for such a technological virtuoso it proved slightly too audacious, however, and part had to be rebuilt in the 1980s.

Nervi was a sensitive artist who largely operated in a tough commercial world with outstanding success. However, the space and openness of his plan for the Turin pavilion was, in execution, somewhat modified by practical considerations.

Palace of Labour, Turin

Pier Luigi Nervi (1891–1979) was one of the most influential architects of the mid-20th century. He was an engineer first, and on many of his most notable buildings he co-operated with other architects. A master of structure, he was a genius in reinforced concrete with a powerful aesthetic sense, qualities first demonstrated in his stadium at Florence (1928).

He ascribed to the undoubtedly correct if logically unjustifiable dictum that a building which looks good aesthetically is good structurally, and vice-versa.

The commission for the Palazzo del Lavoro, like most of Nervi's work, resulted from his submitting a tender that was less expensive and potentially easier to build quickly than other competitors'. It was for a hall honouring the

contribution of labour for an exhibition marking the centenary of Italian independence (1961) in Turin. The terms were challenging. Maximum construction time was 17 months – for a building of over 275,000sq ft (25550sq m) – and the building had to be capable of subsequent conversion into a technical school.

The building is a huge square hall with walls of glass, protected by louvres on the sunny sides, and a roof of steel, which was preferred to concrete because its design promised speedier construction. To avoid the common delays resulting from one operation having to wait for another, the main parts of the structure were made as 16 independent units. They consist of a steel roof section 125-ft (38-m) square, supported by concrete columns 65-ft (20-m) high. A space 6.5-ft (2-m) wide between the squares is glazed to admit light to the centre of the building. Each column is circular at the top of a diameter of 8ft (2.5m), where it meets the tapering steel girders that resemble umbrella spokes. At the bottom it is cross-shaped, 18-ft (5.5-m) across. The shape is dictated by structural considerations, but a dramatic profile results from straight lines drawn between the angles of the cross and the circle. Yet the straight lines are themselves structurally desirable because such members are easier to cast. Around the walls runs a cantilevered mezzanine gallery. The result is – or was, as the building was later altered – not only structurally unique, but visually magnificent.

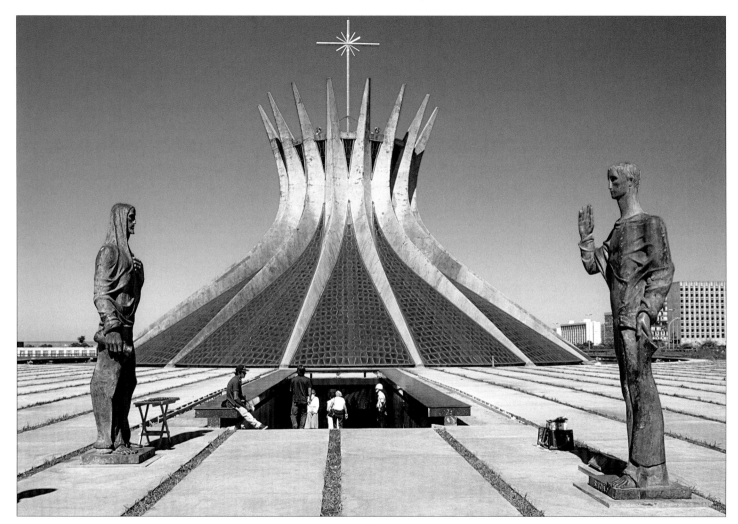

Brasilia Cathedral

The idea of moving the capital of Brazil into the interior was first canvassed as early as 1808 and was enshrined in the constitution of 1889, but it was not until 1956 that a site was chosen and construction begun. Cost apparently was not a problem. The general plan of the new capital was by Lúcio (Luis) Costa, but the presiding genius was the architect Oscar Niemeyer (b. 1907), 'the Brazilian Le Corbusier', with a vigorous creativity to match the master and a similarly cavalier attitude to the strict tenets of Modernism; nearly all the main public buildings in Brasilia were designed by him. At the heart is the monumental Plaza of the Three Powers (1953–60), i.e. buildings of the legislature, judiciary and administration, headed by a giant double slab of offices with, in front, the long low parliament buildings surmounted by two large, shallow domes of which one is turned upside down.

Although the the city's inaugural mass had been held there ten years earlier, the cathedral was not completed until 1970. It is the most interesting building. Niemeyer has often shown himself interested in curving shapes formed with reinforced concrete, which some have traced to an affinity for Brazilian Baroque. The cathedral, which employs sophisticated engineering techniques, is more sculpture than architecture. It takes the form of a crown of thorns, fashioned from 16 hollow concrete ribs, about 100-ft (30-m) high. They slope inwards from the base while expanding in section until they meet near the crown, where they turn outward again and taper off. Some have seen them as hands raised in prayer, others as a flower opening. The spaces between the ribs

are entirely glazed, the leading forming a honeycomb pattern.

The building is entered via a dark Passage of Reflection, from which one emerges into the light and airy space of the circular nave. Being below ground level, it is larger than it appears from the outside and holds 4,000 people. The interior is rather austere. Glass panels in the roof reflect the water in a surrounding pool, which in turn magically reflects shimmering images of nearby buildings.

Like most planned urban utopias, Brasilia failed to realize the hopes of its builders, and tended to develop into two units, the impressive public citadel and the inhuman, fast-deteriorating, geometric slabs of the residential city. It has contributed to the growing dissatisfaction with Modernism.

OPPOSITE
The subterranean entrance to Brasilia Cathedral.

BELOW
Inside, the eye is drawn towards the marble altar and the figures of angels and St Peter suspended from the roof.

Marina City, Chicago

The twin towers, popularly known as corn cobs, of Marina City (1964–67) are the best-known work of Bertrand Goldberg (1913–97) at the culmination of his long career. They were the final manifestation of his belief in the advantages of circular forms: superior aerodynamic qualities, potential offered by a central core, equal distance of units from the centre, etc. It was even possible to find advantages in the fact that internal walls are not parallel. However, the towers of Marina City aroused some derision, especially among high-minded Modernists, when they first appeared and, although they certainly belong to a very different ethos from Mies van de Rohe's classic East Shore Drive Apartments, a close neighbour, it is increasingly difficult to see why. Now that familiarity has made them less startling, however, their structural integrity can be better appreciated.

Built at a time when land prices were rising even faster than buildings, Marina City optimizes a remarkably small riverside site on Chicago's Loop, making the most of the view by placing the lowest apartments, whose semicircular balconies create the corn-cob appearance, on the 21st floor (out of a total of 60 storeys) and by placing the cars of their occupants underneath. There are 450 apartments in each tower, the car park, with its continuous, spiral ramp, accommodating the same number of cars. Theoretically, residents might seldom have to leave the complex, as it also contains offices, shops, restaurants, a theatre between the towers, a gym, even a bowling alley among other amenities, not forgetting the marina. The apartments are grouped around a central core, 35ft (11m) in diameter, containing the services. This powerful core was built first and provided a rising platform for the erection crane, which contributed to the relatively economic construction, matching the economy of space.

When built, Goldberg's towers were said to be the tallest residential buildings in the world and, indeed, the tallest concrete structures. They offer one solution, though perhaps not the most flexible one possible, to the problem of devising the economical, multi-purpose complexes that contemporary cities seem increasingly to demand.

LEFT
The towers of Goldberg's Marina City, which originally failed to attract tenants as easily as was hoped, possibly due to astronomical rents.

OPPOSITE
Chicago with Marina City in the foreground.

Lake Point Tower, Chicago

Although this block was built in 1967–68, its history really begins nearly 50 years earlier, when Mies van der Rohe, stimulated by the burgeoning artistic movements in Europe after the First World War, was going through a particularly creative phase of his development and producing some remarkably varied ideas. Among them were two skyscrapers, the first based on the triangle, the second (1920–21) a glass-clad tower of free, curving forms which was never built, chiefly because finance was not forthcoming, although it was also doubtful if contemporary technology could have coped. All the architects associated with Lake Point (Schipporeit-Heinrich Associates) were former pupils of Mies at the Illinois Institute of Technology, and some of them had also worked in his practice.

Lake Point Tower is an apartment block with various extra amenities, whereas Mies's 1921 design was for an office block. It stands in comparative isolation in Navy Pier Park, then a rather neglected area, at some distance from Chicago's high-rise clusters, which it appears to regard with calm disdain. More recently the pier itself, beyond the park, has been transformed with a $200-million investment of public funds, and in 1996 topped the list of popular attractions in Chicago; but Lake Point has nothing whatever to do with the throngs heading for the amusements on the pier.

The tower is a dizzying 645-ft (197-m) high and contains 900 extremely expensive apartments. It has, strictly speaking, one wall only, a dead-smooth curtain of glass that flows silkily around a three-lobed, clover-leaf plan with a central, triangular core. The view, whether of Lake Michigan or the Chicago skyline, is splendid.

OPPOSITE
The sleek, sophisticated sentinel of Lake Point Tower, the work of former students of Mies van der Rohe who started from a then-practical plan of the master made many years earlier.

RIGHT
Among other amenities, the Tower offers marvellous views.

The Habitat housing complex was the sensation of the Montreal World Fair in 1967. The ingredients are simple but the design is unbelievably complicated.

Habitat, Montreal

The Habitat housing complex on the St Lawrence River was the first major work of the Israeli-Canadian architect Moshe Safdie (b. 1938). Although intended to be permanent, it was designed for 'Expo 67', the Montreal World Fair, and caused a minor sensation. The use of prefabricated reinforced-concrete units was not new, and the Habitat community in many ways reflected the ideas of Gropius and the Bauhaus school in the 1920s. What was new about Safdie's extraordinary block was that 'it lifted the concept of the prefabricated concrete-box unit from a utilitarian technique to the level of emotive architecture' (Gilbert Herbert).

It consists of 554 prefabricated units which are put together to form a single complex. Its form is intricate, a geometric puzzle requiring computer assistance, and superficially looks a jumble, as if someone had thrown a lot of containers together into a pile. The units are put together in different combinations to form,

altogether, 15 different layouts. They are held together with steel cables and connected by internal walkways to make 158 homes with from one to four bedrooms each. The ingenious deployment of projections and recesses provides privacy and a view for each unit, and gives each its own roof garden. As the architect said, the idea was to offer 'privacy, fresh air, sunlight and suburban amenities in an urban setting'.

Originally, 900 apartments had been planned, but no more were ever built; although they had proved more popular than might have been expected, one snag that emerged was the relatively high costs of construction. That may be, partly at any rate, why the Habitat project did not have any obvious successors, although Safdie developed these ideas further in Israel, a region where there is, of course, a tradition of cube-shaped houses; other architects, such as Kisho Kurokawa in Japan, produced similar concepts.

University of East Anglia, Norwich

The British architect Denys Lasdun (1914–2001) was a leading figure of the so-called 'New Brutalist' school of the 1950s–60s, whose commitment was to the 'honest' architecture of Mies van der Rohe and Le Corbusier, where structure and materials are expressed without disguise. In fact the New Brutalists were originally more thoroughly committed to this principle than even Mies, though with time the movement merged with other, sympathetic international influences and acquired other priorities. Lasdun, whose most famous work was the National Theatre in London (1967–76), described his work as 'the combination of the vertical and the horizontal'.

The University of East Anglia was one of the new provincial universities built in something of a rush in England after the Second World War. A popular generic term for them is 'red-brick' (i.e. not ivy-covered stone) but UEA is uncompromising concrete. Locally it is widely dismissed as ugly, the dinginess of rough concrete, stained by the weather, overcoming its 'honesty'. Nevertheless, the campus was in many ways both innovative and successful. Instead of the prevailing dispersed style for a university campus, with the buildings spread out in groups, UEA is highly centralized, with living, teaching and administration accommodation comprising a single mass that is convenient yet not congested. At the same time, the plan made far-sighted allowance for future growth.

Lasdun's greatest success is the terraced accommodation blocks that take the form of ziggurats, with predominantly glass façades on each recessed floor. They exploit a sloping site to provide a fine view for practically every student over the grass and down to what is called, this being Norfolk, a 'broad' (lake). Both individually and as a group, they make a splendid composition, and although the interior has inevitably become shabby and the staircases are very steep, like those in a cross-Channel ferry, the individual rooms are not unreasonably small.

UEA also boasts a notable arts building, the Sainsbury Centre (1977), a typically innovative structure by Norman Foster and Partners.

Though many find its weather-streaked concrete unattractive, the late Sir Denys Lasdun's design for the University of East Anglia is successful both overall and in detail.

Sydney Opera House

The Sydney Opera House (1957–73) was one of those controversial projects whose endless teething troubles seemed to threaten failure; but it has proved a success beyond the city fathers' dreams, and beyond what some of them deserved, since the saga of problems were largely the result of political interference which drove the Danish architect, Jørn Utzon (b. 1918), to pull out before the building was completed. There was also some initial genuine doubt over whether the ambitious design could actually be built. However, the firm of Ove Arup, the outstanding civil engineers, accomplished it in co-operation with Utzon after several contractors had funked the project.

It stands on a small peninsula in Sydney Harbour within nodding distance of the famous bridge. Utzon's design was chosen in an international competition in 1956, allegedly on the basis of a handful of sketches. Utzon, an undoubted genius but not the easiest man to pin down, tended to design, or redesign, as he went along, and no one knows if the building would have taken exactly its present form if he had remained in charge until the end; the interior would probably have been rather more exciting. It contains four theatres altogether, but the building, it is said, is 'all roof'. The structures beneath are substantial enough (the concert hall holds nearly 3,000 people), but the soaring shells, rising to peaks over 200-ft (60-m) high, make them if not invisible, unnoticed. What do these thrilling forms symbolize? They are more suggestive of canvas than concrete, and are often compared with the sails of the boats in Sydney harbour, or with the fins of sharks in the ocean beyond; the Australian gift for a colourful phrase has dubbed them the 'Nuns' scrum'. They have, of course, no practical function and sad to say, while the Opera House is a wonderful place for staging most kinds of entertainment, critics say that classical opera is not among them. The building has not worn well either, though it was revamped for the Olympics in 2000.

Australia's famous Postmodern Opera House sails boldly out into Sydney Harbour in total defiance of the doctrine that function dictates form.

Neue Staatsgalerie, Stuttgart

This addition to the State Gallery in Stuttgart (1977–84) by James Stirling (1926–94) in association with Michael Wilford, ended a decade in which Britain's perhaps most gifted and original architect had been starved of major commissions. Though a thoroughly modern architect, Stirling was far removed from the dogma of the International Modern style, and his later buildings, from about 1971, in which his unconstrained, expressive eclecticism is more evident and geometric abstraction mingles with Neoclassical motifs, are usually classed as Postmodernist. They often manifest a Postmodern jokiness, like the Staatsgalerie's wall lights in the form of a 'fallen' section of cornice, suggesting that architecture should not be treated too solemnly.

Stirling's Staatsgalerie won a competition held in 1977, beating nine German designs. It is skilfully organized as a succession of spaces created by angled surfaces and changing levels. On one hand a display of imaginative invention, it also seemed to provide a kind of collage of contemporary ideas on design. The central unit is a stone-faced drum or rotunda, open to the sky, its wall pierced by openings offering intriguing glimpses of other parts. There is no façade as such. The entrance lobby on one side of the rotunda gives on to the temporary-exhibition hall, with its undulating, green-mullioned glass wall. The masonry walls consist of alternate bands of travertine and sandstone and lend the building a more imposing aspect. That balances the relative frivolity of the poster-paint colours – the bright green floor of the entrance area or the bulky, red, cylindrical handrails of ramps and walkways. The galleries

are on the top floor and are lit from the glazed roof. They are fairly conventional, a succession of plain rooms with a centrally aligned walk-through. Stirling considered the traditional arrangement 'more convincing' than 20th-century alternatives.

The building was a great success from the

start, equally popular with ordinary people and, despite some initial dissent, with Stirling's architectural colleagues. In the year after it opened, the Staatsgalerie moved from 51 to first place in the popularity poll of German museums.

Pompidou Centre, Paris

The idea that a ruler should be commemorated by great works was enthusiastically embraced by Georges Pompidou, president of France (1969–74), no less than Louis XIV, leading him to conceive the idea of the Centre National d'Art et de Culture Georges Pompidou (1971–77), to give it its full title. It was the work of the British architect Richard Rogers (b. 1933), in partnership with the Italian Renzo Piano (b. 1937) and, like the Sydney Opera House, was built by the firm of Ove Arup, in particular, its most brilliant engineer, Peter Rice, also largely responsible for getting the Sydney Opera House up and running. Both architects, who entered the competition for design of the building on the spur of the moment and, being young, little known, and foreign, had little expectation of winning, were devoted to the idea of form defined by function in a Modernist context, as first defined by Louis Sullivan in Chicago in 1896, not of course to the total exclusion of aesthetic considerations, but by abandoning traditional concepts of, for instance, a façade by boldly placing service facilities on the exterior.

The structure, described as a six-storey culture machine, forms a huge transparent box 550-ft (168-m) long, 194-ft (59-m) wide and 138-ft (42-m) high, with a frame of exposed cylindrical steel columns and trusses spanning the entire length. Unsupported spanning beams 157-ft (48-m) long create a highly flexible interior, while steel cantilevers support various service systems outside the columns. They include escalators in transparent plastic tubes, elevators painted red, and further large tubes for air ducts (painted blue), water (green) and electricity (yellow).

The uncompromisingly 'industrial' nature of the design, for a building in an historic district of Paris, not surprisingly caused a good deal of controversy and provoked several blocking actions in the courts. However, if (as someone complained) the outside looks like a half-built factory, by banning service systems to the exterior, the Centre acquires a vast, calm and uncluttered space. The result is that it has proved almost too successful and has become a packed tourist attraction. Offices were moved out to make more room for culture and, only 20 years after it opened, it has had to be temporarily closed for intensive refurbishment.

Full advantage has been taken of the idea that industrial installations can be beautiful, with service elements, usually concealed, comprising the whole aesthetic of the building.

Lloyd's Building, London

Lloyd's of London is an ancient and often misunderstood institution. It is not an insurance company but an association of underwriters in hundreds of syndicates, who between them can insure almost anything anywhere. Its name derives from Lloyd's Coffee House in Lombard Street, where shipowners and marine insurers met from the 1690s. However, after many generations of comparative security and high profit, Lloyd's has experienced troubled times in the last quarter of the 20th century.

Underwriters are generally people of conservative tastes, and many of them were appalled by their dynamic new high-tech building (1978–86) by Richard Rogers, with the engineering firm of Ove Arup. The views of the occupants, however, are not definitive. As the architect has said, 'Though the client's program offers the architect a point of departure, it must be questioned, as the architectural solution lies in the complex and often contradictory interpretation of the needs of the individual, the institution, the place and history.' The design exploited many of the practical devices developed with such success for the Pompidou Centre in Paris; while the framework of the building is built to last, the numerous service systems are built with easy access and future obsolescence in mind. It is perhaps an aesthetically superior structure to the Pompidou Centre, and it is certainly one of the best modern buildings in London.

The structure is mainly concrete with stainless-steel cladding and a great deal of reflective glass. As in Paris, a spacious and flexible interior is achieved by placing the services outside the building: the fast-moving all-glazed lifts offer fine views of London once breath has returned to the body. The main building is rectangular in plan and surrounded by service towers. Its vast central atrium ascends through a series of concentric balconies for the whole height of the 12 storeys. This is 'the Room', where brokers do business, and it can hold about 1,000 of them. In the centre, between four cylindrical columns that also give support to the balconies, an escalator rises in dramatic diagonals within the rectangular space.

The grace of power is again evident in what is perhaps Richard Rogers most successful building to date.

Richard Meier's buildings remain faithful to clarity and order and reject ill-disciplined Postmodernism.

High Museum of Art, Atlanta

The New York architect Richard Meier (b. 1934) was a member of the 'New York Five' who gained prominence through an exhibition at the Museum of Modern Art in 1969, another member being the future Disney architect Michael Graves. All their designs were for family houses, commonly in wood and in the tradition of Le Corbusier and the pre-war International Modern style. All, but especially Meier, displayed a preference for white in their buildings, which helps to account for the unblemished purity of his style. The group of five soon dispersed, but the exhibition led to larger commissions, which for Meier culminated in a succession of prestigious museums, including the High Museum of Art in Atlanta, Georgia (1983), and the vast Getty Center in Los Angeles (1984–97) until, by the end of the 20th century, he was one of the most successful and sought-after international architects.

The Atlanta High Museum, which is part of the Woodrow Arts Center, is perhaps the most striking example of the cool assurance of Meier's buildings, all the more striking in view of his prolific output; the adjective 'high' might almost indicate a moral stance. Meier has emphasized 'the sense of spiritual activity expressed in architectonic forms'.

The design was the unanimous choice of the judges in the competition of 1981. The building is constructed of concrete slabs on a steel frame, with steel columns, and is clad in Meier's characteristic white, porcelain-enamelled steel panels, with a granite plinth. The grid of the panels is echoed by the plinth and the windows. Between cubic wings is the curved,

glazed façade of the atrium, which has circling ramps prompting memories of the New York Guggenheim. The atrium is filled with natural light, like the rest of the building, entering, direct or filtered through skylights, glazed strips,

or through small windows in the galleries. Besides displaying paintings, sculpture, furniture and other objects, the building includes an auditorium, café, shop, members' lounge, and offices.

Commerzbank, Frankfurt

Not many people, given an alternative, would choose to work in run-of-the-mill high-rise office blocks – 'elongated filing cabinets' – as Jonathan Glancey calls them. The design by Norman Foster and Partners for a bank headquarters in Frankfurt is a bold attempt to escape from the anonymous vastness, the monotony and the second-hand air supply of the typical office tower. Some of the devices by which Foster overcame these drawbacks depended on up-to-the-minute technology and the expertise of the near-legendary engineers of the Ove Arup engineering partnership.

Instead of being built around a central core containing lifts and services, the plan of the 57-storey Commerzbank tower (1997), the tallest building in Europe, is an equilateral triangle, with the services placed in the three corners. In the vacant centre, a vast atrium rises about 500ft (150m) from the lobby to a glass roof, with the sky beyond, which acts as a giant ventilation shaft, drawing in fresh air from outside. On the side of the building, but within the outer glass skin, are a series of nine

gardens, strictly speaking conservatories, which rise around the tower in a spiral. Each of the gardens, which individually represents the flora of different parts of the world, is four-storeys-high. There is a view of plants and shrubs from any desk in the office, and the wide windows also give a view of the city. Windows on the inner skin can be opened, tilting from the top, by pressing a button. The outer skin is of course closed, except for air intakes.

The perhaps romantic idea was to replace corporate vastness with a more villagey community. There are 240 people for each garden, working in offices where the view is unrestricted, as in open-plan but with sound sealed off by glass partitions. The absence of columns adds to the sense of space.

The building is less remarkable from the outside, partly due to planning restrictions and partly to economy. Foster's previous bank headquarters, in Hong Kong (1986), where the budget was less limited, had proved notoriously expensive, and the German bankers were understandably wary.

OPPOSITE
The Commerzbank is the tallest building in Europe, designed with many innovations by Norman Foster and Partners to escape the anonymous vastness of the typical office tower.

RIGHT
Interior view of one of the nine conservatories or winter gardens.

OPPOSITE
Built for the Second Reich, the Reichstag Building failed to survive the Third, but the restored version, so everyone hopes, may last much longer in a united, democratic state.

RIGHT
The new glass dome above the debating chamber.

Reichstag, Berlin

The Reichstag was built in rather heavy Neo-Renaissance style in 1884–1894 for the legislature of the new German Empire. The infamous Reichstag fire (1933) seriously damaged it and Hitler's subsequent suspension of the constitution made it redundant. In 1945 Soviet guns all but flattened it and the division of Germany in 1945 left it still without a role, though it was patched up. With the reunification of Germany in 1990, Berlin regained its status as capital, and the old Reichstag building, restored and expanded, became the home of the federal parliament (Bundestag) in 1999. Remarkably, the commission was won by an architect who, though of international stature with a staff of over 500 and possibly the most successful in the world, was British, Sir Norman Foster.

There is a well-known story of how Foster, interviewed about his plan in 1992, told the competition jury, who did not know, what the current running costs of the building were and how they could be vastly reduced. Ecologically, the building is very advanced, using solar power, rapeseed fuel oil and a regeneration system that reduces emission of carbon dioxide by 90 per cent.

The most striking feature is the new glass dome above the debating chamber, the old one having been destroyed. Inside the dome is a large inverted cone containing energy-producing photovoltaic cells and covered with 365 mirrors. It reflects light into the chamber and, from below, a myriad of refracted glimpses of the sky or the people on the spiral ramp that ascends inside the dome to a viewing platform. 'What you see [from the chamber]', Foster explained, 'is the people walking, climbing above the politicians paid to serve them. The people are the masters here, not the politicians.' Undeniably, the dome throws a lot of light on the conduct of the lawmakers.

Though little more than 100-years-old, the Reichstag building has had a momentous history, and Foster and Partners have endeavoured to preserve it. Some of the graffiti made by Soviet soldiers in 1945 are still present.

Petronas Towers, Kuala Lumpur

In the 1980s the Selangor Turf Club, with its race track, was ordered to move out of its site in Kuala Lumpur to reduce traffic congestion on race days. This opened up a vast site in the heart of the Malaysian capital. Originally, it was to be a park, but the government, weighing the advantages of a park that would be expensive to maintain against a commercial development that would bring large profits, opted for the latter. There would still be a small park, but there would also be mixed-purpose development. Petronas, an oil company, became the major investor and planned new headquarters in the Kuala Lumpur City Centre Company, formed to control the whole site. Urged by the forceful prime minister, Dr Mahathir Mohammed, a major monument was planned. This was the genesis of the Petronas Towers (1993–98).

The winning design was by the Argentinian-born US architect, Cesar Pelli (b. 1926), whose earlier buildings included the Canary Wharf Tower in London. It was for twin towers of 88 storeys each, joined midway by a 'sky bridge' and each with an attached cylindrical tower of 44 storeys. An identifiably 'Malaysian' building was called for, and the star-shaped plan of the main towers reflects an Islamic motif, while the profile vaguely suggests Buddhist models.

A great deal of preparation and planning was required before construction could start. Experts around the world gave advice, project managers were sent to study for a year in the USA, geological sampling was carried out down to 330ft (100m) below the surface, complete systems were ordered in advance of construction to prevent costly hold-ups, and with up to 7,000 workers on a site in the middle of a busy city, stringent safety precautions were required.

At a late stage, the height of the pinnacles was increased so that the towers could claim the title of the world's tallest building, at 1,483ft (452m). However, 240ft (73m) of that is taken up by the spire and both the Sears Tower in Chicago and the World Trade Center in New York have more storeys.

Guggenheim Museum, Bilbao

One thing that makes the Bilbao Guggenheim (1993–97) an appropriate building on which to end the 20th century is that it evidently would not have been possible without the aid of the computer. It looks more like a gigantic piece of abstract sculpture, with perhaps a nod towards early movements in modern art, particularly Picasso and Cubism. The assembly of disparate, interconnected forms obey no observable logic. They are mainly clad in titanium, with some glass and stone. The museum has been unhelpfully compared with an unfolding flower or a huge fish, but its design should not have been a total surprise since its Canadian-born, California-based architect, Frank Gehry (b. 1929), had displayed his free-form style ('no-rules architecture') in earlier buildings, including his own house in Santa Monica (1978), though on nothing like this scale.

It arose from a major programme to reinvigorate the run-down Basque city of Bilbao (including a metro system designed by Norman Foster), combined with the desire of the Guggenheim Foundation for a major new museum in Europe for its vast collection of modern art. It was built on a disused industrial site, at a cost of about $100 million (about one-tenth the cost of London's Millennium Dome), and opened in October 1997; an attempt by ETA terrorists to send it off with the wrong sort of bang was forestalled by vigilant security. During its first year, besides hordes of film crews looking for an original backdrop for a TV advertisement, it attracted more visitors than the Prado, Spain's premier museum of art. According to one study, 80 per cent of the visitors admitted they had come to see the museum rather than its contents.

The interior is well adapted to cater for the often very large dimensions of contemporary artworks. The main exhibition gallery is 450-ft (137-m) long and over 150-ft (50-m) high, and there are small spaces for more intimate works. The total exhibition space amounts to about 100,000sq ft (9000sq m), on three floors. Gehry is currently planning another Guggenheim, twice the size of Bilbao, for Manhattan's Lower East Side.

It is an interesting paradox of popular taste that, while almost any modern building provokes disapproval, the most extravagantly unconventional design often excites general enthusiasm, the Sydney Opera House and the Bilbao Guggenheim being cases in point.

adobe: sun-baked clay brick

aisle: one of the lateral divisions in a church

ambulatory: a walkway within or around a building or an apse

apsaras: sculpted female figures on Indian temples

apse: an addition to the east end of (usually) a church, semicircular, square-sided or polygonal

aqueduct: a bridge-like structure carrying a water channel overland

arcade: a row of arches on pillars

arch: a curved structure bridging a space

architrave: the lowest element of an entablature

Art Nouveau: late 19th-century decorative style, characterized by sinuous, plant-like forms and vivid colour

Art Deco: decorative style of the 1920s–1930s based on geometric forms and influenced by streamlining and plastics

Arts and Crafts: movement influenced by John Ruskin and William Morris in Victorian England, favouring the artist-craftsman and hostile to industrialization

ashlar: a hewn stone, blocks of squared stone cut to fit precisely

atlantes: similar to caryatids but with male rather than female figures

atrium: the central courtyard, roofed on the sides, of a Roman villa; hence a similar feature in modern buildings

axial: forming an axis, as in a building with units ranged along a straight line

azulejos: decorative tiles of glazed earthenware characteristic of Iberia and Latin America

bailey: the courtyard of a castle

baldacchino: an ornate canopy, on pillars or suspended, above throne, altar or tomb

baptistery: the part of a church where baptism takes place, often a separate building

barbican: an outlying fortification defending the entrance to a castle

Baroque: the style predominant in 17th–18th-century Europe, characterized by energy, movement and a sense of mass

barrel vault: a vault in the form of a continuous semicircle

basilica: a hall-like building with arcade, aisles and clerestory

bastion: a projecting element in a castle wall, typically at a corner, giving defenders a better view of the walls

battered: of a wall, often the lower wall of a castle, that slopes inward from the ground

battlement: an indented, or crenelated, parapet in a fortified building

bay: a division of a wall, space, or building created by two vertical architectural features, such as pillars

blind arch: a 'filled-in' arch, a decorative feature on a solid wall

boss: a carved, ball-like ornament typically covering the point in a vault where ribs intersect

bracket: a small, weight-bearing platform or shelf, often in the form of volutes

buttress: a solid, vertical feature built against a wall to support it

campanile: a bell tower

cantilever: a horizontal member, such as a beam, projecting beyond its point of support

capital: the top part of a column, above the shaft

caravanserai: a roadside rest house for caravans in the Near East

caryatid: a column in the form of a female figure

cella: the main room of a Classical temple, beyond the portico

centring: the wooden support for an arch during building

central plan: of a building that is more or less symmetrical in all directions

chaitya: A Buddhist sanctuary or shrine

chancel: the eastern arm of a church, containing the altar

château: originally a castle (French); later a grand country house

chhattri (chatri): open, pillared kiosks, often appearing on the roof of a larger building in India

choir: the part of the church occupied by the choir, often used synonymously with chancel

Churrigueresque: lavishly ornamental style in 18th-century Spain derived from the work of the architect José Benito de Churriguera (1665–1725)

Classical: the style of ancient Greece and Rome, often revived (Neoclassicism), the predominant historical influence in Western architecture

clerestory (clearstorey): the wall above the arcade in a basilica-type building, its windows being the main source of light

cloisters: open arcades surrounding a courtyard

coffering: decorative panels in a ceiling

collonnade: a row of columns supporting an entablature, arches or a roof

column: a vertical, cylindrical, supporting member made up of base, shaft and capital

concrete: a stone-like substance made by mixing cement with sand and aggregate, such as gravel

corbel: a projecting block, usually stone, in a wall, providing support for a beam or member

Corinthian: third of the Classical Greek Orders, distinguished by elaborate capitals carved with acanthus leaves

cornice: the topmost section of an entablature; hence, a projecting, ornamental moulding that crowns a wall or building

crenelation: see *battlement*

crockets: small knob-like ornaments in the form of a curling leaf, carved at regular intervals on the angles of Gothic spires, gables, etc.

crossing: in a cruciform church, the area where the arms intersect

cruciform: cross-shaped

cupola: a small dome

curtain wall: in a castle, the main, fortified wall; in modern architecture, the outside, non-load-bearing wall

cusp: the point created by the meeting of two arcs forming part of the inside of an arch or window

Decorated: a style of English Gothic architecture in the late 13th–14th centuries, marked by highly decorated surfaces and extensive use of ogee curves

dome: a curved roof, typically round at the

base and approximately semicircular in section, with infinite variations

donjon: the main building or tower of a castle, often called the keep

Doric: first of the three Classical Greek Orders, characterized by fluted columns with no base and simple capitals

drum: a circular wall supporting a dome; or one of the blocks making up a column

Early English: the earliest style of English Gothic architecture in the late 12th–13th centuries, less determinedly vertical than French

elevation: the plan of a building seen from the side

engaged column: a column attached to a wall

engrailed: decorated with concave arcs, forming cusps

entablature: in Classical architecture, the horizontal elements above the capital of a column, consisting of architrave, frieze and cornice

entasis: the slight outward swell in the shaft of a column

façade: the main front or face of a building

fan vaulting: a complex pattern of ribs fanning out from a single point above the shafts in the walls

finial: an ornamental feature at the top of a gable, pinnacle, etc.

Flamboyant: the final stage of French Gothic architecture, 15th–16th centuries, marked by luxuriant, sinuous tracery

fluting: vertical grooves in the shaft of a column

flying buttress: a buttress attached to the wall by a half-arch, absorbing the thrust of the vault

foliate: in the form of leaves

frieze: the central band of a Classical entablature, or a continuous decorative band around the top of a room or building

gallery: an upper floor open on one side, on the outside of a building or overlooking a courtyard; also the storey above the arcade in a Gothic church

gargoyle: a water spout, throwing rainwater clear of the building, carved as a grotesque head

Gothic: the prevalent style in most of Europe from the late 12th century to the Renaissance, characterized by pointed arches, rib vaults, large windows and flying buttresses

Greek cross: a cross with four arms of equal length

groin vault: a vault formed by four barrel vaults meeting at right angles

gumbaz: a dome

hall church: having nave and aisles of equal length, with no clerestory

horseshoe arch: a rounded arch narrowing towards the bottom

hypostyle: a large interior space in which the roof is supported by many pillars

Ionic: second of the three Classical Greek Orders, characterized by column capitals in the form of volutes

iwan: a large vaulted hall open on one side occupying the centre of the wall on each side of the courtyard of a mosque in eastern Islam

keep: see *donjon*

khan: see *caravanserai*

kiosk: a small open building like a summerhouse, often on pillars, associated chiefly with Iran and Anatolia

lancet window: a narrow, pointed window, a feature of early Gothic

lantern: a small, glazed turret on a dome, tower, etc.

Latin cross: a cross in which the vertical part below the horizontal is longer than the other three parts

lattice: an openwork screen, or a window with glazing bars making a similar pattern

light: the glass between two mullions of a window

lintel: a horizontal slab above a door or window

loggia: an arcaded gallery open at the sides; sometimes an independent structure in a garden

louvre: an air vent, sometimes under a lantern, which can be closed by slats, similar to a venetian blind

machicolation: a projecting parapet on a castle, with holes in the floor for dropping missiles onto attackers

madrasa: a Muslim training college

mahal: a palace

Manueline: the ornamental, late Gothic style in Portugal denoting a style of architecture developed during the reign of Manuel I (1495–1521)

masjid: a mosque

mausoleum: a grand, monumental tomb

metopes: square spaces, often carved, that alternate with triglyphs in a Doric frieze

mezzanine: a low intermediate storey, usually above the ground floor

mihrab: the central prayer niche in the qibla wall of a mosque

minaret: a tall, slim tower in a mosque from which worshippers are called to prayer

minbar: the high pulpit in a mosque

mosaic: decoration of a surface with small glass or stone cubes (*tesserae*) set in cement

moulding: projecting bands decoratively shaped or carved in one of many ways

mullions: the vertical bars dividing a window into lights

muqarnas: carved decoration resembling stalactites on an Islamic vault

nave: the area of a church west of the crossing

obelisk: a tapering, four-sided pillar with pyramid top

oculus: a round window, or circular opening in, for example, the top of a dome

ogee curve: a double curve, like the letter S, a common form of moulding

Order: one of the five Classical categories, three Greek plus two Roman, based mainly on the form of the columns

pagoda: a multi-storey Buddhist temple tower

Palladian: A popular style in early 18th-century Europe, based on the designs of the Renaissance Classical architect Andrea Palladio (1508–80)

pediment: the triangular gable above a Classical entablature

pendentive: a type of spandrel for supporting a dome on a square or polygonal drum, in the form of a concave triangle, with the point at the angle of the walls and the (curved) base at the dome

peristyle: a row of columns around a building or courtyard

Perpendicular: the English Gothic style in the mid-14th–16th centuries, marked by strong emphasis on verticals and huge windows

piazza: a large open space, or square, in a town

pier: a vertical masonry support, like a column but thicker, sometimes in the form of a cluster of engaged pillars

pietra dura: a type of inlaid mosaic incorporating semi-precious stones

pilaster: a rectangular column projecting slightly from a wall of which it forms a decorative part

pillar: a free-standing, vertical support that, unlike a column, need not be cylindrical nor related to the Classical Orders

pilotis: pillars that raise a building from the ground, like stilts

pinnacle: a terminating feature like a small turret, on gables, buttresses, corners, etc.

Plateresque: the lavishly decorative style, resmbling silversmiths' work, of 16th-century Spain

plinth: the projecting, squared-off base of a pedestal or building

podium: the base on which a building, especially a temple, is built

porch: a roofed entrance to a building

portcullis: the iron gate of a castle, raised to open, lowered to close

portico: a substantial entrance or porch, occupying the whole façade in a Classical temple

post-and-lintel: see *trabeate*

precast concrete: concrete elements cast, often in a factory, before being placed in position

presbytery: see *sanctuary*

prestressed concrete: concrete reinforced with tensioned wires which, by imparting tension, cause compression in the tension area of the concrete, thus cancelling out stresses caused when loaded

pylon: a flanking tower of a monumental gateway in ancient Egypt, like an extended, truncated pyramid; hence, similar structures elsewhere

qibla (wall): the wall of a mosque nearest Mecca

quadrangle: a rectangular courtyard surrounded by buildings

quadripartite vault: a vault with four units meeting in a point at the centre of a bay

quoins: cut stones forming the corner of a building, usually arranged to appear alternately long and short

Rayonnant: the classic style of French Gothic architecture in the 13th–14th centuries, marked by the integration of tracery with overall design, refinement of mass and willingness to experiment. The word means 'radiating' and describes the pattern of radiating lights in the rose windows characteristic of the time

reinforced concrete: steel rods intoduced to concrete to compensate for its relative weakness in tension

reredos: a wooden or stone carved screen behind the altar of a church

rib vault: a vault in which the divisions (groins) between the curved units are marked by a raised band or moulding

Rococo: the decorative style of the Late Baroque period, peaking about 1730–60, marked by asymmetrical, boldly curving shapes.

Romanesque: the prevailing style, deriving from ancient Rome, of European architecture up to the mid-12th century, characterized by round arches, hefty piers and thick walls

rondel: a circular form, usually ornamental, like a medallion

rose window: a large circular window, with mullions radiating like spokes of a wheel

rotunda: a circular building, typically with dome and colonnade

rustication: large stone blocks, typically on a lower wall, left rough or boldly textured and with deep joints between them

sanctuary: the holiest part of a church or temple, location of the altar or sacred image

scagliola: imitation marble, plaster- or cement-based, with marble fragments or other material and colouring added

scroll: a curling, ornamental form suggesting a paper scroll unwinding

section: a vertical representation of a building, as if sliced through the middle

sgraffito: 'scratched', a form of decoration of tiles or in plaster, with the design cut through to reveal a contrasting colour underneath

shell (roof): a curved roof or other structure in which the thickness of the material is very thin compared with the surface area

shingles: overlapping wooden tiles on the exterior of a building

sikhara: the main tower, usually over the sanctuary, of an Indian temple

spandrel: the roughly triangular surface between the curve of an arch and the right angle formed by a horizontal drawn from its apex and a vertical rising from its springing; hence also, for example, the space between two arches in an arcade

springing: the point at which an arch 'springs' from its vertical support

squinch arch: a series of expanding concentric arches, usually to cover the interior junction of a square tower and a round or polygonal spire or dome

strapwork: carved decoration in the form of interlacing bands or straps

stucco: plaster

stupa: a domed-shaped Buddhist monument containing sacred relics

stylobate: the top level of the base on which a Classical building stands

tatami: Japanese straw mats whose dimensions provided the unit of measurement for designing interiors

terracotta: baked, unglazed clay, most often used decoratively

torana: gateway to a Buddhist or Hindu temple

trabeate: the method of building with vertical posts and horizontal beams

tracery: intersecting stone framework of Gothic windows; also, similar patterns used on walls, vaults, etc.

transept: the projecting arms of a cruciform church, meeting at the crossing

triforium: the open passageway along the wall of a Gothic church above the level of the nave and below the clerestory; sometimes called the gallery

triglyphs: the fluted, squarish blocks

alternating with metopes in a Doric frieze

truss: a wooden, self-supporting framework bridging a space, as in a roof

tunnel vault: see *barrel vault*

turret: a small tower, usually built above another structure, attached to a corner, etc.

Tuscan: A Roman Order, one of the five Classical Orders, supposedly derived from Etruscan architecture, similar to Doric, but with a base and unfluted columns

tympanum: the semicircle between the lintel and the arch of a doorway; also, the triangular space within a Classical pediment

vault: an arched, masonry ceiling

villa: historically, a large country house

volute: the spiralling, scroll-like form as seen in an Ionic capital

voussoirs: wedge-shaped stones forming the inside curve of an arch

ward: see *bailey*

ziggurat: a monumental building of successively smaller concentric stages, a 'stepped' pyramid

INDEX

Acknowledgements

P.2 A A Photo Library: P.3 AA Photo Library: P 5 A Photo Library: P.6 Edifice: P.7 AA Photo Library: P. 9 AA Photo Library: P. 12 AA Photo Library: P.13 (both) AA Photo Library: P. 14–15 (both) AA Photo Library: P. 16–17 (all) AA Photo Library: P. 18–19 (all) AA Photo Library: P. 20 NW004837 © Nik Wheeler/CORBIS: P. 21 (all) AA Photo Library: P. 22 Sonia Halliday Photographs; Photographer James Wellard: P. 23 Werner Forman Archive: P. 24 (left) AA Photo Library; Photo by Rick Strange: P. 25 (both) AA Photo Library: P. 26 and 27 (both) Werner Forman Archive: P. 30 AA Photo Library: P. 31 AA Photo Library: P. 32 AA Photo Library: P. 33 AA Photo Library: P. 34 AA Photo Library: P. 35 A.F. Kersting: P. 36–37 MN001255 © Michael Nicholson/CORBIS, MN001258 © Michael Nicholson/CORBIS, DB001144 © Dave Barlruffi/CORBIS: P. 38 AA Photo Library: P. 39 AA Photo Library: P. 40–41 (both) AA Photo Library: P. 42 (all) AA Photo Library: P. 43 (all) AA Photo Library: P. 44 and 45 (both) © TRIP/M. Barlow: P. 49 AA Photo Library: P. 50 and 51 (both) A.F. Kersting: P. 52 AH002075 © Angelo Hornak/CORBIS: P. 53 EG001415 © Carmen Redondo/CORBIS: P. 54 AA Photo Library; Photo by Rick Strange: P. 55 AL003030 © Paul Almasy/CORBIS: P.56 (both) AA Photo Library: P. 57 AA Photo Library: P. 58 DC001490 © Dean Conger/CORBIS: P. 59 AW003880 © Adam Woolfit/CORBIS: P. 60 (both) AA Photo Library: P. 61 (both) AA Photo Library: P. 62 and 63 AA Photo Library: P. 64 AA Photo Library: P. 65 VN003319 © Ruggero Vanni/CORBIS: P. 66 IH049930 © Ruggero Vanni/CORBIS: P. 67 (both) AA Photo Library: P. 68 JA006227 © James L Amos/CORBIS: P. 69 (both) A.F. Kersting: P. 70 (both) A.F. Kersting: P. 71 (both) AA Photo Library: P. 72 AW002655 © Adam Woolfit/CORBIS: P. 73 (both) AA Photo Library: P. 74 (both) AA Photo Library: P. 75 CS005110 © Archivo Iconigrafico SA/CORBIS: P. 76 AA Photo Library: P. 77 AL004074 © Paul Almasy/CORBIS: P. 78 and 79 (both) AA Photo Library: P. 80 AL013111 © Paul Almasy/CORBIS: P. 81 AL004358 © Paul Almasy/CORBIS: P. 82 (both) Edifice/Norman: P. 83 © Werner Forman Archive: P. 84 (both) AA Photo Library: P. 85 CJ008459 © Charles & Josette Lenars/CORBIS: P. 86 AL003043 © Paul Almasy/CORBIS: P. 87 A.F. Kersting: P. 88 AA Photo Library: P. 89 (both) AA Photo Library: P. 90 and 91 (both) AA Photo Library: P. 92 AL012901 © Paul Almasy/CORBIS: P. 93 A.F. Kersting: P. 94 and 95 (both) AA Photo Library: P. 96 AA Photo Library: P. 97 (both) AA Photo Library: P. 98 AA Photo Library: P. 99 © TRIP/TH-FOTO WERBUNG: P. 100 AA Photo Library: P.101 (both) AA Photo Library: P. 102 (left) AA Photo Library: P. 102 (right) IH166872 © Richard T. Nowitz/CORBIS: P. 103 JB011287 © Jonathan Blair/CORBIS: P. 104 and 105 (all) AA Photo Library: P. 106 (both) AA Photo Library: P. 107 AW011771 © Adam Woolfit/CORBIS: P. 108 and 109 (both) AA Photo Library: P. 110 (both) AA Photo Library: P. 111 AA Photo Library: P. 112 and 113 (both) AA Photo Library: P. 114 and 115 (all) AA Photo Library: P. 116 and 117 (all) AA Photo Library: P. 118

(left) AA Photo Library: P. 118 (right) WS001869 © Patrick Ward/CORBIS: P. 119 (both) AA Photo Library: P. 120 and 121 (all) AA Photo Library: P. 122 AL003101 © Paul Almasy/CORBIS: P. 123 QU001782 © Chris Lisle: P. 126 AA Photo Library: P. 127 Edifice/Lewis: P. 128 VN002008 © Ruggero Vanni/CORBIS: P. 129 ME001076 G Macduff Everton/CORBIS: P. 130 and 131 (both) A.F. Kersting: P. 132 VU002776 © Sandro Vannini/CORBIS: P. 133 A.F. Kersting: P. 134 EG001331 © Carmen Redondo/CORBIS: P. 135 AA Photo Library: P. 136 MN001278 © Michael Nicholson/CORBIS: P. 137 FC001500 © Francesco Muntada/CORBIS: P. 138 and 139 (all) AA Photo Library: P. 140 and 141 (all) AA Photo Library: P. 142 and 143 (both) AA Photo Library: P. 144 (both) AA Photo Library: P. 145 DS002236 © Leonard de Selva/CORBIS: P. 146 and 147 (all) AA Photo Library: P. 148 A.F. Kersting: P. 149 VN002377 © Ruggero Vanni/CORBIS: P. 150 and 151 (both) AA Photo Library: P. 152 AA Photo Library: P. 153 EL005396 © Elio Ciol/CORBIS: P. 154 and 155 (all) AA Photo Library: P. 156 and 157 (both) AA Photo Library: P. 158–159 CS004571 © Archivo Iconigrafico SA/CORBIS: P. 160 and 161 (both) AA Photo Library: P. 162 DY001456 © Danny Lehman/CORBIS: P. 163 (both) AA Photo Library: P. 164 and 165 (all) AA Photo Library: P. 166 (both) AA Photo Library: P. 167 Edifice/Darley: P. 168 and 169 (both) Edifice/Darley: P. 170 (both) AA Photo Library: P. 171 AA Photo Library; Photo by Tony Souter: P. 172 A.F. Kersting: P. 173 AA Photo Library: P. 174 and 175 (both) AA Photo Library: P. 176 A. F. Kersting: P. 177 A.F. Kersting: P. 178 and 179 (all) AA Photo Library: P. 183 A.F. Kersting: P. 184 and 185 (both) AA Photo Library: P. 186 and 187 (both) Edifice/Darley: P. 188 and 189 (both) A.F. Kersting: P. 190 and 191 (both) A.F. Kersting: P. 192 and 193 (both) A.F. Kersting: P. 194 and 195 (all) Edifice/Darley: P. 196 and 197 (both) AA Photo Library: P. 198–199 HG002428 © Hans Georg Roth/CORBIS: P. 200 AA Photo Library: P. 201 AW025240 © Adam Woolfit/CORBIS: P. 202 and 203 (both) AA Photo Library: P. 204 and 205 (all) Edifice/Lewis: P. 206 and 207 (all) AA Photo Library: Page 208 (both) AA Photo Library: P. 209 A.F. Kersting: P. 210 and 211 (both) AA Photo Library: P. 212 Trip/M. O'Brien: P. 213 AA Photo Library: P. 214 TG004243 © Todd Gipstein/CORBIS: P. 215 (both) AA Photo Library: P. 216 and 217 (both) AA Photo Library: P. 218 Edifice: P. 219 GM004027 © Carl Mooney/CORBIS: P. 220 and 221 (all) AA Photo Library: P. 222 and 223 (all) AA Photo Library: P. 224 and 225 (all) AA Photo Library: P. 226 (both) AA Photo Library: P. 227 (both) AA Photo Library: P. 228 (left) AA Photo Library: P. 228 (right) AA Photo Library; Photo by Tim Woodcock: P. 229 AA Photo Library: P. 230 and 231 (both) AA Photo Library: P. 232 and 233 (both) AA Photo Library: P. 234 HE001602 © Chris Hellier/CORBIS: P. 236 and 237 (all) Glasgow School of Art: P. 238 and 239 (both) AA Photo Library: P. 240 MT000459 © MIT Collection/CORBIS: P. 241 AA Photo Library: P. 245 AA Photo Library © Gordon D.R. Clements/Axiom: P. 246 AA Photo Library: P. 247 AA Photo Library © Gordon D.R. Clements/Axiom: P. 248 and 249 (both) Ffotograff © Patricia

Aithie: P. 250 UB003007 © Patrick Field/CORBIS: P. 251 DC007252 © Dean Conger/CORBIS: P. 252 and 253 (both) © Trip/P. Mitchell: P. 254 and 255 (both) AA Photo Library © Gordon D.R. Clements/Axiom: P. 260 AA Photo Library © 1995 Jim Holmes: P. 264 © Michael Yamashito/CORBIS: P. 266 RH011734 © Robert Holmes/CORBIS: P. 267 UB007000 © Frank Leather/CORBIS: P. 268 RH009883 © Robert Holmes/CORBIS: P. 269 (both) Trewin Copplestone: P. 270 and 271 (all) AA Photo Library © Gordon D.R. Clements/Axiom: P. 272 and 273 (both) © Trewin Copplestone: P. 276 A.F. Kersting: P. 277 A.F. Kersting: P. 278 A.F. Kersting: P. 279 Edifice/Mayer: P. 280 and 281 (both) Edifice/Mayer: P. 282 and 283 (both) A.F. Kersting: P. 284 and 285 (both) A.F. Kersting: P. 286 and 287 (both) A.F. Kersting: P. 288 IH030624 © Sheldon Collins/CORBIS: P. 289 IH033604 © Sheldon Collins/CORBIS: P. 290–291 AA Photo Library: P. 292 AA Photo Library: P. 293 (both) Edifice/Mayer: P. 294 and 295 (both) A.F. Kersting: P. 296 and 297 (both) A.F. Kersting: P. 298 and 299 (both) AA Photo Library: P. 300 © Trip/Trip: P. 301 A.F. Kersting: P. 302 HR003048 © Jeremy Horner/CORBIS: P. 303 A.F. Kersting: P. 304 © Trip, D./Saunders: P. 305 © Werner Forman Archive: P. 306 and 307 (all) AA Photo Library: P. 310 AA Photo Library: P. 311 (right) © HG001174 © Hans Georg Roth/CORBIS: P. 311 (left) TRIP/TRIP: P. 312 AA Photo Library: P. 313 AA Photo Library; Photo by Julian Loader: P. 314 AA Photo Library: P. 315 AA Photo Library; Photo by Michelle Chaplow: P. 316 LJ001213 © Abilio Lope/CORBIS: P. 317 (all) AA Photo Library: P. 318–19 © Trip/J. Sweeney: P. 320 (both) AA Photo Library: P. 321 VN004723 © Gian Berto Vanni/CORBIS: P. 321–322 A.F. Kersting: P. 322–323 A.F. Kersting: P. 324 and 325 (both) AA Photo Library: P. 326 and 327 (both) A.F. Kersting: P. 328 HE002175 © Chris Hellier/CORBIS: P. 329 © Werner Forman Archive: P. 330 and 331 AA Photo Library: P. 332 (both) AA Photo Library: P. 333 AA Photo Library; Photo by Paul Kenward: P. 334 and 335 (all) © Werner Forman Archive: P. 336 RW002460 © Roger Wood/CORBIS: P. 336–337 A.F. Kersting: P. 338 and 339 (both) © Trip/C. Rennie: P. 340 and 341 (both) © TRIP/Tibor Bognar: P. 345 Edifice/Darley: P. 346 and 347 (both) © Thomas A. Heinz: P. 348 and 349 (both) © Thomas A. Heinz: P. 350 TE001916 © Ed Eckstein/CORBIS: P. 351 MK001092 © Michael John Kielty/CORBIS: P. 352 and 353 (all) © Thomas A. Heinz: P. 355 Bildarchiv Foto Marburg: P. 356 and 357 (both) AA Photo Library: P. 358 NB001499 © Neil Beer/CORBIS: P. 359 DH004717 © Dave G. Houser/CORBIS: P. 360 and 361 (both) Edifice/Darley: P. 362 © TRIP/Z. Harasym: P. 363 AA Photo Library: P. 364 and 365 (both) Edifice/Darley: P. 366–367 VN003750 © Ruggero Vanni/CORBIS: P. 368–369 AA Photo Library: P. 370–371 AX001770 © CRDPHOTO/CORBIS: P. 372 and 373 (both) AA Photo Library: P. 374 and 375 (both) © Edifice © Gillian Darley: P. 376 and 377 (both) © Thomas A. Heinz: P. 378 and 379 (both) © Thomas A. Heinz: P. 380 IH166624 © Richard T. Nowitz/CORBIS: P. 381 YM013046 © Michael S. Yamashita/CORBIS: P. 382 and 383 (all) AA Photo Library: P. 384 and 385 (all) AA Photo

Library: P. 386 Edifice/Darley: P. 387 AH002177 © Angelo Hornak/CORBIS: P. 388 and 389 (both) © Thomas A. Heinz: P. 390 © Thomas A Heinz: P. 391 (both) © Trewin Copplestone: P. 392 Edifice © Heini Schneebeli: P. 393 © Sonia Halliday Photographs: P. 394 and 395 (both) Edifice © Heini Schneebeli: P. 396 MA11305A © Francis G. Mayen/CORBIS: P. 397 TG001931 © Todd Gipstein/CORBIS: P. 398 and 399 (both) A.F. Kersting: P. 400 and 401 (both) © Thomas A. Heinz: P. 402–403 VC004260 © Vince Streano/CORBIS: P. 404 KM 003284 © Kelly-Mooney Photography/CORBIS: P. 405 JS1000001 © Joseph Sohm, Visions of America/CORBIS: P. 406 IH027411 © Jeremy Horner/CORBIS: P. 407 AH001754 © Angelo Hornak/CORBIS: P. 408 and 409 (both) Edifice/Darley: P. 410 UB009877 © John Dakars; Eye Ubiquitous/CORBIS: P. 411 UB 004826 © Julia Waterlow; Eye Ubiquitous/CORBIS: P. 412 and 413 (both) © Thomas A. Heinz: P. 414 and 415 (both) © Thomas A. Heinz: P. 416–417 © Thomas A. Heinz: P. 418–419 Edifice/Darley: P. 420–421 AA Photo Library: P. 422 and 423 (both) Edifice/Darley: P. 424 and 425 (both) AA Photo Library: P. 426 DV002351 © WildCountry/CORBIS: P. 427 DV002332 © WildCountry/CORBIS: P. 428 RI002212 © Bob Krist/CORBIS: P. 429 KF001086 © Kevin Fleming/CORBIS: P. 430 Foster & Partners; Photographer Nigel Young: P. 431 Foster and Partners; Photographer Ian Lambot: P. 432 © Edifice/Darley: P. 434 UB010092 ©John Dakars; Eye Ubiquitous/CORBIS: P. 436 © Trewin Copplestone: P. 437 Edifice/Darley.

Kingston Libraries

This item can be returned
or renewed at a Kingston
Borough Library on or
before the latest date
stamped below. If the item
is not reserved by another
reader it may be renewed
by telephone up to a
maximum of three times
quoting your membership
number. Only items issued
for the standard three-week
loan period are renewable.

www.kingston.gov.uk/libraries

Royal
Kingston

ALSO BY ARAVIND ADIGA
FROM CLIPPER LARGE PRINT

The White Tiger

Between the Assassinations

Aravind Adiga

W F HOWES LTD

This large print edition published in 2009 by
W F Howes Ltd
Unit 4, Rearsby Business Park, Gaddesby Lane,
Rearsby, Leicester LE7 4YH

1 3 5 7 9 10 8 6 4 2

First published in the United Kingdom in 2009
by Atlantic Books

A CIP catalogue record for this book is available
from the British Library

ISBN 978 1 40744 220 4

Typeset by Palimpsest Book Production Limited,
Grangemouth, Stirlingshire
Printed and bound in Great Britain
by MPG Books Ltd, Bodmin, Cornwall

For Ramin Bahrani

CONTENTS

ARRIVING IN KITTUR

Kittur is on India's south-western coast, between Goa and Calicut, and almost equidistant from the two. It is bounded by the Arabian Sea to the west, and by the Kaliamma river to the south and east. The terrain of the town is hilly; the soil is black and mildly acidic. The monsoons arrive in June and besiege the town through September. The following three months are dry and cool and are the best time to visit Kittur. Given the town's richness of history and scenic beauty, and diversity of religion, race, and language, a minimum stay of a week is recommended.

DAY ONE (MORNING):
THE RAILWAY STATION

The arches of the railway station frame your first view of Kittur as you arrive as a passenger on the Madras Mail (arrival early morning) or the West Coast Express (arrival afternoon). The station is dim, dirty, and littered with discarded lunch bags into which stray dogs poke their noses; in the evening, the rats emerge.

The walls are covered with the image of a jolly, plump, pot-bellied, and entirely naked man, his genitalia strategically covered by his crossed legs, who floats above a caption in Kannada that says: 'A SINGLE WORD FROM THIS MAN CAN CHANGE YOUR LIFE'. He is the spiritual leader of a local Jain sect that runs a free hospital and lunch-room in the town.

The famous Kittamma Devi temple, a modern structure built in the Tamil style, stands on the site where an ancient shrine to the goddess is believed to have existed. It is within walking distance of the train station

2

and is often the first port of call of visitors to the town.

None of the other shopkeepers near the railway station would hire a Muslim, but Ramanna Shetty, who ran the Ideal Store, a tea-and-samosa place, had told Ziauddin it was okay for him to stay.

Provided he promised to work hard. And keep away from all hanky-panky.

The little, dust-covered creature let its bag drop to the ground; a hand went up to its heart.

'I'm a Muslim, sir. We *don't* do hanky-panky.'

Ziauddin was small and black, with baby fat in his cheeks and an elfin grin that exposed big, white, rabbity teeth. He boiled tea for the customers in an enormous, pitted stainless-steel kettle, watching with furious concentration as the water seethed, overspilled, and sizzled into the gas flame. Periodically, he dug his palm into one of the battered stainless-steel boxes at his side to toss black tea powder, or a handful of white sugar, or a piece of crushed ginger into the brew. He sucked in his lips, held his breath, and with his left forearm tipped the kettle into a strainer: hot tea dripped through its clogged pores into small, tapering glasses that sat in the slots of a carton originally designed to hold eggs.

Taking the glasses one at a time to the tables, he delighted the rough men who frequented the teashop by interrupting their conversations with

3

shouts of 'One-a! Two-a! Three-a!' as he slammed the glasses down in front of them. Later, the men would see him squatting by the side of the shop, soaking dishes in a large trough filled with murky bilge water; or wrapping greasy samosas in pages ripped from college trigonometry textbooks so they could be home-delivered; or scooping the gunk of tea leaves out of the strainer; or tightening, with a rusty screwdriver, a loose nail in the back of a chair. When a word was said in English all work stopped: he would turn around and repeat it at the top of his voice ('Sunday-Monday, Goodbye, Sexy!'), and the entire shop shook with laughter.

Late in the evening, just as Ramanna Shetty was ready to close up, Thimma, a local drunk, who had bought three cigarettes every night, would roar with delight to see Ziauddin, his bum and thighs pressed against the giant fridge, shoving it back into the shop, inch by inch.

'Look at that whippersnapper!' Thimma clapped. 'The fridge is bigger than him, but what a fighter he is!'

Calling the whippersnapper close, he put a twenty-five paisa coin in his palm. The little boy looked at the shopkeeper's eyes for approval. When Ramanna Shetty nodded, he closed his fist, and yelped in English:

'Thanks you, sir!'

One evening, pressing a hand down on the boy's head, Ramanna Shetty brought him over to the

4

drunk and asked: 'How old do you think he is? Take a guess.'

Thimma learned that the whippersnapper was nearly twelve. He was the sixth of eleven children from a farm-labouring family up in the north of the state; as soon as the rains ended his father had put him on a bus, with instructions to get off at Kittur and walk around the market until someone took him in. 'They packed him off without even one paisa,' Ramanna said. 'This fellow was left entirely to his own wits.'

He again placed a hand on Ziauddin's head.

'Which, I can tell you, aren't much, even for a Muslim!'

Ziauddin had made friends with the six other boys who washed dishes and ran Ramanna's shop, and slept together in a tent they had pitched behind the shop. On Sunday, at noon, Ramanna pulled down the shutters, and slowly rode his blue-and-cream-coloured Bajaj scooter over to the Kittamma Devi temple, letting the boys follow on foot. As he entered the temple to offer a coconut to the goddess, they sat on the green cushion of the scooter, discussing the bold red words written in Kannada on the cornice of the temple: 'HONOUR THY NEIGH-BOUR, THY GOD.'

'That means the person in the house next door is your God,' one boy theorized.

'No, it means God is close to you if you really believe in Him,' retorted another.

5

'No, it means, it means—' Ziauddin tried to explain.

But they wouldn't let him finish: 'You can't read or write, you hick!'

When Ramanna shouted for them to come into the temple, he darted in with the others a few feet, hesitated, and then ran back to the scooter: 'I'm a Muslim, I can't go in.'

He had said the word in English, and with such solemnity that the other boys were silent for a moment, and then grinned.

A week before the rains were due to start, the boy collected his bundle and said: 'I'm going home.' He was going to do his duty to his family, and work alongside his father and mother and brothers, weeding or sowing or harvesting some rich man's fields for a few rupees a day. Ramanna gave him an 'extra' of five rupees (minus ten paise for each of two bottles of Thums Up he had broken), to make sure he would return from his village.

Four months later, when Ziauddin came back, he had developed vitiligo, and pink skin streaked his lips and speckled his fingers and earlobes. The baby fat in his face had evaporated over the summer; he returned lean and sunburned, and with a wildness in his eyes.

'What happened to you?' Ramanna demanded, after releasing him from a hug. 'You were supposed to come back a month and a half ago.'

'Nothing happened,' the boy said, rubbing a finger over his discoloured lips.

Ramanna ordered a plate of food at once; Ziauddin grabbed it and stuffed his face like a little animal, and the shopkeeper had to say: 'Didn't they feed you anything back home?'

The 'whippersnapper' was displayed to all the customers, many of whom had been asking for him for months; some who had drifted to the newer and cleaner teashops opening up around the train station came back to Ramanna's place just to see him. At night, Thimma hugged him several times, and then slipped him two 25-paise coins which Ziauddin accepted silently, sliding them into his trousers. Ramanna shouted to the drunk: 'Don't leave him tips! He's become a thief!'

The boy had been caught stealing samosas meant for a client, Ramanna said. Thimma asked the shopkeeper if he was joking.

'I wouldn't have believed it myself,' Ramanna mumbled. 'But I saw it with my own eyes. He was taking a samosa from the kitchen, and—' Ramanna bit into an imaginary samosa.

Gritting his teeth, Ziauddin had begun pushing the fridge into the shop with the back of his legs.

'But . . . he used to be an honest little fellow . . .' the drunk recalled.

'Maybe he had been stealing all along and we just never knew it. You can't trust anyone these days.'

The bottles in the fridge rattled. Ziauddin had stopped his work.

'I'm a Pathan!' He slapped his chest. 'From the

land of the Pathans, far up north, where there are mountains full of snow! I'm not a Hindu! I don't do hanky-panky!'

Then he walked into the back of the shop.

'What the hell is this?' asked the drunk.

The shopkeeper explained that Ziauddin was now spouting this Pathan-Wathan gibberish all the time; he thought the boy must have picked it up from some mullah in the north of the state.

Thimma roared. He put his hands on his hips and shouted into the back of the shop: 'Ziauddin, Pathans are white-skinned, like Imran Khan; you're as black as an African!'

The next morning there was a storm at the Ideal Store. This time Ziauddin had been caught red-handed. Holding him by the collar of his shirt and dragging him out in front of the customers, Ramanna Shetty said: 'Tell me the truth – you son of a bald woman. Did you steal it? Tell me the truth this time and I might give you another chance.'

'I am telling the truth,' Ziauddin said, touching his pink, vitiligo-discoloured lips with a crooked finger. 'I didn't touch even one of the samosas.'

Ramanna grabbed him by the shoulder and pushed him to the ground, kicked him, and then shoved him out of the teashop, while the other boys huddled together and watched impassively, as sheep do when watching one of their flock being shorn. Then Ramanna howled: he raised one of his fingers, which was bleeding.

'He bit me – the animal!'

'I'm a Pathan!' Ziauddin shouted back, as he rose to his knees. 'We came here and built the Taj Mahal and the Red Fort in Delhi. Don't you dare treat me like this, you son of a bald woman, you—'

Ramanna turned to the ring of customers who had gathered around them, and were staring at him and at Ziauddin, trying to make up their minds as to who was right and who was wrong: 'There is no work here for a Muslim, and he has to fight with the one man who gives him a job.'

A few days later, Ziauddin passed by the teashop, driving a cycle with a cart attached to it; large canisters of milk clanged together in the cart.

'Look at me,' he mocked his former employer. 'The milk people trust me!'

But that job did not last long either; once again he was accused of theft. He publicly swore never to work for a Hindu again.

New Muslim restaurants were being opened at the far side of the railway station, where the Muslim immigrants were settling, and Ziauddin found work in one of these restaurants. He made omelette and toast at an outdoor grill, and shouted in Urdu and Malayalam: 'Muslim men, wherever in the world you are from, Yemen or Kerala or Arabia or Bengal, come eat at a genuine Muslim shop!'

But even this job did not last – he was again charged with theft by his employer, who slapped

9

him when he talked back – and he was next seen in a red uniform at the railway station, carrying mounds of luggage on his head and fighting bitterly with the passengers over his pay.

'I'm the son of a Pathan; I have the blood of a Pathan in me. You hear; I'm no cheat!'

When he glared at them, his eyeballs bulged and the tendons in his neck stood out in high relief. He had become another of those lean, lonely men with vivid eyes who haunt every train station in India, smoking their beedis in a corner and looking ready to hit or kill someone at a moment's notice. Yet when old customers from Ramanna's shop called him by his name, he grinned, and then they saw something of the boy with the big smile who had slammed glasses of tea down on their tables and mangled their English. They wondered what on earth had happened to him.

In the end, Ziauddin picked fights with the other porters, got kicked out of the train station too, and wandered aimlessly for a few days, cursing Hindu and Muslim alike. Then he was back at the station, carrying bags on his head again. He was a good worker; everyone had to concede that much. And there was plenty of work now for everyone. Several trains full of soldiers had arrived in Kittur – there was talk in the market that a new army base was being set up on the route to Cochin – and for days after the soldiers left, freight trains followed in their wake, carrying large crates that needed to be offloaded. Ziauddin shut his mouth, and carried the crates off the train and out of the station, where army trucks were waiting to load them.

One Sunday, he lay on the platform of the station, still asleep at ten in the morning, dead tired from the week's labour. He woke up with his nostrils twitching: the smell of soap was in the air. Rivulets of foam and bubble flowed beside him. A line of thin black bodies were bathing at the edge of the platform.

The fragrance of their foam made Ziauddin sneeze.

'Hey, bathe somewhere else! Leave me alone!'

The men laughed and shouted and pointed their lathered white fingers at Ziauddin: 'We're not all unclean animals, Zia! Some of us are Hindus!'

'I'm a Pathan!' he yelled back at the bathers. 'Don't talk to me like that.'

He began shouting at them when something strange happened – the bathers all rushed away from him, crying: 'A coolie, sir? A coolie?'

A stranger had materialized on the platform, even though no train had pulled up: a tall, fair-skinned man holding a small black bag. He wore a clean white business shirt and grey cotton trousers and everything about him smelled of money; this drove the other porters wild, and they crowded around him, still covered in lather, like men with a horrible disease gathering around a doctor who might have a cure. But he rejected

11

them all and walked up to the only porter who was not covered in lather.

'Which hotel?' Ziauddin asked, struggling to his feet.

The stranger shrugged, as if to say: 'Your choice.' He looked with disapproval at the other porters, who were still hovering around, nearly nude and covered in soap.

After sticking his tongue out at the other porters, Zia set off with the stranger.

The two of them walked towards the cheap hotels that filled the roads around the station. Stopping at a building that was covered in signs – for electrical shops, chemists, pharmacists, plumbers – Ziauddin pointed out a red sign on the second floor.

HOTEL DECENT
BOARDING AND LODGING
ALL FOODS AND SERVICES HERE
NORTH INDIAN SOUTH INDIAN
CHINESE WESTERN TIBETAN DISHES
TAXI PASSPORT VISA XEROX TRUNK CALL
FOR ALL COUNTRIES

'How about this one, sir? It's the best place in town.' He put a hand on his heart. 'I give you my word.'

The Hotel Decent had a good deal with all the railway porters: a 'cut' of two and a half rupees for every customer they brought in.

12

The stranger lowered his voice confidentially. 'My dear fellow, is it a good place, though?'

He emphasized the critical word by saying it in English.

'Very good,' Zia said with a wink. 'Very, very good.'

The stranger crooked his finger and beckoned Zia closer. He spoke into Zia's ear: 'My dear fellow: I am a Muslim.'

'I know, sir. So am I.'

'Not just any Muslim. I'm a *Pathan*.'

It was as if Ziauddin had heard a magic spell. He gaped at the stranger.

'Forgive me, sir . . . I . . . didn't . . . I . . . Allah has sent you to exactly the right porter, sir! And this is not the right hotel for you at all, sir. In fact it is a very bad hotel. And this is not the right . . .'

Tossing the foreign bag from hand to hand, he took the stranger around the station to the other side – where the hotels were Muslim-owned and where 'cuts' were not given to the porters. He stopped at one place and said: 'Will this do?'

HOTEL DARUL-ISLAM
BOARDING AND LOGING

The stranger contemplated the sign, the green archway into the hotel, the image of the Great Mosque of Mecca above the doorway; then he put a hand into a pocket of his grey trousers and brought out a five-rupee note.

13

'It's too much, sir, for one bag. Just give me two rupees.' Zia bit his lip. 'No, even that is too much.'

The stranger smiled. 'An honest man.'

He tapped two fingers of his left hand on his right shoulder.

'I've got a bad arm, my friend. I wouldn't have been able to carry the bag here without a lot of pain.' He pressed the money into Zia's hands. 'You deserve even more.'

Ziauddin took the money; he looked at the stranger's face.

'Are you really a *Pathan*, sir?'

The boy's body shivered at the stranger's answer.

'Me too!' he shouted, and then ran like crazy, yelling: 'Me too! Me too!'

That night Ziauddin dreamed of snow-covered mountains and a race of fair-skinned, courteous men who tipped like gods. In the morning, he returned to the guest house, and found the stranger on one of the benches outside, sipping from a yellow teacup.

'Will you have tea with me, little Pathan?'

Confused, Ziauddin shook his head, but the stranger was already snapping his fingers. The proprietor, a fat man with a clean-shaven lip and a full, fluffy white beard like a crescent moon, looked unhappily at the filthy porter, before indicating, with a grunt, that he was allowed to sit down at the tables today.

The stranger asked: 'So you're also a Pathan, little friend?'

Ziauddin nodded. He informed the stranger of the name of the man who had told him he was a Pathan. 'He was a learned man, sir: he had been to Saudi Arabia for a year.'

'Ah,' the stranger said, shaking his head. 'Ah, I see. I see now.'

A few minutes passed in silence. Ziauddin said: 'I hope you're not staying here a long time, sir. It's a bad town.'

The Pathan arched his eyebrows.

'For Muslims like us, it's bad. The Hindus don't give us jobs; they don't give us respect. I speak from experience, sir.'

The stranger took out a notebook and began writing. Zia watched. He looked again at the stranger's handsome face, his expensive clothes; he inhaled the scent from his fingers and face. 'This man is a countryman of yours, Zia,' the boy said to himself. 'A countryman of yours!'

The Pathan finished his tea and yawned. As if he had forgotten all about Zia, he went back into his guest house and shut the door behind him.

As soon as his foreign guest had disappeared into the guest house, the owner of the place caught Ziauddin's eye and jerked his head, and the dirty coolie knew that his tea was not coming. He went back to the train station, where he stood in his usual spot and waited for a passenger to approach him with steel trunks or leather bags to be carried to the train. But his soul was shining with pride, and he fought with no one that day.

15

The following morning, he woke up to the smell of fresh laundry. 'A Pathan always rises at dawn, my friend.'

Yawning and stretching himself, Ziauddin opened his eyes: a pair of beautiful pale blue eyes was looking down on him: eyes such as a man might get when he gazes on snow for a long time. Stumbling to his feet, Ziauddin apologized to the stranger, then shook his hand and almost kissed his face.

'Have you had something to eat?' the Pathan asked.

Zia shook his head; he never ate before noon.

The Pathan took him to one of the tea-and-samosa stands near the station. It was a place where Zia had once worked, and the boys watched in astonishment as he sat down at the table and cried: 'A plate of your best! Two Pathans need to be fed this morning!'

The stranger leaned over to him and said: 'Don't say it aloud. They shouldn't know about us: it's our *secret*.'

And then he quickly passed a note into Zia's hands. Uncrumpling the note, the boy saw a tractor and a rising red sun. Five rupees!

'You want me to take your bag all the way to Bombay? That's how far this note goes in Kittur.'

He leaned back in his chair as a serving-boy put down two cups of tea, and a plate holding a large samosa, sliced into two and covered with watery ketchup, in front of them. The Pathan and Zia

16

each chewed on his half of the samosa. Then the man picked a piece of the samosa from his teeth and told Ziauddin what he expected for his five rupees.

Half an hour later, Zia sat down at a corner of the train station, outside the waiting room. When customers asked him to carry their luggage, he shook his head and said: 'I've got another job today.' When the trains came into the station, he counted them. But since it was not easy to remember the total, he moved further away and sat under the shade of a tree that grew within the station; each time an engine whistled past he made a mark in the mud with his big toe, crossing off each batch of five. Some of the trains were packed; some had entire carriages full of soldiers with guns; and some were almost entirely empty. He wondered where they were going to, all these trains, all these people . . . he shut his eyes and began to doze; the engine of a train startled him, and he scraped another mark with his big toe. When he got up to his feet to go for lunch, he realized he had been sitting on some part of the markings and they had been smudged under his weight; and then he had to try desperately to decipher them.

In the evening, he saw the Pathan sitting on one of the benches outside the guest house, sipping tea. The big man smiled when he saw Ziauddin and slapped a spot on the bench next to him three times.

'They didn't give me tea yesterday evening,' Ziauddin complained, and he explained what had happened. The Pathan's face darkened; Ziauddin saw that the stranger was righteous. He was also powerful: without saying a word he turned to the proprietor and glowered at him; within a minute a boy came running out of the hotel holding a yellow cup and put it down in front of Zia. He inhaled the flavours of cardamom and sweet steaming milk, and said: 'Seventeen trains came into Kittur. And sixteen left Kittur. I counted every one of them just like you asked.'

'Good,' the Pathan said. 'Now tell me: how many of these trains had Indian soldiers in them?'

Ziauddin stared.

'How-many-of-them-had-Indian-soldiers-in-them?'

'All of them had soldiers . . . I don't know . . .'

'Six trains had Indian soldiers in them,' the Pathan said. 'Four going to Cochin, two coming back.'

The next day, Ziauddin sat down at the tree in the corner of the station half an hour before the first train pulled in. He marked the earth with his big toe; between trains he went to the snack-shop inside the station.

'You can't come here!' the shopkeeper shouted. 'We don't want any trouble again!'

'You won't have any trouble from me,' Zia said. 'I've got money on me today.' He placed a one-rupee

18

note on the table. 'Put that note into your money-box and then give me a chicken samosa.'

That evening Zia reported to the Pathan that eleven trains had arrived with soldiers.

'Well done,' said the man.

The Pathan, reaching out with his weak arm, exerted a little pressure on each of Ziauddin's cheeks. He produced another five-rupee note, which the boy accepted without hesitation.

'Tomorrow I want you to notice how many of the trains had a red cross marked on the sides of the compartments.'

Ziauddin closed his eyes and repeated: 'Red cross marked on sides.' He jumped to his feet, gave a military salute, and said: *'Thanks you, sir!'*

The Pathan laughed; a warm, hearty, foreign laugh.

The next day, Ziauddin sat under the tree once again, scrawling numbers in three rows with his toe. One, number of trains. Two, number of trains with soldiers in them. Three, number of trains marked with red crosses.

Sixteen, eleven, eight.

Another train passed by; Zia looked up, squinted, then moved his toe into position over the first of the three rows.

He held his toe like that, in mid-air, for an instant, and then let it fall to the ground, taking care that it not smudge any of the markings. The train left, and immediately behind it another one pulled into the station, full of soldiers, but

Ziauddin did not add to his tally. He simply stared at the scratches he had already made, as if he had seen something new in them.

The Pathan was at the guest house when Ziauddin got there at four. The tall man's hands were behind his back, and he had been pacing around the benches. He came to the boy with quick steps.

'Did you get the number?'

Ziauddin nodded.

But when the two of them had sat down, he asked: 'What're you making me do these things for?'

The Pathan leaned all the way across the table with his weak arm and tried to touch Ziauddin's hair.

'At last you ask. At last.' He smiled.

The guest house proprietor with the beard like the moon came out without prompting; he put two cups of tea down on the table, then stepped back and rubbed his palms and smiled. The Pathan dismissed him with a movement of his head. He sipped his tea; Ziauddin did not touch his.

'Do you know where those trains full of soldiers and marked with red crosses are going?'

Ziauddin shook his head.

'Towards Calicut.'

The stranger brought his face closer. The boy saw things he had not seen before: scars on the Pathan's nose and cheeks, and a small tear in his left ear.

'The Indian army is setting up a base somewhere between Kittur and Calicut. For one reason and one reason only . . .' – he held up a thick finger. 'To do to the Muslims of South India what they are doing to Muslims in Kashmir.'

Ziauddin looked down at the tea. A rippled skin of milk-fat was congealing on its surface.

'I'm a Muslim,' he said. 'The son of a Muslim too.'

'Exactly. Exactly.' The foreigner's thick fingers covered the surface of the teacup. 'Now listen: each time you watch the trains, there will be a little reward for you. Mind – it won't always be five rupees, but it will be something. A Pathan takes care of other Pathans. It's simple work. I am here to do the hard work. You'll—'

Ziauddin said: 'I'm not well. I can't do it tomorrow.'

The foreigner thought about this, and then said: 'You are lying to me. May I ask why?'

A finger passed over a pair of vitiligo-discoloured lips. 'I'm a Muslim. The son of a Muslim, too.'

'There are fifty thousand Muslims in this town.' The foreigner's voice crackled with irritation. 'Every one of them seethes. Every one of them is ready for action. I was only offering this job to you out of pity. Because I see what the Indians have done to you. Otherwise I would have offered the job to any of these other fifty thousand fellows.'

Ziauddin kicked back his chair and stood up.

'Then get one of those fifty thousand fellows to do it.'

Outside the compound of the guest house, he turned around. The Pathan was looking at him; he spoke in a soft voice.

'Is this any way to repay me, little Pathan?'

Ziauddin said nothing. He looked down at the ground. His big toe slowly scratched a figure into the earth: a large circle. He sucked in fresh air and released a hoarse, wordless hiss.

Then he ran. He ran out of the hotel, ran around the train station to the Hindu side, ran all the way to Ramanna Shetty's teashop, and then ran around the back of the shop and into the blue tent where the boys lived. There he sat with his mottled lips pressed together and his fingers laced tightly around his knees.

'What's got into you?' the other boys asked. 'You can't stay here, you know. Shetty will throw you out.' They hid him there that night for old times' sake. When they woke up he was gone. Later in the day he was once again seen at the railway station, fighting with his customers and shouting at them:

'—*don't* do hanky-panky!'

HOW THE TOWN IS LAID OUT

In the geographical centre of Kittur stands the peeling stucco façade of Angel Talkies, a pornographic cinema theatre; regrettably, when the townsfolk give directions, they use Angel Talkies as a reference point. The cinema lies halfway down Umbrella Street, the heart of the commercial district. A significant chunk of Kittur's economy consists of the manufacture of hand-rolled beedis; no wonder, then, that the tallest building in town is the Engineer Beedi Building on Umbrella Street, owned by Mabroor Engineer, reputed to be the town's richest man. Not far from it lies Kittur's most famous ice-cream shop. The Ideal Traders Ice Cream and Fresh Fruit Juice Parlour: White Stallion Talkies, the town's only exclusively English-language film theatre, is another nearby attraction. Ming Palace, the first Chinese restaurant in Kittur, opened on Umbrella Street in 1986. The Ganapati Temple in this street is modelled on a famous temple in Goa and is the site of an annual pooja to the elephant-headed deity.

23

Continue on Umbrella Street north of Angel Talkies and you will reach, via the Nehru Maidan and the train station, the Roman Catholic suburb of Valencia, whose main landmark is the Cathedral of Our Lady of Valencia. The Double Gate, a colonial-era arched gateway at the far end of Valencia, leads into Bajpe, once a forest, but today a fast-expanding suburb. To the south of Angel Talkies, the road goes uphill into the Lighthouse Hill, and down to the Cool Water Well. From a busy junction near the Well begins the road that leads to the Bunder, or the area around the port. Further south from the Bunder may be seen Sultan's Battery, a black fort, which overlooks the road that leads out over the Kaliamma river into Salt Market Village, the southernmost extension of Kittur.

DAY ONE (AFTERNOON):
THE BUNDER

You have walked down the Cool Water Well Road, past Masjid Road, and you have begun to smell the salt in the air and note the profusion of open-air fish stalls, full of prawns, mussels, shrimps and oysters; you are now not far from the Arabian Sea.

The Bunder, or the area around the port, is now mostly Muslim. The major landmark here is the Dargah, or tomb-shrine, of Yusuf Ali, a domed white structure to which thousands of Muslims from across southern India make pilgrimage each year. The ancient banyan tree growing behind the saint's tomb is always festooned in ribbons of green and gold and is believed to have the power to cure the crippled. Dozens of lepers, amputees, geriatrics, and victims of partial paralysis squat outside the shrine begging alms from visitors.

If you walk to the other end of the Bunder, you will find the industrial area, where dozens of textile sweatshops operate in dingy old buildings. The Bunder has the highest crime rate in Kittur, and is the scene of frequent stabbings, police raids, and arrests. In 1987, riots broke out between Hindus and Muslims near the Dargah, and the police shut down the Bunder area for six days. The Hindus have since been moving out to Bajpe and Salt Market Village.

Abbasi uncorked the bottle – Johnnie Walker Red Label blended, the second-finest whisky known to God or man – and poured a small peg each into two glasses embossed with the Air India *maharajah* logo. He opened the old fridge, took out a bucket of ice, and dropped three cubes by hand into each glass. He poured cold water into the glasses, found a spoon and stirred. He bent his head low and prepared to spit into one of the glasses.

Oh, too simple, Abbasi. Too simple.

He swallowed spittle. Unzipping his cotton trousers, he let them slide down. Pressing the middle and index fingers of his right hand together, he stuck them deep into his rectum; then he dipped them into one of the glasses of whisky and stirred.

He pulled up his trousers and zipped them. He frowned at the tainted whisky; now came the tricky part – things had to be arranged so that the right man took the right glass.

He left the pantry carrying the tray.

The official from the State Electricity Board,

26

sitting at Abbasi's table, grinned. He was a fat, dark man in a blue safari suit, a steel ballpoint pen in his jacket pocket. Abbasi carefully placed the tray on the table in front of the gentleman.

'Please,' Abbasi said, with redundant hospitality; the official had taken the glass closer to him, and was sipping and licking his lips. He finished the whisky in slow gulps, and put the glass down.

'A man's drink.'

Abbasi smiled ironically.

The official placed his hands on his tummy.

'Five hundred,' he said. 'Five hundred rupees.'

Abbasi was a small man, with a streak of grey in his beard which he did not attempt to disguise with dye, as many middle-aged men in Kittur did; he thought the white streak gave him a look of ingenuity, which he felt he needed, because he knew that his reputation among his friends was that of a simple-minded creature prone to regular outbreaks of idealism.

His ancestors, who had served in the royal darbars of Hyderabad, had bequeathed him an elaborate sense of courtesy and good manners, which he had adapted for the realities of the twentieth century with touches of sarcasm and self-parody.

He folded his palms into a Hindu's namaste and bowed low before the official. 'Sahib, you know we have just reopened the factory. There have been many costs. If you could show some—'

'Five hundred. Five hundred rupees.'

The official twirled his glass around and gazed

at the Air India logo with one eye, as if some small part of him were embarrassed by what he was doing. He gestured at his mouth with his fingers: 'A man has to eat these days, Mr Abbasi. Prices are rising so fast. Ever since Mrs Gandhi died, this country has begun to fall apart.'

Abbasi closed his eyes. He reached towards his desk, pulled out a drawer, took out a wad of notes, counted them, and placed the money in front of the official. The fat man, moistening his finger for each note, counted them one by one; producing a blue rubber band from a pocket of his trousers, he strapped it around the notes twice.

But Abbasi knew the ordeal was not over yet. 'Sahib, we have a tradition in this factory that we never let a guest depart without a gift.'

He rang the bell for Ummar, his manager, who entered almost at once with a shirt in his hands. He had been waiting outside the whole time.

The official took the white shirt out of its cardboard box: he looked at the design: a golden dragon whose tail spread round onto the back of the shirt.

'It's gorgeous.'

'We ship them to the United States. They are worn by men who dance professionally. They call it "ballroom dancing". They put on this shirt and swirl under red disco lights.' Abbasi held his hands over his head, and spun round, shaking his hips and buttocks suggestively; the official watched him with lascivious eyes.

He clapped and said: 'Dance for me one more time, Abbasi.'

Then he put the shirt to his nose and sniffed it three times.

'This pattern' – he pressed on the outlines of the dragon with his thick finger – 'it is wonderful.'

'That dragon is the reason I closed,' Abbasi said. 'To stitch the dragon takes very fine embroidery work. The eyes of the women doing this work get damaged. One day this was brought to my attention; I thought, I don't want to answer to Allah for the damage done to the eyes of my workers. So I said to them, go home, and I closed the factory.'

The official smiled ironically. Another of those Muslims who drink whisky and mention Allah in every other sentence.

He put the shirt back in its box and tucked it under his arm. 'What made you reopen the factory, then?'

Abbasi bunched his fingers and jabbed them into his mouth. 'A man has to eat, sahib.'

They went down the stairs together, Ummar following three steps behind. When they reached the bottom, the official saw a dark opening to his right. He took a step towards the darkness. In the dim light of the room, he saw women with white shirts on their laps, stitching threads into half-finished dragons. He wanted to see more, but Abbasi said: 'Why don't you go in, sahib. I'll wait out here.'

29

He turned and looked at the wall, while Ummar took the official around the factory floor, introduced him to some of the workers, and led him back out. The official extended his hand to Abbasi just before he left.

I shouldn't have touched him, Abbasi thought, the moment he closed the door.

At 6 p.m., half an hour after the women left the stitching room for the day, Abbasi closed the factory, got into his Ambassador car, and drove from the Bunder towards Kittur; he could think about one thing only.

Corruption. There is no end to it in this country. In the past four months, since he had decided to reopen his shirt factory, he had had to pay off:

The electricity man; the water board man; half the income tax department of Kittur; half the excise department of Kittur; six different officials of the telephone board; a land tax official of the Kittur City Corporation; a sanitary inspector from the Karnataka State Health Board; a health inspector from the Karnataka State Sanitation Board; a delegation of the All India Small Factory Workers' Union; delegations of the Kittur Congress party, the Kittur BJP, the Kittur Communist Party, and the Kittur Muslim League.

The white Ambassador car went up the driveway of a large, whitewashed mansion. At least four evenings a week Abbasi came to the Canara Club, to a small air-conditioned room with a green

30

billiards table, to play snooker and drink with his friends. He was a good shot, and his aim deteriorated after his second whisky, so his friends liked to play long sets with him.

'What's bothering you, Abbasi?' asked Sunil Shetty, who owned another shirt factory in the Bunder. 'You're playing very rashly tonight.'

'Another visit from the electricity department. A real bastard this time. Dark-skinned fellow. Lower-caste of some kind.'

Sunil Shetty purred in sympathy; Abbasi missed his shot.

Halfway through the game, the players all moved away from the table, while a mouse scurried across the floor, running along the walls until it found a hole to vanish into.

Abbasi banged his fist on the edge of the table.

'Where does all our membership money go? They can't even keep the floors clean! You see how corrupt the management of the club is?'

After that, he sat quietly with his back to the sign that said 'RULES OF THE GAMES MUST BE FOLLOWED AT ALL TIMES' and watched the others play, while resting his chin on the end of his cue stick.

'You are tense, Abbasi,' said Ramanna Padiwal, who owned a silk-and-rayon store on Umbrella Street and was the best snooker-shark in town.

To dispel this myth, Abbasi ordered whiskies for everyone, and they stopped playing and held their glasses wrapped in paper napkins as they sipped.

31

As always, what they talked about first was the whisky itself.

'You know that chap who goes around from house to house offering to pay twenty rupees if you sell him your old cartons of Johnnie Walker Red Label,' Abbasi said. 'To whom does he sell those cartons in turn?'

The others laughed.

'For a Muslim, you're a real innocent, Abbasi,' Padiwal, the used-car salesman, said with a laugh. 'Of course he sells them to the bootlegger. That's why the Johnnie Walker Red you buy from the store, even if it comes in a genuine bottle and genuine carton, is bootlegged.'

Abbasi spoke slowly, drawing circles in the air with his finger: 'So I sold the carton . . . to the man who will sell it to the man who will bootleg the stuff and sell it back to me? That means I've cheated myself?'

Padiwal shot a look of wonderment at Sunil Shetty and said: 'For a Muslim, this fellow is a real . . .'

This was a sentiment that was widespread among the industrialists – ever since Abbasi had shut down his factory because the work was damaging the eyesight of his employees. Most of the snooker-players owned, or had invested in, factories that employed women in the same manner; none had dreamed of closing a factory down because a woman here or a woman there went blind.

Sunil Shetty said: 'The other day I read in the

Times of India that the chief of Johnnie Walker said, there is more Red Label consumed in the average small Indian town than is produced in all of Scotland. When it comes to three things' – he counted them off – 'black-marketing, counterfeiting, and corruption, we are the world champions. If they were included in the Olympic Games, India would always win gold, silver, and bronze in those three.'

After midnight, Abbasi staggered out of the club, leaving a coin with the guard who got up from his chair to salute him and help him into his car.

Drunk by now, he raced out of the town and up to the Bunder, finally slowing down when the smell of sea breeze got to him.

Stopping by the side of the road when his house came into view, he decided he needed one more drink. He always kept a small bottle of whisky under his seat, where his wife would not find it; reaching down, he slapped his hand around the floor of the car. His head banged against the dashboard. He found the bottle, and a glass.

After the drink, he realized he couldn't go home; his wife would smell the liquor on him the moment he got past the threshold. There would be another scene. She never could understand why he drank so much.

He drove up to the Bunder. He parked the car next to a rubbish dump and walked across to a teashop. Beyond a small beach the sea was visible; the smell of roasted fish wafted through the air.

A blackboard outside the teashop proclaimed,

in letters of white chalk: 'WE CHANGE PAKISTANI MONEY AND CURRENCY'. The walls of the shop were adorned with a photograph of the Great Mosque of Mecca along with a poster of a boy and a girl bowing to the Taj Mahal. Four benches had been arranged in an outdoor verandah. A dappled white-and-brown goat was tied to a pole at one end of the verandah; it was chewing on dried grass.

Men were sitting on one of the benches. Abbasi touched one of the men on his shoulder; he turned around.

'Abbasi.'

'Mehmood, my brother. Make some room for me.'

Mehmood, a fat man with a fringe beard and no moustache, did so, and Abbasi squeezed in next to him. Abbasi had heard that Mehmood stole cars; he had heard that Mehmood's four sons drove them to a village on the Tamil Nadu border, a village whose only business was the purchase and sale of stolen cars.

Alongside Mehmood, Abbasi recognized Kalam, who was rumoured to import hashish from Bombay and ship it to Sri Lanka; Saif, who had knifed a man in Trivandrum; and a small, white-haired man who was only called the Professor – and who was believed to be the shadiest of the lot.

These men were smugglers, car thieves, thugs, and worse; but while they sipped tea together,

34

nothing would happen to Abbasi. It was the culture of the Bunder. A man might be stabbed in daylight, but never at night, and never while sipping tea. In any case, the sense of solidarity among the Muslims at the Bunder had deepened ever since the riots.

The Professor was finishing up a story of Kittur in the twelfth century, about an Arab sailor named bin Saad who sighted the town, just when he had given up hope of finding land. He had raised his hands to Allah and promised that if he arrived safely on land, he would never again drink liquor or gamble.

'Did he keep his word?'

The Professor winked. 'Take a guess.'

The Professor was always welcome at late-night chit-chats at the teashop because he knew many fascinating things about the port; how its history went back to the Middle Ages, for instance, or how Tippu Sultan had once installed a battery of French-made cannon here to scare away the British. He pointed a finger at Abbasi: 'You're not your usual self. What's on your mind?'

'Corruption,' Abbasi said. 'Corruption. It's like a demon sitting on my brain and eating it with a fork and knife.'

The others drew closer to listen. Abbasi was a rich man; he must have an intimacy with corruption that exceeded theirs. He told them about the morning.

Kalam, the drug-dealer, smiled and said: 'That's

35

nothing, Abbasi.' He gestured towards the sea. 'I have a ship, half full of cement and half full of something else, that has been waiting two hundred metres out at sea for a month. Why? Because this inspector at the port is squeezing me. I pay him and he wants to squeeze me even more, too much more. So the ship is just drifting out there, half full of cement and half full of something else.'

'I thought things would get better with this young fellow Rajiv taking over the country,' Abbasi said. 'But he's let us all down. As bad as any other politician.'

'We need one man to stand up to them,' the Professor said. 'Just one honest, brave man. That fellow would do more for this country than Gandhi or Nehru did.'

The remark was greeted by a chorus of agreement.

'Yes,' Abbasi agreed, stroking his beard. 'And the next morning he would be floating in the Kaliamma river. Like this.'

He mimicked a corpse.

There was general agreement over this too. But even as the words left his mouth, Abbasi was already thinking: is it really true? Is there nothing we can do to fight back?

Tucked into the Professor's trousers, he saw the glint of a knife. The effect of the whisky was wearing off, but it had carried him to a strange place, and his mind was filling up with strange thoughts.

36

Another round of tea was ordered by the car thief, but Abbasi, yawning, crossed his hands in front of him and shook his head.

The next day, he turned up to work at ten-forty, his head throbbing with pain.

Ummar opened the door for him. Abbasi nodded and took the mail from him. With his head down to the floor, he moved to the stairs that led up to his office; then he stopped. At the threshold of the door that led to the factory floor, one of the stitching women was standing staring at him.

'I'm not paying you to waste time,' he snapped.

She turned and fled. He hurried up the stairs.

He put on his glasses, read the mail, read the newspaper, yawned, drank tea, and opened a ledger bearing the logo of the Karnataka Bank; he went down a list of customers who had paid and not paid. He kept thinking of the previous evening's game of snooker.

The door creaked open; Ummar's face popped in.

'What?'

'They're here.'

'Who?'

'The government.'

Two men in polyester shirts and ironed blue bell-bottoms pushed Ummar aside and walked in. One of them, a burly fellow with a big pot belly and a moustache like that of a wrestler in a village fair, said: 'Income Tax Department.'

Abbasi got up. 'Ummar! Don't just stand there! Get one of the women to run and bring tea from the teashop by the sea. And some of those round Bombay biscuits as well.'

The big taxman sat down at the table without being invited. His companion, a lean fellow with arms tied together, hesitated in a fidgety kind of way, until the other gestured him to sit down too.

Abbasi smiled. The taxman with the moustache talked.

'We have just walked around your factory floor. We have just seen the women who work for you, and the quality of the shirts they stitch.'

Abbasi smiled and waited for it.

It came quickly this time.

'We think you are making a lot more money than you have declared to us.'

Abbasi's heart beat hard; he told himself to calm down. There is always a way out.

'A lot, lot, lot more.'

'Sahib, sahib,' Abbasi said, patting the air with conciliatory gestures. 'We have a custom in this shop. Everyone who comes in will receive a gift before they leave.' Ummar, who knew already what he had to do, was waiting outside the office with two shirts. With a fawning smile, he presented them to the two tax officers. They accept the bribes without a word, the lean fellow looking to the big one for approval before snatching his gift.

Abbasi asked: 'What else can I do for you two sahibs?'

The one with the moustache smiled. His partner

also smiled. The one with the moustache held up three fingers.

'Each.'

Three hundred per head was too low; real pros from the income tax office wouldn't have settled for anything under five hundred. Abbasi guessed that the two men were doing this for the first time. In the end, they would settle for a hundred each, plus the shirts.

'Let me offer you a little boost first. Do the sahibs take Red Label?'

The fidgety fellow almost jumped out of his seat in excitement, but the big one glared at him.

'Red Label would be acceptable.'

They've probably never been offered anything better than hooch, Abbasi realized.

He walked into the pantry, took out the bottle. He poured into three glasses with the Air India *maharajah* logo. He opened the fridge. He dropped two ice cubes into each glass and added a thin stream of ice water from a bottle. He spat in two of the glasses and arranged them furthest away on the tray.

The thought fell into his mind like a meteor from a purer heaven. No. Slowly it spread itself across his mind. No, he could not give this whisky to these men. It might be counterfeit stuff, sold in cartons bought under false premises, but it was still a thousand times too pure to be touched by their lips.

He drank one whisky, and then the second, and then the third.

Ten minutes later, he came back into the room with heavy steps. He bolted the door behind him, and let his body fall heavily against it.

The big taxman turned sharply: 'Why are you closing the door?'

'Sahibs. This is the port city of the Bunder, which has ancient traditions and customs, dating back centuries and centuries. Any man is free to come here of his own will, but he can only leave with the permission of the locals.'

Whistling, Abbasi walked to his desk and picked up the phone; he shoved it, like a weapon, right in the face of the bigger taxman.

'Shall I call the income tax office right now? Shall I find out if you have been authorized to come? Shall I?'

They looked uncomfortable. The lean man was sweating. Abbasi thought: my guess is right. They are doing this for the first time.

'Look at your hands. You have accepted shirts from me, which are bribes. You are holding the evidence in your hands.'

'Look here—'

'No! You look here!' Abbasi shouted. 'You are not going to leave these premises alive, until you sign a confession of what you were trying to do. Let us see how you get out. This is the port city. I have friends in all four directions. You will both be dead and floating in the Kaliamma river if I snap my fingers now. Do you doubt me?'

The big taxman looked at the ground, while the

other fellow produced an extraordinary amount of sweat.

Abbasi unbolted the door and held it open. 'Get out.' Then, with a wide smile, he bowed down to them: 'Sahibs.'

The two men scurried out without a word. He heard the thump of their feet on the staircase; and then a cry of surprise from Ummar, who was walking up the stairs with a tray of tea and Britannia biscuits.

He let his head rest on the cool wood of the table and wondered what he had done. Any moment soon, he was expecting that the electricity would be cut off; the income tax officials would return, with more men and an arrest warrant.

He walked round and round the room, thinking: what is happening to me? Ummar stared at him silently.

After an hour, to Abbasi's surprise, there had been no call from the income tax office. The fans were still working. The light was still on.

Abbasi began to hope. These guys were raw – tyros. Maybe they'd just gone back to the office and got on with their work. Even if they had complained, the government officials had been wary of the Bunder ever since the riots; it was possible they would not want to antagonize a Muslim businessman at this point. He looked out of the window at the Bunder: this violent, rotten, garbage-strewn port, crawling with pickpockets and knife-carrying thugs – it seemed the only place where a man was safe from the corruption of Kittur.

'Ummar!' He shouted. 'I'm leaving early today for the club – give Sunil Shetty a call to say that he should come today too. I have great news for him! I beat the income tax office!'

He came running down the stairs and stopped at the last step. To his right, the doorway opened onto the factory floor. In the six weeks since his factory had reopened, he had not once gone through this doorway; Ummar had handled the affairs of the factory floor. But now the doorway to his right, black and yawning, had become inescapable.

He felt he had no option but to go in. He realized now that the morning's events had all been, somehow, a trap: to bring him to this place, to make him do what he had avoided doing since reopening his factory.

The women were sitting on the floor of the dimly lit room, pale fluorescent lights flickering overhead, each at a work station indicated by a numeral in red letters painted on the wall. They held the white shirts close to their eyes and stitched gold thread into them; they stopped when he came in. He flicked his wrist, indicating that they should keep working. He didn't want their eyes looking at him: those eyes that were being damaged, as their fingers created golden shirts that he could sell to American ballroom dancers.

Damaged? No, that was not the right word. That was not the reason he had shunted them into a side room.

Everyone in that room was going blind.

He sat down on a chair in the centre of the room.

The optometrist had been clear about that; the kind of detailed stitchwork needed for the shirts scarred the women's retinas. He had used his fingers to show Abbasi how thick the scars were. No amount of improved lighting would reduce the impact on the retinas. Human eyes were not meant to stare for hours at designs this intricate. Two women had already gone blind; that was why he had shut down the factory. When he reopened, all his old workers came back at once. They knew their fate; but there was no other work to be had.

Abbasi closed his eyes. He wanted nothing more than for Ummar to shout that he was urgently needed upstairs.

But no one came to release him and he sat in the chair, while the women around him stitched, and their stitching fingers kept talking to him: we are going blind; look at us!

'Does your head hurt, sahib?' a woman's voice was asking him. 'Do you want me to get you some Disprin and water?'

Unable to look at her, Abbasi said: 'All of you please go home. Come back tomorrow. But please go home today. You'll all be paid.'

'Is sahib unhappy with us for some reason?'

'No, please. Go home now. You'll all be paid for the whole day. Come back tomorrow.'

He heard the rustle of their feet and he knew, they must be gone now.

They had left their shirts at their work stations and he picked one up; the dragon was half-stitched. He kneaded the cloth between his fingers. He could feel, between his fingers, the fine-spun fabric of corruption.

'The factory is closed,' he wanted to shout out to the dragon. 'There – you happy with me? The factory is closed.'

And after that? Who would send his son to school? Would he sit by the docks with a knife and smuggle cars like Mehmood? The women would go elsewhere, and do the same work.

He slapped his hand against his thigh.

Thousands, sitting in teashops and universities and workplaces every day and every night, were cursing corruption. Yet not one fellow had found a way to slay the demon without giving up his share of the loot of corruption. So why did he – an ordinary businessman given to whisky and snooker and listening to gossip from thugs – have to come up with an answer?

But just a moment later, he realized he already had an answer.

He offered Allah a compromise. He would be taken to jail, but his factory would go on with its work: he closed his eyes and prayed to his God to accept this deal.

But an hour passed and still no one had come to arrest him.

Abbasi opened a window in his office. He could see only buildings, a congested road, and old walls.

44

He opened all the windows, but still he saw nothing but walls. He climbed up to the roof of his building and ducked under a clothesline to walk out onto the terrace. Coming to the edge, he placed a foot on the tiled roof that protruded over the front of his shop.

From here, a man could see the limits of Kittur. At the very edge of the town, one after the other, stood a minaret, a church steeple, and a temple tower, like signposts to identify the three religions of the town to voyagers from the ocean.

Abbasi saw the Arabian Sea stretching away from Kittur. The sun was shining over it. A ship was slowly leaving the Bunder, edging to where the blue waters of the sea changed colour and turned a deeper hue. It was about to hit a large patch of brilliant sunshine, an oasis of pure light.

DAY TWO (MORNING): LIGHTHOUSE HILL

After a lunch of prawn curry and rice at the Bunder, you may want to visit the Lighthouse Hill and its vicinity. The famous lighthouse, built by the Portuguese and renovated by the British, is no longer in use. An old guard in a blue uniform sits at the foot of the lighthouse. If visitors are poorly dressed, or speak to him in Tulu or Kannada, he will say: 'Can't you see it's closed?' If visitors are well-dressed or speak English, he will say: 'Welcome.' He will take them into the lighthouse and up the spiral staircase to the top, which affords a spectacular view of the Arabian Sea. In recent years, the Corporation has begun running a reading room inside the lighthouse: the collection includes Father Basil d'Essa. S.J.'s *Short History of Kittur*. The Deshpremi Hemachandra Rao Park around the lighthouse is named in honour of the freedom-fighter who hung a Congress tricolour from the lighthouse during British rule.

It happens at least twice a year. The prisoner, handcuffs on his wrists, is striding towards the Lighthouse Hill police station with his head held high and a look of insolent boredom on his face; whilst following him, almost scampering to catch up, are the two policemen holding a chain attached to the handcuffs. The odd part is that the man in handcuffs seems to be dragging along the policemen, like a fellow taking two monkeys out for a walk.

In the past nine years, the man known as 'Xerox' Ramakrishna has been arrested twenty-one times on the granite pavement in front of Deshpremi Hemachandra Rao Park for the sale, at discounted rates, of illegally photocopied or printed books to the students of St Alfonso's college. A policeman comes in the morning, when Ramakrishna is sitting with his books spread out on a blue bedsheet; he places his lathi on the books and says: 'Let's go, Xerox.'

The bookseller turns to his eleven-year-old daughter, Ritu, who sells books with him, and says: 'Go home and be a good girl, dear.' Then he holds his hands out for the cuffs.

In jail, Xerox is unchained and put in a cell. Holding on to the bars, he regales the policemen with ingratiating stories. He may tell them a smutty tale about some college girl whom he saw that morning wearing blue jeans in the American style, or a new swear-word in Tulu he has heard on the bus while going to Salt Market Village, or

47

perhaps, if they are in the mood for longer entertainment, he will narrate to them, as he has done so many times before, the story of what his father did for a living all his life – taking the crap out of the houses of rich landlords, the traditional occupation of people of his caste. All day long, his old man would hang around the back wall of the landlord's house, waiting for the smell of human shit; as soon as he smelled that smell, he came up to the house and waited, with bent knees, like a wicket-keeper waits for the ball. (Xerox bent his knees and showed how.) Then, as soon as he heard the 'thud' of the boom-box being shut, he had to pull out the chamber pot through a hole in the wall, empty it into the rosebushes, wipe it clean with his loincloth and insert it back before the next person came to use the toilet. That was the job he did his whole life, can you believe it!

The jailers will laugh.

They bring Xerox samosas wrapped in paper, they offer him chai. They consider him a decent fellow. They let him out at midday; he bows low to them and says: 'Thank you.' Then Miguel D'Souza, the lawyer for the publishers and booksellers on Umbrella Street, will call the station and yell: 'Have you let him off again? Doesn't the law of the land mean anything to you?' The inspector of the station, Ramesh, keeps the receiver at a distance from his ear and reads the newspaper, looking at the Bombay stock-market quotes. That

48

is all Ramesh really wants to do in life: read the stock-market quotes.

By late afternoon, Xerox is back at it. Photocopied or cheaply printed copies of Karl Marx, *Mein Kampf*, published books – and films and albums – and others, are arranged on the blue cloth spread out on the pavement on Lighthouse Hill, and little Ritu sits stiff-backed, with her long unbroken nose and faint moustache, watching as the customers pick up the books and flip through them.

'Put that back in place,' she will say, when a customer has rejected a book. 'Put it back exactly where you picked it up from.'

'*Accounting for Entrance Exams?*' one customer shouts at Xerox. '*Advanced Obstetrics?*' cries another.

'*The Joy of Sex?*'

'*Mein Kampf?*'

'Lee Iacocca?'

'What's your best price?' a young man asks, flipping through the book.

'Seventy five rupees.'

'O, you're *raping* me! It's too much.'

The young man walks away, turns around, comes back, and says, 'What's your final best price, I have no time to waste.'

'Seventy two rupees. Take it or leave it. I've got other customers.'

The books are photocopied, or sometimes printed, at an old printing press in Salt Market Village. Xerox loves being around the machinery.

He strokes the photocopier; he adores the machine, the way it flashes like lightning as it works, the way it whirrs and hums. He cannot read English, but he knows that English words have power, and that English books have aura. He looks at the image of Adolf Hitler from the cover of *Mein Kampf* and he feels his power. He looks at the face of Kahlil Gibran, poetic and mysterious, and he feels the mystery and poetry. He looks at the face of Lee Iacocca, relaxed with his hands behind his head, and he feels relaxed. That's why he once told Inspector Ramesh: 'I have no wish to make any trouble for you or for the publishers, sir; I just love books: I love making them, holding them and selling them. My father took out shit for a living, sir: he couldn't even read or write. He'd be so proud if he could see that I make my living from books.'

Only one time has Xerox really been in trouble with the police. That was when someone called the station and said that Xerox was selling copies of Salman Rushdie's *The Satanic Verses* in violation of the laws of the Republic of India. This time when he was brought to the station in handcuffs there were no courtesies, no cups of chai.

Ramesh slapped him.

'Don't you know, the book is banned, you son of a bald woman? You think you are going to start a riot among the Muslims? And get me and every other policeman here transferred to Salt Market Village?'

50

'Forgive me,' Xerox begged. 'I had no idea that this was a banned book, really . . . I'm just the son of a man who took out shit, sir. He waited all day long for the boom-box to make a noise. I know my place, sir. I wouldn't dream of challenging you. It was just a mistake, sir. Forgive me, sir.'

D'Souza, the booksellers' lawyer, a small man with black oily hair and a neat moustache, heard what had happened and came to the station. He looked at the banned book – a massive paperback with an image of an angel on the front – and shook his head in disbelief.

'That fucking untouchable's son, thinking he's going to photocopy *The Satanic Verses*. What balls.'

He sat at the inspector's desk and shouted at him: 'I told you this would happen, if you didn't punish him! You're responsible for all this.'

Ramesh glared at Xerox, who was lying penitently on a bed, as he had been ordered to do.

'I don't think anyone saw him selling it. Things will be fine.'

To calm the lawyer down, Ramesh asked a constable to go fetch a bottle of Old Monk rum. The two of them talked for a while.

Ramesh read passages out from the book and said: 'I don't get what the fuss is all about, really.'

'Muslims,' D'Souza said, shaking his head. 'Violent people. Violent.'

The bottle of Old Monk arrived. They drank it in half an hour and the constable went to fetch another. In his cell, Xerox lay perfectly still, looking at the ceiling. The policeman and the lawyer went on drinking. D'Souza told Ramesh his frustrations, and the inspector told the lawyer his frustrations. One had wanted to be a pilot, soaring in the clouds and chasing stewardesses, and the other – he had never wanted anything but to dabble in the stock market. That was all.

At midnight, Ramesh asked the lawyer: 'Do you want to know a secret?' Stealthily, he walked the lawyer to the prison and showed him the secret. One of the bars of the cell could be removed. The policeman removed it, and swung it, and then put it back in place. 'That's how the evidence is hidden,' he said. 'Not that that kind of thing happens often at this station, mind you – but that's how it is done, when it is done.'

The lawyer giggled. He loosened the bar and slung it over his shoulder, and said: 'Don't I look like Hanuman now?'

'Just like on TV,' the policeman said.

The lawyer asked that the cell door be opened, and it was. The two of them saw the sleeping prisoner lying on his cot, an arm over his face to keep out the jabbing light of the naked bulb above him. A sliver of naked skin was exposed beneath his cheap polyester shirt; a creeper of thick black hair, which looked to his two onlookers like an outgrowth from his groin, was just about visible.

'That fucking son of an untouchable. See him snoring.'

'His father took out the shit – and this fellow thinks he's going to dump shit on us!'

'Selling *The Satanic Verses*. He'll sell it under my nose, will he?'

'These people think they own India now. Don't they? They want all the jobs, and all the university degrees, and all the . . .'

Ramesh pulled down the snoring man's trousers; he lifted the bar high up, while the lawyer said: 'Do it like Hanuman does, on TV!' Xerox woke up screaming. Ramesh handed the bar to D'Souza. The policeman and the lawyer took turns: he smashed the bar against Xerox's legs, just at the knee-joint, like the monkey god did on TV, and then he smashed the bar against Xerox's legs, just below the knee-joint, like the monkey-god did on TV, and then he smashed it into Xerox's legs, just above the knee-joint, and then, laughing and kissing each other, the two staggered out, shouting for someone to lock the station up behind them.

Periodically through the night, when he woke up, Xerox resumed his screaming.

In the morning, Ramesh came back, was told by a constable about Xerox and said: 'Shit, it wasn't a dream then.' He ordered the constables to take the man in the prison to the Havelock Henry General Hospital, and asked for a copy of the morning paper, so he could check the stock-market prices.

The next week, Xerox arrived, noisily, because he was on crutches, at the police station, with his daughter behind him.

'You can break my legs, but I can't stop selling books. I'm destined to do this, sir,' he said. He grinned.

Ramesh grinned too, but he avoided the man's eyes.

'I'm going up the hill, sir,' Xerox said, lifting up one of his crutches. 'I'm going to sell the book.'

Ramesh and the other cops gathered around Xerox and his daughter and begged. Xerox wanted them to phone D'Souza, which they did. The lawyer came with his wig, along with two assistants, also in black gowns and wigs. When he heard why the policeman had summoned him, D'Souza burst into laughter.

'This fellow is just teasing you,' he told Ramesh. 'He can't possibly go up the hill with his leg like that.'

D'Souza pointed a finger at the middle part of Xerox's body.

'And if you do try to sell it, mind – it won't be just your legs that we break next time.'

A constable laughed.

Xerox looked at Ramesh with his usual ingratiating smile. He bent low with folded palms and said: 'So be it.'

D'Souza sat down to drink Old Monk rum with the policemen, and they settled into another game of cards. Ramesh said he had lost money on the market the past week; the lawyer sucked at his teeth and shook his head, and said that in a big city like Bombay everyone was a cheat or a liar or a thug.

Xerox turned around on his crutches and walked out of the station. His daughter came behind him. They headed for the Lighthouse Hill. The climb took two hours and a half, and they stopped six times for Xerox to drink tea, or a glass of sugar-cane juice. Then his daughter spread down the blue sheet in front of Deshpremi Hemachandra Rao Park, and Xerox lowered himself. He sat on the sheet, stuck his legs out slowly, and put a large paperback down next to him. His daughter sat down too, keeping watch over the book, her back stiff and upright. The book was banned throughout the Republic of India and it was the only thing that Xerox intended to sell that day: *The Satanic Verses*, by Salman Rushdie.

DAY TWO (AFTERNOON): ST ALFONSO'S BOYS' HIGH SCHOOL AND JUNIOR COLLEGE

A short walk from the park rises a massive grey Gothic tower on which is painted a coat of arms and the slogan 'LUCET ET ARDET'. This is the St Alfonso's Boys' High School and Junior College, established 1858, one of the oldest educational establishments in the state of Karnataka. The Jesuit-run school is Kittur's most famous, and many of its alumni have gone on to the Indian Institute of Technology, the Karnataka State Regional Engineering College, and other prestigious universities in India and abroad.

Several seconds, perhaps even a full minute, had passed since the explosion, but Lasrado, the chemistry professor, had not moved. He sat at his desk, his arms spread apart, his mouth open. Smoke was billowing from the bench at the back of the room, a yellow dust like pollen had filled the room, and the stench of fireworks was

56

in the air. The students had all left the classroom by now; they watched from the safety of the door.

Gomati Das, the calculus teacher, arrived from next door with most of his class; then came Professor Noronha, the English and Ancient History man, bringing his own flock of curious eyes. Father Almeida, the principal, pushed his way through the crowd and entered the acrid classroom, his palm over his nose and mouth. He lowered his hand and cried: 'What is the meaning of this nonsense?'

Only Lasrado was left in the classroom; he stood at his desk like the heroic boy who would not leave the burning deck. He replied in a monotone.

'A bomb in class, *Pather*. The bench all the way in the back. It went *opp* during the lecture. About one minute *apter* I began talking.'

Father Almeida squinted at the thick smoke and then turned to the boys: 'The youth of this country have gone to hell and will ruin the names of their fathers and grandfathers!'

Covering his face with his arm, he walked gingerly to the bench, which had toppled over from the blast.

'The bomb is still smoking,' he shouted. 'Shut the doors and call the police.'

He touched Lasrado on the shoulder. 'Did you hear me? We must shut the doors and—'

Red-faced with shame, quivering with wrath, Lasrado turned suddenly, and – addressing principal, teachers, students – yelled: 'You *Puckers! Puckers!*'

In moments the entire Junior College emptied; the boys gathered in the garden, or in the corridor of the Science and Natural History wing, where the skeleton of a shark that had washed up on the beach some decades ago had been suspended from the ceiling as a scientific curiosity. Five of the boys kept apart from all the others, under the shade of a large banyan tree. They were distinguishable from the others by the pleated trousers that they wore, brand-name labels visible on the back-pockets or at the side, and by their general air of cockiness. They were Shabbir Ali, whose father owned the only video rental store in town; the Bakht twins Irfan and Rizwan, children of the black marketeer; Shankara P. Kinni, whose father was a plastic surgeon in the Gulf; and Pinto, the scion of a coffee-estate family.

One of them had planted the bomb. Each of this group had been subjected to multiple periods of suspension from classes for bad behaviour, had been kept back a year because of poor marks, and had been threatened with expulsion for insubordination. If anyone would plant a bomb, it had to be one of this lot.

They seemed to think so themselves.

'Did you do it?' Shabbir Ali asked Pinto, who shook his head.

Ali looked at the others, silently repeating the question. 'I didn't do it either,' he stated at the end.

'Maybe God did it,' Pinto said, and all of them

giggled. Yet they were aware that everyone in the school suspected them. The Bakht twins said they would go down to the Bunder to eat mutton biryani and watch the waves; Shabbir Ali would go to his father's video store, or watch a pornographic movie at home; Pinto would probably tag along with him.

Only one of them remained at the school.

He could not leave yet; he loved it too much, the smoke and confusion. He kept his fist clenched.

He mingled among the crowd, listening to the hubbub, drinking it in like honey. Some of the boys had gone back into the building; they stood out on the balconies of the three floors of the college and shouted down to those on the ground; and this added to the hum, as if the college were a beehive struck with a pole. He knew that it was his hubbub – the students were talking about him, the professors were cursing him. He was the god of the morning.

For so many years the institution had spoken to him – spoken rudely: teachers had caned him, headmasters had suspended and threatened to expel him. (And, he was sure, behind his back, it had mocked him for being a Hoyka, a lower-caste.)

Now he had spoken back to it. He kept his fist clenched.

'Do you think it's the terrorists . . . ?' he heard some boy say. 'The Kashmiris, or the Punjabis . . . ?'

No, you morons! he wanted to shout. It's me! Shankara! The lower-caste!

There – he watched Professor Lasrado, his hair still dishevelled, surrounded by his favourite students, the 'good boys', seeking support and succour from them.

Oddly enough, he felt an urge to go up to Lasrado and touch him on the shoulder, as if to say: 'Man, I feel your grief, I understand your humiliation, I sympathize with your rage', and thus end the long strife between him and the chemistry professor. He felt the desire to be one of the students whom Lasrado trusted at such moments, one of his 'good boys'. But this was a lesser desire.

The main thing was to exult. He watched Lasrado's suffering and smiled.

He turned to his left; someone in the crowd had said: 'The police are coming.'

He hurried to the back yard of the college, opened a gate, and walked down the long flight of stone steps that led to the Junior School. After the new passageway had been opened through the playground, hardly anyone used this route any more.

The road was called Old Court Road. The court had long relocated and the lawyers had moved, and the road had been closed down for years – after the suicide of a visiting businessman here. Shankara had been coming down this road ever since he was a boy; it was his favourite part of town. Even though he could summon his chauffeur up to the college, the man was instructed to wait for him down at the bottom of the steps.

The road was lined with banyan trees; but even strolling in the shade, Shankara had worked up a terrific sweat. (He was always like that, quick to sweat, as if some irrepressible heat were building up inside him.) Most boys had handkerchiefs placed in their pockets by their mothers, but Shankara had never carried one, and to dry himself he had adopted a savage method: he tore large leaves off a nearby tree, and scraped his arms and legs over and over, until the skin was red and raw.

Now he felt dry.

About halfway down the hill, he left the road, parting a growth of trees, and walked into a clearing that was completely hidden except to those who knew it. Inside this bower was a statue of Jesus, made of dark bronze. Shankara had known of this statue for years, ever since stumbling upon it as a boy while playing hide-and-seek. There was something wrong with the statue; with its dark skin, the lopsided expression on its lips, its bright eyes, it seemed more like an icon of the devil than of the Saviour. Even the words at the base – 'I AM THE RESURRECTION AND THE LIFE' – seemed like a taunt to God.

He saw that there was still some fertilizer around the foot of the statue – the remains of the same powder that he had used to detonate his bomb.

61

Quickly he covered the powder with dry leaves. Then he leaned against the base of the Jesus statue. 'Puckers,' he said – and giggled.

But as he did so, he felt as if his great triumph had been reduced to that one giggle.

He sat at the foot of the dark Jesus, and the tension and thrill slowly left him. He always relaxed around images of Jesus. There was a time when he had thought about converting to Christianity; among Christians there are no castes. Every man was judged by what he had done with his own life. But after the way the Jesuit priests had treated him – caning him once on a Monday morning in the assembly grounds, in full view of the entire school – he had sworn never to become a Christian. There was no better institution to stop Hindus from converting to Christianity than the Catholic boys' school.

Waving goodbye to the Jesus, and having checked that there was no fertilizer visible around the base of the statue, he continued downhill.

His chauffeur, a small dark man in a bedraggled khaki uniform, was waiting for him, halfway down the road.

'What are you doing here?' he shouted. 'I told you: wait at the bottom of the hill for me. Never come up this road!'

The driver bent low with his palms folded.

'Sir . . . don't be angry . . . I heard . . . a bomb . . . your mother asked me to make sure you were . . .'

How quickly news had spread. It was bigger than him; it was taking on a life of its own.

'The *bomb* – oh, it was nothing important,' he told the driver, as they walked down. Was that a mistake, he wondered – should he have exaggerated instead?

It was not an appealing irony. His mother had sent the driver to look for him, as if he were a little baby – he, who had exploded the bomb! He gritted his teeth. The driver opened the door of the white Ambassador car for him, but instead of getting into the car, he began shouting.

'You bastard! Son of a bald woman!'

He paused for breath, and then said: 'You *pucker*! You *pucker*!'

Laughing hysterically, he got into the car, while the driver stared at him.

On the way home, he thought how any other master could expect loyalty from his chauffeur. Yet Shankara expected nothing; he suspected his chauffeur of being a Brahmin.

As they paused at a red light, he heard two ladies in an adjacent Ambassador talking about the bomb-blast: '—the police have sealed off the entire school and college now, they say. No one can leave until they find the terrorist.'

It occurred to him he had had a lucky escape; had he stayed any longer, he would have fallen into the trap of the police.

When he got to his mansion, he ran in through the back door and bounded up the steps to his room. He had thought, at one point, of sending a manifesto to the *Dawn Herald*: 'The man Lasrado is a fool and the bomb was burst in his class to prove this to the whole world.' He could not believe he had left it lying on his desk; he tore it up at once. Then, uncertain whether the pieces could be reassembled and the message recreated, he thought about swallowing them all, but decided instead to swallow only some of the key syllables – 'rado', 'bo', 'm', 'class'. The rest he set fire to, with his pocket lighter.

Besides, he thought, slightly sick from the sensation of paper settling into his stomach, that was not the right message to send to the press, because ultimately his anger was not solely directed at Lasrado; it went much deeper. If the police asked him for a statement, what he would say was this: 'I have burst a bomb to end the 5,000-year-old caste system that still operates in our country. I have burst a bomb to show that no man should be judged, as I have been, merely by the accident of his birth.'

And the lofty sentences made him feel better. He was sure he would be treated differently in prison, as a martyr of some kind. The Hoyka Self-Advancement committees would organize marches for him, and the police would not dare touch him. Perhaps, when he was released, large crowds would greet him – he would be launched on a political career.

Now he felt he had to send an anonymous letter

to the newspaper at all costs. He took a fresh piece of paper and began writing, even as his stomach was churning from the paper he had swallowed.

There! He was done. He read it over.

'The Manifesto of a Wronged Hoyka. Why the Bomb was Burst Today!'

But then he reconsidered. It was well-known that he was a Hoyka. Everyone knew it. They gossiped about it, and their gossip was like that faceless buzz out of the black doors of the classrooms today. Everyone in his school, in this entire town, knew that as rich as Shankara Prasad Kinni was, he was only a Hoyka woman's son. If he sent that letter, they would know it was he who had planted the bomb.

He jumped. It was only the cry of the vegetable seller, who had brought his cart right up outside the back wall of the house: 'Tomatoes, tomatoes, ripe red tomatoes, come get your ripe red tomatoes.'

He wanted to go down to the Bunder, book into a cheap hotel, and say he was someone else. No one would ever find him there.

He paced around his room and then slammed the door; he dived into his bed and pulled the sheet over him. Inside the darkness of the bedsheet he could still hear the vendor shouting: 'Tomatoes, ripe red tomatoes, hurry before they all rot!'

In the morning, his mother was watching an old black-and-white Hindi film which she had rented from Shabbir Ali's father's video store. This was how she spent every morning these days, addicted to old melodramas.

'Shankara, I heard there was some brouhaha in school,' she said, turning as she heard him come down. He ignored her and sat at the table. He could not remember the last time he had spoken a full sentence to his mother.

'Shankara,' his mother said, putting toast on the table before him. 'Your Urmila Aunty is coming. Please stay around the house today.'

He bit into the toast, saying nothing to his mother. He found her possessive, and pesky, and hectoring. But he knew that she was in awe of her half-Brahmin son; she felt beneath him, because she was a full-blooded Hoyka.

'Shankara! Please tell me: will you stay around? Will you be nice to me just today?'

Dropping his toast onto his plate, he got to his feet and headed for the stairs.

'Shan-ka-ra! Come back!'

Even as he cursed her, he understood her fears. She did not want to face the Brahmin woman alone. Her sole claim to acceptance, to respectability, was the production of a male child, an heir – and if he wasn't in the house, then she had nothing to show. She was just a Hoyka trespassing into a Brahmin's household.

He thought: it is her own fault if she feels wretched in their presence. Again and again he had told her, mother, ignore our Brahmin relatives.

66

Don't continually humiliate yourself in front of them. If they don't want us, let us not want them.

But she could not do that; she still wanted to be accepted. And her ticket of acceptance was Shankara. Not that he himself was fully acceptable to the Brahmins. They viewed him as the product of a buccaneering adventure on the part of his father; they associated him (he was sure) with an entire range of corruptions. Mix one part premarital sex and one part caste violation in a black pot and what do you get? This cute little satan: Shankara.

Some Brahmin relatives, like Urmila Aunty, had visited him for years, although they never seemed to enjoy fondling his cheeks, or sending flying kisses his way, or doing the other repellent things aunties did to nephews. He got the feeling, around her, that he was being tolerated.

Fuck, he did not like being tolerated.

He had the driver take him to Umbrella Street, gazing blankly out of the window as the car passed its furniture shops and sugarcane juice stands. He got off at White Stallion Talkies. 'Don't wait for me; I'll call you when I'm done with the movie.'

As he was climbing the steps, he saw the owner of a store nearby waving at him vigorously. A relative, on his mother's side. The man flashed him enormous smiles; then he began gesturing for him to come sit in his shop. Shankara was always treated as someone special among his Hoyka relatives; because he was half-Brahmin, and hence so much

67

higher than them in caste terms; or because he was so rich, and hence so much higher than them in class terms. Swearing to himself, he kept going up the stairs. Didn't these stupid Hoykas understand? There was nothing he hated more than their grovelling to him, because of his half-Brahmin-ness. If they had been contemptuous to him, if they had forced him to crawl into their shops to expiate the sin of being half-Brahmin, then wouldn't he have come to see them every day!

There was another reason for him not to visit this particular relative. He had heard a rumour that the plastic surgeon Kinni had kept a mistress in this part of town – another Hoyka girl. He suspected that the relative would know of this woman, that he would be thinking constantly: this fellow Shankara – poor, poor Shankara, little does he know of his father's treachery. Shankara knew all about his father's treachery – this father, whom he had not seen for six years, who no longer even wrote or called over the phone, although he still sent home packages of candies and foreign-made chocolates. Yet, somehow, he felt that his father knew what life was about. A Hoyka mistress near the theatre and another beautiful Hoyka woman for a wife. Now he was leading a life of ease and luxury in the Gulf, fixing the noses and lips of rich Arab women. Another mistress there, for sure. Fellows like his father belonged to no caste or religion or race; they lived for themselves. They were the only real men in this world.

The box office was shuttered up. 'NEXT SHOW 8.30 P.M.' He came down the stairs quickly, avoiding eye-contact with his relative. Turning down a couple of streets in a hurry, he went into the Ideal Traders Ice Cream Shop and ordered a chikoo milkshake.

He sucked it down quickly, and with the sugar in his brain he leaned back and chuckled and said to himself: 'Pucker!'

So he had done it; he had humiliated Lasrado for having humiliated him.

'One more chikoo milkshake!' he shouted. 'With double ice cream!'

Shankara had always been one of the rotten apples at school. Since the age of eight or nine, he had been in trouble. But the most trouble he had ever had was with this chemistry teacher with the speech impediment. One morning, Lasrado had caught him smoking a cigarette in the sugar-cane juice stand outside the college.

'Smoking *bepore* the age of twenty will arrest your development as a normal human being,' Mr Lasrado had shouted. '*Ip* your *pather* were here, and not in the *Gulp*, he would do exactly what I am doing now . . .'

For the rest of that day, Shankara was made to kneel outside the Chemistry class. He kneeled with his eyes to the ground, and thought, over and over again: he is doing this to me because I am a Hoyka. If I were a Christian or a Bunt he would never have humiliated me like this.

69

That night, he lay in bed, and the thought had come to him: since he has hurt me, I will hurt him back. And it came to him, so clearly and succinctly, like a ray of sunlight, like a credo for his entire life. The initial euphoria turned into a restlessness, and he turned from side to side in the bed, saying: Mustafa, Mustafa. He had to meet Mustafa now.

The bomb-maker.

He had heard the name several weeks ago, at Shabbir Ali's place.

They had just – all five of the 'bad boys' gang' – watched another porno at Shabbir Ali's place that night. The woman had been entered from behind; the big black man had stuck his cock into her again and again. Shankara had no idea it could be done that way too; nor did Pinto, who kept squealing with pleasure. Shabbir Ali watched his friends' amusement with detachment; he had seen this video many times and it no longer excited his lust. He lived with such familiarity with evil that nothing excited him any more – neither scenes of fornication nor rape nor even bestiality; a constant exposure to vice had nearly returned him to a state of innocence.

After the video, the boys lay on Shabbir Ali's bed, threatening to jerk off right there, while their host warned them not even to think about it.

Shabbir Ali produced a condom to keep them happy, and they took turns sticking fingers into it.

'Who's this for, Shabbir?'

'My girlfriend.'

'Shut up, you homo.'

'You're the homo!'

The others talked about sex, and Shankara, staring at the ceiling, pretending to be absorbed in himself, listened. He felt he was always being kept out of such discussions, because the others knew he was a virgin. There was a girl in the college who 'talked' to men. Shabbir Ali had 'talked' to her; he implied that he had done much more. Shankara had tried to pretend that he too had 'talked' to women; maybe even screwed a whore on Old Court Road. He knew that the others saw through him.

Ali began passing things around; the condom was followed by a dumb-bell that he kept under his bed; copies of *Hustler*, *Playboy*, and the official NBA magazine.

'Guess what this is,' he said. It was something small and black, with a timer attached to it.

'It's a detonator,' he said, when no one could guess.

'What does it do?' Shankara asked, standing up on the bed and holding the thing to the light.

'It detonates, you idiot.' There was laughter. 'You use it in a bomb.'

'It's the easiest thing on earth, to make a bomb,' Shabbir said. 'Take a bag of fertilizer, and then put this detonator in it, and that's it.'

'Where would you get it?' someone, not Shankara, asked. 'Mustafa gave it to me,' Shabbir Ali said, almost in an aside.

71

Mustafa, Mustafa. Shankara clung tightly to the name.

'Where does he live?' asked one of the twins.

'Down by the Bunder. In the pepper market. Why?' Shabbir Ali poked his questioner. 'You planning on making a bomb?'

'Why not?'

More giggling. And Shankara had said nothing more that evening, saying Mustafa, Mustafa to himself, terrified he would forget the name unless he said nothing else all evening.

As he was stirring his third chikoo shake, two men came and sat down next to him: two policemen. One ordered an orange juice, and the other wanted to know how many types of tea were served at the shop. Shankara got up; then sat down. He knew they would start talking about him. His heart beat faster.

'Only the detonator went off and it blew the fertilizer all round the room. That idiot who made it thought making a bomb is as simple as sticking a detonator into a bag of fertilizer. It's a good thing, otherwise some of those boys would have been killed.'

'What is the youth of this country coming to?'

'These days, it's all sex, sex, and violence. The whole country is going the Punjab way.'

One of the cops caught him staring and stared back. He turned away. Maybe I should have stuck around with Urmila Aunty. Maybe I should have kept indoors today.

But what guarantee that she – even though she was his aunty – wouldn't betray him? You never knew with Brahmins. As a boy, he had been taken to a wedding of one of his Brahmin relatives. His mother never came to such events, but his father put him in the car, and then told him to play with his cousins. The Brahmin boys invited him to join in a competition. An inch of salt sat on a slab of vanilla ice cream; the challenge was for someone to eat it. 'You idiot,' one of the others shouted, when Shankara put his spoon down, a scoop of salty ice cream in his mouth. 'It was just a joke!'

As the years passed, it was always the same. Once, a Brahmin boy in school had invited him home. He took a chance, he liked the fellow, he said yes. The boy and his mother invited Shankara into the drawing room. It was a 'modern' family – they had lived abroad. He saw miniature Eiffel Towers and porcelain milkmaids in the drawing room, and he felt reassured that he would not be ill-treated here.

He was given tea and biscuits and made to feel perfectly at home. But as he left, he turned and saw his friend's mother with a cleaning rag in her left hand. She had begun wiping the sofa where he had been sitting.

His caste seemed to be common knowledge to people who had no business knowing it. One day, when he had gone to play cricket at Nehru Maidan, an old man had stood watching him from the wall of the playground. In the end, he called

73

Shankara over and examined his face, neck, and wrists for several minutes. Shankara had stood helpless during the examination: he just looked at the wrinkles that radiated from the old man's eyes.

'You're the son of Vasudev Kinni and the Hoyka woman, aren't you?'

He insisted that Shankara walk along with him.

'Your father always was a headstrong man. He would never agree to an arranged marriage. One day he found your mother, and he told all the Brahmins: to hell with you. I am marrying this beautiful creature, whether you like it or not. I knew what would happen; you would be a bastard. Neither a Brahmin nor a Hoyka. I told your father this. He would not listen.'

The man patted him on the shoulder. The unselfconscious way in which he touched Shankara suggested that he was not a bigot, not caste-obsessed, but just someone speaking the sad truth of life.

'You too belong to a caste,' said the old fellow. 'The Brahmo-Hoykas, in between the two. They are mentioned in the scriptures and we know that they exist somewhere. They are a people separate entirely from other humans. You should talk to them, and marry one of them. That way everything will be normal again.'

'Yes, sir,' Shankara said, not knowing why he said it.

'Today, there is no such thing as caste,' the man said, with regret. 'Brahmins eat meat. Kshatriyas get educated and write books. And lower-castes convert to Christianity and Islam. You heard what happened at Meenakshipuram, didn't you? Colonel Gaddafi is trying to destroy Hinduism, and the Christian priests are hand in glove with him.'

They walked along for a while, until they came to the bus stop.

'You must find your own caste,' said the man. 'You must find your people.' He lightly embraced Shankara and boarded the bus, where he began to jostle with young men for a seat. Shankara felt sorry for this old Brahmin. He had never in his life had to catch a bus; there was always the chauffeur.

Shankara thought: he is of a higher caste than me, but he is poor. What does this thing mean then, caste?

Is it just a fable for old men like him? If you just said to yourself, caste is a fiction, would it vanish like smoke; if you said, 'I am free', would you realize you had always been free?

He had finished his fourth chikoo milkshake. He felt sick.

As he left the ice-cream shop, all he wanted to do was to go visit Old Court Road. To sit by that statue of the dark Jesus.

He looked around to see if the police were following him. Of course on a day like this he could not go anywhere near the Jesus statue. It was suicide. They would be watching all routes into the school.

He thought of Daryl D'Souza. That was the man to go see! In twelve years in the schooling system, Daryl D'Souza was the only one who had been decent to Shankara.

Shankara had first seen the professor at a political rally. This was the 'Hoyka Pride and Self-Expression Day Rally' held at the Nehru Maidan – the greatest political event in the history of Kittur, the newspaper would say the following day. Ten thousand Hoykas had filled the maidan to demand their rights as a full-fledged community, and to ask for retribution for the five millennia of injustice done to them.

The warm-up speaker talked about the language issue. The official language of the town should be declared Tulu, the language of the common man, and not Kannada, which was the Brahmin language.

A thunderclap of applause followed.

The professor, although not himself a Hoyka, had been invited as a sympathetic outsider; he was sitting next to the guest of honour, Kittur's Member of Parliament, who was a Hoyka, the pride of his community. A three-time MP, and also a junior member of the Cabinet of India – a sign to the entire community of how high they could aim.

Eventually, after many more preliminary speakers, the Member of Parliament got up. He began to shout: 'We, brother and sister Hoykas, were not even allowed into the temple in the old days, did you know? The priest stood at the door, saying: "You low-caste!"'

He paused, to let the insult reverberate among his listeners.

'"Low-caste! Go back!" But ever since I was elected to parliament – by you, my people – do the Brahmins dare do that to you? Do they dare call you "low-caste"? We are ninety per cent of this town! We *are* Kittur! If they hit us, we will hit them back! If they shame us, we will—'

After the speech, someone recognized Shankara. He was led into a small tent where the Member of Parliament was relaxing after the speech, and was introduced as the plastic surgeon Kinni's son. The great man, who was sitting on a wooden chair, a drink in his hand, set his glass down firmly, spilling his drink. He took Shankara's hand in his hand and gestured for him to squat down on the ground beside him.

'In the light of your family situation, your high status in society, you are the future of the Hoyka community,' the MP said. He paused, and belched.

'Yes, sir.'

'You understand what I said?' asked the great man.

'Yes, sir.'

'The future is ours. We are ninety per cent of this town. All that Brahmin shit is finished,' he said, flicking his wrist.

'Yes, sir.'

'If they hit you, you hit them back. If they . . . if they . . .' The great man made circles with his hand, to complete the slurred statement.

Shankara wanted to shout out in joy. 'Brahmin shit!' Yes, that was exactly how he would put it himself; and here was a Member of Parliament, a Cabinet minister in the government of Rajiv Gandhi, talking just as he would!

Then an aide led Shankara from the tent. 'Mr Kinni.' The aide squeezed Shankara's arm. 'If you could make a small donation towards this evening's function. Just a small amount . . .'

Shankara emptied his pockets. Fifty rupees. He gave it all to the aide, who bowed deeply and told him once more that he was the future of the Hoyka community.

Shankara watched. Already hundreds of men were getting into lines, where beer and quarter-litre bottles of rum were being distributed to them, as a bribe for having attended the rally and cheered the speakers. He shook his head with disapproval. He didn't like the idea that he was part of 90 per cent of his town. Now it seemed to him that the Brahmins were defenceless – a former elite of Kittur who now lived in constant fear of being robbed of their homes and their wealth by the Hoykas, the Bunts, the Konkanas, and everyone else in town. The sheer averageness of the Hoykas – whatever they did became the average at once, by definition – repulsed him.

The following morning, he read the newspaper and thought he had been too harsh on the Hoykas. He remembered the professor who had been up on stage and found out from his chauffeur where he lived. He paced backwards and forwards outside the front gate of the professor's house for a while. Finally he opened the gate, approached the house, and pressed the front doorbell.

The professor opened the door. Shankara said: 'Sir, I am a Hoyka. You are the only man in this town whom I trust. I wish to talk with you.'

'I know who you are,' Professor D'Souza said. 'Come in.'

Professor D'Souza and Shankara sat in the living room and had a long talk.

'Who is that Member of Parliament? What is his caste?' the professor asked.

The question confused Shankara.

'He is one of us, sir. A Hoyka.'

'Not quite,' the professor said. 'He is a Kollaba. Have you heard the term? There is no such thing as a Hoyka, my dear fellow. The caste is subdivided into seven sub-castes. You understand the term? Sub-caste? Good. The Member of Parliament is a Kollaba, the top of the seven sub-castes. The Kollabas have always been millionaires. The British anthropologists of Kittur noted this fact with interest even in the nineteenth century. The Kollabas have exploited the other six Hoyka castes for years. And now once again, this man is playing the Hoyka card to get himself re-elected, so he can sit in an office in New Delhi and accept large envelopes filled with cash from businessmen who want to set up garment factories in the Bunder.'

Seven sub-castes? The Kollabas? Shankara had never heard any of this. He gaped.

'This is the big problem with you Hindus,' the professor said. 'You are mysteries to yourselves!'

Shankara felt ashamed to be a Hindu; what a repulsive thing, this caste system that his ancestors had devised. But at the same time he was annoyed with Daryl D'Souza. Who was this man to lecture him on caste? How dare the Christians do this? Hadn't they been Hindus too, at some point? Shouldn't they have remained Hindus and defeated the Brahmins from within, instead of taking the easy way out by converting?

He crushed his annoyance into a smile.

'What do we do about the caste system, sir? How do we get rid of it?'

'One solution is what the Naxalites have done, just to blow up the upper castes entirely,' said the professor. He had a quaint, woman-like habit of dipping his large round biscuit in milk, and then hurrying to eat it before it got too soggy. 'They blow up the entire system; that way you can start from scratch.'

'From scratch' – the American idiom excited Shankar. 'I too think we should start from scratch, sir. I think we should destroy the caste system and start from scratch.'

'My dear boy: you are a nihilist,' the professor

said, with an approving smile. He bit into his soggy biscuit.

They had not met after that; the professor had been travelling, and Shankara had been too shy to barge in on him a second time. But he had never forgotten the conversation. Now, wandering around town in a daze, the sugar from the milk-shakes upsetting his stomach, he thought: he's the only man who'd understand what I've done. I'll confess everything to him.

The professor's house was packed with students. A reporter from the *Dawn Herald* was there, asking the big man questions about terrorism. A black tape recorder sat on the desk. Shankara, who had come to the professor's house by autorickshaw, waited with the students and watched.

'It is an absolute act of nihilism on the part of some student,' the professor was saying, his eyes on the tape recorder. 'He should be caught and thrown into jail.'

'Sir, what does this episode say about today's India, sir?'

'This is an example of the nihilism of our youth,' said Professor D'Souza. 'They are lost and direc-tionless. They have . . .' – a pause – '. . . lost the moral standards of our nation. Our traditions are being forgotten.'

Shankara felt himself choke with rage. He stormed out.

He caught an autorickshaw to Shabbir Ali's

house and rang the bell. A bearded man in a North Indian-style kurta, with his chest hair sticking out, opened the door. It took Shankara some time to recognize him as Shabbir Ali's father, whom he had never before seen.

'He is not allowed to talk to any of his friends,' he said. 'You fellows have corrupted my son.' And he slammed the door in Shankara's face.

So, the great Shabbir Ali, the man who 'talked' to women and played with condoms, was locked up in his house. By his father. Shankara wanted to laugh.

He was tired of moving in autorickshaws; so he called home from a pay-phone and asked for the car to be sent to Shabbir Ali's house to pick him up.

Back home, he bolted the door to his room. He lay in bed. He picked up the phone and put it down and counted to five and then picked it up again. Eventually it worked. In Kittur, that was all you had to do to enter into someone else's world.

He was listening to a crossed line.

The phone line crackled and came to life. A man and woman, possibly husband and wife, were talking. They were speaking in a language he couldn't understand; he thought it might be Malayalam – the speakers must be Muslim, he thought. He wondered what they were talking about – was the man complaining about his health, was she asking for more money for the house-hold? Why were they on the phone, he wondered? Was the man living away from Kittur? Whatever their situation, whatever they were saying in that foreign language, he felt the intimacy of their conversation. It would be nice to have a wife or a girlfriend, he thought. Not to be so alone all the time. Even a single real friend. Even that would have kept him from planting the bomb and getting into all this trouble.

The man's tone changed suddenly. He began to whisper.

'I think someone's breathing on the line,' the man said – or so Shankar imagined.

'Yes, you're right. Some pervert is listening to us,' the woman replied – or so Shankara imagined.

Then the man hung up.

I have the worst of both castes in my blood, Shankara thought, lying in bed, the receiver of the phone still at his ear. I have the anxiety and fear of the Brahmin, and I have the tendency to act without thinking of the Hoyka. In me the worst of both has fused and produced this monstrosity which is my personality.

He was going mad. Yes, he was convinced of that. He wanted to get out of the house again. He worried that the chauffeur was noticing his restlessness.

He went out of the back door and slipped away from the house without the driver observing him.

But he probably doesn't suspect me, he thought. He probably thinks I'm a useless rich brat, like Shabbir Ali.

All these rich fellows like Shabbir Ali, he told himself bitterly, lived out a kind of code. They talked things, but did not do them. They had condoms at home, but did not use them; they kept detonators but did not explode him. Talk, and talk, and talk. That was their life. It was like the salt on the ice cream. The salt was smeared on the slab of vanilla and left there in the open; but no one was meant to lick it! That was only a joke! It was meant to be talk only, all this bomb-exploding stuff. If you knew the code, you understood it was just talk. Only he had taken them seriously; he had thought that they fucked women and blew up bombs. He did not know about the code, because he did not really belong – either to the Brahmins, or to the Hoykas, or even to the gang of spoiled brats.

He was in a secret caste – a caste of Brahmo-Hoykas, of which he had found only one representative so far, himself, and which put him apart from all the other castes of humankind.

He took another autorickshaw to the Junior School, and from there, making sure no one was watching him, walked up Old Court Road with his head to the ground and his hands in his pockets.

He parted the trees, came up to the statue of Jesus, and sat down. The smell of fertilizer was still strong in the air. Closing his eyes, he tried to calm himself. Instead, he began to think about the suicide that had taken place on this road many years ago. He had heard about it from Shabbir Ali. A man had been found hanging from a tree by this road – perhaps even in this spot. A suitcase lay at his feet, broken open. Inside, the police found three gold coins and a note. 'In a world without love, suicide is the only transformation possible.' Then there was a letter, addressed to a woman in Bombay.

Shankara opened his eyes. It was as if he could see the man from Bombay, hanging in front of him, his feet dangling in front of the dark Jesus.

He wondered: was that going to be his fate? Would he end up condemned and hanged?

He remembered again the fateful events. After the conversation at Shabbir Ali's house, he had gone down to the Bunder. He had asked for Mustafa, describing him as a man who sold fertilizers; he had been directed to a market. He found a row of vegetable sellers, asked for Mustafa, and was told: 'Go upstairs.' He climbed stairs. He found himself in a pitch-black space where a thousand men seemed to be coughing at once. He too began to cough. As his eyes got used to the dark he realized he was in a pepper market. Giant gunnybags were stacked up against the grimy walls, and coolies, coughing incessantly, were hauling them around. Then the darkness ended and he arrived in an open courtyard. Once again he asked: 'Where is Mustafa?'

He was directed by a man lying on a cart of old vegetables towards an open door.

He went in and found three men at a round table playing cards.

'Mustafa's not in,' said a man with narrow eyes. 'What do you want?'

'A bag of fertilizer.'

'Why?'

'I am growing lentils,' Shankara said. The man laughed.

'What kind?'

'Beans. Green gram. Horse gram.'

The man laughed again. He put his cards down, went into a room and hauled out an enormous gunnybag, and put it down by Shankara's feet.

'What else do you need to grow your beans?'

'A detonator,' Shankara said.

The men at the table all put down their cards together.

In the inner room of the house, he was sold a detonator; he was told how to turn the dial and set the timer. It would cost more than Shankara had on him at that moment, so he came back the next week with the money, and took the bag and the detonator back with him by autorickshaw, and got off at the bottom of Old Court Road. He had hidden it all near the statue of Jesus.

One Sunday, he went around the school. It was like the movie *Papillon*, one of his favourites, the scene where the hero plans how to escape from jail – it was as exciting as that. He was seeing his

86

school as if for the first time, with all the keenness of a fugitive's eye. After that, on that fateful Monday, he took the bag of fertilizer with him to school, and attached the detonator to it, turned the timer to one hour, left it under the back row, where he knew no one would sit.

Then he waited, counting off the hour minute by minute, like the hero in *Papillon*.

At midnight, the phone began ringing.

It was Shabbir Ali.

'Lasrado wants to see us all in his office, man! Tomorrow, first thing!'

All five of them had to be there in his office. The police would be present.

'He's going to have a lie-detector.' Shabbir paused. Then he shouted: 'I know you did it! Why don't you confess? Why don't you confess at once!'

Shankara's blood went chill. 'Fuck you!' he yelled back and slammed down the phone. But then he thought: my god, so Shabbir knew all along. Of course! Everyone knew all along. Everyone in the bad boys' gang must have known; and by now they must have told the whole town. He thought: let me confess right now. It would be best. Perhaps the police would give him some credit for having turned himself in. He dialled '100', which he thought was the police number.

'I want to speak to the Deputy Inspector General, please.'

'Ha?'

The voice was followed by a shriek of incomprehension.

Thinking he'd get better results, he spoke in English: 'I want to confess. I planted the bomb.'

'Ha?'

'The bomb. It was me.'

'Ha?'

Another pause. The phone was transferred.

He repeated his message to another person on the other line.

Another pause.

'Sorrysorrysorry?'

He put the phone down in exasperation. Damn Indian police – can't even answer a phone call properly; how the hell were they going to catch him?

Then the phone rang again; Irfan, calling on behalf of the twins.

'Shabbir just called us; he says we did it, man. I didn't do it! Rizwan didn't do it, either! Shabbir is lying!'

Then he understood: Shabbir had called everyone and accused them all – hoping to extract a confession! Relief mingled with anger. He had almost been trapped! Now he felt anxious that the police might trace his '100' call back to his phone. He needed a plan, he thought, a plan. Yes, he'd got it; he would say, if they asked, that he was calling to report Shabbir Ali for the crime. 'Shabbir is a Muslim,' he would say. 'He wanted to do this to punish India for Kashmir.'

The following morning, Lasrado was in the principal's office, sitting next to Father Almeida, who was at his desk. The two men stared at the five suspects.

'I have *scientipic* evidence,' Lasrado said. '*Pinger*-prints survive on the black stub of the bomb.' He sensed incredulity among the accused, so he added: '*Pingerprints* have survived even on the loaves of bread *lept* behind in the *Paraoh's* tomb. They are indestructible. We will *pind* the *pucker* who has done this, rest assured.'

He pointed a finger.

'And you, Pinto, a Christian boy – shame on you!'

'I didn't do it, sir,' Pinto said.

Shankara wondered: should he also throw in an interjection of his innocence, just to be safe?

Lasrado looked at them piercingly, waiting for the guilty part to turn himself in. Minutes passed. Shankara understood: he has no fingerprints. He has no lie-detector. He is desperate. He has been humiliated, mocked, and rendered a joke in college, and he wants revenge.

'You *puckers*!' Lasrado shouted. And then, again, in a trembling voice: 'Are you *lapping* at me? Are you *lapping* because I cannot say the letter "*epp*"?'

Now the boys could barely control themselves. Shankara saw that even the principal, having turned his face to the ground, was trying to suppress his laughter. Lasrado knew this; you could see it on his face. Shankara thought: this man has

89

been mocked his whole life because of his speech impediment. That's why he has been such a jerk in class. And now his entire life's work has been destroyed by this bomb; he will never be able to look back on his life with the pride, however false, that other professors do; never be able to say, at his farewell party, 'My students, although I was strict, loved me.' Always there would be someone whispering at the back – yes, they loved you so much they exploded a bomb in your class!

At that moment, Shankara thought, I wish I had just left this man alone. I wish I had not humiliated him, as so many have humiliated me and my mother.

'I did it, sir.'

Everyone in the room turned to Shankara.

'I did it,' he said. 'Now stop bothering these other boys and punish me.'

Lasrado banged his hand on the desk. 'Mother-*pucker*, is this a joke?'

'No, sir.'

'*Op* course it is a joke!' Lasrado shouted. 'You are mocking me! You are mocking me in public!'

'No, sir—'

'Shut up!' Lasrado said. 'Shut up!' He flexed a finger and pointed it wildly around the room.

'*Puckers! Puckers!* Get out!'

Shankara walked out with the four innocent ones. He could see that they did not believe his confession: they too thought he had been mocking the teacher to his face.

'You went too far there,' Shabbir Ali said. 'You really have no respect for anything in this world, man.'

Shankara waited outside the college, smoking. He was waiting for Lasrado. When the door to the staff room opened, and the chemistry professor walked out, Shankara threw the cigarette to the ground and stubbed it out with a scrape of his shoe. He watched his teacher for a while. He wished there were some way he could go up to him and say he was sorry.

DAY TWO (EVENING): LIGHTHOUSE HILL (THE FOOT OF THE HILL)

You are on a road surrounded by ancient banyan trees; the smell of neem is in the air, an eagle glides overhead. Old Court Road – a long, desolate road with a reputation as a hang-out for prostitutes and pimps – leads down from the top of the hill to St Alfonso's Boys' High School and Junior College.

Next to the school you will find a white-washed mosque dating back to the time of Tippu Sultan; according to local legend. Christians from Valencia suspected of being British sympathizers were tortured here. The mosque is the focus of a legal tussle between the school authorities and a local Islamic organization, both of which claim possession of the land on which it stands. Muslim students from the school are allowed, every Friday, to leave classes for an hour to offer namaaz at this mosque, provided they bring a signed note from their fathers, or in case of boys whose fathers are working in the Gulf, from a male guardian. From a bus stop in front of the mosque, express buses go to Salt Market Village.

At least four stalls stand outside the mosque, selling sugarcane juice and Bombay-style bhelpuri and charmuri to passengers at the bus stop.

A flurry of alarm bells rang at ten to nine, warning that this was no ordinary morning. It was a Morning of Martyrs, the thirty-seventh anniversary of the day Mahatma Gandhi had sacrificed his life so that India might live.

Thousands of miles away, in the heart of the nation, in chilly New Delhi, the President was about to bow his head before a sacred torch. Echoing through the massive Gothic edifice of St Alfonso's Boys' High School and Junior College – through thirty-six classrooms with vaulted ceilings, two outdoor lavatories, a chemistry-cum-biology laboratory, and a refectory where some of the priests were still finishing breakfast – the alarm bells announced that it was time for the school to do the same.

In the staff room, Mr D'Mello, assistant head-master, folded his copy of the newspaper, noisily, like a pelican folding its wings. Tossing the paper on a sandalwood table, Mr D'Mello struggled against his paunch to get to his feet. He was the last to leave the staff room.

Six hundred and twenty-three boys, pouring out of classrooms and eventually merging into one long line, proceeded into the Assembly Square. In ten minutes they had formed a geometrical pattern, a tight grid around the flagpole at the centre of the square.

By the flagpole stood an old wooden platform. And next to the platform stood Mr D'Mello, drawing the morning air into his lungs and shouting: 'A-ten-shannn!'

The students shuffled in concert. *Thump!* Their feet knocked the chatter out of the square. Now the morning was ready for the sombre ceremony.

The guest of honour had fallen asleep. From the top of the flagpole, the national tricolour hung, limp and crumpled, entirely uninterested in the events organized for its benefit. Alvarez, the old school peon, tugged on a blue cord to goad the recalcitrant piece of cloth into a respectable tautness.

Mr D'Mello sighed and gave up on the flag. His lungs swelled again: 'Sa-loot!'

The wooden platform began to creak noisily: Father Mendonza, junior school headmaster, was ascending the steps. At a sign from Mr D'Mello, he cleared his throat into the booming mike and launched into a speech on the glories of dying young for your country.

A series of black boxes amplified his nervous voice across the square. The boys listened to their headmaster spellbound. The Jesuit told them the blood of Bhagat Singh and Indira Gandhi fertilized the earth on which they stood, and they brimmed with pride.

Mr D'Mello, squinting fiercely, kept an eye on the little patriots. He knew that the whole humbug would end any moment. After thirty-three years in an all-boys' school, no secret of human nature was hidden from him.

The headmaster lumbered towards the crucial part of the morning's speech.

'It is of course customary on Martyrs' Day for the government to issue every school in the state with Free Film Day tickets for that following Sunday,' he said. It was as if electric current had jolted the square. The boys became breathless with anticipation.

'But this year' – the headmaster's voice quivered – 'I regret to announce that there will be no Free Film Day.'

For a moment, not a sound. Then, the entire square let out one big, aching, disbelieving groan.

'The government has made a terrible mistake,' the headmaster said, trying to explain. 'A terrible, terrible mistake . . . They have asked you to go to a House of Sin . . .'

Mr D'Mello wondered what the headmaster was prattling on about. It was time to bring the speech to an end and send the brats back to class.

'I cannot even find the words to tell you . . . it has been a terrible mix-up. I am sorry. I . . . am . . .'

Mr D'Mello was looking around for Girish, when a movement at the back of the square caught his eye. Trouble had begun. The assistant headmaster, hindered by his massive paunch, struggled to descend from the podium, but then, with a surprising litheness, he slipped through the rows of boys and homed in on the danger zone. Students turned on their toes to watch him as he made his way to the back. His right hand trembled.

A brown dog had climbed up from the playground below the Assembly Square and was loping about behind the boys. Some trouble-makers were trying to persuade it to draw nearer with soft whistles and clicks of their tongue.

'Stop that at once!' D'Mello – he was gasping for breath already – stamped his foot towards the dog. The indulged animal mistook the fat man's advance for another blandishment. The teacher lunged at the dog and it pulled back, but as he stopped to breathe, it raced back towards him.

The boys were laughing openly now. Waves of confusion spread throughout the square. Over the speaker system the headmaster's voice wobbled, with a hint of desperation.

'. . . you boys have no right to misbehave . . . the Free Film Day is a privilege, not a right . . .'

'*Stone it! Stone it!*' someone shouted at D'Mello.

In a moment of panic, the teacher obeyed. Whack! The stone caught the dog on the belly. The animal yelped in pain – he saw a gleam of betrayal in its eyes – before it bounded out of the square and ran down the steps of the playground.

A sensation of sickness tightened in Mr D'Mello's gut. The poor animal had been hurt. Turning around, he saw a sea of grinning boys. One of them had goaded him to stone the animal; he swung around, picked a boy at random – only hesitating for a split second to make sure that it wasn't Girish – and slapped him hard, twice.

When Mr D'Mello walked into the staff room, he found all the other teachers gathered around the sandalwood table. The men were dressed alike, in light-coloured half-sleeve shirts, closely checked, with brown or blue trousers that widened into bell-bottoms, while the few women wore peach or yellow polyester-and-cotton-blended saris.

Mr Rogers, the biology-cum-geology teacher, was reading aloud a schedule of the Free Film Day from the Kannada-language newspaper:

> **'Film One:** Save the Tiger
> **Film Two:** The Importance of Physical Exercise
> **Bonus Reel:** The Advantages of Native Sports (with special attention to Kabbadi and Kho-Kho).'

After that harmless listing, came the bombshell:

> 'Where to send your son or daughter on Free Film Day (1985):
> 1. St Milagres Boys' High School;
>   Surnames A to N, White Stallion
>   Theatre, O to Z Belmore Theatre.

2. St Alfonso's Boys' High School; Surnames A to N, Belmore Theatre, O to Z Angel Talkies.'

'Half our school!' Mr Rogers' voice whistled in excitement. 'Half our school to Angel Talkies!'

Young Mr Gopalkrishna Bhatt, only a year out of the teachers' college in Belgaum, tended to supply the chorus on such occasions. He raised his arms fatalistically: 'What a mix-up! Sending our children to *that* place!'

Mr Pundit, senior Kannada language teacher, scoffed at the naivety of his colleagues. He was a short silver-haired man of startling opinions.

'This is no mix-up, it's deliberate! The Angel Talkies has bribed all those bloody politicians in Bangalore, so they'd send our boys to a House of Sin!'

Now the teachers were divided between those who thought it was a mix-up and those who thought it was a deliberate ploy to corrupt the youth.

'What do you think, Mr D'Mello?' young Mr Bhatt called out.

Instead of replying, Mr D'Mello dragged a cane chair from the sandalwood table towards an open window at the far end of the staff room. It was a sunny morning: he had a blue sky, rolling hills, a private vista of the Arabian sea.

The sky was a dazzling light blue, a thing meant for meditation. A few perfectly formed clouds, like wishes that had been granted, floated through the azure. The arc of Heaven deepened in colour as it stretched towards the horizon and touched a crest of the Arabian Sea. Mr D'Mello invited the morning's beauty into his agitated mind.

'What a mix-up, eh, Mr D'Mello?'

Gopalkrishna Bhatt hopped onto the window ledge, blocking the view of the sea. Dangling his legs gleefully, the young man flashed a gap-toothed smile at his senior colleague.

'The only mix-up, Mr Bhatt,' said the assistant headmaster, 'was made on 15 August 1947, when we thought this country could be run by a people's democracy instead of a military dictatorship.'

The young teacher nodded his head. 'Yes, yes, how true. What about the Emergency, sir – wasn't that a good thing?'

'We threw that chance, away,' Mr D'Mello said. 'And now they've shot dead the only politician we ever had who knew how to give this country the medicine it needed.' He closed his eyes again and concentrated on an image of an empty beach in an attempt to dispel Mr Bhatt's presence.

Mr Bhatt said: 'Your favourite's name is in the paper this morning, Mr D'Mello. Page 4, near the top. You must be a proud man.'

Before Mr D'Mello could stop him, Mr Bhatt had begun reading:

'The Mid-Town Rotary Club announces the Winners of its Fourth Annual Inter-School English Elocution Contest.

Theme: Science – A Boon or Curse for the Human Race?
First Prize: Harish Pai, St Milagres High School (Science as a Boon).
Second Prize: Girish Rai, St Alfonso's High School (Science as a Curse).'

The assistant headmaster pulled the newspaper from the hands of his junior colleague. 'Mr Bhatt—' he snarled, 'I have often said this publicly: I have no favourites among the boys.'

He closed his eyes, but now his peace of mind was gone.

'Second prize' – the words stung him once again. He had worked with Girish all last evening on the speech – its content, its delivery, the boy's posture at the mike, everything! And only second prize? His eyes filled with tears. The boy had got into a habit of losing these days.

There was commotion in the staff room now, and through his closed eyes Mr D'Mello knew that the headmaster had arrived, and all the teachers were running around him sycophantically. He remained in his seat, though he knew his peace would not last long.

'Mr D'Mello,' came the nervous voice. 'It is a terrible mix-up . . . one half of the boys won't get to see the free film this year.'

The headmaster was gazing at him from near the sandalwood table. Mr D'Mello ground his teeth. He folded his copy of the newspaper violently; he

100

took his time getting to his feet, and he took his time turning around. The headmaster was mopping his forehead. Father Mendonza was a very tall, very bald man, with strands of heavily oiled hair combed over his naked pate. His large eyes stared out through thick glasses and an enormous forehead glittered with beads of sweat, like a leaf spotted with dew after a shower.

'May I make a suggestion, Father?'

The headmaster's hand paused with his handkerchief at his brow.

'If we don't take the boys to Angel Talkies, they'll see it as a sign of weakness. We'll only have more trouble with them.'

The headmaster bit his lips.

'But . . . the dangers . . . one hears of terrible posters . . . of evils that cannot be put into words . . .'

'I will take care of the arrangements,' Mr D'Mello said, gravely. 'I will take care of the discipline. I give you my word.'

The Jesuit nodded hopefully. As he left the staff room, he turned to Gopalkrishna Bhatt and the depth of gratitude in his voice was unmistakable: 'You too should go along with the assistant headmaster when he takes the boys to Angel Talkies . . .'

Father Mendonza's words echoing in his mind, he walked to his 11 a.m. class, his first of the morning. *Assistant headmaster.* He knew that he had not been the Jesuit's first choice. The insult still smarted after all this time. The post was his by right of seniority. For thirty years he had taught Hindi and arithmetic to the boys of St Alfonso's, and maintained order in the school. But Father Mendonza, who had recently come down from Bangalore with an oily comb-over and six trunks full of 'modern' ideas, stated his preference for someone 'smart' in appearance. Mr D'Mello had a pair of eyes and a mirror at home. He knew what that remark meant.

He was an overweight man entering the final phase of middle age, he breathed through his mouth, and a thicket of hair poked out of his nose. The centrepiece of his body was a massive pot belly, a hard knot of flesh pregnant with a dozen cardiac arrests. To walk, he had to arch his lower back, tilt his head, and screw his brow and nose together in a foul-looking squint. 'Ogre,' the boys chanted as he passed. 'Ogre! Ogre! Ogre!'

At noon, he ate a dish of red fish curry out of a stainless-steel tiffin-carrier, at his favourite window in the staff room. The smell of the curry did not please his colleagues, so he ate alone. Done, he slowly took his tiffin-carrier to the public tap outside. The boys stopped their games. Since it was out of the question for him to bend forward (the paunch, of course), he had to fill his tiffin-carrier with water and raise it to his mouth. Gargling loudly, he belched out a saffron torrent several times. The boys shrieked with pleasure each time. When he was back in the staff room, they crowded by the tap: little skeletons of fish had piled up at its base, like deposits of a nascent coral reef. Awe and disgust commingled in the voices of the boys and they chanted, in a unison that grew louder and louder: '*Ogreogreogre!*'

'The main problem with selecting Mr D'Mello as my assistant is that he has an excessive penchant for old-fashioned violence,' the young headmaster wrote to the Jesuit Board. Mr D'Mello caned too often, and too much. Sometimes, even as he wrote on the blackboard, his left hand would reach for the duster. He would turn around and send it flying at the last row, and there would be a scream and the bench would topple over under the weight of diving boys.

He had done worse. Father Mendonza reported in detail a shocking story he had heard. Once, many years ago, a small boy had been talking in the front row, right in front of D'Mello. The teacher said nothing. He just sat still and let his anger stew. Suddenly, it was said, there was a moment of blackness in his brain. He snatched the boy from his seat and hoisted him into the air and took him to the back of the class: there he shut him in a cupboard. The boy beat on the insides of the cupboard with his fists for the rest of the class. 'I can't breathe in here!' he shouted. The beating inside the cupboard grew louder and louder; then fainter, and fainter. When the cupboard was finally opened, a full ten minutes later, there was a stench of fresh urine, and the boy fell out in an unconscious heap.

Then there was the little matter of his past. Mr D'Mello had been in training at the Valencia Seminary to be a priest for six years, before leaving suddenly, and on bad terms with his superiors. The rumour was that he had challenged the holy Dogma, and declared that the polices of the Vatican on the matter of family planning were illogical in a country like India – and so walked out, abandoning six years of his life. Other rumours suggested that he was a free-thinker, who did not attend church regularly.

The weeks went on. The Jesuit Board inquired by mail if Father Mendonza had made a decision yet. The young headmaster confessed he had had no time for that. Every morning the padre found that his first duty was to discipline a long line of recalcitrants. The same faces appeared morning after morning. Talking in class. Disfiguring school property. Pinching studious boys.

One day, a foreigner, a Christian woman from Britain who was a generous donor to worthy causes in India, paid a visit to the school. Father Mendonza oiled his surviving strands of hair with special care that morning. He solicited Mr Pundit's assistance in guiding the British lady around the school. With great courtesy, the Kannada teacher explained to the foreigner the proud history of St Alfonso's, its celebrated alumni, its role in civilizing the savage nature of

104

this part of India, once a bare wilderness overrun by elephants. Father Mendonza began to feel that Mr Pundit was as smart a fellow as he was likely to find in this part of the world. Then, all at once, the foreigner began shrieking. The fingers of her hand spread out with horror. Julian D'Essa, the coffee-plantation scion, was standing on the last bench of a giggling classroom, exposing his privates to the world. Mr Pundit rushed at the crazy boy, but the damage had been done. The Jesuit saw the foreign donor step back from him with terror-struck eyes: as if he were the exhibitionist.

An old member of the Board called Father Mendonza from Bangalore that evening to console him. Did the 'reformer' not finally see the truth? Modern ideas of education were fine in Bangalore. But in a backwater like Kittur, miles and miles and miles away from civilization?

'To manage a school filled with six hundred little animals' – the old member of the Board told the sobbing young headmaster – 'you need an ogre now and then.'

Two months after his arrival at St Alfonso's, Father Mendonza summoned Mr D'Mello over to his office one morning. He told Mr D'Mello that he had no option but to ask him to serve as the assistant headmaster. To handle a school like this, the Jesuit declared, he needed a man like Mr D'Mello.

★   ★   ★

Stop for a moment, D'Mello told himself. Catch your breath. He was about to go into the class-room – about to declare war. The plan had worked well so far; he had come the way of the rear entrance. A surprise attack. He had figured that the news of Mendonza's change of mind on Angel Talkies was by now common knowledge. The boys had of course construed it as cowardice on the part of the school authorities. The danger was highest now, but also the opportunity to teach them a lasting lesson.

The class was quiet – too quiet.

D'Mello went in on tiptoe. The last row, where the tall, over-developed boys sat, were clumped together, a soundless knot around a magazine. D'Mello hovered over the boys. The magazine was the usual kind of magazine. 'Julian,' he said gently.

The boys turned around and the magazine dropped to the floor. Julian stood up with a grin. He was the tallest of the tall, the most over-developed of the over-developed. An inverted triangle of chest hair jutted out of his open shirt already, and when he rolled up a sleeve and made a muscle, D'Mello could see his biceps swelling into pale, thick tubers. As the son of a coffee-planting dynasty, Julian D'Essa could never be expelled from the school. But he could be punished. The little demon looked up at D'Mello, with a lecherous grin pasted on his face. In his mind Mr D'Mello heard D'Essa's voice; it goaded him on to do his worst: *Ogre! Ogre! Ogre!*

He heaved the boy out of the seat by his collar. Rip – the collar came off the shirt. D'Mello's shaking elbow straightened out – it connected with the side of the boy's face.

'Get out of the class, you animal . . . and kneel down . . .'

After shoving Julian out of the class, he put his hands on his knees and caught his breath. He picked up the magazine and flipped its pages about for public view.

'So this is the sort of thing you boys want to read, huh? Now you want to go to Angel Talkies? You think you'll see the posters on the wall: those Murals of Sin?'

He walked around the class with his shaking elbow and thundered: even the lechers were ashamed to go into Angel Talkies. They covered themselves in blankets and pushed rupee notes shamefully to the desk attendants. Inside, the walls of the theatre were papered with posters of X-rated films, purveyors of every known depravity. To see a movie in such a theatre was a corruption of body and soul alike.

He hurled the magazine against a wall. Did they think he was frightened to beat them? No! He was not one of these 'new-fashioned' teachers trained in Bangalore or Bombay! Violence was his staple, and his dessert. Spare the rod and spoil the child.

He collapsed onto his chair. He was horribly out of breath. A dull pain spread its roots across his chest. He saw with satisfaction that his speech had

had some effect. The boys were sitting without a squeak. The sight of Julian with his torn collar kneeling outside the class had a quieting effect. But Mr D'Mello knew it was just a matter of time, just a matter of time. At the age of fifty-seven he had no more illusions about human nature. Lust would inflame the boys' hearts with rebellion again.

He ordered them to open the Hindi textbooks. Page 168.

'Who will read the poem?'

The class was silent around one raised arm.

'Girish Rai, read.'

A boy wearing comically large spectacles got to his feet from the first bench. His hair was thick and parted down the middle; his small face was overpowered by pimples. He did not need the textbook, for he knew the poem by heart:

'Nay, said the flower:
Cast me, said the flower,
Not on the virgin's bed
Nor in the bridal carriage
Nor in the Merry Village square.

Nay, said the flower
Cast me but on that lonely path
Where the heroes walk
For their nation to die.'

The boy sat down. The entire class was silent, humbled for a moment by the purity of his enunciation in Hindi, that alien language. 'If only all of you could be like this boy,' Mr D'Mello said quietly.

But he had not forgotten that his favourite had let him down in the Rotary competition. Ordering the class to copy out the poem six times in their notebooks, he ignored Girish for two or three minutes. Then he summoned him with his fingers.

'Girish.' His voice faltered. 'Girish . . . why didn't you get first prize in the Rotary competition? How will we ever get to Delhi unless you win more first prizes?'

'Sorry, sir . . .' the boy said. He hung his head in shame.

'Girish . . . lately you haven't been winning so many first prizes . . . is something the matter?'

There was a worried look on the boy's face. Mr D'Mello panicked.

'Is someone troubling you? One of the boys? Has D'Essa threatened you?'

'No, sir.'

He looked at the tall boys in the back row. He turned to his right and glanced at the kneeling D'Essa, who was grinning hard. The assistant headmaster came to a quick decision.

'Girish . . . tomorrow . . . I don't want you to go to Angel Talkies. I want you to go to Belmore Talkies.'

'Why, sir?'

Mr D'Mello recoiled.

'What do you mean why? Because I say so, that's

why!' he yelled. The class looked at them; had Mr D'Mello raised his voice to his favourite?

Girish Rai reddened. He seemed on the verge of tears, and Mr D'Mello's heart melted. He smiled and patted the small boy on the back.

'Now, now, Girish, don't cry . . . I don't care about the other boys. They've been to the talkies many times – they've read magazines. There isn't anything left to be corrupted. But not you. I won't let you go there. Go to Belmore.'

Girish nodded and went back to his seat in the front bench. He was still on the verge of tears. Mr D'Mello felt his heart melting out of pity; he had been too harsh on the poor boy.

When the class ended, he went up to the front bench and tapped on the desk: 'Girish – do you have any plans for this evening?'

What a terrible day, what a terrible day. Mr D'Mello was walking along the mud road that led from the school to his home in the teachers' colony. That awful *whack* of the stone echoed over and over again in his head . . . the look in the poor animal's eyes . . .

He walked back with his poetry books beneath his armpit. His shirt was now speckled with red curry, and the tips of his collars were curled in, like sunburned leaves. Every few minutes, he stopped to straighten his aching back and catch his breath.

'Are you ill, sir?'

110

Mr D'Mello turned around: Girish Rai, with a huge khaki schoolbag strapped to his back, was following him.

Teacher and pupil walked a few yards side by side, and then Mr D'Mello stopped. 'Do you see that, boy?' he pointed.

Halfway between the school and the teacher's house ran a brick wall with a wide crack yawning down the middle. Both the wall and the crack had been there for years, in that road where no detail had significantly changed since Mr D'Mello had moved to the neighbourhood thirty years ago to take up the quarters assigned to him as a young teacher. Three lamp-posts along the adjacent road were visible through the crack in the wall, and for nearly twenty years now Mr D'Mello had stopped every evening and squinted hard at the three lamp-posts. For twenty years, he had been searching the lamp-posts for the explanation of a mystery. One morning, about two decades ago, while passing the crack he had seen a sentence in white chalk marked on all three lamp-posts:

'Nathan X must die.'

He had squeezed through the crack in the wall to get to the three lamp-posts, and scraped the words with his umbrella, to decipher their mystery. What did the three signs mean? An old man pulled along a cart of vegetables. He tried asking him who Nathan X was, but the vegetable man just shrugged. Ernest D'Mello stood there, with the mist in the trees, and wondered.

111

The next morning the signs were gone. Intentionally wiped out. When he got to school, he scanned the obituary column of the newspaper and couldn't believe his eyes – a man called 'Nathan Xavier' had been murdered the previous night at the Bunder! He was convinced at first that he had come upon some secret society planning a murder. A darker anxiety beset him soon. Maybe Chinese spies had written those words? Years had passed, but the mystery remained, and he thought about it each time he passed that crack.

'Do you think Pakistani spies did it, sir?' Girish said. 'Did they kill Nathan X?'

Mr D'Mello grunted. He felt he shouldn't have revealed the memory to Girish; he felt, somehow, he had compromised himself. Teacher and student walked on.

Mr D'Mello watched as the rays of sunset fell through the banyan leaves in large patches on the ground, like the puddles left behind by a child after a bath. He looked to the sky, and involuntarily spoke a line of Hindi poetry: '*The golden hand of the sun as it grazes the clouds . . .*'

'I know that poem, sir,' a little voice said. Girish Rai repeated the rest of the couplet: '. . . *is like a lover's hand as it grazes its beloved.*'

They walked on.

'So you have an interest in poetry?' D'Mello asked. Before the boy could reply, he confessed another secret to him. In his youth he had wanted

112

to be a poet – a nationalist writer, no less, a new Bharathi or Tagore.

'Then why didn't you become a poet, sir?'

He laughed. 'In this little hole of Kittur, my learned friend, how could a man make a living from poetry?'

The lamps came on, one by one. It was almost night now. In the distance Mr D'Mello saw a lighted door, his quarters. As they got closer to the house, he stopped talking. He could hear the brats from here. What have they smashed today, he wondered.

Girish Rai watched.

Mr D'Mello took off his shirt and left it on a hook on the wall. The boy saw the assistant head-master in his singlet, slowly setting himself down on a rocking chair in his living room. Two girls in identical red frocks were running in circles round the room, bellowing their lungs out. The old teacher ignored them completely. He gazed at the boy for a while, again wondering why, for the first time in his career as a teacher, he had invited a student home.

'Why did we let the Pakistanis get away, sir?' Girish blurted out.

'What do you mean, boy?' Mr D'Mello screwed his nose and brow together and squinted.

'Why did we let the Pakistanis get away in 1965? When we had them in our clutches? You said it in class one day, but you didn't explain.'

'Oh, that!' Mr D'Mello slapped his hand against

his thigh with relish. Another of his favourite topics. The great screw-up of the war of 1965. The Indian tanks had rolled into the outskirts of Lahore when our own government cut the ground beneath their feet. Some bureaucrat had been bribed; the tanks came back.

'Ever since Sardar Patel died, this country has gone down the drain,' he said, and the little boy nodded. 'We live in the midst of chaos and corruption. We can only do our jobs, and go home,' he said, and the little boy nodded.

The teacher exhaled contentedly. He was deeply flattered; in all these years at the school, no student had ever felt the same outrage he had, at that colossal blunder of '65. Lifting himself off the rocking chair, he pulled out a volume of Hindi poetry from a bookshelf. 'I want this back, huh? And in perfect shape. Not one scratch or blotch on it.'

The boy nodded. He looked around the house furtively. The poverty of his teacher's house surprised him. The walls of the living room were bare, save for a lighted picture of the Sacred Heart of Jesus. The paint was peeling, and stout-hearted geckos ran all over the walls.

As Girish flicked through the book, the two girls in red dresses took turns at shrieking into his ears, before screaming away into another room.

A woman in a flowing green dress, patterned with white flowers, approached the boy with a glass of red cordial. The boy was confused by her

114

face and could not answer her questions. She looked very young. Mr D'Mello must have married very late in life, the boy thought. Perhaps he had been too shy to go near women in his young days.

D'Mello frowned and drew nearer to Girish.

'Why are you grinning? Is something funny?'

Girish shook his head.

The teacher continued. He spoke of other things that made his blood boil. Once India had been ruled by three foreigners: England, France, and Portugal. Now their place was taken by three native-born thugs: Betrayal, Bungling, and Backstabbing. 'The problem is here . . .' – he tapped his ribs. 'There is a beast inside us.'

He began to tell Girish things he had told no one – not even his wife. His innocence of the true nature of schoolboys had lasted just three months into his life as a teacher. In those early days, he confessed to Girish, he stayed back after class to read up on the collection of Tagore's poetry in the library. He read the pages carefully, stopping sometimes to close his eyes and fantasize that he were alive during the freedom struggle – in any one of those holy years when a man could attend a rally and see Gandhi spinning his wheel and Nehru addressing a crowd.

When he got out of the library his head would be buzzing with images from Tagore. At that hour, electrolysed by the setting sun, the brick wall around the school became a long plane of beaten gold. Banyan trees grew along the length of the wall; within their deep, dark canopies, tiny leaves glittered in long strings of silver, like rosaries held by the meditating tree. Mr D'Mello passed. The whole earth seemed to be singing Tagore's verses. He passed by the playground, which was set into a pit below the school. Debauched shouts jarred his reveries.

'What is that shouting in the evenings?' he asked a colleague naively. The older teacher helped himself to a pinch of snuff. Inhaling the vile stuff from the edge of a stained handkerchief, he had grinned.

''tripping. That is what is going on.'

''tripping?'

The more experienced teacher winked.

'Don't tell me it didn't happen when you were at school . . .'

From D'Mello's expression he gathered that this was, indeed, not the case.

'It's the oldest game played by boys,' the old teacher said. 'Go down and see for yourself. I don't have the language to describe it.'

He went down the next evening. The sounds became louder and louder as he descended the steps into the playground.

The next morning, he summoned all the boys involved – all of them, even the victims – to his desk. He kept his voice calm with an effort. 'What do you think this is, a moral school run by

116

Catholics, or a whorehouse?' He hit them with such violence that morning.

When he was done, he noticed that his right elbow was still shaking.

The next evening, there was no noise from the playground. He recited Tagore out loud to protect himself from evil: '*Where the head is held high and the mind is without fear . . .*'

A few days later, passing the playground, he saw his right elbow trembling again in recognition. The old, familiar, black noise was rising from the play-ground.

'That was when the scales fell off my eyes,' Mr D'Mello said. 'I had no more illusions about human nature.'

He looked at Girish with concern. The little boy was stirring a large grin into the red cordial.

'They haven't done it to you, have they, Girish – when you play cricket with them in the evening? 'tripping?'

(Mr D'Mello had already let D'Essa and his over-developed gang know: if they ever tried that on Girish, he would skin them alive. They would see what an ogre he really was.)

He watched Girish with anxiety. The boy said nothing.

Suddenly he put his cordial down, stood up, and advanced to his teacher with a folded piece of paper. The assistant headmaster opened it, prepared for the worst.

It was a gift: a poem, in chaste Hindi.

Monsoon:
This is the wet and fiery season,
When lightning follows after thunder.
Each night, the sky shakes, and I wonder,
What could be the reason
God gave us this wet and fiery season?

'Did you write this yourself? Is this what you were blushing about?'

The boy nodded happily.

Good Lord! he thought. In thirty years as a teacher no one had done anything like this for him.

'Why is the rhyming scheme uneven?' D'Mello frowned. 'You should be careful about such things . . .'

The teacher pointed out the flaws of the poem one by one. The boy nodded his head attentively.

'Shall I bring you another one tomorrow?' he asked.

'Poetry is good, Girish, but . . . are you losing interest in quizzes?'

The boy nodded.

'I don't want to go any more, sir. I want to play cricket after class. I never get to play, because of the—'

'You have to go to the quizzes!' Mr D'Mello got up from his rocking chair. He explained: any opportunity for fame in this small town had to be seized at once. Didn't the boy understand?

'First go to the quizzes, become famous, then you'll get a big job, and then you can write poetry.

What will your cricket get you, boy? How will it make you famous? You'll never write poetry if you don't get out of here, don't you understand?'

Girish nodded. He finished his cordial.

'And, tomorrow, Girish . . . You're going to Belmore. I don't want any more discussion about that.'

Girish nodded.

After he left, Mr D'Mello sat in his rocking chair and thought for a long time. It was no bad thing, he was thinking, Girish Rai's newfound interest in poetry. Perhaps he could look out for a poetry contest for Girish to enter. The boy would win, of course – he would come back heaped in gold and silver. The *Dawn Herald* might put a picture of him on the back page. Mr D'Mello would stand with his arms proudly on Girish's shoulders. 'The teacher who nourished the budding genius.' They would conquer Bangalore next, the teacher-and-pupil team that won the all-Karnataka state poetry contest. After that, what else – New Delhi! The president himself would award the two of them a medal. They would take an afternoon off, take a bus to Agra, and visit the Taj Mahal together. Anything was possible with a boy like Girish. Mr D'Mello's heart leaped up with joy, as it had not done for years, since his days as a young teacher. Just before he went to sleep in his chair he pressed his eyes shut and prayed fervently: 'Lord, only keep that boy pure.'

★   ★   ★

Next morning, at ten past ten, by the express order of the state government of Karnataka, a throng of innocent schoolboys from St Alfonso's with surnames from O to Z rushed into the welcoming arms of a theatre of pornography. An old stucco angel crouched over the doorway of the theatre, showering its dubious benediction on the onrushing boys.

Once they got inside, they found they had been tricked.

The walls of Angel Talkies – those infamous murals of depravity – had been covered in black cloth. Not a single picture remained visible to the human eye. A deal had been struck between Mr D'Mello and the theatre management. The children would be shielded from the Murals of Sin.

'Do not stand close to the black cloth!' Mr D'Mello shouted out. 'Do not touch the black cloth!' He had everything planned. Mr Alvarez, Mr Rogers, and Mr Bhatt went among the students to keep them away from the posters. Two attendants from the theatre – presumably the dispensers of tickets to the blanket-covered men – helped in the arrangements. The boys were split into two groups. One group was marched to the upstairs auditorium, one herded downstairs. Before they could react, the boys would be sealed off inside the auditoriums. And so it was done: the plan worked perfectly. The boys were inside Angel Talkies, and they were going to watch nothing but the government films; Mr D'Mello had won.

120

The lights cut out inside the upstairs auditorium; a buzz of excitement from the boys. The screen glowed.

A scratched and fading reel flickered into life.

SAVE THE TIGER!

Mr D'Mello stood behind the seated boys along with the other teachers. He wiped his face with relief. It looked like everything was going to be okay, after all. Leaving him alone in peace for a few minutes, young Mr Bhatt then moved up to the assistant headmaster and tried to make small-talk.

Ignoring young Mr Bhatt, he kept his eyes to the screen. Photos of tiger cubs frolicking together flashed on the screen, and then a caption said: 'If you don't protect these cubs today, how can there be tigers tomorrow?'

He yawned. Stucco angels stared at him from the four corners of the auditorium, long peels of faded paint rising from their noses and ears, like heat-blisters. He hardly went to the films any more. Too expensive; he had to get tickets for the wife and the two little screamers too. But as a boy, hadn't films been his whole life? This very theatre, Angel Talkies, had been one of his favourite haunts; he would cut class and come here and sit alone and watch movies and dream. Now look at it. Even in the darkness the deterioration was unmistakable. The walls were foul, with large moisture-stains. The seats had holes in them. The simultaneous advance of decay and decadence: the story of this theatre was the story of the entire country.

The screen went black. The audience tittered. 'Silence!' Mr D'Mello shouted.

The title-shot of the 'bonus reel' came on.

THE IMPORTANCE OF PHYSICAL WELL-BEING IN THE DEVELOPMENT OF CHILDREN

Images of boys showering, bathing, running, and eating, each appropriately captioned, began flashing one by one. Mr Bhatt came up to the assistant headmaster once again. This time he whispered deliberately: 'It's your turn to go now, if you want.'

Mr D'Mello understood the words, but not the hint of secrecy in the young man's voice. At his own suggestion, the teachers were taking turns to patrol the black-clothed corridor to make sure none of the over-developed boys slipped out to take a peek at the pornographic images. It had just been Gopalkrishna Bhatt's turn to patrol the Murals of Sin. For a moment he was lost – then it all made sense. From the way the young man was grinning, Mr D'Mello realized that he had taken a quick peek himself. He looked around: each of the teachers was suppressing a grin.

Mr D'Mello walked out of the auditorium full of contempt for his colleagues.

He walked past the black-cloth-covered walls without feeling the slightest urge. How could Mr Bhatt and Mr Pundit have been so base to have done it? He walked past the whole length of the black cloth without the least temptation to lift it up.

A light flickered on and off in a stairwell that led to an upper gallery. The walls of this gallery too were covered with black cloth. Mr D'Mello dropped his mouth open and squinted at the upper gallery. No, he was not dreaming. Up there, he could make out a boy, his face averted, walking on tiptoe towards the black cloth. Julian D'Essa, he thought. Naturally. But then the boy's face came into view, just as he lifted up a corner of the black cloth and peered.

'Girish! What are you doing?'

At the sound of Mr D'Mello's voice the boy turned. He froze. Teacher and student stared at each other.

'I'm sorry, sir . . . I'm sorry . . . they . . . they . . .'

There was giggling behind him; and suddenly he vanished, as if someone had dragged him away.

Mr D'Mello rushed up the stairs at once, to the upper gallery. He could climb only two steps. His chest burned. Stomach heaving and hands clutching the balustrade, he rested there for a moment. The naked bulb in the stairwell sputtered on and off, on and off. The assistant headmaster felt dizzy. In his chest the heartbeat felt fainter and fainter, a dissolving tablet. He tried to call to Girish for help, but the words would not come out. Reaching out a hand for help, he caught a corner of the black cloth on the wall. It ripped, and split open: hordes of copulating creatures frozen in postures of rapes, unlawful pleasures, and bestialities, swarmed out and danced around his eyes in a taunting cavalcade, and a world of angelic delights that he had scorned until now flashed at him. He saw everything, and he understood everything, at last.

Young Mr Bhatt found him like that, lying on the stairs.

DAY THREE (MORNING): MARKET AND MAIDAN

The Jawaharlal Nehru Memorial Maidan (formerly King George V Memorial Maidan) is an open ground in the centre of Kittur. In the evenings, it fills up with people playing cricket, flying kites, and teaching their children to ride bicycles. At the edges of the maidan, ice-cream and ice-candy sellers peddle their wares. All major political rallies in Kittur are held there. The Hyder Ali Road leads from the maidan to Central Market, Kittur's largest market for fresh produce. The Town Hall of Kittur, the new law court, and the Havelock Henry General Hospital, and both the premier hotels in Kittur – the Hotel Premier Intercontinental and the Taj Mahal International – are within walking distance of the market. In 1988, the first temple meant exclusively for the use for Kittur's Hoyka community opened for worship in the vicinity of the maidan.

With hair like that, and eyes like those, he could easily have passed himself off as a holy man and earned a living sitting cross-legged on a saffron cloth near the temple. That was what the shopkeepers at the market said. Yet all this crazy fellow did, morning and evening, was crouch on the central railing of the Hyder Ali Road and stare at the passing buses and cars. In the sunset, his hair – a gorgon's head of brown curls – shone like bronze, and his irises glowed. While the evening lasted, he was like a Sufi poet, full of mystic fire. Some of the shopkeepers could tell stories about him: one evening they had seen him on the back of a black bull, riding it down the main road, swinging his hands and shouting, as if the Lord Shiva himself were riding into town on his bull Nandi.

Sometimes, he behaved like a rational man, crossing the road carefully, or sitting patiently outside the Kittamma Devi temple with the other homeless, as they waited for the left-overs of meals from weddings or thread-ceremonies to be scraped into their clustered hands. At other times he would be seen picking through piles of dog shit.

No one knew his name, religion, or caste, so no one made any attempt to talk to him. Only one man, a cripple with a wooden leg who came to the temple in the evenings once or twice a month, would stop to give him food.

'Why do you pretend not to know this fellow?' the cripple would shout, pointing one of his crutches at the fellow with the brown curls. 'You've seen him so many times before! He used to be the king of the number 5 bus!'

For a moment the attention of the market would turn to the wild man; but he would only squat and stare at a wall, his back to them and the city.

Two years ago, he had come to Kittur with a name, a caste, and a brother.

'I am Keshava, son of Lakshminarayana, the barber of Gurupura village,' he had said, at least six times on his way to Kittur, to bus conductors, toll-gatherers, and strangers who asked. This formula, a bag of bedding tucked beneath his arm, and the light pressure of his brother's fingers at his elbow whenever they were in a crowd, were all he had brought with him.

His brother had ten rupees, a bag of bedding that he too tucked under his right arm, and the address of a relative written on a paper chit that he kept crushed in his left hand.

The two brothers had arrived in Kittur on the 5 p.m. bus. They got off at the bus station; it was their first visit to a town. Right in the middle of the Market-Maidan road, in the centre of the biggest road in all of Kittur, the conductor had told them that their six rupees and twenty paise would take them no further. Buses charged around them, with men in khaki uniforms hanging from their doors, whistles in their mouths that they blew on screechingly, shouting at the passengers: 'Stop gaping at the girls, you sons of bitches! We're running late!'

Keshava held on to the hem of his brother's shirt. Two cycles swerved around him, nearly running over his feet; in every direction, cycles, autorickshaws, cars, threatened to crush his toes. It was as if he were at the beach, with the road shifting beneath him like sand beneath the waves.

After a while, they summoned up the courage to approach a bystander, a man whose lips were discoloured by vitiligo.

'Where is Central Market, uncle?'

'Oh, that . . . It's down by the Bunder.'

'How far is the Bunder from here?'

The stranger directed them to an autorickshaw driver, who was massaging his gums with a finger.

'We need to go to the market,' Vittal said.

The driver stared at them, his finger still in his mouth, revealing his long gums. He examined the moist tip of his finger. 'Lakshmi Market or Central Market?'

'Central Market.'

'How many of you?'

And then: 'How many bags?'

And then: 'Where are you from?'

Keshava assumed that these questions were standard in a big city like Kittur, that an autorickshaw driver was entitled to such inquiries.

'Is it a long distance away?' Vittal asked, desperately. The auto driver spat right at their feet.

'Of course. This isn't a village, it's a city. Everything's a long distance from everything else.'

He took a deep breath and sketched a series of

loops with his damp finger in the air, showing them the circuitous path that they would have to take. Then he sighed, giving the impression that the market was incalculably far away. Keshava's heart sank; they had been swindled by the bus driver. He had promised to drop them off within walking distance of Central Market.

'How much, uncle, to take us there?'

The driver looked at them from head to toe, and then from toe to head, as if gauging their height, weight, and moral worth: 'Eight rupees.'

'Uncle, it's too much! Take four!'

The autorickshaw driver said: 'Seven twenty-five', and motioned for them to get in. But then he kept them waiting in the rickshaw, their bundles on their laps, without any explanation. Two other passengers negotiated a destination and a fare and crammed in; one of them sat on Keshava's lap without any warning. Still the rickshaw did not move. Only after another passenger joined them, sitting in the front beside the driver, and with six people crammed into the tiny vehicle that had space for three, did the driver start kicking on his engine's pedal.

Keshava could barely see where they were going, and thus his first impressions of Kittur were of the man who was sitting on his lap; of the scent of castor oil which had been used to grease his hair and the hint of shit that he produced when he squirmed. After dropping off the rider in the front seat, and then the two men at the back, the autorickshaw meandered for some time through a quiet, dark area of town, before turning into another cacophonous street, lit by the glaring white light of powerful paraffin lamps.

'Is this Central Market?' Vittal shouted at the driver, who pointed to a sign:

KITTUR MUNICIPALITY CENTRAL MARKET: ALL MANNER OF VEGETABLES AND FRUIT AT FAIR PRICES AND EXCELLENT FRESHNESS

'Thank you, brother,' Vittal said, overwhelmed with gratitude, and Keshava thanked him too.

When they got out, they found themselves once again in a vortex of light and noise; they kept very still, waiting for their eyes to make sense of the chaos.

'Brother,' Keshava said, excited at having found a landmark that he recognized. He pointed: 'Brother, isn't this where we started out?'

And when they looked round, they realized that they were only a few feet away from where the bus driver had set them down. Somehow they had missed the sign, which had been right behind them all the time.

'We were cheated!' Keshava said, in an excited voice. 'That autorickshaw driver cheated us, brother! He—'

'Shut up!' Vittal whacked his younger brother

on the back of his head. 'It's all your fault! You're the one who wanted to take an autorickshaw!'

The two of them had been brothers for only a few days.

Keshava was dark and chubby; Vittal was tall and lean and fair, and five years older. Their mother had died years ago, and their father had abandoned them; an uncle had raised them and they had grown up amongst their cousins (whom they also called 'brothers'). Then their uncle had died, and their aunt called Keshava and told him to go with Vittal, who was being dispatched to the big city to work for a relative who ran a grocery shop. And that was, really, how they had come to realize that there was a bond between them deeper than that between cousins.

They knew that their relative was somewhere in the Central Market of Kittur: that was all. Taking timid steps, they went into a dark market area where vegetables were being sold, and then, through a back door, they went into a well-lit market where fruits were being sold. Here they asked for directions. Then they walked up steps that were covered in rotting garbage and moist straw to the second floor. Here they asked again: 'Where is Janardhana the store owner from Salt Market Village? He's our kinsman.'

'Which Janardhana – Shetty, Rai, or Padiwal?'

'I don't know, uncle.'

'Is your kinsman a Bunt?'

131

'No.'

'Not a Bunt? A Jain, then?'

'No.'

'Then of what caste?'

'He's a Hoyka.'

A laugh.

'There are no Hoykas in this market. Only Muslims and Bunts.'

But the two boys looked so lost that the man took pity and asked someone, and found out that there were indeed some Hoykas who had set up shop near the market.

They walked down the steps and went out of the market. Janardhana's shop, they were told, displayed a large poster of a muscular man in a white singlet. They couldn't miss it. They walked from shop to shop and then Keshava cried: 'There!'

Beneath the image of the man with the big muscles sat a lean shopkeeper, unshaven, who was reading a notebook with his glasses down on the bridge of his nose.

'We are looking for Janardhana, from Gurupura village,' Vittal said.

'Why do you want to know where he is?'

The man was looking at them suspiciously.

Vittal burst out: 'Uncle, we're from your village. We're your kin.'

The shopkeeper stared. Moistening a tip of his finger, he turned another page in his book.

'Why do you think you're my kin?'

'We were told this, uncle. By our aunty. One-eyed Kamala.'

The shopkeeper put the book down.

'One-eyed Kamala's . . . ah, I see. And what happened to your parents?'

'Our mother passed away many years ago, after Keshava's – this fellow's – birth. And four years ago, our father lost interest in us and just wandered away.'

'Wandered away?'

'Yes, uncle,' Vittal said. 'Some say he's gone to Varanasi, to do yoga by the banks of the Ganga. Others say he's in the holy city of Rishikesh. We haven't seen him in many years; we were raised by our uncle Thimma.'

'And he . . . ?'

'Died last year. We stayed on, and then it was too much for our aunt to support us. The drought was very bad this year.'

The shopkeeper was amazed that they had come all this way, without any prior word, on so thin a connection, just expecting that he would take care of them. He reached down into a counter, bringing out a bottle of arrack, which he uncapped and put to his lips. Then he capped the bottle and hid it again.

'Every day people come from the villages, looking for work. Everyone thinks that we in the towns can support them for nothing. As if we have no stomachs of our own to feed.'

The shopkeeper took another swig of his bottle;

133

his mood improved. He had rather liked their naïve recounting of that story of daddy having gone to 'the holy city of Rishikesh . . . to do yoga'. Old rascal is probably shacked up with a mistress somewhere, and taking care of a brood of bastards, he thought, smiling in approval; how you can get away with anything in the villages. Stretching his hands high above his head as he yawned, he brought them down onto his stomach with a loud whack.

'Oh, so you're orphans now! You poor fellows. One must always stick to one's family – what else is there in life?' He rubbed his stomach: look at the way they are staring at me, as if I were a king, he thought, feeling suddenly important. It was not a feeling he had had often since coming to Kittur.

He scratched his legs. 'So, how are things in the village these days?'

'Except for the drought, everything's the same, uncle.'

'You got here by bus?' the shopkeeper asked. And then: 'From the bus station, you walked over here, I take it?' He got up from his seat: 'Autorickshaw? How much did you pay? Those fellows are total crooks. Seven rupees!' The shopkeeper turned red. 'You imbeciles! Cretins!'

Apparently holding the fact that they had been cheated against them, the shopkeeper ignored them for half an hour.

Vittal stood in a corner, his eyes to the ground, crushed by humiliation. Keshava looked around. Red-and-white stacks of Colgate–Palmolive toothpaste and jars of Horlicks were piled behind the shopkeeper's head, shiny packets of malt-powder hung from the ceiling like wedding bunting; blue bottles of kerosene and red bottles of cooking oil were stacked in pyramids up the front of the shop.

Keshava was a small, lean, dark-skinned boy, with enormous eyes that stared lingeringly. Some of those who knew him insisted he had the energy of a hummingbird and was always flapping around, making a nuisance of himself; others found him lazy and melancholic, liable to sit and stare at the ceiling for hours at a time. He smiled and turned his head away when he was scolded for his behaviour, as if he had no conception of himself and no opinion on the matter.

Again the store owner took out the bottle of arrack, and he sipped a little more. Again this affected his mood for the better.

'We don't drink here like they do in the villages,' he said, returning Keshava's big stare. 'Only a little sip at a time. The customer never finds out that I am drunk.' He winked. 'That's how it is in the city: you can do anything you want, as long as no one finds out.'

After drawing the shutters on his shop, he took Vittal and Keshava around the market. Everywhere men were sleeping on the ground, covered in thin bedsheets; after asking some questions, Janardhana led the boys to an alley behind the market. Men and women and children were sleeping in a long line all the way down the alley. Keshava and Vittal stood back as the store owner began negotiations with one of the sleepers.

'If they sleep here, they will have to pay the Boss,' the sleeper complained.

'What do I do with them, they have to sleep somewhere!'

'Well, you're taking a risk, but if you have to leave them here try the far end.'

The alley ended in a wall that leaked continuously; the drainage pipes had been badly fitted. A large rubbish bin at this end of the alley emitted a horrible stench.

'Isn't uncle going to take us to his house, brother?' Keshava whispered, when the store owner, having given them some advice about how to sleep out in the open, vanished.

Vittal pinched him.

'I'm hungry,' Keshava said, after a few minutes. 'Can we find uncle and ask him for food?'

The two brothers were lying side by side, wrapped in their bedding, next to the garbage bin.

In response, his brother entirely covered himself in his sheet and lay inside, still, like a cocoon.

Keshava could not believe he was expected to sleep here – and on an empty stomach. However bad things had been at home, at least there had always been something to eat. Now all the frustrations of the evening, the fatigue, and confusion combined, and he kicked the shrouded figure hard. His brother, as if he had been waiting for just such a provocation, tore the blanket off; caught Keshava's head in his hands and slammed it twice against the ground.

'If you make one more sound, I swear, I will leave you all alone in this city.' Then he covered himself with his bedding once more and turned his back to his brother.

And though his head had begun to hurt, Keshava was frightened by what his brother had said. He shut up.

Lying there, his head stinging, Keshava wondered, dully, where it was decided that this fellow and this fellow would be brothers; and about how people came into the earth, and how they left it. It was a dull curiosity. Then he began thinking about food. He was in a tunnel, and that tunnel was his hunger, and at the end of the tunnel, if he kept going, he promised himself, there would be a huge heap of rice, covered with hot lentils, with big chunks of chicken.

He opened his eyes; there were stars in the sky. He looked up at them to block the stench of garbage.

When they arrived at the shop the following morning, the shopkeeper was using a long stick to hang plastic bags of malt-powder on hooks in the ceiling.

'You,' the shopkeeper said, pointing to Vittal. He showed the boy how each plastic bag was to be fitted to the end of the pole, and then lifted up and snared on a hook in the ceiling.

'It takes forty-five minutes every morning to do this; sometimes an hour. I don't want you to rush the work. You don't mind working, do you?'

Then, with the redundancy of speech typical of the rich, he said: 'If a man doesn't work, he doesn't eat in this world.'

While Vittal hung the plastic bags from the hooks, the shopkeeper told Keshava to sit behind the counter. He gave him six sheets of paper with the faces of film actresses printed on them, and six boxes of incense-sticks. The boy was to cut out the pictures, put them on the incense-stick boxes, cover them with cellophane quickly, and Scotch-tape the cellophane to the box.

'With pretty girls on them, you can charge ten paise more,' said the storekeeper. 'Do you know who this is?' He showed Keshava the picture he had just cut from the sheet. 'She's famous in Hindi films.'

Keshava began cutting out the next actress from the sheet. In front of them, below the counter, he could see where the store owner had hidden his bottle of hooch.

At noon, the shopkeeper's wife came with lunch. She looked at Vittal, who avoided her gaze, and at Keshava, who stared at her, and said: 'There's not enough food for both of them. Send one of them to the barber.'

Keshava, following instructions he had memorized, made his way through the unfamiliar streets and came to a part of town where he found a barber

138

working on the street. He had set up his barber's stall against a wall, hanging his mirror from a nail hammered between a family planning sign and an anti-tuberculosis poster.

A customer sat in a chair in front of the mirror, draped in a white cloth, and the barber was shaving him. Keshava waited till the customer had left.

The barber scratched his head and inspected Keshava from head to foot.

'What kind of work can I offer you, boy?'

At first the barber could think of nothing for him to do but hold the mirror for his customers to examine themselves after they had been shaved. Then he asked Keshava to clip the toenails and calluses from the customers' feet as he shaved them. Then he told the boy to sweep the hair from the pavement.

'Serve him some food too, he's a good boy,' the barber told his wife, when she arrived with tea and biscuits at four o'clock.

'He's the shopkeeper's boy, he can get food himself. And he's a Hoyka, you want him eating with us?'

'He's a good boy, let him have some food. Just a little.'

It was only as the barber watched the boy wolf down the biscuits that he realized why the shop-keeper had sent the boy to him. 'My God! You haven't eaten all day?'

The next morning, when Keshava showed up,

the barber patted him on the back. He still didn't know exactly what to do with Keshava, but that no longer seemed to be a problem; he knew he could not let this boy, with his sweet face, starve all day at the shopkeeper's place. In the afternoon, Keshava was given lunch. The barber's wife grumbled, but her husband splashed Keshava's plate with large helpings of fish curry.

'He's a hard worker, he deserves it.'

That evening, Keshava accompanied the barber on a round of house-calls; they went from house to house, and waited in the back yards for their customers to come outside. While Keshava set up a small wooden chair in the back yard, the barber threw a white cloth around the customer's neck and asked him how he wanted his hair cut that day. After each appointment, the barber would flap the white cloth hard, dusting off the curlets of hair; as they left the house and went to the next, the barber passed a commentary on the customer.

'That customer can't get it up, you can tell from how limp his moustache is.' Seeing Keshava's blank stare, he said: 'I guess you don't know about that bit of life yet, eh, boy?' Then, regretting that confidence, he whispered to the boy: 'Don't repeat that to my wife.'

Each time they crossed the road, the barber seized the boy's hand by the wrist.

'It's *dangerous* out here,' he said, pronouncing the key word in English, in a tremulous manner, bringing out all the drama in that foreign word. 'One moment of not watching out in this city and your whole life is gone. *Dangerous.*'

In the evening Keshava came back to the alley behind the market. His brother was lying face down on the ground, fast asleep, too tired even to lay out his bedding. Keshava turned Vittal over, unfolded the sheet and covered his face up to his nose.

Since Vittal was already asleep, he pulled his mattress right next to his brother's, so that their arms would touch. He fell asleep gazing at the stars.

A horrible noise woke him in the middle of the night: three kittens, chasing each other, right around his body. In the morning, he saw their neighbour feeding the kittens a bowl of milk. They had yellow flesh, and their pupils were elongated, like claw-marks.

'Have you got the money ready?' the neighbour asked him, when he came over to pet the kittens. He explained that Vittal and Keshava would have to pay a fee to a local 'boss' – one of those who collected payments from the homeless of the streets of Kittur in return for 'protection' – mainly from himself.

'But where is this Boss? My brother and I have never seen him here.'

'You'll see him tonight. That was the word we received. Have the money ready; or he'll beat you.'

Over the next few weeks, Keshava developed a

routine. In the mornings, he worked at the barber's; after his work at the barber's, he was free to do as he wished. He wandered about the market, which seemed to him to be bursting with shining things, expensive things. Even the cows that ate the garbage seemed so much larger in this market than they were back home. He wondered what there was in the garbage here that made the cows so fat. One black cow, an animal with extraordinary horns, walked about like a magical animal from some other land; back in the village he used to ride cows and he wanted to mount this animal, but he was frightened of doing so here in the city. Food seemed to be everywhere in Kittur; even the poor did not starve here. He saw food being scraped into the hands of the poor by the Jain temple. He saw a shopkeeper, trying to sleep in the hubbub of the market, covering his head with a scooter helmet. He saw shops selling glass bangles, white shirts and undershirts in cellophane bags, maps of India with her states marked out.

'Hey! Move out of the way, you village hick!'

He turned. The man was driving a bullock cart laden with cardboard boxes stacked into a pyramid; the boy wondered what was in the boxes.

He wished he had a cycle, to ride fast up and down the main road and stick his tongue out at these haughty fellows riding the bullock carts, who were always rude to him. But most of all he wished he were a bus conductor. They hung from the sides of the buses, shouting at people to get in faster, cursing when a rival bus overtook them; they had their khaki uniforms and their black whistles hanging from the red cords around their necks.

One evening, nearly every bystander around the market looked up to see a monkey walking on a telephone wire that went over their heads. Keshava stared at the monkey in wonder. Its pink scrotum dangled between its legs, and huge red balls whacked against the sides of the wire. It leaped onto a building with a blue sun and spreading rays painted on it, and sat there, looking down indifferently at the crowd.

Suddenly an autorickshaw hit Keshava, flinging him down onto the road. Before he could scramble to his feet, he saw the rickshaw driver in front of him, yelling furiously.

'Get up! You son of a bald woman! Get up! Get up!' The driver had made a fist already, and Keshava covered his face with his hands and begged.

'Leave the boy alone.'

A fat man in a blue sarong stood over Keshava, pointing a stick at the autorickshaw driver. The driver grumbled, but turned away and returned to his vehicle.

Keshava wanted to catch the hands of the man in the blue sarong and kiss them, but the man had melted away into the crowd.

Once again, the cats woke Keshava in the middle of the night. Before he could go back to sleep,

143

there was a loud whistle from the far end of the alley. 'Brother's here!' someone cried. A shuffling of clothes and bedsheets followed; men were getting up all around him. A pot-bellied man in a white singlet and a blue sarong was standing at the head of the alley, his hands on his hips. He bellowed:

'So my little darling dumplings, you thought you could avoid payments to your poor bereaved Brother by coming here to this alley, did you?'

The fat man – the one who called himself Brother – went up to each of the men sleeping in the alley one by one. Keshava started: it was his saviour from the market. With his stick Brother poked every sleeping person and asked.

'How long has it been since you paid me? Huh?'

Vittal was terrified; but a neighbour whispered: 'Don't worry, he'll only make you do some squats, and say sorry, and then he'll be off. He knows there's no money in this lane.'

When he reached Vittal, the fat man stopped and inspected him carefully.

'And you sir, my Maharajah of Mysore, if I may bother you a second,' he said. 'Your name?'

'Vittal, son of the barber from Gurupura village, sir.'

'Hoyka?'

'Yes, sir.'

'When did you arrive in this lane?'

'Four months ago,' Vittal said, blurting out the truth.

'And how many payments have you made to me in that period?'

Vittal said nothing.

The fat man slapped him and he staggered back, tripped on his bedding, and fell on the ground hard.

'Don't hit him, hit me!'

The man in the blue sarong turned to Keshava.

'He's my brother, he's my only relative in the world! Hit me instead. Please!'

The fat man down put his stick; with narrowed eyes he examined the little boy.

'A Hoyka who is so brave? That's unusual. Your caste is full of cowards, that's been Brother's experience in Kittur.'

He pointed at Keshava with his stick and addressed the entire lane: 'Everyone: notice the way he sticks by his brother. Wah, wah. Young fellow, for your sake, I spare your brother's hide tonight.'

He touched Keshava's head with the stick. 'On Thursday, you'll come see me. At the bus station. I have work for brave boys like you there.'

The next morning, the barber was aghast when Keshava told him of his tremendous good fortune.

'But who's going to hold the mirror?' he said.

He caught the boy by the wrist.

'It's *dangerous* with those people in the buses. Stay with me, Keshava. You can come and sleep in my house, so this Brother doesn't bother you any more; you'll be like a son to me.'

145

But Keshava had lost his heart to the buses. Every day, he went straight to the bus station at the end of Central Market to scrub the buses clean with a mop and a bucket of water. He was the most enthusiastic of the cleaners. When he was inside the bus, he would take the wheel and pretend he was driving, vroom-vroom!

'A nice little catch here for us,' Brother told them – and the conductors and drivers laughed and agreed.

As long as he was at the wheel, pretending to be driving, he was loud, and used the coarsest language; but if anyone stopped him and asked: 'What's your name, loudmouth?', he would get confused, and roll his eyes, and slap the top of his skull, before saying: 'Keshava – yes, that's it. Keshava. I think that's my name.' They roared and said: 'He's a bit touched in the head, this fellow!'

One conductor took a liking to him and told him to come along on his 4 p.m. round on the bus. 'Only one round, you understand?' he warned the boy sternly. 'You'll have to get off the bus at 5.15 p.m.'

The conductor returned to the station with Keshava at half past ten.

'He brings good luck,' he said, ruffling the boy's hair. 'We beat all the Christian buses today; a clean sweep.'

Soon all the conductors began inviting him on their buses. Brother, who was a superstitious man, observed this development and declared that

146

Keshava had brought good luck with him from his village.

'A young fellow like you, with ambition!' He tapped Keshava's bottom with his stick. 'You might even become the conductor of a bus one day, loudmouth!'

'Really?' Keshava's eyes widened.

He went with the buses when they roared down the market road at five o'clock, the rush hour, with the number 77 bus right ahead of them.

He was seated up the front, near the driver's seat, a cheering squad of one. 'Are you going to let them beat us?' He asked the driver. 'Let the Christians overtake the Hindu buses?'

The conductor waded his way through the crowd, issuing tickets, collecting money, his whistle in his mouth all the time. The bus picked up speed, just missing a cow. Tearing down the road, the number 5 bus drove parallel to the number 243, as a frightened scooter driver veered leftward for his life, and then – a big cheer from the passengers! – overtook its rival. The Hindu bus had won!

In the evenings, he washed the buses and fixed incense-sticks to the portraits of the gods Ganapati and Krishna by the drivers' rear-view mirrors.

On Sundays, he was free after noon. He explored Central Market from the vegetable sellers at one end, to the clothes sellers at the other end.

He learned to notice what people noticed. He learned what was good value for money in shirts;

147

what was a rip-off; what made for a good dosa, and a bad one. He acquired the connoisseurship of the market. He learned to spit; not like he had in the past, simply to clear his throat or nose, but with some arrogance – some style. When the rains failed again, and more fresh faces arrived at the market from villages, he mocked them: 'O, you hicks!' He came to master life in the market; learned how to cross the road despite the continuous traffic, simply by holding his hand as a stop sign and moving briskly, ignoring the loud honks from the irritated drivers.

When there was a cricket match, the entire market would be abuzz. He went from store to store; each shopkeeper had a small black transistor that emitted a crackly noise of cricket commentary. The entire market was buzzing as if it were a hive, whose every cell secreted cricket commentary.

At night people ate by the side of the road. They chopped firewood and fed it into the stoves, and sat around the fires, burnished by the flickering flames, looking haggard and hard. They cooked broth and sometimes fried fish. He did petty favours for them, like carrying empty bottles, bread, rice, and blocks of ice to nearby shops on the back of his bicycle, and for this he was invited to eat with them.

He hardly saw Vittal any more. By the time he got back to the alley, his brother was wrapped up in his bedsheet and was snoring softly.

★   ★   ★

One evening, he had a surprise: the barber, who worried that Keshava was falling into the influence of the 'dangerous' fellows at the bus station, took him to see a film, holding his hand tightly the whole way to the cinema. When they emerged from the theatre, the barber told him to wait as he went to chat up a friend who sold paan-leaves outside the cinema. As he waited, Keshava heard a drum-beat and yelling, and followed the noise around the corner to the source. A man stood beating a long drum outside a playground; next to him was a metal board painted with the images of fat men in blue underwear grappling with each other.

The drum-beater would not let Keshava in. Two rupees admission, he said. Keshava sighed and turned towards the cinema. On his way back, he saw a group of boys climbing over the side of a wall into the playground; he followed them.

Two wrestlers were in the sandpit in the middle of the playground, one wore grey shorts, the other wore yellow. Six or seven other wrestlers stood by the pit, shaking their legs and arms. He had never seen men with such slender waists and such enormous shoulders before; it was so exciting just to watch their bodies. 'Govind Pehlwan fights Shamsher Pehlwan,' announced a man with a megaphone.

The man with the megaphone was Brother.

Both wrestlers touched the ground and then raised their fingers to their foreheads; then they

149

charged into one another like rams. The one with the grey shorts stumbled and slipped, and the one with the yellow shorts pinned him down; then the situation was reversed. Things continued like this, for some more time, until Brother separated them, saying: 'What a fight that was!'

The wrestlers, covered in dirt, came to the side and washed themselves clean. Under their shorts, to Keshava's surprise, they each wore another pair of shorts and they bathed in these. Suddenly, one of the wrestlers reached over and squeezed the other's buttock. Keshava rubbed his eyes to make sure he had seen what he had seen.

'Next up: Balram Pehlwan fights Rajesh Pehlwan,' came the announcement from Brother.

The pale mud in the pit was now dark in the centre, where the wrestling and fighting had been most intense. Spectators sat on a grassy bank near the pit. Brother walked around the pit, offering commentary on the action. 'Wah, wah,' he cried, whenever a wrestler pinned another one down. A cloud of mosquitoes swirled overhead, as if they too were excited by the match.

Keshava walked among the crowd of spectators; he saw boys who were holding each other's hands, or resting their heads on another's chest. He was envious; he wished he had a friend here too, so he could hold his hand.

'Sneaked in, did you?' Brother had come up to him. He put an arm on Keshava's shoulder and winked. 'Not a good idea – the ticket money comes to me, so you've been swindling me, you rascal!'

'I have to go,' Keshava said, squirming. 'The barber is waiting for me.'

'To hell with the barber!' Brother roared. He sat Keshava next to him and returned to his commentary with the megaphone.

'I too was like you,' Brother told him, during the next break in his commentary. 'A boy with nothing; I wandered here from my village with empty hands. And look what I've done for myself—'

He spread his arms wide, and Keshava saw them embrace the wrestlers, the sellers of peanuts, the mosquitoes, the man with the drum at the gate: Brother seemed like the ruler of all that was important in the world.

That night the barber came down the alley and embraced Keshava, who had lain down to sleep. 'Hey! Where did you vanish after the movies? We thought you were lost.' He put his hand on Keshava's head and ruffled his hair.

'You're like my son, now, Keshava. I'll tell my wife, we must take you into our house. Let her agree, then you come with me. This is your last night here.'

Keshava turned to Vittal, who had pulled down a corner of his blanket to overhear them.

Vittal pulled his blanket over his head and turned the other way. 'Do what you want with him,' he mumbled. 'I have enough work to do, looking after myself.'

★　★　★

One evening, as Keshava was scrubbing the bus, a stick tapped the ground next to him.

'Loudmouth!' It was Brother, in his white singlet. 'We need you for the rally.'

A whole gang of the boys from the bus station were being taken by a number 5 bus to the Nehru Maidan. An enormous crowd had gathered there. Poles had been stuck up over the ground and miniature Congress party flags hung from them.

A huge stage had been erected in the middle of the ground, and above the stage hung the enormous painted image of a man with a moustache and thick black glasses, his arms raised as if in universal benediction. Six men, in white clothes, sat on the stage beneath the painting. A speaker was at a mike: 'He is a Hoyka sits next to the prime minister Rajiv Gandhi and gives him advice! And so the entire world can see that the Hoykas are trustworthy and reliable, despite the falsehoods that the Bunts and other upper castes spread about us!'

After a while, the MP himself – the same man whose face was on the painting – got to the mike.

At once, Brother hissed: 'Start shouting.'

The dozen boys who were standing together at the back of the crowd filled their lungs and bellowed: 'Long live the hero of the Hoyka people!'

They shouted six times, and then Brother told them to shut up.

The great man spoke for over an hour.

'There will be a Hoyka temple. No matter what

152

the Brahmins say; no matter what the rich say; there will be a Hoyka temple in this town. With Hoyka priests. And Hoyka gods. And Hoyka goddesses. And Hoyka doors, and Hoyka bells, and even Hoyka doormats and doorknobs! And why? Because we are ninety per cent of this town! We have our rights here!'

'We are ninety per cent of this town! We are ninety per cent of this town.' Brother instructed the boys to shout. The other boys did as told; Keshava came close to Brother and yelled into his ear: 'But we are not ninety per cent of this town. That isn't true.'

'Shut up and shout.'

After the procession, bottles of liquor were being handed out from trucks, and men jostled each other to grab them.

'Hey,' Brother signalled to Keshava. 'Have a drink, come on, you deserve it.' He slapped him on the back; the others forced the liquor down his throat and he coughed.

'Our star slogan-shouter!'

That night, when Keshava finally got back to the alley, Vittal was waiting for him with his arms folded.

'You're drunk.'

'So what?' Keshava thumped his chest. 'Who are you, my father?'

Vittal turned to the neighbour, who was playing with his cats, and shouted: 'This guy is losing all sense of morality in this city. He can't tell right

153

from wrong any longer. He hangs out with drunks and thugs.'

'Don't say things like that about Brother, I warn you,' Keshava said, in a low voice.

But Vittal continued: 'What the hell do you think you are doing, roaming around the city this late? You think I don't know what kind of animal you've become?'

He swung his fist at Keshava; but his younger brother caught his hand.

'Don't touch me.'

Then, without being entirely aware of what he was doing, he picked up his bedding and walked down the alley.

'Where do you think you're going?' Vittal shouted.

'I'm leaving.'

'And where will you sleep tonight?'

'With Brother.'

He was almost out of the alley, when he heard Vittal shouting his name. Tears were streaming down his face. Calling his name was not enough; he wanted Vittal to come running down, to touch him, to embrace him, to beg for him to come back.

A hand touched his shoulder; his heart leaped. But when he turned around, he saw not Vittal, but the neighbour. A second later, the cats had also come to him and were licking his feet and meowing ferociously.

'You know Vittal didn't mean that! He's worried

about you, that's all: you have been mixing with a dangerous crowd. Just forget everything he said and come back.'

Keshava only shook his head.

It was ten o'clock at night. He walked into the bus-repair shop. In the darkness, two men with masks were cutting metal with a blue flame; fumes, sparks, the smell of acrid smoke, and loud noise.

After a while, one man in a mask gestured upwards with his hand, and not knowing what that meant, Keshava walked right past the buses. He saw a woman crouching on the floor, whom he had never seen before. She was pressing the feet of Brother, who sat bare-chested in a cane chair.

'Brother, take me in, I have nowhere to stay. Vittal has thrown me out.'

'Poor boy!' Without getting up from the chair, Brother turned to the woman pressing his feet. 'You see what is happening to the family structure in our country? Brothers casting brothers out on the street!'

He led Keshava to a nearby building, which, he explained, was a hostel he ran for the best workers at the bus station. He opened a door; inside were rows of beds, and on each bed lay a boy. Brother tore the cover off one bed. A boy was lying asleep with his head on his hands.

Brother slapped the boy awake.

'Get up and get out of this house.'

Without any protest, the boy began scrambling

155

to collect his stuff. He moved into a corner and crouched; he was too confused to know where to go. 'Get out! You haven't showed up to work in three weeks!' Brother shouted.

Keshava felt sorry for the crouching figure, and he wanted to shout out: no, don't throw him out, Brother! But he understood: it was either this boy or him in this bed tonight.

A few seconds later, the crouching figure had vanished.

A long clothesline had been fixed between two of the crossbeams of the ceiling, and the white cotton sarongs of the boys hung from it, over-lapping each other like ghosts stuck together. Posters of film actresses and the god Ayappa, sitting on his peacock, covered the walls. The boys were clustered around the beds, staring at him and taunting him.

Ignoring them, he took out his things: a spare shirt, a comb, half a bottle of hair oil, some Scotch tape, and six pictures of film actresses that he had stolen from his relative's shop. He stuck the pictures up over his bed with the Scotch tape.

At once, the other boys gathered round.

'Do you know the names of these Bombay chicks? Tell us.'

'Here's Hema Malini,' he said. 'Here's Rekha, she's married to Amitabh Bachchan.'

The statement provokes giggles from the boys around him.

'Hey, boy, she's not his wife. She's his *girlfriend.*

156

He sticks it to her every Sunday in a house in Bombay.'

He felt so angry when they said this that he got to his feet and shouted incoherently at them. He lay his face down in bed for an hour after that.

'Moody fellow. Like a lady, so delicate and moody.'

He pulled the pillow over his head; he began thinking of Vittal, wondering where he was right now, why he was not sleeping at his side. He began to cry into the pillow.

Another boy came over: 'Are you a Hoyka?' He asked.

Keshava nodded.

'Me too,' the boy said. 'The rest of these boys are Bunts. They look down on us. You and I, we should stick together.'

He whispered: 'There's something I have to warn you about. In the night, one of the boys walks around tapping guys' cocks.'

Keshava started. 'Which one does that?'

He stayed awake all night, sitting up whenever anyone came anywhere near his bed. Only in the morning, watching the other boys giggling hysterically as they brushed their teeth, did he realize that he had been had.

Inside a week, it seemed as though he had always lived at the hostel.

Some weeks later, Brother came for him.

'It's your big day, Keshava,' he said. 'One of the

157

conductors was killed last night in a fight at a liquor-shop.' He held Keshava's arm up high, as if he had won a wrestling match.

'The first Hoyka bus conductor in our company! He's a pride to his people!'

Keshava was promoted to chief conductor of one of the twenty-six buses that plied the number 5 route. He was issued a brand-new khaki uniform, his own black whistle on a red cord, and books of tickets, marked in maroon, green, and grey, all bearing the number 5.

As they drove, he stood leaning out of the bus, holding on to a metal bar, with his whistle in his mouth, blowing sharply once to tell the driver to stop and twice to tell him not to. As soon as the bus stopped, he jumped down onto the road and shouted at the passengers: 'Get in, get in.' Waiting until the bus moved again, he jumped onto the metal steps that led down from the entrance and hung from the bus, holding on to the rail. Shoving and yelling and pushing his way inside the packed bus, he collected money and gave out tickets. There was no need for tickets – he knew every customer by sight; but it was the tradition for tickets to be issued, and he did so, ripping them out and handing them to the customers, or sending them through the air to inaccesible customers.

In the evenings, the other cleaning boys, awed by his swift promotion, gathered around him at the bus station.

158

'Fix this thing!' He shouted, pointing to the metal bar by which he hung from the bus. 'I can hear it rattling all day long, it's so loose.'

'It's not so much fun,' he said when the work was done and the boys crouched around, gazing at him with star-struck eyes. 'Sure there are girls on the bus, but you can't pester them – you're the conductor, after all. Then there's the constant worry about whether those Christian bastards will beat us and steal the customers. No, sir, it's not all fun at all.'

When the rains started, he had to lower the leather canvas above the windows so that the passengers would remain dry; but water always seeped in anyway and the bus became dank. The front glass of the bus was besmirched with rain; blotches of silvery water clung to the screen like blobs of mercury; the world outside became hazy, and he would grip the bar and lean outside to make sure the driver could find his way.

In the evening, as he lay on his bed in the hostel, having his hair dried with a white towel by one boy and getting his feet massaged by another (these were his new privileges), Brother came to the dormitory, bringing in a rusty old bike behind him.

'You can't go walking around town any more, you're a bigshot now. I expect my conductors to travel in style.'

Keshava pulled the bike to his bed; that night, to the amusement of the other boys, he went to sleep with the bike next to him.

One evening, at the bus station, he saw a cripple sitting and blowing at his tea with his legs crossed, exposing the wooden stub of his artificial leg.

One of the boys chuckled.

'Don't you recognize your patron?'

'What do you mean?'

The boy said: 'That's the man whose bike you ride these days!'

He explained that the cripple had himself once been a bus conductor, like Keshava; but he had fallen from the bus, crushing his legs under a passing lorry, and had to have an amputation.

'And thanks to that, you now have a bike of your own!' he guffawed, slapping Keshava heartily on the back.

The cripple drank his tea slowly, staring at it intensely, as if it were the only pleasure in his life.

When Keshava was not conducting the bus, Brother had a string of bicycle delivery jobs for him; once he had to strap a block of ice on the back of his cycle and ride all the way downtown to drop it off at the house of Mabroor Engineer, the richest man in town, who had run out of ice for his whisky. But in the evenings, he was allowed to ride the bike for his pleasure; which meant, usually, taking it at full speed down the main road next to Central Market. On either side, the shops glowed with the light of paraffin lamps, and all the lights and colour got him so excited that he took both hands off the handlebars and whooped for joy, braking just in time to stop himself running into an autorickshaw.

160

Everything seemed to be going so well for him; yet one morning his neighbours found him lying in bed, staring at the picture of the film actresses and refusing to move.

'He's being morose again,' his neighbours said. 'Hey, why don't you jerk off, it'll make you feel better?'

The next morning he went back to see the barber. The old man was not in. His wife was sitting in the barber's chair, combing her hair. 'Just wait for him, he's always talking about you. He misses you very much, you know.'

Keshava nodded; he cracked his knuckles and walked round the chair three or four times.

That night at the dormitory, the other boys seized him as he was brushing his hair and dragged him out the door.

'This fellow's been morose for days now. It's time for him to be taken to a woman.'

'No,' he said. 'Not tonight. I have to visit the barber. I promised I'd come for—'

'We'll take you to a barber, all right! She'll shave you good!'

They put him in an autorickshaw and drove him down to the Bunder. A prostitute was 'seeing' men in a house by the shirt factories, and though he shouted at them and said he didn't want to do it, they told him that doing it would cure his moods and make him normal like everyone else.

He did seem more normal in the days that followed. One evening, at the end of his shift, he

161

saw a new cleaning boy, one of Brother's recent hires, spit on the ground as he was cleaning the bus; calling him over, Keshava slapped him.

'Don't spit anywhere near the bus, understood?'

That was the first time he ever slapped anyone.

It made him feel good. From then on, he regularly hit the cleaning boys, like all the other conductors did.

On the number 5, he got better and better at his job. No trick escaped him any more. To the schoolboys who tried to get free rides back from the movie theatre on their school passes, he'd say: 'Nothing doing. The passes work only when you're going to class, or going back from class. If it's a joy ride, you pay the full fare.'

One boy was a consistent problem – a tall, handsome fellow, whose friends called him Shabbir. Keshava watched people staring at the shirt enviously. He wondered why this boy was taking the bus at all; people like him had their own cars and drivers.

One evening, when the bus stopped at the women's college, the rich boy went down to the seats earmarked for women and leaned over to one of the girls.

'Excuse me, Miss Rita. I just want to talk to you.'

The girl turned her face towards the window; shifting her body away from him.

'Why won't you just talk to me?' the boy with the Bombay shirt asked, with a rakish grin. His friends up the back whistled and clapped.

Keshava bounded up to him. 'Enough!' He seized the rich boy by the arm and pulled him away from the girl. 'No one pesters women on my bus.'

The boy called Shabbir glared. Keshava glared back at him.

'Did you hear me?' he tore a ticket and flicked it at the rich boy's face to underline the warning. 'Did you hear me?'

The rich boy smiled. 'Yes, sir,' he said, and put out his hand to the conductor as if for a handshake. Confused, Keshava took his hand; the boys in the back row howled with laughter. When the conductor withdrew his hand, he found a five-rupee note in it.

Keshava flung the note at the rich boy's feet.

'Try it again, you son of a bald woman and I'll send you flying out the bus.'

As she stepped down from the bus, the girl looked at Keshava: he saw the gratitude in her eye, and he knew he had done the right thing.

One of the passengers whispered: 'Do you know who that boy is? His father owns that video-lending store and he's best friends with the Member of Parliament. See that insignia that says "CD" on the pocket of his shirt? His father buys those shirts from a shop in Bombay and brings them for his son. Each shirt costs a hundred rupees, or maybe even two hundred rupees, they say.'

Keshava said: 'On my bus, he'd better behave.

There's no rich or poor here; everyone buys the same ticket. And no one troubles the women.'

That evening, when Brother heard this story, he embraced Keshava: 'My valiant bus conductor! I'm so proud of you!'

He raised Keshava's hand up high, and the others applauded. 'This little village boy has shown the rich of this town how to behave on a number 5 bus!'

The following morning, as Keshava was hanging from the metal bar of the bus and blowing his whistle to encourage the driver, the bar creaked – and then it snapped. Keshava fell from the speeding bus, hit the road, rolled, and slammed his head into the side of the kerb.

For some days afterwards, the boarders at the hostel would find him hunched over his bed, on the verge of tears. The bandage had come off his head and the bleeding had stopped. But he was still silent. When they gave him a good shake, Keshava would nod his head and smile, as if to say, yes, he was okay.

'Then why don't you get out and go back to work?'

He said nothing.

'He's morose all day long. We've never seen him like this.'

But then after not turning up at work for four days, they saw him leaning out of the bus, and yelling at the passengers, looking every bit his old self.

Two weeks passed. One morning, he felt a heavy hand on his shoulder. Brother himself had come to see him.

'I hear that you've turned up for work only one day in the last ten. This is very bad, my son. You can't be morose.' Brother made a fist. 'You have to be full of life.' He shook his fist at Keshava, as if to demonstrate the fullness of life.

A boy nearby tapped his head. 'Nothing gets to him. He's touched. That blow on the head has turned him into an imbecile.'

'He always was an imbecile,' said another boarder, combing his hair at a mirror. 'Now he just wants to sleep and eat for free in the hostel.'

'Shut up!' Brother said. He swished his stick at them. 'No one talks about my star slogan-shouter like that!'

He gently tapped his stick on Keshava's head. 'You see what they're saying about you, Keshava? That you're putting on this act just to steal food and bed from Brother? You see the insults they spread about you?'

Keshava began to cry. He drew his knees up to his chest and put his head in them, and cried.

'My poor boy!' Brother himself was almost in tears. He got onto the bed and hugged the boy.

'Someone's got to tell the boy's family,' he said, on the way out. 'We can't keep him here if he's not working.'

'We did tell his brother,' the neighbours replied.

'And?'

165

'He's not interested in hearing about Keshava. He says there's no connection between them any more.'

Brother slammed his fist against the wall.

'You see the extent to which family life has deteriorated these days!' He shook his fist, which was aching from the blow. 'That fellow has to take care of his brother. He has no other option!' He shouted. He whipped his stick through the air: 'I will show that piece of shit! I will force him to remember his duty to his younger brother!'

Although no one actually threw him out, one evening when Keshava came back, someone else was sitting on his bed. The fellow was tracing his finger along the outlines of the actresses' faces, and the other boys were teasing him: 'O, so she's his *wife*, is she? She's not, you idiot!'

It was as if he had always been there, and they had always been his neighbours.

Keshava simply wandered away. He felt no desire to fight to get his bed back.

He sat by the closed doors of the Central Market that night, and some of the streetside sellers recognized him and fed him. He did not thank them; did not even say hello. This went on for a few days. Finally, one of them said to him: 'In this world, a fellow who doesn't work doesn't eat. It's not too late; go to Brother and apologize and beg him to give you your old job back. You know he thinks of you as family . . .'

For a few nights, he wandered outside the

market. One day he drifted back to the hostel. Brother was sitting in the drawing room again, as his feet were massaged by the woman. 'That was a lovely dress Rekha wore in the movie, don't you think . . .' Keshava wandered into the room.

'What do you want?' Brother asked, getting up. Keshava tried to put it into words. He held his arms out to the man in the blue sarong.

'This Hoyka idiot is mad! And he stinks! Get him out of here!'

Hands dragged him for some distance and pushed him to the ground. Leather shoes kicked him in the ribs.

A little later, he heard footsteps, and then someone lifted him up. Wooden crutches tapped on the earth, and a man's voice said: 'So Brother's got no use for you either, eh . . . ?'

He vaguely sensed that he was being offered something to eat. He sniffed; it reeked of castor oil and shit, and he rejected it. He smelled garbage around him, and turned his head towards the sky; his eyes were full of the stars when they closed.

THE HISTORY OF KITTUR (ABRIDGED FROM A SHORT HISTORY OF KITTUR BY FATHER BASIL D'ESSA, S.J.)

'The word "Kittur" is a corruption either of "Kiri Uru". "Small Town", or of "Kittamma's Uru" – Kittamma being a goddess specializing in repelling smallpox whose temple stood near today's train station. A letter from a Syrian Christian merchant written in 1091 recommends to his peers the excellent natural harbour of the town of Kittur, on the Malabar Coast. During the entire twelfth century, however, the town appears to have vanished: Arab merchants who visited Kittur in 1141 and 1190 record only wilderness. In the fourteenth century a dervish named Yusuf Ali began curing lepers at the Bunder; when he died, his body was entombed in a white dome, and the structure – the Dargah of Hazrat Yusuf Ali – has remained an object of pilgrimage to the present day. In the late fifteenth century, "Kittore, also known as the citadel of elephants", is listed in the tax-collection records of the Vijayanagara rulers as one of the provinces of their empire. In 1649, a four-man Portuguese missionary delegation led by Father Cristoforo d'Almeida, S.J., trekked down the coast from Goa to Kittur; it found "a deplorable mess of idolators, Mohameddans, and elephants". The Portuguese drove out the Mohammeddans, pulverized the idols, and distilled the wild elephants into a rubble of dirty ivory. Over the next hundred years, Kittur – now renamed Valencia – passed back and forth between the Portuguese, the Marathas, and the kingdom of Mysore.

In 1780, Hyder Ali, the ruler of Mysore, defeated an army of the East India Company near the Bunder; by the Treaty of Kittur, signed that year, the Company renounced its claims on "Kittore, also called Valencia or The Bunder". The Company violated the treaty after Hyder Ali's death in 1782, by setting up a military camp near the Bunder; in retaliation, Tippu, the son of Hyder Ali, constructed the Sultan's Battery, a formidable fortress of black stone, mounted with French guns. After Tippu's death in 1799, Kittur became Company property and was annexed into the Madras Presidency. The town, like most of South India, took no part in the great anti-British mutiny of 1857. In 1921, an activist of the Indian National Congress raised a tricolour at the old lighthouse: the freedom struggle had come to Kittur.'

DAY THREE (AFTERNOON): ANGEL TALKIES

Nightlife in Kittur centres on the Angel Talkies cinema. Every Thursday morning, the walls of the town are plastered with hand-painted posters featuring a sketch of a full-bodied woman brushing her hair with her fingers; below is the title of the movie: HER NIGHTS, WINE AND WOMEN, MYSTERIES OF GROWTH, UNCLE'S FAULT. The words 'Malayalam Colour' and 'Adults Only' are prominently featured on the posters. By 8 a.m., a long line of unemployed men has queued outside Angel Talkies. Show times are 10 a.m., noon, 2 p.m., 4 p.m. and 7.10 p.m. Seat prices range from Rs 2.20 for a seat at the front to Rs 4.50 for a 'Family Circle' seat up in the balcony. Not far from the theatre is the Hotel Woodside, whose attractions include a famous Paris cabaret, featuring Ms Zeena from Bombay, every Friday, and Ms Ayesha and Ms Zimboo from Bahrain, every second Sunday. A travelling sexologist,

Dr Kurvilla, MBBS, MD, M.Ch., MS, DDBS, PCDB, visits the hotel on the first Monday of every month. Less expensive and seedier in appearance than the Woodside are a nearby series of bars, restaurants, hostels, and apartments. Thanks to the presence of a YMCA in the neighbourhood, however, men of decency also have the option of a moral and clean hostel.

The door of the YMCA swung open at two in the morning; a short figure walked out. He was a small man with a huge protruding forehead, which gave him the look of a professor in a caricature. His hair, thick and wavy like a teenager's, was oiled and firmly pressed down; it was greying around the temples and in the sideburns. He had walked out of the YMCA looking at the ground; and now, as if noticing for the first time that he was in the real world, he stopped for a moment, looked this way and that, and then headed towards the market.

A series of whistles assaulted him at once. A policeman in uniform, cycling down the street, slowed to a halt and put a foot on the pavement.

'What is your name, fellow?'

The man who looked like a professor said: 'Gururaj Kamath.'

'And what work do you do that makes you walk alone at night?'

'I look for the truth.'

'Now don't get funny, all right?'

'Journalist.'

'For which paper?'

'How many papers do we have?'

The policeman, who may have been hoping to uncover some irregularity associated with this man, and hence either to bully or to bribe him, both acts which he enjoyed, looked disappointed, and then rode away. He had hardly gone a few yards when a thought hit him and he stopped again and turned towards to the little man.

'Gururaj Kamath. You wrote the column on the riots, didn't you?'

'Yes,' said the little man.

The policeman looked down at the ground.

'My name is Aziz.'

'And?'

'You've done every minority in this town a great service, sir. My name is Aziz. I want to . . . to thank you.'

'I was only doing my job. I told you: I look for the truth.'

'I want to thank you anyway. If more people did what you do, there wouldn't be any more riots in this town, sir.'

Not a bad fellow after all, Gururaj thought, as he watched Aziz cycle off. Just doing his job.

He continued his walk.

No one was watching him, so he let himself smile with pride.

In the days after the riots, the voice of this

little man had been the voice of reason in the midst of chaos. In precise, biting prose he had laid out for his readers the destruction caused by the Hindu fanatics who had ransacked the shops of Muslim shopkeepers; in a calm, un-emotional tone he had blasted bigotry and stood up for the rights of religious minorities. He had wanted nothing more from his columns than to help the victims of the riots: instead, Gururaj now found himself something of a celebrity in Kittur. A star.

A fortnight ago, he had suffered the greatest blow of his life. His father had passed away from pneumonia. The day after Gururaj returned to Kittur from his ancestral village, having shaved his head and sat with a priest by the water-tank in his ancestral temple to recite Sanskrit verses to bid his father's soul farewell, he discovered that he had been promoted to Deputy Executive Editor, the number two position at the newspaper where he had worked for twenty years.

It was life's way of evening things out, Gururaj told himself.

The moon shone brightly, with a large halo around it. He had forgotten how beautiful a nocturnal walk could be. The light was strong and clean, and it laminated the earth's surface; every object carved sharp shadows in it. He thought it might be the day after a full moon.

Even at this hour of the night, work continued. He heard a low, continuous sound, like the audible respiration of the nocturnal world: an open-back truck was collecting mud, probably for some construction site. The driver was asleep at the wheel; his arm stuck out of one window, his feet out of the other one. As if ghosts were doing the work behind, morsels of mud came flying into the truck from behind. The back of Gururaj's shirt became damp, and he thought: but I will catch a cold. I should go back. That thought made him feel old, and he decided to go on; he took a few steps to his left and began to walk right down the middle of Umbrella Street; it had been a childhood fantasy of his to walk down the middle of a main road, but he had never been able to sneak away from his father's watchful eyes long enough to fulfil the fantasy.

He came to a halt, right in the middle of the road. Then he quickly went into a side alley.

Two dogs were mating. He crouched down and tried to see exactly what was happening.

After completing the act, the dogs separated. One went down the alley and the other headed towards Gururaj, running with postcoital vigour and almost brushing his trousers as it went past. He followed.

The dog came into main road and sniffed at a newspaper. Taking the newspaper in its mouth, it ran back into the alley, and Gururaj ran behind it. Deeper and deeper the dog ran into the side alleys, as the editor followed. Finally, it dropped its bundle; turning, it snarled at Gururaj and then tore the newspaper to shreds.

'Good dog! Good dog!'

Gururaj turned to his right to confront the speaker. He found himself face to face with an apparition; a man in khaki, carrying an old Second World War-era rifle, his yellowish, leathery face covered with nicks and scars. His eyes were narrow and slanting. Drawing closer, Gururaj thought: of course. He's a Gurkha.

The Gurkha was sitting on a wooden chair out on the pavement, in front of a bank's rolled-down shutter.

'Why do you say that?' said Gururaj. 'Why are you praising the dog for destroying a paper?'

'The dog is doing the right thing. Because not a word in the newspaper is true.'

The Gurkha – Gururaj took him for an all-night security guard for the bank – rose from his chair and took a step to the dog.

At once it dropped the paper and ran away. Picking up the torn and mangled and saliva-stained paper with care, the Gurkha turned the pages.

Gururaj winced.

'Tell me what you're looking for: I know everything that's in that newspaper.'

The Gurkha let the dirty paper go.

'There was an accident last night. Near Flower Market Street. A hit and run.'

'I know the case,' Gururaj said. It had not been his story, but he read the proofs of the entire paper every day. 'An employee of Mr Engineer's was involved.'

'The newspaper said that. But it was not the employee who did it.'

'Really?' Gururaj smiled. 'Then who did it?'

The Gurkha looked right into Gururaj's eyes. He smiled and then pointed the barrel of the ancient gun at him. 'I can tell you, but I'd have to shoot you afterwards.'

Looking at the barrel of the rifle, Gururaj thought: I'm talking to a madman.

The next day, Gururaj was in his office at 6 a.m. First to get there, as always. He began by checking the telex machine, inspecting the reels of badly smudged news it was printing out from Delhi and Colombo and other cities he would never visit in his life. At seven he turned on the radio and began jotting down the main points of the morning's column.

At eight o'clock, Ms D'Mello arrived. The chattering of a typewriter broke the peace of the office.

She was writing her usual column, 'Twinkle Twinkle'. It was a daily beauty column; a women's hair salon owner sponsored it and Ms D'Mello answered readers' questions about hair care, offering advice and gently nudging her correspondents in the direction of the salon owner's products.

Gururaj never spoke to Ms D'Mello. He resented the fact that his newspaper ran a paid-for column, a practice he considered unethical. But there was another reason to be cool towards Ms D'Mello: she was an unmarried woman and he didn't want anyone to assume that he might have the slightest interest in her.

Relatives and friends of his father had told Guru for years that he ought to move out of the YMCA and marry, and he had almost given in, thinking that the woman would be needed to nurse his father in his growing senility, when the need for a wife was removed entirely. Now he was determined not to lose his independence to anyone.

By eleven, when Gururaj came out of his room again, the office was full of smoke – the only aspect of his workplace that he disliked. The reporters were at their desks, drinking tea and smoking. The teleprinter machine, off to the side, was vomiting out rolls of smudged and misspelled news reports from Delhi.

After lunch, he sent the office boy to find Menon, a young journalist and a rising star at the paper. Menon came into his room with the top two buttons of his shirt open, a shiny gold necklace flashing at his neck. 'Sit down,' Gururaj said.

He showed him two articles about the car crash on Flower Market Street, which he had dug out of the newspaper's archives that morning. The first (he pointed to it) had appeared before the trial; the second after the verdict.

'You wrote both articles, didn't you?'

Menon nodded.

'In the first article, the car that hits the dead man is a red Maruti Suzuki. In the second, it is a white Fiat. Which one was it, really?'

Menon inspected the two articles.

'I just filed according to the police reports.'

'You didn't bother looking at the vehicle yourself, I take it?'

That night he ate the dinner that the caretaker at the YMCA brought up to his room; she talked a lot, but he was worried she was trying to marry him off to her daughter and he said as little as possible to her.

As he went to sleep he set the alarm for two o'clock.

He woke up with his heart racing fast; he turned on the lights, left his room, and squinted at his clock. It was twenty minutes to two. He put on his trousers, patted his wavy strands of hair back into place, and almost ran down the stairs and out of the gate of the YMCA, and in the direction of the bank.

The Gurkha was there at his chair, with his ancient rifle.

'Listen here, did you see this accident with your own eyes?'

'Of course not. I was sitting right here. This is my job.'

'Then how the hell did you know the cars had been changed in the police—'

'Through the grapevine.'

The Gurkha talks quietly. He explains to the newspaper editor that a network of nightwatchmen passes information around Kittur; every nightwatchman comes to the next for a cigarette and tells him something, and that one visits the next one for a cigarette in turn. In this way, word gets around. Secrets get spread. The truth – what really happened during the daytime – is preserved.

This is insane, this is impossible – Gururaj wipes the sweat from his forehead.

'So what actually happened – Engineer hit a man on his way back home?'

'Left him for dead.'

'It can't be true.'

The Gurkha's eyes flashed. 'You've lived here long enough, sir. You know it *can be*. Engineer was drunk; he was coming back from his mistress's home; he hit the fellow like some stray dog and drove away, leaving him there, with his guts spilled out on the street. In the morning the newspaper boy found him like that. The police know perfectly who drives down that road at night drunk. So the next morning two constables go to his house. Hasn't even washed the blood off the front wheels of the car.'

'Then why—'

'He is the richest man in this town. He owns the tallest building in this town. He cannot be arrested. He gets one of the employees at his factory to say that he was driving the car when it happened. The guy gives the police a sworn affidavit. I was driving under the influence on the night of 12 May when I hit the unfortunate victim. Then Mr Engineer gave the judge six thousand

180

rupees, and the police something less, perhaps four thousand or five, because the judiciary is of course more noble than the police, to keep quiet. Then he wants his Maruti Suzuki back, because it's a new car and a fashion statement and he likes driving it, so he gives the police another thousand to change the identity of the killer car to a Fiat, and he has his car back and he's driving around town again.'

'My God.'

'The employee got four years. The judge could have given him a harsher sentence, but he felt sorry for the bugger. Couldn't let him off for free, of course. So' – the nightwatchman brought down an imaginary gavel – 'four years.'

'I can't believe it,' Gururaj said. 'Kittur isn't that kind of place.'

The foreigner narrowed his cunning eyes and smiled. He looked at the glowing tip of his beedi for a while and then offered the beedi to Gururaj.

In the morning Gururaj opened the only window in his room. He looked down on Umbrella Street, on the heart of the town where he was born, and where he had grown to maturity and where he would almost certainly die. He sometimes thought he knew every building, every tree, every tile on the roof of every house in Kittur. Glowing in the morning light, Umbrella Street seemed to say: *No, the Gurkha's story can't be true.* The clarity of the stencilling on an advertisement, the glistening spokes of the bicycle wheel ridden by the man

181

delivering newspapers, said: *No, the Gurkha is lying*. But as Gururaj walked to his office, he saw the dense dark shade of the banyan tree lying across the road, like a patch of night left unswept by the morning's broom, and his soul was in turmoil again.

Work began. He calmed down. He avoided Ms D'Mello.

That evening, the editor-in-chief of the newspaper summoned him to his room. He was a plump old man, with sagging jowls and thick white eyebrows that looked like frosting and hands that trembled as he drank his tea. The tendons on his neck stood out in deep relief, and every part of his body seemed to be calling out for retirement.

If he did retire, Gururaj would inherit his chair.

'Regarding this story you've asked Menon to reinvestigate . . .' said the editor-in-chief, sipping the tea. 'Forget it.'

'There was a discrepancy over the cars—'

The old man shook his head. 'The police made a mistake on the first filing, that was all.' His voice changed into the quiet, casual tone Gururaj had come to recognize as final. He sipped more tea, and then some more.

The slurping sound of the tea being sipped, the abruptness of the old man's manner, the fatigue of so many nights of broken sleep got on Gururaj's nerves and he said: 'A man might have been sent to jail for no good reason; a guilty man might be walking free. And all you can say is, let's drop the matter.'

The old man sipped his tea; Gururaj thought he could detect his head move, as if in the affirmative.

He went back to the YMCA and walked up a flight of stairs to his room. He lay down on the bed with his eyes open. He was still awake at two in the morning, when the alarm went off. When he emerged, he heard a whistling sound; the policeman, passing by him, waved heartily, as if to an old friend.

The moon was shrinking fast; in a few days it would be entirely dark at night. He walked the same route now, as if it were a ritual formula: first slowly, then crossing to the centre of the road, and then dashing into the side alley until he reached the bank. The Gurkha was in his chair, his rifle on his shoulder, a glowing beedi in his fingers.

'What does the grapevine tell you tonight?'

'Nothing tonight.'

'Then tell me something from a few nights ago. Tell me what else the paper has published that is untrue.'

'The riots. The newspaper got that wrong, completely.'

Gururaj thought his heart would skip a beat. 'How so?'

'The newspaper said that it was Hindus fighting Muslims, see?'

'It was Hindus fighting Muslims. Everyone knows that.'

'Ha.'

The next morning Gururaj did not turn up at the office. He went straight down to the Bunder, the first time since he had come there to talk to the shopkeepers in the aftermath of the riots. He traced every restaurant and fish market that had been burned down in the riots.

He went back to the newspaper, rushed into the office of the editor-in-chief and said: 'I heard the most incredible story last night about the Hindu-Muslim riots. Shall I tell you what I heard?'

The old man sipped his tea.

'I heard that our MP along with the mafia down at the Bunder instigated the riots. And I heard that the hoodlums and the MP have transferred all the burned and destroyed property into the hands of their own men, under the name of a fictitious trust called the New Kittur Port Development Trust. The violence was planned. Muslim goons burned Muslim shops and Hindu goons burned Hindu shops. It was a real-estate transaction masquerading as a religious riot.'

The editor stopped sipping.

'Who told you this?'

'A friend. Is it true?'

'No.'

Gururaj smiled and said: 'I didn't think so, either. Thanks.' He walked out of the room while his boss watched him with concern.

The next morning, he arrived at the office late once again. The office boy turned up at his desk and shouted: 'Editor-in-chief wants to see you.'

'Why didn't you turn up at the City Corporation Office today?' the old man asked him, as he sipped another cup of tea. 'The mayor asked for you to be there; he released a statement on Hindu–Muslim unity and attacking the BJP that he wanted you to hear. You know he respects your work.'

Gururaj pressed his hair down; he had not oiled it this morning and it was unruly.

'Who cares?'

'Excuse me, Gururaj?'

'You think anyone in this office doesn't know that all this political fighting is just make-believe? That in reality the BJP and the Congress cut each other deals and share the bribe money they take on construction projects in Bajpe? You and I have known for years that this is true and yet we pretend to report things otherwise. Doesn't this strike you as bizarre? Look here. Let's just write nothing but the truth and the whole truth in the newspaper today. Just today. One day of nothing but the truth. That's all I want to do. No one may even notice. Tomorrow we'll go back to the usual lies. But for one day I want to report, write, and edit the truth. One day in my life I'd like to be a proper journalist. What do you say to that?'

The editor-in-chief frowned, as if thinking about

it, and then said: 'Come to my house after dinner tonight.'

At nine o'clock, Gururaj walked up Rose Lane, to a home with a big garden and a blue statue of Krishna with his flute in a niche in the front, and rang the bell.

The editor let him into the drawing room and closed the door. He asked Gururaj to sit down, gesturing at a brown sofa.

'You'd better tell me what's bothering you.'

Gururaj told him.

'Let's assume you have proof of this thing. You write about it. You're not only saying that the police force is rotten, but also that the judiciary is corrupt. The judge will call you for contempt of court. You will be arrested – even if what you are saying is true. You and I and people in our press pretend that there is freedom of press in this country but we know the truth.'

'What about the Hindu–Muslim riots? Can't we write the truth about that, either?'

'What is the truth about it, Gururaj?'

Gururaj told him the truth and the editor-in-chief smiled. He put his head in his hands and, in a laugh that seemed to rock the entire night, he laughed his heart out.

'Even if what you're saying is indeed the truth,' the old man said, regaining control of himself, 'and observe that I neither admit nor contradict any of it, there would be no way for us to publish it.'

'Why not?'

The editor smiled.

'Who do you think owns this newspaper?'

'Ramdas Pai,' Gururaj said, naming a businessman in Umbrella Street whose name appeared as proprietor on the front page.

The editor shook his head. 'He doesn't own it. Not all of it.'

'Who does?'

'Use your brains.'

Gururaj looked at the editor-in-chief with new eyes. It was as if the old man had a nimbus around him, of all the things he had learned over the length of his career and could never publish; this secret knowledge glowed around his head like the halo around the nearly full moon. This is the fate of every journalist in this town and in this state and in this country and maybe in this whole world, thought Gururaj.

'Had you never guessed any of this before, Gururaj? It must come from the fact that you are not yet married. Not having had a woman, you have never understood the ways of the world.'

'And you have understood the ways of the world far too well.'

The two men stared, each feeling tremendously sorry for the other.

The following morning, as he walked to the office, Gururaj thought: it is a false earth I am walking on. An innocent man is behind bars and a guilty man walks free. Everyone knows that this is so and not one has the courage to change it.

From then on, every night, Gururaj went down the dirty stairwell of the YMCA, gazing blankly at the profanities and graffiti scribbled on the walls, and walked down Umbrella Street, ignoring the barking and skulking and copulating stray dogs, until he got to the Gurkha, who would lift up his old rifle in recognition and smile. They were friends now.

The Gurkha told him how much rottenness there could be in a small town; who had killed whom in the past few years; how much the judges of Kittur had asked for in bribe money, how much the police chiefs had asked. They talked until it was nearly dawn and it was time for Gururaj to leave, so he could get some sleep before going to work. He hesitated: 'I still don't know your name.'

'Gaurishankar.'

Gururaj waited for him to ask him his name; he wanted to say: 'Now that my father has died, you are my only friend, Gaurishankar.'

The Gurkha sat with his eyes closed.

At four in the morning, walking back to the YMCA, he was thinking: who is this man, this Gurkha? From some reference he had made to being a manservant in the house of a retired general, Gururaj deduced that he had been in the army, in the Gurkha regiment. But how he ended up in Kittur, why he hadn't gone back home to Nepal, all this was still a mystery. Tomorrow I should ask him all this. Then I can tell him about myself.

There was an Ashoka near the entrance to his YMCA, and Gururaj stopped to look at the tree. The moonlight lay on it, and it seemed different somehow tonight; as if it were on the verge of growing into something else.

'They are not my fellow workers; they are lower than animals.'

Gururaj could no longer stand the sight of his colleagues; he averted his eyes as he came into the office, scurrying into his room and slamming his door shut as soon as he got to work. Although he continued to edit the copy he was given, he could no longer bear to look at the newspaper. What especially terrified him was catching his own name in print; for this reason he asked to be relieved from what had been his greatest pleasure, writing his column, and insisted only on editing. Although in the old days he used to stay up to midnight, now he left the office at five o'clock every evening, hurrying back to his apartment to fall on his bed.

At two o'clock sharp, he woke up. To save himself the trouble of finding his trousers in the dark, he had taken to sleeping in all his clothes. He almost ran down the stairs and thrust open the door of the YMCA, so he could speak to the Gurkha.

Then one night, at last, it happened. The Gurkha was not sitting outside the bank. Someone else had taken his chair.

'What do I know, sir?' the new nightwatchman

said. 'I was appointed to this job last night; they didn't tell me what happened to the old fellow.'

Gururaj ran from shop to shop, from house to house, asking every nightwatchman he met what had happened to the Gurkha.

'Gone to Nepal,' one nightwatchman finally told him. 'Back to his family. He was saving money all these years, and now he's gone.'

Gururaj took the news like a physical blow. Only one man had known what was happening in this town, and that one man had vanished to another country. Seeing him gasping for air, the nightwatchmen gathered around him, made him sit down, and brought him cool, clean water in a plastic bottle. He tried explaining to them what had happened between him and the Gurkha all these weeks, what he had lost.

'That Gurkha, sir?' One watchman shook his head. 'Are you sure you talked about these things with him? He was a complete idiot. His brain had been damaged in the army.'

'What about the grapevine? Is it still working?' Gururaj asked. 'Will one of you tell me what you hear now?'

The nightwatchmen stared. In their eyes, he could see doubt turning into a kind of fear. They seem to think I'm mad, he thought.

He wandered at night, passing by the dim buildings, by the sleeping multitudes. He passed by large, still, darkened buildings, each containing hundreds of bodies lying in a stupor. 'I am the

190

only man who is awake now,' he told himself. Once, up on a hill to his left, he saw a large housing block burning with light. Seven windows were lit up and the building blazed; it seemed to him to be a living creature, a kind of monster of light, shining from its entrails.

Gururaj understood: the Gurkha had not abandoned him at all. He had not done what everyone else in his life had done. He had left something behind; a gift. Gururaj would now hear the grapevine on his own. He lifted his arms towards the building burning with lights; he felt full of occult power.

One day as he came into work, late again, he heard a whisper behind him: 'It happened to the father too, in his last days . . .'

He thought: I must be careful that others do not notice this change that is happening inside me.

When he reached his office, he saw that the peon was removing his nameplate from the door. I am losing everything I worked for so many years for, he thought. But he felt no regret or emotion; it was as if these things were happening to someone else. He saw the new nameplate on the door:

KRISHNA MENON
DEPUTY EDITOR
DAWN HERALD
KITTUR'S ONLY AND FINEST NEWSPAPER

'Gururaj! I didn't want to do it, I—'

'No explanation is necessary. In your position, I'd have done the same.'

'Do you want me to speak to someone, Gururaj? We can arrange it for you.'

'What are you talking about?'

'I know you have no father now . . . But we can arrange a wedding for you, with a girl of a good family.'

'What are you talking about?'

'We think you are ill. You ought to know that many of us in this office have been saying that for some time. I insist that you take a week off. Or two weeks. Go somewhere on holiday. Go to the Western Ghats and watch the clouds for a while.'

'Fine. I'll take three weeks off.'

For three weeks he slept through the day and walked through the night. The late-night policeman no longer said 'Hello, editor' as he had before, and Gururaj could see the man's head, as he cycled past, turn and stare at him. The night-watchmen also looked at him oddly; and he grinned – even here, even in this Hades of the middle of the night, I have become an outsider, a man who frightens others. The thought excited him.

He bought a child's square blackboard one day, and a piece of chalk. That night he wrote at the top of the blackboard:

THE TRUTH ALONE SHALL TRIUMPH.
A NOCTURNAL NEWSPAPER
SOLE CORRESPONDENT, EDITOR, ADVERTISER,
AND
SUBSCRIBER:

GURURAJ MANJESHWAR KAMATH, ESQ

Copying out the headline from the morning's newspaper, 'BJP City Councillor blasts Congressman', he rubbed and scratched and rewrote it:

2 October 1989
BJP City Councillor, who needs money in a hurry to build a new mansion on Rose Lane, blasts Congressman. Tomorrow he will receive a brown bag full of cash from the Congress party, and then he will stop blasting the Congressman.

Then he lay in bed and closed his eyes, eager for the darkness to arrive and make his town a decent place again.

One night he thought: there is only one night of my vacation left. The dawn was breaking already and he hurried back to the YMCA. He stopped. He was sure that he was seeing an elephant outside the building. Was he dreaming? What on earth would an elephant be doing, at this hour, in the middle of his town? It was beyond the bounds of reason. Yet it looked real and tangible to his eyes;

193

only one thing that made him think it was not a real elephant – it was absolutely still. He said to himself: elephants move and make some noise all the time, therefore you are not really seeing an elephant. He closed his eyes and walked up to the entrance of the YMCA; and when he opened them again he was staring at a tree. He touched the bark and thought: this is the first hallucination I have had in my life.

When he returned to the office the next day, everyone said Gururaj was back to his old self. He had missed his office life; he had wanted to come back.

'Thank you for your offer to arrange a marriage,' he told the editor-in-chief, as they had tea together in his room. 'But I'm married to my work anyway.'

Sitting in the newsroom with young men just out of college, he edited stories with all his old cheer. After all the young men were gone, he stayed back, digging through the archives. He had come back to work with a purpose. He was going to write a history of Kittur. An infernal history of Kittur – in it every event in the past twenty years would be reinterpreted. He took out old newspapers and carefully read each front page. Then, a red pen in hand, he scratched out and rewrote words, which fulfilled two purposes – one, it defaced the newspapers of the past, and two, it allowed him to figure out the true relationship between the words and the characters in the news

194

events. At first, designating Hindi – the Gurkha's language – as the language of the truth, he rewrote the Kannada-language headlines of the newspaper in Hindi; then he switched to English; and finally he adopted a code in which he substituted each letter of the Roman alphabet for the one immediately after it – he had read somewhere that Julius Caesar had invented this code for his army – and, to complicate matters further, he invented symbols for certain words; for instance, a triangle with a dot inside represented the word 'Bank'. Other symbols were ironically inspired; for instance, a Nazi Swastika represented the Congress party, and the Nuclear Disarmament Symbol the BJP, and so on. One day, looking back over the past week's notes, he found that he had forgotten half the symbols, and he no longer understood what he had written. Good, he thought, that is the way it should be. Even the writer of the truth should not know the truth entire. Every true word, upon being written, is like the full moon, and daily it wanes and then passes entirely into obscurity. That is the way of all things.

When he was done reinterpreting each issue of the newspaper, he deleted the words 'The Dawn Herald' from the headline and wrote in their place: 'THE TRUTH ALONE SHALL TRIUMPH'.

'What the hell are you doing to our newspapers?'

It was the editor-in-chief. He and Menon had sneaked up on Gururaj in the office one evening.

195

The editor-in-chief turned page after page of defaced newspaper in the archives without a word, while Menon tried to peek over his shoulder. They saw pages covered in squiggles, red marks, slashes, triangles, pictures of girls with pigtails and bloody teeth, images of copulating dogs. Then the old man slammed the archive shut.

'I told you to get married.'

Gururaj smiled. 'Listen, old friend, those are symbolic marks. I can interpret—'

The editor-in-chief shook his head.

'Get out of this office. At once. I'm sorry, Gururaj.'

Gururaj smiled, as if to say that no explanation was necessary. The editor-in-chief's eyes were teary, and the tendons of his neck moved up and down as he swallowed again and again. The tears came to Guru's eyes as well. He thought: how hard it has been for this old man to do this. How hard he must have protected me. He imagined a closed-door meeting where colleagues had been baying for his blood and this decent old man alone had defended him to the end. 'I am sorry, my friend, for letting you down,' he wanted to say.

That night, Gururaj walked, telling himself he was happier than he ever been in his life. He was a free man now. When he got back, just before dawn, to the YMCA, he saw the elephant again. This time it did not melt into an Ashoka tree, even when he came close. He walked right up to the beast, saw its constantly flapping ears, which had the colour and shape and movement of a pterodactyl's wing; he walked around and saw that from the back, each of its ears had a fringe of pink and was striped with veins. How can this wealth of detail be unreal? he thought. This creature was real, and if the rest of the world could not see it, then the rest of the world was the poorer for that.

Just make one sound! he pleaded with the elephant. So I know for sure that I am not deluded, that you are for real. The elephant understood; it raised its trunk and roared so loudly that he thought he had been deafened.

'You are free now,' the elephant said, in words so loud they seemed like newspaper headlines to him. 'Go and write the true history of Kittur.'

Some months later, there was news of Gururaj. Four young reporters went to investigate.

They muffled their giggles as they pushed open the door to the municipal reading room in the lighthouse. The librarian had been waiting for them; he ushered them in with a finger to his lips.

The journalists found Gururaj sitting at a bench, reading a newspaper which partially covered his face. The old editor's shirt was in tatters, but he seemed to have gained weight, as if idleness had suited him.

'He won't say a word any more,' the librarian said. 'He just sits there till sunset, holding the paper to his face. The only time he said anything was when I told him I admired his articles on the riots, and then he shouted at me.'

197

One of the young journalists put his finger on the top edge of the newspaper and lowered it slowly; Gururaj offered no resistance. The journalist yelped and stepped back.

There was a moist dark hole in the innermost sheet of the paper. Pieces of newsprint stuck to the corners of Gururaj's mouth, and his jaw was moving.

THE LANGUAGES OF KITTUR

Kannada, one of the major languages of South India, is the official language of the state of Karnataka, in which Kittur is located. The local paper, the *Dawn Herald*, is published in Kannada. Although understood by virtually everyone in the town, Kannada is the mother tongue only of some of the Brahmins. Tulu, a regional language that has no written script – although it is believed to have possessed a script centuries ago – is the lingua franca. Two dialects of Tulu exist. The 'upper-caste' dialect is still used by a few Brahmins, but is dying out as Tulu-speaking Brahmins switch to Kannada. The other dialect of Tulu, a rough, bawdy language cherished for the diversity and pungency of its expletives, is used by the Bunts and Hoykas – this is the language of the Kittur street. Around Umbrella Street, the commercial centre, the dominant language changes to Konkani: this is the language of the Gaud-Saraswat Bratunins, originally from Goa, who own most of the shops here. (Although Tulu – and

Kannada-speaking Brahmins began inter-marrying in the 1960s, the Konkani-Brahmins have so far rejected all marriage proposals from outsiders.) A very different dialect of Konkani, corrupted with Portuguese, is spoken in the suburb of Valencia by the Catholics who live there. Most of the Muslims, especially those in the Bunder, speak a dialect of Malayalam as their mother tongue: a few of the richer Muslims, being descendants of the old Hyderabad aristocracy, speak Hyderabadi Urdu. Kittur's large migrant worker population, which floats around the town from construction site to construction site, is mostly Tamil-speaking. English is understood by the middle class.

It must be noted that few other towns in India can match Kittur's street language for the richness of its expletives, which come from Urdu, English, Kannada and Tulu. The most commonly heard term, 'son of a bald-headed woman', requires explanation. Upper-caste widows were once forbidden to remarry and forced to shave their heads to prevent them from attracting men. A child born of a bald woman was very likely to be an illegitimate one.

DAY FOUR (MORNING): UMBRELLA STREET

If you wish to do some shopping while in Kittur, allow yourself a few hours to wander through Umbrella Street, the commercial centre of town. Here you will find furniture stores, pharmacies, restaurants, sweet-shops, and book-stores. (A few sellers of hand-made wooden umbrellas can still be found here, although most have gone out of business because of cheap metal umbrellas imported from China.) The street houses Kittur's most famous restaurant, the Ideal Traders Ice Cream and Fresh Fruit Juice Parlour, and also the office of the *Dawn Herald*. 'Kittur's only and finest newspaper'.

Every Thursday evening, an interesting event takes place in the Ramvittala Temple near Umbrella Street. Two traditional minstrels sit on the verandah of this temple and recite verses from the Mahabharatha, the great Indian epic of heroism and endurance, all through the night.

201

All the employees of the furniture shop had gathered in a semicircle around Mr Ganesh Pai's table. It was a special day: Mrs Engineer had come to the shop in person.

She had chosen her TV table and now she was approaching Mr Pai's desk to finalize the deal.

His face was smeared with sandalwood and he wore a loose-fitting silk shirt over which a dark triangle of his chest hair stuck out. On the wall behind his chair, he had hung gold tin-foil images of Lakshmi, goddess of wealth, and the fat elephant-god Ganapati. An incense-stick smoked below the images.

Mrs Engineer sat down slowly at the desk. Mr Pai reached into a drawer and then held out four red cards to her. Mrs Engineer paused, bit her lip, and snatched at one of the four cards.

'A set of stainless-steel cups!' Mr Pai said, showing her the bonus card she had selected. 'A truly wonderful gift, Madam. Something you'll treasure for years and years.'

Mrs Engineer beamed. She took out a small red purse, counted off four 100-rupee notes, and put them on the desk before Mr Pai.

Mr Pai, moistening the tip of his finger in a small bowl of water that he kept on his desk for just this purpose, counted the notes afresh; then he looked at Mrs Engineer and smiled, as if expecting something more.

'The balance on delivery,' she said, getting up from her chair. 'And don't forget to send the bonus gift.'

'She may be the wife of the richest man in town, but she's still a stingy old cunt,' Mr Pai said, after he had seen her out of the store, and an assistant laughed behind him. He turned and glared at the assistant – a small, dark, Tamilian boy.

'Get one of the coolies to deliver it, quickly,' Mr Pai said. 'I want the balance before she forgets about it.'

The Tamilian boy ran out of the shop. The cycle-cart pullers were in their usual position – lying on their carts, staring into space, smoking beedis. Some of them were staring with dull avarice at the store on the other side of the road, the Ideal Traders Ice Cream Parlour; fat kids in T-shirts were licking vanilla cones outside the shop.

The boy stuck out his index finger and motioned to one of the men.

'Chenayya – your number is up!'

Chenayya pedalled hard. He had been told to take the direct route to Rose Lane, so he had to go over Lighthouse Hill; he struggled to move the cart with the TV table, which was attached to his cycle. Once he was over the hump of the hill, he let the cycle glide. He slowed down in Rose Lane, found the house number, which he had memorized, and rang the bell.

He was expecting to see a servant, but when a plump, fair-skinned woman opened the door, he knew it was Mrs Engineer herself.

Chenayya carried the TV table into the house and put it down where she indicated.

He went out and returned with a saw. He had walked in holding the thing close to his side, but when he got to the dining room, where he had left the table in two separate pieces, Mrs Engineer watched as he held the tool at an arm's length and suddenly it seemed enormous: eighteen inches long, with a serrated edge, rusty, but with patches of the original metal-grey colour still showing through, like a sculpture of a shark made by a tribal artist.

Chenayya saw the anxiety in the woman's eyes. To dispel her fear, he grinned ingratiatingly – it was the exaggerated, death-mask grin of a person not used to grovelling – then he looked around as if to remind himself where he had left the table.

The legs were not of equal length. Chenayya closed an eye and examined the legs one by one; then he took the saw to each of the legs, creating a fine dust on the ground. He moved the saw so slowly, so precisely that it seemed he was just rehearsing his actions; only the accumulation of wood-dust on the ground was evidence to the contrary. He examined the four legs again with one eye closed to make sure they were even and then dropped his saw. He searched the dirty white sarong he was wearing, which was the only garment on his body, for a relatively clean corner and wiped down the table.

'The table is ready, Madam.' He folded his hands and waited.

With an ingratiating smile, he wiped the table again, to make sure that the lady of the house had noticed the care he had taken with her furniture.

Mrs Engineer had not been watching; she had retreated into an inner room. She returned and counted off seven hundred and forty-two rupees.

Hesitating a moment, she added three rupee notes to it.

'Give me something more, Madam?' Chenayya blurted. 'Give me three more rupees?'

'Six rupees? Nothing doing,' she said.

'It's a long way, Madam.' He picked up his saw and gestured at his neck. 'I had to carry it all that way, Madam, on my cycle-cart. It hurts my neck very much.'

'Nothing doing. Get out – or I'll call the police, you thug – get out and take your big knife with you!'

As he walked out of the house, grumbling and sulking, he folded the money into a wad; then tied it into a knot on the loose dirty white sarong he wore. A neem tree grew near the gate of the house, and he had to duck not to scrape his head against its branches. He had left the cycle-cart near the tree. He threw the saw into the cart. Around his cycle seat he had wrapped a white cotton cloth; he unfastened it and tied it around his head.

A cat went running past his leg; two dogs followed it in full flight. The cat leaped up the neem tree and bounded up the limbs; the dogs waited at the foot of the tree, scraping the base of the tree and barking. Chenayya, who had got onto his seat, lingered to watch the scene. The moment he started pedalling, he would no longer notice such things around him; he would turn into a pedalling machine that was headed straight back to his boss-man's shop. He stood there, watching the animals, enjoying consciousness. He picked up a rotting banana skin and left it draped on the leaves of the neem tree, so that it would startle the owners when they came out.

He was so pleased with himself for this that he smiled.

But he still did not want to start pedalling again, which was like handing over the keys of his personality to fatigue and routine.

About ten minutes later, he was on his bike again, heading back to Umbrella Street. He was cycling, as always, with his butt elevated off the seat, his spine inclined at sixty degrees. Only at crossroads did he straighten himself, relax, and ease back onto the seat. The road, as he drew near to Umbrella Street, was jammed once again; pushing his front wheel into the car ahead of him, Chenayya yelled: 'Son of a bitch, move!'

At last he saw to his right the sign 'GANESH PAI FAN AND FURNITURE STORE' and stopped his cycle.

★   ★   ★

Chenayya felt the money was burning a hole in his sarong; he wanted to hand it over to his employer as soon as possible. He wiped his palm against his sarong, pushed the door open, went into the store, and crouched by a corner of Mr Pai's table. Neither Mr Pai nor the Tamilian assistant paid any attention to him. Untying the bundle in his sarong, he put his hands between his legs and stared at the floor.

His neck was hurting again; he moved it from side to side to relieve the stress.

'Stop doing that.'

Mr Pai motioned for him to hand over the cash. Chenayya got up.

He moved slowly towards to the boss-man's desk and handed the notes over to Mr Ganesh Pai, who moistened his finger in the water bowl and counted off seven hundred and forty-two rupees. Chenayya stared at the water bowl; he noticed how its sides were scalloped to make them look like lotus-petals, and how the artisan had even traced the pattern of a trellis around the bottom of the bowl.

Mr Pai snapped his fingers. He had tied a rubber band around the notes and was holding out his palm in Chenayya's direction.

'Two rupees short.'

Chenayya undid the knot in the side of his sarong and handed over two one-rupee notes.

That was the sum he was expected to hand over to Mr Pai at the end of every delivery; one rupee for the dinner he would be given at around nine o'clock, and one rupee for the privilege of having been chosen to work for Mr Ganesh Pai.

Outside, the Tamilian boy from Mr Pai's shop was giving instructions to one of the cyle-cart pullers, a strong young fellow who had recently joined. He was about to start pedalling a cart with two cardboard boxes on it, and the boy from the store was saying, tapping the two boxes: 'It's a mixie in one box and a four-blade fan in the other. When you take it to the house, you've got to make sure they both get plugged in before you return.' He told the cart puller the address he was to go to; then he made the coolie say it aloud, like a teacher with a slow pupil.

It would be some time before Chenayya's number was called again, so he walked down the road to a spot where a man was sitting at a desk on the pavement, selling bundles of small rectangular tickets that were as colourful as pieces of candy. He smiled at Chenayya; his fingers began flipping through one of the bundles.

'Yellow?'

'First tell me if my number won last time,' Chenayya said. He brought out a dirty piece of paper from the knot on his sarong. The seller found a newspaper and glanced down to the bottom right-hand corner.

He read aloud: 'Winning Lottery Numbers. 17-8-9-9-643-455.'

Chenayya had learned enough about English

numerals to recognize his own ticket number; he
squinted for several moments and then let the
ticket float to the ground.

'People buy for fifteen, sixteen years before they
win, Chenayya,' the lottery seller said, by way of
consolation. 'But in the end, those who believe
always win. That is the way the world works.'

Chenayya hated it when the seller tried to
console him like this; that was when he felt he
was being ripped off by the men who printed the
lottery tickets.

'I can't go on this way for ever,' he said. 'My
neck hurts. I can't go on like this.'

The lottery seller nodded. 'Another yellow?'

Tying the ticket into his bundle, Chenayya staggered back; He collapsed onto his cart. For a while
he lay like that, not feeling refreshed from the rest,
but only numb.

Then a finger tapped on his head.

'Number's up, Chenayya.'

It was the Tamilian boy from the store.

To be delivered to 54 Suryanarayan Rao Lane.
He repeated it aloud: '54, Suryanarayan . . .'

'Good.'

This route took him uphill over the Lighthouse
Hill again. Riding his cart halfway up the hill, he
alighted and began dragging the cart. His sinews
bulged from his neck like webbing; and as he
inhaled, the air burned through his chest and
lungs. You can't go on, said his tired limbs, his
burning chest. You can't go on. But at the same

time, this was when his sense of resistance to his fate waxed greatest within him: and as he pushed, the restlessness and anger that had been within him all day became articulate at last:

You will not break me, motherfuckers! You will never break me!

If the thing to be delivered was light, like a mattress, he was not allowed to take a cycle-cart; it had to be carried on his head. Repeating the address to the Tamilian boy from the shop, he set off with a slow, light step, like a fat man jogging. In a short while, the weight of the mattress had seemed unbearable; it compressed his neck and spine and sent a shaft of pain down his back. He was virtually in a trance.

This morning he was taking a mattress to the railway station. The client turned out to be a North Indian family that was leaving Kittur; the owner, as he had guessed beforehand (from his demeanour, his manner – you can tell which of these rich people have a sense of decency and which don't), refused to pay him the tip.

Chenayya stood his ground. 'You motherfucker! Give me my money!'

It was a triumph for him; the man relented and gave him three rupees. On the way out of the station, he thought: I feel elated, but my customer has done no more than pay me what he owes me. This is what my life has been reduced to.

The odours and the noise of the train station

made him feel sick. Turning around, he squatted down by the tracks and pulled his sarong up and held his breath. As he was squatting there, the train roared by. He turned around; he wanted to shit into the faces of the people on the train. Yes, that would be good; as the train thundered over the motions, he forced out the turds into the faces of the passers-by.

Next to him, he saw a pig, which was doing the same thing.

At once, he thought, God, what am I becoming? He walked to a corner, crawled behind a bush, and defecated there. He told himself: I will never again defecate like this, in a place where I can be seen. There is a difference between man and animal; there is a difference.

He closed his eyes.

The scent of basil from near him seemed like evidence that there were good things in the world. But when he opened his eyes, the earth around was one of thorns and shit and stray animals.

He looked up and took a deep breath. The sky is clean, he thought. There is purity up there. He tore off a few leaves, wiped himself clean with them, then rubbed his left hand against the earth in a bid to neutralize the smell.

At two o'clock, he got his next 'number': the delivery of a giant stack of boxes to an address in Valencia. The Tamilian boy made sure he understood the address exactly: beyond the hospital and down by the Seminary where the Jesuit priests stayed.

'There's a lot of work today, Chenayya,' he said. 'Make sure you go the quick way – over the Lighthouse Hill.'

Chenayya grunted, rose out of the seat, shifted his weight onto the pedals, and was on his way. The rusty iron chain that double-locked the cart to the front wheels of the bicycle began to make a noise as he cycled.

Down the main road, he was stuck in a traffic jam. He stopped, and became aware of his body once again. His neck hurt; the sun seared his back. Once he was conscious of pain, he began to think.

Why are some mornings difficult, some mornings simple? The other cart pullers never had 'good' or 'bad' days; they just did their work like machines. Only he had his moods. He looked down, to relieve his painful neck, and stared at the rusty chain by his feet, wound around the metal rod that joined the cycle to the cart. Time to oil the chain, he told himself. Must not forget.

Uphill again. Leaning forward out of his seat, Chenayya was straining hard; the breath entered his lungs like a hot poker. Halfway up the hill, he saw an elephant walking down towards him with a small bundle of leaves on his back, and a mahout poking its ear with an iron rod.

He stopped; this was unbelievable. He began to shout at the elephant: 'Hey, you, what are you doing with these leaves, take this load from me! It's more your size, motherfucker!'

Cars honked behind him. The mahout turned and gesticulated at him with his iron rod. A passer-by yelled at him not to obstruct the traffic.

'Don't you see that something is wrong with this world,' he said turning around to the driver of the car behind him, who was jabbing at his horn with the fleshy part of his palm. 'When an elephant gets to lounge downhill doing virtually no work at all, and a human being has to pull such a heavy cart?'

They honked and the cacophony grew.

'Don't you see something is wrong here?' he shouted. They honked back. The world was furious at his fury. It wanted him to move out of its way; but he was enjoying being exactly where he was, blocking all these rich and important people.

That evening there were great streaks of pink in the sky. After the shop closed, the coolies moved to the alley behind the store; they took turns buying small bottles of country liquor which they shared amongst themselves, getting giddy and belting out off-key Kannada film songs.

Chenayya never joined them. 'You're wasting your money, you idiots!' he sometimes shouted at them; they simply jeered back.

He would not drink; he had promised himself he would not squander the hard-earned fruits of his labour on alcohol. Yet the smell of liquor in the air made his mouth water; the good humour

213

and bonhomie of the other cart pullers made him lonely. He closed his eyes. A tinkling noise made him open them.

Nearby, on the steps of an unused building, as was usual, a fat prostitute had emerged to ply her trade. She clapped her hands and advertised her presence by striking two coins together. A customer came up; they began haggling over a price. The deal was not concluded; and the man left cursing.

Chenayya, lying in his cart with his feet sticking out, watched the action with a dull grin.

'Hey, Kamala!' he shouted at the prostitute. 'Why not give me a chance this evening?'

She turned her face from him and kept clinking the coins together. He stared at her plump breasts, at the dark tip of her cleavage that showed through the blouse, at her garishly painted lips.

He turned his eyes to the sky: he had to stop thinking of sex. Streaks of pink amidst the clouds. Isn't there a God, or someone there, Chenayya wondered, watching down on this Earth? One evening, at the train station to deliver a parcel, he had heard a wild Muslim dervish talking in a corner of the station about the Mahdi, the last of the Imams, who would come for this Earth and give the evil their due. 'Allah is the Maker of all men,' the dervish had mumbled. 'The poor and the rich alike. And he observes our hurt, and when we suffer He suffers with us. And He will send, at the end of the Days, the Mahdi, on a white

214

horse with a sword of fire, to put the rich in their place and correct all that is wrong with the world.'

A few days later, when Chenayya went to a mosque, he found that Muslims stank, so he did not stay there long. Yet he had never forgotten about the Mahdi; each time he saw a streak of pink in the sky, he thought he could detect some God of Fairness watching over the Earth and glowering with anger.

Chenayya closed his eyes and heard again the tinkling of coins. He turned about restlessly and then covered his face in a rag so the sun wouldn't sting him awake and went to sleep. Half an hour later, he woke up with a sharp pain in his ribs. The police jabbed their lathis into the bodies of the cycle pullers. A truck was entering this part of the market.

All you cycle-cart pullers! Get up and move your carts!

The kite-flying contest took place between two nearby houses. The owners of the kites were hidden; all Chenayya saw, as he brushed his teeth with the stick of neem, were the black and red kites fighting each other in the sky. As always, the kid with the black kite was winning; he was flying his kite the highest. Chenayya wondered about the poor kid with the red kite: why couldn't he ever win?

He spat, and then walked a few feet so he could urinate into the side of a wall.

Behind him he heard jeers. The other pullers were urinating right where they had slept.

He said nothing to them. Chenayya never talked to his fellow cart pullers. He could barely stand the sight of them – the way they bent and grovelled to Mr Ganesh Pai; yes, he might do the same, but he was furious, he was angry inside. These other fellows seemed incapable of even thinking badly of their employer; and he could not respect a man in whom there was no rebellion.

When the Tamilian boy brought out the tea, he reluctantly rejoined the pullers; he heard them talking once again, as they did just about every morning, about the autorickshaws they were going to buy once they got out of here; or the small teashop they were going to open.

'Think about it,' he wanted to tell them, 'just think about it.'

Mr Ganesh Pai allowed them only two rupees for each trip; meaning that, at the rate of three trips a day, they were making six rupees; once you deducted for lotteries, and liquor, you were lucky to save two rupees; Sundays were off, as were Hindu holidays; so at the month's end, they saved forty or forty-five rupees only. A trip to the village, an evening with a whore, an extra-long drinking binge, and your whole month's savings will be dust. Assuming you save everything you can, you're lucky to earn four hundred a year. An autorickshaw would cost twelve, fourteen thousand. A small teashop four times as much. That meant thirty, thirty-five years of such work before they could do anything else. But did they think their bodies would last that long? Did they find a single cart puller above the age of forty around them?

Don't you ever think about such things, you baboons?

Yet when he had once tried to get them to understand this, they had refused to demand more collectively. They thought they were lucky; thousands would take their jobs at a moment's notice. He knew they were right, too.

Despite their logic, despite their valid fears, their sheer spinelessness grated on him. That is why, he thought, Mr Ganesh Pai could be confident that a customer could hand over a cart puller thousands of rupees in cash and know that it will all come to him, every last rupee, without the cycle puller taking a note of it.

Naturally, Chenayya had long planned on stealing the money that a customer gave him one day. He would take the money and leave the town. This much he was certain he would do – someday very soon.

That evening, the men were huddled around. A man in a blue safari suit, an important educated man, was asking them questions; he had a small notepad in his hands. He said he had come from Madras.

He had asked one of the cart pullers for his age. No one was sure; when he said, 'Can you make a rough guess?' they simply nodded. When he said: 'Are you eighteen, or twenty, or thirty – you must have *some* idea', they simply nodded again.

'I'm twenty-nine,' Chenayya called out from his cart.

The man nodded. He wrote something down in his notepad.

'Tell me, who are you?' Chenayya asked. 'Why are you asking us all these questions?'

He said he was a journalist and the cart pullers were impressed; he worked for an English-language newspaper in Madras, and that impressed them even more.

They were amazed that a smartly dressed man was talking to them with courtesy and they begged him to sit down on a cot, which one of them wiped clean with a side of his palm. The man from Madras pulled at the knees of his trousers and sat down.

Then he wanted to know what they were eating. He made a list of everything they ate every day in his notepad; then he went silent and scratched a lot on the pad with his pen, while they waited expectantly.

At the end, he put the notepad down, and, with a wide, almost triumphant grin, he declared: 'The work you are doing exceeds the amount of calories you consume. Every day, every trip you take – you are slowly killing yourselves.'

He held his notepad, with its squiggles and zig-zags and numbers, as proof of his claim.

218

'Why don't you do something else, like work in a factory? Anything else? Why don't you learn to read and write?'

Chenayya jumped off his cart.

'Don't patronize us, you son of a bitch!' he shouted. 'Those who are born poor in this country are fated to die poor. There is no hope for us, and no need of pity. Certainly not from you, who has never lifted a hand to help us; I spit on you. I spit on your newspaper. Nothing ever changes. Nothing will ever change. Look at me.' He held out his palms. 'I am twenty-nine years old. I am already bent and twisted like this. If I live to forty, what is my fate? To be a twisted black rod of a man. You think I don't know this? You think I need your notepad and your English to tell me this? You keep us like this, you people from the cities, you rich fucks. It is in your interest to treat us like cattle! You fuck! You English-speaking fuck!'

The man put away his notepad. He looked at the ground and seemed to be groping for a response.

Chenayya felt a tapping on his shoulder. It was the Tamilian boy from Mr Ganesh Pai's shop.

'Stop talking so much! Your number has come up!'

Some of the other cart pullers began chuckling, as if to say to Chenayya: 'Serves you right.'

You see! He glared at the English-speaker from Madras as if to say: 'Even the privilege of speech is not ours. Even if we raise our voices, we are told to shut up.'

Strangely, the man from Madras was not grinning; he had turned his face away, as if he were ashamed.

As he went up Lighthouse Hill that day, as he forced his cart over the hump, he felt none of his usual exultation. I am not really moving forward, he thought. Every turn of the wheel undid him and slowed him down. Each time he cycled, he was working the wheel of life backwards, crushing muscle and fibre into the pulp from which they were made in his mother's womb; he was unmaking himself.

All at once, right in the middle of traffic, he stopped and got off his cart, possessed by the simple and clear thought: I can't go on like this.

Why don't you do something, work in a factory, anything, to improve yourself?

After all, for years you have delivered things to the gates of factories – it is just a question of getting inside.

The next day, he went to the factory. He saw thousands of men reporting for work and he thought: what a fool I have been, never even to try and get work here.

He sat down and none of the guards asked any questions, thinking he was waiting to collect a delivery.

He waited till noon and then a man came out. From the number of people following him Chenayya thought he must be the big man. He went running past the guard and got down on his knees: 'Sir! I want to work.'

The man stared at him. The guards came running up to drag Chenayya back, but the big man said: 'I have two thousand workers and not one of them wants to work, and here is this man, down on his knees, begging for work. That's the attitude we need to move this country forward.'

He pointed at Chenayya.

'You won't get offered any long-term contract. Understand. Day by day.'

'Anything, anything you want.'

'What kind of work can you do?'

'Anything, anything you want.'

'All right, come back tomorrow. We don't need a coolie right now.'

'Yes, sir.'

The big man took out a pack of cigarettes and lit one.

'Hear what this man has to say,' he said, as a group of other men, who were also smoking, gathered around him.

And Chenayya repeated that he would do anything, under any conditions, for any sort of pay.

'Say it again!' the big man ordered and another group of men came up and listened to Chenayya.

That evening, he came back to Mr Ganesh Pai's shop and shouted at the other workers: 'I've found a real job, you motherfuckers. I'm out of here.'

The Tamilian boy alone cautioned him.

'Chenayya, why don't you wait a day and make sure the other job is good? Then you can quit here.'

'Nothing doing, I quit!' he yelled and walked away.

The next day at dawn, he was back at the factory gate. 'I want to see the big man,' he said, shaking the bars of the gate for attention. 'He told me to come today.'

The guard, who was reading the newspaper, looked up at him fiercely.

'Get out!'

'Don't you remember me? I came—'

'Get out!'

He waited near the gate; after an hour they opened and a car with tinted windows pulled out. Running side by side with the car, he banged on the windows. 'Sir! Sir! Sir!' A dozen hands seized him from behind; he was shoved to the ground and kicked.

When he wandered back to Mr Pai's shop that evening, the Tamilian boy was waiting for him. He said: 'I never told the boss you quit.'

The other rickshaw pullers did not tease Chenayya that night. One of them left him a bottle of liquor, still half full.

The rain fell without pause. He rode his cycle through the downpour, splashing down the road. He wore a long white plastic sheet over his body like a shroud; around the head, a black cloth tied it around his head, giving it the look of an Arab's cape and caftan.

This was the most dangerous time for the coolies. Whenever the road had broken up into a pothole, he had to slow down to avoid tripping his cycle-cart over.

Waiting at the crossroads, he saw to his left a fat kid sitting on the seat of an autorickshaw. The rain made him playful; he stuck his tongue out at the fellow. The boy did likewise, and the game went on for several turns, until the autorickshaw driver chided the boy and glared at Chenayya.

The pain in his neck began biting again. I can't go on like this, he thought.

From across the road, one of the other cart pullers, a young boy, drove his cart alongside Chenayya's. 'Have to deliver this fast and get back,' he said. 'Boss said he's depending on me to be back within an hour.' He grinned and Chenayya wanted to shove his fist into the grin. God, how full of suckers the world is, he thought, counting to ten to calm himself. How happy this man seems to be, to destroy himself with overwork. *You baboon!* he wanted to shout. *You and all the others! Baboons!*

He put his head down and suddenly it seemed a great strain to move the cart.

'You've got no air in one tyre!' the baboon shouted. 'You'll have to stop!' He grinned and rode on.

Stop? Chenayya thought. No, that is what a

baboon would do: not me. Putting his head down, he pedalled on, forcing his flat tyre along:

Move!

And slowly and noisily, rattling its old wheels and its unoiled chains, the cart moved.

It's raining now, Chenayya thought, lying in his cart that night, a plastic sheet over him to protect him from the rain. That means half the year is over. It must be June or July. I must be nearly thirty now.

He pulled the sheet down and lifted his head to relieve the pain in his neck. He could not believe his eyes: even in this rain, some mother-fucker was flying a kite! It was the kid with the black kite. As if taunting the heavens, the lightning, to come strike him. Chenayya watched and forgot his pain.

In the morning, two men in khaki uniforms came into the alley: autorickshaw drivers. They had come to wash their hands at the tap at the end of the alley. The cart pullers instinctively moved to one side and let the two men in uniforms through. As they washed their hands, Chenayya heard them talk about an autorickshaw driver who had been locked up by the police for hitting a customer.

'Why not?' one autorickshaw driver said to the other. 'He had every right to hit that man! I only wish he had gone further and killed that bastard before the police got to him!'

After brushing his teeth, Chenayya went to the

lottery seller. A boy, a total stranger, was sitting at the desk, kicking his legs merrily.

'What happened to the old fellow?'

'Gone.'

'Gone where?'

'Gone into politics.'

The boy described what had happened to the old seller. He had joined the campaign of a BJP candidate for the Corporation elections. His candidate was likely to win in the elections. Then he would sit on the verandah of the candidate's house; if you wanted to see the politician, you would have to pay him fifty rupees first.

'That's the politician's life – it's the fastest way to get rich,' the boy said. He flipped through his coloured paper pieces. 'What'll you have, uncle? A yellow? Or a green?'

Chenayya turned away without buying any of the coloured tickets.

Why, he thought at night, can't that be me – the fellow who goes into politics to get rich? He did not want to forget what he had just heard, so he pinched himself sharply at the ankle.

It was Sunday again. His free day. Chenayya woke up when it got too hot, then brushed his teeth lazily, looking up to see if kites were flying in the sky. The other pullers were going to see the new Hoyka temple that the Member of Parliament had opened, just for Hoykas, with their own Hoyka deity and Hoyka priests.

'Aren't you coming, Chenayya?' the others shouted to him.

'What has any god ever done for me?' he shouted back; they giggled at his recklessness.

Baboons, he thought, as he lay down in the cart again. Going to worship some statue in a temple, thinking it'll make them rich.

Baboons!

He lay with one arm over his face; then he heard the tinkling of coins.

'Come over, Kamala,' he called out to the prostitute, who was in her usual spot, playing with the coins. When he taunted her for the sixth time, she snapped: 'Get lost, or I'll call Brother.'

At this reference to the kingpin who ran the brothels in this part of town, Chenayya sighed and turned over in his cart.

He thought: perhaps it is time for me to get married.

He had lost contact with all his relatives; plus he did not actually want to get married. Bring children – into what future? That was the most baboon-like thing the other coolies did; to procreate, as if to say, they were satisfied with their fate, they were happy to replenish the world that had consigned them to this task.

There was nothing in him but anger, and if he married he thought he would lose his anger.

As he turned around in his cart, he noticed the welt on his foot. He frowned, trying hard to remember how he had got it.

The next morning, returning from a delivery, he made a diversion and rode his cart to the office of the Congress party in Umbrella Street. He crouched on the verandah of the office and waited for someone important-looking to come out.

A sign outside showed Indira Gandhi raising her hand, with the slogan: 'Mother Indira will protect the poor.' He smirked.

Were they completely nuts? Did they really think that anyone would believe a politician would protect the poor?

But then he thought: maybe this woman, Indira Gandhi, had been someone special; maybe they were right. In the end, she was shot dead, wasn't she? That seemed evidence to him that she had wanted to help people. Suddenly it seemed that the world did have good-hearted men and women – he felt he had cut himself off from all of them by his bitterness. Now he wished he hadn't been so rude to that journalist from Madras . . .

A man in loose white clothes appeared, followed by two or three hanger-ons; Chenayya rushed up to him and got down on his knees with his palms folded.

All the following week, whenever he knew his number was not going to be called for a while, he rode around on his cycle, sticking up posters of the Congress candidates in all the Muslim-dominated streets, shouting: 'Vote for Congress – the party of Muslims! Defeat the BJP!'

The week passed. The elections took place, the

results were declared. Chenayya rode his cycle to the Congress party, parked it outside, went to the doorkeeper and asked to see the candidate.

'He's a busy man now; just wait out here a moment,' said the doorkeeper. He placed a hand on Chenayya's back. 'You really helped us do well in the Bunder, Chenayya. The BJP defeated us everywhere else, but you got the Muslims to vote for us!'

Chenayya beamed. He waited outside the party headquarters and watched the cars arrive and disgorge rich and important men, who hurried in to see the candidate. He saw them and thought: this is where I will wait to collect money from the rich. Not much. Just five rupees from everyone who comes to see the candidate. That should do.

His heart beat from excitement. An hour passed.

Chenayya decided to go into the waiting room, to make sure that he too got to see the Man when he finally emerged. There were benches and stools in the waiting room; a dozen other men were waiting. Chenayya saw an empty chair and wondered if he should sit down. Why not, had he not worked for the victory too? He was about to sit down, when the doorkeeper said: 'Use the floor, Chenayya.'

Another hour passed. Everyone in the waiting room was told to go in and see the Big Man; but Chenayya was still squatting outside, his face between his palms, waiting.

Finally, the doorkeeper came up to him with a box full of round yellow sweets. 'Take one.'

Chenayya took a sweet, almost put it in his mouth, and then put it back. 'I don't want a sweet.' His voice rose quickly. 'I hung posters all over this town! Now I want to see the Big Man! I want to get a job with—!'

The doorkeeper slapped him.

I am the biggest fool here, Chenayya thought, back at his alley: the other pullers were lying in their carts, snoring hard. It was late that night and he was the only one who could not sleep. *I am the biggest fool; I am the biggest baboon here.*

On the way to his first assignment the next morning, there was another traffic jam in front of Umbrella Street – the biggest one he had ever seen.

He slowed down, spitting on the road every few minutes to help himself pass the time.

When he finally got to his destination, he found that he was delivering to a foreign man. He insisted on helping Chenayya unload the furniture, which confused Chenayya terribly. The whole time, the foreigner spoke to Chenayya in English, as if he expected everyone in Kittur to be familiar with the language.

He held his hand out at the end to shake Chenayya's hand, and gave him a fifty-rupee note.

Chenayya was in a panic – where was he expected

to get change? He tried to explain, but the European just grinned and shut the door.

Then he understood. He bowed deeply to the closed door.

When he returned to the alley with two bottles of liquor, the other cart pullers jeered at him.

'Where did you get money for that from, Chenayya?'

'None of your business.'

He drank a bottle dry; then drank the second. Then he went over to the liquor shop and bought another bottle of hooch; when he woke next morning he realized he had spent all his money on liquor.

All of it.

He put his face in his hands and began to cry.

On an assignment to the train station, he went to the tap to drink; nearby, he overheard autorickshaw drivers talking about that driver who had hit his customer.

'A man has a right to do what he has to do,' one said. 'The condition of the poor is becoming intolerable here.'

But they were not poor themselves, Chenayya thought, slathering his dry forearm with water; they lived in houses, they owned their vehicles. You have to attain a certain level of richness before you can complain about being poor, he thought. When you are this poor, you are not given the right to complain.

'Look – that's what the rich of this town want to turn us into!' the autorickshaw man said, and Chenayya realized that he was being pointed at. 'They want to swindle us out of our money until we turn into that!'

He cycled out of the train station, but he could not stop hearing their words. He could not switch off his mind. Like a tap it dripped. Think, think, think. He passed by a statue of Gandhi and he began thinking again. Gandhi dressed like a poor man – he dressed like Chenayya did. But what did Gandhi do for the poor?

Did Gandhi even exist? he wondered. These things – India, the river Ganga, the world beyond India – were they even real?

How would he ever know?

Only one group was lower than he was. The beggars. One misstep and he would be down with them, he thought. One accident. And that would be him. How did the others deal with this? They did not. They preferred not to think.

When he stopped at a crossroads that night, an old beggar put his hands in front of Chenayya.

He turned his face away and rode down the road back to Mr Ganesh Pai's shop.

The following morning, he was going over the hill again, with five cardboard crates piled up one above the other in his cart, thinking: because we let them. Because we do not dare run away with that wad of fifty thousand rupees – because we

231

know other poor people will catch us and drag us back before the rich man. We poor have built the prison around ourselves.

In the evening, he lay down exhausted. The others had built a fire. Someone would come and give him some rice. He was the hardest worker, so the boss-man had let it be known that he ought to be fed regularly.

He saw two dogs humping. There was no passion in what they were doing: it was just a release. That is all I want to do right now, he thought: hump something. But instead of humping, I have to lie here, thinking.

The fat prostitute sat outside. 'Let me come up,' he said. She did not look at him; she shook her head.

'Just one time. I'll pay you next time.'

'Get out of here, or I'll call Brother,' she said, referring to the don who ran the brothel and took a cut from the women every night. He gave in; he bought a small bottle of liquor and he began drinking.

Why do I think so much? These thoughts are like thorns inside my head; I want them out. And even when I drink, they're there. I wake up in the night, my throat burning, and I find all the thoughts still in my head.

He lay awake, lying in his cart. He was sure he had been hounded by the rich even in his dreams, because he woke up furious and sweating. Then he heard the noise of coitus nearby. Looking around, he saw another cart puller humping the prostitute. Right next to him. He wondered: why not me? why not me? He knew the fellow had no money; so she was doing it out of charity. Why not me?

Every sigh, every groan of the coupling pair was like a chastisement; and Chenayya couldn't take it any more.

He got off his cart, walked around till he found a puddle of cowdung on the ground, and scooped a handful. He flung the shit at the lovers. There was a cry; he rushed up to them and dabbed the whore's face with shit. He put his shit-smeared fingers into her mouth and kept them there, even though she bit them; the harder she bit the more he enjoyed it, and he kept his fingers there until the other pullers descended on him and dragged him away.

One day he was given an assignment that took him right out of the city limits, into Bajpe; he was delivering a doorframe to a construction site.

'There used to be a big forest here,' one of the construction workers told him. 'But now that's all that's left.' He pointed to a distant clump of green.

Chenayya looked at the man and asked: 'Is there any work here for me?'

On his way back, he took a detour off the road and went to the patch of green. When he got there, he left his bike and walked around; seeing a high rock, he climbed up and looked at the trees around him. He was hungry, because he had not eaten all day, but he felt all right. Yes, he could live out here. If only he had a little food, what more would he want? His aching muscles could be rested. He put his head on the rock and looked at the sky.

He dreamed of his mother. Then he remembered the thrill with which he had come to Kittur from his village, at the age of seventeen. That first day, he was taken around by a female cousin who pointed out some of the main sights to him, and he remembered the whiteness of her skin, which doubled the charms of the city. He never saw that cousin again. He remembered what came next: the terrible contraction, the life that got smaller and smaller by the day in the city. The realization came to him now, that the first day in a city was destined to be the best: you had already been expelled from paradise, the moment you walk into the city.

He thought: I could be a sanyasi. Just eat bushes and herbs and live with the sunrise and sunset. The wind picked up; the trees nearby rustled, as if they were chuckling at him.

It was night-time when he cycled back. To get to the shop faster, he took the route down the Lighthouse Hill.

As he was coming down, he saw a red light and then a green light attached to the back of a large silhouette moving down the road; a moment later he realized it was an elephant.

It was the same elephant he had seen earlier;

234

only now it had red and green traffic lights tied with string to its rump.

'What's the meaning of this?' he shouted to the mahout.

The mahout shouted back: 'Well, I have to make sure no one bumps into us from behind at night – there are no lights anywhere!'

Chenayya threw his head up and laughed; it was the funniest thing he had ever seen: an elephant with traffic lights on its rump.

'They didn't pay me,' the mahout said. He had tied the beast to the side of the road and was chatting to Chenayya. He had some peanuts and he didn't want to eat them alone, so he was glad to share a few with Chenayya.

'They made me take their kid on a ride and they didn't pay me. You should have seen them drink and drink. And they wouldn't pay me fifty rupees, which was all I asked for.'

The mahout slapped the side of his elephant. 'After all that Rani did for them—'

'That's the way of the world,' Chenayya said.

'Then it's a rotten world.' The mahout chewed a few more peanuts. 'A rotten world.' He slapped the side of his elephant. Chenayya looked up at the beast.

The behemoth's eyes gazed sidelong at him; they glistened darkly, almost as if they were tearing. The beast also seemed to be saying: 'Things should not be this way.'

The mahout pissed against the wall, turning his

head up, arching his back, and exhaling in relief, as if it were the happiest thing he had done all day.

Chenayya kept looking at the elephant, its sad wet eyes. He thought: I am sorry I ever cursed you brother, as he rubbed its trunk.

The mahout stood at the wall, watching Chenayya talking to the elephant, a sense of apprehension rising within him.

Outside the ice-cream shop, two kids were licking ice lollies and staring right at Chenayya. He lay sprawled on his cart, dead tired after another day's work.

'Don't you see me?' Chenayya wanted to shout out over the traffic. His stomach was grumbling; he was tired and hungry, and there was still an hour before the Tamilian boy from Mr Ganesh Pai's shop would come out with dinner.

One of the kids across the street turned away, as if the fury in the cycle puller's eyes had become tangible; but the other one, a fat light-skinned fellow, stayed put, licking his tongue up and down his ice-cream stick, staring nonchalantly at Chenayya.

Don't you have any shame, any sense of decency, you fat fuck?

He turned around in his cart and began talking aloud to calm his nerves. His gaze fell on the rusty saw lying at the end of his cart. What stops me now, he said aloud, crossing the street and slashing that boy into shreds?

Just the thought made him feel powerful.

A finger began tapping on his shoulder. If it is the fat motherfucker with his ice-cream stick, I will pick up that saw and slice him in two, I swear to God.

It was the Tamilian assistant from the store.

'Your turn, Chenayya.'

He took his cart to the entrance of the store, where the boy handed him a small package, wrapped in newspaper and tied in white string.

'It's to the same place you went a while back to deliver the rose table. Mrs Engineer's house. We forgot to send the bonus gift and she's been complaining.'

'Oh, no,' he groaned. 'She doesn't tip at all. She's a complete cunt.'

'You have to go, Chenayya. Your number came up.'

He cycled there slowly. At every crossroads and traffic light he looked at the saw in his cart.

Mrs Engineer opened her door herself: she said she was on the phone and told him to wait outside.

'The food at the Lion's Club is so fattening,' he heard her saying. 'I've put on ten kilos in the past year.'

He looked around quickly. No lights were on in the neighbours' houses. There seemed to be a nightwatchman's shed at the back of the house, but that too was dark.

He snatched the saw and went in. She had her back to him; he saw the whiteness of her flesh in the gap between her blouse and her skirt; he smelled the perfume of her body. He went closer.

She turned round; then covered the receiver with her hand. 'Not in here, you idiot! Just put it on the floor and get out!'

He stood confused.

'On the floor!' she screamed at him. 'Then get out!'

He nodded and dropped the saw on the floor and ran out.

'Hey! Don't leave that in here! O, my God!'

He ran back, picked up the saw, then left the house, ducking low, to avoid the neem tree leaves. He tossed the saw into the cart: a loud clatter. The bonus gift . . . where was it? He grabbed the package, ran into the house, left it somewhere and slammed the door.

There was a startled meow. A cat was sitting up on a branch of the tree, watching him closely. He went close to it. How beautiful its eyes were, he thought. Like a jewel that had fallen off the throne, a hint of a world of beauty beyond his knowledge.

He reached up to it and it came to him.

'Kitty, kitty,' he said, stroking its fur. It wriggled in his arms, restless already.

Somewhere, I hope, a poor man will strike a blow against the world. Because there is no God watching over us. There is no one coming to release us from the jail in which we have locked ourselves.

He wanted to tell all this to the cat; maybe it could tell it to another cart puller; the one who would be brave enough to strike the blow.

He sat down by the wall, still holding on to the cat and stroking its fur. Maybe I can take you along, kitty. But how would he feed it? Who would take care of it when he was not around? He released it. He sat with his back to the wall and watched it walking cautiously up to a car, and then slinking under it; he craned his neck to see what it was doing down there, when he heard a shout from above. It was Mrs Engineer, yelling at him from a window at the top of her mansion: 'I know what you're up to, you thug – I can read your mind! You won't get another rupee out of me! Get moving!'

He was no longer angry; and he knew she was right. He had to go back to the store. His number would come up again soon. He got on his cart and pedalled.

There was a traffic jam in the city centre and Chenayya had to go over the Lighthouse Hill again. Traffic was bad here too. It moved a few inches at a time, and then Chenayya had to stop mid-hill and clamp his foot down on the road to hold his cart in its place. When the horns began to sound, he rose from his seat and pedalled; behind him, a long line of cars and buses moved, as if he were pulling the traffic along with an invisible chain.

DAY FOUR (AFTERNOON): THE COOL WATER WELL JUNCTION

The old Cool Water Well is said never to dry up, but it is now sealed and serves only as a traffic roundabout. The streets around the Well house a number of middle-class colonies. Professional people of all castes – Bunts, Brahmins, and Catholics – live side by side here, although the Muslim rich keep to the Bunder. The Canara Club, the most exclusive club in town, is located here, in a large white mansion with lawns. The neighbourhood is the 'intellectual' part of town: it boasts a Lion's Club, a Rotary Club, a Freemasons' Lodge, a Baha'i educational group, a Theosophist Society, and a branch of the Alliance Francaise of Pondicherry. Of the numerous medical institutions located here, the two best-known are the Havelock Henry General Hospital and Dr Shambhu Shetty's Happy Smile orthodontic clinic. The St Agnes Girls' High School, Kittur's most sought-after girls-only school, is also located

close by the junction. The poshest part of
the Cool Water Well Junction area is the
hibiscus-lined street known as Rose Lane.
Mabroor Engineer, believed to be Kittur's
richest man, and Anand Kumar, Kittur's
Member of Parliament, have mansions here.

I t's one thing to take a little ganja, roll it inside
a chappati and chew it at the day's end, just
to relax the muscles – I can forgive that in a
man, I really can. But to smoke this drug – this
smack – at seven in the morning, and then lie in
a corner with your tongue hanging out, I tolerate
that in no man on my construction site. You understand me? Or do you want me to repeat this in
Tamil or whatever language your people speak?'

'I understand, sir.'

'What did you say? What did you say, you son
of . . . ?'

Holding her brother by the hand, Soumya
watched as the foreman chastized her father. The
foreman was young, so much younger than her
father – but he wore a khaki uniform that the
construction company had given him, and twirled
a lathi in his left hand, and she saw that the
workers, instead of defending her father, were
listening quietly to the foreman. He was sitting in
a blue chair on an embankment of mud; a gas
lamp buzzed noisily from a wooden pole driven
into the ground next to the chair. Behind him was

241

the crater around the half-demolished house; the inside of the house was filled with rubble, its roof had mostly fallen in, and its windows were empty. With his baton and his uniform, and his face harshly illuminated by the incandescent paraffin lamp, the foreman looked like a ruler of the underworld, at the gate of his kingdom.

A semi-circle of construction workers had formed below him. Soumya's father stood apart from the others, looking furtively at Soumya's mother, who was muffling her sobs in a corner of her sari. In a tear-racked voice she said: 'I keep telling him to give up this *smack*. I keep telling—'

Soumya wondered why her mother had to complain about her father in front of everyone. Raju pressed her hand.

'Why are they all scolding Daddy?'

She pressed back. Quiet.

All at once the foreman got up from his chair, took a step down the embankment, and raised his stick over Soumya's father. 'Pay attention, I said' – he brought his stick down.

Soumya shut her eyes and turned away.

The workers had returned to their tents, which were scattered about the open field around the dark, half-demolished house. Soumya's father was lying on his blue mat, apart from everyone else; he was snoring already, his hands over his eyes. In the old days she would have gone to him and snuggled against his side.

Soumya went up to her father. She shook him

by his big toe, but he did not respond. She went to where her mother was making rice and lay down beside her.

Mallets and sledgehammers woke her up in the morning. Thump! Thump! Thump! Bleary-eyed, she wandered over to the house. Her father was up on the bit of the roof that remained, sitting on one of the black iron crossbeams; he was cutting it with a saw. Two men swung at the wall below with sledgehammers; clouds of dust rose up and covered her father as he sawed. Soumya's heart leaped.

She ran to her mother and cried: 'Daddy's working again!'

Her mother was with the other women; they were coming down from the house, carrying large metal saucers on their heads filled to the brim with rubble. 'Make sure Raju doesn't get wet,' she said, as she passed Soumya.

Only then did Soumya notice it was drizzling.

Raju was lying on the blanket where his mother had been; she woke him up and took him into one of the tents. Raju began whimpering, saying he wanted to sleep some more. She went to the blue mat; her father had not touched the rice from last night. Mixing the dry rice with the rainwater, she squeezed it into a gruel and stuffed morsels into Raju's mouth. He said he didn't like it and bit her fingers each time.

The rain fell harder and she heard the foreman roar: 'You sons of bald women, don't slow down!'

The moment the rain stopped, Raju wanted to be pushed on the swing. 'It's going to start raining again,' she said, but he wouldn't change his mind. She carried him in her arms to the old truck tyre swing near the compound wall and put him on it, and gave him a push, shouting: 'One! Two!'

As she pushed, a man appeared before her.

His dark, wet skin was coated in white dust and it took an instant for her to recognize him.

'Sweetie,' he said, 'you must do something for Daddy.'

Her heart was beating too fast for her to say a word. She wanted him to say 'sweetie' not like he was saying it now – as if it were just a word, air that he were breathing out – but like before, when it came from his heart, when it was accompanied by his pulling her to his chest and hugging her deeply and whispering madly into her ear.

He went on speaking, in the same strange, slow, slurred way, and told her what he wanted her to do; then he walked back to the house.

She found Raju, who was cutting an earthworm into smaller bits with a piece of glass he had stolen from the demolition site, and said: 'We have to go.'

Raju could not be left alone, even though he would be a real nuisance on a trip like this. Once she had left him alone and he had swallowed a piece of glass.

'Where are we going?' he asked.

'To the Bunder.'

'Why?'

'There is a place by the Bunder, a garden, where Daddy's friends are waiting for him to come. Daddy cannot go there – because the foreman will hit him again. You don't want the foreman to beat Daddy again in front of all the world, do you?'

'No,' Raju said. 'And when we get to this garden, what do we do?'

'We give Daddy's friends at this garden ten rupees and they will give us something Daddy *really* needs.'

'What?'

She told him.

Raju, already shrewd with money, asked: 'How much will it cost?'

'Ten rupees, he said.'

'Did he give you ten rupees?'

'No. Daddy said we'll have to get it ourselves. We'll have to beg.'

As the two of them walked down Rose Lane, she kept her eyes on the ground. Once she had found five rupees on the ground – yes, five! You never know what you'd find in a place where rich people live.

They moved to the side of the lane; a white car paused for a moment to go over a bump on the road and she shouted at the driver: 'Where is the port, uncle?'

'Far from here,' he shouted back. 'Go to the main road and take a left.'

The tinted windows in the back of the car were

rolled up, but through the driver's window Soumya caught a glimpse of a passenger's hand covered with gold bangles; she wanted to knock on the window. But she remembered the rule that the foreman had laid down for all the workers' children. No begging in Rose Lane. Only on the main road. She controlled herself.

All the houses were being demolished and rebuilt in Rose Lane. Soumya wondered why people wanted to tear down these fine, large, whitewashed houses. Maybe houses became uninhabitable after some time, like shoes.

When the lights on the main road turned red, she went from autorickshaw to autorickshaw, opening and closing her fingers.

'Uncle, have pity, I'm starving.'

Her technique was solid. She had got it from her mother. It went like this: even as she begged, for three seconds she kept eye contact; then her eye would begin to wander to the next autorickshaw. 'Mother, I'm hungry' (rubbing her tummy) 'give me food' (closing her fingers and bringing them to her mouth).

'Big brother, I'm hungry.'

'Grandpa, even a small coin would—'

While she did the road, Raju sat on the ground and was meant to whimper when anyone well-dressed passed by. She did not count on him to do much; at least if he sat down he would stay out of other kinds of trouble, like running after cats, or trying to pet stray dogs that might be rabid.

Towards noon, the roads filled with cars. The windows had been rolled up against the rain, and she had to raise both her hands to the glass and scratch like a cat, to get attention. The windows in one car were rolled down and she thought her luck had improved.

A woman in one of the cars had beautiful patterns of gold painted on her hands and Soumya gaped at them. She heard the woman with the gold hands say to someone else in the car: 'There are beggars everywhere these days in the town. It never used to be like this.'

The other person leaned forward and stared for a moment. 'They're so *dark* . . . Where are they from?'

'Who knows?'

Only fifty paise, after an hour.

Next she tried to get on the bus when it stopped at the red light and beg there, but the conductor saw her coming and stood at the door: 'Nothing doing.'

'Why not, uncle?'

'Who do you think I am, a rich man like Mr Engineer? Go ask someone else, you brat!'

Glaring at her, he raised the red cord of his whistle over his head as if it were a whip. She scrambled out.

'He was a real cock-sucker,' she told Raju, who had something to show her: a sheet of wrapping plastic, full of round buttons of air that could be popped.

Making sure the conductor couldn't see, she got down on her knees and put it on the road right in front of the wheel. Raju crouched: 'No, it's not right. The wheels won't go over it,' he said. 'Push it to the right a little.'

When the bus moved again, the wheels ran over the plastic sheets and the buttons exploded, startling the passengers; the conductor poked his head out of the window to see what had happened. The two children ran away.

It began raining again. The two of them crouched under a tree; coconuts came crashing down and a man who had been standing next to them with an umbrella jumped up and swore at the tree, and ran. She giggled, but Raju was worried they would get hit by a falling coconut.

When the rain stopped, she found a twig and scratched on the ground, drawing a map of the city, as she imagined it. Here – was Rose Lane. Here – was where they had come, still close to Rose Lane. Here – was the Bunder. And here – the garden inside the Bunder that they were looking for.

'Do you understand all of this?' she asked Raju. He nodded, excited by the map.

'To get to the Bunder, we have to go' – she drew another arrow – 'through the big hotel.'

'And then?'

'And then we go to the garden inside the Bunder . . .'

'And then?'

'We find the thing Daddy wants us to get.'

'And then?'

The truth was, she had no idea if the hotel was on the way to the port or not: but the rain had driven the vehicles away from the road, and the hotel was the only place where she might be able to beg for the money right now.

'You have to ask for money in English from the tourists,' she teased Raju as they walked to the hotel. 'Do you know what to say in English?'

They stopped outside the hotel to watch a group of crows bathing in a puddle of water. The sun was shining on the water, and the black coats of the crows turned glossy as scintillas of water flew from their shaking bodies; Raju declared it was the most beautiful thing he had ever seen.

The man with no arms and legs was sitting in front of the hotel; he yelled curses from the other side of the road.

'Go away, you devil's children! I told you never to come back here!'

She shouted back: 'To hell with you, monster! We told you: never come back here!'

He was sitting on a wooden board with wheels. Whenever a car slowed down at the traffic light in front of the hotel, he rolled up on his wooden board and begged from one side; she begged from the other side of the car.

Raju, sitting on the pavement, yawned.

'Why do we need to beg? Daddy is working today. I saw him cutting those things . . .' He moved his legs apart and began sawing at an imaginary crossbeam below him.

'Quiet.'

Two taxis slowed down near the red light. The man with no arms and legs rushed on his wooden board to the first taxi; she ran to the second one and put her hands into the open window. A foreigner was sitting inside. He stared at her with an open mouth: she saw his lips making a perfect pink 'O'.

'Did you get any money?' Raju asked, when she came back from the car and the white man.

'No. Get up,' she said and dragged the boy to his feet.

By the time they had crossed two red lights, however, Raju had figured it out. He pointed to her clutched fist.

'You got money from the white man. You have the money!'

She went up to an autorickshaw parked by the side of the road: 'Which way is the Bunder?'

The driver yawned. 'I don't have any money. Go away.'

'I'm not asking for money. I'm asking for directions to the Bunder.'

'I told you, I'm not giving you anything!'

She spat at his face. Then she grabbed Raju by the wrist and they ran like mad.

The next autorickshaw driver they asked was a

kind man. 'It's a long, long way. Why don't you take a bus? The number 343 will get you there. Otherwise, it'll be a couple of hours at least, by foot.'

'We don't have money, uncle.'

He gave them a rupee coin and asked: 'Where are your parents?'

They got onto a bus and paid the conductor. 'Where are you getting off?' he shouted.

'The port.'

'This bus doesn't go to the port. You need the number 343. This is the number—'

They got out and walked.

They were near the Cool Water Well Junction now. They found the one-armed, one-legged boy working there, as he always did; he went hopping about from car to car, begging before she could get to them. Someone had given him a radish today, so he went about begging with a large white radish in his hand, tapping it on the windscreens to get the attention of the passengers.

'Don't you dare do your begging here, you sons of bitches!' he shouted at them, waving the radish threateningly.

The two of them stuck their tongues out at him and shouted: 'Freak! Disgusting freak!'

Raju began crying after an hour and refused to walk any more, so she picked in a rubbish can for some food. There was a carton with two biscuits and they had one each.

They walked some more. After a while, Raju's nostrils began bubbling.

'I can smell the sea from here.'

She could, too.

They walked faster. They saw a man painting a sign in English by the side of the road; two cats fighting on the roof of a white Fiat; a horse-cart, loaded with chopped wood; an elephant, walking down the road with a mound of neem leaves; a car that had been smashed up in an accident; and a dead crow with its claws drawn in stiffly to its chest, its belly open and swarming with black ants.

Then they were at the Bunder.

The sun was setting over the sea and they went past the packed markets, looking for a garden.

'There are no gardens here in the Bunder. That's why the air is so bad here,' an old Muslim peanut-seller told them. 'You've got the wrong directions.'

Looking at their crestfallen faces, he offered them a handful of peanuts to munch on.

Raju whined. He was hungry . . . to hell with the peanuts! He thrust them back at the Muslim man, who called him a devil.

That made Raju so angry he left his sister and ran, and she ran after him until Raju came to a stop.

'Look!' he shrieked, pointing at a row of mutilated men with bandaged limbs, sitting in front of a building with a white dome.

Gingerly they walked around the lepers. And

then she saw a man lying down on a bench, his palms crossed over his face, breathing heavily. She came near the bench and saw, right at the water's edge, fenced off by a small stone wall, a little green park.

Raju was quiet now.

When they got to the park, there was shouting. A policeman was slapping a very dark man. 'Did you steal the shoes? Did you?'

The very dark man shook his head. The policeman hit him harder. 'Son of a bald woman, you take these drugs and then you steal things, and you – son of a bald woman, you—!'

Three white-haired men, hiding in a bush near her, gestured to Soumya to come and hide with them. She took Raju into the bush and they waited there for the policeman to leave.

She whispered to the three white-haired men: 'I'm the daughter of Ramachandran, the man who smashes rich people's houses in Rose Lane.'

None of the three knew her father.

'What do you want, little girl?'

She said the word, as well as she could remember: ' . . *ack*.'

One of the men, who appeared to be their leader, frowned: 'Say it again.'

He nodded when she said the strange word the second time. Taking a pouch made of newspaper-skin out of his pocket, he tapped it: white powder, like crushed chalk, poured out. He took out a cigarette from another pocket, sliced it open, tapped out the tobacco, filled the paper with the white powder, and rolled it tight. He held the cigarette up in the air and gestured with his other hand to Soumya.

'Twelve rupees.'

'I've got only nine,' she said. 'You'll have to take nine.'

'Ten.'

She gave them the money; she took the cigarette. A horrible doubt seized her.

'If you're robbing me, if you're cheating me – Raju and I'll come back with Daddy – and beat you all.' The three men crouched together. They began shaking, and they were laughing together. Something was wrong with them. She grabbed Raju by the wrist and they ran.

Glimpses of the scene to come flashed through her mind. She would show Daddy what she had brought for him from so far away. 'Sweetie,' he would say – the way he used to say it – and hold her in a frenzy of affection, and the two would go mad with love for each other.

Her left foot began to burn after a while, and she flexed her toes and stared at them. Raju insisted on being carried; but fair enough, she thought – the little fellow had done well today.

It began raining again. Raju cried. She had to threaten to leave him behind three times; once she actually left him and walked a whole block before he came running after her, telling her of a giant dragon that was chasing him.

They got onto a bus.

'Tickets,' the driver shouted, but she winked at him and said: 'Big brother, let us on for free, please . . .'

His face softened and he let them stay near the back.

It was pitch black when they got back to Rose Lane. They saw the lamps lit up in all the mansions. The foreman was sitting under his gas lamp, talking to one of the workers. The house looked smaller: all the crossbeams had been sawed off.

'Did you go begging in this neighbourhood?' the foreman shouted, when he saw the two of them.

'No, we didn't.'

'Don't lie to me! You were gone all day – and doing what? Begging on Rose Lane!'

She raised her upper lip in contempt.

'Why don't you ask if we begged here, before accusing us!'

The foreman glared at them, but kept quiet, defeated by the girl's logic.

Raju ran ahead, screaming for his mother. They found her asleep, alone, in her rain-dampened sari. Raju ran up to her, butted his head into her side, and began rubbing against her body for warmth, like a kitten; the sleeping woman groaned and turned over to the other side. One of her arms began swatting Raju away.

'Amma,' he said, shaking her. 'Amma! I'm hungry! Soumya gave me nothing to eat all day! She made me walk and walk and take this bus and that, and no food! A white man gave her a hundred rupees but she never gave me anything to eat or drink.'

'Don't lie!' Soumya hissed. 'What about the biscuits?'

But he kept shaking her: 'Amma! Soumya gave me nothing to eat or drink all day!'

The two children began wrestling each other. Then a hand lightly tapped Soumya's shoulder.

'Sweetie.'

When he saw their father, Raju began to simper; he turned and ran away to his mother. Soumya and her father walked to one side.

'Do you have it, sweetie? Do you have the thing?'

She drew air. 'Here,' she said and put the packet into his hands. He lifted it up to his nose, sniffed, and then put it under his shirt: she saw his hands reach through his sarong into his groin. He took his hand out. She knew it was coming now: his caress.

He caught her wrist; his fingers cut into her flesh.

'What about the hundred rupees that the white man gave you? I heard Raju.'

'No one gave me a hundred rupees, Daddy. I swear. Raju is lying, I swear.'

'Don't lie. Where is the hundred rupees?'

He raised his arm. She began screaming.

When she came to lie down next to her mother, Raju was still complaining that he had not eaten all day long, and had been forced to walk from here to there and then from there to another place and then back to here. Then he saw the red marks on his sister's face and neck and went silent. She fell to the ground, and went to sleep.

KITTUR: BASIC FACTS

TOTAL POPULATION (1981 CENSUS):
193,432 residents

CASTE AND RELIGIOUS BREAK-DOWN
(as percentage of total population)

HINDUS
Upper castes
Brahmins:
   Kannada-speaking: 4 per cent
   Konkani-speaking: 3 per cent
   Tulu-speaking: less than 1 per cent
Bunts: 16 per cent
Other upper castes: 1 per cent

Backward castes
Hoykas: 24 per cent
Miscellaneous backward castes and tribals: 4
per cent

Dalits (formerly known as untouchables): 9
per cent

MINORITIES
Muslims
Sunni: 14 per cent
Shia: 1 per cent
Ahmediya, Bohra, Ismaili: less than 1 per cent
Catholics: 14 per cent
Protestants (Anglicans, Pentecostals, Jehovah's
Witnesses, Mormons): 3 per cent

Jains: 1 per cent

Other religions (including Parsi, Jew, Buddhist, Brahmo Samaji, and Baha'i): less than 1 per cent

89 residents declare themselves to be without religion or caste.

DAY FIVE (MORNING): VALENCIA (TO THE FIRST CROSSROADS)

Valencia, the Catholic neighbourhood, begins with Father Stein's Homeopathic Hospital, which is named after a German Jesuit missionary who began a hospice here. Valencia is the largest neighbourhood of Kittur: most of its inhabitants are educated, employed, and owners of their homes. The handful of Hindus and Muslims who have bought land in Valencia have never encountered any trouble, but Protestants looking to live here have sometimes been attacked with stones and slogans. Every Sunday morning, men and women in their best clothes pour into the Cathedral of Our Lady of Valencia for mass. On Christmas Eve, virtually the entire population crams into the cathedral for midnight mass; the singing of carols and hymns continues well into the early hours.

When it came to troubles seen and horrors experienced, Jayamma, the advocate's cook, wanted it known that her life had been second to none. In the space of twelve years her dear mother had given birth to eleven children. Nine of them had been girls. Yes, nine! Now *that's* trouble. By the time Jayamma was born, number eight, there was no milk in her mother's breasts – they had to feed her an ass's milk in a plastic bottle. An ass's milk, yes! Now *that's* trouble. Her father had saved enough gold only for six daughters to be married off; the last three had to remain barren virgins for life. Yes, for life. For forty years she had been put on one bus or the other, and sent from one town to the next to cook and clean in someone else's house. To feed and fatten someone else's children. She wasn't even told where she would be going next; it would be night, she'd be playing with her nephew – that rolypoly little fellow Brijju – and what would she hear in the living room but her sister-in-law tell some stranger or the other: 'It's a deal, then. If she stays here, she eats food for nothing; so you're doing us a favour, believe me.' The next day Jayamma would be put on the bus again. Months would pass before she saw Brijju again. This was Jayamma's life, an instalment plan of troubles and horrors. Who had more to complain about on this earth?

But at least one horror was coming to an end. Jayamma was about to leave the advocate's house.

She was a short, stooped woman in her late fifties, with a glossy silver head of hair that seemed to give off light. A large black wart over her left eyebrow was the kind that is taken for

261

an auspicious sign in an infant. There were always pouches of dark skin shaped like garlic cloves under her eyes, and her eyeballs were rheumy from chronic sleeplessness and worry.

She had packed up her things: one big brown suitcase, the same one she had arrived with. Nothing more. Not a paise had been stolen from the advocate, although the house was sometimes in a mess and there surely had been the opportunity. But she had been honest. She brought the suitcase to the front porch and waited for the advocate's green Ambassador. He had promised to drop her off at the bus station.

'Goodbye, Jayamma. Are you leaving us for real?'

Shaila, the little lower-caste servant girl at the advocate's house – and Jayamma's principal tormentor of the past eight months – grinned. Although she was twelve and would be ready for marriage the following year, she looked only seven or eight. Her dark face was caked with Johnson and Johnson's Baby Powder, and she batted her eyelids mockingly.

'You lower-caste demon!' Jayamma hissed. 'Mind your manners!'

An hour late, the advocate's car pulled into the garage.

'Haven't you heard yet?' he said, when Jayamma came towards him with her bag. 'I told your sister-in-law we could use you a bit longer, and she agreed. I thought someone would have informed you.'

262

He slammed his car door shut. Then he went to take his bath, and Jayamma took her old brown suitcase back into the kitchen and began preparing for dinner.

'I'm never going to leave the advocate's house, am I, Lord Krishna?'

The next morning, the old woman was standing over the gas burner in the kitchen, stirring a lentil stew. As she worked, she sucked in air with a hiss, as if her tongue were on fire.

'For forty years I've lived among good Brahmins, Lord Krishna: homes in which even the lizards and the toads had been Brahmins in a previous birth. Now you see my fate, stuck among Christians and meat-eaters in this strange town, and each time I think I'm leaving, my sister-in-law tells me to stay on some more . . .'

She wiped her forehead and went on to ask: what had she done in a previous life – had she been a murderess, an adulteress, a child-devourer, a person who was rude to holy men and sages – to have been fated to come here, to the advocate's house, and live next to a lower-caste?

She sizzled onions, chopped coriander and threw them in, then stirred in red curry powder and monosodium glutamate from little plastic packets.

'Hai! Hai!'

Jayamma started and dropped her ladle into the broth. She went to the grill that ran along the rear end of the advocate's house and peered.

Shaila was at the outer wall of the compound, clapping her hands, while next door in the Christian neighbour's back yard, thick-lipped Rosie, a cleaving knife in her hand, was running after a rooster in her background. Slowly unbolting the door, Jayamma crept out into the back yard, to take a better look. 'Hai! Hai! Hai!' Shaila was shouting in glee, as the rooster clicked and clucked, and jumped on the green net over the well, where Rosie finally caught the poor thing and began cutting its neck. The rooster's tongue stuck out and its eyes almost popped out. 'Hai! Hai! Hai!'

Jayamma ran through the kitchen, straight into the dark prayer room, and bolted the door behind her. 'Krishna . . . My Lord Krishna . . .'

The prayer room doubled as a storage room for rice, and also as Jayamma's private quarters. The room was seven feet by seven feet; the little space in between the shrine and the rice bags, just enough to curl up in and go to sleep at night, was all Jayamma had asked from the advocate. (She had refused point-blank to take up the advocate's initial suggestion that she share a room with the lower-caste in the servants' quarters.)

She reached into the prayer shrine and took out a black box which she opened slowly. Inside was a silver idol of a child god – crawling, naked, with shiny buttocks – the god Krishna, Jayamma's only friend and protector.

'Krishna, Krishna,' she chanted softly, holding

the baby god in her hands again and rubbing its silver buttocks with her fingers. 'You see what goes on around me – me, a high-born Brahmin woman!'

She sat down on one of three rice bags lined up against the wall of the prayer room, and surrounded by yellow moats of DDT. Folding her legs up on the rice bag, and leaning her head against the wall, she took in deep breaths of the DDT – a strange, relaxing, curiously addictive aroma. She sighed; she wiped her forehead with the edge of a vermilion sari. Spots of sunlight, filtering through the plantain trees outside, played along the ceiling of the little room.

Jayamma closed her eyes. The fragrance of DDT made her drowsy; her body uncoiled, her limbs loosened, she was asleep in seconds.

When she woke up, fat little Karthik, the advocate's son, was shining a torchlight on her face. This was his way of rousing her from a nap.

'I'm hungry,' he said. 'Is anything ready?'

'Brother!' The old woman sprang to her feet. 'There's black magic in the back yard! Shaila and Rosie have killed a chicken – and they're doing black magic.'

The boy switched off the torchlight. He looked at her sceptically.

'What are you talking about, you old hag?'

'Come!' The old cook's eyes were large with excitement. 'Come!'

She coaxed the little master down the long hallway into the servants' quarters.

They stopped by the metal grille which gave them a view of the back yard. There were short coconut trees, and a clothes-line, and a black wall beyond which began the compound of their Christian neighbour. There was no one around. A strong wind shook the trees, and a loose sheet of paper was swirling around the back yard, like a dervish. The boy saw the white bedsheets on the clothes-line swaying eerily. They too seemed to suspect what the cook suspected.

Jayamma motioned to Karthik: be very, very quiet. She pushed the door to the servants' quarters. It was bolted shut.

When the old woman unlocked it, a stench of hair oil and baby powder wafted out, and the boy clamped his nostrils.

Jayamma pointed to the floor of the room.

A triangle in white chalk had been marked inside a square in red chalk, dried coconut flesh crowned the points of the triangle. Withered, blackening flowers were strewn about inside a circle. A blue marble gleamed from its centre.

'It's for black magic,' she said, and the boy nodded.

'Spies! Spies!'

Shaila stood athwart the door of the servants' room. She made a finger at Jayamma.

'You – you old hag! Didn't I tell you never to snoop around my room again?'

The old lady's face twitched.

'Brother!' she shouted. 'Did you see how this lower-caste speaks to us Brahmins?'

Karthik made a fist at the girl. 'Hey! This is my house and I'll go wherever I want to, you hear!'

Shaila glared at him: 'Don't think you can treat me like an animal, okay . . .'

Three loud honks ended the fighting. Shaila flew out to open the gate; the boy ran into his room and opened a textbook; Jayamma raced around the dining room in a panic, laying the table with stainless-steel plates.

The master of the house removed his shoes in the entrance hall and threw them in the direction of the shoe rack. Shaila would have to rearrange them later. A quick wash in his private bathroom and he emerged into the dining room, a tall, mustachioed man who cultivated flowing side-burns in the style of an earlier decade. At dinner he was always bare-chested, except for the Brahmin caste-string winding around his flabby torso. He ate quickly and in silence, pausing only once to gaze into a corner of the ceiling. The house was put in order by the motions of the master's jaws. Jayamma served. Karthik ate with his father. In the car shed, Shaila hosed down the master's green Ambassador and wiped it clean.

The advocate read the paper in the television room for an hour, and then the boy began searching for the black remote control in the mess of papers and books on the sandalwood table in the centre of the room. Jayamma and Shaila scrambled into the room and squatted in a corner, waiting for the television to come on.

267

At ten o'clock, all the lights in the house went out. The master and Karthik slept in their rooms.

In the darkness, a vicious hissing continued in the servants' quarters:

'Witch! Witch! Black-magic-making lower-caste witch!'

'Brahmin hag! Crazy old Brahmin hag!'

A week of non-stop conflict followed. Each time Shaila passed by the kitchen, the old Brahmin cook showered vengeful deities by the thousand down on that oily lower-caste head.

'What kind of era is this when Brahmins bring lower-caste girls into their household?' she grumbled as she stirred the lentils in the morning. 'Where have the rules of caste and religion fallen today, O Krishna?'

'Talking to yourself again, old virgin?' The girl had popped her head into the kitchen; Jayamma threw an unpeeled onion at her.

Lunch. Truce. The girl put out her stainless-steel plate outside the servants' living room and squatted on the floor, while Jayamma served out a generous portion of the lentil soup over the mounds of white rice on the girl's plate. She wouldn't starve anyone, she grumbled as she served, not even a sworn enemy. That's right: not even a sworn enemy. It wasn't the Brahmin way of doing things.

After lunch, putting on her glasses, she spread a copy of the newspaper just outside the servants' quarters. Sucking air in constantly, she read loudly and slowly, piecing letters into words and words into sentences. When Shaila passed by, she thrust the paper at her face.

'Here – you can read and write, can't you? Here, read the paper!'

The girl fumed; she went back into the servants' quarters and slammed the door.

'Do you think I've forgotten the trick you played on the advocate, you little Hokya? He's a kind-hearted man, so that's why, that evening you went up to him with your simpering lower-caste face and said, Master, I can't read. I can't write. I want to read. I want to write. Doesn't he, immediately, drive out to Shenoy's Book Store in Umbrella Street and buy you expensive reading-and-writing books? And all for what? Were the lower-castes meant to read and write?' Jayamma demanded of the closed door. 'Wasn't that all just a trap for the advocate?'

Sure enough, the girl lost all interest in her books. They lay in a heap in the back of her room, and one day when she was chatting up the thick-lipped Christian next door, Jayamma sold them all to the scrap-paper Muslim. Ha! Showed her!

As Jayamma narrated the story of the infamous reading-and-writing scam, the door to the servants' quarters opened; Shaila's face popped out and she screamed at Jayamma at the top of her voice.

That evening the advocate spoke during dinner: 'I hear there's been some disturbance or other in the house every day this week . . . it's important to keep things quiet. Karthik has to prepare for his exams.'

Jayamma, who had been carrying away the lentil stew using the edge of her sari against the heat, put the stew down on the table.

'It's not me making the noise, Master – it's that Hoyka girl! She doesn't know our Brahmin ways.'

'She may be a Hoyka . . .' the advocate licked the rice grains clinging to his fingers – '. . . but she is clean and works well.'

As she cleared the table after dinner, Jayamma trembled at the reproach.

Only once the lights were off in the house, and she lay in the prayer room with the familiar fumes of DDT about her, and opened the little black box, did she calm down. The baby God was smiling at her.

O, when it came to troubles and horrors, Krishna, who had seen what Jayamma had seen? She told the patient deity the story of how she first came to Kittur; how her sister-in-law had commanded her: 'Jayamma, you have to leave us and go, the advocate's wife is in a hospital in Bangalore, someone has to take care of little Karthik' – that was supposed to be just a month or two. Now, it had been eight months since she had seen her little nephew Brijju, or held him in her arms, or played cricket with him. Oh yes, these were troubles, Baby Krishna.

The next morning, she dropped her ladle in the lentils again. Karthik had poked her midriff from behind.

She followed him out of the kitchen and into the servants' room. She watched the boy as he looked at the diagram on the floor and the blue marble at the centre of it.

In his eyes the old servant saw the gleam – the master's possessive gleam that she had seen so many times in forty years.

'Look at that,' Karthik said. 'The nerve of that girl, drawing this thing in my own house . . .'

The crouching pair sat down by the yellow grille and watched Shaila move along the far wall of the compound towards the Christian's house. A wide well, covered with green netting, made a bump in the back of the house. Hens and roosters, hidden by the wall, ran around the well and clucked incessantly. Rosie was standing at the wall. Shaila and the Christian talked for a while. It was a brilliant, flickering afternoon. As the light emerged and retreated at rapid intervals, the glossy green canopies of the coconut trees blazed and dimmed like bursts of fireworks.

The girl wandered aimlessly after Rosie left. They saw her bending by the jasmine plants to tear off a few flowers and put them in her hair. A little later, Jayamma saw Karthik begin to scratch his leg in long, shearing strokes, like a bear scratching the sides of a tree. From his thighs, his rasping fingers moved upward towards his groin. Jayamma watched with a sense of disgust. What would the boy's mother say, if she could see what he was doing right now?

271

The girl was walking by the clothes-line. The thin cotton sheets hung out to dry turned incandescent, like cinema screens, when the light emerged from the clouds. Inside one of the glowing sheets, the girl made a round, dark bulge, like a thing inside a womb. A keening noise rose from the white sheet. She had begun singing:

'A star is whispering
Of my heart's deep longing
To see you once more,
My baby-child, my darling, my king.'

'I know that nursery rhyme . . . My brother's wife sings it to Brijju . . . my little nephew . . .'
'Quiet. She'll hear you.'
Shaila had re-emerged from the hanging clothes. She drifted towards the far end of the back yard, where neem trees mingled with coconut palms.
'Does she think about her mother and sisters often, I wonder . . .' Jayamma whispered. 'What kind of a life is this for a girl, away from her family?'
'I'm tired of this waiting!' Karthik grumbled.
'Brother, wait!'
But he was already in the servants' room. A triumphant shriek: Karthik came out with the blue marble.

In the evening, Jayamma was on the threshold of the kitchen, winnowing rice. Her glasses had slid halfway down her nose and her brow was furrowed. She turned towards the servants' room, which was bolted from the inside, and from which came the sound of sobbing, and shouted: 'Stop crying. You've got to get tough. Servants like us, who work for others, have to learn to be tough.'

Swallowing her tears audibly, Shaila shouted back through the bolted door: 'Shut up, you self-pitying Brahmin hag! You told Karthik I had black magic!'

'Don't accuse me of things like that! I never told him you did black magic!'

'Liar! Liar!'

'Don't call me a liar, you Hoyka! Why do you draw triangles on the ground, if not to practise black magic! You don't fool me for a minute!'

'Can't you see those triangles were just part of a game? Are you losing your mind, you old hag?'

Jayamma slammed down the winnow; the rice grains were splattered about the threshold. She went into the prayer room and closed the door.

She woke up and overheard a sob-drenched monologue: it was coming from the servants' quarters, and so loud that it had penetrated the wall of the prayer room.

'I don't want to be here . . . I didn't want to leave my friends, and our fields, and our cows, and come here. But my mother said: "You have to go to the city and work for the advocate Panchinalli, otherwise, where will you get the gold necklace? And who will marry you without a gold necklace?" But

273

ever since I came, I've seen no gold necklace – just trouble, trouble, trouble!'

Jayamma shouted into the wall at once: 'Trouble, trouble, trouble – see how she talks like an old woman! This is nothing, your misfortune. I've seen real trouble!'

The sobbing stopped. Jayamma told the lower-caste a few of her own troubles. At dinner, Jayamma came with the trough of rice to the servants' living room. She banged on the door, but Shaila would not open.

'Oh, what a haughty little miss she is!'

She kept banging on the door, until it opened. Then she served the girl rice and lentil stew, and watched to make sure that it was eaten.

The next morning, the two servants were sitting at the threshold together.

'Say, Jayamma, what's the news of the world?'

Shaila was beaming. Flowers in her hair, and Johnson's powder on her face again. Jayamma looked up from the paper with a scornful expression.

'Oh, why do you ask me, you can read and write, can't you?'

'C'mon, Jayamma, you know we lower-castes aren't meant to do things like that . . .' The little girl smiled ingratiatingly. 'If you Brahmins don't read for us, where will we learn anything . . .'

'Sit down,' the old woman said haughtily. She turned the pages over slowly and read out from the news items that interested her.

'They say that in Tumkur district, a holy man

has mastered the art of flying through willpower, and can go seventeen feet up in the air and bring himself down too.'

'Really?' The girl was sceptical. 'Has anyone actually seen him do this, or are they simply believing him?'

'Of course they saw him do it!' Jayamma retorted, tapping on the news item as proof. 'Haven't you ever seen magic?'

Shaila giggled hysterically; then she ran into the back yard and dashed into the coconut trees; and then Jayamma heard the song again.

She waited till Shaila came back to the house and said: 'What will your husband think, if he sees you looking like a savage? Your hair is a mess.'

So the girl sat down on the threshold, and Jayamma oiled her hair and combed it into gleaming black tresses that would set any man's heart on fire.

At eight o'clock the old lady and the girl went together to watch TV. They watched till ten, then returned to their rooms when Karthik switched it off.

Halfway through the night, Shaila woke up to see the door to her room pushed open.

'Sister . . .'

Through the darkness Shaila saw a silver-haired head peering in.

'Sister . . . let me spend the night here . . . there are ghosts outside the storage room, yes . . .'

Almost crawling into the servants' quarters,

Jayamma, breathing hard and sweating profusely, propped herself against a wall of the room and sank her head between her knees. The girl went out to see what was happening in the storage room; she came back giggling.

'Jayamma . . . those aren't ghosts, those are just two cats, fighting in the Christian's house . . . that's all . . .'

But the old lady was already asleep, her silver hair spread out on the ground.

From then on, Jayamma began to come to sleep in Shaila's room whenever she heard the two screeching cat-demons outside her room.

It was the day before the Navaratri festival. Still no word from home, nor from the advocate, about when she might be going home. The price of jaggery had gone up again. So had kerosene. Jayamma read in the papers that a holy man had learned to fly from tree to tree in a grove in Kerala – but only if the trees were areca nut trees. There was going to be a partial solar eclipse the following year, and that might signal the end of the earth. V. P. Singh, a member of the Union Cabinet, had accused the prime minister of corruption. The government could fall any day and there was going to be chaos in Delhi.

That night, after dinner, Jayamma proposed to the advocate that on the holy day she take Karthik to the Kittamma Devi temple near the train station.

'He should not fall out of the habit of prayer now that his mother is no more, should he?' she said meekly.

'That's a good idea . . .' The advocate picked up his newspaper.

Jayamma breathed in for courage.

'If you could give me a few rupees towards the rickshaw . . .'

She knocked at the little girl's room. She opened her fist triumphantly.

'Five rupees! The advocate gave me five rupees!'

Jayamma took a bath in the servants' toilet, lathering herself thoroughly in sandalwood soap. Changing from her vermilion sari to her purple one, she walked up to the boy's room relishing the fragrance of her own skin, feeling like someone important.

'Get dressed, brother – we'll miss the five o'clock pooja.'

The boy was on his bed, punching at the buttons of a small hand-held electronic game – Bip! Bip! Bip!

'I'm not coming.'

'Brother – it's a temple. We should go!'

'No.'

'Brother . . . What would your mother say if she were . . .'

The boy put his game down for a second. He walked up to the door of his room and slammed it in Jayamma's face.

She lay in the storage room, seeking comfort in

the fumes of DDT and the sight of the baby Krishna's silver buttocks. The door creaked open. A small black face, coated in Johnson and Johnson's Baby Powder, smiled at her.

'Jayamma – Jayamma – take me to the temple instead . . .'

The two of them sat quietly in the autorickshaw.

'Wait here,' Jayamma said at the entrance to the temple. She bought a packet of flowers with fifty paise of her own money.

'Here.' She guided the girl to place the basket in the hands of the priest when they were in the temple.

A throng of devotees had gathered around the silver linga. Little boys jumped high to strike the temple bells around the deity. They struggled in vain and then their fathers hoicked them up. Jayamma caught Shaila leaping high at a bell.

'Shall I lift you up?'

At five, the pooja got under way. A bronze plate; flames rose from camphor cubes. Two women blew giant conches; a brass gong was struck, faster and faster. Then, one of the Brahmins rushed out with a copper plate that burned at one end and Jayamma dropped a coin into it, while the girl reached forward with her palms for the holy fire.

The two of them sat out on the verandah of the temple, on whose walls hung the giant drums that were played at weddings. Jayamma remarked on the scandal of a woman decked in a sleeveless blouse heading towards the temple gate. Shaila thought the sleeveless style was quite 'sporty'. A screaming child was being pulled along by her father to the temple door. She quietened down when Jayamma and Shaila both began to pet her.

The two servants left the temple reluctantly. Birds rose up from the trees as they waited for a rickshaw. Bands of incandescent cloud piled up one above the other like military decorations as the sun set. Jayamma began fighting with the rickshaw driver over the price to go home, and Shaila giggled the whole time, infuriating the old woman and the driver alike.

'Jayamma – have you heard the Big News?'

The old lady looked up from the newspaper spread out on the threshold. She removed her glasses and blinked at the girl.

'About the price of jaggery?'

'No, not that.'

'About the man in Kasargod who gave birth?'

'No, not that, either.' The girl grinned shyly. 'I'm getting married.'

Jayamma's lips parted. She turned her head down, took off her glasses, rubbed her eyes.

'When?'

'Next month. The marriage has been fixed. The advocate told me this yesterday. He will send my gold necklace directly to my village.'

'So you think you're a queen now, huh?' Jayamma snapped. 'Because you're getting hitched to some village bumpkin!'

She saw Shaila run to the compound wall to spread the tidings to the thick-lipped Christian. 'I'm getting married, I'm getting married,' the girl sung sweetly all day long.

Jayamma cautioned her from the kitchen: 'You think it's any big deal being married? Don't you know what happened to my sister, Ambika?'

But the girl was too full of herself to listen. She just sang all day: 'I'm getting married, I'm getting married!'

So at night, it was the baby Krishna who got to hear the story of the luckless Ambika, punished for her sins in a previous life:

Ambika, the sixth daughter and the last to be married, was the family beauty. A rich doctor wanted her for his son. Excellent news! When the groom came to see Ambika, he left for the bathroom repeatedly. 'See how shy he is,' the women all giggled. On the wedding night, he lay with his back turned to Ambika's face. He coughed all night. In the morning, she saw blood on the sheets. He notified her that she had married a man with advanced tuberculosis. He had wanted to be honest, but his mother would not let him. 'Someone has put black magic on your family, you wretched girl,' he said, as his body was racked by fits of coughing. A month later, he was dead on a hospital bed. His mother told the village that the girl, and all her sisters, were cursed; and no one would agree to marry any of the other children.

'And that's the true story of why I'm a virgin,' Jayamma wanted the infant Krishna to know. 'In fact, I had such thick hair, such golden skin, I was considered a beauty, you know that?' She raised her eyebrows archly, like a film actress, suspecting that the little god did not entirely believe her. 'Sometimes I thank my stars I never married. What if I too had been deceived, like Ambika? Better a spinster than a widow, any day . . . And yet that little lower-caste can't stop singing about it every minute of the morning . . .' Lying in the dark, Jayamma mimicked the little lower-caste's voice for the baby god's benefit: 'I'm getting married, I'm getting married . . .'

The day came for Shaila's departure. The advocate said he would himself drive the girl home in his green Ambassador.

'I'm going, *Jayamma*.'

The old lady was brushing her silver hair on the threshold. She felt that Shaila was pronouncing the name with deliberate tartness. 'I'm going to get married.' The old lady kept brushing her hair. 'Write to me sometime, won't you, Jayamma? You Brahmins are such fine letter writers, the best of the best . . .'

Jayamma tossed the plastic comb into a corner of the storage room. 'To hell with you, you little lower-caste vermin!'

The weeks passed. Now she had to do the girl's work too. By the time dinner was served and the dishes cleaned, she was spent. The advocate made no mention of hiring a new servant.

She understood that, from now on, it was up to her to perform the lower-caste's work too.

In the evenings, she took to wandering in the back yard with her long silver hair down at the sides. One evening, Rosie, the thick-lipped Christian, waved at her.

'What happened to Shaila? Did she get married?'
Thrown into confusion, Jayamma grinned.
She started to watch Rosie. How carefree those Christians were – eating whatever they wanted, marrying and divorcing whenever they felt like it.

One night the two demons came back. She lay paralysed for many minutes, listening to the screeching of the spirits, which had disguised themselves as cats once again. She clutched the idol of baby Krishna, rubbing its silver buttocks while sitting on a bag of rice surrounded by the moat of DDT; she began to sing:

'A star is whispering
Of my heart's deep longing
To see you once more,
My baby-child, my darling, my king . . .'

That next evening, the advocate spoke to her at dinner. He had received a letter from Shaila's mother.

'They said they were not happy with the size of the gold necklace. After I spent two thousand rupees on it, can you believe it?'

'Some people are never satisfied, Master . . . what can be done?'

He scratched at his bare chest with his left hand and belched. 'In this life, a man is always the servant of his servants.'

That night she could not go to sleep from anxiety. What if the advocate cheated her out of her pay too?

'For you!' One morning, Karthik tossed a letter onto the rice-winnower. Jayamma shook the grains of rice off it and tore it open with trembling fingers. Only one person in the world ever wrote her letters – her sister-in-law in Salt Market Village. Spreading it out on the ground, she put together the words one by one.

'The advocate has let it be known that he intends to move to Bangalore. You, of course, will be returned to us. Do not expect to stay here long; we are already looking for another house to dispatch you to.'

She folded the letter slowly and tucked it into the midriff of her sari. It felt like a slap to her face: the advocate had not bothered to tell her the news. 'Well, let it be, who am I to him, just another servant woman.'

A week later, he came into the storage room and stood at the threshold, as Jayamma got up hurriedly, trying to put her hair in order. 'Your money has been sent already, to your sister-in-law in Salt Market Village,' he said.

This was the usual agreement anywhere

283

Jayamma worked; the wages never came to her directly.

The advocate paused.

'The boy needs someone to take care of him . . . I have relatives in Bangalore . . .'

'I only hope for the best for you and for Master Karthik,' she said, bowing before him with slow dignity.

That Sunday, she had collected all her belongings over the past year into the same suitcase with which she had come to the house. The only sad part was saying goodbye to the baby Krishna.

The advocate was not going to drop her off; she would walk to the bus stop herself. The bus was not due till four o'clock, and she walked about the back yard, amidst the swaying garments on the clothes-line. She thought of Shaila – that girl had been running around this back yard, her hair loose, like an irresponsible brat; and now she was a married woman, the mistress of a household. Everyone changed and moved up in life, she thought. Only I remain the same: a virgin. She turned to the house with a sombre thought: this is the last time I will see this house, where I have spent more than a year of my life. She remembered all the houses she had been sent to, these past forty years, so that she could fatten other people's children. She had taken back nothing from her time at all those houses; she was still unmarried, childless, and penniless. Like a glass from which clean water had been drunk, her life showed no trace of the years that had passed – except that her body had grown old, her eyes were weak, and her knee joints ached. Nothing will ever change for me till I die, thought old Jayamma.

All at once, her gloom was gone. She had seen a blue rubber ball, half hidden by a hibiscus plant in the back yard. It looked like one of the balls Karthik played cricket with; had it been left out here because it was punctured? Jayamma had brought it right up to her nose for a good examination. Although she could not see a hole anywhere, when she squeezed it next to her cheek, she felt a tickling hiss of air on her skin.

With a servant's instinct for caution, the old cook glanced around the garden. Breathing in deep, she tossed the blue ball to the side of the house; it smacked against the wall and came back to her with a single bounce.

Good enough!

Jayamma turned the ball over and examined its skin, faded but still with a nice blue sheen. She sniffed at it. It would do very nicely.

She came to Karthik, who was in his room, on the bed: Bip! Bip! Bip! She thought how much he resembled the image of his mother in photographs when he beetled his brow to concentrate on the game; the furrow in his brow was like a bookmark left there by the dead woman.

'Brother . . .'

'Hm?'

'I'm leaving for my brother's home today . . .

I'm going back to my village. I'm not coming back.'

'Hm.'

'May the blessings of your dear mother shine on you always.'

'Hm.'

'Brother . . .'

'What is it?' his voice crackled with irritation. 'Why are you always pestering me?'

'Brother . . . that blue ball out in the garden, the one that's punctured, you don't use it, do you?'

'Which ball?'

'. . . Can I take that with me for my little Brijju? He loves playing cricket, but sometimes there's no money to buy a ball . . .'

'No.'

The boy did not look up. He punched at the buttons on his game.

Bip!

Bip!

Bip!

'Brother . . . you gave the lower-caste girl a gold necklace . . . can't you give me just a blue ball for Brijesh?'

Bip!

Bip!

Bip!

Jayamma thought with horror of all the food she had fed this fat creature, how it was the sweat of her brow, dripping into the lentil broth in the heat of that little kitchen, that had nourished him until here he was, round and plump, like an animal bred in the back yard of a Christian's house. She had a vision of chasing this fat little boy with a meat-cleaver; she saw herself catch him by the hair and raise the cleaver over his pleading head. Bang! She brought it down – his tongue spread out, his features bulged out, and he was . . .

The old lady shuddered.

'You are a motherless child, and a Brahmin. I don't want to think badly of you . . . farewell, brother . . .'

She went out into the garden with her suitcase, shooting a final glance at the ball. She went to the gate and stopped. Her eyes were full of the tears of the righteous. The sun mocked her from between the trees.

Just then, Rosie came out of the Christian's house. She stopped and looked at the suitcase in Jayamma's hand. She spoke. For a moment Jayamma couldn't understand a word, then the Christian's message sounded loud and clear in her mind:

Take the ball, you Brahmin fool!

Swaying coconut palms rushed past. Jayamma was on the bus back to Salt Market Village, sitting next to a woman who was returning from the sacred city of Benares. Jayamma could pay no attention to the holy lady's stories about the great temples she had seen . . . her thoughts were all on the thing she was concealing in her sari, tucked against her tummy . . . the blue ball with the small hole . . . the one she had just stolen . . . She could not believe that she, Jayamma, the daughter of good Brahmins of Salt Market Village, had done such a thing!

Eventually the holy woman next to her fell asleep. The snoring filled Jayamma with fear for her soul. What would the gods do to her, she wondered, as the bus rattled over the dirt road; what would she be in the next life? A cockroach, a silver-fish that lived in old books, an earthworm, a maggot in a pile of cowshit, or something even filthier.

Then a strange thought came to her: maybe if she sinned enough in this life, she would be sent back as a Christian in the next one . . .

The thought made her feel light-headed with joy; and she dozed off almost at once.

DAY FIVE (EVENING): THE CATHE-DRAL OF OUR LADY OF VALENCIA

It cannot be easily explained why the Cathedral of Our Lady of Valencia still remains incomplete, despite so many attempts to finish the work in recent years and so much money sent by expatriates working in Kuwait. The original baroque structure dating to 1691 was entirely rebuilt in 1890. Only one bell tower was left incomplete, and it remains incomplete to the present day. Scaffolding has covered the north tower almost continuously since 1981; work resumes fitfully and stops again, either because of a lack of funds, or the death of a significant priest. Even in its incomplete state, the cathedral is considered Kittur's most important tourist attraction. Of particular interest are the frescoes of the miraculously preserved corpse of St Francis Xavier painted on the ceiling of the chapel, and the colossal mural entitled *Allegory of Europe Bringing Science and Enlightenment into the East Indies* behind the altar.

George D'Souza, the mosquito-man, had caught himself a princess. Evidence for this claim would be produced at sunset, when work ended on the cathedral. Until then George was only going to suck on his watermelon, drop hints to his friends, and grin.

He was sitting on a pyramid-shaped mound of granite stones in the compound in front of the cathedral, with his metal backpack and his spray-gun to one side.

Cement mixers were growling on both sides of the cathedral building, crushing granite stones and mud, and disgorging mounds of black mortar. On a scaffolding, bricks and cement were being hoisted up to the top of the northern bell tower. George's friends Guru and Michael poured water from plastic one-litre bottles into the cement mixer. As the machines dripped into the red soil of the compound, rivulets of blood-red water cascaded down from the cathedral, as if it were a heart left on a piece of newspaper to drain.

When he was done with his melon, George smoked beedi after beedi. He closed his eyes and at once construction workers' children began to spray each other with pesticide. He chased them for a while, then returned to the pyramid of stones and sat on it.

He was a small, lithe, dark fellow who seemed to be in his early forties – but since physical labour accelerates ageing, he might have been younger, perhaps even in his late twenties. He had a long scar under his left eye, and a pockmarked face which suggested a recent bout of chickenpox. His biceps were long and slender: not the glossy rippling kind bulked up in expensive gyms, but the hewed-from-necessity sinews of the working poor, stone hard and deeply etched from a lifetime of having to lift things for other people.

At sunset, firewood was piled up in front of George's stone pyramid, a flame lit, and rice and fish curry cooked in a black pot. A transistor radio was turned on. Mosquitoes buzzed. Four men sat around the flickering fire, their faces burnished, smoking beedis. Around George were his old colleagues – Guru, James, and Vinay; they had worked with him on the construction site before his dismissal.

Taking his green notebook from his pocket, he opened it to the middle page, where he had kept something pink, like the tongue of an animal he had caught and skinned.

It was a twenty-rupee note. Vinay fingered the thing in wonder; even after it was gently prised away from him by Guru, he could not take his eyes off it.

'You got this for spraying pesticide in her house?'

'No, no, no. She saw me do the spraying and I guess she was impressed, because she asked me to do some gardening work.'

'If she's rich, doesn't she have a gardener?'

'She does – but the fellow is always drunk. So I did his work.'

George described it – removing the dead log from the path of the gutter in the back yard and carrying it a few yards away, removing the muck that had been sedimented in the gutter, allowing the mosquitoes to breed. Then trimming the hedges in the front yard with a giant clipper.

'That's all?' Vinay's jaw dropped. 'Twenty rupees for that?'

George blew smoke into the air with a luxuriant wickedness. He put the twenty-rupee note back in the notebook, and the notebook in his pocket.

'That's why I say: she's my princess.'

'The rich own the whole world,' said Vinay, with a sigh that was half in rebellion and half in acceptance of this fact. 'What is twenty rupees to them?'

Guru, who was a Hindu, generally spoke little and was considered 'deep' by his friends. He had been as far as Bombay and could read signs in English.

'Let me tell you about the rich. Let me tell you about the rich.'

'All right: tell us.'

'I'm telling you about the rich. In Bombay, at the Oberoi Hotel in Nariman Point, there is a dish called 'Beef Vindaloo' that costs five hundred rupees.'

'No way!'

'Yes, five hundred! It was in the English news-paper on Sunday. Now you know about the rich.'

'What if you order the dish and then you realize

you made a mistake and you don't like it? Do you get your money back?'

'No, but it doesn't matter to you if you're rich. You know what the biggest difference is, between being rich and being like us? The rich can make mistakes again and again. We make only one mistake and that's it for us.'

After dinner, George took everyone else out to drinks at the arrack shop. He had drunk and eaten off their generosity since being fired from the construction site: the mosquito-spraying, which Guru had arranged for him through a connection in the city Corporation, was only a once-a-week job.

'Next Sunday,' Vinay said, as they headed out of the arrack shop at midnight, dead drunk. 'I'm coming to see your fucking princess.'

'I'm not telling you where she lives,' George cried. 'She's my secret.' The others were annoyed, but didn't press the issue. They were happy enough to see George in a good mood, which was a rare thing, since he was a bitter man.

They went to sleep in tents at the back of the cathedral construction site. Since it was September, there was still the danger of rain, but George slept out in the open, looking at the stars and thinking of the generous woman who had made this day a happy one for him.

The following Sunday, George strapped on his metal backpack, connected the spray-gun to one of its nozzles, and walked out into Valencia. He stopped at every house along his route, and wherever he saw a gutter or puddle, and at sewage holes he found, he fired his gun: tzzzk . . . tzzzk . . .

He walked the half-kilometre from the cathedral and then turned left, into one of the alleys that slide downhill from Valencia. He took the route down, firing his gun into the gutters by the side of the road: tzzzk . . . tzzzk . . . tzzzk . . .

The rain had ended and muddy raucous torrents no longer gushed downhill, but the twinkling branches of roadside trees and the sloping tiled roofs of the houses still dripped into the road, where the loose stones braided the water into shining rivulets that flowed into the gutters with a soft music. Thick green moss coated the gutters like a sediment of bile, and reeds sprouted up from the bedrock, and small swampy patches of stale water gleamed out of nooks and crannies like liquid emeralds.

A dozen women in colourful saris, each with a green or mauve bandana around her head, were cutting the grass at the sides of the road. Swaying in concert as they sang strange Tamil songs, the migrant workers were down in the gutters, where they scraped the moss and pulled the weeds out from between the stones with violent tugs, as if they were taking them back from children, while others scooped out handfuls of black gunk from the bottom of the gutters and heaped it up in dripping mounds.

He looked at them with contempt and he thought: but I have fallen to the level of these people myself!

He grew moody; he began to spray carelessly; he even avoided spraying a few puddles deliberately.

By and by, he got to 10A, and realized that he was outside his princess's house. He unlatched the red gate and went in.

The windows were closed; but close to the house he could hear the sound of water hissing inside. She is taking a shower in the middle of the day, he thought. Rich women can do things like this.

He had immediately guessed, when he saw the woman the previous week, that her husband was away. You could tell, after a while, with these women whose husbands work in the Gulf: they have an air of not having been around a man for a long time. Her husband had left her well compensated for his absence: the only chauffeur-driven car in all of Valencia, a white Ambassador in the driveway, and the only air conditioner in the lane, which jutted out of her bedroom and over the jasmine plants in her garden, whirring and dripping water.

The driver of the white Ambassador was nowhere around.

He must be off drinking somewhere again, George thought. He had seen an old cook somewhere in the back the previous time. An old lady and a derelict driver – that was all this lady had in the house with her.

A gutter led from the garden into the back yard and he followed its path, spraying into it: tzzzk . . . tzzzk . . . The gutter was blocked again. He got down into the filth and muck of the blocked gutters, carefully applying his gun at different angles, pausing periodically to examine his work. He pressed the mouth of the spray-gun against the side of the gutter. The spraying sound stopped. A white froth, like the one that is produced when a snake is made to bite on a glass to release its venom, spread over the mosquito larvae. Then he tightened a knob on his spray-gun, clicked it into a groove on his backpack canister, and went to find her once again with the book she had to sign.

'Hey!' a woman peeped out a window. 'Who are you?'

'I'm the mosquito-man. I was here last week!'

The window closed. Sounds came from various parts of the house, things were unbolted, slammed, and shut, and then she was before him again – his princess. Mrs Gomes, the woman of house 10A, was a tall woman, approaching her forties now, who wore bright red lipstick and a Western-style gown that exposed her arms nine-tenths of the way up her shoulder. Of the three kinds of women in the world – 'traditional', 'modern', and 'working' – Mrs Gomes was an obvious member of the 'modern' tribe.

'You didn't do a good job last time,' she said

and showed him red welts on her hands, then stepped back and lifted up the edge of her long green gown to expose her ravished ankles. 'Your spraying didn't do any good.'

He felt hot with embarrassment, but he also did not dare take his eyes off what he was being shown.

'The problem is not my spraying, but your back yard,' he retorted. 'Another twig has blocked the gutters, and I think there's a dead animal of some kind, a mongoose maybe, blocking the flow of water. That's why the mosquitoes keep breeding. Come and see if you don't believe me,' he suggested.

She shook her head. 'The back yard is filthy. I never go there.'

'I'll clean it up again,' he said. 'That will get rid of the mosquitoes better than my spray-gun.'

She frowned. 'How much do you want to do this?'

Her tone annoyed him, so he said: 'Nothing.'

He went around to the back yard, got into the gutter, and began attacking the gunk. How these people think they can buy us like cattle! – How much do you want to do this? How much for that?

Half an hour later, he rang the bell with blackened hands; after a few seconds he heard her shout: 'Come over here.'

He followed the voice to a closed window.

'Open it!'

He put his blackened hands to a small crack between the two wooden shutters of the window and pulled them apart. Mrs Gomes was reading in her bed.

He stuck his pencil into the book and held it out.

'What should I do with the book?' she asked, bringing the smell of freshly washed hair with her to the window.

He held his dirty thumb on one line. House 10A: Mr Roger Gomes.

'Do you want some tea?' she asked, as she forged her husband's signature on his book.

He was dumbfounded; he had never been offered tea before on his job. Mostly out of fear of what this rich lady might do if he refused, he said yes.

An old servant, perhaps the cook, came to the back door and regarded him with suspicion as Mrs Gomes asked her to get some tea.

The old cook came back a few minutes later, a glass of tea in her hand; she looked at the mosquito-man with scorn and put the glass down on the threshold for him to pick up.

He came up the three steps, took the cup, and then went back down and took another three steps further back, before he began to sip.

'How long have you been doing this job?'

'Six months.'

He sipped the tea. Seized by a sudden inspiration, he said: 'I have a sister in my village whom I have to support. Maria. She is a good girl, Madam. She can cook well. Do you need a cook, Madam?'

The princess shook her head. 'I've got a very good cook. Sorry.'

George finished his tea and put the glass down at the foot of the steps, holding it an extra second, to make sure it didn't fall over as he left it.

'Will the problem in my back yard start again?'

'For sure. A mosquito is an evil thing, Madam. It causes malaria and filaria,' he said, telling her of Sister Lucy in his village, who got malaria of the brain. 'She said she was going to flap-flap-flap her wasted arms like a hummingbird until she got to Holy Jerusalem'; using his arms, and gyrating around the parked car, he showed her how.

She let out a sudden wild laugh. He seemed a grave and serious man, so she had not expected this burst of levity from him; she had never heard a person of the lower classes be so funny before. She looked him over from head to toe, feeling that she was seeing him for the first time.

He noticed that she laughed heartily, and snorted, like a peasant woman. He had not expected this; women of good breeding were not meant to laugh so crudely and openly, and her behaviour confused him.

In a weary voice, she added: 'Matthew is supposed to clean the back yard. But he's not even here often enough to do the driving, forget about the back yard. Always out, drinking.'

Then her face lit up with an idea: 'You do it.' she said. 'You can be a part-time gardener for me. I'll pay you.'

George was about to say yes, but something within him resisted, disliking the casual way the job had been offered.

'That's not my kind of work. Taking shit out of back yards. But I will do it for you, Madam. I will do anything for you, because you are a good person. I can see into your soul.'

She laughed again.

'Start next week,' she said, vestiges of the laugh still rippling on her face, and closed the door.

When he was gone, she opened the door to her back yard. She rarely went out there: it was strong with the smell of fecund black soil, overgrown with weeds, the air tinged with sewage. She smelled the pesticide; it drew her out of the house. She heard a sound and recognized that the mosquito-man was still somewhere in her neighbourhood.

Tzzzk . . . tzzzk; in her mind she followed it as it sounded from round the neighbourhood – first at the Monteiros' house; then to Dr Karkada's compound; then at the Valencia Jesuit Teachers' College and Seminary: tzzzk . . . tzzzk . . . tzzzk – before she lost track of it.

George was on the pile of stones, waiting for other men who felt about their work as he did, and then they would move together to an arrack shop close by, to start drinking.

'What's got into you?' the other guys asked him later that evening. 'Hardly a word out of you.'

After an initial hour of raucousness, he had

become sullen. He was thinking of the man and the woman – the ones he had seen on the cover of his princess's novel. They were in a car; the wind was blowing through the woman's hair and the man was smiling. In the background, there was an aeroplane. Words in English, the title of the novel, in silver letters, hovered over the scene, like a benediction from the God of good living.

He thought of the woman who could afford to spend her days reading such books, in the comfort of her home, with the air conditioner on at all times.

'The rich abuse us, man. It's always, here, take twenty rupees, kiss my feet. Get into the gutter. Clean my shit. It's always like that.'

'There he goes again,' Guru chuckled. 'It was this talk that got him fired in the first place, but he hasn't changed at all. Still so bitter.'

'Why should I change? Am I lying?' George shouted back: 'The rich lie in bed reading books, and live alone without families, and eat five-hundred-rupee dishes called . . . what was that thing called? Vindoo? Vindiloo?'

That night he could not sleep. He left the tent and went to the construction site, gazing at the unfinished cathedral for hours and thinking about that woman in 10A.

The next week it was clear to him she had been waiting for him. When he came to her house, she stuck her arm out, rotating it from side to side until he had seen the flesh from 360 degrees.

'No bites,' she said. 'Last week was much better. Your spray is finally working.'

He took charge of her back yard. First, walking with his spray-gun out and his left hand adjusting a knob on his backpack canister, he went down on his knees and drizzled germicide over her gutters. Then, as she watched, he put some order into her long-neglected yard: he dug, and sprayed, and cut, and cleaned for an hour.

That evening, the guys at the construction site could not believe the news.

'It's a full-time job now,' George said. 'The Princess thinks I'm such a good worker she wants me to stay there and sleep in a shed in the back yard. She's paying me double what I get now. And I don't have to be a mosquito-man any more. It's perfect.'

'We'll never see you again, I bet,' Guru said, flicking his beedi to the ground.

'That's not true,' George protested. 'I'll come down to drink every evening.'

Guru snorted. 'Sure, you will.'

And he was right: they did not see much of George after that.

Every Monday, a white woman dressed in North Indian salwar kameez arrived at the gate and asked him, in English: 'Madam is in?'

He opened the gate, and bowed, and said: 'Yes. She is in.'

She was from England; she had come to teach

yoga and breathing to Madam. The air conditioner was turned off and George heard the sound of deep breathing from the bedroom. Half an hour later, the white woman emerged and said: 'It's amazing, isn't it? Me having to teach you yoga.'

'Yes, it's sad. We Indians have forgotten everything about our own civilization.'

Then the white woman and Madam walked around the garden for a while. On Tuesday mornings, Matthew, his eyes red and his breath reeking of arrack, drove Madam to the Lion Ladies' meeting at the club on Rose Lane. That seemed to be the extent of Mrs Gomes's social life. When they drove out, George held the gate open: as the car passed him, he saw Matthew turn and glare.

He's frightened of me, George thought, as he went back to trimming the plants in the garden. Does he think I will try to take over from him as driver one day?

It was not a thought he had entertained until then.

When the car came back, he looked at it with disapproval: its sides were filthy. He hosed it down and then wiped the outsides with a dirty rag, and the insides with a clean rag. The thought came to him as he worked that cleaning the car was not his job, as gardener, he was doing something extra – but of course Madam wouldn't notice. They never have any gratitude, the rich, do they?

'You've done a very good job with the car,' Mrs Gomes said in the evening. 'I am grateful.'

George was ashamed of himself. He thought: this rich woman really was different from other rich people.

'I'll do anything for you, Madam,' he said.

He kept a distance of about five or six feet between them whenever they talked; sometimes, in the course of conversation, the distance contracted, perfume made his nostrils expand, and he would automatically, with little backward steps, re-establish the proper radius between mistress and servant.

The cook brought him tea in the evenings and chatted to him for hours. He had not yet gone inside the house, but from the old woman he came to realize that its share of wonders went far beyond an air conditioner. That enormous white box he saw whenever the back door opened was a machine that did washing – and drying – automatically, the old cook said.

'Her husband wanted her to use it and she didn't. They never agreed on anything. Plus,' she said in a conspiratorial whisper, 'no children. That always causes problems.'

'What drove them apart?'

'That way she laughs,' the old woman said. 'He said she laughed like a devil.'

He had noticed it, too: high-pitched, savage, like the laugh of a child or an animal, gloating and wanton. He always stopped work to listen when it ricocheted from her room; and he often heard it elsewhere even in the creak made by the opening

304

of a door, or the particular cadence of an unusual bird-cry. He understood what her husband had meant.

'Are you educated, George?' Mrs Gomes asked one day, in a surprised tone. She had found him reading the newspaper.

'Yes and no, Madam. I studied till the tenth standard, Madam, but I failed the SSLC.'

'Failed?' she asked with a smile. 'How can anyone fail the SSLC? It is such a simple exam . . .'

'I could do all the sums, Madam. I passed Mathematics with sixty marks out of hundred. I only failed Social Studies, because I could not mark Madras and Bombay on the map of India that they gave me. What could I do, Madam? – we had not studied those things in class. I got thirty-four in Social Studies – one mark fail!'

'Why didn't you take the exam again?' she asked.

'Take it again?' He uttered the words as if he did not understand them. 'I began working,' he said, because he did not know how to answer her. 'I worked for six years, Madam. The rains were bad last year and there was no agriculture. We heard there were jobs for Christians at the construction site – the cathedral, I mean – and a bunch of us from the village came up here. I was working as a carpenter there, Madam. Where was the time to study?'

'Why did you leave the construction site?'

'I have a bad back,' he said.

'Should you be doing this kind of work, then?' she

asked. 'Won't it hurt your back? And then you'll say that I broke your back, and make a fuss about it!'

'My back is fine, Madam. My back is fine. Don't you see me bent over and working every day?'

'So why did you say your back was bad?' she demanded. He said nothing, and she shook her head and said: 'Oh, you villagers are impossible to understand!'

The next day he was waiting for her. When she came out into the garden after her bath, wiping her wet hair dry with a towel, George approached her and said: 'He slapped me, Madam. I slapped him back.'

'What are you talking about, George? Who slapped you?'

He explained: he had got into a fight with his foreman. George pantomimed the exchange of palms, hoping to impress upon her how fast it had been, how reflexive.

'He said I was making eyes at his wife, Madam. But that was untrue. We are honest people in my family, Madam. We used to plough in the village, Madam,' he said. 'And we would find copper coins. These are from the time of Tippu Sultan. They are over a hundred years old. And those coins were taken from me and melted down for copper. I wanted so much to keep them, but I handed them over to Mr Coelho, the landlord. I am not dishonest. I do not steal, or look at another man's woman. This is the truth. Go to the village and ask Mr Coelho. He'll tell you.'

306

She smiled at this; like all villagers, his manner of defending his character was naïve, circuitous, and endearing.

'I trust you,' she said and went in, without locking the door. He peered into the house and saw clocks, red carpets, wooden medallions on the walls, potted plants, things of bronze and silver. Then the door closed again.

She brought tea out herself that day. She put the glass down on the threshold and he scampered up the steps with a bowed head, picked it up, and scampered back down.

'Ah, Madam, but you people have it all and we people have nothing. It's just not fair,' he said, sucking on the tea.

She let out a little laugh. She did not expect such directness from the poor; it was charming.

'It's just not fair, Madam,' he said again. 'You even have a washing machine that you never use. That's how much you have.'

'Are you asking me for more money?' She arched her eyebrows.

'No, Madam, why should I? You pay very well. I don't do things in a roundabout way,' he said. 'If I want it, I'll ask for money.'

'I have problems you don't know about, George. I have problems too.' She smiled and went in. He stood outside, hoping vainly for an explanation.

A little later it began to rain. The foreign yoga teacher came, with an umbrella, through the heavy rain; he ran up to the gate to let her in and then sat in the garage, by the car, eavesdropping on the sound of deep breathing from Madam's bedroom. By the time the yoga session was over, the rain had ended and the garden was sparkling in the sun. The two women seemed excited by the sun – and the garden's carefully tended condition. Mrs Gomes talked to her foreign friend with an arm on her hip; George noticed that, unlike the European woman, his employer had retained her maidenly figure. He supposed it was because she did not have any children.

The lights came on in her bedroom at around six-thirty, and then the noise of water flowing. She was taking a bath; she took a bath every night. It was not necessary, since she bathed again in the morning, and anyway she smelled of wonderful perfume, yet she bathed twice – in hot water, he was sure, coating herself in lather and relaxing her body. She was a woman who did things just for her pleasure.

On Sunday, George walked uphill to attend mass at the cathedral; when he came back, the conditioner was still purring. 'So she does not go to church,' he thought.

Every other Wednesday afternoon, the Ideal Mobile Circulating Library came to the house on a Yamaha motorbike; the librarian-cum-driver of the bike, after pressing the bell, would untie a metal box of books strapped to the back of his motorbike, and place it on the back of the car for her to inspect. Mrs Gomes peered over the books and picked out a couple. When she had made her selection and paid, and gone back inside, George went up to the librarian-cum-driver, who was retying the box to the back of his Yamaha, and tapped him on the shoulder.

'What sort of books does Madam take?'

'Novels.'

The librarian-cum-driver stopped and winked at him. 'Dirty novels. I see dozens like her every day: women with their husbands abroad.'

He bent his finger and wiggled it.

'It still scratches, you know. So they have to read English novels to get rid of it.'

George grinned. But when the Yamaha, kicking up a cloud of dust, turned in a circle and left the garden, he ran to the gate and shouted: 'Don't talk of Madam like that, you bastard!'

At night he lay awake; he wandered about the back yard quietly, making no noise. He was thinking. It seemed to him, when he looked back on it, that his life consisted of things that had not said yes to him, and things that he could not say no to. The SSLC had not said yes to him, and his sister he could not say no to. He could not imagine, for instance, abandoning his sister to her own fate and trying to go back and complete his SSLC examination.

He went out, he walked up the lane and along the main road. The unfinished cathedral was a dark shape against the blue coastal night sky. Lighting a beedi, he walked in circles around the mess of the construction site, looking at familiar things in an unfamiliar way.

The next day, he was waiting for her with an announcement: 'I've stopped drinking, Madam,' he told her. 'I made the decision last night – never another bottle of arrack.'

He wanted her to know; he had the power now, to live any way he wanted. That evening, as he was out in the garden, trimming the leaves on the rose plant, Matthew unlatched the gate and came in. He glared at George, then he walked away into the back yard, to his quarters.

Half an hour later, when Mrs Gomes needed to be driven to the Lion Ladies' meeting, Matthew was nowhere to be seen, even after she yelled into the back yard six times.

'Let me drive, Madam,' he said.

She looked at him sceptically: 'Do you know how to drive?'

'Madam, when you grow up poor, you have to learn to do everything, from farming to driving. Why don't you get in and see for yourself how well I drive?'

'Do you have a licence? Will you kill me?'

'Madam,' he said, 'I would never do anything to put you in the slightest danger.' A moment later he added: 'I would even give my life for you.'

She smiled at that; then she saw that he was saying it in earnest and she stopped smiling. She got into the car and he started the engine, and he became her driver.

'You drive well, George. Why don't you work full-time as my new driver?' she asked him at the end.

'I'll do anything for you, Madam.'

Matthew was dismissed that evening. The cook came to George and said: 'I never liked him. I'm glad you're staying, though.'

George bowed to her. 'You're like my elder sister,' he said and watched her beam happily.

In the mornings he cleaned and washed the car, and sat on Matthew's stool, his legs crossed, humming merrily, and waiting for the moment Madam would command him to take her out. When he drove her to the Lion Ladies' meetings, he wandered about the flagpole in front of the Club, watching the buses go by, around the municipal library. He looked at the buses and the library differently: not as wanderer, a manual worker who got down into gutters and scooped out earth – but like someone with a stake in things. He drove her down to the sea once. She walked towards the water and sat by the rocks, watching the silver waves, while he waited by the car, watching her.

As she got out of the car, he coughed.

'What is it, George?'

'My sister Maria.'

She looked at him with a smile, encouraging him.

'She can cook, Madam. She is clean, and hard-working, and a good Christian girl.'

'I have a cook, George.'

'She's not good, Madam. And she's old. Why don't you get rid of her and have my sister over from the village?'

Her face darkened.

'You think I don't know what you're doing? Trying to take over my household! First you get rid of my driver and now my cook!'

She got in and slammed the door. He smiled; he was not worried. He had planted the seed in her mind; it would germinate, in a little time. He knew now how this woman's mind worked.

That summer, during the water shortage, George showed Mrs Gomes that he was indispensable. He was up at the top of the hill, waiting for the water-tanker to come along; he brought the buckets down himself, filling up her flush and commodes so she did not have to go through the humiliation of rationing her flushes, like everyone else in the neighbourhood. As soon as he heard a rumour that the Corporation was going to release water through the taps for a limited time (they sometimes gave half an hour of water every two or three days), he would come rushing into the house, shouting: 'Madam! Madam!'

She gave him a set of the keys to the back door, so that he could come into the house anytime he heard that the water was going to be on and fill up the buckets.

Thanks to his hard work, at a time when most people couldn't bathe even once every other day,

Madam was still taking her twice-a-day pleasure baths.

'How absurd,' she said, one evening, coming to the back door with her hair wet and falling down her shoulders, rubbing it vigorously with a white towel. 'That in this country, with so much rain, we still have water shortages. When will India ever change?'

He smiled, averting his eyes from her figure and her wet hair.

'George, your pay will be increased,' she said and went back inside, closing the door firmly.

There was more good news for him too, a few evenings later. He saw the old cook leaving, a bag under her arm. She looked at him with baleful eyes as their paths crossed and hissed: 'I know what you're trying to do to her! I told her you'll destroy her name and reputation! But she's fallen under your spell.'

A week after Maria joined the household of 10A, Mrs Gomes came to George as he was tinkering with the engine of the car.

'Your sister's shrimp curry is excellent.'

'Everyone in our family is hard-working, Madam,' he said and got so excited he jerked up his head, whacking it against the bonnet. It stung, but Mrs Gomes had begun to laugh – that sharp, high-pitched animal laugh of hers – and he tried to laugh along with her, while rubbing the red bump on his skull.

Maria was a small, frightened girl who came

with two bags, no English, and no knowledge of life beyond her village. Mrs Gomes had taken a liking to her and allowed her to sleep in the kitchen.

'What do they talk about, inside the house, Madam and that foreign woman?' George asked her, when Maria came to his one-room quarters with his evening meal.

'I don't know,' she said, ladling out his fish curry.

'Why don't you know?'

'I wasn't paying attention,' she said, her voice small, scared, as always, of her brother.

'Well, pay attention! Don't just sit there like a doll, saying "Yes, Madam" and "No, Madam"! Take some initiative! Keep your eyes open!'

On Sundays, he took Maria along to mass at the cathedral; construction stopped in the morning, to let people in, but as they emerged, they could see the contractors getting ready to resume work in the evening.

'Why doesn't Madam come to mass? Isn't she a Christian too?' Maria asked, as they were leaving church.

He took a deep breath. 'The rich do as they want. It's not for us to question them.'

He noticed Mrs Gomes talking to Maria; with her open, generous nature, which did not distinguish between rich and poor, she was becoming more than just a mistress to Maria, but a good friend. It was exactly as he had hoped.

In the evenings he missed his drink, but he filled

the time by walking about, or by listening to a radio and letting his mind drift. He thought: Maria can get married next year. She had a status now as a cook in a rich woman's house. Boys would line up for her back home in the village.

After that, he figured, it would be time for his own marriage, which he had put off so long, out of a combination of bitterness, poverty, and shame. Yes, time for marriage, and children. Yet regret still gnawed at him, created by his contact with this rich woman, that he could have done so much more with his life.

'You're a lucky man, George,' Mrs Gomes said one evening, watching him rub the car with a wet cloth. 'You have a wonderful sister.'

'Thank you, Madam.'

'Why don't you take Maria around the city? She hasn't seen anything in Kittur, has she?'

He decided that this was a clear opportunity to show some initiative. 'Why don't we all three go together, Madam?'

The three of them drove down to the beach. Mrs Gomes and Maria went for a walk along the sand. He watched from a distance. When they returned, he was waiting with a paper cone filled with roasted groundnuts for Maria.

'Don't I get some too?' Mrs Gomes demanded, and he hurried to pour some nuts out, and she took them from his hands, and that was how he touched her for the first time.

★ ★ ★

It was raining again in Valencia, and he knew he had been at the house almost a year. One day, the new mosquito-man came for the back yard. Mrs Gomes watched as George directed the fellow around the gutters and canals in the back, to make sure not a spot was missed.

That evening, she called him to the house and said: 'George, you should to do it yourself. Please spray the gutter yourself, like last year.'

Her voice became sweet, and though it was the same voice she used to make him move mountains for her, this time he stiffened. He was offended that she would still ask him to perform such a task.

'Why not?' She raised her voice, angrily. She shrieked. 'You work for me! You do what I say!'

The two of them stared at each other, and then, grumbling and cursing her, he left the house. He wandered aimlessly for some time, then decided to visit the cathedral again, to see how the old fellows were doing.

Nothing much had changed in the field by the cathedral. The construction had been held up, he was told, because of the rector's death. It would start again soon.

His other friends were missing – they had left the work and returned to the village – but Guru was there.

'Now that you're here, why don't we—' Guru made the gesture of a bottle being emptied down a throat.

They went to an arrack shop and there was some fine drinking, just like in old times.

'So how are things with you and your princess?' Guru asked.

'Oh, these rich people are all the same,' George said, bitterly. 'We're just trash to them. A rich woman can never see a poor man as a man. Just as a servant.'

He remembered his carefree days, before he was tied down to a house, and to Madam – and he became resentful at having lost his freedom. He left early, shortly before midnight, saying that he had something to take care of, at the house. On the way back, he staggered drunkenly, singing a Konkani song; but another pulse had started to throb beneath the lighthearted film number.

As he drew near the gate, his voice dropped down and died out, and he realized he was walking with exaggerated stealth. He wondered why and felt frightened of himself.

He opened the latch of the gate soundlessly and walked towards the back door of the house. He had been holding the key in his hand for some time; bending down to the lock, and squinting at the keyhole, he inserted it. Opening it carefully and quietly, he walked into the house. The heavy washing machine lay in the dark, like a night-watchman. In the distance wisps of cool air escaped from a crack in the closed door of her bedroom.

George breathed slowly. His one thought, as he

staggered forward, was that he must avoid walking into the washing machine.

'O God,' he said, suddenly. He realized that he had banged his knee into the washing machine and the damn machine was reverberating.

'O God,' he said again, with the dim, desperate consciousness that he had spoken too loudly.

There was a movement; her door opened and a woman with long loose hair emerged.

A cool air-conditioned breeze thrilled his entire body. The woman pulled the edge of a sari over her shoulder.

'George?'

'Yes.'

'What do you want?'

He said nothing. The answer to the question was at once vague and full of substance, half-obscure but all too present, just as she herself was. He almost knew what he wanted to say; she said nothing. She had not screamed or raised the alarm. Perhaps she wanted it too. He felt that it was now only a matter of saying it, or even of moving. Just do *something*. It will happen.

'Get out,' she said.

He had waited too long.

'Madam, I—'

'Get out.'

It was too late now; he turned around and walked quickly.

The moment the back door closed on him, he felt foolish. He thumped it with his fist so hard that it hurt. 'Madam, let me explain!' He pounded the door harder and harder. She had misunderstood him – completely misunderstood!

'Stop it,' came a voice. It was Maria, looking at him fearfully through the window. 'Please stop it at once.'

At that moment, the immensity of what he had done struck George. He was conscious the neighbours might be watching. Madam's reputation was at stake.

He dragged himself up to the construction site and fell down there to sleep. The next morning, he discovered he had been lying, just as he had done months before, on top of a pyramid of crushed granite.

He came back, slowly. Maria was waiting for him by the gate.

'Madam,' she called, as she went into the house. Mrs Gomes came out, her finger deep into her latest novel.

'Maria, go to the kitchen,' Mrs Gomes ordered, as he walked into the garden. He was glad of that; so she wanted to protect Maria from what was coming. He felt gratitude for her delicacy. She was different from other rich people; she was special. She would spare him.

He put the key to the back door on the ground.

'It's okay,' she said. Her manner was cool. He understood now that the radius had increased; it was pushing him back every second he stood. He did not know how far back to go; it seemed to him he was already as far back as he could be and hear what she was saying. Her voice was distant and small and cold. For some reason, he could not take his eyes off the cover of her novel; a man was driving a red car, and two white women in bikinis were sitting inside.

'It's not anger,' she said. 'I should have taken greater precautions. I made a mistake.'

'I've left the key down here, Madam,' he said.

'It doesn't matter,' she said. 'The lock is being changed this evening.'

'Can I stay, until you find someone else?' he blurted out. 'How will you manage with the garden? And what will you do for a driver?'

'I'll manage,' she said.

Until then, all his thoughts had been for her – her reputation in the neighbourhood, her peace of mind, the sense of betrayal she must feel – but now he understood: she was not the one who needed taking care of.

He wanted to speak his heart out to her and tell her all this, but she spoke first.

'Maria will have to leave as well.'

He stared at her, his mouth open.

'Where will she sleep tonight?' His voice was thin, and desperate. 'Madam, she left everything she had in our village and came here to live with you.'

'She can sleep in the church, I suppose,' Mrs Gomes said calmly. 'They let people in all night, I've heard.'

'Madam,' he folded his palms. 'Madam, you're Christian like us, and I'm begging you in the name of Christian charity, please leave Maria out of—!'

She closed the door; then he heard the sound of it being locked, and then double-locked.

He waited for his sister at the top of the road, and looked in the direction of the unfinished cathedral.

DAY SIX (MORNING):
THE SULTAN'S BATTERY

The Sultan's Battery, a large black rectangular fort, appears high up to your left as you go from Kittur to Salt Market Village. The best way explore the fort is to ask someone in Kittur to drive you up here; your host will have to park the car by the main road, and then the two of you have to walk uphill for half an hour. When you pass through the arched doorway, you find that the fort is in an advanced state of decay. Although a plaque of the Archeological Survey of India declares this a protected site, and speaks of its role in 'enshrining the memory of the patriot Tippu Sultan, Tiger of Mysore', there is no evidence of any attempt to preserve the ancient structure from the onslaught of creepers, wind, rain, erosion, and grazing animals. Giant banyan trees have germinated on the walls of the fort; their roots smash between the stones like gnarled fingers reaching into a mouse-hole. Avoiding the thorns and piles of goat droppings, you should walk to one of the loopholes in the walls of the fort; here, hold an imaginary gun in your hands, close an eye, and pretend that you are Tippu himself, firing down on the English army.

He walked quickly towards the white dome of the Dargah, a fold-up wooden stool under one arm, and in the other a red bag with his album of photographs and seven bottles full of white pills. When he reached the Dargah, he walked along the wall, not paying any attention to the long line of beggars: the lepers sitting on rags, the men with mutilated arms and legs, the men in wheelchairs and the men with bandages covering their eyes, and the creature, with little brown stubs like a seal's flippers where he should have had arms, a normal left leg, and a soft brown stump where he should have had the other leg, who lay on his left side, twitching his hip continuously, like an animal receiving galvanic shocks, and intoning, with blank, mesmerized eyes: 'Al-lah! Al-laaaah! Al-lah! Al-laaah!'

He walked past this sorrowful parade of humanity and went behind the Dargah.

Now he walked past the vendors squatting on the ground in a long line that extended for half a mile. He passed rows of baby shoes, bras, T-shirts bearing the logo 'New York Fucking City', fake Ray-Ban glasses, fake Nike shoes and fake Adidas shoes, and piles of Urdu and Malayalam magazines. He spotted an opening between a counterfeit-Nike seller and a counterfeit-Gucci seller, unfolded his stool there, and placed on it a glossy black sheet of paper with gold lettering.

The golden words read:

RATNAKARA SHETTY
SPECIAL INVITEE
FOURTH PAN-ASIAN CONFERENCE ON
SEXOLOGY
HOTEL NEW HILLTOP PALACE NEW DELHI
12–14 APRIL 1987

The young men who had come to pray at the Dargah, or to eat lamb kebabs in one of the Muslim restaurants, or simply to watch the sea, began making a semi-circle around Ratna, watching, as he added to the display on the stool, the photo album and the seven bottles of white pills. With grave ceremony, he then rearranged the bottles, as if their position had to be exactly right for his work to begin. In truth, he was waiting for more onlookers.

They came. Standing in pairs or alone, the crowd of young men had now taken on the appearance of a human Stonehenge; some stood with their hands folded on a friend's shoulder; some stood alone; and a few crouched to the ground, like fallen boulders.

All at once, Ratna began to talk. Young men came quicker, and the crowd became so thick that it was two or three men deep at each point; and those at the back had to stand on their toes to get even a partial glimpse of the sexologist.

He opened the album and let the young men see the photos in plastic folders inside. The onlookers gasped.

Pointing at his photographs, Ratna spoke of abominations and perversions. He described the consequences of sin: he demonstrated the passage of venereal germs up the body, touching his nipples, his eyes, and then his nostrils, and then closing his eyes. The sun climbed the sky and the white dome of the Dargah shone more brightly. The young men in the semi-circle pressed against each other, straining to get closer to the photographs. Then Ratna went in for the kill: he shut the book and held up a bottle of white pills in both of his hands. He began shaking the pills.

'With each bottle of pills you will receive a certificate of authenticity from Hakim Bhagwandas of Daryaganj in Delhi. This man, a greatly experienced doctor, has studied the wise books of the pharaohs, and has used his scientific equipment to create these magnificent white pills that will cure all your ailments. Each bottle costs just four rupees and fifty paise! Yes, that is all you need to pay to atone for sin and earn a second chance in this life! Four rupees and fifty paise!'

In the evening, dead-tired from the heat, he boarded the 34B bus with his red bag and fold-up stool. It was packed at this hour, so he held on to a strap and breathed in and out slowly. He counted to ten, to recover his strength, then dipped a hand into the red bag, taking out four green brochures, each of which bore the image of three large rats on the cover. He held the brochures up high in one hand, in the manner of a gambler holding up his cards, and spoke at the top of his voice:

'Ladies and gentlemen! All of you know that we live in a rat race, where there are few jobs, and many job applicants. How will your children survive, how will they get the jobs you have? For life in this day and age is a veritable rat race. Only in this booklet will you find thousands of useful general knowledge data, arranged in question and answer form, that your sons and daughters need to pass the civil service entrance examination, the bank entrance examination, the police entrance examination, and many other exams which are needed to win the rat race. For instance' – he took a quick breath – 'the Mughal Empire had two capitals; Delhi was one of them. Which was the other? Four capital cities of Europe are built on the banks of one river. Name that river. Who was the first king of Germany? What is the currency of Angola? One city in Europe has been the capital of three different empires. Which city? Two men were involved in the assassination of Mahatma Gandhi. Nathuram Godse was one of them. Name the other man. What is the height of the Eiffel Tower in metres?'

Holding the pamphlets with his right hand, he staggered forward, bracing himself as the bus bumped over the potholes of the road. One passenger asked for a pamphlet and handed him a rupee. Ratna walked back and waited near the exit door; when the bus slowed down, he dipped his head in silent thanks to the conductor and got off.

Seeing a man waiting at the bus stop, he tried to sell him a collection of six coloured pens, first at a rupee a pen; then at two pens a rupee; finally offering three for a rupee. Although the man said he would not buy, Ratna could see the interest in his eyes; he took out a large spring that could give much amusement to children, and a geometrical set that could make wonderful designs on papers. The man bought one of the geometrical sets for three rupees.

Ratna headed away from from the Sultan's Battery, taking the road towards Salt Market Village.

Once he got to the village, he went to the main market, took out a handful of change and sorted it out on the flat of his palm as he walked; he left the coins on the counter of a shop, taking in exchange a packet of Engineer beedis, which he put into his suitcase.

'What are you waiting for?' The boy in charge of the shop was new to the job. 'You have your beedis.'

'I usually get two packets of lentils too, included in the price. That's the way it's done.'

Before entering his house, Ratna ripped open one of the packets with his teeth and poured its contents onto the ground near his door. Seven or eight of the neighbourhood dogs came running and he watched them crunch the lentils loudly. When they began digging at the earth, he tore open the second packet with his teeth and scattered its contents on the ground too.

He walked into his house without waiting to see the dogs devour this second lot of lentils. He knew they would still be hungry, but he could not afford to buy them a third packet every day.

He hung his shirt on a hook by the door, as he scratched his armpits and hairy chest. He sat down on a chair, exhaled, muttered: 'O Krishna, O Krishna', and stretched out his legs; even though they were in the kitchen, his daughters knew at once that he was there – a powerful odour of stale feet went through the house like a warning cannon shot. They dropped their women's magazines and busied themselves with their work.

His wife emerged from the kitchen with a tumbler of water. He had begun smoking the beedis.

'Are they working in there – the maharanis?' he asked her.

'Yes,' the three girls, his daughters, shouted back from the kitchen. He did not trust them, so he went in to check.

The youngest, Aditi, crouched by the gas stove, wiping the leaves of the photo album with a corner of her sari. Rukmini, the oldest sister, sat beside a mound of white pills, which she was counting off and pouring into bottles; Ramnika, who would be married off after Rukmini, pasted a label on each bottle. The wife was in the kitchen, making noise with plates and pots. After he had smoked his second beedi, and his body had visibly relaxed, she built up the courage to approach him: 'The astrologer said he would come at nine.'

'Uhm.'

He burped, and then lifted a leg and waited for the fart. The radio was on; he placed the set on his thigh and slapped his palm against his other leg to the beat of the music, humming all the while and singing the words whenever he knew them.

'He's here,' she whispered. He turned off the radio, as the astrologer came into the room and folded his palms in a namaste.

Sitting down in a chair, he took off his shirt, which Ratna's wife hung for him on the hook next to Ratna's. While the women waited in the kitchen, the astrologer showed Ratna the choice of boys.

He opened an album of black and white photos; they gazed at the faces of one boy after another, who looked back at them out of tense, unsmiling portraits. Ratna scraped one with his thumb. The astrologer slid the photo out of the album.

'Boy looks okay,' Ratna said, after a moment's concentration. 'The father does what for a living?'

'Owns a firecracker shop on Umbrella Street. A very good business. Boy inherits it.'

'His own business,' Ratna exclaimed, with genuine satisfaction. 'It's the only way ahead in the rat race: being a salesman is a dead end.'

His wife dropped something in the kitchen; she coughed and dropped something else.

'What's going on?' he asked.

A timid voice said something about 'horoscopes'.

'Shut up!' Ratna shouted. He gestured at the kitchen with the photo – 'I have three daughters to marry off and this damn bitch thinks I can be choosy?' – and he tossed the photo into the astrologer's lap.

The astrologer drew an 'X' across the back of the photo.

'The boy's parents will expect something,' he said. 'A token.'

'Dowry.' Ratna gave the evil its proper name in a soft voice. 'Fine. I've saved money for this girl.' He breathed out. 'Where I'll get dowry for the next two, though, God alone knows.'

Gritting his teeth in anger, he turned towards the kitchen and yelled.

The following Monday, the boy's party came. The younger girls went around with a tray of lemon juice, while Ratna and his wife sat in the drawing room. Rukmini's face was whitened by a thick layer of Johnson's Baby Powder, and garlands of jasmine decorated her hair; she plucked the strings of a veena and sang a religious verse, while looking out of the window at something far away.

The prospective groom's father, the firecracker merchant, was sitting on a mattress directly opposite Rukmini; he was a huge man in a white shirt and a white cotton sarong, with thick tufts of glossy, silvery hair sticking out of his ears. He moved his head to the rhythm of the song, which Ratna took as an encouraging sign. The prospective mother-in-law, another enormous and fair-skinned creature, looked around the ceiling and the corners of the room. The groom-to-be had his father's fair skin and features, but he was much smaller than either of his parents, and seemed more like the family's domestic pet than the scion. Halfway through the song, he leaned over and whispered something into his father's hairy ears.

The merchant nodded. The boy got up and left. The father held up his little finger and showed it to everyone in the room.

Everyone giggled.

The boy came back and squirmed into place between his fat father and his fat mother. The two younger girls came with a second tray of lemon juice, and the fat firecracker merchant and his wife took glasses; as if only to follow them, the boy also took a glass and sipped. Almost as soon as the juice touched his lips, he tapped his father and whispered into his hairy ear again. This time the old man grimaced; but the boy ran out.

As if to distract attention from his son, the

331

firecracker merchant asked Ratna, in a rasping voice: 'Do you have a spare beedi, my good man?'

Searching in the kitchen for his packet of beedis, Ratna saw, through the grille in the window, the bridegroom-to-be, urinating copiously against the trunk of an Ashoka tree in the back yard.

Nervous fellow, he thought, grinning. But that's only natural, he thought, feeling already a touch of affection for this fellow, who was soon going to join his family. All men are nervous before their weddings. The boy appeared to be done; he shook his penis and stepped away from the tree. But then, he stood as if frozen. After a moment he craned his head back and seemed to gasp for air, like a drowning man.

The matchmaker returned that evening to report that the firecracker merchant seemed satisfied with Rukmini's singing.

'Fix the date soon,' he told Ratna. 'In a month, the rental rates for wedding halls will start to . . .' – he gestured upwards with his palms.

Ratna nodded, but he seemed distracted.

The next morning, he took the bus to Umbrella Street, walking past furniture and fan shops until he found the firecracker merchant's place. The fat man with the hairy ears sat on a high stool, in front of a wall of paper bombs and rockets, like an emissary of the God of Fire and War. The groom-to-be was also in the shop, sitting on the floor, licking his fingers as he turned the pages of a ledger.

The fat man kicked his son gently.

'This man is going to be your father-in-law, aren't you going to say hello?' He smiled at Ratna: 'The boy is a shy one.'

Ratna sipped tea, chatted with the fat man, and kept an eye on the boy all the time.

'Come with me, son,' he said, 'I have something to show you.'

The two men walked down the road, neither of them saying a word, till they got to the banyan tree that grew beside the Hanuman temple on Umbrella Street; Ratna indicated that they should sit down in the shade of the tree. He wanted the boy to turn his back to the traffic, so that they faced the temple.

For a while Ratna let the young man talk, only observing his eyes, ears, nose, mouth, and neck.

Suddenly, he seized the fellow's wrist.

'Where did you find this prostitute that you sat with?'

The boy wanted to get up, but Ratna increased the pressure on his wrist to make it clear that there would be no escape. The boy turned his face to the road, as if pleading for help.

Ratna increased the pressure on the boy's wrist.

'Where did you sit with her? At the side of a road, in a hotel, or behind a building?'

He twisted harder.

'By the side of a road,' the boy blurted out; then he looked at Ratna with his face close to tears. 'How do you know?'

Ratna closed his eyes; breathed out and let go of the boy's wrist. 'A truckers' whore.' He slapped the boy.

The boy began to cry. 'I only sat with her once,' he said, fighting back his sobs.

'Once is enough. Do you burn when you pass urine?'

'Yes, I burn.'

'*Nausea?*'

The boy asked what the English word meant, and said yes once he understood.

'What else?'

'It feels like there is something large and hard – like a rubber ball – between my legs all the time. And then I feel dizzy sometimes.'

'Can you get hard?'

'Yes. No.'

'Tell me what your penis looks like. Is it black? Is it red? Are the lips of your penis swollen?'

Half an hour later, the two men were still sitting at the foot of the banyan tree, facing the temple.

'I beg you . . .' The boy folded his palms. 'I beg you.'

Ratna shook his head.

'I have to cancel the wedding, what else can I do? How can I let my daughter get this disease too?'

The boy stared at the ground, as if he had simply run out of ways to beg. The drop of moisture at the tip of his nose gleamed like silver.

'I'll ruin you,' he said quietly.

Ratna wiped his hands on his sarong. 'How?'

'I'll say that the girl has slept with someone. I'll say that she's not a virgin. That's why you had to cancel the wedding.'

In one swift motion, Ratna seized the boy's hair, yanked back his head, held it for a moment, and then slammed it against the banyan tree. He stood up and spat at the boy.

'I swear by the god who sits in this temple before us, I will kill you with my own hands if you say that.'

He was in fiery form that day at the Dargah; thundering, as the young men gathered round him, about sin, and disease, and about how germs rise from the genitalia, through the nipples, into the mouth, and eyes, and ears, until they reach the nostrils. Then he showed them his photos: images of rotten and reddened genitalia, some of which were black, or distended, or even appeared charred, as if acid-burned. Above each photo was one of the face of the victim, his eyes covered by a black rectangle, as if he were a victim of torture or rape. Such were the consequences of sin, Ratna explained: and expiation and redemption could come only in the form of magic white pills.

Three months or so went by. One morning, he was at his spot behind the white dome, bellowing at the Stonehenge of worried young men, when he saw a face that made his heart stop.

Afterwards, when he was done with his lecture, he saw the face again, right in front of him.

'What do you want?' he hissed. 'It's too late. My daughter's married now. Why have you come here now?'

Ratna folded the stool under his arm, dropped his medicines into his red bag, and walked fast. A flurry of footsteps followed him. The boy – the firecracker merchant's son – panted as he spoke.

'Things are becoming worse by the day. I can't piss without my penis burning. You must do something for me. You must give me your pills.'

Ratna gnashed his teeth. 'You sinned, you bastard. You sat with a prostitute. Now pay for it!'

He walked faster, and faster, and then the footsteps behind him were gone and he was alone.

But the following evening, he saw the face again and the quick steps followed him all the way to the bus stop, and the voice said, again and again: 'Let me buy the pills from you', but Ratna did not turn around.

He boarded the bus and counted to ten; producing his brochures, he spoke to the passengers of the rat race. As the dark outline of the fort appeared in the distance; the bus slowed down and then stopped. He got down. Someone else got down with him. He walked away. Someone walked behind him.

Ratna spun around and seized his stalker by the collar. 'Didn't I tell you? Leave me alone. What has got into you?'

The boy pushed Ratna's hands away, and

straightened his collar, and whispered: 'I think I'm dying. You have to give me your white pills.'

'Look here, none of those young men is going to be cured by anything I sell. Don't you get it?'

There was a moment of silence and then the boy said: 'But you were at the Sexology Conference . . . the sign in English says so . . .'

Ratna raised his hands to the sky.

'I found that sign lying on the platform of the station.'

'But the Hakim Bhagwandas of Delhi . . .'

'Hakim Bhagwandas, my arse! They're white sugar pills that I buy wholesale from a chemist on Umbrella Street – right next to where your father has his shop; my daughters bottle them and stick labels on them at my house!'

To prove his point, he opened his leather case, unscrewed the top from a bottle, and scattered the pills across the ground, as if broadcasting seed on the earth. 'They can do nothing! I have nothing for you, son!'

The boy sat on the ground, took a white pill from the earth, and swallowed it. He got down on all fours and scooped up the white pills, which he began swallowing in a frenzy, along with any dirt attached to them.

'Are you mad?'

Getting down on his knees, Ratna gave the boy a good shake and asked the same question again and again.

And then, at last, he saw the boy's eyes. They

had changed since he had last observed them; teary and red, they were like pickled vegetables of some kind.

He relaxed his grip on the boy's shoulder.

'You'll have to pay me, all right, for my help? I don't do charity.'

Half an hour later, the two men got off a bus near the railway station. They walked together through streets that become progressively narrower and darker, until they reached a shop whose awning was marked with a large red medical cross. From inside the shop, a radio blared out a popular Kannada film song.

'Buy something here and leave me alone.'

Ratna tried to walk away, but the boy clutched his wrist.

'Wait. Pick the medicine for me and then go.'

Ratna walked quickly in the direction of the bus stop, but again he heard the footsteps behind him. He turned, and there was the boy, arms laden with green bottles.

Regretting that he had ever agreed to bring him here, Ratna walked faster. Still he heard the light, desperate footsteps again, as though a ghost were following him.

For several hours that night Ratna lay awake, turning in his bed and disturbing his wife.

The next day, in the evening, he took the bus into the city, back into Umbrella Street. When he reached the firecracker shop he stood at a distance, with his arms folded, waiting until the boy saw him.

The two of them walked together in silence for a while and then sat down on a bench outside a sugarcane juice stall. As the machines turned, crushing the cane, Ratna said: 'Go to the hospital. They'll help you.'

'I can't go there. They know me. They'll tell my father.'

Ratna had a vision of that immense man with the tufts of white hair growing out of his ears, sitting in front of his arsenal of firecrackers and paper bombs.

The following day, as Ratna was folding his wooden stand and packing his case, he was conscious of a shadow on the ground in front of him. He walked round the Dargah; past the long line of pilgrims waiting to pray at the tomb of Yusuf Ali, past the rows of lepers, and past the man with one leg lying on the ground, twitching from the hip and chanting: 'Al-lah, Allaaah! Al-lah!'

He looked up at the white dome for a moment.

He went down to the sea, and the shadow followed him. A low stone wall ran along the sea's edge and he put his right foot up on it. The waves were coming in violently; now and then water crashed against the wall, and thick white foam rose up into the air and spread out, like a peacock's tail emerging from the sea. Ratna turned around.

'What choice do I have? If I don't sell those boys the pills, how will I marry off my daughters?'

The boy, avoiding his gaze, stared at the ground and shifted his weight uncomfortably.

The two of them caught the number 5 bus and took it all the way into the heart of the city, descending near Angel Talkies. The boy carried the wooden stool, and Ratna searched up and down the main road, until he located a large billboard of a husband and a wife standing together in wedding clothes:

HAPPY LIFE CLINIC
CONSULTING SPECIALIST: DOCTOR
M. V. KAMATH
MBBS (MYSORE), B.MEC. (ALLAHABAD),
DBBS (MYSORE), M.CH. (CALCUTTA),
G.COM. (VARANASI).
SATISFACTION GUARANTEED

'You see those letters after his name?' Ratna whispered into the boy's ear. 'He's a *real* doctor. He'll save you.'

In the waiting room, a half-dozen lean, nervous men sat on black chairs, and in a corner one married couple. Ratna and the boy sat down between the single men and the couple. Ratna looked curiously at the men. These were the same ones who came to him – older, sadder versions; men who had been trying to shake off venereal disease for years, who had thrown bottle after bottle of white pills at it, to find no improvement – who were now at the end of a long journey of despair, a journey that led from his booth at the Dargah, through a long trail of other hucksters, to this doctor's clinic, where they would be told at last the truth.

One by one, the lean wasted men went into the doctor's room, and the door shut behind them. Ratna looked at the married couple and thought: at least they are not alone in this ordeal. At least they have each other.

Then the man got up to see the doctor; the woman stayed back. She went in later, after the man had left. Of course they are not husband and wife, Ratna told himself. When he gets this disease, this disease of sex, every man is alone in the universe.

'And who are you in relation to the patient?' the doctor asked.

They had taken their seats, at last, at his consulting desk. On the wall behind the doctor a giant chart depicted a cross-section of a man's urinary and reproductive organs. Ratna looked at it for a moment, marvelling at the diagram's beauty, and said: 'His uncle.'

The doctor made the boy take off his shirt; then he sat next to him, made him put his tongue out, peered into his eyes, and put his stethoscope to the boy's chest, pressing it to one side and then the other.

Ratna thought: to get a disease like this, on his very first time! Where was the justice in that?

After examining the boy's genitals, the doctor

moved to a washbasin with a mirror above; he pulled a cord and a tube-light flickered to life above the mirror.

Letting the water run in the basin, he gargled and spat, and then turned off the light. He wiped a corner of the basin with his palm, lowered a blind over the window, inspected his green plastic wastebasket.

When he ran out of things to do, he returned to his desk, looked at his feet, and practised breathing for a while.

'His kidneys are gone.'

'Gone?'

'Gone,' the doctor said.

He turned to the boy, who was trembling hard in his seat.

'Are you unnatural in your tastes?'

The boy covered his face in his hands. Ratna answered for him.

'Look, he got it from a prostitute, there's no sin in that. He's not an unnatural fellow. He just didn't know enough about this world we live in.'

The doctor nodded. He turned to the diagram and put his finger on the kidneys, and said: 'Gone.'

Ratna and the boy went to the bus station together at six in the morning, the following day, to catch the bus to Manipal; he had heard that there was a doctor at the Medical College who specialized in the kidneys. A man with a blue sarong, sitting on the bench in the station, told them that the bus to Manipal was always late, maybe fifteen minutes, maybe thirty, maybe more. 'Everything's been falling apart in this country since Mrs Gandhi was shot,' the man in the blue sarong said, kicking his legs about. 'Buses are late. Trains are late. Everything's falling apart. We'll have to hand this country back to the British or the Russians or someone, I tell you. We're not meant to be masters of our own fate, I tell you.'

Telling the boy to wait for a moment by the bus stop, Ratna returned with peanuts in a paper cone which he had bought for twenty paise, and said: 'You haven't had breakfast, have you?' But the boy reminded him that the doctor had warned against eating anything spicy; it would irritate his penis. So Ratna went back to the vendor and exchanged the peanuts for the unsalted kind. They munched together for a while, until the boy ran to a wall and began to throw up. Ratna stood over him, patting his back, as the boy retched again and again. The man in the blue sarong watched with greedy eyes; then he came up to Ratna and whispered: 'What's the kid got? It's serious, isn't it?'

'Nonsense; he's just got a flu,' Ratna said. The bus arrived at the station an hour late.

It was late on the way back as well. The two of them had to stand in the densely crowded aisle for over an hour, until a pair of seats became empty beside them. Ratna slid into the window seat and motioned for the boy to sit down next to him.
'We got lucky, considering how crowded the bus is,' Ratna said with a smile.

Gently, he disengaged his hand from the boy's.

The boy understood too; he nodded, and took out his wallet, and threw five-rupee notes, one after the other, into Ratna's lap.

'What's this for?'

'You said you wanted something for helping me.'

Ratna thrust the notes into the boy's shirt pocket. 'Don't talk to me like that, fellow. I have helped you so far; and what did I have to gain from it? It was pure public service on my part, remember that. We aren't related: we have no blood in common.'

The boy said nothing.

'Look! I can't keep on going with you from doctor to doctor. I've got my daughters to marry off, I don't know where I'll get the dowry for—'

The boy turned, pressed his face into Ratna's collarbone and burst into sobs; his lips rubbed against Ratna's clavicles and began sucking on them. The passengers stared at them, and Ratna was too bewildered to say a word.

It took another hour before the outline of the black fort appeared on the horizon. The man and the boy got off the bus together. Ratna stood by the main road and waited as the boy blew his nose and shook the phlegm from his fingers. Ratna looked at the black rectangle of the fort and felt a sense of despair: how had it been decided, and by whom, and when, and why, that Ratnakara Shetty was responsible for helping this firecracker merchant's son fight his disease? Against the black rectangle of the fort, he had a vision, momentarily, of a white dome, and he heard a throng of mutilated beings chanting in unison. He put a beedi in his mouth, struck a match and inhaled.

'Let's go,' he told the boy. 'It's a long walk from here to my house.'

DAY SIX (EVENING): BAJPE

Bajpe the last area of forested land in Kittur, was marked out by the founding fathers as one of the 'cleansing lungs of the town, and for this reason was for thirty years protected from the avarice of real-estate developers. The great forest of Bajpe, which stretched from Kittur right up to the Arabian Sea, was bordered on the town side by the Ganapati Hindu Boys School and the small adjacent temple of Ganesha. Next to the temple ran Bishop Street, the only part of the neighbourhood where houses had been allowed. Beyond the street stood a large wasteland, and beyond that began a dark lattice of trees – the forest. When relatives from the centre of town visited, the residents of Bishop Street were usually up on their terraces or balconies, enjoying the cool breezes that blew from the forest in the evening. Guests and hosts together watched as herons, eagles, and king-fishers flew in and out of the darkening mass of trees, like ideas circulating around an immense brain. The sun which had by now

346

plunged behind the forest, burned orange and ochre through the interstices of the foliage as if peering out of the trees, and the observers had the distinct impression that they were being observed in return. At such moments guests were wont to declare that the inhabitants of Bajpe were the luckiest people on earth. At the same time, it was assumed that if a man built his house on Bishop Street, he had some reason to want to be so far from civilization.

Giridhar Rao and Kamini, the childless couple on Bishop Street, were one of the hidden treasures of Kittur, all their friends declared. Weren't they a marvel? All the way out in Bajpe, on the very edge of the wilderness, this barren couple kept alive the all-but-dead art of Brahmin hospitality.

It was another Thursday evening, and the half a dozen or so members of the Raos' circle of *intimates* were making their way through the mud and slush of Bishop Street for their weekly get-together. Ahead of the pack, moving with giant strides, came Mr Anantha Murthy, the philosopher. Behind him was Mrs Shirthadi, the wife of the Life Insurance Company of India man. Then Mrs Pai, and then Mr Bhat, and, finally, Mrs Aithal, always the last to descend from her green Ambassador.

The Raos' house was all the way down at the end of Bishop Street, just yards away from the trees.

Sitting right on the forest's edge, the house had the look of a fugitive from the civilized world, ready to spring into the wilderness at a moment's notice.

'Did everyone hear that?'

Mr Anantha Murthy turned around. He put a hand on his ear and raised his eyebrows.

A cool breeze was blowing in from the forest. The *intimates* came to a halt, trying to hear what Mr Murthy had heard.

'I think it's a woodpecker, somewhere in the trees!'

An irritated voice boomed down: 'Why don't you get up here first and listen to the woodpeckers later! The food has been prepared with a lot of care and it's getting cold!'

It was Mr Rao, leaning down from the balcony of his house.

'Okay, okay,' Mr Anantha Murthy grumbled, picking his way down the muddy track again. 'But it's not every day a man gets to hear a woodpecker.' He turned to Mrs Shirthadi. 'We tend to forget everything that's important when we live in towns, don't we, Madam?'

She grunted. She was trying to make sure she didn't get mud on her sari.

The philosopher led the *intimates* into the house. When they had done scraping their chappals and shoes on the coconut-fibre mat, the visitors found old Sharadha Bhatt squinting at them. She was the proprietor of the place, a widow whose only son lived in Bombay. It was understood that the Raos stayed on in their cramped apartment, so far from the heart of town, partly out of concern for Mrs Bhatt – she was a distant relative. A suggestion of intense religiosity clung to the old lady. The visitors heard the drone of M. S. Subbalakshmi singing Suprabhatam from a small black tape recorder in her room. Sitting with her legs folded on a wooden bed, she struck at her thighs alternately with the front and back of her left palm as she followed the rhythm of the holy music.

Some of the visitors remembered her husband, a celebrated teacher of Carnatic music who had performed on All India Radio, and paid their respects, politely nodding towards her.

Done with their obligation to the ancient lady, they hurried up a wide stairwell to the Raos' quarters. The childless couple occupied a crushingly small space. Half the living area consisted of a single drawing room, cluttered with sofas and chairs. In a corner, a sitar was propped up against the wall, its shaft having slid down to a 45 degree angle.

'Ah! It's our *intimates* once again!'

Giridhar Rao was neat, modest, and unpretentious in appearance. You could tell at once that he worked in a bank. Since his transfer from Udupi – his hometown – he had been the deputy branch manager at the Corporation Bank's Cool Water Well Branch for nearly a decade now. (The *intimates* knew that Mr Rao could have risen much higher had he not repeatedly refused to be transferred to Bombay.) His wavy hair was flattened with coconut oil and parted to one side. A handlebar moustache – the one anomaly in his demure appearance – was neatly combed and curled at the ends. Mr Rao had now thrown a short-sleeved shirt over his singlet. The fabric of the shirt was thin: inside its dark silk, the thick singlet glowed like a skeleton in an X-ray.

'How are you, Kamini?' Mr Anantha Murthy asked in the direction of the kitchen.

The drawing room furniture was a motley mix – green metal seats discarded from the bank, a torn old sofa, and three fraying cane chairs. The *intimates* headed for their favourite seats. The conversation began haltingly; perhaps they sensed, once again, that they were as haphazard a collection of people as the furniture was. None was aware of any blood relation to the other. By day, Mr Anantha Murthy was a chartered accountant catering to Kittur's rich. In the evenings he became a committed philosopher of the Advaita school. He found Mr Rao a willing (if silent) listener to his theories of the Hindu life – and that was how he had become part of the circle. Mrs Shirthadi, who usually attended without her busy husband, had been educated in Madras and espoused several 'liberated' views. Her English was exceptionally fine, a marvel to listen to. Mr Rao had asked her to speak on the subject of Charles

Dickens at the bank a few years ago. Mrs Aithal and her husband had met Kamini at a violin concert the previous May. The two of them were originally from Vizag.

The *intimates* knew that the Raos had selected them for their distinction – for their delicacy. They realized that they bore a responsibility upon entering that cosy little garret. Certain topics were taboo. Within the wide circumference of acceptable conversation – world news, philosophy, bank politics, the relentless expansion of Kittur, the rainfall this year – the *intimates* had learned to meander freely. Forest breezes came in from a balcony, and a transistor radio precariously balanced on the edge of the parapet emitted a steady patter of the BBC's evening news service.

A late arrival – Mrs Karwar, who taught Victorian literature at the university – threw the house into chaos. Her vivacious five-year-old, Lalitha, charged up the stairs shrieking.

'Look here, Kamini' – Mr Rao shouted at the kitchen – 'Mrs Karwar has smuggled your secret lover into the house!'

Kamini rushed out of the kitchen. Fair-skinned and shapely, she was almost a beauty. (Her forehead was protuberant and her hair thinnish at the front.) She was famous for her 'Chinese' eyes: narrow slits that were half closed beneath the curve of heavy eyelids, like prematurely opened lotus buds. Her hair – she was known to be a 'modern' woman – was cut short in the Western style. Ladies admired her hips, which, never having been widened by childbirth, still sported a girlish slimness.

She went up to Lalitha. She hoisted the little girl into the air, kissing her several times.

'Look, let's wait till my husband's back is turned, and then we'll get on my moped and drive away, huh? We can leave that evil man behind us and drive away to my sister's house in Bombay, okay?'

Giridhar Rao put his hands to his waist and glared at the giggling girl.

'Are you planning on stealing my wife? Are you really her "secret lover"?'

'Hey, keep listening to your BBC,' Kamini retorted, leading Lalitha by the hand into the kitchen.

The *intimates* acknowledged their keen delight in this pantomime. The Raos certainly did not lack the skill to keep a child happy.

The voices of the BBC continued from the radio outside – a gravy of words that the *intimates* dipped into when their conversation ran dry. Mr Anantha Murthy broke one long pause by declaring that the situation in Afghanistan was getting out of hand. One of these mornings the Soviets would come streaming over Kashmir with their red flags. Then the country would regret having missed its chance to ally itself with America back in 1948.

'Don't you feel this way, Mr Rao?'

Their host had never anything more to express than a friendly grin. Mr Murthy did not mind.

He acknowledged that Mr Rao was not a 'man of many words' – but he was a 'deep' fellow all the same. If you ever wanted to check little details of world history – like for instance, who was the American president who dropped the bomb on Hiroshima – not Roosevelt, but the little man with the round glasses – then you turned to Giridhar Rao. He knew everything; he said nothing. That kind of fellow.

'How is it you remain so calm, Mr Rao, despite all this chaos and killing that the BBC is always telling you about? What is your secret?' Mrs Shirthadi asked him, as she often did.

The bank manager smiled.

'When I need peace of mind, Madam, I just go to my private beach.'

'Are you a secret millionaire?' Mrs Shirthadi demanded. 'What's this private beach you keep talking about?'

'Oh, nothing, really.' He gestured towards the distance. 'Just a little lake, with some gravel around it. It's a very soothing place.'

'And why haven't we all been invited there?' demanded Mr Murthy.

The guests sat up. A triumphant Mrs Rao entered the drawing room bearing a plastic tray whose multiple compartments brimmed with the evening's first offerings: dried walnuts (which looked like little shrunken brains), juicy figs, sultana raisins, chopped almonds, slices of desiccated pineapple . . .

Before the guests had recovered, the next assault followed: 'Dinner is ready!'

They went into the dining room – the only other room in the house (it led into a little alcove-kitchen). An enormous bed, plump with cushions, lay in the middle of the dining room. There was no pretending not to see the conjugal site. It lay there, brazenly open to view. A small table was pulled up right next to it, and three of the guests hesitantly took their seats there. Their embarrassment disappeared almost immediately. The informality of their hosts, the voluptuous softness of the bedding beneath them – these things soothed their nerves. Then dinner rolled out of Kamini's little kitchen. Course after course of fine tomato saaru, idli, and dosas flowed out of that factory of gustatory treats.

'This kind of cooking would amaze people even in Bombay,' proposed Mr Anantha Murthy, when Kamini's pièce de résistance – fluffy North Indian rotis, lined inside with chilli powder – arrived on the table. Kamini beamed and protested: he was all wrong, she had so many inadequacies as a cook and a housewife!

When the guests rose, they realized that their buttocks had left wide, warm, and deep markings on the bed, like an elephant's footprints in clay. Giridhar Rao brushed aside their apologies: 'Our guests are like gods to us; they can do no wrong. That's the philosophy in this house.'

They stood in line outside the washroom, where water flowed from a green rubber pipe twisted

354

into a loop around the tap. Then back to the drawing room for the highlight of the evening – almond kheer.

Kamini brought out the dessert in breathtakingly large tumblers. The shake – served warm or cold, according to each guest's pleasure – was so full of almonds that the guests protested that they had to *chew* the drink! When they looked into their tumblers, they held their breath in wonder: shiny flecks, strands of real saffron, floated between the pieces of almond.

They left the apartment silently, heeding Mr Rao's request not to disturb the sleeping Sharadha Bhatt. (The old lady turned restlessly on her wooden bed as they departed; in the background the religious music droned on.)

'Do come next week!' Mr Rao had said from the terrace. 'It's the week of the Satya Narayana Pooja! I'll make sure Kamini does a better job with the cooking next week, unlike tonight's disaster!' He turned into the house and raised his voice: 'Did you hear that, Kamini? The food had better be good next time, or you're divorced.'

There had been a laugh and a high-pitched scream from inside: 'You'll be the one to get divorced, unless you shut up!'

Once at a safe distance, the *intimates* burst into chatter.

What a pair! The man and woman such complete opposites! He was 'bland'; she was 'spicy'. He was 'conservative', she was 'modern'. She was 'quick', he was 'deep'.

Still picking their way along the muddy road, they began to discuss the forbidden topic, with all the excitement and eagerness of people who were discussing it for the first time.

'It's obvious,' said one of the women, Mrs Aithal or Mrs Shirthadi, 'Kamini is the one "at fault". She wouldn't have *the operation. No wonder her life is racked by guilt. Don't you see how she throws herself on any available child in a storm of frustrated maternity, showering them with kisses and blandishments and caramel chocolates? What does that signify, if not guilt?*'

'And why did she refuse the operation?' demanded Mr Anantha Murthy.

Obstinacy. The women were sure of it. Kamini simply refused to acknowledge that the fault was hers. Some of Kamini's stubbornness, to be sure, came from her privileged background. She was the youngest of four sisters, all fair as buttermilk, the darling children of a famous eye-surgeon in Shimoga. How she must have been spoiled as a child! The other sisters had married well – a lawyer, an architect, and a surgeon, and they all lived in Bombay. Giridhar Rao was the poorest of the brothers-in-law. You could be sure that Kamini was not the kind of woman to let him forget this. Haven't you seen how defiantly she rides about town in her Hero Honda moped, as if she were the lord of their household?

356

Mr Anantha Murthy raised several objections. Why were all the womenfolk so suspicious of Kamini's 'sportiness'? How rare to find such a free-thinking woman! The fault was surely *his*. Haven't you seen him refuse promotion after promotion just because he would have to move to Bombay? What does that tell you? The man is lethargic.

'If only he would show . . . some more *initiative* . . . the problem of childlessness could easily be solved . . .' Mr Murthy said, giving his bald head a sad philosophical shake.

He even claimed to have given Mr Rao the names of doctors in Bombay who could solve his lack of 'initiative'.

Mrs Aithal reacted indignantly. Mr Rao had more than enough 'spunk' in him! Didn't he have such thick facial hair? And didn't he ride an entirely masculine red Yamaha motorcycle to the bank every morning?

The women enjoyed romanticizing Mr Rao. Mrs Shirthadi irritated Mr Murthy by suggesting that the modest little bank manager was also in secret 'a philosopher'. Once she had caught him reading the 'religious issues of the day' column on the last page of *The Hindu*. He seemed embarrassed at this discovery, and parried her inquiries with jokes and puns. Still, the feeling had grown that beneath all his joking, he was undeniably 'philosophical'.

'How else can he be so calm all the time, even without children?' Mr Aithal demanded.

'He has a secret of some kind, I'm sure,' Mrs Murthy suggested.

Mrs Karwar coughed and said: 'Sometimes I fear that she might be thinking of divorcing him' – and everyone looked concerned. The woman certainly was 'modern' enough to think of trying something like that . . .

But they had reached their cars now, and the group broke up, and drove away one after the other.

Later in the week, though, the Raos were observed as they circled the Cool Water Well Junction on his Yamaha bike. Kamini sat on the backseat holding on to her husband tightly, and the observers were surprised to see how the two of them looked like a real couple just then.

Next Thursday, when the *intimates* returned to the Raos' residence, they found Sharadha Bhatt herself opening the door for them. The old woman's silver hair was disarrayed and she glared at her tenants' guests.

'She's having trouble with Jimmy – you know, her architect son in Bombay. She's asked him again if she can come to stay with him, but his wife won't allow it,' Kamini whispered, as she led them up the stairs.

Because of the anticipation of an extraordinary meal this evening, Mr Shirthadi was putting in a rare appearance alongside his wife. He spoke passionately about the ingratitude of today's children, and said he sometimes wished he had stayed childless. Mrs Shirthadi sat nervously – her husband had almost crossed the invisible circumference.

Then Mrs Karwar arrived with Lalitha, and there was the usual shouting and shrieking between Kamini and the 'secret lover'.

After the sherbet, Mr Anantha Murthy asked Mr Rao to confirm a piece of gossip – had he turned down another offer to be posted to Bombay?

Mr Rao confirmed this with a nod.

'Why don't you go, Giridhar Rao?' demanded Mrs Shirthadi. 'Don't you want to rise in the bank?'

'I'm happy out here, Madam,' Mr Rao said. 'I have my private beach, and my BBC in the evenings. What more does a man need?'

'You are the perfect Hindu man, Mr Giridhar,' said Mr Murthy, who was growing restless for dinner. 'Which is to say, you are almost completely contented with your fate on earth.'

'Well, would you still be contented if I ran away with Lalitha?' Kamini shouted from the kitchen.

'My dear, if you ran away, then I'd be truly contented,' he retorted.

She shrieked out in mock outrage and the *intimates* applauded.

'Well, what about this private beach that you keep talking about, Mr Rao – when are we going to see it, exactly?' Mrs Shirthadi asked.

Before he could reply, Kamini came scampering out of the kitchen and leaned over the bannister.

A stertorous breathing grew louder. Sharadha Bhatt's face became visible, as she limped up, one stair at a time.

Kamini was agitated.

'Should I help you up the stairs? Should I do something?'

The old woman shook her head. Half out of breath, she stumbled onto a chair at the top of the stairs.

The conversation stopped. This was the very first time the old woman had joined the weekly diners.

In a few minutes the *intimates* had learned to ignore her.

Mr Anantha Murthy clapped his hands when Kamini came out with the appetizer tray.

'So, what's this I hear about your taking up swimming?'

'And if I am?' she snapped, putting a hand to her waist. 'What's wrong with that?'

'I hope you are not going to wear a bikini like a Western woman?'

'Why not? If they do it in America, why can't we? Are we less than them in any way?'

Lalitha giggled furiously as Kamini announced plans for the two of them to buy the scandalous swimsuits right away.

'And if Mr Giridhar Rao doesn't like it – then the two of us are going to run away and live together in Bombay, aren't we?'

Giridhar Rao glanced nervously at the old woman, who was gazing at her toes.

'All this "modern" talk isn't getting you upset, is it, Sharadhaamma?'

The old lady breathed heavily. She curled her toes and stared at them.

Mr Anantha Murthy ventured a comparison between the barfi that Kamini had put out on the appetizer tray and the barfi served in the best café in Bombay.

Then the old lady spoke in a hoarse voice: 'It is written in the Scriptures . . .' She paused for a long time. The room went silent. '. . . that a man . . . a man who has no son may not aspire to enter the gates of Heaven.' She breathed out. 'And if a man doesn't enter Heaven, neither can his wife. And here you are talking of bikinis and wikinis, and cavorting with "modern" people, instead of praying to God to forgive your sins!'

She breathed heavily for another moment, then got to her feet and hobbled down the stairs.

When the *intimates* left – it was a truncated evening – they found the old lady outside the house. Sitting on a suitcase bursting with clothes, she was bellowing at the trees.

'Yama Deva, come for me! Now that my son has forgotten his mother, what more is there for me to live for?'

As she called to the Lord of Death, she struck at her forehead with the stems of her fists, and her bangles jangled.

Feeling Giridhar Rao's hand on her shoulder, the old woman burst into tears.

The *intimates* saw Giridhar Rao gesture for them to leave. The old lady had exhausted her histrionics. Her head sank onto Kamini's breast and she convulsed in sobs.

'Forgive me, mother . . . The gods have given us each our punishment. They gave you a uterus of stone, and they have smashed the heart in my son's chest . . .'

After they had put the old lady to bed, Mr Rao let his wife climb the stairs first. When he joined her, she was lying on the bed, with her back turned towards him.

He walked onto the verandah and turned the radio off.

She said nothing as he picked up his helmet and headed back down the stairs. The kick-starting of his engine rent the quiet of Bishop Street.

In a few minutes, he was heading down the road that went through the forest towards the sea. On either side of the speeding bike, serried silhouettes of coconut palms bristled against the blue coastal night. Hanging low over the trees, a bright moon looked as though it had been cleaved by an axe. With its top right corner sliced off, it hung in the sky like an illustration of the idea of 'two-thirds'. After a quarter of an hour, the Yamaha bike swerved off the road into a muddy track, thundering over stones and gravel. Then its engine went dead.

A lake, a small circle of water inside the forest,

came into view, and Giridhar Rao stopped his bike, leaving his helmet on the seat. Fishermen had cleared a small shore around the lake, which was bounded on the far side by more coconut trees. At this hour, there would be nets all over the lake, but there was not another soul to be seen. A heron, walking through the shallow water at the edge of the lake, was the only other living thing in sight. Giridhar had stumbled upon his lake years ago, on a drive through the forest at night. He had no idea why no one came here; but a small town is like that, full of hidden treasures. He walked beside the lake for a few minutes, then sat down on a rock.

The water, its glossy surface broken by black ripples, looked like sheets of molten glass settling one on top of another.

The heron flapped its wings and rose into the air. Now he was all alone. He hummed softly, a tune from his bachelor days in Bangalore. A yawn expanded his face. He looked up. Three stars had emerged from the tatters of a grey cloud; together with the two-thirds moon they composed a quadrilateral. Mr Rao admired the structure of the night sky. It pleased him to think that the elements of our world were not cast about at random. Something stood behind them: an order.

He yawned again and stretched his legs out from the rock.

His peace was broken. It had begun to drizzle. He wondered if he had remembered to fasten the windows above their bed; the rain might strike her face.

Leaving his private beach behind, he sprinted to his motorbike, donned his helmet, and kicked the machine to life.

One morning in 1987, all of Bishop Street woke to hear the dull thack-thack-thack of axes hacking away at the trees. In a few days, chainsaws were buzzing, and cranes were scooping up huge portions of black earth. And that was the end of the great forest of Bajpe. In its place, the inhabitants of Bishop Street now saw a giant pit filled with cranes, lorries, and an army of bare-chested migrant workers carrying stacks of bricks and cement bags on their heads like ants moving grains of rice. A giant sign in Kannada and Hindi proclaimed that this was to be the site of the 'Sardar Patel Iron Man of India Sports Stadium. A Dream Come True for Kittur'. The racket was incessant, and dust swirled up from the pit like steam from a geyser. Outsiders who returned to Bajpe thought the neighbourhood had become a dozen degrees warmer.

DAY SEVEN: SALT MARKET VILLAGE

If you want a servant you can trust, a cook who won't steal sugar, a driver who doesn't drink, you go to Salt Market Village. Although it has formed part of Kittur Corporation since 1988, Salt Market remains largely rural and much poorer than the rest of the town.

If you visit in April or May, you must stay to watch the local festival known as the 'rat hunt' – a nocturnal ritual in which the women of the suburb march through the rice fields bearing burning torches in one hand, as they pound the earth with hockey sticks or cricket bats in the other hand, shouting all the time at the tops of their voices. Rats, mongooses, and shrews, terrified by the noise, run into the centre of the field, where the women pound the encircled rodents to death.

The only tourist attraction of Salt Market Village is an abandoned Jain basadi, where early Kannada epics were written by the poets Harihara and Raghuveera. In 1990, a portion of the Jain basadi was acquired by the Mormon Church of Utah, USA, and turned into an office for its evangelists.

Murali, waiting in the pantry for the tea to boil, took a step to his right and peeped through the doorway.

Comrade Thimma, who was sitting beneath the framed Soviet poster, had begun to grill the old woman.

'Do you understand the exact nature of the doctrinal differences between the Communist Party of India, the Communist Party of India (Marxist), and the Communist Party of India (Marxist-Maoist)?'

Of course she doesn't know, Murali thought, stepping back into the pantry and switching off the kettle.

No one on earth did.

He put his hand into a tin box full of sugar biscuits. A moment later, he was out in the reception area with a tray holding three cups of tea and a sugar biscuit next to each cup.

Comrade Thimma was looking up at the wall opposite him, where it was pierced by a grilled window. The evening light illuminated the grille; a block of light glowed on the floor, like the tail of an incandescent bird perched in the grille.

The Comrade's manner strongly suggested that the old woman, considering her state of complete doctrinal ignorance, was unworthy to receive assistance from the Communist Party of India (Marxist-Maoist), Kittur branch.

The woman was frail and haggard; her husband had hanged himself two weeks ago from the ceiling of their house.

Murali placed the first cup before Comrade Thimma, who picked it up and sipped the tea. This improved his mood.

Once again looking high up at the glowing grille, the Comrade said: 'I will have to tell you of our *dialectics*; if you find them acceptable, we can talk about help.'

The farmer's wife nodded, as if the word 'dialectics', in English, made perfect sense to her.

Without taking his eyes from the grille, the Comrade bit into one of the sugar biscuits; the crumbs fell around his chin, and Murali, after handing the old woman her tea, went back to the Comrade and wiped the crumbs off with his fingers.

The Comrade had small, sparkling eyes, and a tendency to look high up and far away, as he delivered his words of wisdom, which he always did with a feeling of suppressed excitement. This gave him the air of a prophet. Murali, as prophets' sidekicks often are, was physically the superior specimen: taller, broader, with a large and heavily creased forehead, and a kind smile.

'Give the lady our brochure on *dialectics*,' the Comrade said, speaking straight to the grille.

Murali nodded and moved purposefully towards one of the cupboards. The reception area of the Communist Party of India (Marxist-Maoist) was furnished with an old tea-stained table, a few decrepit cupboards, and a desk for the secretary-general, behind which hung a giant poster, from the early days of the Soviet Revolution, depicting a group of proletarian heroes climbing a ladder up into heaven. The workers bore mallets and sledgehammers, while a group of oriental gods cowered at their advance. After digging into two of the cupboards, Murali found a pamphlet with a big red star on the cover. He brushed it with a corner of his shirt and brought it to the old woman.

'She can't read.'

The soft voice came from the woman's daughter, who was sitting in the chair next to her, holding on to her teacup and untouched sugar biscuit. After a moment's hesitation Murali let the daughter have the brochure; keeping the teacup in her left hand, she held the pamphlet between two fingers of her right, as if it were a soiled hand-kerchief.

The Comrade smiled at the window grille; it was not clear if he was reacting to the events of the past few minutes. He was a thin, bald, dark-skinned man with sunken cheeks and gleaming eyes.

'In the beginning we had only one party in

India, and it was the true party. It made no compromise. But then the leaders of this true party were seduced by the lure of bourgeois democracy; they decided to contest elections. That was their first mistake and the fatal one. Soon the one true party had split. New branches emerged, trying to restore the original spirit. But they too became corrupted.'

Murali wiped the cupboard shelves and tried to realign the loose hinge of its door as well as he could. He was not a peon; there was no peon – Comrade Thimma would not allow the exploitative hiring of proletarian labour. Murali was certainly not proletarian – he was the scion of an influential landowning Brahmin family – so it was okay for him to perform all kinds of menial work.

The Comrade took a deep breath, took off his glasses and rubbed them clean with a corner of his white cotton shirt.

'We alone have kept the faith – we the members of the Communist Party of India (Marxist-Maoist). We alone remain true to the dialectics. And do you know what the strength of our membership is?'

He put his glasses back on and inhaled with satisfaction.

'Two. Murali and me.'

He gazed at the grille with a wan smile. He appeared to be done; so the old woman placed her hands on her daughter's head and said: 'She is unmarried, sir. We are begging of you some money to marry her off, that is all.'

Thimma turned to the daughter and stared; the girl looked at the ground. Murali winced. I wish he'd have more delicacy sometimes, he thought.

'We have no support,' the old woman said. 'My family won't even talk to me. Members of our own caste won't—'

The Comrade slapped his thigh with his palm.

'This caste question is only a manifestation of the class struggle: Mazumdar and Shukla definitively established this in 1938. I refuse to accept the category of "caste" in our discussions.'

The woman looked at Murali. He nodded his head, as if to say: 'Go on.'

'My husband said, the Communists were the only ones who cared about people like us. He said that if the Communists ruled the earth there would be no hardships for the poor, sir.'

This seemed to mollify the Comrade. He looked at the woman and the girl for a moment, and then sniffed. His fingers seemed to lack something. Murali understood. As he went to the pantry to boil another cup of tea, he heard the Comrade's voice continue behind him: 'The Communist Party of India (Marxist-Maoist) is not the party of the poor – it is the party of the proletariat. This distinction has to be understood, before we discuss assistance or resistance.'

After turning the kettle on once more, Murali was about to toss the tea leaves in; then he wondered why the daughter had not touched her tea. He was seized by the suspicion that he had put too much tea into the kettle – and that the way he had been making tea for nearly twenty-five years might have been wrong.

Murali got off the number 67c bus at the Salt Market Village stop and walked down the main road, picking his way through a bed of muck, while hogs sniffed the earth around him. He kept his umbrella up on his shoulder, like a wrestler keeps his mace, so that its metal point wouldn't be sullied by the muck. Asking a group of boys playing a game of marbles in the middle of the village road for directions, he found the house: a surprisingly large and imposing structure, with rocks placed on the corrugated tin roof, to stabilize it during the rains.

He unlatched the gate and went in.

A handspun cotton shirt hung on a hook on the wall next to the door; the dead man's, he assumed. As if the fellow were still inside, taking a nap, and would come outside and put it on to greet his visitor.

At least a dozen framed multi-coloured images of gods had been affixed to the front wall along with one of a pot-bellied local guru with an enormous nimbus affixed to his head. There was a bare cot, its fibres fraying, for visitors to sit down on.

Murali left his sandals outside and wondered if he should knock on the door. Too intrusive for a place like this – where death had just entered – so he decided to wait until someone came out.

Two white cows were sitting in the compound of the house. The bells round their necks tinkled during their rare movements. Lying in front of them was a puddle of water in which straw had been soaked to make a gruel. A black buffalo, snippets of fresh green all over its moist nose, stood gazing at the opposite wall of the compound, chewing at a sack full of grass that had been emptied on the ground in front of it. Murali thought: these animals have no concern in the world. Even in the house of a man who has killed himself, they are still fed and fattened. How effortlessly they rule over the men of this village, as if human civilization had confused masters and servants. Murali was transfixed. His eyes lingered on the fat body of the beast, its bulging belly, its glossy skin. He smelled its shit, which had caked on its backside; it had been squatting in puddles of its own waste.

Murali had not been to Salt Market Village in decades. The previous time was twenty-five years ago, when he had come searching for visual details to enrich a short story on rural poverty that he was writing. Not much had changed in a quarter-century; only the buffaloes had grown fat.

'Why didn't you knock on the door?'

The old woman emerged from the back yard; she walked around him with a big smile and went into the house and shouted: 'Hey, you! Get some tea!'

In a moment the girl came out with a tumbler of tea, which Murali took, touching her wet fingers as he did so.

The tea, after his long journey, felt like heaven. He had never mastered the art of making tea, even though he had been boiling it for Thimma for nearly twenty-five years now. Maybe it was one of those things that only women can truly do, he thought.

'What do you need from us?' the old woman asked. Her manner had become more servile; as if she had guessed the purpose of his visit only now.

'To find out if you are telling the truth,' he replied, calmly.

She summoned the neighbours so he could interview them. They squatted around the cot; he insisted that they sit on the same level as him but they remained where they were.

'Where did he hang himself?'

'Right here, sir!' said one old villager with broken, paan-stained teeth.

'What do you mean right here?'

The old man pointed to the beam of the roof. Murali could not believe it: in full public view, he had killed himself? So the cows had seen it; and the fat buffalo too.

He heard about the man whose shirt still hung from the hook. The failure of his crops. The loan from the moneylender. At 3 per cent per month, compounded.

'He was ruined by the first daughter's wedding. And he knew he had one more to marry off – this girl.'

The daughter had been lingering in a corner of the front yard the whole time. He saw her turn her face away, in slow agony.

As he was leaving, one of the villagers came running after him: 'Sir . . . sir . . . I mean, an aunt of mine committed suicide two years ago . . . I mean, just a year ago, sir, and she was virtually a mother to me . . . can the Communist Party . . .'

Murali seized the man's arm and pressed his fingers deeply into the flesh. He peered into the man's eyes: 'What is the name of the daughter?'

Slowly he walked back to the bus station. He let the tip of his umbrella trail in the earth. The horror of the dead man's story, the sight of those fat buffaloes, the pain-stricken face of that beautiful daughter – these details kept churning in his mind.

He thought back twenty-five years, when he had come to this village with his notebook and his dreams of becoming an Indian Maupassant. As he walked down the twisting streets, crowded with streetchildren playing their violent games, fatigued day-labourers sleeping in the shade, and with thick, still, glistening pools of effluent, he was reminded of that strange mixture of the strikingly beautiful and the filthy which is the nature of every Indian village – and the simultaneous desire to admire and to castigate that had been inspired in him from the time of his first visits.

He felt the need, as he had before, to take notes.

Back then, he had visited Salt Market Village every day for a week, jotting down painstakingly detailed descriptions of farmers, roosters, bulls, pigs, piglets, sewage, children's games, religious festivals, intending to juggle them into a series of short stories that he crafted in the reading room of the municipal library at night. He was not sure if the Party would approve of his stories, so he sent a bundle of them under a nom de plume – 'The Seeker of Justice' – to the editor of a weekly magazine in Mysore.

After a week, he received a postcard from the editor, summoning him from Kittur for a meeting. He took the train to Mysore and waited half a day for the editor to call him into his office.

'Ah, yes . . . the young genius from Kittur.' The editor searched his table for his glasses and pulled the folded bundle of Murali's stories from their envelope, while the young author's heart beat violently.

'I wanted to see you' – the editor let the stories

fall on the table – 'because there is talent in your writing. You have gone into the countryside and seen life there, unlike ninety per cent of our writers.'

Murali glowed. It was the first time anyone had mentioned the word 'talent' when speaking of him.

Picking up one of the stories, the editor silently scanned the pages.

'Who is your favourite author?' He asked, biting at a corner of his glasses.

'Guy de Maupassant.'

Murali corrected himself: 'After Karl Marx.'

'Let's stick to literature,' the editor retorted. 'Every character in Maupassant is like this . . .' – he bent his index finger and wiggled it. 'He wants, and wants, and wants. To the last day of his life he wants. Money. Women. Fame. More women. More money. More fame. Your characters' – he unbent his finger – 'want absolutely nothing. They simply walk through accurately described village settings and have deep thoughts. They walk around the cows and trees and roosters and think, and then walk around the roosters and trees and cows and think some more. That's it.'

'They do have thoughts of changing the world for the better . . .' Murali protested. 'They desire a better society.'

'They *want* nothing!' the editor shouted. 'I can't print stories of people who want nothing!'

He threw the bundle of stories back at Murali. 'When you find people who want something, come back to me!'

Murali had never rewritten those stories. Now, as he waited for the bus to take him back to Kittur, he wondered if that bundle of stories was still somewhere in his house.

When Murali got off the bus and walked back to the office, he found Comrade Thimma with a foreigner. It was not unusual for there to be strangers in the office; lean, fatigued men with paranoid eyes who were on the run from nearby states going through one of their routine purges of radical Communists. In those places radical Communism was a real threat to the state. The fugitives would sleep and take tea at the office for a few weeks, until things cooled down and they could return home.

But this man was not one of those hunted ones; he had blond hair and an awkward European accent.

He sat next to Thimma, and the Comrade was pouring his heart out, as he gazed at the distant light in the grille up on the wall. Murali sat down and listened to him for half an hour. He was magnificent. Trotsky had not been forgiven, nor had Bernstein been forgotten. Thimma was trying to show the European that even in a small town like Kittur men were up to date with the theory of dialectics.

The foreigner had nodded a lot and written every-thing down. At the end, he capped his ballpoint pen and observed: 'I find that the Communists have virtually no presence in Kittur.'

Thimma slapped his thigh. He glared at the grille. The Socialists had had too much influence in this part of South India, he said. The question of feudalism in the countryside had been solved; big estates had been broken up and distributed among peasants.

'That man Devraj Urs – when he was leader of the Congress – created some kind of revolution here,' Thimma sighed. 'Just a pseudo-revolution, naturally. The falsehood of Bernstein once again.'

Murali's own land had been subjected to the socialist policies of the Congress government. His father had lost his land; in return, the government had allocated compensation. His father went to the municipal office to receive his compensation, but he found that someone, some bureaucrat, had forged his signature and run away with his money. When Murali heard this, he had thought: my old man deserves this. I deserve this. For all that we have done to the poor, this is fit retribution. He realized, of course, that his family's compensation had not been stolen by the poor, but by some corrupt civil servant. Nevertheless this was justice of a kind.

Murali went about his regular end-of-day tasks. First he swept the pantry. As he reached with his broom under the sink, he heard the foreigner say:

'I think the problem with Marx is that he assumes human beings are too . . . decent. He rejects the idea of original sin. And maybe that is why Communism is dying everywhere now. The Berlin Wall . . .'

Murali crawled under the sink to the hard-to-reach places; Thimma's voice resonated oddly in the enclosed space beneath the sink: 'You have completely misunderstood the dialectical process!'

He paused, and waited under the sink for Comrade Thimma to come up with a better response.

He swept the floor, closed the cupboards, turned off the unwanted lights to save on the electricity bill, tightened the taps to save on the water bill, and went to the bus station to wait for the number 56B to take him home.

Home. A blue door, one fluorescent lamp, three naked electric bulbs, ten thousand books. The books were everywhere; waiting for him like faithful pets on either side of the door when he walked in, coated in dust on the dinner table, stacked against the old walls as though to buttress the structure of the house. They had taken all the best space in the house and had left him a little rectangular area for his cot.

He opened the bundle that he had brought home with him: 'Is Gorbachev straying from the

True Path? Notes by Thimma swami, BA (Kittur), MA (Mysore), secretary-general, Kittur regional politburo, Communist Party of India (Marxist-Maoist)'.

He would add them to the notes he was collecting on Thimma's thoughts. The idea was to publish them one day and hand them out to the workers as they left their factories.

This evening, Murali could not write for long; the mosquitoes bit him and he swatted them. He lit a coil to keep the mosquitoes away. Even then he could not write; and then he realized it was not the mosquitoes that were disturbing him.

The way she had averted her face. He would have to do something for her.

What was her name? – Ah, yes. Sulochana.

He began to rummage in the mess around his bed, until he found the old collection of short stories that he had written all those years ago. He blew the dust off the pages and began to read.

The photograph of the dead man hung on the wall, beside the portraits of the gods who had failed to save him. The guru with the big belly, perhaps taking all the blame, had now been dismissed.

Murali stood at the door, waited, and knocked slowly.

'They're working in the fields,' the old neighbour with the broken red teeth shouted.

The cows and the buffalo were missing from the courtyard; sold for cash, no doubt. Murali thought it was appalling. That girl, with her noble looks, working in the fields like a common labourer?

I've come just in time, he thought.

'Run and get them!' he shouted at the neighbour. 'At once!'

The state government had a scheme to compensate the widows of farmers who had killed themselves under duress, Murali explained to the widow, making her sit down on the cot. It was one of those well-intentioned rural improvement schemes that never reached anyone, because no one knew about it – until people from the city, like Murali, told them about it.

The widow was leaner, and sunburned; she sat there wiping her hands constantly against the back of her sari; she was ashamed of the dirt on them.

Sulochana brought out the tea. He was amazed that this girl, who had been working in the fields, had still found time to make him tea.

When he took the cup from her, touching her fingers, he quickly admired her features. Having just come from a day's hard labour in the fields, she was still beautiful – in fact, more beautiful than ever before. There was that simple, unpainted elegance to her face. None of the make-up, lipstick or false eyebrows you see in cities these days.

How old was she? he wondered.

'Sir . . .' The old woman folded her hands. 'Will the money really come?'

'If you sign here,' he said. 'And here. And here.'

The old lady held the pen and grinned idiotically.

'She can't write,' Sulochana said; so he placed the letter on his thigh and he signed for her.

He explained that he had brought another letter; one to be delivered to the central police station near the Lighthouse Hill, demanding prosecution of the moneylender for his role in instigating the man's death through usury. He wanted the old woman to sign that too, but she joined her palms together and bowed to him.

'Please, sir, don't do that. Please. We don't want any trouble.'

Sulochana stood by the wall, looking down, silently reinforcing her mother's plea.

He tore up the letter. As he did so, he realized that he was now the arbiter over this family's fate; he was the patriarch here.

'And her marriage?' he said, indicating the girl leaning against the wall.

'Who will marry this one? And what am I to do?' the old woman wailed as the girl retreated into the dark of the house.

It was on the way back to the bus station that the idea came to him.

He pressed the metal tip of his umbrella to the ground and trailed a long, continuous line through the mud.

And then he thought: why not?

She had no other hope, after all . . .

He boarded the bus. He was still a bachelor, at fifty-five. After his time in jail his family had disowned him, and none of his aunts or uncles had tried to fix an arranged marriage for him. Somehow, in the midst of distributing pamphlets and spreading the word to the proletariat and collecting Comrade Thimma's speeches, he had never found time to marry himself off. He had not had any great desire to do so, either.

Lying in bed, he thought: but this is nowhere for a girl to live. It is a filthy house, filled with old editions – books by veterans of the Communist Party and nineteenth-century French and Russian short-story writers – that no one reads any more.

He had not realized how badly he had been living until he tried to imagine living with someone else. But things would change; he felt a great hope. If she came into his life everything could be different. He lay down on his cot and stared at the ceiling fan. It was switched off; he rarely turned it on, except in the most oppressive summer heat, so that he wouldn't increase the electricity bill.

All his life he had been dogged by a restlessness, a feeling that he was meant for some greater endeavour than could be found in a small town. After his law degree from Madras, his father had expected him to take over his law practice. Instead,

Murali had been drawn to politics; he had begun attending Congress party meetings in Madras, and continued doing so in Kittur. He took to wearing a Nehru cap and keeping a photo of Gandhi on his desk. His father noticed. One day there was a confrontation and shouting, and Murali had left his father's house and joined the Congress party as a full-time member. He knew what he wanted to do with his life already: there was an enemy to overcome. The old, bad India of caste and class privilege – the India of child marriage, of ill-treated widows; of exploited subalterns – it had to be overthrown. When the state elections came, he campaigned with all his heart for the Congress candidate, a young lower-caste man named Anand Kumar.

After Anand Kumar won, he saw two of his fellow Congress workers sitting outside the Party office every morning. He saw men approach them with letters addressed to the candidate; they took the letters and a dozen rupees from each supplicant.

Murali threatened to report them to Kumar. The two men turned grave. They stepped aside and invited Murali to go right in.

'Please complain at once,' they said.

As he went and knocked on Kumar's door, he heard laughter behind him.

Murali joined the Communists next, having heard that they were incorruptible. The larger factions of the Communists turned out to be

384

just as rotten as the Congress; so he changed his membership from one Communist Party to the other, until one day he entered a dim office and saw, beneath the giant poster of heroic proletarians climbing up to heaven to knock out the gods of the past, the small dark figure of Comrade Thimma. At last – an incorruptible. Back then the party had seventeen member-volunteers; they ran women's education programmes, population control campaigns, and proletarian radicalization drives. With a group of volunteers, he went to the sweatshops near the Bunder, distributing pamphlets with the message of Marx and the benefits of sterilization. As the membership of the party dwindled, he found himself going alone; it made no difference to him. The cause was a good one. He was never strident like the workers from the other Communist parties; quietly, and with great perseverance, he stood by the side of the road, holding out pamphlets to the workers and repeating the message that so few of them ever took to heart: 'Don't you want to find out how to live a better life, brothers?'

He thought that his writing, too, would contribute to that cause – although he was honest enough to admit that perhaps only his vanity made him think so. The word 'talent' was now lodged in his mind, and that gave him hope; but even as he was wondering how to improve his writing, he was sent to jail.

The police came for Comrade Thimma one day. This was during the Emergency.

'You are right to arrest me,' Thimma had said, 'as I freely and openly support all attempts to overthrow the bourgeois government of India.'

Murali had asked the policemen: 'Would you mind arresting me as well?'

Jail had been a happy time for him. He washed Thimma's clothes and hung them out to dry in the mornings. He had hoped all the free time in jail would concentrate his mind, and help him reshape his fiction, but he had no time for that. In the evenings, he took notes as Thimma dictated. Thimma's responses to the great questions of Marxism. The apostasy of Bernstein. The challenge of Trotsky. A justification for Kronstadt.

He collected the responses faithfully; then he pulled a blanket over Thimma's face, leaving his toes out in the cool air.

He shaved him in the morning, as Thimma thundered to the mirror about Khrushchev's defiling of the legacy of Comrade Stalin.

It was the happiest period of his life. But then he had been released.

With a sigh, Murali rose from his bed. He paced around the dark house, looking at the mess of the books, at the decaying editions of Gorky and Turgenev, and saying to himself, again and again: what do I have to show for my life? Just this broken-down house . . .

386

Then he saw the face of the girl again and his whole body lit up with hope, and joy. He took out his bundle of short stories and read them again. With a red-ink pen he began to delete details of his characters, quickening their motives, their impulses.

It came to Murali one morning, on his way to Salt Market Village: 'They're avoiding me. Both mother and daughter.'

Then he thought: no, not Sulochana – it's only the old woman who's gone cold.

For two months now, he had been catching the bus to Salt Market Village on a variety of fictitious premises, only to see Sulochana's face again, only to touch her fingers when she brought him his cup of scalding-hot tea.

He had tried to put it to the old lady that they should marry – hints could be delivered, and the topic would insinuate itself into the woman's mind. That had been his hope. Then, purely out of social responsibility, he would agree, despite his advanced age, to marry her.

But the old lady had never divined his desire.

'Your daughter is excellent in the household,' he had said once, thinking that enough of a hint.

The following day, when he arrived, a strange young girl came out to meet him. The widow had moved up in life; she had now hired a servant.

'Is Madam in?' he asked. The servant nodded.

'Will you go and get her?'

A minute passed. He thought he heard the sound of voices behind the door; then the servant came out and said: 'No.'

'No what?'

She turned her gaze towards the house again. 'They . . . are not here. No.'

'And Sulochana? Is she in?'

The servant girl shook her head.

Why shouldn't they avoid me, he thought, trailing his umbrella on the ground as he returned to the bus station. He had done his work for them; he was not needed any more. This is how people in the real world behaved. Why should he be hurt?

In the evening, pacing around his gloomy home, he felt he had to agree with the old woman's judgement: surely this is no fit habitation for a young girl like Sulochana. How could he bring a woman into it?

Yet the next day, he was back on the bus to Salt Market Village, where, once again, the servant girl told him that no one was home.

On the way back, he rested his head against the grille and thought: the more they snub me, the more I want to fall down before that girl and propose marriage.

At home he tried writing a letter. 'Dear Sulochana: I have been searching for a way to tell you. There is so much to say . . .'

He went back every day for a week, and was refused entry every day. 'I will never come back,' he promised himself on the seventh evening, as he had for six evenings before. 'I really will never come back. This is disgraceful behaviour. I am exploiting these people.' But he was also angry with the old woman and Sulochana for treating him like this.

On the journey home, he stood up and shouted to the conductor: 'Stop!' He had remembered, out of the blue, a story he had written twenty-five years ago, about a matchmaker who worked in the village.

He asked the children playing marbles for the matchmaker; they directed him to the shop-keepers. It took an hour and a half to find the house.

The matchmaker was an old, half-blind man sitting in a chair smoking a hookah; his wife brought a chair for the Communist to sit in.

Murali cleared his throat and cracked his knuckles. He wondered what to say, what to do. The hero in his story had walked around the matchmaker's house and then left; he had never come this far.

'There is a friend of mine who wishes to marry that girl. Sulochana.'

'The daughter of the fellow who . . . ?' The matchmaker pantomimed a hanging.

Murali nodded.

'Your friend is too late, sir. She has money now, and so she has a hundred offers,' the matchmaker said. 'That is the way of life.'

'But . . . my friend . . . my friend has set his heart on her . . .'

'Who is this friend?' the matchmaker asked, and with a dirty, omniscient gleam in his eyes.

He caught the bus in the mornings, as soon as his work was over at the Party office, and waited for her at the market. She came in the evenings to buy vegetables. He would follow her slowly. He looked at the bananas, at the mangoes. He had been buying fruit for Comrade Thimma for decades. He was expert at so many women's tasks; his heart skipped a beat when he saw her choose an over-ripe mango; when the vendor tricked her, he wanted to run over and yell at him and protect her from his avarice.

In the evenings, he stood waiting for the bus back to Kittur. He observed the way people lived in villages. He saw a boy cycling furiously, a block of ice strapped to the back of his bicycle. He had to make it in time before the ice melted; it was already half gone, and he had no aim in life but to deliver the rest of the ice in time. A man came with bananas in a plastic bag and looked around; there were large black spots on the bananas already, and he had to sell them before they rotted. All these people sent Murali a message. To want things in life, they were saying, is to recognize that time is limited.

He was fifty-five years old.

He did not take the bus back that evening; instead, he walked to the house. Rather than approach the front door, he entered through the back. Sulochana was winnowing rice; she looked at her mother and went inside.

The servant went in to bring a chair, but the old woman said: 'Don't.'

'Look here; you want to marry my daughter?' she asked.

So she had found out. It was always like this; you make an effort to conceal desire and then it is out in the open. The greatest fallacy: that you can hide from others what you want from them.

He nodded, avoiding her eyes.

'How old are you?' she asked.

'Fifty.'

'Can you give her children at your age?'

He tried to respond.

The old woman said: 'Why would we want to get you into our family, in any case? My late husband always told me, Communists are trouble.'

His jaw dropped. Was this the same husband who had praised the Communists? Had this woman just made all that up?

Murali understood now; her husband had said nothing about the Communists. In their wanting they became so cunning, these people!

He said: 'I bring many advantages to your family. I am a Brahmin by birth; a graduate of—'

'Look here!' The widow got up. 'Please leave –
or there will be trouble.'

Why not? Maybe I can't give her children, at my
age, but I can make her happy, certainly, he
thought, on the bus back home. We can read
Maupassant together.

He was an educated man, a graduate of the
Madras University; this was no way to treat him.
Tears flooded his eyes.

He sought out books of fiction and poetry,
but it was the words of a film song he had heard
on the bus which seemed to express his feelings best. So this is why the proletariat go to
the cinema, he thought. He bought a ticket
himself.

'How many?'

'One.'

The ticket-seller grinned. 'Don't you have any
friends, old man?'

After the movie, Murali wrote a letter and posted
it to her.

The next morning he woke up wondering if she
would ever read it. Even if it reached the house,
wouldn't her mother throw it away? He should
have hand-delivered it!

It is not enough to make an honest attempt.
That was enough for Marx and Gandhi – to have
tried. But not for the real world, in which he
suddenly found himself.

After considering the matter for an hour, he
wrote the letter again. This time he paid an urchin

three rupees to deliver the message into the girl's hands.

'She knows you come here to look for her,' the vegetable seller said, the next time he came to the market. 'You've scared her away.'

She is avoiding me – his heart felt a pang. Now he understood so many more film songs. This is what they meant, the humiliation of being avoided by a girl you have come a long way to see . . .

He thought the vegetable sellers were all laughing at him.

Even ten years ago – in his forties – there would have been nothing unseemly about approaching such a girl, he thought, as he headed home. Now he was a dirty old man; he had become the stock figure whom he had worked into several of his stories – the lecherous old Brahmin, preying on an innocent girl of a lower caste.

But those fellows were just caricatures, class-villains; *now* he could flesh them out so much better. When he climbed into bed at night, he took a piece of paper and wrote: 'Some thoughts that a lecherous old Brahmin might *actually* have.'

Now I know enough, Murali thought, looking at the words he had written. I can become a writer at last.

The next morning order and reason returned. There were the comb on his hair, the breathing exercises before the mirror, the slow steady gait out the front door, the business of cleaning the Party headquarters and making tea for Thimma.

But, by afternoon, he was on the bus to Salt Market Village again.

He waited for her to come to the market and then walked behind her, examining potatoes and brinjals and stealing glances at her. All the time he could see the vendors mocking him: dirty old man, dirty old man. He thought with regret of a man's traditional prerogative in India – in the old, bad India – to marry a younger woman.

The next morning, back in the pantry at the Party headquarters, boiling tea for Thimma, everything around him seemed dingy, and dark, and unbearable – the old pots and pans, the filthy spoons, the dirty old tub out of which he scooped sugar for the tea: the embers of a life that had never flared, never flamed.

'You've been fooled,' everything in the room said to him. 'You've wasted your life.'

He thought of all his advantages: his education, his sharper wit, his brains, his gift for writing. His 'talent' – as that Mysore editor had said.

All of that, he thought as he brought the tea out into the reception area, wasted in the service of Comrade Thimma.

Even Thimma had wasted himself. He had never remarried after his wife's early death; he had dedicated himself to his life's goal – uplifting the proletariat of Kittur. Ultimately it was not Marx; it was Gandhi and Nehru who were to blame. Murali was convinced of that. A whole generation of young men, deluded by Gandhianism, wasting their lives running around organizing free eye clinics for the poor and distributing books for rural libraries, instead of seducing those young widows and unmarried girls. That old man in his loincloth had turned them mad. Like Gandhi you had to withhold all your lusts. Even to know what you wanted in life was a sin; desire was bigotry. And look where the country was, after forty years of idealism? A total mess! Maybe if they had all become bastards, the young men of his generation, the place would be like America by now!

That evening he forced himself not to take the bus to the village. He stayed on, cleaning the Party headquarters twice over.

No – he thought, as he strained to clean under the sink the second time – it was not a waste! The idealism of young men like him had changed Kittur and the villages around it. Rural poverty was halved, smallpox had been eradicated, public health was a hundred times improved, literacy was up. If Sulochana could read, it was because of volunteers like him, because of those free library projects . . .

He paused in the darkness under the sink. A voice growled inside him: 'Fine, she can read – and what does that do for you, you idiot?'

395

He rushed back into the light, into the reception area.

The poster now came to life. The proletarians climbing up to heaven to overturn the gods began to melt and change form. He saw them for what they were: a subaltern army of semen, blood, and flesh rebelling inside him. A revolution of the body proletariat, long suppressed, but now becoming articulate, saying:

We want!

The Communists were finished. The European visitor had said as much; and all the newspapers were saying the same thing. The Americans had somehow won. Comrade Thimma would talk on and on. But there would soon be nothing to talk about; because Marx had become mute. Dialectics had become Dust. So had Gandhi; so had Nehru. Out in the streets of Kittur, the young people were driving brand-new Suzuki cars, blaring pop music from the West; they were licking raspberry ice-cream cones with red tongues and wearing shiny metal watches.

He picked up the pamphlet and threw it at the Soviet poster, startling a gecko that had been hiding behind it.

Do you think privilege has no place in Indian life? Do you think a Madras University man – a Brahmin – can be tossed aside so lightly?

In his hand, as the bus rocked, Murali held a letter from the state government of Karnataka that announced that another instalment of the money was due to arrive for the widow of the farmer Arasu Deva Gowda, provided she signed. Eight thousand rupees.

Asking for directions, he found the house of the moneylender. He saw it: the biggest construction in the village, with a pink façade and pillars up the front supporting a portico – the house that 3 per cent interest, compounded monthly, had built.

The moneylender, a fat, dark man, was selling grain to a group of farmers; by his side, a fat, dark boy, probably his son, was making a note in a book. Murali stopped to admire it all: the sheer genius of exploitation in India. Sell a farmer your grain. Get rid of your bad stock this way. Then charge him a loan for buying that grain. Make him pay it back at 3 per cent a month. Thirty-six per cent a year. No, even more – much more! Compound interest! – how diabolical, how brilliant! And to think, Murali smiled, that he had assumed that Communists had brains.

When Murali went up to him, the moneylender was sticking his hand deep into the grain; when he brought it out, the chocolate-coloured skin was coated with a fine yellow dust, like a bird's pollen-covered beak.

Without wiping his arm, he took the letter from Murali. Behind him, in an alcove in the wall of his house, sat a giant red statue of the pot-bellied

Ganesha. A fat wife, with fat children around her, was sitting on a charpoy. And from behind them wafted the odour of a feeding, defecating beast: a water buffalo, without doubt.

'Did you know that the government has paid the widow another eight thousand rupees?' Murali told him. 'If you have debts outstanding, you should collect them now. She is in a position to pay.'

'Who are you?' the moneylender asked, with small suspicious eyes.

Hesitating for a moment, Murali said: 'I am the 55-year-old Communist.'

He wanted them to know. The old woman and Sulochana. They were both in his power now. They had been in his power from the day they had walked into his office.

When he returned to his house, there was a letter from Comrade Thimma under the door. Probably hand-delivered, since there was no one else to deliver anything now.

He tossed it away. He realized, as he did it, that he was casting away for good his membership of the Communist Party of India (Marxist-Maoist). Comrade Thimma, his mouth thirsting for tea, would deliver lectures alone, in that dim hall, denouncing him. He joined Bernstein and Trotsky and the long line of apostates.

At midnight he was still awake. He lay staring at the ceiling fan, whose fast-rotating blades were chopping the light from the halogen streetlamps outside the bedroom into sharp white glints: they showered down on Murali like the first particles of wisdom he had received in his life.

He stared at the brilliant blur of the fan's blades for a long time: then, with a jerk, he got up from the bed.

CHRONOLOGY

1984
31 October
News reaches Kittur via the BBC that Mrs Indira Gandhi, prime minister of India, has been assassinated by her own bodyguards. The town shuts down in mourning for two days. Mrs Gandhi's cremation, broadcast live, proves a major boost to the number of TVs sold in Kittur.

November
General elections. Anand Kumar, the Congress (I) candidate and a junior minister in Indira Gandhi's cabinet, retains his seat. His majority of 45,457 votes over Ashwin Aithal, his BJP opponent, is the largest in Kittur's history.

1985
Reflecting the growing interest in the stock market, the Dawn Herald begins publishing a daily report on the activities of the Bombay Stock Exchange on page 3.

Dr Shambhu Shetty opens Happy Smile Clinic. Kittur's first orthodontic clinic.

1986
A giant rally held by the Hoyka community in Nehru Maidan pledges to build the first temple 'for, by, and of Backward Castes' in Kittur.

The first video lending library opens in Umbrella Street.
Construction of the north bell tower, delayed for over a century, is resumed at the Cathedral of Our Lady of Valencia.

1987
The Cricket World Cup is held in India and Pakistan. Interest in Cricket proves a major boost to the demand for colour TVs.

Riots break out between Hindus and Muslims in the Bunder. Two people are killed. Dawn-to-dusk curfew in the port.

Kittur is reclassified by the state government of Karnataka from 'town' to 'city', and the town municipality becomes a 'City Corporation'. The first act of the new Corporation is to authorize the cutting down of the great forest of Bajpe.

The arrival of migrant Tamil workers, drawn by the construction boom in Bajpe and Rose Lane, is believed to be the cause of a severe outbreak of cholera.

1988
Mabroor Ismail Engineer, generally believed to be the richest man in town, opens the first Maruti-Suzuki car showroom in Kittur.

The Rashtriya Swayamsevak Sangh (RSS) holds a march from Angel Talkies to the Bunder. Marchers call for India to be declared a Hindu nation, and for a return to traditional social values.

Elections held to the City Corporation. The BJP and the Congress divide the seats almost exactly.

Construction of the north bell tower, delayed for a year by the death of the rector, is recommenced at the Cathedral of Our Lady of Valencia.

1989
General elections. Ashwin Aithal, the BJP candidate, upsets cabinet minister and Congress candidate Anand Kumar to become the first non-Congress candidate ever to win the seat of Kittur.

The Sardar Patel Iron Man of India Stadium opens in Bajpe. The construction of houses in the neighbourhood proceeds rapidly, and by the year's end the old forest is almost entirely gone.

1990

A bomb explodes during a chemistry class at St Alfonso's Boys' High School and Junior College, leading to its temporary closure. The *Dawn Herald* runs a frontpage editorial asking: 'Does India need martial law?'

The first computer lab in Kittur is opened at St Alfonso Boys' High School and Junior College. Other schools follow within the year.

The Gulf War breaks out, leading to the loss of expatriate remittances from Kuwait. A severe economic crisis follows. However, the broadcast of the war on CNN, available only to those TVs with a dish antenna, proves a great boost to sales of satellite TV dish antennas in Kittur.

With its funding frozen, construction work on the north bell tower of the cathedral once again comes to a halt.

1991
21 May
News reaches Kittur via CNN of the assassination of Rajiv Gandhi. The town is shut down in mourning for two days.